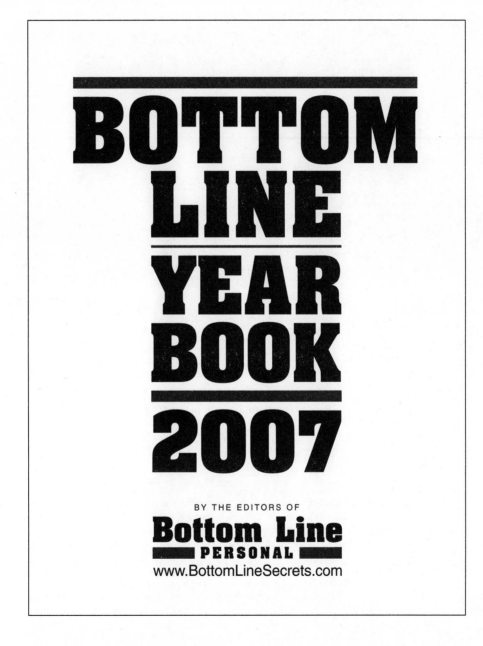

BOTTOM LINE YEAR BOOK 2007

BY THE EDITORS OF

Bottom Line
PERSONAL

www.BottomLineSecrets.com

Contents

10 • INVESTMENT ADVISER

11 • THE SAVVY SHOPPER

PART THREE: YOUR FINANCIAL FUTURE

12 • WORRY-FREE RETIREMENT

13 • ESTATE PLANNING ANSWERS

PART FOUR: YOUR LEISURE

14 • BON VOYAGE

15 • FUN TIMES

16 • A SMOOTH RIDE

PART FIVE: YOUR LIFE

17 • HOME AND FAMILY MATTERS

1

Health Watch

Dangerous Medical Myths: Protect Yourself And Loved Ones

Most people unintentionally increase their risk for sickness, premature aging and even death just because they lack key facts about their own bodies.

Problem: Because doctors don't have time to educate patients about everything that could possibly go wrong with their health, you need to have a basic understanding of what kinds of symptoms to watch for...and which medical advice can be trusted.

Some of the most commonly held beliefs are the most dangerous...

Myth: **Ulcers are not contagious.** Nearly all ulcers are caused by *Helicobacter pylori* (H. pylori), a spiral-shaped bacterium which penetrates the stomach lining. A blood test can detect H. pylori in people with ulcer symptoms,

including pain in the abdominal area just above the navel. Doctors can successfully eradicate H. pylori with a two-week course of antibiotics, but ulcers often return.

Reason: Kissing can transmit the bacterium. Even when an ulcer patient is successfully treated with antibiotics, he/she can later reacquire the bacterium—and the ulcer—from H. pylori-infected saliva.

Recommendation: If you or your spouse or partner has ulcers due to H. pylori, ask your doctor about *both* of you taking antibiotics to avoid reinfecting one another. Also, get a new toothbrush to avoid reinfecting yourself.

Myth: **High blood pressure begins only at 140/90.** Until recently, doctors didn't consider

Michael F. Roizen, MD, chief of the division of anesthesiology, critical care medicine and comprehensive pain management at The Cleveland Clinic.

Mehmet C. Oz, MD, medical director of the Integrative Medicine Center and director of the Heart Institute at New York–Presbyterian Hospital—Columbia University in New York City.

Dr. Roizen and Dr. Oz are coauthors of *You: The Owner's Manual* (HarperCollins) and *You: The Smart Patient* (Free Press).

blood pressure to be elevated unless it climbed above 140/90. According to the National Heart, Lung and Blood Institute, a patient with a reading as low as 120/80 has *prehypertension*—and is at an increased risk for heart disease.

Optimal blood pressure is 115/76. The difference of just a few points might seem insignificant, but patients who maintain blood pressure readings at this level or lower have *half* the cardiovascular risk of those at the higher level.

Recommendation: Because many physicians don't flag blood pressure readings that are only slightly elevated, ask the nurse/technician taking your blood pressure what your reading is. If it is above 115/76, ask your doctor how to bring it down.

Slight elevations can almost always be controlled with lifestyle changes, such as losing just five to 10 pounds, exercising and increasing fruit and vegetable intake.

Myth: **If your cholesterol levels are normal, you won't have a heart attack.** Most heart attack sufferers have normal cholesterol levels. Few people realize that heart attacks are typically caused by blood clots that form on top of irritated, inflamed areas of plaque (a mixture of cholesterol and other substances) on artery walls. When these clots grow, they can lodge in an artery and cause a heart attack.

Lowering LDL "bad" cholesterol creates a less favorable environment for clot formation. If your doctor says your LDL cholesterol is elevated, implement lifestyle changes, such as diet and exercise.

Still, some researchers speculate that statins, such as *atorvastatin* (Lipitor), work not so much by lowering cholesterol but rather by reducing the arterial inflammation that promotes clots. In fact, studies have shown that statins reduce heart attack risk even in patients with normal cholesterol levels.

Important: Do *not* take more than 100 milligrams (mg) of vitamin C or 100 international units (IU) of vitamin E daily if you are taking a statin, as these vitamins inhibit the drug's anti-inflammatory effects.

In addition to statins, these natural strategies help prevent inflammation and clots…

Recommendation 1: Care for your teeth. Brush *and* floss daily. Get a professional cleaning twice a year. The bacteria that cause gum disease also can promote inflammation and plaque in the arteries.

Recommendation 2: Consider aspirin therapy. Ask your doctor about taking two 81-mg "baby" (or half an adult) aspirin daily to reduce arterial inflammation and inhibit clots.

Helpful: Buy regular, cheap aspirin. Drink one-half glass of water before and after taking the aspirin. This will aid absorption and make the aspirin less likely to cause gastrointestinal bleeding.

Important: Some recent studies have questioned whether aspirin really does help prevent heart disease, but we recommend this therapy for patients who are candidates because it also helps curb the risk for colon, breast, prostate and other cancers.

Myth: **Fiber prevents colon cancer.** Eating fruits and vegetables can help to prevent colon malignancies and other cancers, but research shows that it isn't the fiber in these foods that does the trick—it's the antioxidants.

Although there are many reasons to get plenty of dietary fiber—for example, it prevents constipation, improves digestion and helps lower LDL cholesterol levels—other approaches have been proven to be more effective at preventing colon cancer.

Recommendation 1: Ask about aspirin. Two baby (or half of an adult) aspirin daily reduces your risk for colon cancer by 40%, possibly due to its anti-inflammatory effect. Ask your doctor if aspirin is right for you. It should not be taken with blood thinners.

Recommendation 2: Boost intake of folate and calcium. People who take at least 400 micrograms (mcg) of folate daily and/or 500 mg of calcium twice daily reduce their colon cancer risk by 30%. The reason for this effect is unknown, but researchers believe these supplements may slow the harmful breakdown of DNA that is associated with cancer.

Myth: **The more you exercise, the better your health.** The human body isn't designed to withstand constant stress. People who exercise vigorously more than about an hour a day don't live longer or healthier lives than those who exercise at moderate levels.

Recommendation: Get one hour a day of moderate exercise—fast walking, swimming, bicycling, etc. Research shows that this level of activity can make you feel and behave younger.

Regular physical activity will promote weight loss, improve cardiovascular conditioning and bone strength and decrease the risk for diabetes. Exercising for more than one hour at a time doesn't provide additional health benefits, however, it does increase the risk for muscle, bone or joint damage.

Myth: Diarrhea should run its course. A common misconception is that it's best not to treat diarrhea in order to promote the removal of organisms/toxins that lead to this potentially dangerous condition.

Not true. Untreated diarrhea is more than just uncomfortable. It can remove quarts of water from the body and cause dangerous dehydration within 24 hours, especially in children and older adults.

Recommendation: Eat chicken soup with rice. The broth and rice provide protective sugars to cells that line the intestine. Drink two quarts of water or juice daily to prevent dehydration. Also, take readily absorbable, calcium-containing tablets (such as Tums) several times daily. Calcium slows down muscular movements in the intestine.

 # Seven Big Cancer Myths

Gregory Pennock, MD, a medical oncologist who specializes in lung cancer, sarcoma (cancer of the soft tissue) and melanoma (skin cancer). He is medical director of clinical research at the MD Anderson Cancer Center in Orlando, FL, *www.mdandersonorlando.org,* which has an international reputation for exceptional cancer care and research.

Despite all of the medical information in the media now, many people are misinformed about the realities of cancer. These misconceptions can prevent people from getting appropriate treatment. *Here, the truth behind common myths about cancer…*

Myth: Cancer usually is fatal. In a recent American Cancer Society (ACS) survey, 68% of respondents said that they believe the risk of dying of cancer is increasing. Not true. Though the number of Americans diagnosed with cancer has increased (because the US population is increasing and getting older), the risk of dying of cancer has decreased due to early detection and improved treatment. More than half of people diagnosed with cancer survive the disease—and for some cancers, such as lymphoma and leukemia, the cure rate is between 70% and 80%.

Cancer isn't a single disease. It includes many types of tumors, all of which behave differently. Some tumors, such as those found in the breast, respond very well to chemotherapy and to other treatments. Lung tumors are more resistant to treatment. The likelihood of a cure depends not only on the type of tumor but how far advanced it is at the time of diagnosis.

Myth: Cancer runs in families. Only about 8% of cancers are genetically linked. These usually are cancers that occur in younger patients, such as sarcoma or early-onset colon cancer. But, the vast majority of cancers occur without a known cause or are related to lifestyle.

A family history does increase risk for certain cancers. For example, when a woman has a first-degree relative (such as a mother or sister) who developed the BRCA1 form of breast cancer at an early age, her risk for getting that cancer is increased.

However, only about 10% to 20% of women diagnosed with breast cancer have a family history of the disease. That's why it's important for every woman to undergo regular mammograms and do breast self-exams on a regular basis.

Myth: Stress causes cancer. There's a long-standing belief that people who experience a lot of stress or lack a positive attitude are more prone to cancer. One survey of long-term breast cancer survivors in Canada found that 42% attributed their cancer to stress. This causes many people with cancer to blame themselves or feel that they always have to be upbeat to prevent a recurrence.

There's no evidence that stress or a negative attitude triggers cancer. In a study reported in the journal *Cancer,* 8,500 people were scored on factors such as fatigue, irritability, etc. After following the participants for almost nine years on average, researchers found no link between emotional distress and cancer risk.

However, positive thinking may play a role in recovery. Patients with a positive attitude are more likely to do things that improve outcomes, such as following medical instructions and maintaining a healthy lifestyle.

Myth: **Surgery causes cancer to spread.** In the ACS survey, 41% of respondents said they believe that cancer spreads through the body during surgery. But, in reality, the risk of cancer spreading during surgery is close to zero. This myth probably started in the days before early detection of cancer. It was common for doctors to find advanced cancers during surgery—even in patients who may have had only mild symptoms. Patients and their families concluded that the surgery itself made the disease worse.

Some cancers in the abdomen or ovaries produce large amounts of malignant fluid. In those cases, it's theoretically possible for cancer cells to spread if the fluid leaks into the abdomen during surgery, but there is no actual evidence of that happening.

Myth: **Injuries cause cancer.** More than one-third of respondents in the ACS survey thought that injuries such as a bruised breast or a hard fall could cause cancer later in life.

These types of injuries don't cause cancer. But, what may happen is that people hurt a part of the body, see a doctor about the injury and then learn that they have a tumor, but the tumor was already there. The injury just triggered the discovery.

That said, a few cancers are caused by certain types of injuries. A serious sunburn during childhood, for example, does increase the risk of skin cancer later in life. And, chronic reflux disease (heartburn) can burn the esophagus and increase the risk of esophageal cancer.

Myth: **It's okay to keep smoking after a lung cancer diagnosis.** Some people believe that because the damage is done, they do not have to quit smoking—but those who do continue to smoke after a lung cancer diagnosis have significantly poorer outcomes than those who quit. There is also evidence that the chemicals in cigarette smoke interfere with radiation and chemotherapy. People with lung cancer who quit smoking respond better to the treatments.

Important: Lung cancer is the leading cause of cancer deaths in men and women. Lung tissue gradually returns to normal when people quit smoking. Ten years after quitting, lung cancer risk is reduced to one-third of what it was.

Myth: **Cell phones trigger brain cancer.** Large population studies have shown no evidence that cell phones cause any kind of cancer, including brain cancer.

Cell phone use today is vastly higher than it was a decade ago. If there were any truth to the cancer/cell-phone link, we would be seeing an increased incidence of brain cancers by now, but that hasn't happened.

A Lung Cancer Vaccine Is on the Way

Lung cancer kills more than 150,000 Americans every year. Current treatment involves surgery and/or chemotherapy.

Recent study: The vaccine wiped out lung cancer in some patients and slowed its spread in others.

It could be presented to the FDA for approval by 2007.

John Nemunaitis, MD, oncologist at Baylor/Sammons Cancer Center, Mary Crowley Medical Research Center in Dallas, and leader of a study of 43 lung cancer patients, reported in the *Journal of the National Cancer Institute.*

New Hope for a Pancreatic Cancer Vaccine

A new cancer vaccine causes the immune system to destroy pancreatic cancer cells that remain after surgery. In a preliminary study, the vaccine—combined with radiation and chemotherapy—boosted one-year survival rates to 88% versus 63% without the vaccine.

The Johns Hopkins University School of Medicine, 733 N. Broadway, Baltimore, MD 21205.

A Surprising Cause Of Cancer

Julie Parsonnet, MD, a professor of infectious diseases and the George DeForest Barnett professor of medicine at Stanford University School of Medicine in Stanford, CA. She is editor of *Microbes and Malignancy: Infection as a Cause of Human Cancers* (Oxford University).

People tend to think that cancer is caused only by unhealthful habits, such as smoking, or by environmental factors, including exposure to asbestos or excessive sunlight. They don't realize that cancer often is triggered by an infectious disease.

The shocker: At least 25% of malignancies are caused by viruses, bacteria and parasites. After smoking, infection is the number-one cause of cancer.

Although millions of Americans are infected with organisms that cause cancer at some point during their lives, most of these people do not develop cancer as a result. There are additional risk factors that work in tandem with infectious microbes to trigger the biological changes that lead to cancer.

THE INFECTION LINK

Viruses are the main cancer-causing organisms, followed by bacteria and parasites.

Primary ways that these organisms can cause cancer…

•**Genetic changes.** Viruses can't replicate on their own. When viruses enter your body, they inject their own genetic material into your cells and take over the cells' inner workings.

Some viral genes, known as oncogenes, cause cells to divide much more rapidly than usual. Rapid cell division increases the odds of genetic "mistakes" that can lead to cancer. Viruses also inhibit our body's natural ability to destroy damaged cells, which may otherwise just continue to grow and divide in ways that make us more vulnerable to cancer.

•**Chronic inflammation.** Some organisms, such as those that cause stomach and liver cancer, irritate tissues and trigger persistent inflammation. Inflammation causes cells to divide at a faster rate than normal, increasing the likelihood that they will mutate and undergo changes that lead to cancer.

CANCER-CAUSING INFECTIONS

Numerous cancers are believed to be caused, in part, by infectious organisms. *The most common cancer-causing infections—and steps you can take to protect yourself…*

•**Helicobacter pylori.** Between 30% and 40% of all Americans are infected with *Helicobacter pylori,* a screw-shaped bacterium that burrows into the stomach lining and causes chronic inflammation. About 20% of these people eventually develop ulcers, and another 5% will develop stomach cancer.

Infection with H. pylori is a very strong risk factor for cancer, presumably because the bacterium causes inflammation and cell proliferation. More than 80% of stomach cancer cases are caused by H. pylori. Infection with this bacterium increases your risk of developing stomach cancer by at least eightfold.

Self-defense: Ulcer patients are routinely tested for H. pylori and treated with antibiotics if infection is present. Once the bacterium is eliminated, the risk for ulcers drops significantly. It is not yet known if treating bacteria will help prevent stomach cancer. Patients with a family history of stomach cancer should talk to their doctors about getting tested for H. pylori.

Also helpful: Eat a nutritious diet that is rich in fruits and vegetables and low in salt and food preservatives known as nitrates. Such a diet may reduce cancer risk.

•**Epstein-Barr virus.** The Epstein-Barr virus (EBV) causes infectious mononucleosis, which leads to extreme fatigue and other flu-like symptoms. EBV is found in the tumors of a significant number of patients with Hodgkin's disease (a form of lymphoma that strikes most often between the ages of 15 to 35 and after age 55).

The risk that an individual patient who has had mononucleosis will go on to develop Hodgkin's disease—or get non-Hodgkin's lymphoma, which also is associated with the EBV virus—is still very low.

The main risk for non-Hodgkin's lymphoma appears to be in those patients with severely compromised immune systems—for example, those who have undergone transplant surgery and/or are taking immune-suppressing drugs.

5

Self-defense: Transmission of EBV is impossible to prevent because many healthy people can carry and spread the virus for life. People who receive transplants and immune-suppressing drugs should ask their doctors about symptoms of EBV-related malignancies. Decreasing immunosuppression can often reverse lymphoma when caught early.

•**Hepatitis B.** The hepatitis B virus (HBV) is spread by contact with body fluids of an infected person, including blood, saliva, vaginal secretions and semen.

At greatest risk: People who have sex with infected partners…as well as drug users who share needles.

Most HBV cases are acute, lasting six months or less. This form of hepatitis is not linked to cancer. However, the chronic form of HBV, which is almost always acquired in childhood and lasts for more than six months, greatly increases the risk for cirrhosis (destruction of normal liver tissue) as well as liver cancer.

Self-defense: All newborns are now given the vaccine for HBV. It is also recommended for children ages 18 years or younger who weren't previously vaccinated. Adults don't require the vaccine for cancer prevention—but it is recommended for those in high-risk groups because it can reduce the risk for long-term liver disease.

Among those who should get the HBV vaccine: Health-care workers…those who are sexually active with people who may have HBV and/or have household contact with them…and dialysis patients.

•**Hepatitis C.** Most people with the hepatitis C virus (HCV) were infected by tainted blood transfusions prior to 1992, when blood-screening tests first became available. HCV also can be transmitted through intercourse with a person who is infected…sharing contaminated hypodermic needles…and receiving nonsterile tattoo or body-piercing procedures.

About 5% of patients with HCV will develop liver cancer. A much higher percentage will develop cirrhosis or other chronic liver diseases—usually decades after the initial exposure.

Self-defense: In addition to the high-risk practices mentioned above, you shouldn't share razors, toothbrushes or nail clippers in households

with an HCV-infected person. Patients who received a blood transfusion prior to 1992, or who engage in high-risk practices, should get tested for HCV.

Treatment depends on the type and extent of the HCV infection. For example, a combination of *interferon* (such as PEG-Intron) and an antiviral drug called *ribavirin* (Rebetol) can eliminate infection in 50% to 80% of cases.

•**Human papilloma virus.** The majority of sexually active women in America will be exposed to one of the numerous strains of human papilloma virus (HPV) at some time during their lives. HPV is a sexually transmitted infection that may cause no symptoms itself but increases the risk for cervical cancer.

Fortunately, only a small percentage of women with HPV go on to develop cervical cancer. There also are relatively harmless forms of HPV, such as those that cause genital warts—these do *not* increase cancer risk.

The use of condoms as well as other safe-sex practices aren't very effective at preventing the spread of HPV. That's because condoms may not cover enough of the penis to prevent exposure. The virus also can be transmitted by hand-to-genital contact.

Self-defense: Women should get regular Pap tests to look for precancerous changes in the cervix. The American Cancer Society new recommends an HPV test in addition to a Pap smear for women ages 30 and older. The cure rate for cervical cancer is about 90% when it's detected at an early stage.

New: A new HPV vaccine, *Gardasil*, appears to be extremely effective, but is not intended to replace regular Pap smears. It was approved by the FDA in June 2006.

Processed Meats Are Linked to Pancreatic Cancer

In a new finding, people who ate large amounts of processed meats—hot dogs, bacon, sausage and luncheon meats—over a seven-year period had a 67% greater risk of pancreatic cancer than those who ate little or none. Eating large amounts of red meat increased risk by 50%.

Other pancreatic cancer risk factors: Diabetes, obesity, smoking and family history.

Ute Nothlings, DrPH, postdoctoral research fellow at the Cancer Research Center of Hawaii, University of Hawaii, Honolulu. His analysis of 190,545 men and women was presented at the American Association for Cancer Research's annual meeting.

Does Teflon Really Cause Cancer?

Ronald Melnick, PhD, senior toxicologist with National Institute of Environmental Health Sciences, a division of the National Institutes of Health, Research Triangle Park, NC. He is currently conducting experiments on chemicals related to PFOA.

Teflon has not been found to cause cancer. *Perfluorooctanoic acid* (PFOA), a chemical used in the synthesis of Teflon, has been labeled a "likely carcinogen" by a panel advising the Environmental Protection Agency. But Teflon pans do not emit PFOA when used properly.

Teflon cookware might emit a small amount of PFOA when it's heated to extreme temperatures—for example, when a Teflon frying pan has been left empty on a heated burner for an extended period. Even then, it has not been established that overheated Teflon produces a dangerous amount of PFOA. Still, it wouldn't be unreasonable to dispose of a Teflon pan that has been left empty on a heated burner.

Approximately 95% of the US population has some amount of PFOA in their bloodstream—but most of this PFOA likely comes from stain- and water-repelling treatments used on carpets and on fabrics. Grease-resistant food packaging, such as the microwave popcorn bags and cardboard fast-food boxes, also might contain small amounts of PFOA.

The fact that PFOA is in our bodies does not mean that we are all going to die from PFOA-related cancers. Individuals who have worked in factories producing PFOA, and perhaps some people who live in neighboring areas, seem to have the highest levels of PFOA.

High Blood Sugar Increases Cancer Risk

People with the highest levels of fasting glucose—blood sugar that is measured eight to 12 hours after the last meal—had higher cancer risk than people with lower fasting-glucose levels. Diabetics also had higher cancer risk.

Possible reason: Higher insulin levels may cause cancer cells to reproduce more quickly.

Self-defense: Reduce blood sugar through proper diet, exercise, weight control and, if necessary, medication.

Jonathan M. Samet, MD, professor and chair, department of epidemiology at the Bloomberg School of Public Health, Johns Hopkins University, Baltimore, and leader of a study of cancer causes and deaths, published in *The Journal of the American Medical Association*.

When a Fever Might Mean Cancer

Fever of unknown origin may signal the presence of cancer.

New finding: Patients hospitalized with fever of 101.5°F or more for which a cause never was determined were twice as likely to be diagnosed with cancer within the next year as the general population. The increased risk was high for cancers of the liver, brain, kidney, colon and/or pancreas as well as sarcoma (cancer of soft tissue).

Reason: Cancer can cause fever through inflammation and infection.

Self-defense: If you are hospitalized because of a fever of unknown origin, ask your doctor whether cancer could be a cause.

Henrik Toft Sorensen, MD, professor, department of clinical epidemiology, Aarhus University Hospital, Denmark.

Hot Cancer Treatment

Heating tumors after radiation is more effective than radiation alone. One study of patients with breast, melanoma or other cancers found that radiation plus heat destroyed tumors in 66% of patients, compared with 42% of those getting just radiation.

Science News, 1719 N St. NW, Washington, DC 20036.

 # The Facts on Sunscreen

David Herschthal, MD, dermatologist, Tamarac, FL, *www.drherschthal.com*.

Sunscreen is important for skin cancer prevention and wrinkles. *Get the facts on how to use it correctly...*

• **Use daily**—including on rainy days and in winter. Even brief exposure adds up over time.

• **UVA and UVB rays are harmful**—they cause skin cancer and premature aging. UVA tans skin. UVB burns it. Both cause wrinkles. SPF ratings do not refer to UVA rays, so be sure your sunscreen also includes UVA block, such as transparent minimum 6% zinc oxide.

• **Sunscreen with higher numbers is not much more effective.** SPF 15 blocks 93% of UVB rays...SPF 30 blocks 97%. The difference matters most to people who tan or burn easily.

• **Use adequate amounts of sunscreen.** An eight-ounce bottle of SPF 15, if applied properly, is enough for a weekend at the beach.

• **Waterproof sunscreen protects you for about 80 minutes while you are in the water.** So reapply if you are in the water longer and after you towel off.

Don't Mix Sunscreen And DEET

In a new study, combining the insect repellent DEET with certain sunscreens causes skin to absorb DEET three times faster than it would otherwise. DEET is safe and has a low risk of side effects on its own.

Edward A. Ross, MD, associate professor of medicine, University of Florida, Gainesville, and leader of a study of DEET absorption, published in *Drug Metabolism and Disposition*.

How to Use Statins Safely

Jay S. Cohen, MD, adjunct associate professor of family and preventive medicine and of psychiatry at the University of California, San Diego. He is the author of *What You Must Know About Statin Drugs & Their Natural Alternatives* (Square One). Dr. Cohen has published more than 15 journal articles on the safety of medication. His Web site is *www.medicationsense.com*.

In the fight against heart disease, statin drugs are heavy artillery. Their cholesterol-lowering power has the potential to reduce heart disease, stroke and cardiac deaths by 25%.

Yet these medications aren't for everyone. In two recent surveys, both published in *The Journal of the American Medical Association,* 60% to 75% of 100,000 people who started taking statins said they discontinued them within an average of eight months.

What goes wrong? When a patient has no insurance, cost is a factor—a month's supply of some statins exceeds $300. More often, people discontinue this medication because of side effects, which are largely avoidable—if the drugs are prescribed properly.

STATINS AND SIDE EFFECTS

To reduce cholesterol levels, statins alter liver metabolism. Cholesterol is manufactured in the liver, and statins inhibit an enzyme needed for cholesterol production. These drugs also prevent the inflammation that lodges cholesterol deposits inside arteries.

Although statins have fewer side effects than other cholesterol-lowering drugs, an estimated 15% to 30% of people taking them experience abdominal discomfort, muscle or joint pain, muscle weakness and/or memory problems.

More serious side effects occur in 1% to 2% of statin users, whose liver enzymes rise—a warning of possible liver damage when uncorrected.

Rhabdomyolysis, a breakdown of muscle tissue, is an extremely rare side effect but can be fatal. Approximately one in 2,000 long-term (more than five years) statin users develops a painful nerve condition known as peripheral neuropathy.

These adverse effects—both uncomfortable and dangerous—are dosage-related. The more powerful the statin and the greater the dosage, the greater the risk.

The side effects can be minimized, if not avoided altogether, by following a simple principle: Take the lowest effective dosage.

MORE ISN'T BETTER

Many people are now getting excessive doses of statins because of the way the FDA assesses new drugs for approval. To gain FDA approval, a drug manufacturer must show that its medication works for the majority of people who take it—so manufacturers design clinical trials with doses high enough to meet that benchmark.

But people respond very differently to medication. Women may need less of a particular drug than men, and people who weigh less often don't need as much as those who weigh more. Older people often respond to lower dosages. And some people need less—or more—just because everyone's biochemistry is different.

Result: Many people could do well on far less than the "recommended" dosage that was proven to be most effective in clinical trials.

What's more, not everyone needs the same amount of cholesterol reduction.

PRECISION PRESCRIBING

The main question in prescribing a statin is, how much cholesterol reduction do you need? Depending on your risk for heart disease, aggressive treatment with statins may—or may not—be a good idea.

To determine your optimum cholesterol level, check with your doctor. National Institutes of Health guidelines advise LDL "bad" cholesterol levels of 100 to 160, depending on cardiovascular risk factors, such as family history of heart disease, age, HDL "good" cholesterol below 40 milligrams per deciliter (mg/dl), etc.

Regardless of your LDL level, it's prudent to make lifestyle changes. A diet that is low in saturated fats (10% or less of total calories) and high in fruits and vegetables (at least nine daily servings) and whole grains often can lower cholesterol as much as a moderate statin. Regular exercise also helps. Walking 45 minutes per day reduces cardiac mortality by 50%. And if you do go on medication, a healthy diet and regular exercise will enable you to use a lower dosage.

To be sure that you are being prescribed the appropriate amount of medication, ask your doctor what percentage of LDL cholesterol reduction you need. Then look at the statin doses chart in my book with your doctor to determine what statin dosage is best for you.

Example: Your LDL cholesterol is 165, and your target is 130 (a 21% reduction). A daily 10-mg dose of *lovastatin* (Mevacor) or *pravastatin* (Pravachol) is a good place to start.

After one month, have your cholesterol tested again. If it hasn't dropped enough, you may need to increase the statin dosage. Or, if it has decreased to desired levels, particularly if you also have made dietary changes, you may be able to decrease your dosage.

This approach can identify your lowest effective dosage and minimize side effects.

WHICH STATIN?

All statins work the same way, so the key difference among them is potency. LDL reductions of 50% to 60% are possible if using *atorvastatin* (Lipitor) and *simvastatin* (Zocor), compared with an average of about 40% with older statins, such as lovastatin, pravastatin and *fluvastatin* (Lescol). The newest, strongest statin, *Rosuvastatin* (Crestor) is also the riskiest. There have been reports of rhabdomyolysis, kidney damage and kidney failure in some patients taking this drug. I recommend it only if no other drug lowers cholesterol adequately.

If you do need a significant reduction in cholesterol, particularly if you currently have heart disease or risk factors, one of the high-potency statins makes sense.

For a more modest reduction, you may well consider an older, less powerful drug. Lovastatin is a particularly attractive choice if cost is a factor—it is the only statin that's available in generic form and costs up to four times less than the other statins.

Statin Helper

Boost the effect of cholesterol-lowering statins by adding a B vitamin.

New finding: Taking 1 g of Niaspan ER, a prescription formulation of the B vitamin niacin, boosted HDL "good" cholesterol levels by 21% in patients taking a statin. This is the first study to show that the combination therapy can have benefits over taking a statin alone.

Self-defense: If your HDL level is lower than 40 mg/dl (for men) or 50 mg/dl (for women), ask your doctor about prescription niacin.

Allen J. Taylor, MD, director, cardiovascular research, Walter Reed Army Medical Center, Washington, DC.

If You Take a Blood Thinner...

Anticoagulants, including *warfarin* (Coumadin), aspirin, *clopidogrel* (Plavix) and *dipyridamole* (Persantine), all prevent blood clots by thinning the blood. Taking one of these drugs with a supplement that also affects clotting may lead to bleeding in the brain or gastrointestinal tract. Provide your doctor with a list of all the over-the-counter supplements and prescription medications that you are taking, and discuss this with him/her. A number of supplements do have blood-thinning effects.

Ahmed Hasan, MD, program administrator, Thrombosis and Hemostatis Scientific Research Group at the National Heart, Lung and Blood Institute, Bethesda, MD.

Best Time to Take Your Aspirin

Heart attack prevention may be enhanced by taking low-dose aspirin in the late evening. Heart attacks occur most often in the early morning, when platelet activity (tendency for clotting) increases because of the body's natural circadian (24-hour) rhythm. If your doctor has prescribed aspirin therapy, taking it around 10 pm provides peak anticlotting action by early morning.

Jack M. Rosenberg, PharmD, PhD, director of the International Drug Information Center at the Arnold and Marie Schwartz College of Pharmacy Health Sciences at Long Island University, Brooklyn, NY.

Best Way to Lower Blood Pressure

To lower blood pressure, a combination of drugs is best for most people. Studies have tried to show that one or another class of drugs is better, but the best combination varies from patient to patient. Lowering blood pressure is important. Studies have shown that "borderline" levels (120 to 140 over 80 or 90) are associated with higher risk of heart attack and stroke.

Steven E. Nissen, MD, cardiologist, The Cleveland Clinic Foundation.

Blood-Pressure Medication Warning

Women on certain blood-pressure medications are at increased risk of dying from heart disease. When used together with diuretics in women with hypertension but no history of heart disease, calcium channel blockers—a class of drugs that includes *diltiazem* (Cardizem) and *amlodipine* (Norvasc)—increased risk more than a beta-blocker or ACE inhibitor taken with a diuretic. Calcium channel blockers used alone also increased risk of dying from heart disease, compared with diuretics used alone.

Self-defense: Consult your physician. Don't stop taking any blood pressure medication on your own.

Sylvia Wassertheil-Smoller, PhD, professor and head of epidemiology, Albert Einstein College of Medicine, Bronx, NY, and leader of a study of 30,219 women, published in *The Journal of the American Medical Association.*

Painkillers Linked to High Blood Pressure

In a three-year study, women ages 34 to 77 who took an average daily dose of 500 mg of *acetaminophen* (Tylenol) were twice as likely to develop hypertension as those who did not take the drug. Risk increased by 60% to 80% for those who took more than 400 mg per day of nonsteroidal anti-inflammatory drugs (NSAIDs), such as *ibuprofen* (Advil) or *naproxen* (Aleve).

Theory: These drugs increase blood pressure by interfering with the blood vessels' ability to relax.

Aspirin, however, was not found to elevate blood pressure.

John Phillip Forman, MD, instructor of medicine, Harvard Medical School, Boston.

A Special Breathing Device to Lower High Blood Pressure

William Elliott, MD, PhD, professor of preventive medicine, internal medicine and pharmacology, Rush University Medical College in Chicago. His Resperate study was published in *The Journal of Clinical Hypertension*.

The FDA-approved *Resperate* device takes people through deep-breathing exercises. As breathing slows, muscles surrounding the small blood vessels relax, so that the blood flows more freely and blood pressure drops.

The device includes a sensor belt to monitor breathing, a handheld computer and headphones. Musical tones delivered through these headphones indicate when to inhale and to exhale. Resperate should be used for 15 minutes at least three times a week.

Results after eight weeks: The people who used the device for an average of 23 minutes per week saw a 15-point decrease in blood pressure. The effect was greater in elderly patients and people with extreme hypertension. Most people who used the device also took blood pressure medication.

Cost: $299,* may be covered by insurance.

Information: 877-988-9388, *www.resperate. com*.

*Price subject to change.

Predict Heart Disease With a Simple Blood Test

In a study of more than 72,000 women without infection, those with the highest levels of white blood cells (WBCs)—from 6,700 to 15,000—were twice as likely to die from heart disease as women with the lowest levels. Researchers believe this link also applies to men.

Theory: WBC levels, which typically rise in response to infection, also can be a marker for inflammation, which weakens blood vessels and may trigger blockages leading to heart attack or stroke.

Self-defense: Request a WBC count with your next blood test. A level above 6,700 may indicate increased heart disease risk.

Karen L. Margolis, MD, associate professor of medicine, University of Minnesota, Minneapolis.

Heart Attack Symptoms and Women

Women may experience heart attack warning symptoms more than a month before the attack. The most common symptom is overwhelming fatigue, reported by 71% of women. Other reported symptoms are sleep disturbance (48%), shortness of breath (42%), indigestion (39%) and anxiety (35%). Only 30% experience chest discomfort.

Self-defense: If you are experiencing these or any suspicious symptoms, contact your doctor.

Jean McSweeney, PhD, RN, professor at the University of Arkansas for Medical Sciences, Little Rock, and lead researcher of a survey of 515 female heart attack survivors, published in *Circulation*.

Common Bacteria Causes Heart Attacks

Chlamydia pneumoniae brings on a flu-like upper-respiratory infection that can develop into pneumonia. People who are infected with it produce antibodies called IgA and IgG.

New finding: Men ages 30 to 50 with high levels of IgA antibody to chlamydia pneumoniae are more likely to have serious heart attacks. The more recent the bacterial infection, the more likely a heart attack.

Christine M. Arcari, PhD, assistant professor of population health sciences, University of Wisconsin Medical School, Madison, and leader of a study of 300 male soldiers, ages 30 to 50, who had heart attacks, published in *Clinical Infectious Diseases.*

CPR Training at Home

Up to 80% of heart attacks occur at home, with a survival rate of only 5%. Cardiopulmonary resuscitation (CPR) saves lives, but most people do not know how to do it. The American Heart Association provides a complete training kit—a mannequin, a 22-minute DVD and a booklet—for $29.95.* To order, 877-242-4277 or *www.cpranytime.org.*

American Heart Association, 7272 Greenville Ave., Dallas, TX 75231, *www.americanheart.org.*

*Price subject to change.

How to Survive a Heart Attack

Richard Stein, MD, director of preventive cardiology at Beth Israel Medical Center, New York City, and author of *Outliving Heart Disease* (Newmarket).

Choosing the right hospital to go to in the event of a heart attack can be the key to surviving a heart attack.

To find the best hospital in your area, check out the Hospital Compare heart attack statistics at *www.hospitalcompare.hhs.gov.* Do it now *before* an emergency. Call the hospital cardiology departments to determine which perform emergency angioplasty to open up blocked arteries and if it is done less than 90 minutes after arrival at the hospital. (Medication can be used instead, but angioplasty generally is more effective if done soon after arrival.) If possible, choose a hospital where your doctor has admitting privileges.

HEART ATTACK SURVIVAL CHECKLIST

•**Know the symptoms.** The classic heart attack symptoms are chest pain or discomfort that may also be felt in the neck or left arm and may be accompanied by nausea. Women are more likely than men to have atypical symptoms—shortness of breath, profound fatigue, sweating, racing heart, burning stomach.

•**Call 911 for an ambulance** to take you to the hospital immediately if you experience symptoms. Don't let embarrassment or concern that it is something minor prevent you from getting checked.

•**Chew two full-strength aspirin.**

•**Tell ambulance and hospital staff that you think you're having a heart attack.** Do not minimize your symptoms.

•**Have the appropriate tests,** including an electrocardiogram (EKG) and blood testing to measure certain cardiac enzymes. Women with the atypical symptoms cited above may need to be assertive to get these tests.

Accurate diagnosis may require several EKGs and/or blood tests within the first few hours. In 2000, Vice President Dick Cheney experienced chest and shoulder pain. The initial EKG and blood tests showed no evidence of a heart attack. Several hours later, the second set of tests revealed that he had indeed suffered a minor heart attack.

•**Get the proper treatment.** *Treatment should begin even before all test results are in...*

•Aspirin right away if you did not take it at home.

•One of the beta-blockers, such as *metoprolol* (Lopressor) or *propranolol* (Inderal), should be given to most patients to decrease the heart's need for oxygen-rich blood and minimize damage to the heart.

•Nitroglycerin, prescribed for chest pain or if the heart is short of blood, dilates blood vessels.

•ACE inhibitor to decrease blood pressure and the heart's workload.

•Clot-busting therapies, such as the drug tPA, and/or angioplasty.

Save this article so that you can take it with you to the ER.

Lifesaving Heart Therapy

A new study reports that more than one-third of heart attack patients whose hearts had completely stopped survived when their bodies were quickly cooled to 93.2°F, and they were then revived with a heart-lung bypass machine.

Nihon University School of Medicine, Tokyo.

Good News for Heart Patients

People recovering from minor heart attacks do just as well with drugs as with invasive procedures. Many minor heart attacks are treated with bypass surgery or angioplasty—a surgical procedure in which a small balloon is used to clear blockages.

New study: Patients who were given clot-reducing medicine after their heart attacks and underwent surgery only if symptoms persisted fared just as well as patients who were treated more aggressively.

Robbert J. de Winter, MD, PhD, director of the cardiac catheterization laboratory, Academic Medical Center, Amsterdam, The Netherlands. His study of 1,200 heart attack patients was published in *The New England Journal of Medicine*.

Better Bypass Surgery

Heart patients are usually told to stop taking aspirin, which has a blood-thinning effect, seven to 10 days before bypass surgery to reduce risk for excess bleeding.

New finding: Patients who continued aspirin therapy up to the time of surgery had less lung damage from the heart–lung machine (which performs the functions of the heart and lungs during surgery). Patients also were able to come off the machine six hours sooner.

Theory: Aspirin decreases *thromboxane* (a substance that constricts blood vessels and is released abundantly during heart surgery).

If you are scheduled for bypass surgery using a heart-lung machine: Ask your doctor about continuing aspirin therapy.

Important: Discontinuing aspirin treatment before eye surgery and many other surgeries is still recommended.

Rabin Gerrah, MD, cardiothoracic surgeon, Massachusetts General Hospital, Boston.

Pacemaker Alert

Pacemakers can harm as well as help. They can put extra stress on the heart.

Recent study: There were 53% more deaths attributed to heart failure among people with pacemakers than among those without.

Self-defense: Have your pacemaker checked every few months—its timing may need to be adjusted or a different type implanted.

Also: Contact your cardiologist if you develop heart failure symptoms, such as fatigue or shortness of breath.

Ronald Freudenberger, MD, an associate professor of medicine and director of heart failure and transplant cardiology, Robert Wood Johnson Medical School, University of Medicine & Dentistry of New Jersey in New Brunswick. His study of more than 22,000 men and women was published in *The American Journal of Cardiology*.

High Salt Intake Increases Stroke Risk

In a new finding, people who consumed 4,000 mg or more of sodium every day were 84% more likely to suffer a stroke than those who got 2,400 mg or less. This link existed independent of blood pressure levels, age, diabetes, ethnicity and smoking history.

Theory: Sodium adversely affects blood vessels, which can lead to stroke.

Self-defense: Restrict daily sodium intake to 2,400 mg (one teaspoon of salt). Because most dietary sodium comes from prepared foods, opt for lower sodium products.

Armistead D. Williams, MD, postdoctoral fellow, Neurological Institute, Columbia University Medical Center in New York City.

Better Treatment for Stroke Victims

S troke patients often don't get the appropriate treatment quickly enough. Those treated with tissue plasminogen activator (tPA)—which will dissolve stroke-causing clots—within three hours of the onset of symptoms are three times as likely to have a good outcome as those who are not given tPA. Yet only about 3% of stroke patients receive this treatment.

Reasons: Victims and bystanders might not call for help immediately because they don't recognize the stroke symptoms. Hospital phone operators may not recognize stroke symptoms and so discourage callers from coming in for help. Ambulances take people to the nearest hospital instead of one equipped for tPA treatment.

Larry B. Goldstein, MD, professor of neurology, Duke University Medical Center, Durham, NC.

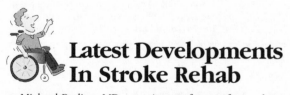 ## Latest Developments In Stroke Rehab

Michael Reding, MD, associate professor of neurology at Weill Medical College of Cornell University, New York City. He is chief of Cerebral Vascular Disease Service at The Burke Rehabilitation Hospital, one of the premier rehabilitation centers in the country, White Plains, NY.

M ost stroke patients require rehabilitation to recover their physical skills and to regain the ability to live independently.

Recent developments in stroke rehabilitation are helping patients recover better and faster, perhaps even several years after the stroke.

The following six treatments are the latest approaches to stroke recovery. Check the stroke centers in your area for what is available.

ARMS AND LEGS

Stroke patients often require physical therapy for arm or leg weakness or immobility. Repetitive physical movements prevent muscle atrophy and enhance brain cells in the area surrounding the stroke damage. *Breakthrough therapies…*

•**Robotic therapy.** MIT researchers have developed the tabletop robot MIT-Manus, which significantly improves arm mobility—and may even be more effective than conventional physical therapy.

How it works: First, a patient puts his/her lower arm and wrist into a brace attached to the robot. A video screen prompts the patient to perform arm exercises, such as connecting dots on the screen. The robot monitors movement and increases or decreases resistance as required—and even moves the arm if the patient is not able to do so. The robot can move the arm thousands of times in a single session and detects (and responds to) movements and muscle tension that are too subtle for the patient to notice.

Patients who use robotic therapy have muscle strength scores that are about twice as high as those undergoing traditional physical therapy.

Most patients enjoy the interactive nature of this "video game" therapy. It offers immediate feedback and boosts their motivation to keep trying. Between 18 and 36 sessions are needed.

•**Bilateral arm training with rhythmic auditory cueing (BATRAC).** When patients move both the damaged arm and the healthy arm together (bilateral movement), the healthy side of the brain promotes better functioning in the side damaged by stroke.

How it works: The patient works with an occupational therapist for about an hour several days per week. He performs movements to the beat of a metronome or another auditory device. He moves both arms simultaneously—for example, moving arms away from the body, then moving them back in. Early studies indicate that patients treated with BATRAC have greater improvements in upper-extremity motor function than those treated with conventional therapy.

•Constraint-induced movement therapy. When a victim of stroke has trouble moving a limb, damage to the brain's sensory cortex may cause him to lose awareness of that hand, arm or leg—and he stops moving it entirely.

How it works: In constraint-induced therapy, placing the healthy limb in a sling forces the patient to use the disabled limb and thereby regain movement control. This approach requires the patient to practice for up to six hours a day for several weeks. He might be asked to pick up a block of wood, sweep floors, throw balls or draw pictures repeatedly.

The therapy is performed in a clinic setting, often in groups to encourage participation and enhance motivation. Studies show that this approach results in improvements in motor function and muscle strength.

WALKING

Patients in conventional rehabilitation programs will typically use canes or leg braces for support. For safety reasons, they walk slowly, and they may not reach their optimal level of recovery.

•Body weight support. With body weight support, patients can more than double their speed. Faster walking hastens recovery and prepares patients for the types of movements they will need in daily life, such as quickly crossing a street.

How it works: The patient is suspended in a harness attached to a weight-support system. The harness prevents the patient from falling, so he can increase the speed of the treadmill and push himself harder. The harness adjusts to support more or less of the patient's body weight, depending on his progress.

SWALLOWING

Many patients experience difficulty swallowing (dysphagia). Traditionally, speech therapists teach patients how to initiate normal swallowing movements.

•VitalStim therapy. Electricity applied to the neck stimulates the muscles involved in swallowing to activate at the appropriate times. This approach is effective in as little as one week.

How it works: Electrodes are placed on the neck. Electrical currents stimulate muscles in the throat to contract. The treatment, lasting 20 to 30 minutes, may be repeated 10 or more times over a week. It retrains the brain to stimulate involuntary swallowing movements.

Drawbacks: This does not work for all patients. Many do require speech therapy sessions. Also, the treatment may be uncomfortable—it causes a feeling of tightness around the neck, as though one is being grabbed by the throat.

VISION

•Visual retraining. Stroke victims who suffer vision damage can gain significant improvement from a technique called visual retraining, or vision restoration therapy.

How it works: The patient fixes his eyes on a spot on a monitor, then clicks a button when he becomes aware that another dot has appeared in the periphery. This stimulates neurons in the visual center of the brain. Sessions usually are 30 minutes, twice daily, for six months.

One study presented at the American Stroke Association International Conference in 2005 reported that patients were able to detect 62% of the peripheral dots after six months, compared with 54% when they began. Follow-up studies show that 70% of patients maintain the improvement more than a year later.

BEWARE OF DEPRESSION

Depression is common in stroke patients in the first year. One study found that patients who suffer poststroke depression are 3.5 times more likely to die within 10 years than those who are not depressed.

Stroke patients should be evaluated for depression and, if diagnosed, given the appropriate treatment—therapy and/or antidepressants. Treatment can greatly improve patients' motivation and increase their rate of recovery.

The Diabetes Epidemic: You May Already Have It—and Not Even Know

Anne Peters, MD, professor of clinical medicine, Keck School of Medicine of the University of Southern California in Los Angeles, and director of the USC Westside Center for Diabetes, Beverly Hills. She is author of *Conquering Diabetes—A Cutting-Edge, Comprehensive Program for Prevention and Treatment* (Hudson Street).

The US is now in the midst of a diabetes epidemic. Twenty million Americans currently have type 2 (adult-onset) diabetes, putting them at risk for such serious complications as blindness, kidney failure, heart disease, nerve damage and circulatory failure leading to amputation.

Another 41 million have prediabetes, which can turn into full-blown diabetes. The problem is that people with high blood sugar levels often don't feel any different—which is why one out of three Americans with diabetes don't even know they have the disease.

Primary reason for this epidemic: More Americans are now overweight and physically inactive, both of which make the body less responsive to insulin, the chemical that transports sugar from the bloodstream into the body's various cells. This condition, known as insulin resistance, forces the body to produce more and more insulin in an effort to keep blood sugar within normal limits. Among those with genetic vulnerability (including many people who aren't overweight), this eventually causes the insulin-producing cells of the pancreas to "burn out," leaving the body unable to produce enough insulin to control blood sugar.

The result: Soaring blood sugar levels.

The good news: Complications can be avoided by catching insulin resistance early and then taking basic steps to bring your blood sugar levels within normal limits.

GET A FASTING BLOOD SUGAR TEST

The best way to learn whether you have insulin resistance is a fasting blood sugar test—a simple blood draw, taken 10 to 12 hours after you've last eaten. It should be included in your annual physical. If you have not had a fasting blood sugar test within the past year, call your primary care physician and schedule one—*especially* if you have a family history of diabetes.

A fasting blood sugar level of 126 milligrams per deciliter (mg/dl) or higher indicates diabetes, while a result between 100 and 125 mg/dl indicates prediabetes.

I always recommend a second test to confirm a high reading. If your test result is below 100, your blood sugar is within normal range, but you still may have early-stage insulin resistance—particularly if you are overweight or have close relatives with diabetes. If you and your doctor suspect this may be the case, you should follow the steps outlined below.

TEST FOR CARDIOVASCULAR RISK FACTORS

Since insulin resistance is associated with significantly increased risk for heart disease, it is important that your doctor order a cholesterol (lipid) panel and check both your blood pressure and body mass index (BMI). BMI is a measurement that indicates how your weight/height ratio stacks up against the general population.

Triglyceride (one type of blood lipid) levels above 150 mg/dl and HDL (good) cholesterol levels below 50 (for women) or 40 (men), blood pressure of more than 120/80 and a BMI over 25 are all signs that you may be at risk for both heart disease and prediabetes/diabetes.

DEVELOP A TREATMENT PLAN WITH YOUR DOCTOR

Some doctors still believe that there's nothing to worry about as long as your blood sugar is less than 126. However, if one of my patients has a fasting blood sugar above 100 (or less than 100, but with other risk factors for insulin resistance or a family history of diabetes), I generally treat that patient as if he/she already has diabetes.

Reason: The damage from insulin resistance begins long before blood sugar reaches "diabetic" levels.

This is why I urge everybody to ask their doctors for copies of their blood test results, rather than take a doctor's word that everything is OK. If your blood sugar is above 100, you need to discuss setting up a treatment plan with your doctor, or find another doctor if yours is not being responsive.

This plan should include five elements…

•Lose weight and exercise.

•Decrease cardiac risk associated with diabetes. This includes taking a baby aspirin daily to reduce risk of heart attack and stroke, and, if your test results warrant, a statin drug to lower high cholesterol (Lipitor, Zocor, Crestor), fibric acid derivatives (Lopid, Tricor) to lower triglycerides and ACE inhibitors (Lotensin, Vasotec, Zestril, Altace) or the angiotensin receptor blockers (Avapro, Cozaar, Hyzaar, Diovan) to treat high blood pressure.

•Test blood sugar regularly. If your fasting blood sugar test is above 100, I recommend getting another fasting blood sugar test every three months. If your blood sugar test is above 125, you'll need to test more often. My diabetic patients do home blood tests every day, including first thing in the morning and two hours after each meal, and also get an A1C blood test every three months. This test shows what your average blood sugar level was for the previous several months. The goal is to keep your A1C below 7, and preferably between 4 and 6.

•Consider a diabetes medication. If your blood sugar levels continue to be high despite weight loss and exercise, you and your doctor might consider a *glitazone* medication, either *pioglitazone* (Actos) or *rosiglitazone* (Avandia), to increase your body's sensitivity to insulin.

Your doctor may also prescribe *metformin* (which will reduce the liver's glucose production and can be used with glitazones) and/or alpha-glucosidase inhibitors, such as *acarbose* (Precose) or *miglitol* (Glyset), which can decrease the amount of carbohydrates absorbed by the intestines. (Unfortunately, they also tend to produce large amounts of intestinal gas.) Also, the new injected drug *exenatide* (Byetta) can help lower blood sugar level and decrease weight at the same time.

If all else fails, your doctor can prescribe daily insulin doses to supplement your body's natural insulin production.

•Test for complications of insulin resistance. Since cell damage from diabetes begins early, I also recommend regular tests for complications, even if your blood sugar is only slightly elevated.

Reason: Diabetes-related complications may be treatable early on, but once the damage becomes serious, treatment becomes difficult or impossible.

Tests include: An annual dilated eye exam by an ophthalmologist…a yearly urine test for microalbuminuria (an early sign of kidney damage)…yearly cholesterol and triglyceride tests… a check for normal foot sensation at every doctor's visit, and if any numbness is detected, twice daily home foot exams for cuts or sores that you can't feel.

Moderate Drinking May Cut Diabetes Risk

In a recent finding, people who consume one or two standard alcoholic drinks per day are about 30% less likely to develop type 2 diabetes than people who did not drink at all. The risk reduction was the same whether a person has one or two drinks.

Caution: Drinking more than three alcoholic beverages a day raises diabetes risk. Ask your doctor if daily alcohol is right for you.

Lando L.J. Koppes, PhD, a researcher at VU University Medical Center, EMG Institute in Amsterdam, the Netherlands, and leader of a meta-study analyzing data from 15 studies involving alcohol use and diabetes risk in nearly 370,000 people, published in *Diabetes Care*.

Stop Alzheimer's Before It's Too Late

Zaldy S. Tan, MD, MPH, director of the Memory Disorders Clinic at Beth Israel Deaconess Medical Center and instructor in medicine at Harvard Medical School, both in Boston. He is the author of *Age-Proof Your Mind: Detect, Delay and Prevent Memory Loss—Before It's Too Late* (Warner).

Alzheimer's disease, the dread destroyer of memory, doesn't happen all at once. Like heart disease and many other serious ailments, it's years in the making.

Only recently have medical researchers nailed down the early warning signs for Alzheimer's. People who exhibit a condition known as mild cognitive impairment (MCI), which marks the transitional stage between normal aging and dementia, are highly likely to develop Alzheimer's. According to a Mayo Clinic study, 15% of people with MCI have Alzheimer's one year later, compared with 1% to 2% of those without MCI. Within four years, 50% of people with MCI will have Alzheimer's…after five years or longer, it's 80% to 90%.

Can this downward spiral be stopped? As yet, the jury still is out, but there is good reason to be hopeful. After all, 10% to 20% of people who have MCI do *not* fall victim to Alzheimer's. What protects them?

A growing body of scientific evidence suggests that remaining mentally active, exercising regularly and eating well can help to preserve memory—and slow down or perhaps even halt the progression of MCI.

NORMAL AGING OR MCI?

People with MCI have the same kind of lapses in short-term memory—forgetting facts, names, appointments, etc.—that most of us experience as we progress through our 50s, 60s and beyond…but many more such instances.

They still remember how to perform everyday activities, such as driving, reading, typing and cooking. In addition, their ability to reason, solve math problems and control emotions is left intact.

A key criterion for identifying MCI is "subjective" memory loss—that is, the person notices the lapses and thinks that they are troublesome and too frequent. Still, people differ widely in their sensitivity to their own memory performance. Often, friends and family become aware of memory problems before the person experiencing them does. Perhaps the most reliable indicator is performance on memory tests administered by a psychologist, psychiatrist, geriatrician or neurologist.

Should you be tested? Try this—ask someone to read aloud a list of four unrelated words, pausing one second between each. For example, flower, truck, valor, dentist. After memorizing the list, perform an unrelated task. Five minutes later, say the words to your companion. If you missed some, have him/her read them to you again. Five minutes later, repeat the words out loud again and note your score. Do the same 20 minutes after that. Most people will remember all or three of the words. There's no "passing grade" on this test. But, take the test again four to six months later. If your ability to perform the test declines—particularly if you're aware of memory problems in the meantime—seek an evaluation.

BRAIN TO SPARE

MCI progresses to Alzheimer's when enough brain cells are affected to seriously compromise the brain's ability to function. The more densely interconnected your brain cells are, the greater your "brain reserve." This allows your brain to keep on working well even if some cells have been affected.

Researchers now know that new *synapses*—connections between brain cells—can be formed throughout life. Mental activity builds synapses the same way physical activity builds muscle. If you are concerned about your memory, it's critical to challenge your mind.

Self-defense: Spend at least one hour daily performing a rigorous mental activity. Read books on subjects that demand concentration… do crossword puzzles at a level you find difficult…take an adult education course in a new discipline…work conscientiously to master a foreign language.

YOU CAN HALT MENTAL DECLINE

Mental activity is only part of the story. The same lifestyle and diet changes that are recommended to reduce the risk for heart attack, cancer and other serious diseases maximize brain reserve as well by maintaining brain cells and stimulating connections between them.

•**Exercise.** Physical activity keeps brain cells well nourished and supplied with the oxygen they require to survive. A six-year study of 345 Californians age 55 or older found significantly less mental decline among those who were more physically fit than the others.

Self-defense: Any regular exercise you enjoy, even 30 minutes of brisk walking daily, will help.

Ideal: Physical activities that also challenge your mind, such as ballroom dancing or learning a new sport.

•**Limit calories.** One source of free radicals (high-energy oxygen molecules that are known to damage cells in the brain) is the conversion of food to energy. The more you eat, the more toxic molecules are created. Human population studies have linked calorie restriction to slower aging. In one study conducted at Columbia University, those who ate the fewest calories had the lowest risk of developing Alzheimer's.

Self-defense: If you're moderately active, aim for 1,800 to 2,200 calories per day.

•**Get your fruits and vegetables.** Foods rich in antioxidant vitamins and similar plant-based chemicals appear to protect brain cells against harmful free radicals.

In one Dutch study, people who consumed more than 23 international units (IU) per day of vitamin E had a 43% reduction in Alzheimer's risk. Similar protection was found in those who consumed 133 milligrams (mg) or more daily of vitamin C.

Self-defense: Include in your daily diet foods rich in antioxidants, such as spinach (one cup provides 10 IU of vitamin E)…or frozen peaches (one cup contains 235 mg of vitamin C). There is less evidence that antioxidants in supplement form are protective.

•**Eat fish.** Like the heart, the brain benefits from the omega-3 fatty acids found in fish. In a Rush University study of more than 800 older adults, the Alzheimer's risk in those who ate fish at least once weekly was 60% lower than in those who did not.

Self-defense: Eat cold-water fish that is high in omega-3 fatty acids—halibut, mackerel or salmon, for example—at least once weekly.

PROTECTIVE MEDICATION?

Research now suggests that inflammation—the same process that triggers many diseases, such as rheumatoid arthritis—can destroy brain cells. Inflammation-fighting drugs may protect against Alzheimer's disease.

Studies from Mayo Clinic have found a significantly lower incidence of Alzheimer's among those who took nonsteroidal anti-inflammatory drugs (NSAIDs), such as *ibuprofen* (Advil), regularly for at least two years. Other studies suggest that people who take cholesterol-lowering statin drugs are also less likely to develop Alzheimer's disease.

The evidence is still too weak to justify regular use of NSAIDs or statins for everyone. These drugs have risks—NSAIDs can cause gastrointestinal bleeding and statins can cause side effects, such as muscle pain and liver problems. If you have MCI, however, the drugs' potential benefits may outweigh the risks. Talk to your doctor.

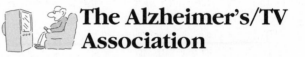

The Alzheimer's/TV Association

Risk of Alzheimer's disease increases by 30% for each hour of daily TV viewing. Watching TV doesn't cause Alzheimer's, but it is a marker of an inactive lifestyle, which can contribute to the disease. Both mental and physical activities enhance brain health and help to prevent diseases associated with aging.

Robert Friedland, MD, professor of neurology at Case Western Reserve University in Cleveland, and leader of a study of activity level and Alzheimer's incidence in 551 people, presented at the International Conference on Alzheimer's Disease and Related Disorders.

New Hope for Alzheimer's Disease

Alzheimer's may be slowed with cholesterol-lowering drugs. In one three-year study of 300 Alzheimer's patients, the disease progressed more gradually (loss of 1.5 points in a 30-point mini mental status exam, or MMSE) in people who took a cholesterol-lowering drug than it did in those not taking the medication (loss of 2.5 points in MMSE).

Theory: High cholesterol levels increase the deposition of proteins which can impair brain function.

Florence Pasquier, MD, PhD, professor of neurology, University Hospital, Lille, France.

New Ways to Deal with Knee Injuries

Knee injuries can be diagnosed with powerful MRI scans, eliminating the need for exploratory surgery.

Recent study: The 3-Tesla MRI machine detected all knee injuries that were found through conventional scans and exploratory surgery combined. This may help identify patients who can recover with rehabilitation alone.

Talk to your doctor about availability of the 3-Tesla MRI in your area.

Thomas Magee, MD, director, department of radiology, Neuroskeletal Imaging, Merritt Island, FL, and leader of a study of 130 knee surgery patients, presented at a recent meeting of the American Roentgen Ray Society.

Chronic Pain Can Shrink the Brain

In a new study, MRIs on 26 people who had suffered lower back pain for at least one year showed a loss of brain tissue in several areas involved in pain perception. Those who experienced pain the longest lost the most brain tissue. This atrophy may contribute to impaired cognition. The damage may be reversible, so it is important to decrease pain intensity as much as possible through drug therapy, surgery, etc.

A. Vania Apkarian, PhD, associate professor of physiology, Northwestern University Medical School, Chicago, and leader of the study, published in *Journal of Neuroscience.*

Better Pain Relief For Arthritis

In one new study, osteoarthritis patients who applied 40 drops of a topical version of the nonsteroidal anti-inflammatory drug (NSAID) *diclofenac* (Pennsaid) to their affected knees four times daily for 12 weeks experienced a 45.7% reduction in pain.

Bonus: Topical diclofenac appears to be as effective at relieving pain as the oral form of the drug, with minimal risk of side effects.

Topical diclofenac has not yet been approved by the FDA. It is already available in Europe and Canada. You'll need a prescription, but you can buy the topical drug at *www.canadapharmacy. com,* 800-891-0844 or *www.canadadrugs.com,* 800-226-3784.

J. Zev Shainhouse, MD, attending physician, internal medicine/infectious diseases at The Scarborough Hospital, Toronto.

Fibromyalgia Help

Fibromyalgia may improve with the Parkinson's drug *pramipexole* (Mirapex).

New finding: Patients who have fibromyalgia, a condition resulting in muscle pain, stiffness and fatigue, who took pramipexole for 14 weeks indicated an average of 36% less pain, compared with a 9% pain reduction in patients who were in a placebo group.

Theory: Pramipexole decreases the brainstem arousal that fragments sleep and contributes to fatigue and pain.

Although the side effects such as upset stomach and weight loss were common, the recent pramipexole clinical trial showed that it was the single most effective prescription medication tested for fibromyalgia pain so far.

If you have fibromyalgia: Ask your doctor about trying pramipexole.

Andrew J. Holman, MD, rheumatologist, Pacific Rheumatology Associates, Seattle.

New Treatment for Gout

In the past 35 years, no new treatments have been introduced to relieve gout (an inflammatory joint disease resulting from excess levels of urates, deposits of uric acid salts).

New finding: After treatment with *febuxostat,* a new gout drug awaiting FDA approval, 81% of patients had healthy urate levels of less than 6 mg/dl, compared with only 39% who took 300 mg per day of *allopurinol,* the drug most often prescribed for gout.

Michael A. Becker, MD, professor of medicine in the rheumatology section at the University of Chicago Medical Center.

Caffeine Warning

Caffeine may increase risk for developing kidney stones.

New finding: After drinking the amount of caffeine found in two cups of coffee, men and women with a history of kidney stones excreted more calcium in their urine than those without a history of the condition. Increased calcium in the urine along with low fluid intake promote the formation of some types of kidney stones.

If you are at risk for kidney stones: Limit caffeinated beverages to less than two eight-ounce cups daily and drink eight glasses of fluids per day to keep urine diluted.

Linda K. Massey, PhD, RD, professor of human nutrition, Washington State University, Spokane.

Foods and Beverages Do Not Cause Ulcers

A recent analysis of diet and ulcer research found no link between spicy foods, alcohol or caffeine and the development of ulcers. Stomach ulcers are typically caused by overuse of nonsteroidal anti-inflammatory drugs (NSAIDs), such as *ibuprofen* (Advil)…or by the bacterium *Heliocobacter pylori,* which may enter the blood via food and water. Most H. pylori–related ulcers (detected by an antibody test, breath analysis or endoscopy) are treated with antibiotics.

Helpful: A high-fiber diet (at least 25 g daily) could reduce ulcer risk.

Milly Ryan-Harshman, PhD, RD, nutrition consultant at FEAST Enterprises, Oshawa, Ontario, Canada.

Heartburn Drug Danger

Medications for heartburn and reflux disease such as *esomeprazole* (Nexium), *lansoprazole* (Prevacid), *cimetidine* (Tagamet) and *ranitidine* (Zantac) suppress the stomach acid that fights bacteria.

Side effect: A two- to threefold increase in risk of a *Clostridium difficile* bacterial infection, which can cause diarrhea, colitis and other intestinal problems.

Self-defense: If you use a heartburn or reflux medication, be meticulous about washing your hands, which will kill *C. difficile* bacteria.

Consult your physician if you have frequent diarrhea containing mucus or blood. *C. difficile* infections are treated with antibiotics.

Sandra Dial, MD, director of respiratory medicine, McGill University, Montreal, Quebec, and leader of a study, published in *Journal of the American Medical Association.*

Medical Breakthroughs For Aging Eyes

Neil F. Martin, MD, FACS, an ophthalmologist in private practice in Chevy Chase, MD, *www.washingtoneye. com,* and a clinical correspondent for the American Academy of Ophthalmology.

As we get older, our vision can be affected by a number of conditions, including cataracts, glaucoma, macular degeneration and diabetes-related eye damage as well as presbyopia (age-related farsightedness) and insufficient tear production (dry eyes). Catching and treating these problems early is the key to preventing long-term vision loss.

NEW EYE TREATMENTS

A number of new drugs and lens technologies are making it much easier to treat a variety of age-related eye ailments. *The following treatments have become available just within the last several years…*

•Restasis eyedrops for dry eyes. The drug *cyclosporine A* (Restasis), used to prevent rejection in heart and kidney transplants, also relieves tear-deficiency syndrome (dry eyes) when used as eyedrops by decreasing inflammation in the tear glands. The drops are applied twice a day to increase tear production. Some people may experience slight stinging at first. Anyone with an active eye infection (such as conjunctivitis) shouldn't use the drops.

•Improved glaucoma treatments. A new eyedrop medication, *latanoprost* (Xalatan), reduces fluid buildup better than older eyedrops. (Glaucoma eyedrop treatments work by enhancing the eye's natural filtering process.) While very safe, latanoprost can cause occasional redness, tends to make eyelashes grow longer and may turn light-colored irises brown over time.

Other new treatments include selective laser trabeculoplasty (SLT), which uses a cool laser to enhance the eye's natural drainage canal and improve flow out of the eye without invasive surgery. SLT uses less energy than its predecessor, argon laser trabeculoplasty, lowering the risk of damaging surrounding tissue. SLT is so effective and safe that it may even become a first-line treatment for glaucoma, in place of using eyedrops.

•Eyeglasses that have progressive lenses. Progressive lenses are made by a computer. It "morphs" one lens setting in the upper half of the eyeglasses (for far objects) into another in the lower half (for close objects). Progressive lenses have been available for awhile, but the newest lenses are a vast improvement over what was available just a few years ago.

Reason: Advanced computer designs allow a smoother transition from far to near.

•Improved Lasik. Lasik surgery utilizes an "excimer" laser that can be focused very precisely to reshape the cornea to correct nearsightedness or farsightedness.

The most recent version, the Allegretto Wave, uses tiny pulses of laser light adjusted by computer to match your eye's specific curvature. It can be used for treating more severe cases of nearsightedness, farsightedness and astigmatism, previously untreatable by laser, and also causes fewer side effects (such as seeing halos around car headlights at night), with less need for corrective follow-up treatments. (To locate a doctor who uses the Allegretto Wave, go to *www. allegrettowave.com.*)

•New replacement lenses for cataract patients. Cataract surgery, in which the cataract-clouded natural lens is removed and replaced with an artificial lens, has long been effective at restoring distance vision. Now, several new types of replacement lenses provide improved near and intermediate vision. Each has its own strengths and weaknesses. *Discuss with your doctor which is best for you…*

•The Crystalens from Eyeonics combines the distance vision of a traditional lens implant with an ability to flex slightly and turn into a lens for near vision when the eye muscles focus on closer objects. It's particularly good at providing clear intermediate vision.

•The ReZoom lens from Advanced Medical Optics employs alternating rings of near- and far-distance lenses.

•The AcrySof ReSTOR lens from Alcon Laboratories has a series of tiny ridges that diffract light (instead of refracting it, like an ordinary lens), enhancing near and intermediate vision. This lens may be the best of the three for focusing on very close objects.

Note: Cataract surgery is extremely safe, with a success rate of more than 95% and a complication rate of less than 2%. Most complications, such as minor swelling of the cornea or retina, increased pressure in the eye or a droopy eyelid, generally resolve themselves with treatment and time. Rarely, cataract surgery can lead to severe visual loss as the result of surgery-related infection, bleeding in the eye or retinal detachment.

•New intraocular contact lenses. For those too nearsighted for Lasik, the FDA recently approved the first intraocular contact lens—Myopic VISIAN ICL from Staar Surgical. The lens is implanted directly in front of your own lens through a tiny incision. This procedure is safe, and the lens can be surgically removed if necessary. A similar lens specifically for farsightedness and astigmatism is in clinical trials.

iPod Danger

If played too loudly, iPods can trigger hearing loss and tinnitus (ringing in the ears). To protect your hearing, these and other personal stereo devices using earphones should not be audible to anyone standing near you. No matter what sort of earpiece you use, set the volume at about the level of a conversation with someone near you—the music should never get so loud that it causes discomfort and you have to turn down the volume.

Richard Tyler, PhD, an audiologist and professor of otolaryngology and speech pathology and audiology, University of Iowa, Iowa City.

A Once-a-Month Osteoporosis Medication

The first once-monthly drug for osteoporosis, *ibandronate* (Boniva), increases bone-mineral density. *Alendronate* (Fosamax), the most commonly prescribed osteoporosis drug, can be taken once a week.

Important: To maximize absorption of the medication and protect against heartburn and ulcers, patients must sit or stand for 60 minutes after taking ibandronate or 30 minutes after taking alendronate.

Robert Recker, MD, director, Osteoporosis Research Center, Creighton University School of Medicine, Omaha.

The New Antidepressants

David L. Ginsberg, MD, clinical associate professor of psychiatry at New York University and the director of outpatient psychiatry for Tisch Hospital, New York University Medical Center, both based in New York City. He regularly writes psychopharmacology reviews for the peer-reviewed monthly journal *Primary Psychiatry.*

Antidepressants have been getting negative reviews lately. Pharmaceutical companies have been called to task for the credibility of their research, and new fears have emerged that these drugs may increase suicide risk—especially among teenagers.*

In the face of such controversy, why would anyone want to take an antidepressant?

Problem: Up to 19 million Americans suffer from depression. However, self-help strategies, such as exercise, diet and natural remedies, do not help everyone.** For many people suffering from depression, medication offers the best hope for relief.

Good news: Drugs that relieve depression without causing intolerable side effects now are available.

DO YOU NEED AN ANTIDEPRESSANT?

Depression affects both the mind and the body. Emotionally, you feel sad or "numb" much of the time. You may no longer enjoy things that once pleased you (including hobbies, seeing friends and shopping)…feel unmotivated…find it difficult to concentrate…experience decreased libido…feel guilty or worthless. You might be more prone to abuse alcohol or drugs and might even think of suicide.

Physically, you may experience fatigue, too little (or too much) sleep, changes in appetite and/or a sense of slowing down. In some people, depression manifests as headaches and/or backaches.

If you have several such symptoms, see your doctor or a mental health professional to determine whether depression is to blame. This is especially true if your symptoms have caused trouble in your relationships and/or at work.

When depression is relatively mild—especially if it seems linked to a situation (a bad job or troubled marriage, for example) or traumatic event (such as a death in the family)—it may be worthwhile to try psychotherapy first. But if depression interferes seriously with your life, particularly if you or any family members have had depression

*Antidepressants now carry a warning label because research shows increased suicidal thoughts (not actual suicides) in children and adolescents taking these drugs. When taking an antidepressant, call your doctor if you experience agitation or physical restlessness or have suicidal thoughts.

**To read about natural treatments for depression, see page 93 of this book and log onto *www.bottomlinesecrets. com/depression.*

and/or anxiety before, medication combined with psychotherapy may be a better choice.

A GROWING ARSENAL

For nearly 50 years, doctors have prescribed tricyclic antidepressants, such as *amitriptyline* (Elavil) and *imipramine* (Tofranil)…and monoamine oxidase inhibitors (MAOIs), such as *tranylcypromine* (Parnate). They are not widely used today, largely because of side effects, such as weight gain, sedation and dietary restrictions.

Over the last 18 years, antidepressants known as the selective serotonin reuptake inhibitors, or SSRIs, have received significant attention. They work by increasing the activity of serotonin, a brain chemical linked with depression. SSRIs include *fluoxetine* (Prozac), *sertraline* (Zoloft), *paroxetine* (Paxil) and *citalopram* (Celexa). During 2002, *escitalopram* (Lexapro) joined the group.

Drugs that work on other brain chemicals instead of—or in addition to—serotonin include *bupropion* (Wellbutrin), *venlafaxine* (Effexor), *mirtazapine* (Remeron) and the newest, *duloxetine* (Cymbalta), which was introduced in 2004.

FINDING THE RIGHT MEDICATION

Individuals respond differently to antidepressants. You may do better on Drug A while another person does better on Drug B. This is largely due to differences in individual biology. Any antidepressant will substantially relieve symptoms in about two-thirds of the people who take it.

Regardless of the drug being used, you may begin to feel better in a week or two, but it takes four to six weeks to substantially improve symptoms. If you're still depressed after six to eight weeks, your doctor may suggest increasing the dosage or trying a different antidepressant.

SIDE EFFECTS

All medication, including antidepressants, may affect the body in undesired ways.

Example: SSRIs can cause sexual problems (decreased desire, difficulty with arousal or orgasm) in many people. Such problems are least likely with bupropion or mirtazapine.

Many people fear that an antidepressant will change their personalities or muffle their emotions. With the right medication, however, this should not occur.

If side effects are troublesome, it may be necessary to reduce the dose of the antidepressant or switch to another. *If the medicine is otherwise working well, talk to your doctor about trying the following strategies to reduce these side effects…*

Nausea: Split the dose or take the medication at bedtime. Or take the pill with food.

Daytime sleepiness or fatigue: If nighttime sleep is adequate, consider taking the antidepressant at night. Your doctor also may consider lowering the dosage, adding a low-dose stimulant, such as *modafinil* (Provigil), or switching to another drug.

Weight gain: Diet and exercise are essential—but an antidepressant may lower metabolism, leading to weight gain. Consider one of the antidepressants that's least likely to affect weight, such as bupropion.

THE LONG HAUL

Once an antidepressant relieves depression symptoms, most people want to stop taking it. But stopping too soon increases the risk for recurrence.

If this is your first episode of depression: Talk to your doctor about staying on the drug for at least one year after you feel better.

If this is your second bout, or if depression runs in your family: Consider continuing medication for two years or longer.

If you've had three or more episodes of depression: The risk for recurrence is more than 90%. Many doctors advocate medication indefinitely—the way a diabetic takes insulin.

Important: If you stop taking an antidepressant, do so gradually—and under your doctor's supervision.

Good News for Depression Sufferers

Leptin, a hormone that is involved in weight regulation, may play a role in treating depression. In preliminary studies, animals given leptin stayed more active and coped better with chronic stress.

MedPage Today, Overlook at Great Notch, 150 Clove Rd., Little Falls, NJ 07424, *www.medpagetoday.com*.

Migraine and Depression Are Linked

In a recent study of patients newly diagnosed with depression, 49% also reported suffering migraines. The risk for migraines increased with the severity of depression. Also, depression side effects, such as anxiety and chronic pain, occurred in 72% of those who had both depression and migraines, compared with only 29% of the depression-only group.

Theory: A decrease in the brain chemicals *serotonin* and *norepinephrine* contributes to migraine and depression.

If you suffer from migraines: Get screened for depression—and if you suffer from depression and headaches, get screened for migraines.

Gary E. Ruoff, MD, clinical professor of family practice, Michigan State University College of Medicine, East Lansing, MI.

Bird Flu Update

William Schaffner, MD, chairman of the department of preventive medicine at Vanderbilt University School of Medicine in Nashville, TN. He is a Fellow of the Infectious Diseases Society of America, a liaison member of the Advisory Committee on Immunization Practices of the Centers for Disease Control and Prevention and an associate editor of *The Journal of Infectious Diseases*.

The avian flu pandemic (global epidemic) may be coming, though it could be years away. *Infectious disease authority William Schaffner, MD, answers questions regarding the avian flu below…*

●**What does a pandemic look like in its early stages? How will we know when it's here?** The early stages of this pandemic will look like any other outbreak of a pneumonic respiratory illness. Large numbers of people in one specific region will come down with flu symptoms, but doctors there won't initially know that they're dealing with the deadly avian flu. That should become apparent within a few days, when they recognize the severity of the illness. The flu usually sends only a small percentage of victims to the hospital—this one probably will be worse.

This initial outbreak is most likely to occur in Southeast Asia, where birds suffering from the dangerous strain of avian flu are most common. It's probable, but not certain, that word of this initial outbreak will reach the US before the virus itself does. The bird flu virus has not yet been detected in North and South America.

●**How serious will it be, really?** It all depends on how readily the virus transfers from person to person—and we can't know that until the virus has mutated into a form suited to human hosts and the outbreak begins. Right now, the virus still cannot be transmitted among humans.

If the initial outbreak reaches a major city before doctors figure out that it is under way, that's a clue that the mutated virus is easily transmitted from person to person and will spread quickly. If the outbreak is still contained to a rural community near poultry farms when it's discovered, a slower course is more probable, which could mean a lower death toll.

●**Can't science stop the pandemic?** Science will not be able to prevent this pandemic, but it might be able to blunt its impact and reduce the death toll.

●**What can be done to prepare for and protect yourself from avian flu pandemic?** The Centers for Disease Control and Prevention as well as state health departments are creating specific guidelines for the public. For example, if human transmission does occur, we will need to isolate ourselves as much as possible to avoid contracting the disease. Avoidance of all crowds will be recommended. To prepare, buy enough nonperishable food and water (one gallon per person daily) to tide you over for at least several days. You may want to buy special masks, such as those meeting the N95 standard (with sealed sides that help to prevent transmission). These inexpensive masks, available at medical-supply stores or on-line, have not been proven to prevent the illness but may help.

If there is a pandemic, influenza vaccine will be available based on need—members of your family may qualify if they have impaired immune systems or other underlying medical problems, such as lung or heart disease. People who are overweight or who have diabetes, high blood pressure or other medical problems are at most risk for the serious complications of influenza. Do what you can now to get these medical matters under control.

.If the pandemic does hit, would it be helpful to have an air purifier in my home? No. Home air purifiers will not filter out viruses. Even a high-end, hospital-quality air purification system would not keep your entire home virus-free.

Avian Flu Vaccine Shows Promise

A new avian flu vaccine tested in animals gives 100% protection against avian flu. Unlike traditional vaccines, it is produced in cell cultures rather than fertilized chicken eggs.

Advantages: It can be produced in almost unlimited supplies in as little as one month.

A clinical trial in humans is being planned.

The University of Pittsburgh Graduate School of Public Health, 130 DeSoto St., Pittsburgh, PA 15261, *www.public health.pitt.edu.*

Infection Cure: "A Croc"?

A ustralian researchers report that crocodile antibodies kill bacteria that is resistant to penicillin—and may form the basis for new antibiotics. Crocodiles rarely get infections—even

after savage fights that result in torn flesh—due to a powerful immune system.

CNN.com.

Apple Alert

E ven washed, blemish-free apples can harbor disease-causing bacteria. Studies show that, in rare cases, *E. coli, salmonella* and other pathogens can find their way into apple cores, perhaps entering near the end opposite the stem.

Self-defense: Avoid eating apple cores, and wash and rinse all fruit and vegetables vigorously with water.

Larry Beuchat, PhD, research professor at the Center for Food Safety, University of Georgia, Griffin.

Vegetable Oil Warning

E xtended heating of some vegetable oils can produce toxic compounds.

New finding: When vegetable oils, such as soybean and corn, are heated to frying temperature (365°F) for at least one-half hour, they start to produce a toxic compound that's known as *4-hydroxy-trans-2-non-enal* (HNE). HNE has been linked to atherosclerosis, stroke, Parkinson's, Alzheimer's and many other diseases.

Self-defense: Avoid high-temperature frying for more than 30 minutes and do *not* reuse oil.

A. Saari Csallany, DSc, professor of food chemistry and nutritional biochemistry at the University of Minnesota in St. Paul.

2

Taking Charge of Your Health Care

Five Questions Your Doctor Should Ask—but Won't

In the US, the typical doctor's office visit lasts seven to 10 minutes. During that time, the doctor will review your medical history, ask questions about your symptoms, perform an exam and order tests, if they are necessary.

This approach can be effective for emergencies or acute illnesses, such as earaches, bronchitis or chest pain. It doesn't work as well for chronic diseases, such as diabetes, arthritis, asthma or fatigue.

Reason: Doctors don't ask questions that reveal the key facts about a person's life that can significantly affect the development and progression of disease.

Example: One of my patients had severe rheumatoid arthritis. She failed to improve even with the latest and most powerful drugs. None

of her doctors thought to ask about her diet, which was triggering the release of inflammatory chemicals that exacerbated her symptoms.

I ask all my patients to complete a 20-page questionnaire before their initial visit with me. In many cases, their answers provide important clues to an accurate diagnosis. Even if your doctor doesn't ask the questions listed below, you should bring up these issues with him/her during your appointment.

Questions that your doctor should ask—but may not...

•Have you ever felt better after avoiding particular foods? Up to 40% of *healthy* Americans indicate having an intolerance to one or more foods.

Why it matters: Millions of Americans react to wheat, dairy or other specific foods or food

Leo Galland, MD, director of the Foundation for Integrated Medicine in New York City. He has held faculty positions at Rockefeller University and at Albert Einstein College of Medicine, both in New York City, and at the State University of New York, Stony Brook. He is author of *The Fat Resistance Diet* (Broadway) and *The Four Pillars of Healing* (Random House).

27

groups. Food intolerance is a frequent cause of diarrhea and other digestive problems. It also can cause fatigue and headache. Patients often suffer for years without being accurately diagnosed. The quality of a person's diet can have a significant impact on the risk for chronic or recurrent disease…energy levels, mood and body weight…recovery from infection…and the control of chronic disorders such as diabetes and high blood pressure.

What you can do: If you have unexplained symptoms, such as headache or diarrhea, keep a food diary to record everything you eat and drink over a three-day period, including spices and condiments, such as pepper and mustard. The most common culprits are milk products, wheat, corn, yeast, sugar, artificial colors and flavors and spices. Eliminate a suspected problem food from your diet for five to seven days. Do your symptoms improve when you avoid the food? Do they get worse when you reintroduce it? If you find a problem food, ask your doctor whether you may have a food intolerance.

•**What are the major sources of stress in your life?** Our bodies' nerves, hormones and immune cells work together to help us cope with emotional stress. In people who suffer chronic stress, this network becomes overwhelmed and stops working efficiently.

Why it matters: The body is designed to respond to stress and often benefits by becoming stronger. However, when people experience high levels of stress on a daily basis, the cost of responding to stress exceeds the benefit. This results in an increased risk for cardiovascular disease, infection, depression and other illnesses.

What you can do: It's impossible to eliminate stress altogether, but we all can learn to manage it more efficiently. For example, daily exercise—30 minutes of walking at a moderate to brisk pace—diminishes the effects of stress-related hormones.

•**Do you feel close to your family and/or friends?** Physicians are often reluctant (or too busy) to inquire about patients' personal lives. However, personal relationships are among the most important factors in preventing and treating disease.

Why it matters: Patients who are diagnosed with serious illnesses, including cancer and heart disease, live longer when they have a strong social network. Research also shows that people who are active in their communities or close to family and friends are less likely to get sick in the first place. A social support network also eases depression and protects you from the effects of daily stress.

What you can do: Take stock of your relationships with other people and nourish them by spending time with people you care about. If you are isolated, get involved in activities that help others.

•**How much personal control do you believe you have over your health?** There are two primary ways that you can approach your health—you can rely on your doctor to tell you what to do…or you can actively participate in your health care.

Why it matters: Research shows that people are healthier and have better medical outcomes when they take responsibility for their own care…make important lifestyle changes…and generally put themselves in charge of their own health.

What you can do: The first step is to motivate yourself and make a commitment to yourself and those you love that you will be proactive in advocating for your own health. The second step is to learn what you can about the health conditions that affect you.

•**Do you have physical problems or certain personality traits that remind you of someone in your family?** Your family medical history can help identify diseases that you may be predisposed to develop. Family history is an especially important risk factor for depression, heart disease, diabetes, high blood pressure and allergic and autoimmune disorders. Most cancers are not due to genetic risk factors, but to environmental exposures or diet.

Why it matters: A family history of a disease doesn't mean that you will develop that illness—but knowing your history, or just noticing similarities, makes it easier to predict and to prevent future problems. For instance, if you suffer from unexplained fatigue, weight gain or mood disturbances, and there is a history of thyroid problems in a close family member, such as a parent or sibling, your symptoms may be thyroid-related.

What you can do: Maintain a family tree that includes the health status and cause of death of grandparents, parents, aunts, uncles and siblings—and show it to your doctor. See the next article for complete details on how to construct a family medical history.

Secret to Improving Your Family's Health

Louise Acheson, MD, MS, professor of family medicine and associate professor of oncology and reproductive biology, Case Western Reserve University, Cleveland.

Your family's health history offers a gold mine of clues that you can use to tailor your health care and possibly lower your risk of illness. A family health history can uncover whether you're susceptible to conditions such as heart disease and diabetes. It also can determine whether early screening for diseases such as cancer is warranted...and highlight behavioral risk factors, including smoking or lack of exercise, that may influence you to make lifestyle changes.

Bonus: It is an opportunity to connect with your relatives.

Draw a diagram of your family tree, starting with your immediate family and moving on to grandparents, aunts, uncles and cousins. Ideally, your tree will span three generations. The US Surgeon General's Family History Initiative at *www.hhs.gov/familyhistory* and the National Society of Genetic Counselors at *www.nsgc.org/consumer/familytree/index.cfm* have free downloadable tools.

For each person, include birth date and presence of major illnesses, such as cancer, heart disease and diabetes. If possible, provide information on health habits, such as physical activity, diet and smoking. If the person has died, note the date and cause of death.

Also give his/her ethnic information because some disorders are more prevalent in certain populations. For example, Northern Europeans have a higher incidence of cystic fibrosis, and African-Americans are at higher risk for sickle cell anemia.

Family holiday gatherings and reunions can be a good time to reach out to relatives, or a private phone call or an e-mail can elicit more information. Prepare yourself beforehand with a list of open-ended questions that prompt more than yes or no responses.

Examples: Could you tell me about any medical conditions that run in the family?...Why did Uncle Pat need a wheelchair?...Do you remember at what age Grandma was diagnosed with breast cancer?

If a relative is deceased or if you are having trouble getting information, you can use government records or access genealogy resources on-line or at the library.

When you have completed your family tree, make note of disease patterns. Also give a copy to your physician, who may see connections that you missed. Obtain your relatives' permission to share the history with other family members. Keep the diagram in a safe place and update it every few years.

Best Time for Kids' Checkups

Schedule children's medical checkups during doctors' slow months, usually between April and September. Between October and March, their offices are overrun with sick children. For the same reason, avoid scheduling a checkup on a Monday morning, when the office is crowded with kids who got sick over the weekend.

Also: Prepare a list of questions about your child's health, behavior and development beforehand, as well as any other topics you want to discuss.

Lynette Padwa, a publishing consultant and self-help writer in Los Angeles, and author of *Say the Magic Words: How to Get What You Want from the People Who Have What You Need* (Penguin).

Great Second Opinions— Without Leaving Home

Rebecca Shannonhouse, editor of *Bottom Line/Health*, Boardroom Inc., 281 Tresser Blvd., Stamford, CT 06901.

What if you had a type of cancer or other disease that local doctors had little experience treating? You would need a second opinion—but the quality of that opinion would vary widely in different communities. The Internet now makes it possible for patients to get second opinions from world-class specialists.

The specialists at The Cleveland Clinic and the Harvard-affiliated teaching facilities Brigham and Women's Hospital and Massachusetts General Hospital now offer second opinions on the Internet. Top-rated radiologists, pathologists, etc., review computed tomography (CT) scans, pathology slides and other laboratory and imaging tests. Then they share their findings with the patient's primary care physician.

"A doctor in a local hospital or even a regional medical center may see only a few cases of a particular disease in his/her entire career. With on-line programs, a primary care physician can tap the expertise of specialists who see several cases a *day*," explains Joseph C. Kvedar, MD, the founder and director of Harvard's on-line second-opinion program, Partners Telemedicine.

A first-year analysis of the Harvard program found that specialists arrived at different diagnoses in 5% of cases and recommended different treatments—such as newer drugs or more up-to-date approaches—90% of the time.

Typical cost: $350 to $750.* Insurance may cover some of this cost.

Visit eCleveland Clinic, *www.eclevelandclinic. org* or Partners Telemedicine, *www.telemedicine. partners.org* to learn more.

*Prices subject to change.

More from Rebecca Shannonhouse...

Premium Medical Care

If you are tired of crowded waiting rooms and rushed doctor appointments, you're definitely not alone.

Latest approach: Concierge medicine, in which physicians drastically reduce their patient loads in order to offer personalized attention, including longer office visits...same- or next-day appointments...and 24/7 availability by phone, e-mail or pager.

Doctors in concierge practices charge each patient a fixed annual fee, ranging from $1,500 to $20,000* per year. In addition, patients retain their usual insurance coverage and pay for services just as they would in a traditional doctor's practice.

Not long ago, Richard Goldman, MD, an internist and founder of a concierge medical practice in Wellesley, Massachusetts, handled 3,500 to 4,000 patients a year in an HMO. "Now I see 300 to 400 patients," he says. "This is the way medicine used to be practiced."

There are about 100 concierge medical practices in the US. *This type of service isn't practical (or affordable) for everyone, but it can be a solution for people who...*

•**Maintain hectic schedules** and cannot afford to spend time in a waiting room.

•**Feel rushed and depersonalized in an HMO.**

•**Suffer from chronic conditions** that require frequent care and/or want 24-hour access to their physicians.

To find a concierge medical practice in your area, consult the Society for Innovative Medical Practice Design's Web site, *simpd.org*.

*Prices subject to change.

Do You Believe In Miracles?

In a survey of 1,100 physicians of varying religious backgrounds, 74% said they believe in medical miracles—and more than half said they have actually witnessed miracles when treating patients.

American Family Physician, American Academy of Family Physicians, Box 11210, Shawnee Mission, KS 66207-1210, *www.aafp.org/afp*.

Lifesaving Medical Tests Doctors Too Often Overlook

David Sandmire, MD, an associate professor in the department of biological sciences at the University of New England in Biddeford, ME. He is coauthor of *Medical Tests That Can Save Your Life: 21 Tests Your Doctor Won't Order ...Unless You Know to Ask* (Rodale).

A 50-year-old man I knew went for an annual checkup. His doctor pronounced him in excellent health. Eight months later, the man suffered a major heart attack and died.

His death could have been prevented. If the doctor had talked to the patient at length, he would have discovered that one of his relatives had hemochromatosis, a dangerous condition in which the body retains too much iron, causing heart problems. A simple $35 blood test would have confirmed the condition—and the patient could have been treated and still be alive today.

Dozens of screening options can diagnose deadly diseases in the earliest stages, when treatment has the greatest chance of success—but doctors, pressured by increasing patient loads and hamstrung by what insurers will cover, don't always order them when they should.

KEY TESTS

The following conditions can be detected with simple tests. *These tests may not be covered by insurance—check with your insurer—but consider paying for them even if they're not...**

•**Diabetes.** Type 2 diabetes affects 17 million American adults and children, yet close to one-third don't know they have it because symptoms might not appear for a decade. Almost 200,000 people die every year from complications of type 2 diabetes. Hundreds of thousands more suffer blindness, kidney failure and/or nervous system damage.

Test: A fasting blood glucose test is taken after you have not eaten for at least eight hours. If your results are above 110 milligrams per deciliter (mg/dl), you should have the more definitive oral glucose tolerance test. After you ingest a high sugar drink, your blood glucose level is

*Test costs vary based on facility and region, and are subject to change.

measured every hour for three hours. If your glucose level rises more than is expected and doesn't return to normal by the third hour, you have diabetes.

Who should consider testing: Obese people with a body mass index (BMI) of 30 and above (to calculate BMI, go to *www.diabetes.org*) ...African-Americans, Latinos and Native Americans over the age of 45...anyone with a close relative who has type 2 diabetes.

Cost: About $12 for a fasting blood glucose test...approximately $25 for an oral glucose tolerance test.

•**Coronary heart disease (CHD).** In CHD, the walls of the coronary arteries are narrowed or blocked by a buildup of fatty plaque. CHD is the single largest killer of men and women in the US. A traditional CHD blood test measures *C-reactive protein* (CRP) in the blood. Elevated C-reactive protein levels are a sign of inflammation and are a better predictor of heart disease in women than LDL (bad) cholesterol levels.

Test: The new high-sensitivity C-reactive protein test measures levels more accurately than the old test. This is vital because studies now show that any reading above 1 mg/l puts you at above-average risk for CHD. (The older test wasn't able to detect a level that low.) It used to be thought that only readings above 5 mg/l put you at risk.

Who should consider testing: Anyone with high cholesterol or high blood pressure...people with diabetes...people whose parents or siblings have or had CHD...smokers.

Cost: $25 to $50.

•**Hemochromatosis.** This disease will cause the body to absorb too much iron, resulting in heart problems, arthritis and reduced life expectancy. One out of 10 Americans has the single mutated gene that causes secondary hemochromatosis, a milder form of the disease.

Test: A percent transferrin saturation blood test screens for abnormal metabolism that signals a propensity to over-accumulate iron. If the test is positive, a genetic blood test for hereditary hemochromatosis should be performed.

Who should consider testing: Male Caucasians of Northern European descent, particularly of Celtic ancestry...individuals with relatives who have had hemochromatosis.

31

Cost: $20 to $50 for percent transferrin saturation test…$125 to $165 for genetic testing.

• **Hepatitis C virus (HCV).** About four million Americans are infected with HCV, but less than 30% are diagnosed because most sufferers have no symptoms. Left untreated, HCV can lead to cirrhosis and liver cancer.

Test: An enzyme-linked immunosorbent assay (ELISA) blood test can detect the presence of hepatitis C antibodies. If the test results are positive, you'll need to have an HCV RNA (ribonucleic acid) test to determine how recently you were exposed to the virus and how much of it is in your blood.

Who should consider testing: People who received blood transfusions or organ transplants before 1992 (when the blood supply was not screened for HCV)…health-care workers who suffer accidental needle sticks…intravenous drug users…those who have had multiple sex partners.

Cost: $70 to $100 for an ELISA test…about $100 for an HCV RNA test.

• **Pancreatic cancer.** The five-year survival rate of this deadly disease is just 4% because symptoms rarely appear until the tumor grows large enough to interfere with the function of nearby organs, such as the stomach, small intestine and liver. Early detection can raise the five-year survival rate to nearly 40%.

Test: Endoscopic retrograde cholangiopancreatography (ERCP) can detect abnormalities of the pancreas, including a precancerous condition known as dysplasia, about 90% of the time. A physician guides an endoscope down through your stomach and small intestine to inject a dye into the ducts in the pancreas. X-rays are taken and examined. If anything suspicious is seen, a biopsy is performed.

Who should consider testing: People who now have pancreatitis, an inflammatory condition that occurs when digestive enzymes attack the pancreas itself instead of breaking down food in the small intestine. Symptoms include mild to severe abdominal pain, often with nausea, vomiting and fever. People with an inherited defect in the BRCA2 gene also should be tested. This is found in about 1% of Ashkenazi Jews and in some women who have a family history of breast cancer.

Cost: $1,500 to $2,000.

YOUR RISK PROFILE

The more informed a doctor is about your health and risk factors, the more likely he/she is to order tests that could save your life. You can help by developing your own detailed risk profile. *Include…*

• **Personal medical history**—major diseases, injuries and operations you have had and any residual effects. Patients often forget childhood illnesses, so ask close relatives. Also list allergies, including those to medications.

• **Genetic makeup**—your racial and ethnic background.

• **Extended family medical history**—diseases that family members suffer from or have died from, such as type 2 diabetes, cancer and coronary artery disease. Also include family conditions such as obesity and depression.

• **Lifestyle.** Be honest with yourself and with your doctor about smoking, alcohol consumption, diet and exercise. Ask family and friends for objective opinions.

How to Ensure Accurate Results From a Biopsy

Thomas M. Wheeler, MD, interim chair of the department of pathology and professor of pathology and urology at Baylor College of Medicine in Houston, TX. He is an attending pathologist at Houston's Ben Taub General Hospital and is on the Board of Governors of the College of American Pathologists.

A biopsy is required to diagnose virtually all types of cancer as well as many other potentially serious medical problems, including hepatitis (inflammation of the liver).

A biopsy starts with the removal of tissue or individual cells from a patient. The sample is preserved and sent to a pathologist (a doctor who specializes in identifying diseases by studying cells and tissues under a microscope).

Biopsies vary considerably in the amount of tissue removed, and this will dictate whether anesthesia is needed and if so, if it is local or general. If a doctor orders a biopsy, most patients simply comply—without fully understanding why the test is required or how it is done. But this can be a mistake. In most cases, it is important to ask whether a less invasive biopsy could be used to diagnose the particular condition.

What you need to know about the most common types of biopsies…

FINE (THIN) NEEDLE ASPIRATION

Used to diagnose: Cancer affecting superficial (near the skin surface) masses, such as the thyroid or a lymph node, or a deeper organ, like the liver or pancreas.

How it's done: A thin needle, about the same size as one used to draw blood from the arm for routine blood work, is inserted into a superficial mass, such as a lymph node, and cells are drawn into a syringe. If a biopsy of a deep organ, such as the pancreas, is needed, the procedure is done by a radiologist with a longer needle of the same diameter. Imaging equipment, such as a computed tomography (CT) scan or ultrasound, is used to precisely locate the area. Since the needle is so thin, the procedure is virtually painless and anesthesia is not necessary. The fine needle biopsy is the least invasive and least expensive of all the biopsies.

CUTTING NEEDLE

Used to diagnose: Cancer of the prostate, lung, breast or other organs…and inflammatory conditions, such as hepatitis or cirrhosis of the liver.

How it's done: This type of biopsy uses a larger-diameter, hollow needle. Since it can be painful, a local anesthetic typically is given to numb the area. The needle is inserted into the organ and tissue, rather than just cells, is extracted. The tissue specimen looks like a thin piece of pasta, up to one inch in length.

INCISIONAL

Used to diagnose: Tumors or other conditions occurring deep in the abdominal or chest cavity (in a lung, the liver, pancreas, etc.)… lumps in breast or skin tissue…and lymphoma.

This type of biopsy is used when a larger sample is needed than a needle biopsy will provide, for example, but the surgeon is not planning to remove the whole tumor or mass, as in some cases of lymphoma, lung or breast tumors.

How it's done: Patients are given either a local or general anesthetic, depending on the location of the suspicious area. With a scalpel, laser or electrocautery knife (in which an electrical current heats the tissue and causes less bleeding), a surgeon makes an incision into the area or organ of interest to obtain a sample. If cancer is diagnosed, the patient may later undergo surgery to remove the whole tumor.

EXCISIONAL

Used to diagnose: Tumors of a superficial or deep organ (such as the lung or pancreas) that need to be removed whole for an accurate diagnosis and/or treatment…and/or surrounding tissue which also could potentially harbor cancer cells.

How it's done: Patients who require excisional biopsies near the skin surface usually are given a local anesthetic. General anesthesia may be required when surgery is needed to access tumors or organs deep inside the body, such as in the abdominal cavity.

After the patient is anesthetized, the surgeon makes an excision and removes the whole abnormality. In some instances in which the whole tumor is removed, no further treatment is necessary. If the tumor is malignant, the patient may be treated with further surgery, radiation and/or chemotherapy.

SPECIAL BIOPSIES

A number of specialized biopsies have been developed. Dermatologists will frequently use a *punch biopsy* to diagnose skin rashes or small lumps just beneath the skin. A sharp tool that resembles a spherical "cookie cutter" is used to cut through the skin and remove cylindrical plugs of skin ranging from about 2 millimeters (mm) in diameter—about the size of pencil lead—to 6 mm or more in diameter. A smaller biopsy usually will heal on its own, but a larger punch biopsy may require one or two stitches to bring the sides of the wound together.

An *endoscopic biopsy,* used to diagnose conditions affecting the intestines, bladder, abdomen or bronchial system, is taken through an endoscope, a fiber-optic tube that is introduced into the body to allow these structures to be seen. If the physician performing this procedure sees an abnormality, he/she can introduce biopsy forceps to take a "snip" of the abnormality.

These biopsies are usually no more than 3 mm in size.

A similar type of biopsy, a *colposcopic biopsy,* is typically performed by a gynecologist to evaluate abnormal-looking areas of the cervix. The area is viewed with a colposcope (a magnifying lens that looks like a microscope), and an incisional biopsy is taken.

Important: If your doctor recommends a biopsy, insist that it be reviewed by a board-certified pathologist who practices in a laboratory accredited by the College of American Pathologists (CAP). To locate an accredited lab in your area, contact CAP at 800-323-4040 or go to its Web site at *www.cap.org.*

How Drug Companies Are Turning Us All into Patients

Alan Cassels, a drug policy researcher at University of Victoria, British Columbia. He has spent the last decade studying how clinical research about prescription drugs is communicated to policymakers, doctors and consumers. He is coauthor of *Selling Sickness: How the World's Biggest Pharmaceutical Companies Are Turning Us All into Patients* (Nation).

How many pills did you and your family take today? It seems that there is a prescription drug for every condition now, no matter how benign. In fact, the US has become the most medicated society in the world. We constitute 5% of the world's population, but we buy 50% of all prescription medicine. Conflicts of interest abound—from your doctor, who may be on the payroll of a pharmaceutical firm, to your favorite celebrity, who may get a kickback for hawking powerful meds.

Alan Cassels, the esteemed pharmaceutical policy researcher, believes that we need to protect ourselves from a culture which insists on "medicalizing" every problem in our lives. *He answers some important questions below…*

●**Why has our society become overmedicated?** We all want a quick fix, even if we aren't sick but just feel vulnerable or at risk. The trouble is that vast commercial forces are exploiting this

desire. Much of the health information that we get is distorted so that drugs are the first choice we consider for, say, depression, high cholesterol or high blood pressure—even if there are safer effective alternatives, such as exercise or a healthy diet.

Drug ads use statistical gimmicks to exaggerate benefits. I saw an ad that claimed a certain pill would lower your risk of a heart attack by 33%. Technically, that's correct, but the actual clinical study indicated a drop in risk from 3% to 2%. That's only a one-percentage-point reduction, in absolute terms.

●**What's an example of a drug that is prescribed too often?** Look at the multibillion-dollar sales of antidepressants in the past few years. If you walk into a doctor's office complaining of mild to moderate depression, you often are given a prescription for a selective serotonin reuptake inhibitor (SSRI), such as Paxil, Prozac or Zoloft—drugs that may have significant side effects—despite evidence that behavioral and talk therapy can be equally effective.

What has happened is that marketing campaigns from pharmaceutical firms have transformed the way we think about physical and mental health, convincing us that our problems are best cured with medication. Alternative views of the illness and treatment get short shrift.

●**Are the drug companies really the problem?** Drug companies make wonderful products that extend lives and ameliorate suffering. However, they are now aggressively targeting the healthy as well as the sick in pursuit of profits. One of their strategies is to broaden the boundaries of what constitutes an illness.

For instance, back in the 1990s, only about 13 million Americans warranted treatment under the US National Institutes of Health's cholesterol guidelines. Then, in 2003, one panel of experts rewrote these guidelines and lowered them so much that now 36 million more people have "high" cholesterol. Many of the doctors on that panel had served as paid speakers, consultants or researchers for large pharmaceutical companies that manufacture cholesterol-lowering drugs known as statins.

It's not surprising that high cholesterol has become an obsessive concern for everyone. We all know our "numbers," but high cholesterol isn't an illness. It's just one of many risk factors for heart disease. While there's extensive evidence that statins are valuable for people who have had heart attacks, there often are cheaper, safer and equally effective treatments for the rest of us, like better diet, more exercise and not smoking.

Even more insidious is the fact that the drug companies do not just market blockbuster pills through advertising—they market the conditions for their medications to cure. For example, Paxil used to be one of many popular antidepressants on the market, but in the past five years, its manufacturer, GlaxoSmithKline, took a rare psychiatric condition known as "social anxiety disorder" and helped transform it into an often-diagnosed condition for which Paxil is the cure.

•**Who is the primary target for this kind of advertising?** Every segment of the population is targeted. Women are told that they should take medication for "illnesses" such as menopause and premenstrual syndrome, which actually are natural cyclical changes. Children who simply can't sit still or who drift off in class are diagnosed with attention deficit hyper-activity disorder (ADHD) and given Ritalin. Older people who don't have high blood pressure are told they have a condition called "prehypertension" (a systolic blood pressure of 120 to 139, or a diastolic pressure of 80 to 89) that may warrant drug intervention. There's now no evidence that giving medication to patients with this level of blood pressure will result in any alteration of the length or quality of life. "Prehypertension" is a verbal strategy designed to cast the net wider, creating more patients and selling more pills.

Maybe we should rename life itself and call it "predeath." Then we would all need to be taking drugs of some kind.

•**Aren't these drugs helpful and warranted in many cases?** Of course. I'm not saying that you should ignore symptoms or that every diagnosis is being blown out of proportion. There may be many times in your life when you need drug intervention, but we have become too comfortable popping pills. We assume that as long as it's advertised on TV or recommended by our doctors, it must be safe.

•**Isn't my doctor supposed to be the gatekeeper for all this information? Can't he or she see through all the marketing tactics?**

Doctors may be very responsible and hard to manipulate, but they still are under enormous pressure to prescribe drugs. Patients ask for the drugs that they see advertised on TV. Pharmaceutical representatives bombard doctors with sales pitches—the typical physician averages at least one visit from a rep every day.

•**What should I be doing to protect myself as a patient?** Be skeptical. Ask your doctor if a drug has been tested on people like yourself (your age, sex and physical condition). What are the benefits and dangers? Would lifestyle changes work instead? *Also, seek out reputable sources of independent information, including…*

•Consumer Reports' free Web site, *www.crbestbuydrugs.org,* which provides information for making cost-effective prescription drug choices.

•The Medical Letter, a publication for physicians and other health-care professionals which publishes critical appraisals of new drugs and comparative reviews of older drugs. 26 issues. $89/yr.* 800-211-2769, *www.medicalletter.org.*

•Public Citizen, a nonprofit advocacy organization that has information on hundreds of drugs in its book, *Worst Pills Best Pills,* as well as on its free Web site, *www.worstpills.org.*

•**Is overmedicating the wave of the future?** Not necessarily. The thousands of lawsuits pending against pharmaceutical giant Merck over the side effects of its painkiller Vioxx may have a profound effect on our public and private regulatory systems. The Food and Drug Administration already has tightened its protocols.

Influential medical journals now are calling for an international clinical trial medical registry. This is crucial. Right now, a pharmaceutical company can conduct a dozen trials for a new drug…only make known the positive-result trials…then use those as evidence for drug approval or marketing. Drug companies should have to register every study in a central database and publish all results so that we can judge for ourselves what to allow into our medicine cabinets.

*Price subject to change.

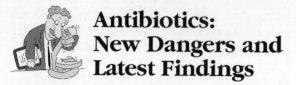

Antibiotics: New Dangers and Latest Findings

Stuart Levy, MD, a professor of medicine, molecular biology and microbiology, and director of the Center for Adaptation Genetics and Drug Resistance, both at Tufts University School of Medicine in Boston. He is founder and president of the nonprofit Alliance for the Prudent Use of Antibiotics, *www.apua.org,* and author of *The Antibiotic Paradox* (Perseus).

By now, we've all heard about the growing threat of antibiotic-resistant bacteria. We know not to ask our doctors to prescribe an antibiotic unnecessarily, and we have been instructed that frequent handwashing can cut down on the transmission of bacterial infections. With such strong warnings, you might assume that antibiotic resistance is going away. It isn't.

Increasingly, bacteria that are responsible for sinusitis, ear and urinary tract infections as well as many types of pneumonia are resistant to one or more antibiotics. This means that many infections that were once easily cured by taking an antibiotic for a few days now can linger much longer—and even become life-threatening.

How antibiotic-resistance develops: Bacteria can become resistant to antibiotics by mutating to become insensitive to the drug. The surviving resistant organisms then multiply and create new strains of bacteria that don't respond to the antibiotics that were previously effective. Emergence of resistance is enhanced when patients do not finish a full course of an antibiotic—or when antibiotics are overused or misused in general. *Latest developments…*

LAX HANDWASHING

What's new: Many people *still* aren't washing their hands. While 91% of American adults claim to wash their hands after using the restroom, only 83% actually do so, according to the American Society for Microbiology.

What this means for you: Since many viruses and bacteria are spread from hands to the mucous membranes of your mouth, nose or eyes, dirty hands are a prime means of transmitting infection.

Self-defense: In addition to washing both your hands after using the restroom and before eating or preparing food, it's also important after handling garbage…playing with a pet…changing a diaper…blowing your nose, sneezing or coughing…and inserting or removing contact lenses.

What to do: Using soap and warm, running water, rub your hands together for at least 10 seconds. Don't forget the wrists and backs of your hands. Dry with a clean or disposable towel. Pocket-sized bottles of hand-sanitizing gels and disposable towelettes that contain alcohol are convenient ways to wash when water is not available.

MORE DRUG-RESISTANT STRAINS

What's new: The number of drug-resistant and multidrug-resistant strains of bacteria is up sharply from just a few years ago. About 70% of the bacteria that cause infections in hospitals are now resistant to at least one common antibiotic.

What this means for you: If you are hospitalized, you're now at increased risk of contracting an infection that can be difficult to treat and may even result in death. Recent studies show that 5% to 10% of hospital patients in the US get an infection during their stay, and nearly 100,000 die annually as a result. This compares with about 13,000 deaths from hospital-acquired infections in 1992.

Self-defense: Keep hospital stays as short as possible. Visitors and hospital staff should wash their hands before and after contact with you. With some infectious diseases, such as tuberculosis, visitors and staff may need to wear a mask, gown and gloves to prevent the spread of the infection.

ANTIBIOTIC BAN FOR POULTRY

What's new: In July of 2005, the FDA announced a ban on the use of the animal antibiotic *enrofloxacin* (Baytril) in poultry. Enrofloxacin is a *fluoroquinolone* antibiotic in the same class as *ciprofloxacin* (Cipro). The ban followed the finding that fluoroquinolone-resistant bacteria that infected poultry were becoming increasingly less responsive to Cipro in human infections caused by the same bacteria. This was the first time the FDA had banned an antibiotic used in animal health because of a potential harm posed to people by the emergence of drug-resistant bacteria.

What this means for you: Greater attention is being given to antibiotic use in agriculture, animals and people. Europe has instituted a ban on the use of all growth-promoting antibiotics. In the US, antibiotics are still given to poultry to increase growth. The FDA is currently reviewing the issue, and many experts believe the US should also ban growth-promoting antibiotics.

Self-defense: Although the FDA ban on enrofloxacin went into effect last September, poultry producers still can use growth-promoting antibiotics. To find poultry that is totally free of antibiotics, check with your local butcher or at a natural-food store.

NEW STAPH INFECTIONS

What's new: A drug-resistant strain of *staphylococcus* bacterium, community-acquired methicillin-resistant *Staphylococcus aureus* (CA-MRSA), formerly found only in hospitals, is now increasingly being detected within communities.

What this means for you: This particular staph bacterium does seem to be more virulent and spreads from person-to-person, especially through the skin-to-skin contact sports, such as football and wrestling.

Self-defense: To help prevent infection, wash well with soap and water immediately after any contact sports, being especially careful to clean any cuts. Never share towels or washcloths in a gym.

CIPRO RESISTANCE

What's new: *Ciprofloxacin* (Cipro), one of the first-line antibiotics to treat anthrax (a leading bioterror weapon), is becoming increasingly ineffective against other infections.

What this means for you: For now, other antibiotics can fill the gap for ear, sinus and urinary tract infections. Experts do not believe that Cipro's effectiveness against anthrax has been compromised—but this could change in the future if the antibiotic is overused.

Self-defense: Some experts do believe that doctors are too quick to prescribe Cipro when another antibiotic would do. If your physician does prescribe Cipro, ask if another antibiotic could be used.

LATEST ANTIBIOTICS

What's new: *Tigecycline* (Tygacil), the first in a new class of antibiotics called *glycylcyclines*, was introduced in June 2005. It was approved by the FDA as a first-line treatment for hospital-based skin and soft tissue infections caused by bacteria that are resistant to other antibiotics. A new class of antibiotics called *diarylquinolones*, which treats drug-resistant tuberculosis, is now in clinical trials.

What this means for you: Despite these new drugs, antibiotic research is getting short shrift. That's because many major pharmaceutical companies have found that it is more profitable to fund research and development for new drugs that treat chronic illnesses, such as diabetes, arthritis and high cholesterol.

Self-defense: Write to your representatives in Congress and tell them that you support efforts to increase incentives (via tax credits and other means) for pharmaceutical companies to develop new antibiotics. To write to your congressional representatives on-line, go to *www.firstgov.gov*. This Web site also provides mailing addresses and phone numbers for your congressional representatives.

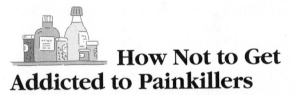

How Not to Get Addicted to Painkillers

Allen H. Lebovits, PhD, a psychologist and professor in the department of anesthesiology and psychology at New York University Medical Center and codirector of the NYU Pain Management Center, both in New York City.

Radio personality Rush Limbaugh made headlines in 2004 when he admitted that he was addicted to prescription painkillers. His announcement may have discouraged people with chronic pain from getting appropriate treatment, but Limbaugh is not typical. Addiction is rare when prescription painkillers are used appropriately. The most powerful class of painkillers—opioids, such as *codeine, morphine* and *oxycodone* (Oxycontin)—are all potentially addictive, but less than 1% of pain patients ever become addicted.

People who take these drugs can develop a drug tolerance and then require higher doses. They may experience the withdrawal symptoms, such as heightened anxiety and pain, if they stop taking the drug, but they rarely exhibit the hallmark signs of addiction.

Warning signs of addiction...

- **Diminished ability to concentrate.**

- **Fixation on the drug.**

- **Watching the clock until the next dose.**

- **Hiding drug use from friends and family members.**

To prevent addiction, first try to achieve pain relief through the nonsteroidal anti-inflammatory drugs (NSAIDs), such as aspirin and ibuprofen. *If these aren't effective or cause stomach bleeding or other side effects...*

- **Ask your doctor about other non-opioid drugs that help pain.** Many anti-depressants, including *amitriptyline* (Elavil), are effective at very low doses for chronic pain. The anticonvulsant *gabapentin* (Neurontin) works for nerve pain. These drugs are not addictive.

- **Try pain-relief therapies such as acupuncture and biofeedback.** The nondrug approaches often permit patients to take lower doses of painkillers or discontinue them.

Helpful: Get treatment at a multidisciplinary center. Specialists at these centers are familiar with a wide range of therapies. For information, contact the American Pain Foundation (888-615-7246, *www.painfoundation.org*).

If these approaches don't work, a pain specialist may recommend opioid drugs. *If you take an opioid...*

- **Limit use.** The risk of addiction tends to rise when a patient takes a prescription painkiller for a year or more.

- **Take a long-lasting drug.** Sustained-release opioids such as MS Contin can stay in the bloodstream for 12 hours and are less likely to cause addiction than shorter-acting drugs such as Percocet. Methadone also is long-lasting and a good choice for chronic pain.

- **Talk to your doctor immediately if you notice any addiction warning signs**—especially if you have a personal or family history of alcoholism or addiction.

When Are Bacon, Broccoli and Muffins Dangerous?

Earl Mindell, RPh, PhD, emeritus professor of nutrition at Pacific Western University in Los Angeles. He is also the author of more than 50 books, including *Natural Remedies for 150 Ailments* (Basic Health) and *Bottom Line's Prescription Alternatives* (Bottom Line Books at *www.bottomlinesecrets.com*).

Some foods can interact with medications in potentially dangerous ways. Foods, like drugs, are complex mixtures of chemical compounds. When some drugs and foods are taken simultaneously, the combination may increase or decrease blood levels of the drug in the body or speed or slow the drug's absorption into the bloodstream.

Example: Thiazide diuretics, a category of drugs used to treat high blood pressure and other conditions, cause the body to excrete potassium and magnesium. Taking them and eating salty foods can increase mineral loss and result in deficiencies.

Drug instruction sheets provide minimal information. They usually are limited to whether to take the medications with food (to protect the stomach) or with an empty stomach (to speed absorption). That's why it's important to always ask your doctor or pharmacist if certain foods should be avoided when taking a medication.

MAIN OFFENDERS

- **Broccoli, cabbage and leafy greens.** These are high in vitamin K, which can promote blood clotting and counteract the effects of blood thinners such as *warfarin* (Coumadin).

It's fine to eat small quantities—say, two or three weekly servings—of vitamin K–rich foods when taking an anticoagulant, but check with your doctor about eating more than that.

- **Grapefruit.** Both the juice and the whole fruit block liver enzymes that break down and clear drugs from the body. Eating grapefruit if you're on certain medications is like taking a higher dose, which can result in excessive levels of the drug in the blood.

Don't combine grapefruit with the statin drugs *lovastatin* (Mevacor) or *simvastatin* (Zocor)...

calcium channel blockers, such as *amlodipine* (Norvasc) and *diltiazem* (Cardizem)…benzodiazepine tranquilizers (such as Valium)…or the antihistamine *loratadine* (Claritin). After taking any of these drugs, wait one to two hours before having grapefruit or grapefruit juice.

•Bran muffins, whole-grain cereals and other high-fiber foods. Fiber slows the absorption of *penicillin, ampicillin* and other antibiotics. In some cases, it binds to drugs in the intestine and prevents most of the active ingredient from entering the blood.

Warning: Fiber also can block the absorption of the heart drug *digoxin* (Lanoxin). Don't consume high-fiber foods or fiber supplements within two hours of taking this drug.

•Dairy. The calcium in dairy foods reduces the absorption of the antibiotic tetracycline. If you are taking *tetracycline* for an infection, take it one hour before or two hours after consuming dairy foods or taking a calcium supplement.

•Tyramine-rich foods. Numerous cheeses (like American, cheddar, blue and Parmesan), cured meats (such as salami, bacon and pepperoni), liver, red wine and beer contain *tyramine*. It's a chemical compound that can cause a potentially fatal rise in blood pressure in people who take older-generation antidepressants called monoamine oxidase inhibitors (MAOs).

People who take MAOs, such as *phenelzine* (Nardil) and *procarbazine* (Matulane), should never eat foods that contain tyramine. Ask your doctor or pharmacist for a complete list of foods that contain it.

•Soft drinks. All the carbonation, sugar and phosphoric acid in soft drinks can greatly speed absorption and increase blood levels of *ketoconazole* (Nizoral), an oral drug taken for fungal infections. Avoid regular and diet sodas while taking this drug.

•Rhubarb contains natural chemicals that increase blood pressure and can reduce the effects of antihypertensive drugs.

Ask your doctor about: Eating five medium stalks of celery daily when taking antihypertensive drugs. Celery lowers blood pressure and can make the treatment more effective.

The Worst Time to Fill Prescriptions

Don't fill prescriptions at the beginning of the month. Deaths due to mistakes—the wrong drug, the wrong dose—tend to rise by as much as 25% at the start of any month. This is probably due to a surge in orders received by pharmacies when government assistance payments are made to seniors and Medicaid patients.

Self-defense: Review your prescriptions with your doctor—know drug names, dosages and purposes. At your drugstore, double-check the information with the pharmacist, including your name and address.

David P. Phillips, PhD, professor of sociology, University of California, San Diego, LaJolla, and leader of a study of medication deaths, published in *Pharmacotherapy*.

Cosmetic Surgery Trap

Fast-growing demand for plastic surgery is attracting many new practitioners. But, beware. In most states, it is legal for any MD to perform plastic surgery—including those whose training is in a different field and who have no experience with it.

Safety: Check a doctor's experience and credentials before committing to a procedure. Get references from other patients, and verify the doctor's certifications with the American Board of Medical Specialties at *www.abms.org*.

Steven G. Wallach, MD, FACS, plastic surgeon in New York City.

More Music, Less Anesthesia

Listening to music during surgery reduces the need for anesthesia.

New study: Patients who were able to control the amount of anesthesia they received during surgery listened to music of their choice through headphones, white noise through headphones or operating room noise.

Result: Those who listened to music needed less anesthesia.

Theory: Music helps to activate areas in the brain that release painkilling chemicals known as endorphins.

If you are scheduled for surgery and will be awake during the procedure: Ask your doctor if you can bring headphones to play your favorite music.

Zeev N. Kain, MD, professor and vice chairman of clinical affairs, department of anesthesiology, Yale University School of Medicine, New Haven, CT.

Safer Surgery

To reduce risk of infection from surgery, antibiotics should be administered one hour or less before the procedure.

Recent study: Antibiotics are given within this ideal time frame only about 55% of the time.

Self-defense: Patients should talk to their physicians about measures to prevent wound infections and confirm that the hospital has a protocol to ensure that antibiotics are delivered just before an incision is made.

Dale W. Bratzler, DO, MPH, principal clinical coordinator at the Oklahoma Foundation for Medical Quality, Oklahoma City, and leader of a study of 34,000 surgical patients, reported in *Archives of Surgery*.

Avoiding Unnecessary Surgery

Charles B. Inlander, a health-care consultant and president of the nonprofit People's Medical Society, a consumer health advocacy group in Allentown, PA. He is the author of more than 20 books on consumer health issues, including *Take This Book to the Hospital with You: A Consumer Guide to Surviving Your Hospital Stay* (St. Martin's).

Few things are worse than having an unnecessary surgical procedure. Yet every year, millions of Americans have operations they do not need. In fact, the Congressional Committee on Energy and Commerce reports that 20% of all surgeries performed in the US are unnecessary. *Surgeries you may not need...*

•**Removal of the prostate.** The most common treatment for prostate cancer is removal of the prostate gland, but clinical studies show that the operation is of little benefit to men who have a life expectancy of 10 years or less because the cancer grows very slowly. This means that most men over age 75 have nothing to gain and may suffer from side effects of the surgery, such as incontinence and infection. Regardless of a man's age, he should seek several medical opinions (including that of a urologist who does not perform surgery).

•**Cataract removal.** More than a decade ago, the Agency for Healthcare Policy and Research warned that many of the operations performed to remove a cataract were not necessary. The National Institutes for Health suggests that cataract removal is best performed if your vision has been reduced to at least 20/150—even with eyeglasses.

And yet each year, hundreds of thousands of Americans have the surgery even though their eyesight is far better than that. In many cases, surgery will not improve sight and can cause infection. For a more impartial view, get a second opinion from an optometrist (a health-care provider licensed to provide a broad range of eye-care services), rather than a surgical ophthalmologist (a medical doctor who specializes in eye disease).

•**Gallbladder removal.** Since the late 1980s, the number of gallbladder operations has increased by about 40%. The reason is the advent of minimally invasive laparoscopic surgery. This procedure can be done in an outpatient setting and is quicker (conventional surgery typically requires three days in the hospital), more convenient and more profitable for doctors. But it is often not necessary. Before agreeing to gallbladder removal, consult an experienced internist about nonsurgical options, such as a special diet or the gallstone-dissolving medication *ursodiol* (Actigall).

•**Wisdom tooth extraction.** This procedure is the granddaddy of all unnecessary surgeries, as about half of all wisdom tooth extractions are unnecessary. For decades, major dental organizations and journals have criticized the removal of wisdom teeth that are symptom free. To protect yourself, any time a dentist recommends having your wisdom teeth removed, get a second opinion from another dentist. If wisdom teeth are impacted, infected or are causing other teeth to shift, surgery may be necessary. But many times they will not cause any problems, and you can save yourself a lot of time, money and pain.

More from Charles Inlander…

Unexpected Sources of Lethal Infections

According to the Centers for Disease Control and Prevention (or CDC), infections that are acquired in the hospital kill approximately 100,000 patients every year, seriously harm almost 2 million additional people and add more than $5 billion to annual health-care costs. The CDC also estimates that up to half of these infections are preventable, if only hospital personnel would take infection control more seriously—primarily by washing their hands.

However, hospitals aren't the only place that an unsuspecting medical consumer can acquire a deadly infection. You also can get an infection from outpatient surgical and emergency centers, nursing homes, assisted-living facilities—even in your doctor's office.

Not one single state routinely inspects non-hospital medical facilities for infection-control practices, nor do states require these facilities to report infections that might have been caused by treatments received there. That means it's up to you—the patient—to take steps that will lower your risk for infection. *Best strategies…*

•**Check for clean hands.** You may have heard it before, but you cannot afford to ignore this advice. In fact, the CDC reports that staff not washing their hands is the number-one reason that infections spread. Do not let anyone—not even a doctor or a nurse—touch you unless he/she has washed his hands in your presence. If a health-care worker comes into the examining room with gloves on, ask him to remove those gloves, wash his hands and put on new gloves.

It has been found that, in rare cases, personnel wear the same gloves all day long!

•**Insist on clean equipment.** For example, make sure a doctor or nurse wipes the flat surface (diaphragm) of his stethoscope with alcohol before listening to your chest. Studies show that stethoscopes can be contaminated with *staphylococcus aureus* and other deadly bacteria if the equipment is not cleaned.

•**Beware of urinary catheters.** Infections triggered by urinary catheters are a problem, especially in nursing homes and assisted-living facilities. The longer the catheters stay in, the greater the risk for infection. Too often catheters are inserted in patients for the convenience of the staff, simply because they do not have the time (or desire) to bring a bedpan or change a diaper. Unless there is a medical reason for a urinary catheter, insist on a bedpan or diaper. It can save your life—or that of a loved one.

•**Ask about presurgical antibiotics.** When it comes to infection, outpatient surgery is just as risky as inpatient surgery. Research now shows that many patients should be given an antibiotic within one hour of surgery. Unfortunately, busy health-care workers often forget to administer it. So when your surgery is scheduled, talk to your doctor about receiving a presurgical antibiotic. If it is recommended, ask about the antibiotic as soon as you arrive at the facility.

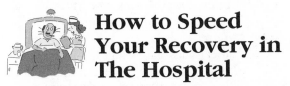

How to Speed Your Recovery in The Hospital

Pam Hagan, RN, a nurse for more than 25 years and chief programs officer, American Nurses Association, *www.nursingworld.org*.

There is much a patient can do to help—or occasionally hinder—recovery. Take the simple act of breathing, for example. When patients are sedentary, lung secretions may build up, resulting in pneumonia. I encourage patients to cough frequently and vigorously—even when they don't feel the need.

Some hospital patients are given an inspirometer to help with breathing. Request it if you're not given one. The deeper you breathe, the higher the ball in the inspirometer rises. Use it often—your lungs will thank you for it.

I also urge patients confined to bed to flex their feet, do ankle rotations and perform other simple exercises. Ask a nurse or a physical therapist for suggestions.

Other things you can do…

•**Ring for assistance getting out of bed.** More than a million falls occur each year in US hospitals, at least 30% resulting in moderate to severe injuries. The biggest risks are falling when attempting to get to the bathroom or in the bathroom. Ask for help before the need is urgent. Painkillers, diuretics, laxatives, sedatives and other drugs can increase the risk of falling.

Also helpful: Keep the bed in a low position.

•**Drink to stay hydrated**—to help prevent blood clots and increase the flow of secretions.

•**Eat nutritiously.** Poor nutrition can suppress the immune system, increasing the likelihood of medical complications. Ms. Hagan encourages all patients to request foods they like, as long as they comply with doctor-ordered limitations on salt and other restrictions. Ask to speak with the hospital dietitian if you have concerns. *Among the situations you may encounter…*

•If you don't like what you get—the meal, the flavor of your protein shake—request something else.

•If you are hungry between meals or want more of something, ask.

•**Get better sleep.** Sleep is a great healer, but hospital patients often don't get enough. *To get better shut-eye…*

•Wear earplugs and/or an eye mask.

•Ask the night nurse to help get you into a comfortable sleeping position and turn off lights.

•Make the nursing staff aware of your normal sleep schedule. They may be able to adjust the timing of your medications or other nighttime interruptions.

•If you feel you do need a sleeping pill, ask your physician for one. Talk with the nursing staff about pain medication, too. Day or night, *preventing* pain is easier than relieving it.

Have you noticed how frequently the word "ask" shows up on this page? Optimal recovery

requires a partnership between hospital professionals and patients. Communication is key.

US Integrative Care Centers

Consortium of Academic Health Centers for Integrative Medicine, 420 Delaware St. SE, Minneapolis 55455, *www.imconsortium.org*.

The following medical centers provide a combination of conventional and alternative care…

EAST

•**Continuum Center for Health & Healing at Beth Israel Medical Center, New York City,** 646-935-2257, *www.healthandhealingny.org*.

•**Thomas Jefferson University Hospital's Jefferson-Myrna Brind Center of Integrative Medicine, Philadelphia,** 215-955-2221, *www.jeffersonhospital.org/cim*.

•**University of Maryland School of Medicine's Center for Integrative Medicine, Baltimore,** 410-448-6361, *www.compmed.umm.edu*.

MIDWEST

•**Evanston Northwestern Healthcare's Integrative Medicine Program, Illinois,** 847-657-3540, *www.enh.org/healthandwellness/clinicalservices/integrative*.

•**University of Michigan Integrative Medicine, Ann Arbor,** 734-998-6649, *www.med.umich.edu/umim*.

WEST

•**The Scripps Center for Integrative Medicine, La Jolla, California,** 858-554-3300, *www.scrippsintegrativemedicine.com*.

•**University of Arizona Program in Integrative Medicine, Tucson,** 520-626-6417, *integrativemedicine.arizona.edu*.

•**University of Colorado Hospital's Center for Integrative Medicine, Aurora,** 720-848-1090, *www.uch.edu/integrativemed*.

For a complete list, go to the Web site *www.imconsortium.org*.

3

Simple Solutions for Common Ailments

Natural Healing Remedies To Treat Fatigue, Heartburn and More

It is a little-known truth that an estimated 50% of all hospital admissions are currently the result of adverse reactions to prescription drugs, and over-the-counter medications as well.

But aren't drugs the only alternative for some medical conditions? Certainly—but not as often as you might think.

Many natural remedies are effective, inexpensive *and* safe. Dietary supplements, herbs and simple lifestyle changes are available for most health problems.*

Important: Some natural remedies can bring immediate relief, but others may take weeks. Be

*To find a naturopathic physician in your area to monitor your use of natural remedies, contact the American Association of Naturopathic Physicians, 866-538-2267, *www. naturopathic.org. Please note:* Pregnant and breast-feeding women should avoid many natural remedies.

prepared to wait up to one month to experience the full effect.

To see what works best for you, try one of the following remedies, available in health-food stores, for two weeks. If you don't begin to see a beneficial effect during that time, try a different remedy for the condition.

FATIGUE

A persistent lack of energy is common in our age of too little sleep, too much stress, lack of exercise and inadequate nutrition.

Natural approach: The dietary supplement coenzyme Q10 (60 milligrams [mg] daily) fights off fatigue by strengthening the heart muscle... and dehydroepiandrosterone (DHEA), taken as a supplement first thing in the morning (25 mg for women and 50 mg for men daily), increases energy, because levels of this hormone naturally

Earl Mindell, RPh, PhD, emeritus professor of nutrition at Pacific Western University in Los Angeles. He is also the author of more than 50 books, including *Natural Remedies for 150 Ailments* (Basic Health) and *Bottom Line's Prescription Alternatives* (Bottom Line Books at *www.bottomlinesecrets. com*).

decline after age 40. If you are over age 40, ask your doctor to measure your DHEA level with a saliva test to confirm that you are deficient. This hormone should not be taken by people with a hormone-sensitive cancer, such as breast or prostate cancer.

Also helpful: The herbs astragalus and ginseng are natural energy boosters. Drink a cup of astragalus or ginseng tea daily.

GLAUCOMA

This condition is caused by increased pressure within the eyeball. Regular eye exams should include a check for glaucoma. If it is detected, you may need prescription eyedrops and should be under an ophthalmologist's care.

Natural approach: When glaucoma is detected early, dietary supplements can help to reduce eyeball pressure. I recommend to my patients a combination dietary supplement of methylsulfonylmethane (MSM)—1,000 mg daily—and vitamin C for its anti-inflammatory effect. I also advocate two additional dietary supplements— alpha lipoic acid (50 mg daily), which protects against free radicals that can exacerbate eye pressure…and L-arginine (1,500 mg, twice daily) to increase circulation.

Also helpful: The herbs grape seed extract (200 mg daily) and green tea extract (200 mg daily), both of which help prevent eye damage.

HEARTBURN

This fiery pain behind the breastbone is caused by stomach acid backing up into the esophagus. There are drugs that can shut down stomach acid production, but a natural approach aims to improve digestion.

Natural approach: The probiotic acidophilus (one to three capsules before each meal) adds "friendly" bacteria that fight heartburn by aiding digestion…and the hydrochloric acid supplement betaine (150 mg once daily, with a meal) increases stomach acid levels in people who have a deficiency. Both supplements help the body break down protein and other food elements.

Also helpful: Aloe vera juice (one tablespoon, twice daily with meals) heals the intestinal lining, which helps prevent heartburn.

If heartburn develops, chew one to three papaya tablets or eat fresh papaya for quick relief.

HEMORRHOIDS

These inflamed veins in the rectum can be painful and often bleed.

Keep bowel movements regular to prevent straining on the toilet, which worsens hemorrhoids. Get at least 25 grams (g) of fiber in your daily diet. In addition to eating plenty of fruits and vegetables, add unprocessed wheat bran to soups, stews and salads…or take a fiber tablet. Be sure to drink eight to 10 glasses of water daily—otherwise, fiber can be constipating.

Natural approach: Vitamin C (500 to 1,000 mg daily) helps strengthen capillaries, including those in the rectum. Acidophilus (one to three capsules before each meal) aids bowel regularity.

Also helpful: Apply vitamin E oil or cream to hemorrhoids to ease the discomfort and promote healing.

PSORIASIS

The scaling, itchiness and inflammation from psoriasis can be tormenting, but dietary supplements bring substantial relief for many people.

Natural approach: Fish oil capsules (500 mg, twice daily) and selenium (100 to 200 micrograms [mcg] daily) have been shown to reduce symptoms of psoriasis. Natural mixed carotenoids—5,000 international units (IU) to 10,000 IU daily—which convert to vitamin A in the body, if it is needed, and vitamin D (400 to 800 IU daily) promote healthy skin and protect against infection. Allow 30 days for this program to take effect.

Also helpful: Aloe vera gel, applied twice daily, soothes affected skin and relieves itching.

TINNITUS

This incessant ringing or buzzing in the ears is often worse at night and frequently interferes with sleep.

Natural approach: Calcium (500 mg daily) and magnesium (200 mg daily) help to promote sleep if taken before bedtime…coenzyme Q10 (60 mg, twice daily) and a multivitamin-mineral complex rich in antioxidants protects against cell breakdown that can worsen the condition.

Also helpful: The herb ginkgo biloba (60 mg, three times daily) reduces tinnitus by improving circulation to the inner ear.

Bananas Fight Heartburn, Depression and More

Ara DerMarderosian, PhD, professor of pharmacognosy (the study of natural products utilized in medicine) and Roth chairman of natural products at the University of the Sciences in Philadelphia. He also is the scientific director of the university's Complementary and Alternative Medicines Institute and has published two books, as well as more than 100 scientific papers.

Most people know that bananas are an excellent resource for potassium (one ripe banana supplies more than 10% of an adult's daily requirement of the mineral). That's important because people with a low dietary intake of potassium are 28% more likely to suffer a stroke than those who consume higher levels, according to a study conducted at Tulane University.

Lesser-known medicinal uses of bananas…

• **Depression.** Bananas are a good source of *tryptophan* (a precursor to *serotonin,* a chemical in the brain that helps regulate mood).

• **Diarrhea.** Unripened bananas and plantains (high-starch, green bananas which are typically cooked) are a rich source of *tannins,* astringent plant compounds that help stop water accumulation in the intestines, thus diminishing diarrhea.

• **Heartburn and ulcers.** Bananas neutralize acidity and soothe and coat esophageal tissue with pectin (a substance used as a thickener and stabilizer in jellies).

Important: In rare cases, bananas may trigger an allergic reaction. Bananas with blackened skin can increase blood sugar levels. Because bananas have high levels of potassium, people with kidney problems should check with their doctors before eating this fruit.

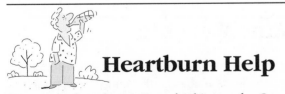

Heartburn Help

Prone to heartburn? Stop drinking soda. Consumption of carbonated beverages is a risk factor for nighttime heartburn—which can cause more damage to the esophagus than daytime heartburn. Acid that comes up into the esophagus is not cleared as easily by the body during sleep. Even people who usually don't have heartburn should stop drinking soda at least three hours before bedtime to reduce the chance of nighttime acid reflux.

Stuart F. Quan, MD, professor of medicine, University of Arizona, Tucson, and coauthor of a recent study of 3,806 people with nighttime heartburn, published in *Chest.*

A Cure for Stomach Flu

Jamison Starbuck, ND, a naturopathic physician in family practice and a lecturer at the University of Montana, both in Missoula. She is past president of the American Association of Naturopathic Physicians and a contributing editor to *The Alternative Advisor: The Complete Guide to Natural Therapies and Alternative Treatments* (Time Life).

"Doctor, this is my third bout this winter! What can I do to get over it for good?" Ken was in obvious distress, holding his belly and rocking back and forth. Ken had "stomach flu"—a catchall phrase for *gastroenteritis,* an acute inflammation of the lining of the stomach and intestines that is characterized by nausea, vomiting, discomfort in the abdomen and diarrhea. It is usually caused by a viral or bacterial infection. He was suffering yet another episode of these acute symptoms after following the advice of his medical doctor. Now he was ready to try a natural approach.

When the medical doctors treat stomach flu, they recommend bed rest, bland food and lots of fluids. They also usually prescribe antibiotics when patients have high fevers. After a few days of symptoms, most people recover—or so they think. If gastroenteritis is treated conventionally, you may fail to *fully* recover.

Here's why: The organisms that cause the infection also inflame the intestinal membranes, and vomiting and diarrhea may have eliminated both the "bad" and "good" bacteria found in the intestines. This is a setup to make you more susceptible to repeat infections.

My naturopathic approach…

• **Limit your diet.** To rest the gastrointestinal tract and speed healing, drink chicken or vegetable broth and eat baked apples and/or pears (the pectin in these fruits soothes the stomach and helps stop the diarrhea) until your symptoms abate. Avoid dehydration by consuming at least 72 ounces of water per day while you have the flu. Also, drink chamomile, peppermint, ginger, black or green tea—all have antinausea and antivomiting properties. Brew a strong tea using two tea bags per 12 ounces of water. Drink three to six cups daily, on an empty stomach.

•**Use a mustard poultice.** This will relieve nausea and vomiting.

What to do: Combine one tablespoon of mustard powder with one cup of flour. Stir in enough water to make a smooth paste. Saturate a piece of cotton cloth about the size of a facecloth with hot water from the faucet, wring it out and spread the paste over the cloth. Place it (paste-side up) over your abdomen. Cover with a dry cotton cloth, and then a hot water bottle or heating pad. Leave the poultice in place for 30 minutes. Apply twice a day.

•**Take an herbal tincture.** The clinical trials confirm that the herbs Oregon grape root and geranium have antimicrobial properties, while slippery elm and licorice reduce inflammation and promote growth of tissue in the intestine. Make a mixture of equal parts of these tinctures, which are sold individually at most health-food stores. Take 60 drops of the combined tinctures in two ounces of water, on an empty stomach, four times per day for up to five days.

•**Try probiotics.** *Lactobacillus acidophilus* and *Bifidobacterium bifidum* replenish "friendly" bacteria in the bowels. Probiotics are available at health-food stores in powder, liquid or capsules. Take 10 billion colony-forming units (CFUs) each of L. acidophilus and B. bifidum in four divided doses daily for the duration of the illness and for three weeks after your symptoms have resolved.

Shorter Flu Recovery

In a new study, flu patients who were given elderberry extract four times daily for five days recovered in four days compared with eight days for those given a placebo.

Theory: Elderberry helps prevent the flu virus from attaching to cells, which stops the virus from replicating.

Self-defense: Take four tablespoons of elderberry extract or four elderberry lozenges daily at the onset of flu symptoms and for the duration of the illness.

Vivian Barak, PhD, head of the immunology lab for tumor diagnosis at Hebrew University-Hadassah Medical School, Jerusalem.

The Best Tea For a Sore Throat

A sore throat occurs when the mucous membranes of your throat become inflamed and irritated. One natural anti-inflammatory, marshmallow root, is particularly effective in soothing sore throat pain. Use one heaping teaspoon of marshmallow root pieces in one cup of boiling water. Let steep for 20 minutes and strain. Drink up to six cups daily.

For sore throats accompanied by cold and flu symptoms, try peppermint or ginger tea. Peppermint reduces fever by helping you to sweat, and ginger alleviates chills and aching muscles, and relieves nausea. Use one teaspoon of dried ginger root or dried peppermint leaves per cup of water. For greater convenience, tea bags also can be used. Drink three to six cups daily.

Brigitte Mars, herbalist in private practice in Boulder, CO, *www.brigittemars.com,* and author of *Healing Herbal Teas* (Basic Health Media).

Zinc Warning

Zinc cold remedies should be used cautiously. There is evidence that zinc can diminish a cold's severity, but zinc products should be used only two or three times a day, primarily in the first 48 hours after symptom onset—not every three hours, as indicated on labels. Also, do not use zinc lozenges *and* nasal spray—choose one.

High concentrations of zinc can cause nausea and diarrhea.

Neil Schachter, MD, professor of pulmonary medicine and medical director of respiratory care, Mount Sinai Medical Center, New York City.

Do Antibiotics Cure Bronchitis?

In a recent study, after 640 bronchitis patients first saw their doctors, coughing lasted for 11 days whether they received antibiotics or not. Other symptoms, such as increased phlegm and shortness of breath, cleared up less than one day sooner in those who took antibiotics.

Bottom line: Most bronchitis is caused by viruses, not bacteria—and antibiotics are ineffective against viral infections.

Self-defense: Talk to your physician about taking *acetaminophen* (Tylenol), which reduces fever and relieves sore throat and muscle pain. Inhaling steam for five minutes three times per day also may be effective.

Paul Little, MD, professor of primary care research, University of Southampton, England.

Help for Kids with Frequent Ear Infections

Kids with recurrent ear infections may benefit from seeing an osteopathic physician (DO) trained to perform osteopathic manipulation to relieve pressure in the eustachian tube. Osteopaths are licensed to practice medicine just as MDs are.

Recent finding: Children who received osteopathic manipulations in addition to routine care—antibiotics, ibuprofen, ear tubes, etc.— had fewer ear infections and were less likely to need antibiotics or surgery than ones given routine pediatric care only.

Miriam V. Mills, MD, clinical assistant professor of pediatrics, College of Osteopathic Medicine, Oklahoma State University, Tulsa.

Food Allergy Breakthrough

Food allergies soon may be treated with the bacteria *Listeria*. Animal studies show that allergies to peanuts, milk and wheat improved by twentyfold when subjects were given a shot of the offending food combined with heat-killed *Listeria*. Human trials are being planned.

Dale T. Umetsu, MD, PhD, professor of pediatrics at Children's Hospital Boston, and leader of a study of using heat-killed *Listeria* to treat severe allergies in dogs, published in *Allergy*.

Alleviate Allergies with Breakfast in Bed

Allergy sufferers are sensitive to temperature changes. That's why they cough and sneeze when they leave a warm bed. Drinking hot tea in bed warms the body and prevents this reaction. Caffeinated or decaffeinated tea increases the speed of nasal cilia, tiny hairs in the mucous membranes, to rid the nose of allergy-triggering dust that has accumulated during sleep.

Helpful: Fill a thermos with hot tea at night and drink a cup in the morning.

Murray Grossan, MD, otolaryngologist and head and neck surgeon at Cedars-Sinai Medical Center, Los Angeles, *www.ent-consult.com.*

Asthma Symptoms Eased By Biofeedback

In a new finding, when asthmatics practiced biofeedback (using electronic instruments to control physiological responses) twice daily for 20 minutes, they needed 22% less medication than those who did not practice biofeedback.

Theory: Biofeedback helps prevent asthma attacks by slowing breathing, which makes sufferers less reactive to both physical and emotional stressors.

To find a biofeedback practitioner, contact the Biofeedback Certification Institute of America, 303-420-2902, *www.bcia.org.*

Paul Lehrer, PhD, professor of psychiatry, The University of Medicine and Dentistry of New Jersey–Robert Wood Johnson Medical School, Piscataway, NJ.

Pain Reliever Linked to Asthma

A study of more than 13,000 Americans found that those who took *acetaminophen* (Tylenol) regularly (six to 29 times per month) were at an increased risk for asthma and chronic obstructive pulmonary disease (COPD).

Theory: Regular use of acetaminophen may deplete levels of glutathione, an antioxidant that helps protect the lungs.

Tricia M. McKeever, PhD, lecturer, division of epidemiology, University of Nottingham, England.

Drug-Free Headache Relief: Small Changes Mean a Lot

Mark V. Wiley, OMD, PhD, doctor of Oriental medicine at Optimal Acu-Therapy in Philadelphia. He is also a board member of the International Association of Optimal Acupuncture and Clinical Chinese Medicine and the author of *Outwitting Headaches, The Eight-Part Program for Total and Lasting Headache Relief* (Lyons).

For the 41 million plus Americans who suffer from headaches every year, powerful drugs—many with quite dangerous side effects—are the standard treatment. Fortunately, there are other options available. However, you probably won't hear about them from your medical doctor.

The first step is to consult your primary care physician to rule out any underlying medical cause, such as meningitis or a brain tumor. Then try my seven drug-free steps, which I created to treat my own chronic headaches. Most people start to see results by the end of the first week. If you cut out all triggers, your headaches, including tension headaches and migraines, should be gone after two weeks.

●**Breathe deeply.** Most of us breathe shallowly. The resulting low oxygen levels force blood vessels to widen in an effort to allow more blood to flow through them, which can trigger headaches. *To bring fresh air deep into your lungs, practice an abdominal breathing exercise three times every day…*

What to do: Lie on your back, knees bent and feet flat on the floor about a foot away from your buttocks. Rest the lower back on the floor. Inhale deeply, allowing your abdomen to rise. Exhale, fully expelling air from your lungs as your abdomen sinks. Repeat 12 times.

●**Drink plenty of water.** Keeping the body well-hydrated helps cleanse the colon and flush the kidneys, clearing headache-inducing toxins from the body. Only water can do this—not caffeinated coffees and teas, herbal teas or sugary sodas and fruit drinks.

However: Not all water is fit to drink. Tap water may contain heavy metals, chemical toxins or naturally occurring contaminants, so stick to bottled spring or filtered water.

What to do: Aim to drink two quarts of bottled or filtered water daily. This should keep your urine light-colored or clear.

●**Eliminate food triggers.** Certain foods are well-known as headache triggers—alcohol (especially red wine)…caffeine…dairy products…processed and preserved meats (cold cuts, beef jerky)…dried fruits…foods containing the amino acid *tyramine* (aged cheese, pickled foods)…chocolate…and the sweetener aspartame.

What to do: Eliminate all suspected food triggers from your diet for two weeks. Add them back one at a time, waiting a day before adding each new one. If you develop a headache, eliminate the food indefinitely.

Also helpful: Eat smaller, frequent meals—a one-third–sized portion every three hours—to prevent headaches due to overeating and extreme blood-sugar fluctuations. Also, take a daily multivitamin that includes the B vitamins, which help prevent headaches.

•**Flush out toxins.** When we take in more chemicals from food, water and drugs than our bodies can handle, they build up (causing constipation) and interfere with proper functioning of the liver, colon, kidneys and lungs. The result can be headaches.

What to do: Avoid constipation by eating more whole grains, fruits and vegetables and drinking plenty of water.

Also helpful: Fast up to four times a year to give your digestive system a rest. A fast typically lasts one to three days and includes only liquids—water…fresh, organic fruit or vegetable juices…and/or broth.

Important: You may experience a headache on the first or second day of the fast. Be patient, it will pass.

•**Tame stress with meditation.** Stress is a potent headache trigger. It also provokes lifestyle choices that cause chronic headaches—eating unhealthful foods, drinking alcohol and/or caffeine and taking painkillers. To short-circuit the damaging effects of stress, I practice mindfulness meditation.

What to do: Sit or lie with your spine straight and head aligned. Close your eyes and take a deep breath through your nose. Then focus on your breath as it passes into and out of your nose. Repeat a few times. If thoughts enter your mind, release them without passing judgment. Practice this daily for at least 15 minutes.

•**Stay active.** Exercise reduces stress and improves blood flow, which helps prevent headaches. *Recommended exercises…*

•Brisk walking. Set aside some time each day, preferably up to 30 minutes, to walk at a brisk pace. Keep your mind clear of stressful thoughts by focusing on your breathing or on the sensation of your big toe lifting off the ground.

•Qigong standing. For this ancient Chinese exercise, which increases blood flow and strengthens muscle, stand with your legs shoulder-width apart and knees slightly bent. Bend both arms at the elbow, creating a 90-degree angle. Keep your forearms parallel to the ground, palms facing down. Visualize that your arms are floating on water. Quiet your mind by letting thoughts pass without judgment. Breathe at a steady pace.

Perform for five minutes, working up to a total of 40 minutes.

What to do: Perform each exercise daily until your headaches stop. Then do one or the other each day as a preventive strategy.

•**Cultivate a deep sleep.** To battle insomnia, eliminate caffeinated drinks after 6 pm and keep a notepad by your bed. When your mind races with things that need to be done, write them down. This should make it easier to let them go until morning. Also, practice progressive relaxation at bedtime.

What to do: While lying on your back with arms at your sides, inhale fully for four seconds and exhale for eight seconds. Repeat 10 times, then resume normal breathing.

Mentally focus on the toes of one leg. Will each toe to relax, maintaining your focus until the toe relaxes—it may begin to tingle or feel numb. Then relax the sole, ankle, calf and so on up to the hips. Do the same with the other leg—and with each part of the body.

Herbal Relief for Low-Back Pain

In an analysis of 12 studies involving more than 1,000 people, devil's claw relieved back pain as effectively as the standard dose of *rofecoxib* (Vioxx), the COX-2 inhibitor that was taken off the market due to increased risk for cardiovascular complications.

Theory: Devil's claw contains iridoid glycosides, substances believed to have strong anti-inflammatory effects.

Self-defense: Take 60 mg daily of harpagoside, the active compound in devil's claw. It is available in most health-food stores.

Caution: Do not use devil's claw if you currently take a blood thinner or you have a clotting disorder.

Joel J. Gagnier, ND, postgraduate fellow, Institute of Medical Sciences, University of Toronto.

Alleviate Neck and Back Pain with Fish Oil Supplements

In a new finding, when neck and back pain sufferers took a fish-oil supplement (1,200 mg daily) for 75 days, 60% reported significant pain relief that allowed them to decrease or discontinue use of painkillers.

Theory: The omega-3 fatty acids found in fish oil block the inflammation that can lead to neck and back pain. Fish oil also may help relieve joint pain.

If you have neck or back pain: Ask your doctor about taking fish oil.

Caution: Do not use fish oil if you take *warfarin* (Coumadin) or any other blood thinner.

Joseph Maroon, MD, vice chairman of neurological surgery, University of Pittsburgh.

Help for Carpal Tunnel Syndrome

Carpal tunnel syndrome can be relieved without having surgery. Steroid injections are just as effective as surgery at treating the condition, which causes pain and numbness in the hands and wrists.

José-Luis Andreu, MD, PhD, rheumatologist, department of rheumatology, Clinica Puerta de Hierro, Madrid, Spain, and leader of a study of 101 patients with carpal tunnel syndrome, published in *Arthritis & Rheumatism*.

Say Cheese!

Eat cheese after sweets to stabilize the pH levels in your mouth. This helps to fight plaque buildup and cavities.

Best cheeses to prevent cavities: Aged Cheddar, Gouda, Monterey Jack and mozzarella.

Even better: Rinse your mouth with water after consuming sweets.

Best: Floss and brush after eating.

Sheldon Nadler, DMD, dentist in private practice, New York City.

Yogurt Stops Bad Breath

In a new finding, the amount of odor-producing bacteria in people with halitosis was reduced by more than half after having six ounces of unsweetened yogurt daily for six weeks.

Theory: Ingredients in yogurt, which include two common bacteria—*Streptococcus thermophilus* and *Lactobacillus bulgaricus*—produce an unfavorable environment for the bacteria that coat the tongue.

Best: Eat unsweetened yogurt that contains live active cultures.

Kenichi Hojo, MS, researcher, department of oral bacteriology, Tsurumi University, Yokahama, Japan, and lead researcher of a study of the effect of sugar-free yogurt on halitosis, presented at a recent meeting of the International Association for Dental Research.

Natural Mosquito Repellents

For years, the Centers for Disease Control and Prevention (CDC) has recommended only DEET-containing products to protect against mosquitoes, which could carry West Nile virus.

New finding: Repellents that contain oil of lemon eucalyptus or the chemical *picaridin* can provide protection against these insects similar to that of low-concentration (7% to 10%) DEET products.

New products: Spectrum Cutter Advanced, BugNix and OFF! Botanicals.

Be aware that the mosquito season lasts until the first heavy frost.

Lyle Petersen, MD, MPH, director of CDC's division of vector-borne infectious diseases, Atlanta, *www.cdc.gov*.

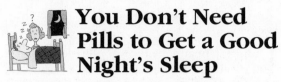

You Don't Need Pills to Get a Good Night's Sleep

Peter Hauri, PhD, a consultant emeritus to the Sleep Disorders Center at the Mayo Clinic in Rochester, MN. He is coauthor of *No More Sleepless Nights* (Wiley). Dr. Hauri is one of the founders of the American Sleep Disorders Association, now the American Academy of Sleep Medicine, *www.aasmnet.org.*

More Americans than ever are now taking sleeping pills. Last year, about 42 million prescriptions for sleep medication were filled.

Insomnia is more than an annoyance. It can wreak havoc on the immune system, contributing to serious illnesses.

The newer sleep medications, such as *zolpidem* (Ambien), *zaleplon* (Sonata), *ramelteon* (Rozerem) and *eszopiclone* (Lunesta), are believed to be safe.

However: Even these medications can cause headaches, daytime drowsiness, dizziness and other adverse symptoms. Older adults, who are most likely to use sleeping pills, are particularly sensitive to them.

Is there a better alternative? Absolutely. New studies have found that natural treatments are just as effective as sleep medication for mild to moderate insomnia.

GETTING STARTED

Most people require eight hours of sleep per night to feel refreshed and to stay healthy, but some of us need as many as 10 hours and others as little as four.

If you have trouble getting to sleep, staying asleep or regularly awaken much earlier than you'd like, schedule an appointment with your primary care physician. Medical problems, including thyroid disorders, pain and allergies, can compromise sleep. Treating such conditions can improve sleep.

Depression, anxiety, a panic disorder or even everyday stress also can disturb sleep. If you suspect that psychological issues may be causing sleeplessness, mention it to your doctor and consider consulting a mental health professional.

If your doctor can't find a medical problem, you can begin a natural self-help treatment plan.

To determine whether natural approaches will be effective, you must try them for at least one or two weeks—one at a time.

Helpful: Keep a log of your sleep quality for at least a week, preferably two. Use a rating scale from one to 10, with 10 being optimal. Rate your sleep each night—preferably about a half hour after you get out of bed in the morning.

When you introduce one of the strategies described below, rate your nightly sleep again for about a week or two. If the ratings improve, then you know that the technique you're trying works for you.

BEHAVIORAL APPROACHES

During my 40-year career, I've treated thousands of adults with sleep complaints. *Here are the simple strategies that I've found to be most successful...*

•**Create a sleep-inducing environment.** Keep your bedroom at a temperature that is comfortable for you (cooler is typically better)...turn out all the lights (darkness promotes the body's production of a sleep-promoting hormone called melatonin)—some people, however, sleep better with a night-light...and, if necessary, adjust your sound level—some people like total quiet, while others prefer soft background noise, such as a radio or a "white noise" machine.

•**Go to bed at about the same time each night so that your body gets into a rhythm.** Some insomniacs are kept awake all night worrying what time it is, so putting a clock where you cannot see or reach it is often helpful. It is counterproductive to lie in bed desperately trying to fall asleep. Distract your mind by reading.

•**Get more physical activity.** Physically fit people tend to sleep more deeply. If you have been sedentary, start performing aerobic exercise, such as brisk walking or bicycling, three times a week.

Some sleep research indicates that it's best to exercise four to six hours before going to bed. If you exercise too close to bedtime, your body may be too stimulated for you to fall asleep.

•**Meditate.** Studies indicate that a period of meditation during the day or the early evening helps fight insomnia by promoting physical relaxation and/or slowing the mind.

SUPPLEMENTS

If the behavioral approaches described above don't work as well as desired, consider also trying a sleep-promoting supplement (available at health-food stores).* *Effective supplements…*

•**Melatonin** has been shown to help restore a more normal sleep cycle—but it rarely lengthens the amount of time you sleep. If you have problems falling asleep, take it two hours before bedtime. If you wake up too early or in the middle of the night, take it when you awaken.

Recommended dose: Three milligrams (mg) once per day. If this doesn't work, gradually increase the dosage over a month to a maximum of 9 mg daily.

Possible side effects: Headache, digestive upset and depression. Long-term use of melatonin has not been studied, so consult your doctor if you need to use this hormone for more than a few months or you develop side effects.

•**Valerian** helps many people fall asleep faster and stay asleep longer.

Recommended dose: Take one-half to one teaspoon of liquid extract or 300 to 500 mg in capsule form 20 minutes before bedtime.

Possible side effects: Stomach upset.

•**5-hydroxytryptophan (5-HTP)** is a compound derived from the seed of an African plant called griffonia. 5-HTP is best known for treating mild to moderate depression. The scientific evidence on 5-HTP's efficacy as a sleep aid is inconclusive at this time, however, the compound may be worth trying if you don't get relief from the other supplements listed above. 5-HTP has helped some of my patients.

Recommended dose: Ask your doctor.

Possible side effects: Mild nausea.

•**Vitamin B-12 and/or calcium** can help improve your sleep if you have a deficiency. Both vitamin B-12 and calcium calm the nervous system and have a mild sedative effect in some.

Recommended dose: Ask your doctor.

Possible side effects: None are known.

Important: If you are taking any medications, including prescription sleeping pills, consult your doctor before taking these supplements.

*The FDA does not regulate herbal and other natural supplements. Do not take these supplements if you are pregnant or nursing.

Help for Snoring

The best treatment for snoring depends on the cause. Snoring can occur because of a blockage anywhere from the tip of the nose to the back of the throat.

Common cause: Being overweight. Losing weight should relieve the problem.

Other causes: Deviated septum, sinus infection, floppy uvula (the fleshy lobe that hangs from the back of the soft palate). These may require surgery or, when infection is present, treatment for the infection.

Best: A physician who looks at the whole patient.

Example: An overweight smoker with allergies who complains of snoring may need to see an allergist, an acupuncturist to help stop smoking and a dietitian for weight loss.

If snoring continues, the cause can be narrowed down and treated directly—surgery for a deviated septum, for example.

Jordan S. Josephson, MD, a scientist and snoring, ear, nose and throat-endoscopic sinus specialist in private practice, New York City, *www.drjjny.com.*

12 Powerful Ways To Boost Your Energy

Kenneth H. Cooper, MD, MPH, a pioneer in the fields of preventive medicine and physical fitness. He is president of Cooper Aerobics Center, Dallas, *www.cooperaero bics.com* and the author of 18 books, including *Regaining the Power of Youth at Any Age* (Nelson). His books have sold more than 30 million copies worldwide.

As we get older, we often complain that we're "running on empty." I call this age-related loss of energy *youth drain*—but we don't have to be victims of it. At 74 years of age, I work 60 hours a week, travel widely and still feel energetic.

Youth drain can be caused by a variety of factors, including obesity…chronic medical problems, such as anemia, diabetes, emphysema or an underactive thyroid gland…depression…cancer…use of sedatives and sleeping pills…menopause…poor diet…inadequate sleep…and stress. These factors batter us over the years and drain our vitality—unless we learn how to respond to them and counter their effects.

Here, 12 revitalizing strategies for us all…

•**Eat less but more frequently.** Consuming large meals (more than 1,000 calories in one sitting) makes you feel sluggish, since your body's resources are directed toward digesting all that food. Instead, have small meals and snacks that contain a mix of carbohydrates and protein (but little fat) to provide a steady stream of fuel.

Examples: Yogurt smoothie…peanut butter and banana sandwich…fruity cottage cheese.

•**Exercise.** Many people tell me they continue to exercise year after year because it makes them feel good and gives them more energy. I recommend at least 30 minutes of sustained activity five times a week. The best activities tend to be brisk walking, jogging, swimming, cycling and aerobic dance.

•**Take a multivitamin.** In a clinical trial, people who took multivitamins daily not only had improved immunity against infectious diseases but also had more energy. In general, it is best to get vitamins from food, but many people don't get the necessary amounts, so I suggest taking a multivitamin/mineral supplement daily.

•**Prevent dehydration.** Consuming an inadequate amount of fluids, particularly if it's hot outside or you're exercising, can deplete energy and lead to weakness, dizziness and headaches. Drink at least six to eight eight-ounce glasses of water daily. On days that you exert yourself to the point of perspiring, drink up to 13 glasses.

•**Watch what you drink.** Drink no more than one caffeinated beverage a day. Coffee, tea, cola and other caffeinated beverages provide a temporary energy boost, but energy levels plunge when the stimulant's effects wear off.

Caffeinated drinks also have a diuretic effect, which may cause you to lose fluids because you urinate more frequently.

And, have no more than one alcoholic drink a day—any more can lead to fatigue.

•**Practice the "relaxation response."** This technique, developed by Herbert Benson, MD, of Harvard University, has been shown to reduce blood pressure and heart rate. For me, doing this for just five minutes in the middle of the day is rejuvenating.

How to do it: Sit in a chair in a quiet room. Close your eyes. Starting with your feet, begin to relax your muscles, progressively moving up the body to the top of the head. While you do this, breathe in slowly and naturally through your nose and out through your mouth. As you exhale, silently repeat a focus word or phrase that has meaning for you, such as "peace." Push away distracting thoughts by focusing on your breathing and the word you have chosen to repeat.

For more information, read *The Relaxation Response* by Herbert Benson, MD (HarperTorch).

•**Take naps.** Surveys show that most Americans don't get as much sleep as they need (most of us require seven to eight hours a night). Daily naps of 15 to 20 minutes are energizing—and longer naps can help if you are sleep-deprived.

•**Don't immerse yourself in bad news.** Negative information can hurt the psyche, causing stress and fatigue. Reduce the amount of time you spend watching, listening to or reading the news, and focus on things that bring you joy.

•**Be social.** Studies show that isolation can lead to depression and early death. We gain energy by being with others (both humans and animals). Make time for family, friends and pets.

•**Explore your creativity.** Boredom leads to a lack of motivation and energy. Finding a creative outlet that absorbs you is invigorating. Developing your creativity also challenges your brain and leads to the release of endorphins. Take up a new pastime or take on an unusual project at work.

•**Laugh.** Laughter appears to release endorphins just as creative pursuits do. By improving your outlook, you'll feel more energetic and ready to tackle life. Watch funny movies…read cartoons…share humorous stories with friends.

•**Think young.** Your mindset can determine how much energy you have. When you expect the worst, you are likely to feel tired and unwell. If you expect to stay vital, you'll fight off disease that can sap energy—and you'll add years to your life.

Reduce Stress in Minutes

Millie Grenough, a clinical instructor of psychiatry, Yale University School of Medicine, New Haven, CT, and author of *Oasis in the Overwhelm* (Beaver Hill).

After a near-fatal bicycling accident, I developed simple strategies to elevate my mood and decrease stress during recovery. *A lot of people know about deep breathing, but here are some of my unusual methods for destressing…*

•**Sanity stone.** Hold a shell, one quarter or some other small object, and focus all your attention on it. As you take 10 slow, deep breaths, notice its color, pattern, texture and other characteristics. Then gradually let your eyes and attention move out to your surroundings.

My clients use sanity stones in traffic jams, before (and after) tough conversations and even when they are trying to stay away from a tempting dessert.

•**Gut reaction.** Whenever you experience discomfort, notice where you feel it—churning stomach, sweaty hands, a pounding headache. *Ask yourself…*

•What is the distress signaling to me? Anger? Anxiety? Frustration? And…exactly what situation is causing this discomfort? Is there anything that I can—and want—to do about it now?

If the answer is yes, take the action right away. If not, change your "emotional channel" by asking yourself what emotion you want to let go of—and which emotions you want to invite in. *Examples:* To switch from fear to calm, you might picture a peaceful outdoor scene. Let go of worry and think of something that is good about life—that the sun is shining, that you can walk, see, etc. In this way, you can retrain your brain to slide easily into positive emotions.

•**Four-direction stretch.** Stretching can improve mood, enhance blood flow and reduce stress. The following instructions may sound a little corny, but they will energize.

•Stand and relax your body. Stretch your arms and body upward, yelling, "North!" Return to starting position.

•Bend at the waist, letting your head and upper body drop toward the floor as you yell out, "South!"

•Stand back up. Stretch both arms in front of you. Extend and wiggle your fingers. Swing your arms and upper body to the right, yelling, "East!"

•Return to center. Extend your arms and upper body to the left, wiggle your fingers and yell out, "West!"

Variations on the four-direction stretch: If you prefer, substitute words such as "Canada," "South America," "Paris" and "Hawaii" for the four directions. During a long meeting or flight, do the exercise moving only your feet. If stuck in traffic, just move your head. In public, say the words internally and visualize them. Using words—aloud or silently—adds energy to this stretch.

Each of these exercises takes only a minute. They are well worth the time in this too, too fast-paced world.

Soothing Sounds

We are surrounded by noise—the rush of traffic, airplanes overhead, humming refrigerators, etc.—all of which can contribute to your anxiety and stress.

Five-minute healer: Listen to relaxing classical music (such as Bach, Vivaldi and Gregorian chants). Or spend a few minutes in nature. Sit by a fountain in a park…listen to the rustling of leaves…tune in to the rushing sounds of wind.

A study at a New York hospital showed that hypertensive patients obtained normal systolic blood pressure after listening to classical music or nature sounds for approximately three minutes. Other studies have shown that soothing sounds can reduce the need for pain medication by up to 30%.

Mary Capone, a founder of the Living School of Sound, and an instructor of sound, movement and breath healing techniques in Longmont, CO, *www.marycapone.com.* She is a coauthor of *The Five Minute Healer: Self-Healing Techniques for Busy People* (Johnson).

4

Quick and Easy Fitness

The Lose Weight Forever Diet

Weight loss is not only, or even mainly, about fewer calories. Surprisingly, we put on weight when natural weight-control mechanisms are disrupted by an inflammatory response caused by unwise diet choices and environmental toxins.

When people gain weight, the extra fatty tissue produces *leptin,* a hormone that suppresses appetite and speeds metabolism. In theory, this should cause people to lose the extra weight.

Instead, inflammation in fat tissue and blood vessels stimulates the production of anti-inflammatory chemicals. These chemicals disable leptin's ability to suppress appetite and speed metabolism. This is called *leptin resistance.*

To combat leptin resistance, I have developed a fat-resistance diet based on cutting-edge research at premier institutions such as Harvard, Johns Hopkins and Rockefeller universities. Eating the proper

foods can eliminate chronic inflammation and re-program the body's weight-loss mechanisms.

ANTI-INFLAMMATORY FOODS

The focus of the diet isn't calorie reduction. The idea is to eat foods that supply anti-inflammatory nutrients. The major problem with most weight-loss diets is the use of artificial sweeteners and fat substitutes to reduce calories. Substituting these products for real foods deprives your body of key anti-inflammatory nutrients. *Main principles…*

•**Eat fish at least three times weekly.** The omega-3 fatty acids in fish have powerful anti-inflammatory properties. Fish that are rich in the omega-3s and relatively low in mercury include anchovies, conch, herring (fresh or pickled, not the creamed), mackerel (Atlantic only), sablefish,

---

Leo Galland, MD, director of the Foundation for Integrated Medicine in New York City. He has held faculty positions at Rockefeller University and at Albert Einstein College of Medicine, both in New York City, and at the State University of New York, Stony Brook. He is author of *The Fat Resistance Diet* (Broadway) and *The Four Pillars of Healing* (Random House).

salmon (that's fresh, canned or smoked, wild or farmed), sardines (Atlantic), sturgeon and tuna (fresh or canned bluefin—not albacore).

•**Balance essential fatty acids.** The optimal ratio of omega-6 fatty acids to omega-3s is about 4:1. The ratio in the average American diet is closer to 20:1. A relative excess of omega-6 fats in tissues leads cells to produce excessive levels of pro-inflammatory chemicals called *prostanoids.* The best approach is to decrease intake of omega-6s and increase intake of omega-3s.

Foods high in omega-3s: Fish, flaxseed, walnuts and beans—navy, kidney and soybeans.

Foods high in omega-6s: Red meat, chicken, milk, eggs and most vegetable oils, including corn, sunflower and safflower.

•**Cut back on unhealthy fats.** Saturated fat—primarily found in beef, pork, lamb, dairy products and poultry skin—should be limited to no more than 10% of total calories. Don't eat any trans fat—this means avoiding any foods made with hydrogenated or partially hydrogenated vegetable oil. These include most commercial baked goods and some fast foods. Both saturated fat and trans fat greatly increase levels of inflammatory chemicals.

•**Get 25 grams (g) of fiber daily.** A high-fiber diet helps control appetite and reduce inflammation. A study by the Centers for Disease Control and Prevention found that people who consume the most fiber have lower levels of *C-reactive protein* (CRP), which indicates the presence of inflammatory chemicals in the body. All plant foods contain some fiber. Among the best sources are beans, whole grains and vegetables.

•**Eat colorful fruits and vegetables.** Get at least nine servings daily. Produce with deep colors and intense flavors is high in flavonoids and carotenoids, chemical compounds that have anti-inflammatory effects.

Important: Have at least one serving of blueberries, cherries or pomegranates a day. These all contain *anthocyanins,* which are among the most potent anti-inflammatory agents.

•**Choose alliums and crucifers.** Crucifers are stronger-flavored vegetables, including broccoli, cauliflower, cabbage and kale. The alliums include onions and garlic. Both classes of vegetables reduce chronic inflammation and lower the risk of cancer, particularly breast cancer. Eat at least one serving of each daily.

•**Use only egg whites or unbroken egg yolks.** The cholesterol in yolks has relatively little effect on cholesterol in the blood—but if the yolk is broken, the cholesterol is oxidized and produces inflammatory by-products. Poached or boiled whole eggs are fine to eat. Avoid scrambled eggs and whole-egg omelettes.

•**Favor herbs and spices that are potent anti-inflammatories.** These include basil, cardamom, cilantro, cinnamon, clove, ginger, parsley and turmeric. Use them every day. Avoid chiles, cayenne pepper and jalapeños, which can trigger inflammation.

THREE STAGES

The diet progresses in phases...

•**Stage 1.** Eat as much as you want of such foods as arugula, bell peppers, broccoli, cabbage, carrots, leeks, onions, romaine lettuce, scallions, shiitake mushrooms, spinach and tomatoes—as well as blueberries, cherries, grapefruit and pomegranates.

Eating three four-ounce servings of high-protein foods each day helps suppress appetite and maintain muscle mass. Choose fish, egg whites, poultry and plain, fat-free yogurt. The meat lovers can eat red meat twice a week but should marinate beef with cherry or pomegranate concentrate (this decreases the inflammatory chemical compounds produced throughout cooking). You can have a tablespoon or two each day of nuts or seeds (especially flaxseed, walnuts and almonds). During this stage, get 25 g of fiber, primarily from vegetables.

Avoid all grains, even whole grains, because they tend to raise insulin levels, increasing leptin resistance.

Most people stay in this stage for two weeks and lose six to 10 pounds.

•**Stage 2.** This is the long-term weight-loss portion of the diet. Stay on this until you reach your goal weight. Expect to lose one to two pounds per week.

In addition to the Stage 1 foods, add some whole grains, such as oats and brown rice, and beans, lentils and other legumes (about two to three cups a week of each).

•Stage 3. This is the lifelong maintenance part. Increase variety by adding potatoes, pasta and whole-grain breads.

Soup's On!

In a study of 147 men and women who ate a reduced-calorie diet for a year, those who consumed 10.5 fluid ounces of low-fat, low-calorie soup twice a day lost 50% more weight than those who ate healthful but carbohydrate-rich snacks, such as baked chips or pretzels.

Theory: Although the soup had the same calories as the other snacks, the soup's greater weight and volume made study participants feel full enough to eat less for the rest of the day.

Self-defense: Consume one large mugful of a broth-based, low-fat, low-calorie and low-sodium soup that's rich in vegetables and/or beans as a first course twice daily.

Barbara Rolls, PhD, professor and Guthrie Chair in Nutrition, Pennsylvania State University, University Park. She is author of *The Volumetrics Eating Plan* (HarperCollins).

More from Barbara Rolls, PhD...

The Salad Trick

Large salads help you consume fewer calories. A recent study found that diners who have a large low-calorie salad before the main course of their meal consume 12% fewer total calories at the meal than those who have nothing before the main course at all.

Why: Salad takes the edge off your appetite and helps fill you up.

Does the Breakfast Cereal Diet Really Work?

The breakfast cereal diet calls for eating one serving (about one cup) of any ready-to-eat cereal (with ⅔ cup of skim milk and a small banana, two cups of strawberries or some other

100-calorie serving of fruit) for breakfast and another for either lunch or dinner. A normal meal is eaten at the remaining meal time.

In a recent study, obese or overweight people who followed this plan for two weeks—whether they ate one single brand of cereal or a variety of cereals—lost about three to four pounds during that period. The study participants who ate normally lost less than two-tenths of a pound. This diet is one option that may be effective for people who have trouble limiting portion size. Consult your doctor or dietitian for advice.

Richard D. Mattes, MD, MPH, RD, professor of foods and nutrition, Purdue University, Lafayette, IN.

Looking for a Low-Sugar Cereal?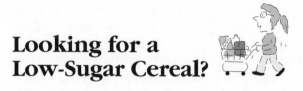

Check the ingredients list of cereals for words that mean added sugar. Look for the words dextrose, sucrose, maltose, cane juice, corn syrup and honey.

Good low-sugar dry cereals: General Mills' regular Cheerios and Wheat Chex…Post Grape-Nuts and Grape-Nuts Flakes…puffed Kashi… and all brands of unfrosted shredded wheat.

Good hot cereals: Old-fashioned rolled oats, unsweetened regular or instant…Ralston 100% Wheat…Wheatena…and 7 Grain cereal made by Arrowhead Mills.

Healthier ways to add sweetness: Mix in sliced bananas, peaches, strawberries, blueberries or chopped dried fruit.

Suzanne Havala Hobbs, DrPH, RD, clinical assistant professor, School of Public Health, University of North Carolina at Chapel Hill.

Weight-Loss Trap

Consuming too few calories slows metabolism. It actually is harder to lose weight on a super-low-calorie diet than on a moderate calorie regimen. To find your calorie minimum, multiply your weight in pounds by 10. That will give you the minimum number of calories your body needs to maintain its metabolism. Reduce your intake to that number—but not less.

Example: If you're 150 pounds, you should consume no less than 1,500 calories a day.

Neal Barnard, MD, founder and president, Physicians Committee for Responsible Medicine, Washington, DC.

Vitamins May Fight Food Cravings

In a recent study, people who had taken multivitamins, B vitamins or chromium regularly for the past 10 years gained less weight than people who did not take them.

Possible reason: The body's craving for certain essential nutrients may cause hunger. Vitamin/mineral supplements may lessen hunger by supplying nutrients that would have been supplied by food.

Best: Take a multivitamin/mineral that provides chromium and the daily recommended intake of B-6 and B-12.

Emily White, PhD, epidemiologist at Fred Hutchinson Cancer Research Center, Seattle, and coleader of a survey of 15,000 men and women, presented at a recent meeting of the American Association of Naturopathic Physicians.

Weight-Loss Surgery: Is It for You?

Neil Hutcher, MD, a bariatric surgeon in private practice and associate clinical professor of surgery at Virginia Commonwealth University, both based in Richmond. He has performed more than 4,000 weight-loss surgeries in the past 32 years. Dr. Hutcher is president of the American Society for Bariatric Surgery.

An estimated two-thirds of all American adults are overweight, and one-third of those are "obese"—that is, their weight puts their health in jeopardy. Most have tried to slim down with diets and/or exercise—but have failed.

Not surprisingly, the popularity of weight-loss surgery has soared. In 2004, more than 140,000 people had such surgery in the US—eight times as many as in 1998.

Weight-loss (technically known as "bariatric") surgery works for the majority of people who have it, often with dramatic health benefits. But it's not for everyone.

ARE YOU A CANDIDATE?

The critical issue, says the National Institutes of Health (NIH), is body mass index (BMI), a measure of the relationship between height and weight. According to NIH guidelines, surgery should be considered when BMI exceeds 40, or 35 for people with a weight-related medical condition, such as diabetes or heart disease. For these people, the benefits of weight-loss surgery generally outweigh the risks.

To calculate your BMI: Multiply your height in inches by itself. Divide your weight in pounds by this number. Multiply by 703. Or go to the National Heart, Lung, and Blood Institute's Web site, *www.nhlbisupport.com/bmi/bmicalc.htm.*

Examples: A 5' 10" man who weighs more than 280 lbs., or a 5' 5" woman who tops 240 lbs., has a BMI over 40.

HOW IS IT DONE?

Weight-loss surgery changes the way the digestive system holds and processes food. There are two approaches—*restrictive* and *malabsorptive* procedures.

Restrictive procedures reduce the amount of food the stomach can hold and, therefore, the amount you can eat. Malabsorptive procedures reroute the passage of food and digestive enzymes through the small intestine, so less will be absorbed.

•**Gastric bypass** combines both approaches and accounts for 80% to 85% of bariatric operations in the US. With this procedure, a small pouch is created from part of the stomach just below the esophagus, separated from the rest of the stomach by a line of staples, thus reducing the capacity of the stomach from football-sized to egg-sized. Digestive juices from the liver and pancreas are diverted to bypass some of the small intestine, so less of the food you eat is digested and absorbed.

Advantages: Appetite is reduced along with eating capacity. Weight loss is usually swift—one-half to one pound a day, for the first two to three months.

Drawbacks: Malnutrition is possible if diet and supplement guidelines aren't followed.

OTHER PROCEDURES

•**Vertical banded gastroplasty** is a purely restrictive approach that creates a pouch similar to gastric bypass, but this procedure leaves the intestine unchanged.

•**Adjustable gastric band** is a new procedure in which an inflatable silicone band, placed around the upper part of the stomach, is tightened to form the pouch.

Advantages: These operations are simpler than gastric bypass and have less risk for complications. The adjustable gastric band can be placed laparoscopically (using a lighted scope that requires smaller incisions than traditional surgery) as an outpatient procedure.

Drawbacks: These surgeries reduce eating capacity but not the desire to eat. One possible reason is that unlike a gastric bypass, banding does not decrease the secretion of the appetite stimulating hormone ghrelin. Many do complain that they never feel satisfied. It's consequently less effective—about 40% of those having purely restrictive surgery lose less than half of their excess body weight.

•**Biliopancreatic diversion** is similar to gastric bypass, but it is more extreme. The surgeon removes three-fourths of the stomach and restructures the small intestine so that even less absorption takes place.

Advantages: Patients are able to eat more food than with other procedures, and lose more weight due to greater malabsorption. Studies show that patients drop 75% to 85% of excess weight after five years.

Drawbacks: The complications are more frequent, and the risk for nutritional deficiencies, gastric ulcer and gallstones is greater.

BENEFITS

A report published in *The Journal of the American Medical Association* analyzed 136 studies involving 22,094 surgical patients. They had lost, on average, 61% of their excess weight.

Diabetes was essentially cured in more than three-fourths of those who had weight-loss surgery and improved in a total of 86%. High blood pressure normalized in 62% of affected individuals, while cholesterol improved in 70%. Usually, these benefits appeared within six months—in the case of diabetes, sometimes within *days*.

REDUCE THE RISK

Because the people who undergo weight-loss surgery are obese and frequently have medical conditions, such as diabetes, they are particularly prone to complications, such as venous thrombosis (a blood clot in a vein), infections and respiratory failure.

Within 30 days of the surgery, the risk of death from these complications is highest (one in 90) for those who have the most extensive types of surgery, such as biliopancreatic diversion. It's lowest (one in 1,200) for patients who have purely restrictive procedures, such as gastric banding. For gastric bypass, it falls in between (one in 200).

Important: Have surgery in a facility which performs at least 125 such procedures a year, by a surgeon who performs 50 or more procedures each year.*

A LIFETIME COMMITMENT

Most people are out of the hospital in one to three days—but the surgery is just the beginning of a whole new way of life.

You need to learn how to eat slowly, chew thoroughly and pause between swallows. This is important in order to give the body time to signal that it is getting full, so you do not overeat. Because you'll be eating less, your diet must be rich in nutrients, particularly protein. Supplements—including folic acid, vitamin B-12, vitamin D, iron and calcium—are essential.

Many health insurance plans, including Medicare, pay for weight-loss surgery in cases of medical necessity.

*To locate a bariatric surgeon in your area, contact the American Society for Bariatric Surgery, 352-331-4900, *www.asbs.org*.

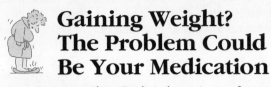

Gaining Weight? The Problem Could Be Your Medication

Lois M. Jessen, PharmD, clinical associate professor of pharmacy and vice chair of the department of pharmacy practice and administration in the School of Pharmacy at Rutgers State University of New Jersey in Piscataway. She lectures extensively in the areas of psychopharmacology and obesity.

If you have put on more than a few pounds and can't figure out why, look in your medicine chest. Dozens of prescription drugs can cause weight gain. It's not unusual for patients to gain at least five pounds after they start taking certain medications. *A few common offenders…*

•**Antidepressants.** Many of the selective serotonin reuptake inhibitors (SSRIs) cause an average weight gain of 7%. Recent data shows that this generally doesn't occur when patients take them for less than six months. Some SSRIs, such as *paroxetine* (Paxil), are more likely to cause weight gain than others.

These drugs increase brain levels of *serotonin*, a neurotransmitter that is involved in appetite and satiety. Patients who take them may feel hungrier in general and not feel full after eating.

What to do: Try another drug in the same class. A chemically similar drug such as *sertraline* (Zoloft) is less likely to cause weight gain as a side effect. Or ask your doctor about a non-SSRI antidepressant, such as *bupropion* (Wellbutrin) or *venlafaxine* (Effexor).

•**Hormones.** The hormones used in birth control pills and to relieve menopausal discomfort (hormone replacement therapy, or HRT) appear to cause weight gain in about 25% of patients. And, the contraceptive injection Depo-Provera triggers weight gain in up to 70% of users. *Estrogen* and *progestin* promote fluid retention and may increase levels of androgens, male hormones that can trigger weight gain.

What to do: Most women taking these drugs gain only a few pounds. Lifestyle changes, such as eating less and exercising more, usually can offset weight gain and are the best choice for women undergoing HRT.

Women who take oral contraceptives can try nonhormonal methods, such as a diaphragm or condoms. Women who prefer birth control pills can try OrthoTri-Cyclen. One month's supply of pills has variable dosing—different concentrations of hormones that mimic the body's cycle, which may minimize weight gain.

•**Evista.** *Raloxifene* (Evista) helps prevent osteoporosis and can reduce bone fractures by up to 50% in postmenopausal women—but a small percentage of women who take it gain weight.

What to do: Ask your doctor about *alendronate* (Fosamax), which builds bone and is less likely to cause weight gain.

•**Steroids.** *Prednisone, cortisone* and other steroid medications are used to treat dozens of conditions, including asthma, lupus and cancer. They frequently cause weight gain because they increase appetite and promote fluid retention.

What to do: Try to eat smaller portions of food and exercise more. Substituting other drugs is rarely an option.

Exception: Patients who gain weight while taking prednisone may want to ask their doctors about switching to *dexamethasone*. It has similar therapeutic effects but is less likely to cause significant weight gain.

The Super 12-"Stop" Program for Weight Loss From a US Governor

Mike Huckabee, governor of Arkansas and the second-longest-serving governor in the US. Two years after committing to weight-loss and fitness changes, he now weighs 175 pounds. He is author of *Quit Digging Your Grave with a Knife and Fork: A 12-Stop Program to End Bad Habits and Begin a Healthy Lifestyle* (Center Street).

Mike Huckabee, the long-time governor of Arkansas, knows something about the urge to shovel in calories to take the edge off a stress-filled day. He knows about gargantuan portions served the Southern way, dredged in cornmeal and fried in hot grease. And, just like millions of Americans, he knows about the disappointment of trying, and often failing, to lose weight.

It wasn't until his weight topped out at more than 280 pounds—and his doctor diagnosed him with type 2 diabetes—that Huckabee realized he had to discard bad habits before establishing healthier ones.

Example: Focusing on weight rather than long-term health. People whose only goal is to lose weight generally fail because they start to abandon their efforts as soon as they reach their target weight.

The big weight-loss challenge isn't to change actions temporarily, but to permanently change attitudes. *Governor Huckabee's 12-"stop" plan...*

STOP 1: STOP PROCRASTINATING

People will always come up with a reason why now is not the right time to diet, exercise more, etc. They often say they are too busy to make a serious life change.

We don't find time, we *make* time. No matter how busy you are, once you start, you will find that you're more productive because you have less fatigue and more energy. *To get started...*

•**Set a specific start date within the next two weeks.**

•**Share your start date with family and friends.** That makes it harder to make excuses.

Example: I told my immediate staff about the changes I was trying to make. When we went out to eat, everyone was watching to see what I'd do...like order the cheesecake. A little social pressure helps you make the right decisions.

STOP 2: STOP MAKING EXCUSES

Nearly everyone has excuses to justify weight-loss failure. "I'm genetically predisposed." "I've tried every diet, and none have worked." "I'm large boned."

All these are not legitimate excuses. Anyone who tries hard enough can lose weight. If you've failed in the past, it means that you will have to try harder—cutting more calories, avoiding more desserts, exercising more, etc.

STOP 3: STOP SITTING ON THE COUCH

The hardest part of losing weight is getting active after years of being sedentary. Exercising does not feel good initially—and a common mistake is to attempt more than is reasonable or realistic.

Example: I started out exercising for 30 to 60 minutes the first day, the amount doctors recommend. I could hardly get out of bed the next day—and gave up.

Helpful: Commit to no more than 12 minutes a day—walking, swimming, biking, etc. Everyone can set aside that much time, and you won't get hurt (or bored). Every week, add a little more time as you get in better shape. (Of course, talk to your doctor before starting any exercise program.)

STOP 4: STOP IGNORING BODY SIGNALS

Your body will tell you when you are out of shape. You might fatigue easily, be short of breath, have trouble sleeping or experience depression, headaches or joint or muscle pain.

Pay attention to these feelings: They'll remind you how important it is to change bad habits into good ones.

Bonus: You'll get the satisfaction of feeling aches and pains—and negative feelings—disappear as you change your life.

STOP 5: STOP LISTENING TO DESTRUCTIVE CRITICISM

It's amazing how many well-intentioned people say things that undermine your motivation.

Examples: "You don't need to lose weight, you're fine the way you are," or "You've lost too much weight, you have to put some back on."

We all have doubts about our ability to succeed. Listening to destructive criticism makes it hard to stay focused and motivated. Ignore it.

STOP 6: STOP EXPECTING IMMEDIATE SUCCESS

Most people can quickly lose weight initially, then get discouraged when they hit a plateau and the pounds refuse to come off. This happens to almost everyone, and it's a serious motivation drain.

Important: Keep your focus on your real goals—adding years to your life and having a better quality of life. Fitness involves more than what's revealed on the bathroom scale. It also includes mental sharpness...staying flexible and strong...and feeling energized.

STOP 7: STOP WHINING

People who complain that they hate watching calories or giving up certain foods almost always fail. If dieting seems hateful, you won't stick with it.

Helpful: Rather than dwell on what you can't eat, make a list of all the things you can eat and can do. You'll find that the "cans" greatly outnumber the "can'ts"—and that focusing on the positive will help you to stay motivated.

STOP 8: STOP MAKING EXCEPTIONS

Nearly everyone is tempted to cheat "just a little" after a few days or weeks of starting new behaviors. Don't do it. An ex-smoker cannot afford the luxury of having "just one" cigarette, and people who are trying to get fit can't afford to have the extra-rich chocolate cake. There are some things you have to walk away from. Otherwise, you'll find yourself slipping back into unhealthy habits.

STOP 9: STOP STORING PROVISIONS FOR FAILURE

One of the hardest habits for me to break was stockpiling "provisions," such as candy bars in a desk drawer or chips in the cabinet. I told myself that I would only eat them in an "emergency." I had a lot of emergencies.

If you keep the bad-for-you foods on hand, you're going to eat them. You have to stop buying them. Keep them out of the house—and out of the car and office, too.

STOP 10: STOP FUELING WITH SWEETS AND PROCESSED FOODS

Sugar and processed foods, in any amount, simply are not good for you. Sugar is addictive. The more you eat, the more you crave. Giving up sweets entirely may be the only way to get the cravings out of your system.

Good news: Cravings for sugar almost always disappear within a few weeks.

Other foods nutritionists suggest avoiding…

•**Refined grains,** such as white bread. As far as your body's concerned, they are almost the same as eating sugar.

Better choice: Whole grains, such as brown rice, whole-wheat bread and whole-grain cereals. They're high in fiber as well as health-protecting antioxidants.

•**Deep-fried fast foods.** They're loaded with artery-clogging saturated fat.

•**Fatty meats,** also high in saturated fat.

Better choice: Lean cuts, such as flank steak or chicken without the skin.

•**Hydrogenated fats used in many margarines and commercial baked goods.** Studies indicate that these fats are even worse for your heart than saturated fat.

STOP 11: STOP ALLOWING FOOD TO BE A REWARD

A lot of us "reward" ourselves with special foods or meals after completing difficult tasks. (I did it after reaching my target weight!) This reinforces the idea that eating is the same as happiness—and that giving up certain foods is punishment. No one wants to spend a lifetime feeling punished.

Find ways to reward yourself—or friends or family members—that don't involve food.

Examples: Treat yourself to a movie after a hard week's work…give your child a CD when he/she brings home good grades…plan a special trip when you finally reach one of your fitness goals.

STOP 12: STOP NEGLECTING YOUR SPIRITUAL HEALTH

Most 12-*step* programs include the affirmation that we are destined to fail without assistance from a higher power. The belief that your body was created by God or some kind of higher power can motivate you to take better care of this special gift.

I believe that we tend to take better care of ourselves when we feel accountable not only to ourselves, but to the higher power that designed our bodies for optimal performance and health.

Laugh Away The Pounds

A recent study of students who watched comedy clips found that laughing for 10 to 15 minutes can burn 10 to 40 calories.

Implication: Ten to 15 minutes of laughing daily could result in weight loss of about four pounds a year.

American Family Physician, American Academy of Family Physicians, Box 11210, Shawnee Mission, KS 66207-1210, *www.aafp.org/afp.*

Yoga May Slow Midlife Weight Gain

In a recent finding, people in their 50s who regularly practiced yoga lost about five pounds over 10 years, while those who did not practice yoga gained about 13 pounds. Most yoga exercises do not burn enough calories to account for the weight loss, but some practitioners believe that yoga keeps people aware of their bodies and eating habits.

Alan Kristal, DrPH, researcher, Fred Hutchinson Cancer Research Center, Seattle, and leader of a study of 15,550 people, published in *Alternative Therapies in Health and Medicine.*

Thin Body, Fatter Wallet

A 15-year study of 7,300 people ages 21 to 28 found that those who lost enough weight to go from the middle of the overweight category—body mass index (BMI) of 27.5—to the middle of the normal category—BMI of 21.7—increased their wealth by an average of $4,085 over the research period. Weight gainers had an 8% decrease in wealth.

Ohio State University, Columbus, OH 43210, *ohio.stateuni versity.com.*

Walk Your Way to Great Health

Mark Fenton, associate director of the advocacy group America Walks, *www.americawalks.org.* Based in Scituate, MA, Mr. Fenton was former host of the PBS series *America's Walking* and is author of several books on walking, including *Walk It Off: The Complete Guide to Walking for Health, Weight Loss, and Fitness* (Lyons).

Most people know that walking is one of the most healthful of exercises. The problem is that walking has the reputation of being boring.

Wrong! People who do lots of walking know that it's not just good for you—it's also fun.

Nordic walking, for instance, is an activity that has been around for many years in Europe and is now growing in popularity in the US.

Nordic walkers use two poles that assist in balance, especially on rough terrain, and provide additional exercise for the upper body. Walking poles usually cost $70 to $140* a pair in sporting-goods stores.

Information: Exel at 802-524-4770 or on the Web at *www.nordicwalker.com.*

To aim at an even higher fitness level, try power walking or race walking, which require moving at more than four miles per hour.

In both activities, you stand upright, push off with your toes, bend your arms about 90 degrees at the elbow and take quicker, though not shorter, steps.

We normally walk at a pace of about 120 steps per minute. Power walkers take 140 to 160 steps per minute, and race walkers take more than 170 per minute. But there's a big difference between walking and running. Walkers never take both feet off the ground at the same time, and competitive rules require their legs to be straight when the foot hits the ground.

Information: Contact your local recreation department or the North American Racewalking Foundation (626-795-3243, *www.philsport.com/narf*) or visit the Web site *walking.about.com.*

THE PAYOFF

According to The Cooper Institute, a research institute dedicated to advancing the understanding of the relationship between living habits and health, in Dallas, Nordic walking, power walking and race walking all improve circulation and burn more calories than ordinary walking does.

Everyday walking also has big health benefits, say the Harvard School of Public Health, the US Surgeon General's office and the American Heart Association.

Proof: Researchers have shown that light exercise—which includes walking—cuts the risk of diabetes, heart disease, obesity, stroke, several types of cancer, high blood pressure, osteoporosis and depression. It does not take much walking to see huge benefits—for the average person, only about 30 minutes more a day than he/she normally walks.

*Prices subject to change.

MAKING IT FUN

Unlike many other activities, walking can be a solitary or a group activity. Thousands of walking events held throughout the US are great for meeting and socializing with other walkers.

The American Hiking Society (301-565-6704 or *www.americanhiking.org*) and the American Volkssport Association (800-830-9255, *www.ava. org*) keep track of the clubs and events, as does *walking.about.com*. City or county recreation departments usually know of local clubs.

Many events are five-kilometer walks (about three miles), which is well within the ability of most amateur walkers.

By joining a walking club, you can easily meet others who take regular walks. Clubs have already mapped out accessible and interesting routes—through historic areas, along rivers or to other places where you'll enjoy a leisurely visit.

Ask people you know to join you on a daily walk. If you're still working, invite coworkers. Lunchtime strolls can go a long way in reducing workday stress. If you have children or grandchildren who are students, think about walking them to and/or from school.

When you travel, look into walking tours that let you see areas that many tourists never have a chance to visit.

Examples: If you enjoy the French Riviera, you'll get a spectacular view of the Mediterranean by strolling along one of the many walking paths on the coast in Provence. The Italian Riviera and parts of the English countryside also have terrific sites for walkers. Check with your travel agent for overseas walking tours.

In the US, most large cities and many small ones have walking tours that are easy to find through local tourist offices and chambers of commerce.

SET GOALS

Even though walking can be fun, overscheduling often makes it hard to maintain any activity on a regular basis. Setting goals is an effective way to keep on track.

As a general rule, it is more effective to set goals for what you intend to do instead of the results you hope to achieve.

Example: Aim to walk 30 minutes every day instead of, say, setting a goal to lose 10 pounds in three months.

Recommended: Set a goal of walking a certain length of time each day or a certain number of miles each week or month.

Helpful: Maintain a log of how often or far you walk.

Or reward yourself with a present after maintaining a streak of walking every day for a certain time—two months, for instance.

Pedometers, which keep track of the number of steps you take, are also good motivators, especially if you're just beginning to walk on a regular basis. They're available at most sporting-goods stores.

Typical price: $15 to $30.

Wear a pedometer for about a week to see how many steps you average per day. Then set a goal to gradually increase them.

Most people over age 50 take 2,000 to 4,000 steps a day, according to The Cooper Institute, which says many walkers start experiencing health benefits after an increase of only 1,000 steps a day. This is a half mile or about 10 minutes of walking for someone who has an average stride.

A good plan is to increase your average daily steps by no more than 20%. If you now take an average of 3,000 steps a day, for instance, 600 more steps will require five to six minutes of additional walking.

Although an extra 30 minutes of walking is enough for many health benefits, it usually takes 60 to 90 minutes of walking per day to achieve substantial weight loss, if that's what you would like to achieve.

Regardless of your goals, it helps to wear shoes specifically designed for walking. Today, nearly all major manufacturers have them, including Adidas, Asics, New Balance and Nike. Prices are in the $60 to $80 range.

If you plan a walking tour, wear rugged walkers that give your feet added support and protection. Major manufacturers include Merrell, Timberland and Tecnica.

Typical price: $70 to $90.

Essential: Consult your doctor before beginning a walking regimen or any other type of exercise program.

Antiaging Workout— Especially for People Over Age 50

Karl Knopf, EdD, an exercise physiologist and executive director of the Fitness Educators of Older Adults Association in Sunnyvale, CA. He is the author of five books, including *Weights for 50 Plus: Building Strength, Staying Healthy and Enjoying an Active Lifestyle* (Ulysses).

Most people know that cardiovascular exercise, such as walking and swimming, helps promote good health. Unfortunately, many neglect strength training.*

People who do not perform regular strength exercises will lose 50% of their muscle mass and muscular strength by age 65. In fact, *sarcopenia* (age-related muscle loss) is one of the main reasons that many older adults become unable to live independently.

The following simple program, designed especially for those over age 50, is easily done at home using a stretchable rubber exercise band (about $15**)…ankle weights ($10 per pair)… and dumbbells ($1 to $2 a pound). These products are available at sporting-goods stores.

Most of the following exercises recommend beginning with one- to two-pound dumbbells or ankle weights. Increase the weight when you can perform 15 repetitions easily. By performing this 30-minute full body workout two to three times a week, in addition to your regular cardiovascular exercise routine four to five times a week, you can enhance your energy, strength— and even your independence.

SIT TO STAND

Purpose: Strengthens the front leg muscles that are used to get up from a seated position.

What to do: Sit toward the front of a sturdy chair, with your feet flat on the floor. Lean slightly forward. Inhale. Exhale slowly as you stand up. If it's possible, do not use your hands. Cross your arms in front of your chest. Inhale and

*Consult your doctor before beginning this or any new exercise routine.

**Prices subject to change.

Exercise illustrations by Shawn Banner.

lower yourself slowly into the chair. Do six to 15 repetitions. When you can complete 15 repetitions easily, try holding a one- to two-pound dumbbell in each hand.

LUNGES

Purpose: Strengthens the legs and helps with balance.

What to do: Stand with your feet shoulder-width apart, arms at your sides, holding a one- to two-pound dumbbell in each hand. Inhale. Keeping your left leg in place, exhale and lunge forward with your right leg as far as you comfortably can while keeping your right knee in line with your right ankle. Inhale as you step back to the initial position. Do six to 15 repetitions. Repeat with your left leg.

Modification: If you find this exercise too difficult, do it without weights, and place your hands on your hips instead. If balance is an issue, hold on to a chair when lunging.

LATERAL ARM RAISES

Purpose: Strengthens the shoulders and upper back.

What to do: Stand straight, feet shoulder-width apart and knees relaxed. Place your arms at your sides and hold a one- to two-pound dumbbell in each of your hands. To protect your lower back, keep your torso very steady by contracting your abdominal muscles and not arching your back. Inhale as you slowly lift your arms out to each side, no higher than at shoulder level. Hold for one second. Exhale as  you slowly return to the starting position. Do six to 15 repetitions.

Modification: If doing this exercise with the arms straight is too difficult, bend your elbows and lift them out from your sides.

Caution: If this exercise causes pain and/or a clicking sound in the shoulder area, stop right away. Consult your doctor.

MODIFIED PUSH-UPS

Purpose: Strengthens the upper body.

What to do: While on your hands and knees, move your hands forward so your torso is slanted at a comfortable angle and your hands are shoulder-width apart. Keep your back straight and pull your abdominal muscles in. Inhale. Exhale as you  bend your elbows to lower your chest toward the floor. Keep your elbows close to your body. Go only as far as you comfortably can. Inhale as you return to the starting position. Do six to 15 repetitions.

TRICEPS BAND EXTENSIONS

Purpose: Strengthens the backs of the arms.

What to do: Stand straight and drape an exercise band over your left shoulder, placing your right hand on the band to secure it (begin with the easiest resistance band and work up as you  get stronger). Keeping your left elbow next to your body, grasp the band with your left hand to achieve a 90-degree angle with your arm, keeping the band taut at all times. Inhale. Then exhale as you slowly pull the band by extending your left arm downward. Inhale and slowly return to the starting position. Do 15 repetitions. Repeat with your right arm.

POSTURE STRENGTHENER

Purpose: Strengthens upper body muscles to improve posture.

What to do: Hold your exercise band out straight in front of your body and at shoulder-height, one end in each hand. Ex-  tend both of your arms to the sides, stretching the exercise band, squeezing your shoulder blades together and making a "T" with your body. Hold for two seconds, and then return to the arms-in-front position. Do 15 repetitions.

SEATED LEG EXTENSIONS

Purpose: Strengthens the front muscles of the legs.

Note: If you have long legs, roll up a towel and place it under your knees.

What to do: Strap a one- to two-pound ankle weight to each ankle and sit with your back against the back of a chair. Place your hands in a comfortable position. Inhale. Exhale and slowly extend your left leg until it is almost straight (but do not lock the knee). Hold it for two seconds. Inhale and slowly return your leg to the starting position. Do 15 repetitions. Repeat with the right leg.

Modification: If you find this exercise too difficult, try it without weights.

Best Heart Workout

Barry A. Franklin, PhD, director of the Cardiac Rehabilitation Program and Exercise Laboratories at the William Beaumont Hospital in Royal Oak, MI. He has served as president of the American Association of Cardiovascular and Pulmonary Rehabilitation and the American College of Sports Medicine. He is coauthor of *Take a Load Off Your Heart* (Workman).

We all know that regular physical activity plays an important role in preventing heart problems and stroke. But new studies indicate that just being active isn't enough—moderate to vigorous regular exercise is better.

UNDERSTANDING METs

One metabolic equivalent (MET) equals the amount of oxygen your body uses when resting. Walking at a leisurely pace uses just two to three METs. Jogging requires eight to 10. The average healthy adult has an aerobic capacity of eight to 12 METs. People who have heart failure, are sedentary or are morbidly obese could have a capacity as low as three. Elite athletes are usually in the range of 20 to 25 METs.

New studies indicate that for each one-point increase in MET, people with or without known heart disease can reduce their chances of dying from a heart attack by about 10%.

Example: A person who increases his/her MET capacity from five to nine could reduce the risk of dying from heart disease by approximately 40%.

Most people can increase their MET capacity by 10% to 20% within just three months of starting an exercise program.

A treadmill test is the best way to assess MET capacity, but you can estimate METs by determining how far you can walk and/or jog in 12 minutes. In this test, developed by aerobics guru Ken Cooper, MD, an individual who can cover a mile in 12 minutes with only slightly labored breathing has an estimated aerobic capacity of seven METs. If you can cover 1.25 miles, your aerobic capacity is 9.5 METs. If you can do 1.5 miles, it's 12 METs.

EXERCISE GUIDELINES

People who exercise at moderate to vigorous intensity for 30 to 60 minutes most days of the week will achieve the greatest MET gains. Fast treadmill walking or using a stationary bike that works the arms and legs simultaneously increases aerobic capacity more efficiently than bench presses or other forms of weight training. As a rule of thumb, breathing should be slightly labored when you're exercising in the moderate-to-vigorous range.

I recommend only exercise that you enjoy doing and can do on a regular basis. Swimming, biking, fast walking and jogging all are effective.

Important: Get your physician's approval to perform vigorous exercise if you have been sedentary, have been diagnosed with a cardiac condition or have exertion-related symptoms such as chest pain.

Want to Exercise at Home? Here's the Best Equipment to Buy...

Colin Milner, a health and fitness expert for more than 23 years, and chief executive officer of the International Council on Active Aging, in Vancouver, British Columbia, which promotes healthier lifestyles and provides information about fitness equipment, *www.icaa.cc.*

Today, men and women of every age are benefiting from treadmills, dumbbells and other home-exercise equipment.

Bulging biceps are no longer the main objective, though building up arm strength can indeed be helpful to people over age 50. Exercise equipment can also help improve your cardiovascular system, strengthen respiratory functions and help you lose weight.

Exercising on home equipment can have big advantages for people who don't enjoy the atmosphere of health clubs or for those without a club nearby. It's also a plus for people who live in areas with cold winters, where outdoor sports—or even walking—are difficult.

And, home equipment has the benefit of convenience. It allows you to exercise in the middle of the night, before breakfast or any other time.

Important: Be sure to consult your physician before you start an exercise program.

BUILDING A HOME GYM

Do not make the mistake of buying lots of equipment right away. Start with basic devices to gain strength, and then—if you still enjoy exercising at home—work up to more demanding and sophisticated equipment. *Road map...*

Step 1: If you haven't exercised regularly in a few years, start again by increasing your strength. That type of exercise is relatively easy, the equipment is inexpensive and building strength will give you the ability to go to the next step—cardiovascular exercise.

Resistance bands are the simplest variety of upper-body equipment. These are bands of expandable materials with hand clasps at both ends. Stretching the band builds up strength in your arms and upper body. Dumbbells are also effective in building up muscles in this area, and they're usually preferable to barbells.

Reason: Dumbbells are weights lifted individually by each arm. Since you're probably stronger in one arm than the other, a dumbbell lets you concentrate on the weaker arm.

That's nearly impossible with a barbell, which is one long bar with weights at each end. Moreover, if you lose control of a barbell, it could fall on your chest and even roll back on your throat. If you have problems lifting a dumbbell, you can simply drop it on the floor.

Weight-lifting guideline: Begin with about 70% of the greatest amount of weight you can lift. Then increase this amount very slowly—one pound a week, for example.

As you improve your fitness, also consider a "multigym," a device with one or two weight stacks, plus attachments that let you exercise arms as well as legs in many different ways.

Step 2: Once you've increased your upper-body strength, work also on improving your cardiovascular system.

•**Pedometers** aren't usually thought of as a piece of gym equipment, but they can serve in that role by encouraging you to take more steps, even around the house.

Some pedometers, including Digi-Walker, record the number of steps you take and estimate how many calories you burn. Most people over 50 take about 2,000 to 4,000 steps a day, and only 1,000 steps more are known to improve heart and lung functions.

•**Treadmills** can be an even better way to burn calories and improve the cardiovascular system. You can adjust a treadmill to move at varying speeds, so you can start at, say, one mile per hour (mph) and slowly increase the pace and/or the length of your exercise.

•**Stationary bicycles and recumbent steppers** (which exercise your muscular and cardiovascular systems from a sitting position) also help improve the cardiovascular system. They are safer than treadmills, which entail the risk—however slight—of falling.

General rule: If you have a problem with balance or have not exercised in several years, opt for a stationary bike or recumbent stepper.

•**Elliptical machines** (motion is similar to a bike but you pedal while in a standing position) are a good addition to your home gym once you've worked out for several months—or if you're already physically fit. By requiring you to move in elliptical patterns, this device gives you the opportunity to improve your cardiovascular system while also getting a particularly safe workout as you stand.

If you doubt that you're exercising at the right level, use the "talk test." If you cannot talk comfortably while exercising, you're probably pushing yourself too hard.

TEST, THEN BUY

With so many different types of exercise equipment on the market, it's easy to spend big bucks for a device that winds up as a coatrack. The solution is to visit retailers that sell exercise apparatus, and try out different types of equipment.

Look for equipment that challenges you but doesn't cause pain or require exertion that you cannot perform. Be cautious of machines with expensive gadgets that you're unlikely to use, such as a treadmill device that tells you "how far you've gone." All you really need is a timer and speed indicator so that you can pace yourself at, say, four mph for 20 minutes.

But, if you enjoy using gadgets, they could be valuable motivators that inspire you to work out more often.

Don't fall into the trap of buying equipment that is difficult to use on the premise that you won't benefit much without a major challenge. In fact, equipment that's overly demanding often falls into disuse. Instead, consider devices that let you start with easy exercises and then work up to more demanding ones.

Example: A weight-training machine that starts at 10 or 15 pounds and allows you to work up in five-pound increments.

What about exercise equipment advertised on TV? The problem is that you can't test it like you can at a store where you can compare three or four types of equipment.

My advice: Never buy anything advertised on TV unless you have the right to return it and get a complete refund, including shipping charges.

Helpful: More information on evaluating fitness equipment can be seen at my organization's Web site: *www.icaa.cc/facilitylayouts/equipment needs.htm.*

Regardless of where you shop, the cheapest equipment will rarely be as long-lasting as more expensive models, but the most costly devices will probably have unneeded bells and whistles. Even though you don't need to buy the most expensive equipment you can find, it's still worth investing in good quality. So expect to pay up to $2,000 or $3,000 to get something durable that has what you need.

Make sure that you have room for the equipment in your home. It's easy to underestimate the space you'll need, especially when you try out equipment on a large showroom floor. For a treadmill, make sure that you have at least five feet between the device and the wall behind it. That will prevent the treadmill from pinning you against the wall in case you should fall down on it.

5

Better Health Naturally

How to Add 20 Wonderful Years to Your Life

Everyone knows that a healthful lifestyle—eating right, exercising, not smoking, etc.—is the key to disease prevention. What people may not realize is that each healthful change can add years to your life. By making several changes, you may be able to add 20 years or more.

Most chronic diseases are almost entirely due to lifestyle factors. About 71% of colon cancer cases are avoidable, as are 82% of heart disease cases and 91% of diabetes cases.

People don't have to completely turn their lives around to get significant benefits.

Example: Someone who exercises for 30 minutes six times per week can gain 2.4 years of life, even if he/she remains overweight or doesn't adequately control his blood pressure.

Making multiple changes can give exponential (rather than just additive) gains. Studies have

shown that if you eat nuts regularly, you add 2.5 years to your life, and if you reduce high blood pressure, you gain 3.7 years. Add that to the 2.4 years you gain from exercising, and the total is 8.6 years—but the increase in life span can be even greater.

Not smoking is probably the most important change. Men who smoke a pack a day lose an average of 13 years of life, while women lose 14 years.

The earlier in your life that you start to make changes, the better—but it is never too late. *Important steps...*

NUTS

Studies show that eating one-quarter cup of nuts five times a week can add years to your life. Tree nuts and peanuts (though technically a legume) are high in beneficial fats, antioxidants

Steven G. Aldana, PhD, professor of lifestyle medicine in the department of exercise sciences at Brigham Young University in Provo, UT. He is author of *The Culprit & the Cure: Why Lifestyle Is the Culprit Behind America's Poor Health* (Maple Mountain). Go to *www.culpritandcure.com* for more information.

and other protective phytochemicals. One study found that women who ate peanut butter five or more times a week had a 21% reduction in diabetes risk.

A nut-rich diet can lower LDL cholesterol by about one-third, the same amount achieved with some statin drugs.

Eat a variety—walnuts, pecans, almonds and other nuts—to get a greater number of protective chemical compounds.

Lengthens life by... 2.5 years.

FRUITS AND VEGETABLES

People who can boost their consumption of fruits and vegetables from two to five servings a day can reduce by half the risk of many cancers—including pancreatic, colorectal and endometrial cancers. Produce also greatly reduces the risk of heart disease, diabetes, hypertension and Alzheimer's disease.

The fiber in produce will bind to potential carcinogens in the intestine and prevent them from entering the bloodstream. Fruits and vegetables are the best sources of antioxidants and other phytochemicals that inhibit oxidation and inflammation—triggers that cause normal cells to become cancerous.

Have a serving of fruit with breakfast every day…snack on a handful of dried fruit…eat carrot sticks at lunch…and have a vegetable salad with dinner.

Lengthens life by... 2 to 4 years.*

FIBER

For every 10 grams (g) of fiber you consume per day, your risk of heart attack goes down by 14% and risk of death from heart disease drops by 27%. People who eat as little as two servings of fiber-rich whole grains daily can reduce their risk of stroke by 36%.

Fiber-rich foods also reduce colon cancer risk. Fiber speeds digested food through the intestine and reduces the time that the colon is exposed to carcinogens. It also binds to excess estrogen and promotes its excretion in stool—this is important for preventing estrogen-dependent breast cancers. Fiber causes a drop in LDL cholesterol and reduces the risk of atherosclerosis, blockages in the arteries that can lead to heart disease.

*Numbers with asterisks are estimates. Numbers without asterisks are based on actual studies.

Get at least 25 to 30 g of fiber daily. Whole grains are good sources.

Example: Two slices of whole-grain bread plus one cup of whole-grain cereal can provide up to 10 g of fiber.

Lengthens life by... 2 to 4 years.*

"GOOD" FATS

People who increase their intake of mono- and polyunsaturated fats and cut back on saturated fat can achieve drops in cholesterol that are comparable to those accomplished by using statin drugs. Improvements in cholesterol translate into a 12% to 44% reduction in the risk of heart disease and stroke.

Mono- and polyunsaturated fats, along with the omega-3 fatty acids in cold-water fish such as salmon appear to reduce blood vessel inflammation that causes clots, the cause of most heart attacks.

Get 20% of total daily calories from healthful fats (in olive oil, nuts, fish, etc.). Limit saturated fat (in butter, red meat, whole milk, etc.) to 10% or less.

Important: Eliminate trans fats (often called "partially hydrogenated" fat and found in many margarines and in commercially baked goods). Americans get an average of 3% of total calories from trans fats. If we cut that percentage to 1%, the risk of heart disease would be reduced by half—and there would be 347,000 fewer deaths each year.

Lengthens life by... 3 to 5 years.*

WEIGHT LOSS

Excess weight will greatly increase the risk of cancer, diabetes and hypertension. A person who is 20 pounds over his/her ideal weight is 50% more likely to develop heart disease—and the risk increases as weight increases.

In addition to regular exercise…

•**Eat most meals at home.** Restaurant food tends to be higher in calories.

•**Drink water instead of soda.** The sugar in soft drinks is a main contributor to weight gain—and artificial sweeteners have not been proven safe.

•**Don't eat in front of the TV.** Studies show that people who engage in "mindless" eating take in far more calories.

•**Weigh yourself weekly to monitor your progress**—or identify backsliding.

Lengthens life by... 11 years. (The difference in life span between obese and normal-weight adults.)

EXERCISE

Vigorous exercise is ideal, but it's not realistic for many of the 78% of Americans who describe themselves as sedentary. People who engage in moderate exercise at least three to five times a week can reduce their blood pressure by an average of 10 points and dramatically lower their risk of diabetes.

Studies show that even mild exercise, such as walking for 30 minutes a day, can increase life span by two to five years. Any kind of exercise, even working in the yard, is beneficial.

Lengthens life by... 2 to 5 years.

Antiaging Formula

Bruce Ames, PhD, professor of biochemistry and molecular biology at the University of California at Berkeley and a senior scientist at the Children's Hospital Oakland Research Institute in Oakland, CA. Dr. Ames is best known for developing the Ames Test, a widely used procedure for identifying potential carcinogenic substances.

Wouldn't it be great if you could take a pill that would help to protect you against all serious ailments, including cancer and heart disease?

You can. Dozens of studies have shown that taking a daily multivitamin/mineral supplement is one of the simplest and best ways to help fight age-related disease. But it has to be the *right* multi to get the job done. Unfortunately, only one in three American adults consistently takes a multivitamin.

ARE YOU GETTING ENOUGH?

There's no question that a balanced diet consisting of whole grains, vegetables, fruits, fish, dairy and lean meats is our best source of the nearly 40 vitamins, fatty acids, minerals and amino acids that are essential to human health.

While most Americans consume enough of these micronutrients to avoid acute deficiency diseases, such as scurvy (vitamin C deficiency) or anemia (iron deficiency), research shows that up to 10% of us consume less than half of the recommended levels of each key micronutrient —a dangerously low level. *Also...*

•**Up to 25% of premenopausal American women** consume less than half of the recommended intake of iron.

•**More than half of Americans** aren't getting enough magnesium or calcium.

•**Up to 80% of American adults with darker skin** (African-Americans, people from India and some Hispanics)—particularly those who live in northern states, where sun exposure tends to be limited—are deficient in vitamin D. Fair-skinned people who don't get much sun exposure and don't get vitamin D from a supplement also are at risk.

All these nutritional deficiencies are serious threats to our health—on par with smoking or obesity. Even a marginal deficiency of only one key nutrient can significantly change our cells in a way that can lead to cancer and other serious diseases.

THE SCIENTIFIC EVIDENCE

At our laboratory at the Children's Hospital Oakland Research Institute in Oakland, California, we study nutritional deficiencies in human cells by limiting vitamins or minerals and examining how the cells respond.

Our findings: When cells are grown so that one of the vitamins (biotin or B-6) or minerals (iron, zinc, magnesium or copper) is limited, the cells' chromosomes undergo significant damage, changes that are linked to the development of cancer.

An abundance of research shows that inadequate levels of folic acid are linked to breast, pancreatic and colon cancers...low consumption of vitamin B-6 is implicated in colorectal cancer...insufficient vitamin D increases the risk for colorectal cancer and may double the risk for prostate cancer...low zinc appears to heighten the risk for esophageal cancer...and low magnesium increases colorectal cancer risk.

If this isn't reason enough to get your daily vitamins and minerals, there's even more evidence. Nutrient deficiencies appear to disrupt the normal functioning of *mitochondria,* the tiny "engines" inside our cells that convert fuel (starches and fats) into energy. This process normally produces a small number of "free radicals," oxidized molecules that contribute to cellular aging.

However, when zinc, iron, copper, biotin or other key nutrients are in short supply, we've observed that mitochondria mass-produce free radicals. In the body, this may lead to premature aging and a raft of degenerative diseases, affecting everything from our hearts and brains to our bones.

Antioxidant nutrients may help stave off the damage, but supplying the missing nutrient is the key. In a recent Johns Hopkins University study, older people taking vitamins E and C were found to be less likely to develop Alzheimer's disease. In studies at The Cooper Institute in Dallas, patients who took multivitamins for six months had significantly lower blood levels of C-reactive protein, a marker for cardiovascular disease.

YOUR BEST DEFENSE

A multivitamin/mineral is a very convenient way to fill any nutritional gaps in your diet. An expensive brand-name supplement isn't necessary. I recently bought a year's supply for about $10 at one of the big national discount stores.

Just make sure to choose a multivitamin/mineral supplement that contains close to 100% (as listed below) of the Daily Value (recommended daily intake) of most vitamins and minerals.

Vitamin A	5,000 IU
Vitamin C	60 mg
Vitamin D	400 IU
Vitamin E	30 IU
Thiamin	1.5 mg
Riboflavin	1.7 mg
Niacin	20 mg
Vitamin B-6	2 mg
Folic acid	400 mcg
Vitamin B-12	6 mcg
Pantothenic acid	10 mg
Copper	2 mg
Manganese	2 mg

Men and women age 50 and older who eat some red meat should choose an iron-free formulation—most adults do get sufficient amounts of this mineral from their food. Premenopausal women, who lose their iron through menstruation, should choose a supplement with iron.

Be cautious about any supplements providing "megadoses" (five to 10 times the recommended daily intake) of specific vitamins and/or minerals. In my opinion, there's very little scientific evidence showing that the use of more than the recommended daily intake of any nutrient is beneficial for the general public (though future studies may change that). What's more, certain vitamins, especially vitamin A, and many of the minerals, including iron, manganese and selenium, are toxic at high doses.

Some manufacturers are now advertising multivitamins that offer a "bonus" ingredient—for example, the herb ginkgo to bolster memory… or the sugar-cane derivative policosanol to lower cholesterol. These combination products are generally safe, but most lack sufficient research to prove that they are actually any better for you—or whether the added benefits are worth the additional costs. Talk to your doctor before starting a multivitamin with added ingredients, especially if you're taking medications.

Important: A multivitamin should be taken with food to help promote the body's absorption of fat-soluble vitamins, such as vitamins D and E.

OTHER IMPORTANT NUTRIENTS

In addition to a basic multivitamin, I also recommend a calcium/magnesium supplement. Because calcium and magnesium are bulky, most of the multivitamin/mineral supplements have no more than a small percentage of the recommended daily intake (otherwise the pills would be too big to swallow). Look for a product that offers a 2:1 ratio of calcium to magnesium—your body can't effectively use one without the other. And be sure your multivitamin contains 400 international units (IU) of vitamin D to aid absorption of these minerals.

Unless you eat three meals of cold-water fish (such as salmon, halibut, mackerel) weekly, I advise taking a fish-oil supplement with omega-3 fatty acids. These essential fatty acids promote brain and heart health.

If you feel your energy or cognition slumping, try taking these lesser-known nutrients—acetyl-L-carnitine and alpha lipoic acid. In animal studies, these biochemicals lower oxidant levels caused by aging and improve physical and mental performance. Twenty-four clinical trials have shown these nutrients to be safe.

Good choice: The supplement Juvenon (*www.juvenon.com*) contains both.

Healing Herbs

Mark Blumenthal, founder and executive director of the American Botanical Council (ABC), *www.herbalgram. org,* an Austin, TX–located independent, nonprofit organization dedicated to disseminating reliable information about herbs and medicinal plants. He is senior editor of the English translation of *The Complete German Commission E Monographs—Therapeutic Guide to Herbal Medicines* (Integrative Medicine Communications), a clinical guide on the safety and efficacy of herbal medicines, and senior editor of *The ABC Clinical Guide to Herbs* (ABC).

It was headline news when *The New England Journal of Medicine* published a study that cast doubt on the effectiveness of echinacea. The message to the countless consumers spending more than $300 million annually on the purported cold-fighting herb? *Save your money.*

University of Virginia School of Medicine researchers had found echinacea to be no more effective than a placebo at combating cold and flu symptoms. But don't clear out your herbal medicine chest just yet.

What went largely unreported was that study participants received only 900 milligrams (mg) of echinacea daily—less than one-third of the dosage recommended by the World Health Organization for combating upper-respiratory infections. That's akin to expecting one-third of a dose of aspirin to relieve a headache.

What's the other side of the story? Dozens of clinical studies corroborate echinacea's effectiveness, including an August 2004 Canadian trial in which volunteers who took echinacea at the onset of colds experienced 23% milder, shorter symptoms, such as sore throat, stuffy nose, chills and headache, than those taking a placebo—a benefit that researchers linked to a marked increase in circulating white blood cells and other cells of the immune system.

More research is needed to identify the optimal echinacea species (supplements are commonly derived from *E. purpurea, E. pallida* or *E. augustifolia*) and the most potent plant parts (roots, stems, leaves or flowers).

Meanwhile, best results have been achieved by taking 3,000 mg daily of an echinacea product that combines one of the above-mentioned species and parts at the first sign of cold or flu until symptoms resolve.

Caution: If you're allergic to ragweed, avoid the echinacea supplements derived from stems, leaves or flowers since they may contain pollen and bring on a reaction. Use an echinacea root supplement.

Five other herbs with scientific evidence on their side…

GARLIC

What it does: Helps prevent and possibly reverse arterial plaque buildup (atherosclerosis), which can lead to heart attack and stroke…reduces risk for stomach and colorectal cancers… and acts as a blood thinner to reduce the risk for blood clots.

Scientific evidence: In one recent German study, 152 patients with advanced atherosclerosis who took 900 mg daily of garlic powder for four years experienced a 3% decrease in existing arterial plaques in their neck (carotid) and thigh (femoral) arteries. Those taking a placebo experienced more than a 15% *increase* in arterial plaques.

Potential side effects: Bad breath and indigestion. Because garlic has a blood-thinning effect, it should not be used if you take aspirin regularly or an anticoagulant drug, such as warfarin (Coumadin). To minimize bleeding risk, ask your doctor about discontinuing garlic supplements at least one week before undergoing elective surgery.

Typical dose: One clove of fresh, minced garlic daily, or 200 to 300 mg of standardized garlic powder, taken in pill or tablet form, three times daily.

GINKGO

What it does: Improves memory and concentration in people who have early-stage senile dementia or Alzheimer's disease, as well as in healthy adults, by increasing blood flow to the brain. May also relieve tinnitus (ringing in the ears), vertigo and altitude sickness, as well as vascular problems such as intermittent claudication, a painful calf condition caused by decreased circulation to the legs.

Scientific evidence: An overwhelming majority of ginkgo trials have shown positive results. At least 33 randomized, controlled trials have shown this herb to enhance mental functioning or slow cognitive deterioration in older patients with dementia, while another 13 controlled studies have shown ginkgo to enhance memory and cognitive performance in healthy adults.

Potential side effects: Stomach upset, headache, rash and/or dizziness. Like garlic, ginkgo should not be taken with aspirin or a prescription blood thinner such as *warfarin.* The herb was previously believed to increase the effects of monoamine oxidase inhibitor (MAOI) antidepressants, such as *phenelzine* (Nardil), but this has been refuted.

Typical dose: 120 mg daily. Nearly all positive ginkgo trials have used one of three formulations that are produced in Germany and sold in health-food stores in the US under the brand names Ginkoba by Pharmaton Natural Health Products…Ginkgold by Nature's Way…and Ginkai by Abkit Inc.

MILK THISTLE

What it does: Because of its strong antioxidant activity, milk thistle detoxifies the liver and may help regenerate liver cells. It may be appropriate for patients with alcohol-related liver damage or infectious or drug-induced hepatitis, as well as anyone who is regularly exposed to industrial pollutants.

Scientific evidence: At least 19 out of 21 clinical studies (a total of 2,200 people out of 2,400) have shown milk thistle to protect the liver against invasive toxins and possibly even stimulate the generation of new liver cells.

Potential side effect: Loose stools.

Typical dose: Take 140 mg of milk thistle three times daily.

SAW PALMETTO

What it does: Relieves the symptoms of benign prostatic hyperplasia (BPH), a noncancerous swelling of the prostate gland, which causes frequent and/or weak urination and is common in men over age 50.

Scientific evidence: In almost two dozen clinical trials, saw palmetto has proven almost equal to prescription drugs, such as *finasteride* (Proscar) and *terazosin* (Hytrin), for relieving the symptoms of BPH. Unlike prescription prostate medications, which can cause side effects, including diminished libido, saw palmetto causes only minor adverse effects. Saw palmetto does not inhibit the production of prostate specific antigen (PSA), a protein that, when elevated, serves as an early warning for prostate cancer. (Conventional BPH drugs suppress PSA, complicating prostate cancer screening.)

Potential side effects: Stomach upset or nausea if taken on an empty stomach.

Typical dose: 320 mg daily. It requires four to six weeks to take effect.

VALERIAN

What it does: The root combats insomnia and acts as a mild sedative to relieve anxiety or restlessness.

Scientific evidence: All of the nearly 30 clinical studies to date have shown the herb to be effective against insomnia and anxiety. In a recent German trial, taking 600 mg of valerian root extract every day proved as effective as the prescription tranquilizer *oxazepam* (Serax) for improving sleep quality, but with fewer side effects. Unlike prescription sleep aids, valerian isn't habit-forming, won't leave you feeling groggy the next morning and doesn't diminish alertness, reaction time or concentration.

Potential side effects: None known. It is best to avoid combining valerian with any conventional sedatives, such as *diazepam* (Valium), since the herb may exacerbate the drug's sedating effects.

Typical dose: 2 to 3 g of the dried crushed root, infused as a tea…or 400 to 800 mg in supplement form, taken one-half hour before going to bed.

How to Stress-Proof Your Personality…and Reduce Your Risk for Major Illness

Redford Williams, MD, director of the Duke University Behavioral Medicine Research Center in Durham, NC. He is coauthor of *In Control: No More Snapping at Your Family, Sulking at Work, Steaming in the Grocery Line, Seething in Meetings, Stuffing Your Frustrations* (Rodale).

Nobody escapes stress, but some fortunate people seem to be able to negotiate the shallows of life with apparent ease. They take setbacks in stride and do not waste a lot of time or inflame their arteries by flaring up unnecessarily. They enjoy loving relationships and supportive friendships.

While their talent for living may seem mysterious, it is actually a matter of skill. Like the musician who knows how to draw lovely music from a violin, they know how to bring happiness and harmony to themselves and others.

These people have skills that put them in control of their emotions and relationships. Fortunately, these skills can be learned—at any age.

THE ADVANTAGE OF BEING IN CONTROL

Research conducted over the past three decades has shown that psychological stress increases the risk for heart disease and for other major illnesses, such as depression and anxiety. Higher mortality rates are particularly linked to hostility, which can manifest as a cynical mistrust of others, a low threshold for anger and/or a high level of aggression.

New finding: A study recently published in the *American Heart Journal* found that coronary-bypass patients who underwent a training program to increase control of their emotions showed significantly less depression, anger and stress, along with more social support and satisfaction, compared with healthy people who received no training.

The trained participants' pulses slowed, and their blood pressure reacted less to stress after the training—clear signs that they were taking strain off their hearts. These factors remained unchanged or worsened in the other group.

SHORT CIRCUIT STRESS

You can't deal with stress properly unless you recognize it. *How to cope when a negative situation arises…*

Step 1. Ask yourself, how important is it? The goal is to know how to separate trivial situations that are outside your control from those that are worth getting worked up over.

Helpful: Step back and decide whether you should allow yourself to react to a setback, annoyance or obstacle. Is there anything you actually can do about it? Is it important enough to go to the mat over?

Step 2. Change your reaction. If your evaluation of the stressful situation tells you that it's not that important, practice turning off the negative thoughts and calming the bad feelings.

Helpful: When you're alone and feel irritated, tell yourself to *STOP!* in a sharp voice. Repeat the command silently when stressful situations arise in public.

During a calm time, write up a list of topics that make you feel good when you think about them—a beloved relative…a pleasant vacation spot. When you're stressed or upset, close your eyes and picture items from your list.

Step 3. Take action. If your analysis leads you to conclude that the stressful situation is worth acting on, take *positive* steps.

Helpful: Problem-solve in a systematic way. Define the problem…list the possible solutions …make a decision…and implement it.

Example: Max was not comfortable driving at night. When he found out he had a book club meeting scheduled for 8 pm in a neighboring town, he at first became anxious. After considering his options (having a friend pick him up and drive him home…not going at all), he settled on calling a taxi.

IMPROVE RELATIONSHIPS

Intimate relationships, friendships and pleasant encounters with coworkers and acquaintances provide social support—a buffer against life's difficulties.

You can improve your relationships by being considerate, treating others with respect, offering help when needed, etc. One of the best strategies is to become a good listener. People appreciate you and like you better when they feel heard and understood.

To improve your relationships, practice these important skills…

•Keep silent while others are speaking. Suppress your desire to add information, ask questions, give advice or steer the conversation to yourself. Limit your input to the occasional nod or "Uh-huh." If your mind wanders, refocus on the other person's words. Your turn will come…wait for it.

•Use appropriate body language. To show interest, maintain a relaxed but attentive facial expression. Relax your shoulders, uncross your arms and lean slightly forward.

•**Repeat what the other person says.** Before you comment, summarize what you think you heard, focusing on facts or feelings.

Example: "It sounds like you had a great time with your grandkids last weekend."

•**Be open.** This doesn't mean that you must change your mind, only that you are receptive to the possibility. When your mental attitude is open rather than rigid, it shows. You may even learn something useful.

ACCENTUATE THE POSITIVE

Several years ago, a University of Washington study found that marriages last longer when positive communications (compliments, affectionate touching, smiling, sharing enthusiasm) outnumbered the negative ones (criticism, nasty looks, withdrawal) by a ratio of five to one.

Use the same principle in all your relationships—make a conscious effort to distribute five times as many compliments as criticisms.

Most important, apply the five-to-one ratio to yourself. Overwhelm negative self-talk ("I'm unprepared...my nose is too big...their house is nicer than mine") with positive messages.

Helpful: List your five best traits and count five of your blessings. Also, become aware of your five biggest self-criticisms and pledge to stop them.

What Your Doctor Won't Tell You About High Blood Pressure

Aggie Casey, RN, director of the Cardiac Wellness Program at the Mind/Body Medical Institute, *www.mbmi.org,* and associate in medicine at Harvard Medical School, both in Boston.

Herbert Benson, MD, founding president of the Mind/Body Medical Institute and associate professor of medicine at Harvard Medical School.

They are the coauthors of *The Harvard Medical School Guide to Lowering Your Blood Pressure* (McGraw-Hill).

High blood pressure (hypertension) has long been known as "the silent killer." That is because it generally causes no symptoms, but it sets the stage for stroke, heart attack and serious kidney damage.

Hypertension is indicated by a blood pressure reading of 140/90 millimeters of mercury (mm/Hg) or higher.

Now: Data compiled from several studies indicates that risk for death from heart disease and stroke starts to increase with a blood pressure above 115/75 mm/Hg.

After reviewing more than 30 clinical trials, the National Heart, Lung and Blood Institute recently created a new category of hypertension called "prehypertension"—a systolic (top number) blood pressure of 120 to 139 mm/Hg and/or a diastolic (bottom number) blood pressure of 80 to 89 mm/Hg.

Result: An estimated 90 million Americans—including 40 million who previously were considered not to be at risk—are now said to have prehypertension or hypertension. *Medication is the most common treatment, but you can avoid medication or reduce the dosage by following these important but often-overlooked strategies...*

TAKE STRESS SERIOUSLY

When treating hypertension, doctors rarely pay attention to stress, but that's a mistake. Stress hormones, such as *epinephrine* and *norepinephrine,* make the heart beat faster and blood vessels constrict, significantly raising blood pressure.

The stress response can be triggered by driving in traffic...waiting in a long line...or arguing with a family member, friend or colleague. Many studies have demonstrated that emotional stress can contribute to high blood pressure.

Solution: Allocate time each day to elicit the relaxation response. This is a quiet state which can be brought forth by meditation or breathing exercises. Start with five or 10 minutes several days a week, and gradually increase it to 20 minutes daily.

For optimal benefit, add a "minirelaxation" exercise whenever you feel stress building.

Examples: Count slowly from 10 to zero, inhaling and exhaling slowly with each number. Or sit quietly and focus on your breathing for one minute. With every inhalation, repeat *I am* to yourself. With each exhalation, repeat *at peace.*

Important: Activities that people often perceive as "relaxing," such as watching TV, do *not* have a quieting effect on the mind and body.

LOW PRESSURE EATING

Most people know all the basics of a healthful diet—unsaturated fats, whole grains, low-fat dairy and at least five servings of fruits and vegetables daily. But there's more.

In the landmark 1997 Dietary Approaches to Stop Hypertension (DASH) study, 459 men and women with high blood pressure were divided into three groups—one group followed the typical American diet...one added more fruits and vegetables...and the third followed a diet designed specifically for the program.

The DASH diet incorporated four daily servings of fruits, four servings of vegetables, two to three servings of low-fat dairy foods and a moderate intake of fish, poultry and nuts, along with a decreased intake of saturated and total fats. Blood pressure dropped most significantly in the DASH group—by an average of 11.4 mm/Hg systolic and 5.5 mm/Hg diastolic.

Researchers are unsure why the DASH diet helps control blood pressure so effectively, but they speculate that it may be the potassium, calcium and magnesium that it contains...the antioxidant compounds...and/or the fiber.

Also, most Americans still are consuming too much salt. The usual recommendation for daily sodium intake is 2,400 milligrams (mg) [approximately one-half teaspoon of salt] or less, but most Americans consume 3,300 mg or more daily.

For the 50% of people who are sensitive to salt (they experience an increase in their blood pressure after eating salty foods), even 2,400 mg daily is too high.

DASH research found that cutting sodium intake back to 1,500 mg daily decreased blood pressure by 12 mm/Hg systolic and 6 mm/Hg diastolic.

Surprisingly, only 15% of an average person's sodium intake comes from the salt shaker. Processed foods are the biggest source.

To detect sources of hidden sodium, it's crucial to read food labels. A snack should have no more than 200 mg per serving and a meal entrée no more than 500 mg. Less is even better.

Unexpected sodium sources...

•**Processed food** that's labeled as "healthy" or "lean." A serving may be low in calories, cholesterol and saturated fat but include up to half your daily sodium quota.

•**Packaged meats** and meat substitutes that are soy-based.

•**Canned foods,** including beans, tomatoes and other vegetables as well as tuna (even if it's packed in water).

•**Breakfast cereals,** including some "heart-healthy," high-fiber or whole-grain varieties.

Also important: Weight loss is an underused weapon against hypertension. If you are more than 10% above your ideal body weight, your blood pressure will drop an average of 1 mm/Hg systolic and diastolic for each two pounds you lose.

Helpful site: To determine your ideal body weight, go to *www.healthstatus.com/calculate/iwc,* the Web site of Health Status, which provides health calculations and assessments.

AN ACTIVE APPROACH

Few people—doctors included—appreciate just how much difference exercise can make. In a study of 44 men and women with hypertension, those who performed 30 minutes of aerobic exercise every day for six months experienced a reduction of 4.4 mm/Hg systolic and 4.3 mm/Hg diastolic.

Target: Thirty to 60 minutes of exercise three to five days per week, incorporating aerobic, strength and flexibility workouts, such as stretching and yoga.*

WORK WITH YOUR DOCTOR

Tracking your own blood pressure shows how it fluctuates in the course of a day, which adds valuable information to the reading taken in your doctor's office.

To obtain the most from home monitoring, check your blood pressure daily or as often as your health-care provider has recommended—rotating your readings in the morning, afternoon and evening.

A blood pressure monitor that uses an arm cuff, such as the Omron Digital BP, rather than a wrist cuff, is the most accurate. You can take your monitor to your doctor's office to check its accuracy.

For a reliable reading, avoid caffeine for a half hour, sit quietly for five minutes and then take

*Have a medical checkup first—particularly if you are over age 45, have been sedentary or take heart or blood pressure medication.

your blood pressure with your arm resting on a table or other flat surface.

Record your readings and review them with your health-care provider at your office visit. It will help him/her suggest ways to reduce the peaks and/or adjust your dosage if you take medication.

Lower Blood Pressure With a Vegetarian Diet

Recent findings have shown that people who eat a vegetarian diet have hypertension rates that are as much as 20% lower than people who eat a traditional diet.

Also: Substituting vegetable products for animal products lowers blood pressure in people with or without high blood pressure.

Possible reasons: Plant foods thin the blood, provide pressure-lowering potassium and are less fattening than other types of foods—obesity contributes to hypertension.

Susan E. Berkow, PhD, nutritionist, and Neal D. Barnard, MD, president, Physicians Committee for Responsible Medicine, Washington, DC, and leaders of an analysis of 80 scientific studies, published in *Nutrition Reviews.*

Grapefruit Lowers Cholesterol

In a new study, men and women whose elevated cholesterol levels did not respond to cholesterol-lowering drugs ate balanced meals with one red grapefruit, one white grapefruit or no grapefruit daily.

Result: Total cholesterol dropped by 15.5% in those who ate red grapefruit and by 7.6% in the white grapefruit group. Cholesterol did not drop in those who did not eat grapefruit. Grapefruit juice also may confer this benefit.

Theory: Antioxidants found in grapefruit lower cholesterol levels.

Caution: Grapefruit can interact with some drugs. Consult your doctor.

Shela Gorinsten, PhD, chief scientist, Hebrew University of Jerusalem.

Kiwi Cure

There's new evidence that eating kiwifruit can help prevent a heart attack.

New study: People who ate two to three kiwifruits daily for 28 days reduced their platelet aggregation response (potential for blood clot formation) by 18% and their blood triglyceride (fat) levels by 15% compared with people who ate no kiwi.

The fruit is rich in polyphenols (antioxidant plant chemicals), vitamins C and E, magnesium, potassium and copper, all of which protect the blood vessels and heart. Kiwifruits are available in grocery stores year-round and can be peeled, sliced and added to green or fruit salads.

Asim K. Duttaroy, PhD, professor of nutritional medicine, department of nutrition, University of Oslo, Norway.

Tomatoes for the Heart

Recent research indicates that drinking tomato juice protects the heart.

New finding: People with type 2 diabetes or impaired glucose tolerance (a precursor to diabetes) who drank 8.5 ounces of tomato juice a day for three weeks experienced a 30% to 40% reduction in platelet aggregation, a key to the clot formation that can trigger heart attack. This benefit is believed to apply to healthy people as well.

Bonus: Tomato juice also reduces the risk for deep vein thrombosis (DVT), dangerous blood clots that can occur after sitting for long hours.

Helpful: Drink 8 ounces of low-sodium tomato juice each day.

Manohar L. Garg, PhD, associate professor of nutrition and dietetics, University of Newcastle, Australia.

Boost Magnesium for Heart Health

Heart disease is associated with low levels of magnesium.

New finding: Adults who got less than 309 mg of magnesium daily from food sources were 55% more likely to have elevated *C-reactive protein* (CRP) levels (a marker of chronic inflammation that may lead to heart disease), compared with those who met the recommended daily intake of 400 mg.

Self-defense: Aim for 400 mg of magnesium daily, from supplements or from foods such as pumpkin seeds (187 mg per one-quarter cup)… spinach (151 mg per cup)…or navy beans (107 mg per cup). Ask your physician if you should have your CRP level checked.

Dana E. King, MD, associate professor, department of family medicine, Medical University of South Carolina in Charleston.

Natural Way to Low Triglycerides

John A. Merenich, MD, endocrinologist and director of population management programs for Kaiser Permanente in Denver.

In addition to both exercising and eating a high-fiber diet to decrease your triglyceride level—try taking omega-3 fatty acid supplements. Two grams (g) every day of the omega-3 fatty acids *docosahexaenoic acid* (DHA) and *eicosapentaenoic acid* (EPA) have been shown to reduce triglycerides by 30%. Although cold-water fish is rich in omega-3s, you would have to eat two to three daily servings, which also can be high in mercury and other toxins, to get this amount of the fatty acid.

Better: Take 2 g of DHA/EPA every day, the amount typically found in about six or seven fish oil capsules (check the label), for two to four weeks and then have your triglyceride level checked again.

Caution: Do not take fish oil if you are taking a blood thinner, such as *warfarin* (Coumadin).

Good news: Tests conducted by Consumer-Labs.com, an independent evaluator of dietary supplements, discovered that the 41 commercially available omega-3 products they analyzed did not contain mercury, dioxins or polychlorinated biphenyls (PCBs).

Lower Cholesterol Naturally

A derivative of the B vitamin *pantothenic acid, pantethine,* lowers LDL ("bad") cholesterol and triglycerides and increases HDL ("good") cholesterol. It also boosts immune function, improves energy and protects against mental and physical stress. Pantethine is found in such high-cholesterol foods as eggs, meat and dairy products, so people trying to lower their cholesterol may prefer to get it through supplements.

Dosage: One 300-mg capsule, taken two to four times daily.

Robert C. Rountree, MD, a family physician in private practice, Boulder, CO.

Sleep Tight!

Men who changed their sleeping positions from their backs to their stomachs experienced significant drops in blood pressure, as high as 15 points systolic (top number) in some instances.

Researchers theorize that sleep position is an underrecognized risk factor for nighttime cardiovascular events, including heart attack.

Important: Avoid sleeping on your stomach if you have back pain.

American Heart Association, 7272 Greenville Ave., Dallas, TX 75231, *www.americanheart.org.*

Natural Stroke Care

Rebecca Shannonhouse, editor of *Bottom Line/Health*, Boardroom Inc., 281 Tresser Blvd., Stamford, CT 06901.

A friend of mine who suffered a stroke is doing everything he can to improve his odds for a total recovery. That includes taking certain nutritional supplements.

This is smart. Naturopathic physician Andrew Rubman, ND, medical director of the Southbury Clinic for Traditional Medicine, Southbury, Connecticut, believes that more people could benefit from the use of supplements to help prevent and treat stroke.

My friend's stroke recovery program includes regular visits to his neurologist…a physical and occupational therapy regimen…and the use of anticoagulant medication. *In addition, he takes the following nutritional supplements, which are available at health-food stores…*

•**L-carnitine.** This vitamin-like nutrient may have a beneficial effect on brain function.

•**Calcium/magnesium butyrate.** This is a single product that contains a highly absorbable form of calcium and magnesium. These minerals prevent arteries from going into spasm, potentially causing more brain damage.

•**Omega-3 fatty acids.** These "good" fats help to curb the inflammation associated with "mini-strokes," known as transient ischemic attacks (TIAs)—a significant danger for first-time and recurrent stroke sufferers.

•**B-12 and B-complex.** These vitamins help to support neurological function.

Before using supplements to help prevent or treat stroke, be sure to consult a naturopathic physician who will work with your neurologist or primary care physician to create a full treatment regimen.

Magnesium Helps Fight Diabetes

In a new study, the more magnesium women consumed in their diets, the lower their risk for diabetes.

Theory: The mineral helps the body deliver glucose from the bloodstream to the cells. Diabetes results from the body's inability to utilize glucose properly.

Self-defense: Eat a balanced diet which includes up to 320 mg per day of magnesium-rich foods, such as oat bran (221 mg per cup) or spinach (163 mg per cup).

Other studies have shown comparable results in men.

Yiqing Song, MD, research fellow, division of preventive medicine, Brigham and Women's Hospital, Boston.

Better Diabetes Control

In a new finding, 24% of 716 people with diabetes who took an alpha-lipoic acid supplement daily for three weeks felt an improvement in pain, burning and numbness in their feet due to diabetic neuropathy (nerve damage caused by high blood sugar) compared with 16% of 542 diabetics taking a placebo.

Theory: Alpha-lipoic acid neutralizes the damage caused by small molecules that accumulate when blood sugar is elevated.

If you suffer from diabetic neuropathy: Ask your doctor about taking 1,200 to 1,800 mg daily of controlled-release alpha-lipoic acid, available at health-food stores. Taking it may alter insulin or drug requirements.

Ira Goldfine, MD, professor of endocrinology, University of California, San Francisco.

The Anticancer Diet: Cut Your Risk in Half

Diana Dyer, RD, a nutritionist based in Ann Arbor, MI. She is a cancer survivor and the author of *A Dietitian's Cancer Story* (Swan). Her Internet site at *www.cancerrd. com* provides links to cancer-research organizations and anticancer menus.

For the first time, researchers have announced that a large, randomized and placebo-controlled study—thought to be one of the highest standards of scientific research—*proves* that diet reduces cancer rates.

In this study, 2,437 women who had early-stage breast cancer were randomly chosen to follow a low-fat diet (33.3 grams [g] of fat daily) or a higher-fat diet (51.3 g daily). After five years, there was a reduction of more than 20% in breast cancer recurrence in the low-fat group.

The study didn't prove that a low-fat diet can reduce cancer in women without a history of the disease. Nor did it look at other nutritional factors, such as the consumption of fiber, fruits and vegetables, etc.

But more and more oncologists are convinced that future research will continue to demonstrate that good nutrition can help guard against most types of malignancies.

A CANCER-PROTECTION PLAN

Diana Dyer, a registered dietitian and three-time cancer survivor, has reviewed all the latest studies and interviewed top researchers to create an anticancer nutrition plan.

Even if you consume ample amounts of fiber (25 to 30 g daily) and try to eat broccoli and other cruciferous vegetables as often as possible, you may be surprised to learn that there is much more you can do to curb your cancer risk.

PRODUCE: NINE A DAY

For years, US dietary guidelines recommended five daily servings of fruits and vegetables. Now five to nine daily servings (one-half cup equals one serving) are recommended.

In addition to providing fiber, fruits and vegetables are the best resources for antioxidants and other plant chemicals that inhibit damage of a cell's DNA and fight the inflammation that causes normal cells to become cancerous.

What most people don't know: Only about 22% of all Americans eat five servings of fruits and vegetables daily. If you're getting only two daily servings but increase your intake to five daily servings, you could potentially reduce the risk for some cancers, such as esophageal and colorectal, by 20% to 50%. More daily servings provide even greater protection. *To maximize the cancer-fighting effect, eat produce with the highest levels of antioxidants...*

•**Vegetables.** Kale, beets, red peppers, broccoli, spinach, sweet potatoes and corn. Try a stir-fry with olive oil and many of these veggies...or top a pizza with them.

•**Fruits.** All berries, including blueberries and strawberries, plums, oranges, red grapes and pink grapefruit.

FAT: IT MUST BE THE RIGHT KIND

The average American diet includes 33% fat. Excessive fat—especially the saturated fat found in lunch meats, prime rib and other red meats and full-fat dairy products, such as butter, milk, cheese and sour cream—produces carcinogens that increase cancer risk.

What most people don't know: To maximize the absorption of fat-soluble—and cancer-fighting—phytochemicals and nutrients found in vegetables and fruits, 16% to 18% of your diet *should* be from healthful fat, such as monounsaturated fat.

Helpful: To add healthful monounsaturated fat to your diet, use olive oil for salads, sautéing, etc.

Avoid saturated fat altogether, or follow these suggestions...

•**Buy only very lean meats.** Limit portion sizes to two to three ounces (about the size of a deck of cards) per meal.

•**Always use reduced-fat or fat-free dairy products.**

•**Minimize the use of margarine,** shortening and liquid vegetable oils.

FISH: IT FIGHTS CANCER, TOO

The omega-3 fatty acids found in wild salmon, light tuna and other cold-water fish are known to protect the heart.

What most people do not know: Omega-3s interact with other molecules in the body to help reduce inflammatory changes that can promote cancer. Aim for two to three servings of fish weekly. Or use one to two tablespoons of ground flaxseed meal daily. It's high in alpha-linolenic acid (ALA), a beneficial omega-3.

Caution: Avoid all blackened fish. High-heat cooking and grilling produce carcinogens that increase cancer risk. If you do grill, marinate fish or meats in vinegar, lime juice, teriyaki sauce or other marinades, and turn once a minute. This reduces the production of carcinogens by approximately 90%.

USE HERBS AND SPICES OFTEN

Garlic, anise and other herbs as well as ginger and other spices used in cooking contain high levels of anticancer phytochemicals. To increase flavor, add herbs and spices to your foods instead of salt, sugar or fat.

What most people don't know: Cutting or smashing fresh garlic 10 minutes before cooking will preserve higher levels of its anticancer compounds.

SOY: A LITTLE GOES A LONG WAY

Soybeans contain numerous anticarcinogenic compounds, including the phytoestrogen genistein. Phytoestrogens are plant chemicals that mimic the effects of natural estrogen—and help prevent it from causing cancerous changes in cells in women and men.

Just one daily serving of soy (one cup of soy milk, one-half cup of tofu, one-half cup of soybeans) may reduce the risk for some breast and prostate cancers.

What most people don't know: Soy foods, such as soybeans, tofu and tempeh, also are good sources of cancer-fighting omega-3s.

Caution: Soy foods may *increase* the risk for hormone-sensitive cancers, such as some breast or prostate malignancies—or reduce the effects of the anticancer drug *tamoxifen* (Nolvadex). Patients diagnosed or at risk for these types of cancers should ask their doctors or a registered dietitian whether soy foods are appropriate.

Add Some Spice To Your Burger

In a new finding, adding fresh rosemary leaves to ground beef decreased the production of cancer-causing compounds during cooking by up to 60%.

Theory: Antioxidants in rosemary reduce levels of *heterocyclic amines,* known carcinogens found in protein-rich meat that has been grilled, broiled or fried. Basil, oregano and thyme also are believed to confer this benefit.

J. Scott Smith, PhD, professor, Animal Sciences & Industry, Food Science Institute, Kansas State University in Manhattan, KS.

A Red-Hot Cancer Fighter

Red chili pepper contains *capsaicin,* an anti-inflammatory that is effective against cancer cells. In tests, capsaicin caused cancer cells to die without damaging normal ones. Though clinical trials are needed before a recommendation to eat chili pepper can be made, it can be enjoyed as part of your regular diet.

Sanjay K. Srivastaya, PhD, assistant professor of pharmacology, University of Pittsburgh School of Medicine, and leader of a study of capsaicin and pancreatic cancer cells.

Honey May Fight Cancer

In a recent study, cancerous mice that were fed honey, royal jelly (produced by bees as food for larvae) or propolis (a substance used in the hive) had tumors that grew more slowly than those in mice who received no special food.

Nada Orsolic, PhD, assistant professor of animal physiology, faculty of science, University of Zagreb in Croatia, and leader of a study of the use of honeybee products in preventing and/or treating cancerous tumors, reported in *Journal of the Science of Food and Agriculture.*

Raspberries May Prevent Oral Cancer

The pulp of black raspberries contains antioxidants and anti-inflammatory acids that may slow the growth of—or even eliminate—cancerous lesions in the mouth. Researchers now are testing a raspberry-based gel for treatment of lesions. Oral cancer, generally associated with alcohol and tobacco use, causes 8,000 deaths in the US each year.

Russell J. Mumper, PhD, vice chair and associate professor of pharmaceutical sciences at the University of Kentucky, Lexington.

Drinking Coffee Cuts Liver Cancer Risk

In a new finding, adults from ages 40 to 69 who drank coffee (one to four cups daily) had half the risk of liver cancer as those who rarely drank coffee.

Theory: Coffee contains large quantities of specific disease-combatting antioxidants, such as *chlorogenic acid,* which may inhibit the development of liver cancer.

The study did not distinguish between caffeinated and decaffeinated coffees.

Manami Inoue, MD, section head, epidemiology and prevention division, Japanese National Cancer Institute, Tokyo.

Vitamin A vs. Cancer

John Erdman, PhD, professor of food science and human nutrition in the division of nutritional sciences at the University of Illinois in Urbana. Dr. Erdman has participated in more than 100 scientific studies and authored 140 scientific publications on vitamin A and other areas of nutrition.

Vitamin A has traditionally been known for its role in helping to prevent night blindness (a condition in which you cannot see well in dim light).

In fact, that's why carrots, which are rich in beta-carotene (a vitamin A precursor), are said to be so good for your eyes.

Now, scientists are identifying new healthful benefits of the vitamin.

Recent finding: Researchers at the Harvard School of Public Health analyzed the diets of 450 men without prostate cancer. Among those under age 65, the men with the highest dietary intake of beta-carotene were 36% less likely to develop prostate cancer than those who had the lowest intake.

How vitamin A could potentially help you...

WHAT VITAMIN A DOES

Vitamin A was discovered in 1920. As one of the first known vitamins, it was designated by the first letter of the alphabet.

Vitamin A helps prevent night blindness because it is a crucial component of *rhodopsin,* a light-sensitive molecule in the eye. It also helps maintain the health of the cornea (the front of the eye), guarding against the development of blindness, especially in children.

In addition to its beneficial effects on vision, vitamin A helps keep almost all the surfaces of the body healthy—the skin, the mucous membranes and the linings of the respiratory, urinary and intestinal tracts.

Vitamin A also improves the function of the immune system by supporting the action of a variety of infection-fighting immune cells, such as neutrophils, macrophages and natural killer cells. In addition, it assists with reproduction, aiding the production of sperm and the development of eggs.

WHERE VITAMIN A IS FOUND

Foods of animal origin (like egg yolks, liver and milk products) contain a preformed version of vitamin A known as *retinol.* Some fortified foods, such as low-fat milk and breakfast cereals, are supplemented with this highly usable form of vitamin A.

Vitamin A also can be produced in the body through the consumption of foods that contain *beta-carotene,* including sweet potatoes, pumpkin, mangoes, cantaloupe, apricots, tomatoes, red peppers, peas, peaches, papayas, winter squash, spinach and kale.

HOW MUCH DO YOU NEED?

The federal government sets a daily recommended dietary allowance (RDA) for vitamin A. This amount includes vitamin A derived from retinols (found in foods of animal origin) and carotenoids, such as beta-carotene (derived from brightly colored fruits and vegetables).

For women age 19 and older, the RDA is 2,310 international units (IU). For men age 19 and older, it is 3,000 IU. The RDA for pregnant women is 2,565 IU...for lactating women, it's 4,300 IU.

Approximately 56% of all Americans do not meet the RDA for vitamin A, according to the US Department of Agriculture. This segment of the population is believed to have a generally poor diet that includes significant amounts of fast foods and other low-nutrient food products.

Because vitamin A is *fat-soluble* (that is, it is stored in the liver and does not dissolve in water), it takes longer for a deficiency to develop than it would with a water-soluble vitamin, such as vitamin C.

Many Americans may suffer from a *subclinical* deficiency, a low level of vitamin A that has no observable symptoms. This type of deficiency could diminish a person's ability to recover from significant stress, such as a major illness or operation.

People who have illnesses that inhibit the absorption of nutrients, such as Crohn's disease (an inflammatory bowel disorder) and celiac disease (an intolerance to gluten, a protein found in barley, wheat and rye), should ask their doctors whether they would benefit from a vitamin A supplement. Vegans, who consume no foods derived from animals, including eggs and dairy products, also may need a vitamin A supplement. A multivitamin typically is a good choice.

CAN YOU GET TOO MUCH?

Vitamin A toxicity has been well studied by scientists.

Most important findings…

•**Vitamin A and bones.** A handful of studies over the past five years have shown that postmenopausal women who took approximately twice the RDA of vitamin A were at greater risk for osteoporosis and had an increased rate of hip fractures compared with women who received the RDA. A study from Sweden showed the same result in men.

It is important to remember, however, that while these studies do show an association between increased intake of vitamin A and bone problems, they do not prove that the nutrient causes bone loss.

Best advice: Postmenopausal women who are concerned about vitamin A-related bone loss should make sure that the nutritional supplements they take do not contain a total amount of vitamin A that exceeds the RDA.

•**Vitamin A and lung cancer.** By the 1990s, 24 out of 25 epidemiological studies of various populations had shown that smokers who consumed the most beta-carotene–rich fruits and vegetables had the lowest incidence of lung cancer. The researchers theorized that the nutrient functioned as an antioxidant, protecting lungs from cellular damage.

To test the theory, in two studies conducted a decade ago, men at high risk for lung cancer (those who smoked a pack a day or more for decades…and/or were exposed to lung-damaging asbestos) were given 20 to 30 milligrams (mg) daily of supplemental beta-carotene for approximately six years. *More* of these men got lung cancer than similar men who did not get beta-carotene supplements.

Researchers explain this increased lung cancer risk by noting that the high-risk men who were studied had received 80 times more of a highly absorbable variety of supplemental beta-carotene than the amount generally consumed from fruits and vegetables in a typical diet found in the epidemiological studies. As the study participants' bodies attempted to break down and eliminate this high dose of beta-carotene, harmful by-products were created that promoted the development of cancer in the lung.

Best advice: Get beta-carotene from food.

VITAMIN A AS MEDICINE

•**Acne and psoriasis.** Retinoids (synthetic derivatives of vitamin A) are used to treat acne, psoriasis and other skin disorders.

Caution: The acne drug *isotretinoin* (Accutane) can trigger severe side effects, including birth defects, and should be used only under the close supervision of a doctor.

•**Breast cancer.** Another synthetic derivative of vitamin A—*4-hydroxyphenylretinamide* (4-HPR)—is being used experimentally to prevent the recurrence of breast cancer.

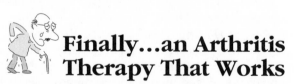

Finally…an Arthritis Therapy That Works

Vijay Vad, MD, a sports medicine physician and researcher specializing in minimally invasive arthritis therapies at the Hospital for Special Surgery in New York City. He is an assistant professor of rehabilitation medicine at Weill Medical College of Cornell University, also in New York City, and author of *Arthritis Rx* (Gotham).

Only about half of the people who suffer from osteoarthritis pain obtain significant relief from aspirin, *ibuprofen* (Advil) or other nonsteroidal anti-inflammatory drugs (NSAIDs)—and each year, an estimated 16,000 Americans die from gastrointestinal bleeding or other side effects from these medications.

New approach: Up to 80% of people who have osteoarthritis can experience a significant improvement in pain and mobility—and reduce their need for medication and surgery—when they combine dietary changes, supplement use and the right kind of exercise. This program provides significant relief within six weeks.

DIET Rx

Inflammation in the body has been implicated in heart disease, diabetes and kidney disease—and it also contributes to osteoarthritis.

The incidence of arthritis has steadily risen since the early 1900s, when processed foods, such as packaged crackers, cereals, bread and snack foods, began to dominate the American diet—and more people started becoming obese. Most of these foods actually promote inflammation, which can cause joint and cartilage damage and aggravate arthritis pain.

Studies suggest that adding more foods with anti-inflammatory effects to the average American diet—and reducing the foods that promote inflammation—can reduce inflammation by approximately 20% to 40%.

Best anti-inflammatory foods…

•**Apricots and berries** contain large amounts of antioxidants, chemical compounds that reduce inflammation.

•**Almonds** have fiber, vitamin E and monounsaturated fats to curb inflammation.

Other important steps…

•**Increase omega-3s.** These inflammation-fighting essential fatty acids are mainly found in cold-water fish, such as salmon, tuna, mackerel and sardines. At least three three-ounce servings of fish per week provide adequate levels of omega-3s.

People who don't like fish, or don't eat it often, can take fish-oil supplements or flaxseed oil.

My advice: Use 2 to 3 grams (g) daily of a fish-oil supplement which contains *eicosapentaenoic acid* (EPA) and *docosahexaenoic acid* (DHA)… or one to three tablespoons daily of flaxseed oil.

Caution: Because fish oil taken at this dosage can trigger a blood-thinning effect, check with your doctor if you take a blood-thinning medication, such as *warfarin* (Coumadin).

•**Reduce omega-6s.** Most Americans get far too many of these inflammation-promoting fatty acids in their diets. A century ago, the ratio of omega-6 to omega-3 fatty acids was about 2:1 for the typical American. Today, it's about 20:1. This imbalance boosts levels of a chemical by-product, *arachidonic acid*, that triggers inflammation.

My advice: Because the omega-6s are found primarily in red meats, commercially processed foods (described earlier) and fast foods, anyone with arthritis should avoid these foods as much as possible.

•**Give up nightshades.** Although the reason is unknown, tomatoes, white potatoes, eggplant and other foods in the nightshade family have been found to increase arthritis pain. It has been estimated that up to 20% of arthritis patients get worse when they eat these foods.

My advice: If you eat these foods and have arthritis pain, give them up completely for six months to see if there's an improvement.

SUPPLEMENT Rx

Americans spend billions of dollars annually on supplements to ease arthritis pain, but many of them are ineffective. *Best choices…*

•**Ginger.** The biochemical structure of this herb (commonly used as a spice) is similar to that of NSAIDs, making it a powerful anti-inflammatory agent. A study of 250 patients at the University of Miami School of Medicine found that ginger, taken twice daily, was as effective as prescription and over-the-counter drugs at controlling arthritis pain.

My advice: Add several teaspoons of fresh ginger to vegetables, salads, etc., daily or take a daily supplement containing 510 milligrams (mg) of ginger.

Caution: Ginger thins the blood, so consult with your physician if you take blood-thinning medication.

•**Glucosamine and chondroitin.** Taken in a combination supplement, such as Cosamine DS, these natural anti-inflammatories inhibit enzymes that break down cartilage and enhance the production of *glycosaminoglycans*, molecules that stimulate cartilage growth.

My advice: Take 1,500 mg of glucosamine and 1,200 mg of chondroitin daily. Or consider using a product called Zingerflex, which contains both glucosamine and chondroitin as well as ginger.

Caution: If you have diabetes, consult your doctor before using glucosamine. It can raise blood sugar. Do not take glucosamine if you are allergic to shellfish.

EXERCISE R_x

Osteoarthritis pain weakens muscles, which diminishes joint support. The result is more inflammation and pain, and faster progression of the underlying disease.

Common exercises, including both running and traditional forms of yoga, actually can *increase* pain by putting too much pressure on the joints. Patients will benefit most from medical exercise, which includes modified variations of common strengthening and stretching exercises, supervised by a physical therapist.*

It's best to perform medical exercises under the guidance of a physical therapist for one to two months before beginning an exercise program at home. *Best choices...*

• **Medical yoga** improves joint strength and flexibility by strengthening muscles and moving joints through their full range of motion. Unlike conventional yoga, it does not require poses that put undue stress on the joints.

• **Pilates** combines yoga-like stretching and breathing control to strengthen the "core" muscles in the lower back and abdomen, as well as muscles in the hips. Like medical yoga, it puts very little pressure on the joints. A move called One-Leg Circle is typical of the Pilates exercises that are recommended for arthritis patients.

To perform One-Leg Circle...

• Lie on your back with your arms at your sides and your palms down. Tighten the abdominal muscles, press the lower back toward the floor and raise your right leg up toward the ceiling, while pointing your toes.

*To locate a physical therapist in your area, contact the American Physical Therapy Association at 800-999-2782 or *www.apta.org.*

Exercise illustration by Shawn Banner.

• Rotate your right leg clockwise, breathing in during half the rotation, then exhale during the other half. Then rotate the leg in the other direction. Repeat the sequence four times. Repeat with your left leg.

• **Healthy breathing.** Most of us take shallow breaths from the upper lungs—a breathing pattern that increases levels of stress hormones and heightens pain.

Better: Deep breathing, which promotes the release of pain-relieving chemicals known as endorphins. Patients who breathe deeply for five minutes daily have less pain for several hours afterward. Practice deep breathing in addition to a regular exercise program.

Here's how...

• Sit in a chair with both feet flat on the floor. Close your mouth, place one hand on your stomach and breathe deeply through your nose until you can feel your stomach expanding. Hold your breath for 10 seconds.

• Exhale through your nose, contracting your stomach until you've expelled as much air as possible. Hold the "emptiness" for a moment before inhaling again.

• Repeat the cycle for at least five consecutive minutes daily.

Fight Osteoarthritis with Pomegranate Juice

Pomegranate juice has antioxidants and an anti-inflammatory effect that can block enzymes involved in cartilage deterioration by up to 68%. It also may protect against cancer and heart disease. Pomegranate juices are available at health-food stores.

Best: Mix at least two tablespoons of 100% pomegranate juice with another juice or seltzer every day.

Tariq Haqqi, PhD, professor of medicine and director of rheumatology research at Case Western Reserve University in Cleveland. His study was published in the *Journal of Nutrition.*

Herb Alert

Herbal supplements raise risks from arthritis medications.

Examples: Echinacea can increase risk of liver toxicity in people taking the arthritis drug *methotrexate*. Ginkgo biloba, garlic and devil's claw can increase the risk of bleeding problems in those people also taking nonsteroidal anti-inflammatory drugs, such as aspirin, ibuprofen and naproxen.

Self-defense: Be sure your doctor and pharmacist know everything you take—prescription and over-the-counter drugs as well as herbal supplements.

Erin Arnold, MD, rheumatologist, Bone Joint Institute, Morton Grove, IL.

Exercise May Help Prevent Arthritis In Knees

Osteoarthritis of the knee is a leading cause of disability among seniors—but a new study suggests that moderate exercise may be the best "medicine."

Facts: Persons with a history of knee surgery who faced high risk of osteoarthritis were divided into two groups, one that exercised their knees three times a week for four months and another that did not.

Result: The exercisers reported fewer joint symptoms and better knee functioning, while the MRI scans of their knees showed improved quality and strengthening of their cartilage not found in the nonexercisers.

Key: Like muscle and bone, cartilage also responds to the stress of exercise by increasing its content of supportive building blocks (or matrix molecules).

Leif Dahlberg, MD, PhD, department of clinical sciences, Malmö University Hospital, Malmö, Sweden, and Ewa M. Roos, PT, PhD, Lund University, Lund, Sweden.

Fish Oil Eases Lupus Symptoms

Lupus, an autoimmune disease related to arthritis most often strikes women of childbearing age. Symptoms include facial rashes, fatigue and joint pain. One study found that some patients got symptom relief by taking a three-gram capsule of fish oil daily for six months. Nearly half of the participants had at least some improvement.

Emeir Duffy, MD, a lecturer in human nutrition, School of Biomedical Sciences, University of Ulster, Londonderry, Northern Ireland, and leader for research examining the impact of fish oil supplements on lupus, published in *The Journal of Rheumatology.*

Pain Relief Magic—Takes Three Minutes a Day

Joseph Weisberg, PhD, a physical therapist and dean of Touro College School of Health Sciences in New York City and Bay Shore, NY, and founder and owner of North Shore Rehabilitation in Great Neck, NY. He is coauthor of *3 Minutes to a Pain-Free Life* (Atria).

Conventional treatments for chronic pain in the back, hips, neck and wrist, such as medication and surgery, mainly aim to relieve symptoms of pain, including spasm and inflammation—not the *cause* of the pain. That's like adding grease to squeaky shock absorbers on a car. The noise may disappear temporarily, but the underlying problem is still there—and the squeaks return.

Good news: Most chronic pain can be prevented—or relieved—with a movement therapy program. Unlike drugs, surgery or other conventional treatments, this approach corrects the causes of pain by lengthening muscles and allowing joints to move through their full range of motion.

UNDERLYING CAUSES OF PAIN

Few cases of chronic musculoskeletal pain are due to serious injuries.

Main cause: A sedentary lifestyle. The body's muscles and joints must be moved in their full range to remain stretched and lubricated.

However, most Americans remain inactive for long periods of time while at work, watching television, etc. As a result, muscle fibers shorten and joint movement becomes restricted. Common and unavoidable positions and movements, such as sitting, reaching, gripping and bending over, cause *microtraumas* to muscles—minute tears that are so subtle that they cause no pain initially and fail to trigger the body's own healing mechanisms.

After years or decades, the microtraumas can accumulate and trigger pain. Patients begin to curtail their normal range of motion by taking shorter steps, getting up slowly from chairs, not bending down, etc. to minimize discomfort.

THERAPEUTIC MOVEMENTS

Most people can reverse this cycle with a program of six 30-second exercises that target the musculoskeletal system.* Performed daily for a total of only three minutes, these movements increase joint lubrication and lengthen and strengthen muscle fibers. This reduces your likelihood of developing microtraumas, thus eliminating the underlying causes of most chronic pain.

1: BOW

Primary areas worked: Spine, shoulders, hips, knees and ankles.

How it helps: The spine is essential to most common movements, including standing, sitting, bending and raising and lowering the head. However, the spine is rarely taken through its full range of motion. The Bow mobilizes all of the spinal joints and stretches the paraspinal muscles—layers of muscles that run along the spine and are involved in most cases of back pain.

What to do: Kneel on the floor, and sit back  on your heels. Bend over and reach your arms out as far forward as you can. Place your palms flat on the floor, arms shoulder-width apart and fingers spread out. Hold for 30 seconds.

2: ARCH

Primary areas worked: Spine, neck, wrists, hands, fingers and abdomen.

*Check with your physician before beginning this—or any—exercise program.

Exercise illustrations by Shawn Banner.

How it helps: This movement also targets the spine and takes the neck through its full range of motion. The movement of arching both upward and downward causes the abdominal muscles to contract and then relax, strengthening these muscles to better stabilize and support the lower back.

What to do: Begin in a kneeling position, with your palms flat on the floor under  your shoulders. Spread your fingers wide and keep both your back and head straight. Gradually arch your back upward while lowering your head. Then reverse this movement and arch your back downward while raising your head. The upward and downward movements should take approximately three seconds. Repeat 10 times for a total of 30 seconds.

3: LIZARD

Primary areas worked: Spine (especially spinal discs) and lower back.

How it helps: Disc problems are among the main causes of chronic pain. Prolonged sitting and frequent bending can cause discs in the lower back to bulge or rupture (herniate). The Lizard extends the spine and can push discs back into their normal positions.

What to do: Lie on your stomach. Place your palms flat on the floor, slightly more than shoulder-width apart. Flex both your ankles so that your toe pads are on the floor. Very slowly raise your head and shoulders until your elbows are straight, and look up toward the ceiling. Keep your lower stomach on the floor throughout the movement. Hold for 30 seconds.

Important: If the movement triggers pain, modify it a bit by not quite straightening your elbows, which will reduce the stretch.

4: NATURAL SQUAT

Primary areas worked: Lower back and pelvis.

How it helps: Sitting is among the main causes of back, leg and hip pain. The Natural Squat stretches the entire lower back...reduces pressure on the spinal discs…and stretches the pelvis, hips, knees and ankles.

 What to do: With your feet shoulder-width apart, squat down, keeping your heels flat on the floor. You can wrap your arms around your knees or hold them straight in front of you. Hold for 30 seconds.

5: SPLIT

Primary areas worked: Hips, inner thighs, groin and knees.

How it helps: The hips are designed to abduct (moving the legs away from the body), but this movement is rarely performed in daily life. The inner thigh muscles are also underutilized. The Split works the inner thigh and groin muscles and stretches the hamstring (back of thigh) muscles. Strengthening and stretching these muscles reduces knee and hip strain and injury.

What to do: While standing, spread your legs as far as you comfortably can while keeping the feet parallel and the knees straight. Hold this position for 15 seconds. Then, bending at the hips, lean forward as far as you can, but keeping your knees straight. Your hands may touch the floor, but they don't have to. Hold for 15 seconds.

6: SKY REACH

Primary areas worked: Spine, shoulders, forearms, elbows, wrists, hands and fingers.

How it helps: The Sky Reach improves posture. It also works muscles in the upper extremities, including the rotator cuffs in the shoulders. These are among the most-used muscles in the body—and most prone to injury. The forearm muscles, which support the elbows, hands and fingers, are also stretched. And the wrists are exercised in their full range of motion.

What to do: Sit on the floor with your legs comfortably crossed. Interlace the fingers of your hands. Keeping your back straight, lift your arms up and over your head. With palms facing upward, reach up as high as you can. Hold for 30 seconds.

Natural Migraine Help

In a new study, 10 of 21 people with recurring migraines who tried 100 mg of the supplement coenzyme Q10 (CoQ10) three times a day for three months had at least a 50% reduction in frequency of monthly headaches. Only three of 21 people in a placebo group got relief.

Theory: CoQ10, already shown to improve heart health, may ward off migraines by boosting your body's energy reserves.

Self-defense: Talk to your doctor about taking 300 mg per day of CoQ10 as an alternative to other migraine prevention therapies.

Peter S. Sandor, MD, head of research, headache and pain unit, University Hospital Zurich, Switzerland.

Melatonin Relieves Migraines

In a recent finding, when people who averaged two to eight migraines per month took 3 mg of the hormone melatonin a day, they had significant pain relief during migraine episodes and a 50% to 100% drop in frequency by the end of the third month. Eight of the 32 people studied stopped having migraines entirely.

Mario F. Peres, MD, PhD, director of São Paulo Headache Center, Brazil, and leader of the study, published in *Neurology*.

Lift Weights for Your Eyes

In a recent study, men and women who performed three sets of 10 repetitions of either leg or chest presses lowered the fluid pressure within their eyes, known as intraocular pressure (IOP), by 13% and 15%, respectively. High IOP can damage the optic nerve, leading to reduced peripheral vision and glaucoma, a potentially blinding eye disease. More studies are under way to determine whether the benefit is long term. Until then, perform a weight-lifting program that includes all the major muscle groups at least twice a week to decrease your risk for IOP disorders.

Caution: People with glaucoma or chronically high IOP should not lift heavy weights.

Joseph Chromiak, PhD, assistant professor of kinesiology, Mississippi State University, Starkville.

Remember to Eat Your Broccoli

The naturally occurring antioxidant that's in broccoli and broccoli sprouts, *sulforaphane,* protects the eye from damage caused by the sun's ultraviolet rays. This damage is believed to be the primary cause of age-related macular degeneration.

Paul Talalay, MD, professor of pharmacology and molecular sciences at Johns Hopkins University School of Medicine, Baltimore, and coauthor of a study of antioxidant protection in cells, published in *Proceedings of the National Academy of Sciences of the USA.*

Eggs Protect Eyesight

Lutein in eggs helps fight age-related macular degeneration, the leading cause of blindness among older Americans.

Recent study: The lutein in eggs is absorbed two to three times better than lutein from other sources, such as spinach or supplements.

One egg a day can double your lutein intake.

Elizabeth Johnson, PhD, a research scientist and assistant professor, Carotenoids and Health Laboratory, Jean Mayer USDA Human Nutrition Research Center on Aging, Tufts University, Boston, and leader of a study of lutein bioavailability, published in *Journal of Nutrition.*

Omega-3 Fats Fight Dry Eye Syndrome

People naturally produce fewer tears as they age. This often leads to dry eye syndrome, which can cause irritation and light sensitivity. Omega-3s help maintain normal tear quality. Get them from salmon, chunk light tuna, walnuts and flaxseeds.

Neil F. Martin, MD, FACS, ophthalmologist in private practice, Chevy Chase, MD, *www.washingtoneye.com.*

Soy for Your Bones

A study of soy consumption in 24,403 post-menopausal women over four and a half years found that those who ate 13 g or more of soy protein daily were 37% less likely to break a bone than those who consumed less than 5 g daily.

Theory: Soy slows bone breakdown.

Self-defense: Postmenopausal women should aim to get at least 5 g of soy protein in their diets daily.

Sources: Soy milk (10 g per eight ounces) and tofu (13 g per four ounces).

Xianglan Zhang, MD, MPH, research instructor of medicine at Vanderbilt University School of Medicine in Nashville, TN.

Osteoporosis Risk Reduced by Vitamin B-12

In a new finding, men and women who had the highest blood levels of vitamin B-12 had higher bone mineral density than those with the lowest levels of the vitamin.

Theory: B-12 stimulates production of osteoblasts, cells that build and repair bone.

Problem: The stomach acid needed to absorb B-12 from food declines as we age.

If you are age 50 or older: Get 25 micrograms (mcg) of vitamin B-12 daily from readily absorbed forms found in fortified foods, such as cereals, or in a supplement.

Katherine Tucker, PhD, director of the epidemiology and dietary assessment program, Jean Mayer USDA Human Nutrition Research Center on Aging, Tufts University, Boston.

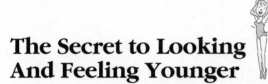

The Secret to Looking And Feeling Younger

Paul D'Arezzo, MD, a board-certified emergency physician and posture-alignment specialist practicing in Colorado Springs, *www.posturealignment.com*. He is author of *Posture Alignment: The Missing Link in Health and Fitness* (Marcellina Mountain).

You can take years off your appearance and ease pain in your muscles and joints without expensive surgery, cosmetics or even highly demanding exercise routines.

All you need to do is spend a few minutes a day focusing on one of the most important—and neglected—aspects of a youthful appearance and an optimally functioning body…posture.

Think of your body as if it were a stack of building blocks. If the blocks are lined up unevenly, the structure is weak and is more likely to collapse. If they're carefully lined up one on top of the other, the structure is strong.

When the body is misaligned, it fails to function as efficiently as possible. Bad posture contributes to arthritis, muscle pain and injuries. These aches and pains cause us to avoid activities that we once enjoyed.

What went wrong here? Modern society has evolved in such a way that we're no longer required to move as much during our day-to-day activities. And whenever we do move, we do so in the same repetitive ways, not utilizing all of our muscles or our full range of motion. Certain muscles get strong while others get weak—and we lose correct alignment.

WHAT IS BAD POSTURE?

• **A rounded back** and/or shoulders.

• **A pelvis that is tilted too far forward** or backward.

• **Too much or too little curve in the lower back.**

• **A head that droops** or protrudes too far forward.

• **A shoulder, hip or other body part that is higher** or more forward than the same part on the other side of the body.

• **A foot, knee or ankle that points to one side.**

BETTER ALIGNMENT

By performing the following simple exercises to correct and maintain posture, you can begin to achieve maximum physical function as you age. The following four exercises will strengthen and stretch specific muscles in the body that hold us upright and stabilize us—muscles that usually aren't worked by standard aerobic and strength-training exercises.

Optimally, this alignment program should be practiced at least every other day as an adjunct to your usual aerobic, stretching and strength-training regimen. Although it can take weeks to change posture, you'll feel a difference in your alignment after doing the exercises only once.

GROIN STRETCH

Purpose: Stretches and aligns the groin muscles. Over time, it will align your hips and allow your shoulders and back to return to a more anatomically correct position.

What you need: A chair, coffee table or ottoman that is the right height so that when you lie on the floor on your back, one leg can rest on top of the object and form an approximate 90-degree angle.

What to do: Lie on your back, bend your left leg and place it on top of your "platform." Your left calf muscle should be resting on the platform. Stretch your right leg straight out on the floor, toes pointed toward the ceiling. Place your arms out to the sides, palms up. Rest in this pose for five minutes, allowing gravity to do the work, relaxing and letting the muscles stretch. Repeat with your right leg.

TABLE STRETCH

Purpose: Counteracts the tendency to hunch and roll shoulders forward.

Exercise illustrations by Shawn Banner.

What you need: A table, desk, counter or back of a chair.

What to do: Stand a few feet from the table, with feet hip-width apart and pointing straight ahead. Lean forward and  place your hands, palms down, on the surface so that your legs and torso form a 90-degree angle. Relax. Let your head fall forward between your shoulders, and let gravity do all the work for you. Hold for one to two minutes.

CATS AND DOGS

Purpose: Increases flexibility and movement in the pelvis and lower back.

What you need: A carpet, exercise mat or other comfortable floor surface.

What to do: Get on your hands and knees so that your back forms a small table. Place your hands directly below your shoulders, fingers pointing forward. Knees should be in line with your hips. Exhale and slowly arch your back upward like a cat, pressing your chin toward your chest. Hold for five seconds.

Then arch in the opposite direction (the way dogs do when they stretch), pulling your head and neck upward and your upper and lower back downward while lifting your buttocks into the air. Hold for five seconds. Smoothly transition from "cat" to "dog" for 10 complete cycles.

FACE THE WALL

Purpose: Stretches and aligns the muscles of the chest, shoulders and pelvis.

What you need: A wall.

What to do: Stand facing the wall with  feet hip-width apart, toes turned inward and touching (pigeon-toed). Your chest and nose should almost touch the wall.

Lift your arms straight above your head, shoulder-width apart. Place the backs of your hands on the wall, and hold for one minute, eventually working up to three minutes. You will feel a stretch in your pelvis and shoulders.

At first you only may be able to reach the wall with the sides of your hands. As your muscles align and stretch, you will be able to work up to reaching the wall with the backs of your hands.

Helpful: This may be uncomfortable at first, but after a minute your shoulders will begin to loosen and relax.

How to Give Yourself Radiant Skin the Natural Way

Jamison Starbuck, ND, a naturopathic physician in family practice and a lecturer at the University of Montana, both in Missoula. She is past president of the American Association of Naturopathic Physicians and a contributing editor to *The Alternative Advisor: The Complete Guide to Natural Therapies and Alternative Treatments* (Time Life).

Everyone would love to have vibrant skin, but few people know how. First, it's important to recognize the many functions of this complex organ. Your skin not only aids elimination (through perspiration), but also is involved in sensation, protection against injury and disease, regulation of temperature, the prevention of dehydration and the synthesis of vitamin D.

In traditional Chinese medicine, the skin is linked to lung health. In naturopathic medicine, it's linked to liver health. Although there's no clear-cut answer, both of these theories make sense. Like skin, the lungs and liver protect us from external toxins and are part of our elimination system. Whenever these organs are overworked, the skin will suffer. That's why the skin of longtime smokers has a wrinkled, yellowed look, while the faces of heavy drinkers generally appear ruddy and/or blotchy.

Some soaps, cosmetics and topical medicines temporarily improve the skin, but to have true, long-lasting skin health, you've got to take care of it from the inside out. *Here's how...**

•**Get your vitamin A.** One of the most important skin nutrients, vitamin A protects overall

*If you have a chronic skin condition, such as psoriasis or eczema, consult your doctor.

skin health and promotes wound healing. Carotene, a water-soluble nutrient found in many foods, is converted into vitamin A in the intestines. I recommend the carotene-rich vegetables and fruit, such as kale, spinach, carrots, apricots, cantaloupe and papaya.

●**Improve your circulation.** Walking, yoga, saunas, massage and dry skin brushing are excellent ways to improve skin health. All of these practices increase circulation to bring blood to the skin, which supplies nutrients and stimulates growth of new cells, and help slough off dead skin cells. Dry skin brushing can easily be done at home. Purchase a loofah (a sponge consisting of the fibrous skeleton of this tropical plant) or a long-handled skin brush. Each day before you shower, brush your entire body (except your face), using small, circular motions.

●**Take omega-3 fatty acids.** Found in fish, flax, borage and evening primrose oils, these nutrients help the skin stay moist and supple. With a daily dose of 1,500 milligrams (mg) of any one of these oils, people generally notice improved skin health within two weeks. A few people develop acne from fish oil, while some get eczema from plant oils. If you experience adverse reactions to one of these oils, discontinue it and use another type.

●**Try botanical medicine.** Burdock, Oregon grape, yellow dock, sarsaparilla and nettle have anti-inflammatory properties, are rich with vitamins and minerals, and assist the liver and kidneys with elimination. Use the herbs in a tincture as a skin restorative. Combine one part burdock and one part Oregon grape with ½ part each of yellow dock, sarsaparilla and nettle. Take ¼ teaspoon of tincture, in two ounces of water, twice daily for one month.

Natural Prevention for Varicose Veins

P revent and alleviate both varicose and spider veins with moderate exercise. Varicose veins are caused when blood backs up or collects in veins rather than flows forward to the heart. The resulting congestion causes the veins to enlarge. Moderate exercise promotes good blood circulation and so counters varicose veins.

Good exercises: Swimming and walking—the leg motion helps to push the blood forward through the veins.

Caution: Avoid all high-impact exercises that put stress on the legs, such as running and strenuous cycling. High-impact motions can push the blood the wrong way, putting stress on the veins and worsening vein conditions.

Robert J. Min, MD, Weill Medical College, Cornell University, New York City.

Relieve Depression and Stress...Without Drugs

David Servan-Schreiber, MD, PhD, a clinical professor of psychiatry at the University of Pittsburgh. He is author of *The Instinct to Heal: Curing Stress, Anxiety, and Depression Without Drugs and Without Talk Therapy* (Rodale). His Web site is *instincttoheal.org.*

W hen we are faced with emotional difficulties, doctors will often recommend drugs or psychotherapy—but drugs have side effects, and some people aren't comfortable with psychotherapy.

There is another way. If you suffer from anxiety, depression or the effects of stress, you can help your mind regain balance by applying methods proven to trigger its own healing powers.

CALM THE HEART

As the nervous system adapts to changing conditions inside and outside the body, the heart rate adjusts, speeding up and slowing down. Under stressful conditions, it becomes chaotic, like the driving of someone who shifts incessantly between the brake and the accelerator. You can train your heart to run smoothly, and researchers have found that smoothing out its rhythm calms the brain.

Example: In one Stanford University study of people with heart failure, stress declined by 22% and depression by 34% after six weeks of cardiac coherence training (CCT). CCT involves biofeedback to control the moment-to-moment changes in heart rate.

Exercise to calm your heart: Take slow, deep breaths, and center your attention on your heart. Imagine that you are breathing in and out through your heart…imagine how each inhalation brings in oxygen to nourish your body and each exhalation dispels waste.

Visualize your heart floating in a lukewarm bath. Be aware of a warm feeling in your chest. Focus on it and also encourage it with slow, deep breaths.

Even when you're not under stress, practice this exercise so that you can easily do it whenever you need to. I find that 10 minutes before bed is a good time.

SYNCHRONIZE BODY RHYTHMS

Our ancestors followed the rhythms of nature, rising with the sun and resting when it got dark. Electric lights changed all that. Now our busy lives often follow "unnatural" schedules.

The brain thrives on regularity. Try to go to bed and get up at the same time each day. It is important to awaken naturally. Being startled out of sleep, perhaps in the midst of a dream, sends you into the world off balance. Keep your shades open, and rise with the sun.

If that's not practical, use a dawn simulator, a timer that gradually turns on your bedroom light. Set it to begin 30 to 45 minutes before you need to get up, to ease the transition from sleep to wakefulness. These devices cost $40 to $160.* Companies that distribute them include Natural Emporium (866-286-3227 or *www.naturalemporium.com*) and Light Therapy Products (800-486-6723 or *www.lighttherapyproducts.com*).

MAXIMIZE OMEGA-3s

Today, the average American diet has at least 10 times as much omega-6 fatty acids (a component of many vegetable oils) as the omega-3s (found in fish and certain leafy vegetables). The imbalance plays a role in heart disease, arthritis, Alzheimer's disease and depression.

A study in *The Lancet* found that people who eat fish more than twice a week are less likely than others to feel depressed. Other research has shown that supplements rich in omega-3s reduce depression, moodiness and other emotional ills.

*Prices subject to change.

To get more omega-3s…

• **Eat ocean fish,** such as mackerel, herring, tuna and salmon, two to three times a week.

• **Eat dark-green, leafy vegetables,** particularly spinach and watercress.

• **Substitute oils rich in omega-3s,** such as flaxseed and walnut oil, for those that are particularly high in the omega-6s, such as soy, corn and sunflower oils.

• **Take a fish-oil supplement daily.** It should contain one gram of omega-3s. Be sure to check with your doctor—especially if you're taking aspirin or a blood thinner.

INCREASE ACTIVITY

Exercise is as important for the mind as it is for the body. Research has shown that it promotes relaxation, reduces anxiety and increases energy. Active people cope with stressful situations better than people who are sedentary.

Example: In one Duke University Medical Center study, middle-aged people who suffered from depression gained as much benefit from 30 minutes of walking three times a week as a comparison group did from an antidepressant.

Exertion will spur the release of endorphins, natural opiate-like brain chemicals that bring on feelings of pleasure. It interrupts the cascade of negative thoughts that perpetuates depression. Regular exercise also may raise levels of chemicals that promote the growth of new brain cells.

Exercise intensity matters less than regularity. Aim to walk briskly, run, cycle or swim for at least 30 minutes a day, three times a week.

Natural Immunity Boosters

J.E. Williams, doctor of oriental medicine (OMD) and academic dean of East West College of Natural Medicine in Sarasota, FL. He is author of *Viral Immunity: A 10-Step Plan to Enhance Your Immunity Against Viral Disease Using Natural Medicines* (Hampton Roads).

E ven people who pay close attention to their health often could be doing more to boost their immunity.

Your body's immune system consists of specialized cells and chemicals that kill and/or inactivate viruses and other invaders. When viruses invade your body, they not only can bring on colds and the flu, they also can cause various types of hepatitis and have been implicated in certain cancers.

Latest development: Immunity researchers are confirming the profound importance of eating a healthful diet—and finding other helpful ways for you to protect yourself from the viruses that are all around us.

BEST DEFENSE

Some people forget that good nutrition is as important for strong viral immunity as it is for the health of your heart and arteries. And despite all the talk about eating healthfully, most people fall short in at least one key food group.

Best immunity-boosting diet…

•**Complex carbohydrates** should account for about 50% to 60% of your daily calories.

Good choices: Whole grains, such as brown and basmati rice, and legumes.

•**Vegetables and fruits** (preferably organic)— have one or two servings at each meal.

Good choices: Papaya, pineapple or peaches with breakfast…garden salad with fresh tomatoes with lunch…and steamed carrots and broccoli with dinner.

•**Fats** should account for 20% to 25% of your daily calories. Choose unsaturated oils that are rich in omega-3 fatty acids.

Good sources: Cold-water fish, such as salmon, mackerel and sardines…avocados…nuts (in particular walnuts and almonds) and seeds (particularly flax).

•**Protein** should make up about 20% of your diet.

Good choices: Protein from animal sources, such as fish, poultry, lean meat, low-fat milk and eggs. The vegetable protein found in grains and legumes (beans) also is nourishing. However, if you do eat mostly plant-based proteins, take 12 grams (g) daily of whey protein (milk protein without fats or lactose) as a supplement.

When it's difficult to maintain this daily diet, I recommend taking supplements to compensate for any missing nutrients. In addition to a daily multivitamin, take 200 to 500 milligrams (mg) of vitamin C…400 international units (IU) of vitamin E*…200 micrograms (mcg) of selenium… and 15 mg of zinc.

IMMUNITY-BOOSTING LIFESTYLE

Other ways to maximize your body's virus-fighting power…

•**Avoid fried foods.** Even an occasional serving of french fries or fried chicken can compromise your body's immunity. That's because fats are oxidized during the frying process, creating compounds that damage all cells, including those that fight viruses.

My advice: For optimal benefit from a generally healthful diet, avoid all fried foods. Grill (with low heat), boil, steam or bake your food.

•**Limit alcohol consumption.** Alcohol can depress immune function. Studies have linked excessive alcohol to susceptibility to a variety of lung infections, including bacterial pneumonia and tuberculosis.

My advice: Drink alcohol in moderation (up to one drink daily for women…two for men)— or not at all.

•**Drink pure water.** Most people don't consume enough water—or the right type. Water is one of the simplest ways to effectively flush toxins from the body and introduce the minerals as well as trace minerals that have been shown to support immune function.

Even though some experts don't believe that it's necessary to drink as many as eight eight-ounce glasses of water daily, I do stand by this advice. If you exercise—even if you don't sweat—you need even more water because greater amounts of it are lost from the lungs due to exhalation. During winter, excessively heated rooms also deplete water from your body.

My advice: Don't include soda, juice or other sugary beverages in your daily water quota. Drink pure spring water, such as Evian or Volvic, or filtered tap water. It helps flush viruses from your body without the immune-depressing effects of sugar and other additives.

*Due to the possible interactions between vitamin E and various drugs and supplements as well as other safety considerations, be sure to talk to your doctor before taking vitamin E.

•**Get enough sleep.** A study published in *Nature Reviews Immunology* in 2004 showed that insufficient sleep inhibits the production of chemicals, such as cytokines, which help to boost the body's immunity. Not surprisingly, sleep deprivation is associated with increased rates of infection.

My advice: Most people need at least eight hours of sleep a night to restore normal body functions. If you feel rundown or are battling the early stages of a cold or other viral infection, try to get even more sleep.

Important: Just being in bed for eight hours does not count if you're having trouble falling asleep or are waking up during the night. If this occurs, ask your doctor for advice on improving the quality of your sleep.

•**Exercise—but not too much.** Regular exercise has been shown to neutralize inflammatory chemicals and improve the function of the body's natural killer cells—both key players in viral immunity.

But overly strenuous workouts, such as running a marathon, can have the opposite effect, triggering the production of *cortisol, adrenaline* and other stress hormones that suppress immune function and increase your odds of contracting an infection.

My advice: Up to one hour a day of moderate exercise (such as brisk walking, bicycling or swimming) is right for most people. Let your body be your guide—if you feel exhausted and generally worse after you exercise, cut back.

•**Take a sauna.** Dangerous chemicals from the environment, including the pesticides that we consume in nonorganic foods, cause an imbalance in the immune cells that fight viral infections. A sauna helps your body to release these chemicals via perspiration.

My advice: Take a dry sauna once or twice weekly. Don't exceed 20 minutes, and drink at least an extra quart of pure water to compensate for what you lose through perspiration.

Caution: Saunas may not be safe for people over age 65 or anyone who is weak or has a fever.

IMMUNITY-BOOSTING PLANTS

The leaves, stems and roots of some plants are concentrated sources of powerful antiviral compounds. Unless you have a chronic viral infection, such as chronic hepatitis, it's usually best not to take these on a regular basis.

However, if you're under considerable stress, feel rundown or are exposed to viral illnesses, consider using one or more of the following supplements throughout cold and flu season…*

•**Astragalus.** Prized in Chinese medicine for its ability to restore the body's energy, this herb strengthens antiviral defenses by stimulating the production of *interferon*, a substance that inhibits viral growth.

Typical dose: As a tea, drink one cup twice daily.

To prepare: Simmer 30 g of dried astragalus root in one cup of water for 20 minutes. Or take two to three 500-mg capsules twice daily.

•**Ginseng.** This herb is known as an energy tonic, but it also stimulates the immune system.

Typical dose: Take a 250-mg capsule twice daily (choose a standardized extract containing 30% of the active ingredient *ginsenosides* per 250 mg).

Caution: Do not take ginseng if you have high blood pressure, a fever or an active infection. This herb also should be avoided by people who take a monoamine oxidase inhibitor (MAOI) antidepressant, like *phenelzine* (Nardil) or *tranylcypromine* (Parnate).

•**Acemannan.** This aloe vera extract has been shown to increase the activity of virus-killing T-cells and stimulate the release of *interleukin-1*, an important immune system messenger chemical. Acemannan is available at most health-food stores in a product called Manapol, manufactured by Carrington Labs.

Typical dose: An 80-mg capsule one to three times daily.

*If you use prescription medication, are pregnant, nursing or have a chronic disease, such as diabetes or heart, liver or kidney disease, do not take any of these supplements without consulting your doctor.

6

Strictly Personal

Sex After 50 Can Be Better Than Ever

Most older Americans grew up not talking about sex. Through others' silence, they were taught to believe that sex was shameful and taboo. Any mention of sex between "old folks," in particular, made people shudder.

Sexual activity is a natural and healthy part of life. In fact, you can get better at sex and enjoy it more—at any age. I treat couples in their 80s and 90s who would not dare tell their children or grandchildren that they're seeing a sex therapist. Typically, whatever the state of their sex life, therapy improves it. You can learn how the aging body works differently from its younger self, what pleases you individually and how to please each other in new ways.

PRACTICAL MATTERS

Yes, bodies change with age. Many women start to feel old and asexual at menopause. Men may develop erectile problems. But most difficulties can be overcome.

Physical change: Chronic conditions, such as diabetes, thyroid disease, cancer, Parkinson's disease and depression, can affect sexual function. With heart disease, sex can trigger chest pain, and with asthma, breathlessness.

Remember, intercourse is the equivalent of walking two city blocks. Check with your doctor first.

Physical change: Joint pain and stiffness from arthritis makes sex difficult.

Solution: Relax in a Jacuzzi or bath before sex…vacation together in a warm climate…find new positions that won't stress your sore spots.

Physical change: Many drugs—antidepressant, hypertension, heart disease and some cancer

Dagmar O'Connor, PhD, a sex therapist in private practice located in New York City. The first woman trained in New York City by Masters and Johnson, she has been practicing for more than 30 years and gives workshops throughout the world. She is the creator of a self-help sex therapy video and book packet: *How to Make Love to the Same Person for the Rest of Your Life—and Still Love It* (Dagmedia, 800-520-5200).

medications, as well as alcohol—can affect sexual function.

Solution: If your sex drive is down or you're having other sexual problems, ask your doctor whether your medications could be the cause and if switching might help.

Physical change: After menopause, vaginal tissue becomes less elastic, the vaginal opening becomes smaller and lubrication decreases.

Result: Discomfort during intercourse.

Solution: Don't avoid sex—increase it. The more tissue is exercised, the more it stretches and the more you relax your muscles. Using your finger or a dildo, gently widen the vaginal opening every day. If the problem persists for more than two months, see a gynecologist or sex therapist.

Meanwhile, smooth the way with a nonprescription water-based lubricant, such as Astroglide or K-Y Jelly.

Not as good: Oil-based lubricants or petroleum products such as Vaseline. They may linger in the vagina and irritate it.

Bonus: Applying lubricant may get you in the mood for sex. Or let your partner apply it as part of lovemaking. Good foreplay makes lubrication flow naturally.

Physical change: With age, men do require more manual stimulation for erections, take longer to ejaculate and have a longer refractory period—the amount of time between an orgasm and the next erection.

Solution: Patience. All these changes are an invitation to discover the slow, loving sex that many women, in particular, have always wanted but haven't received.

Erectile problems can be treated medically, as well. Discuss the situation with your doctor. You may be referred to a urologist for medication or other treatment. For more information on impotence, see the article on page 99.

BEYOND INTERCOURSE

Couples in their 60s and 70s and older often ask me what to do about erectile problems and other issues that interfere with intercourse. I tell them to slow down—expand their sexual horizons, develop new sexual habits and start all over again. The goal is simply to *feel more.*

Our society fears low-level arousal—pleasurable excitement that doesn't lead to penetration or orgasm. But those who have always resisted "just touching" become gluttons for such physical connection once they realize how great it is.

Exercise: During the day or with a light on at night, one partner lies back and is touched by the other—but *not* on the breasts or genitals—for 15 minutes to an hour. The partner being touched stipulates what's wanted in a nonverbal way. If you would like your partner to touch more slowly, put your hand over your partner's and slow it down. When the "touchee" is finished, switch places.

Simple interludes set a loving, sensual tone and encourage you both to overcome shyness about requesting what pleases you. Prolonged sensual touching without genital contact removes sexual anxieties…helps you become relaxed, sensitized and responsive…revives a feeling of trust and well-being that you may not have experienced since you were stroked as a child.

You will emerge from these interludes feeling wonderful about each other. Resentments and recriminations will evaporate. Making sensual, uninhibited love often follows naturally. If not, there is always next time.

LOVE YOUR BODY AS IT IS

The US culture presumes that only the young and the skinny are (or should be) sexually active. As a result, many older people avoid sex out of embarrassment about spotted skin, a protruding stomach, wrinkles and flab. (Do remember that while you are ashamed of your wrinkles and a protruding belly, your partner's eyesight has probably also diminished!) A mastectomy or other surgery can interfere with self-esteem, too, especially with a new partner.

Your body is miraculous. Learn to love it the way it really looks. One woman attending my sexual self-esteem workshop said, "I did not learn to love my body until I lost it." But your body at any age is a gift. Value it for itself…not as it compares with anyone else's or to how you looked when younger.

Exercise: Stand together before a full-length mirror. Say what you like about your own body out loud. Do this exercise alone at first, before you share it with your partner. Then try out the exercise with your partner, taking turns. Listen, but don't respond.

To learn to appreciate your body, admire it often. Come away from this event loving five things about your body.

If you look better, you'll feel better. I recommend exercise—walking, swimming, Pilates—to couples of all ages. Getting stronger makes both women and men look better and feel more powerful...more sexual.

EDUCATE YOUR PARTNER

The young body works without thought. As you grow older, you can—and may need to—benefit from learning more about your body and your lover's. The key to intimacy is to express your needs—once you have learned what they are—and to insist on knowing the needs of your partner so that you can try to fulfill them.

Special note to women: If you rarely initiated sex but would like to, take baby steps. Try asking for different ways of being touched, or take his hand and show him how you like to be touched.

Exercise: Turn up the thermostat, and hang out nude together. Sleep nude in the same bed even if you haven't done so for years.

Latest Ways to Prevent and Treat Impotence

Irwin Goldstein, MD, editor in chief of *The Journal of Sexual Medicine*. He is former professor of urology and gynecology and former director of The Institute for Sexual Medicine and the Center for Sexual Medicine at Boston University School of Medicine. His Web site is *www.irwin goldsteinmd.com*.

The majority of men who have difficulty initiating or maintaining erections have underlying physical problems. Many of the same conditions that increase the risk of heart disease and stroke also increase the risk of erectile dysfunction by inhibiting blood flow to the penis.

When a man is sexually aroused, blood flows into spongelike structures in the penis and produces an erection. The main artery in the penis is only about one-half millimeter in diameter. Even small accumulations of fatty deposits (plaques) can inhibit blood flow.

Other common causes of erection problems include low testosterone...nerve damage from diabetes...and use of medications that interfere with nerve signals and/or blood flow.

Warning: Because erectile dysfunction may be an early sign of cardiovascular disease, men experiencing impotence should get a complete cardiovascular workup. This is particularly important if they have risk factors for heart disease, such as smoking, hypertension, diabetes or family history.

LIFESTYLE CHANGES

For most men, impotence can be prevented —and in some instances reversed—by making the same changes that promote cardiovascular health. *Best strategies...*

•**Control cholesterol.** Men whose total cholesterol level is 200 or higher are more likely to suffer from impotence than men whose levels are lower.

According to new government guidelines, the optimal level of LDL ("bad") cholesterol is 100 to 129. HDL ("good") cholesterol should be 60 or above. Some patients can achieve these levels through dietary changes, such as eating less saturated fat and increasing fiber consumption.

Many patients, however, do need cholesterol-lowering drugs called statins. The starting dose of 10 milligrams (mg) of *atorvastatin* (Lipitor) or *pravastatin* (Pravachol) can lower LDL by as much as 40%. If a man already is experiencing erectile dysfunction, taking a statin may restore his ability to achieve erections.

•**Get checked for diabetes and hypertension.** Diabetes, which can damage nerves and blood vessels, is thought to contribute to almost half of impotence cases. More than 40% of men with hypertension (high blood pressure) also suffer from impotence.

•**Ask about drug side effects.** Virtually all blood pressure–lowering drugs and many drugs for treating diabetes can cause impotence as a side effect. So can some antihistamines (such as Benadryl and Banophen) and potentially hundreds of prescription drugs, including sedatives (such as Valium), antipsychotics, antidepressants and pain medications (particularly narcotic analgesics, such as codeine).

Drug side effects are very individual. Switching to a different drug, even one from the same category of drugs, could reverse your problem. Ask your doctor to review all the medications you currently are taking.

•**Prevent cycling injuries.** Men who regularly bike may experience arterial trauma that impairs blood flow and causes erectile dysfunction. Consider replacing a narrow bicycle seat with a wider one that has a prominent "nose." This distributes weight over a wider area and can reduce damage to blood vessels.

•**Test testosterone.** Levels of this hormone naturally decline with age. Men who have very low levels may experience declines in libido and difficulty getting erections. Every man who suffers from erectile dysfunction should have a blood test that measures levels of testosterone. Restoring normal testosterone levels with skin patches or other treatments can be effective.

•**Stop smoking.** Smoking damages the inner lining of blood vessels in the penis and elsewhere and increases risk of plaque build-up. Studies indicate that men who smoke one pack of cigarettes or more per day have a 60% higher risk of erectile dysfunction than those who never smoked.

TREATMENTS

Men have many options for treating erectile dysfunction. If it is the result of a medical condition, the cost of treatment may be covered by insurance. Check with your insurer.

•**Oral drugs** relax blood vessels in the penis and promote better circulation. Almost 70% of patients are able to achieve erections with oral medications. The three drugs below share many similarities but have differences as well. Talk to your doctor about the best option for you. Side effects may include headache, facial flushing and/or nasal congestion.

•Viagra (*sildenafil*) takes about one hour to work. The ability to achieve an erection lasts about four hours. High-fat meals interfere with Viagra's effectiveness (unlike with the other two drugs).

•Levitra (*vardenafil*) is the fastest-acting oral drug. An erection can occur within 10 minutes in 30% to 40% of men or within 30 minutes in 60%

of men. The ability to achieve an erection lasts 10 to 14 hours.

•Cialis (*tadalafil*) is the longest-acting drug. Men who take it have the ability to get erections for up to 36 hours. An erection can occur 30 to 60 minutes after taking it.

•**Vacuum devices** can be a good alternative when oral drugs aren't effective. A hollow plastic tube is placed over the penis. The man uses a pump to create a vacuum in the tube, which pulls blood into the penis. The blood is held in place by slipping a rubber tension ring around the base of the penis. After orgasm, the ring is removed and the erection subsides.

Cost: $300 to $500.*

Caution: Devices sold over the Internet may cause damage to the penis.

•**Injections.** The drug *alprostadil* (Caverject, Edex) is injected into the penis with a very fine needle and can cause an erection in five to 20 minutes. Doctors recommend injections when oral drugs or vacuum devices aren't effective.

Alternative: A combination of drugs—*prostaglandin E, papaverine* and *phentolamine*—can be compounded by a pharmacist. It can be injected in place of the single-drug injection. The combination isn't yet approved by the FDA, but it is much more effective—and can forestall surgery in men who suffer severe impotence. Talk to your doctor.

•**Penile implants.** In an outpatient procedure, a surgeon implants either inflatable tubes or semirigid rods into the penis (implants do not interfere with an ejaculation). The inflatable tubes are more expensive than the rods, but they are the best choice for most men because they can be inflated or deflated as needed. Recovery takes two to four weeks, and the tubes or rods can last more than a decade.

*Prices subject to change.

More from Dr. Irwin Goldstein...

Orgasm Helper

Diminished orgasms can originate from several different causes. *Check the following list...*

•**Medications** can affect brain chemicals involved with sexual satisfaction.

Examples: Beta-blocker heart drugs, such as *carvedilol* (Coreg) and *atenolol* (Tenormin)... SSRI antidepressants, such as *fluoxetine* (Prozac) and *sertraline* (Zoloft).

•**Low testosterone levels,** which commonly occur soon after age 50 or from medications, such as those used to treat prostate cancer.

•**Nerve damage**—from long-term bicycle riding or other perineal injuries—may lessen sensation. In addition, diabetics and alcoholics may experience less sensation.

•**Stress, anxiety and depression** can interfere with satisfaction.

Best course of action: Consult a physician who specializes in sexual medicine. Your primary care provider or local hospital may be able to recommend a sexual medicine clinic in your area.

Treatment may include sex therapy, medications to increase hormone levels or the antidepressant *bupropion* (Wellbutrin).

Viagra Warning

A very small percentage of men who have taken Viagra (*sildenafil*), Cialis (*tadalafil*) or Levitra (*vardenafil*) have suffered sudden, permanent vision loss. Men who have diabetes, hypertension or high cholesterol and/or triglyceride levels are at greatest risk.

Theory: The drug alters the blood supply to the optic nerve.

Self-defense: Ask your ophthalmologist to check your optic nerve and its "cup-to-disc" ratio. A ratio of 0.2 or less increases vulnerability.

Howard Pomeranz, MD, PhD, associate professor of ophthalmology, neurology and neurosurgery and director of the neuro-ophthalmology service, University of Minnesota, Minneapolis.

Cell Phone Use May Impact Fertility

Excessive cell phone use may affect a man's sperm production.

Recent finding: Radio waves such as those emitted by cell phones damaged sperm DNA in mice.

DNA damage in sperm correlates to reduced fertility and increased rates of miscarriage and childhood disease, including cancer. More study is needed to determine the effects in humans.

R. John Aitken, PhD, ScD, director, Australian Research Council Centre of Excellence in Biotechnology and Development, discipline of biological sciences, School of Life and Environmental Sciences, University of Newcastle, Callaghan, New South Wales, and leader of a study of 22 mice, published in the *International Journal of Andrology.*

Natural Help for PMS

Prevent premenstrual syndrome (PMS) with vitamin D and calcium.

Recent finding: Women who had about four servings a day of skim or low-fat milk or low-fat dairy foods—which contain vitamin D and calcium—and/or calcium-fortified orange juice were 40% less likely to experience such classic PMS symptoms as anxiety, depression, cramps and headaches.

Elizabeth R. Bertone-Johnson, ScD, assistant professor of epidemiology, School of Public Health & Health Sciences, University of Massachusetts at Amherst, and leader of a 10-year study of 3,025 women aged 27 to 44 years, published in the *Archives of Internal Medicine.*

A Very Simple Hot Flash Cure

Most menopausal women are awakened by hot flashes in the first half of the night.

Reason: Rapid eye movement (REM) activity, which suppresses hot flashes, is less frequent at this time.

In a new study, turning the thermostat to 64°F reduced the occurrence of hot flashes by 68%.

North American Menopause Society, 5900 Landerbrook Dr., Mayfield Hts., OH 44124, *www.menopause.org.*

Natural Ways to Ease Menopause Symptoms

Ann Louise Gittleman, PhD, nutritionist based in Post Falls, ID, and author of 25 books, including *Hot Times: How to Eat Well, Live Healthy, and Feel Sexy During the Change* (Avery).

For decades, women relied on hormone replacement therapy (HRT) to relieve symptoms from menopause—hot flashes, sleep disturbance, anxiety and mood swings. But several large studies have linked long-term HRT with increased risk of breast cancer, dementia, heart attack and stroke.

Fortunately, there are safer, natural alternatives to HRT.

MORE THAN JUST ESTROGEN

People typically attribute menopausal symptoms to the declining production of the female hormones *estrogen* and *progesterone*. But poor eating and lifestyle habits also play a role, by overtaxing the adrenal glands. For women who are going through menopause, the adrenal glands are nature's backup system. When the ovaries decrease their production of estrogen and progesterone, the adrenals have the ability to produce hormones to compensate. Poor diet and lifestyle choices put stress on the adrenals, creating an imbalance in body chemistry and contributing to the uncomfortable symptoms that we associate with menopause.

If you are a woman with menopausal symptoms, adopting healthier habits can help to even out these imbalances.

If you are a man and the woman you love is going through menopause, you can help by understanding that she is experiencing a profound physiological change. Your kindness and patience can ease her transition through a time that is confusing—for her as well as for you.

Common symptoms and natural solutions...

HOT FLASHES

As many as 80% of women experience hot flashes during menopause. One theory is that the hypothalamus, which controls body temperature, is triggered in some way by hormonal fluctuations.

●**Avoid spicy foods.** Foods containing cayenne or other peppers have a thermogenic effect, meaning that they raise body temperature.

●**Cook with garlic, onion, thyme, oregano and sage.** These seasonings contain very small amounts of phyto-estrogens (plant-based estrogens such as lignans and isoflavones that occur naturally in certain foods) and can help restore hormone balance.

●**Cut down on caffeine.** Caffeine stimulates the adrenal glands, leading to a spike in blood sugar levels followed by a plunge in blood sugar to even lower levels than before. This stresses the body and aggravates menopause woes.

If you don't want to give up coffee completely, have one cup per day with food. Don't use coffee as a stimulant between meals. Instead, eat frequent small meals for energy.

Better than coffee: Green, white and black teas have less caffeine and are high in disease-fighting antioxidants. Try substituting tea for coffee. Then transition to herbal tea or hot water with lemon.

●**Add flaxseed.** Ground flaxseed contains lignans, which seem to help modulate fluctuating estrogen and progesterone levels. Aim for two tablespoons a day. Ground flaxseed has a pleasant nutty flavor—sprinkle it on cereal, yogurt and salads.

Bonus: Flaxseed reduces cholesterol, helps prevent certain cancers and relieves constipation (be sure to drink plenty of water).

●**Eat soy foods in moderation.** Some countries with diets high in soy report low rates of menopausal symptoms and breast cancer. But I'm cautious regarding soy. Preliminary research suggests that while isoflavones in soy appear to protect against some breast cancers, they may stimulate growth of other types of breast cancer.

I'm especially concerned about isolated soy protein, which often is added to protein powder, energy bars and supplements. This puts far more soy isoflavones into the diet than other cultures typically consume—and these higher amounts may not be healthful.

If you enjoy soy foods, limit your consumption to two servings a week, and eat them in their whole-food form—as tofu, tempeh, miso and edamame.

•**Be wary of herbal remedies.** I'm cautious about black cohosh, red clover and other plant remedies with estrogenlike properties. Research has not demonstrated clearly that they help, and some can have harmful side effects if not properly monitored. However, some women do report good results from these remedies. Check with your doctor first. If you don't notice a clear change in symptoms after two to three weeks of trying a new remedy, ask your doctor about trying something else.

What men can do: Buy a dual-control electric blanket so that you both will be comfortable. Make her a cup of herbal tea. Join her in eating flaxseed—it is beneficial for both your colon and prostate.

INSOMNIA

During menopause, increased levels of the stress hormone cortisol make it difficult to fall asleep and can trigger intermittent awakening throughout the night. *Natural sleep aids...*

•**Wild yam cream.** This topical cream extracted from yams grown in Mexico is a source of natural progesterone. It is available at most health-food stores and in some pharmacies. Applying small amounts of wild yam cream daily may help to balance cortisol levels and enhance sleep. (The cream also helps reduce anxiety and hot flashes.)

Apply one-quarter teaspoon once in the morning and once at night. Gently rub the cream into areas where you notice capillaries, such as the wrist, back of the knee and neck—these are the places where skin is thinnest and the cream is easily absorbed. Alternate where you apply the cream on a daily basis.

•**Magnesium.** Levels of magnesium, a natural sleep aid, are depleted when you consume too much coffee, cola, alcohol, sugar or salt. Foods that have magnesium include halibut…whole-wheat bread…leafy green vegetables such as spinach…nuts…and dried beans (soaked and cooked). If your diet is low in magnesium, take 200 to 400 milligrams (mg) in supplement form at bedtime.

•**Zinc.** This mineral can help quiet an overactive mind. Foods rich in zinc include poultry, red meat and nuts, but it is hard to get enough zinc from food. Take 25 mg to 45 mg in supplement form before bed.

•**Exercise.** One study discovered that women over age 50 who walked, biked or did stretching exercises every morning fell asleep more easily. Try to get a half-hour of exercise most mornings. Avoid working out in the evening—you may have trouble winding down. And don't go to extremes. Overexercising (more than two hours of strenuous, nonstop activity every day) can lead to hormonal imbalance.

What men can do: Exercise with her in the morning. Make sure there is a bottle of magnesium tablets by the bedside at home and when traveling.

MOOD SWINGS

Drinking less coffee and eating frequent small meals will go a long way toward balancing your moods by reducing spikes in blood sugar and stress on adrenals. *In addition...*

•**Eat a balanced diet.** The emotional and mental stress of menopause can lead to a vicious cycle in which stress depletes important mineral stores, further taxing the adrenals.

Among the minerals depleted by stress are copper, calcium, magnesium, potassium, sodium and zinc. To restore these minerals, eat an adrenal-supportive diet rich in brightly colored fruits and vegetables, legumes, lean meats and whole grains. Avoid all sugar and other refined carbohydrates.

Recommended: Sea vegetables, such as nori, arame, wakame and hijiki. These are especially high in the key minerals. Health-food stores sell them in dried form. They can be crumbled into soup and over fish, salad and vegetables.

•**Get the right kind of fat.** Though you should avoid saturated fats (found in pork, beef and high-fat dairy products) and hydrogenated fats (in margarine, shortening and many packaged baked goods), certain fats are necessary for hormonal regulation and proper functioning of the nervous system. Known as *essential fatty acids* (EFAs), these healthy fats help to stabilize blood sugar.

Strive to consume two tablespoons a day of healthy oil (use it in cooking, salad dressings, etc.). Olive, sesame, almond, macadamia and flaxseed oils are especially high in EFAs. (Flax-seed oil does not cook well.)

●**Take the B-complex vitamins.** B vitamins are known as the antistress vitamins because they nourish the adrenals. Good sources of B vitamins include whole grains and dried beans (soaked and cooked). Most diets are too low in these vitamins, so supplements usually are needed to make up the deficit. Take 50 to 100 mg of a vitamin-B complex daily.

What men can do: Make it easy for her to avoid sugar and caffeine by cutting back on them yourself—your health will benefit, too. If she seems distant or on edge, don't take it personally. Remind yourself that it is not you—it is her biochemistry that is acting up.

WEIGHT GAIN

One reason why so many women gain weight during menopause is that the ovulation process burns calories—as many as 300 per day during the first 10 days of the menstrual cycle. When ovulation stops, fewer calories are burned and metabolism slows.

Foods that can help counter the slowdown…

●**Protein.** Increasing protein intake can raise the body's metabolic rate by as much as 25%. Aim for three to four ounces of lean protein from fish, poultry, beef or lamb twice a day. Eggs and beans also are good sources.

●**Healthy carbohydrates.** Whole grains, vegetables and fruits metabolize slowly and give you energy throughout the day. Try to consume daily at least two servings of fruits, three servings of vegetables and three servings of whole grains.

What men can do: Don't nag her about her weight. Support her by not buying high-calorie foods, such as potato chips and rich desserts.

The Good News on Breast Cancer

Carolyn M. Kaelin, MD, MPH, FACS, director, Comprehensive Breast Health Center at the Brigham and Women's Hospital, surgical oncologist at the Dana Farber Cancer Institute and assistant professor of surgery at Harvard Medical School, all in Boston. In the summer of 2003, Dr. Kaelin, then 42, discovered she had breast cancer. She since has had three lumpectomies, a mastectomy, chemotherapy and reconstructive surgery. She is the author of *Living Through Breast Cancer* (McGraw-Hill).

Every three minutes a woman in the US is diagnosed with breast cancer. And, breast cancer incidence in women has increased from one in 20 in 1960 to one in eight today. However, the good news is that the death rate from the disease has declined. The vast majority of women with breast cancer go on to lead full, normal lives.

Several recent studies highlight the most recent breakthroughs in breast cancer treatment and prevention…

New finding: **Standard treatments can extend life even longer.** Two standard medical treatments for breast cancer are chemotherapy (medicines that kill cancer cells) and hormonal therapy (medicines that stop *estrogen* from stimulating cancer cells to reproduce). Scientists have known that these treatments can improve the survival rates of patients treated for breast cancer at the five- and 10-year marks, but they didn't know whether the treatments could extend the life of a breast cancer survivor by more than that.

A new study published in *The Lancet* shows that women who have nonmetastatic breast cancer (the disease has not spread to other parts of the body) who receive chemotherapy and/or hormonal therapy after surgery outlive women who don't—beyond the 10-year mark. The study found that after 15 years, the survival rate for women who had chemotherapy and *tamoxifen,* an antiestrogen drug, was 85.3% for those ages 50 to 69 and 88.4% for those under age 50, versus 75% for women who did not have chemotherapy or hormonal therapy.

New finding: **Herceptin reduces recurrence.** As much as 20% of women with breast cancer have cells with an overabundance of the growth-related protein that is called *HER2.* This substance makes their tumors particularly fast-growing and deadly. The medication herceptin has been developed to block HER2, slowing the duplication of cancer cells. Previous studies have shown that herceptin improves the survival rates in HER2-positive women who have early-stage breast cancer (confined to the breast and adjacent lymph nodes) and metastatic breast cancer (the disease has spread to other parts of the body).

A study reported at the 2005 American Society of Clinical Oncology meeting confirms the big benefits of herceptin. HER2-positive women who were given herceptin after surgery, along with standard chemotherapy, had a 52% lower rate of tumor recurrence than women who weren't given the drug. Women with invasive breast cancer routinely have tumor cells tested for HER2.

New finding: **Exercise fights breast cancer.** Previous research showed that physical activity—a 30-minute walk, five days a week—can help prevent breast cancer, cutting risk by 20%. A recent study published in *The Journal of the American Medical Association* shows that exercise helps prevent a recurrence. Researchers at Harvard Medical School looked at 3,000 women who had been diagnosed with breast cancer, matching their levels of physical activity against recurrence over 10 years. They found that women who walked three to five hours a week at a moderate pace of two to three miles an hour cut their risk of recurrence in half.

They also found that exercise improved the overall chance of survival. After 10 years, 92% of those who walked three to five hours per week were alive, versus 86% of those who walked less than one hour per week.

Exercise may cut the risk of cancer in many different ways, including decreasing the levels of circulating estrogen, a cancer-promoting hormone, and decreasing *leptin,* a molecule associated with cellular proliferation in breast tissue.

Related finding: Exercise after chemotherapy increases the activity of infection-fighting T cells, perhaps helping the immune system recover from the damage caused by powerful anticancer drugs, according to researchers at Penn State University. For those who feel particularly fatigued, walking for five minutes several times a day is an option.

New finding: **A low-fat diet may help.** In another study reported at the annual meeting of the American Society of Clinical Oncology, scientists at UCLA followed more than 2,000 postmenopausal women with cancer of the breast who were treated with surgery, hormonal therapies and, in some cases, chemotherapy. The women went on one of two low-fat diets—one diet had about 30% of calories from fat, the other, 20%. (The typical American diet is 40% to 45% calories from fat.) Over five years, the women with the lower level of dietary fat had a significantly lower level of recurrence—9.8%, compared with 12.4% for the group consuming more fat.

This study, which was widely reported in the media, is provocative but not definitive. There are what scientists call "confounding factors" in the data—factors other than a low-fat diet that may account for the results. The most important of these is that the women on the lowest-fat diet lost an average of four pounds. That is very unusual for women being treated for breast cancer—they usually gain five to 30 pounds. Did the low-fat diet prevent recurrence—or did the weight loss? Also, because the women ate less fat, they may have been eating more fruits and vegetables, which contain anticancer nutrients.

What this means: Women who have been treated for cancer in the breast don't necessarily need a low-fat diet, but they should be thoughtful about what they eat and always maintain a healthy weight.

Another Benefit of Olive Oil

Olive oil may help stop some types of breast cancer cells from growing and dividing. Olive oil is already known to be good for heart health—it boosts HDL (good) cholesterol and lowers LDL (bad) cholesterol. To get more olive oil in your diet, sauté vegetables in olive oil instead of butter, and use salad dressing containing olive oil.

Ruth Lupu, PhD, director, Breast Cancer Translational Research at Evanston Northwestern Research Institute in Evanston, IL.

Better Treatment For Breast Cancer

In a new study of more than 9,000 postmenopausal women with early-stage breast cancer, women who took *anastrozole* (Arimidex) were less likely to have their cancer recur, develop in the other breast or spread elsewhere in the body than those taking *tamoxifen* (Nolvadex). Anastrozole works by interfering with estrogen production—unlike tamoxifen, which prevents estrogen from entering the cells.

Bonus: Anastrozole caused fewer side effects, such as gynecologic problems, stroke and blood clots in the lungs, than tamoxifen.

Anthony Howell, MD, senior lecturer, school of medicine, University of Manchester in England. His five-year study was published in *The Lancet.*

Better Ovarian Cancer Detection

Ovarian cancer has been known as a "silent" killer—a disease that can progress without warning. However, research shows that nearly all ovarian cancer patients have some symptoms in the disease's early stages, such as bloating, increased abdominal size, fatigue, bladder problems (including frequent urination) and pain in the stomach and pelvic area.

Self-defense: If you experience any of these symptoms for more than three weeks, see your doctor and ask for a pelvic exam, which may include a pelvic ultrasound.

Barbara Goff, MD, professor and codirector, gynecologic oncology, department of obstetrics and gynecology, University of Washington, Seattle.

Cervical Cancer Vaccine

In two large-scale, placebo-controlled studies, a cervical cancer vaccine, known as *Gardasil,* was 100% effective after a 17-month follow-up when three doses were given over six months (as recommended by the vaccine maker) and 97% effective after an average two-year follow-up when one dose was given.

The vaccine blocks infection caused by both *human papilloma virus* (HPV) 16 and 18, the two types of HPV that together cause 70% of all cervical cancers. It is not intended to replace regular Pap smears to screen for cervical cancer. Gardasil was approved by the FDA in June 2006.

Kevin Ault, MD, associate professor of obstetrics and gynecology, Emory University School of Medicine, Atlanta.

A Double Whammy For BPH

For *benign prostatic hyperplasia* (BPH), an enlargement of the prostate gland that can cause difficulty urinating, *finasteride* (Proscar) reduces the prostate size. And the drug *tamsulosin* (Flomax) improves symptoms by relaxing the prostatic muscles. Now it has been shown that a long-term combination of these two medications is an effective and safe way to reduce the bothersome symptoms of prostate enlargement while lowering the long-term risks for urinary retention and the need for invasive surgery.

Sheldon Marks, MD, associate clinical professor of urology, University of Arizona College of Medicine, Tucson.

Cholesterol-Lowering Drugs Reduce Risk for Prostate Cancer

In a new finding, men who took cholesterol-lowering drugs, including statins, cut their risk for advanced prostate cancer in half.

Theory: Statins may stall tumor growth or reduce inflammation that can lead to cancer.

More research is needed before statins can be prescribed for prostate cancer prevention.

Elizabeth Platz, ScD, MPH, assistant professor of epidemiology at Johns Hopkins Bloomberg School of Public Health, Baltimore.

Green Tea May Help Prevent Prostate Cancer

In a recent study, men who had premalignant prostate lesions took 200 mg of a green tea supplement or a placebo three times daily for one year.

Result: Only 3% of the men in the green tea group developed prostate cancer, compared with 30% in the placebo group.

Theory: Green tea contains *catechins*, chemicals that inhibit a key molecule involved in the development of prostate cancer.

Drinking green tea is not practical—20 cups would be needed to get the level of catechins found in the supplement.

Saverio Bettuzzi, PhD, associate professor of biochemistry, department of experimental medicine, University of Parma, Italy.

Reverse Prostate Cancer

Prostate cancer can be slowed, stopped or even reversed with intensive lifestyle changes.

Recent finding: Men who adhere to a strict vegetarian diet, meditate and exercise regularly lower their prostate specific antigen (PSA) levels by 4% after one year, compared with men who do not make these lifestyle changes. (Elevated PSA levels indicate increased risk of prostate cancer.) Also, tumor growth was inhibited by 70% in those who made lifestyle changes, compared with 9% in those who didn't make changes.

Dean Ornish, MD, president of the Preventive Medicine Research Institute, Sausalito, CA, clinical professor of medicine, University of California, San Francisco, and leader of a study involving 93 prostate cancer patients, published in *The Journal of Urology.*

 # Prostate Cancer Surgery Can Prolong Life

In a study of 841 men with prostate cancer that had spread beyond the prostate, the 15-year survival rate for those who underwent radical prostatectomy (removal of the prostate gland plus some surrounding tissue) was 79%. The 15-year survival rate for patients treated with radiation was 67%.

Self-defense: Ask your doctor whether radical prostatectomy is right for you.

Horst Zincke, MD, PhD, director of urooncologic surgery, Mayo Clinic, Rochester, MN.

Lower Colon Cancer Risk

In a study of 1,520 people, those who ate the most chicken (an average of four servings daily) had a 21% lower risk for colorectal adenomas (growths that can be precursors of colon cancer) than those who ate the least chicken (less than one serving daily).

Theory: Chicken eaters may consume smaller amounts of processed meat, which has been found to increase colon cancer risk.

Self-defense: Substitute chicken for processed meats, such as cold cuts and hot dogs.

Douglas J. Robertson, MD, MPH, assistant professor of medicine, Dartmouth Medical School, Hanover, NH.

Reduce Colorectal Cancer Risk

High magnesium consumption may help to prevent colorectal cancer. In a new analysis of 61,433 women ages 40 to 75, those with the highest daily intakes of the mineral had a 40% lower risk of developing the disease than those with the lowest daily intakes.

Theory: Magnesium lowers levels of insulin (a hormone produced in the pancreas that regulates blood glucose). Elevated insulin levels are associated with colorectal cancer risk.

Self-defense: Eat food containing 300 to 400 mg of magnesium daily. Good sources, which contain 50 mg of magnesium in each serving, include one cup of cooked or one-half cup of raw spinach…one large banana…one-half cup of cooked oatmeal…two slices of whole-grain bread…and one-half cup of beans. If you include magnesium-rich foods in your diet, there is no need to take a magnesium supplement.

Susanna C. Larsson, researcher, division of nutritional epidemiology, National Institute of Environmental Medicine, Karolinska Institute, Stockholm, Sweden. Her study was published in the *Journal of the American Medical Association*.

Hope for IBS Sufferers

After years of uncertainty, the cause of irritable bowel syndrome (IBS) for a majority of patients has been determined. "Friendly" bacteria from the large intestine (colon) make their way up into the small intestine to ferment the food we eat. This small intestinal bacterial overgrowth, or SIBO, triggers the bloating, cramps, gas, diarrhea and/or constipation of IBS, which afflicts about 11% to 14% of all Americans. Research is currently under way to develop treatments for SIBO. In the meantime, antibiotics can temporarily eradicate the bacterial overgrowth problem and resolve symptoms of IBS.

Henry Lin, MD, gastroenterologist and associate professor of medicine, division of gastrointestinal and liver disease, University of Southern California, Los Angeles.

The Best Treatments for Thinning Hair

Robert M. Bernstein, MD, associate clinical professor of dermatology at Columbia University College of Physicians and Surgeons in New York City, and medical director, Bernstein Medical Center for Hair Restoration in Fort Lee, NJ, *www.bernsteinmedical.com.*

Many people experience thinning hair as they age. *Here are some products that will help make thinning hair appear thicker…*

•**Couvré masking lotion,** applied to the scalp and at the base of the hair, eliminates the contrast between hair and scalp that can make thinning hair obvious. Comes in a tube with a special applicator…eight colors…will wash out with shampoo but holds through wind, sweating and swimming. One tube lasts three to four months. Spencer Forrest, Inc., 800-416-3325, *www.couvre.com.*

•**DermMatch** is a hard-packed powder that coats thin hairs, thickens them and helps them to stand up and spread out for better coverage. It also colors the scalp, causing bald spots to disappear. It is available in eight colors. It withstands sweat, wind and swimming. DermMatch, Inc., 800-826-2824, *www.dermmatch.com.*

•**Toppik** consists of thousands of microfibers of keratin, the protein that hair is made of. If shaken over the thinning area, the microfibers bond via static electricity with the hair and stay in place through wind and rain—but not swimming. Spencer Forrest, Inc., 800-416-3325, *www.toppik.com.*

Help for Alcoholism

The findings of a new study show that people who took a special kudzu extract and then were allowed to drink beer at will consumed, on average, 50% fewer beers during 90 minutes of watching TV than when they took a placebo.

Theory: Kudzu increases blood alcohol levels and turns off your desire for more alcohol.

The extract used for this research is not yet commercially available. Heavy drinkers (typically drinking four to five drinks per day) also can ask their doctors about FDA-approved medications, such as *disulficam* (Antabuse), *naltrexone* (Revia) or *acamprosale* (Campral) for treatment of alcoholism and attend Alcoholics Anonymous meetings.

Scott Lukas, PhD, director, Behavioral Psychopharmacology Research Laboratory, McLean Hospital, Boston.

7

Money Management Made Simple

There's an Extra $300/ Month Waiting for You

Finding extra cash each and every month is a great idea, but the most popular ways to save money and cut costs often are not the best...

POPULAR MISTAKES

●**Refinancing your mortgage.**

Problem: Closing costs can be thousands of dollars, so refinancing generally is worthwhile only if your new rate is at least one percentage point less than your current one or if you can get a truly no-cost streamlined refinance deal.

●**Consolidating debt with a home-equity loan.**

Problem: While these loans can reduce interest costs, about one-third of people who use them for this purpose incur heavy credit card debt all over again. Even worse, they put their homes at risk.

SMART MONEYSAVERS

Try several of the following painless ways to free up $300 or more every month...

●**Ask your credit card company to reduce your interest rate.** This works for more than half of callers. *Steps to take...*

●Gather up all the recent preapproved credit card offers you have received in the mail. Call your current card issuer and ask for a rate reduction. Specify which company is offering a better deal.

●Be prepared to counter objections from customer service agents.

Scenario #1: The agent says, "Your card has a fixed rate. It can't be changed."

Your response: "A fixed rate means only that my rate doesn't vary with the prime rate. In fact, your company could raise my rate at any time just by giving me 15 days' notice, right? So, if you want, you can choose to lower my rate today."

Jean Chatzky, New York City–based financial editor for NBC's *Today* show and an editor-at-large at *Money* magazine. Her latest book is *Pay It Down! From Debt to Wealth on $10 a Day* (Portfolio). Her Internet site is at *www.jean chatzky.com.*

Scenario #2: The agent says, "I'm not authorized to lower your rate."

Your response: Ask to speak with a supervisor. Say to him/her, "If I transfer my balance to a new card, your bank probably is going to send me offers to come back at the same lower rate. Why not save the company the cost of that effort by reducing my rate now?"

Potential monthly savings: $20 to $60, assuming an average credit card balance of $8,000 and a rate reduction of three to nine percentage points.

•Refinance your car loan. Since there are no closing costs, this strategy can be worthwhile even if you will save only a small amount. *Steps to take...*

•Find out how much your car is currently worth based on its value in Kelley Blue Book, available at most libraries or on-line at *www.kbb.com*. You won't be able to refinance if you owe more than your car's resale value.

•Try to obtain a better interest rate by calling several lenders or checking with *www.bankrate.com*, which pinpoints the best rates in your area.

Potential monthly savings: $35, assuming a car loan of $14,000 and a rate reduction of three percentage points.

•Haggle for services, not just goods. Ask for price breaks from your plumber, veterinarian, painter, landscaper—even your doctor. In most cases, it helps to gather prices from several comparable service providers. Then ask your usual provider to match the lowest one. *Other steps to take...*

•Offer to give cash at the time of service. Remind the service provider that he/she won't have to bill you or pay a transaction fee to a credit card company.

•Negotiate a group rate. For example, if you need your chimney cleaned, recruit several neighbors to have theirs done at the same time for a group discount.

Potential monthly savings: $15 to $200.

•Pay your bills as soon as they arrive rather than near their due dates. This way, you'll be sure to avoid late fees. These fees have grown so steep that they easily offset any interest you could earn by holding on to your money a bit longer. Typically, a single late credit card payment now

means a $35 penalty...an increase in your interest rate to the maximum that the card company charges...maybe even rate hikes on your other credit cards. Of course, if you are wrongly charged a late fee, ask to have it rescinded.

Potential monthly savings: $35 or more.

•Increase your automatic savings. Most people never miss the money taken out of their paychecks for 401(k)s. You can use this same technique for personal savings with an automatic investment plan through a mutual fund firm.

•Stop spending money on high-cost, low-priority items. Sure, you have fixed costs, but you could probably cut back on some of your habitual spending elsewhere. *Low-priority items might include...*

•Restaurants/take-out food.

Potential monthly savings: $100 and up.

•Unused memberships. Ask your health club to put your membership on hold. In the meantime, take brisk walks...or borrow workout DVDs from the library and exercise at home with a friend. Or decide if paying on a per-class basis would be more cost-effective.

Potential monthly savings: $15 or more.

•A second car. Even if you are done paying for the car, getting rid of it will save on insurance, maintenance and gasoline. Several cities, including New York, offer car-sharing programs, an alternative to rentals in which members can use a car for as little as an hour at a time. Check at *www.zipcar.com* and *www.flexcar.com*.

Potential monthly savings: $100.

•Cell phone calling plans that provide more than you need. On average, people pay for nearly twice as many minutes as they use. *Better:* Gather your recent cell phone bills, and look closely at your calling habits. Then go to *www.myrateplan.com*, *www.saveonphone.com* or *www.letstalk.com* to find a better rate for your level of usage.

Potential monthly savings: $25 and up.

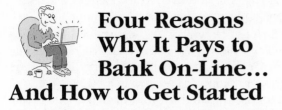

Four Reasons Why It Pays to Bank On-Line... And How to Get Started

Jim Bruene, the editor and publisher of *Online Banking Report,* a trade publication located in Seattle. He has spent over 15 years working in interactive financial services, and helped develop US Bancorp's pioneering on-line banking program in the early 1990s.

On-line banking is no longer a novelty. Every major US bank, and many small ones, provide this free service. In just five years, ING Direct—the largest Internet-only bank, with savings account yields nearly 20% higher than the national average—has garnered $40 billion in assets.

Why on-line banking is appealing...

•It is much faster and more convenient than going to a bank branch.

•You can pay bills, transfer money from one account to another, apply for loans, and view statements and canceled checks from the privacy of your own computer at home—or any computer connected to the Internet.

•Yields on interest-earning accounts and CDs can be higher when they are purchased on the Internet.

•Customer security has been ramped up to meet 2006 guidelines from federal regulators.

What you need to know...

HOW ON-LINE BANKING WORKS

It's easy to get started. If you already have an account with a land-based bank, go to its secure Web site to register for on-line banking services. There you will be asked to create a user name and password to access your account. No special software or hardware is required, just the computer's Web browser, such as *Internet Explorer* or *Firefox.*

On-line instructions will tell you how to view your accounts and do your banking. For example, in many cases, you can sign up with your monthly service providers—credit card issuers, phone company, etc.—to have them bill you electronically, then schedule your bank to automatically debit your account each month for the amounts. This saves time and eliminates the risk of incurring late fees. (You also can pay bills on-line one by one, if you prefer.) If, for some reason, you want to suspend automatic payments—even temporarily—just contact the creditor and your bank (see page 113 for more information).

CHOOSING THE RIGHT BANK

•Make sure that your bank has the on-line services you need. *Look for these features...*

•Free automatic on-line payment of bills and guarantees that the bank will pay the penalties in the event that it sends payments in late or misdirects them.

•Money transfers to and from other banks and brokerages, including automatic debiting to make regular contributions to, say, an IRA at a mutual fund company.

•E-mail alerts when your balance is low, a bill is due or someone tries to access your account with an incorrect password.

•Electronic statements going back at least six months.

•Ability to stop payments on checks, for a charge, and view scanned images (both front and back) of canceled checks.

•Rebates to your checking account if you are charged a fee to use another bank's ATMs. In most cases, there is no fee from your bank and a rebate on up to six fees from other banks each month.

•Some banks offer budgeting reports that organize your expenditures—any payments that you make by check or directly from your bank account, including credit card bills—into specific categories, such as "groceries," "restaurants" and "lodging." Many of these budgeting reports are compatible with on-line features of popular financial software programs, such as *Quicken* and *Microsoft Money.* The reports can help small businesses track tax-deductible expenses.

•Compare the interest rates on savings accounts and certificates of deposit at *www.bank rate.com.* They are also listed in *Barron's,* the financial weekly. Also review the Web sites of various banks for promotions. For example, the London-based global banking giant HSBC is offering US residents an on-line savings account with a 5.05%* annual percentage yield (APY).

*Rates subject to change.

●**Consider an Internet-only bank.** These banks provide a variety of traditional banking products but they have no land-based customer branches. You contact bank representatives by e-mail or by calling an 800 number. Checks are deposited by mail and cash can be withdrawn through ATMs.

Where to stash your cash: Internet banks typically provide better deals on interest-bearing accounts, CDs and mortgages and other loans. For example, E*trade offers a one-year CD with a 5.30% APY. And, ING Direct's Orange Savings Account offers 4.40% APY.

Biggest Internet banks: *www.etrade.com… www.ingdirect.com.*

Even if you decide on an Internet-only bank, you should also maintain an account with a local bank. You may want free use of the local ATMs or face-to-face interaction—for example, if you need to cash a check. Some Internet-only banks *require* you to have a traditional account at another bank.

CAUTION

Don't fall for phishing scams. Con artists send authentic-looking e-mails that appear to come from your financial institution. The messages attempt to trick you into providing account numbers and passwords by claiming to have found "suspicious activity" or warning of the "impending suspension" of your account.

Delete these messages, and never click on the Web links or pop-up ads they include.

No legitimate institution will ask you to supply personal information by e-mail. If you have doubts about any e-mail you receive, look up your bank's phone number and call it. Don't use any phone number in the e-mail—it could be fake.

On-Line Banking Pitfall

Electronic banking and bill paying is convenient and increasingly popular—but it can leave you without paper statements and receipts that later may be needed to document transactions and prove that bills were paid.

Safety: Download all statements and electronic copies of canceled checks, and save all e-mail confirmations of bill payments. Keep them on your computer and also in a backup file you keep safely apart from your main computer so it will be safe if your main computer fails or is damaged.

Good news: Studies show that those who bank entirely on-line reduce their risk of identity theft by about 10%.

Edward Mrkvicka, Jr., president of Reliance Enterprises, Inc., Marengo, IL, and author of Your Bank Is Ripping You Off *(St. Martin's).*

More from Edward Mrkvicka, Jr....

Pass on the Overdraft Protection

Bounce protection for checks is not worthwhile. Banks typically charge about $30 per check and possibly a small transaction fee to prevent a check from being rejected or to let a depositor withdraw more from an ATM than is in the account.

Example: Your bank deposits $50 to cover an overdraft and charges you a $5 transaction fee as well as a $30 bounce-protection fee. You have paid $35 to borrow $50 for one day.

Self-defense: Ask that your bank "red-flag" your account. At no cost to you, the bank will call you if you are overdrawn. You will have until the end of business that day to deposit whatever is needed to cover the overdraft.

Hidden Deals on Bank CDs

Unadvertised higher rates on bank CDs are available. Sometimes a bank will boost CD rates for a week, a day or even a few hours. Ask your bank if it has a special rate and when it will be offered.

Alternative: Keep cash in a money market account or money market mutual fund.

Best low-cost funds: Vanguard Prime Money Market Fund (VMMXX) and Vanguard Federal Money Market Fund (VMFXX), both yielding over 5%.*

Ray Martin, CFP, enrolled agent, personal finance expert for *The Early Show* on CBS and president of CitiStreet Advisors, an investment advisory company that's located in Quincy, MA.

*Rate subject to change.

To Stop Automatic Bill Paying...

To stop an automatic bill-payment agreement in which you grant a company permission to debit your bank account, notify the company that is debiting your account in writing. It can take 10 days to process this change. Keep records in case there is a problem.

If you switch banks and want to continue automatic debits, ask your new bank if it offers a kit to simplify the process of notifying all companies on your automatic-debit list.

Gerri Detweiler, president of Ultimate Credit Solutions, Inc., Sarasota, FL, *www.ultimatecredit.com.*

More from Gerri Detweiler...

How to Fight Credit Card Disputes

Web sites that will tackle credit card disputes on your behalf can charge hefty fees. Sites such as *www.disputemycharge.com* work on a contingency basis. If they succeed in getting a charge removed from your bill, you may have to pay as much as half the disputed charge.

Better: Handle the matter yourself.

The federal *Fair Credit Billing Act* allows you to dispute a charge and withhold payment if the item you requested is different than what you received or if it is not delivered as agreed. You must submit your dispute in writing to the card issuer within 60 days from the mailing date of the statement on which the charge appeared. Include any documentation of your side of the dispute. If you phone in the dispute, follow up with written confirmation. Send your letter with return receipt requested.

Beware of Late Fees

Late fees on credit cards have nearly tripled over the past decade. They have risen from an average of $12.55 to $34.31. Grace periods have shrunk from an average of nearly 27 days 10 years ago to 20 days today. Be on the lookout for universal default provisions—your card provider can impose a higher rate on your account even if you are late with a payment to *another* creditor.

Statistics from CardData, payment card information network, Frederick, MD.

Make the Most of Credit Card Rewards

Maximize credit card rewards by using the same card all of the time and charging everyday items, like your groceries, gasoline and on-line purchases. Find a card with the type of rebate that works best for you—some offer cash back, others give points redeemable for a variety of goods and services. Look for credit cards that have partnerships with more than one company. Finally, always pay your bills in full every month—otherwise, finance charges will cost more than the rebate program gives you.

Curtis Arnold, founder and public relations director, CardRatings.com, which reviews and rates credit card offers, Little Rock, AR.

Best Way to Cancel A Credit Card

Even if the card issuer lets you cancel a credit card over the phone, always get confirmation by e-mail or in writing. If you get a confirmation number, keep it with your records. Note the customer service agent's name and the date and time. Be sure the confirmation states that the account was closed at your request.

A month or so later, request a copy of your credit report to verify that the account is closed and the reason for closing it is accurate. You can get one free credit report annually from each of the three credit bureaus—Experian, TransUnion and Equifax—from *www.annualcreditreport.com* or by calling 877-322-8228.

Caution: Do not cancel unused credit cards if you plan to buy a house or car soon. Cancelling a large amount of unused credit may lower your credit score.

Jessica Cecere, president, Consumer Credit Counseling Service, a nonprofit debt management agency, West Palm Beach, FL, *www.cccsatl.org*.

The Best Way to Boost Your Credit Rating

Stephen Snyder, founder of the nonprofit After Bankruptcy Foundation, which educates Americans with poor credit, Fishers, IN. It publishes the free e-newsletter *Life After Bankruptcy,* available at *www.lifeafterbankruptcy.com/subscribe*. He is also the author of *Credit After Bankruptcy* (Bellwether).

Poor credit makes borrowing difficult—and bankruptcy taints your credit rating for 10 years—but you don't have to wait to get a new credit card, car loan or mortgage. There are attractive credit options available to you now.

The quicker you are able to get new credit after a bankruptcy or another serious financial problem, the sooner you can start rebuilding a damaged credit rating.

CREDIT CARDS

It's possible to get a "secured" credit card at a competitive interest rate. (If you're bankrupt, you must wait until your debts are discharged.) "Secured" means that you will have to deposit several hundred dollars with the bank that issues the card—and you can charge only up to that amount. If you pay all of your bills on time, you might be able to upgrade to an unsecured account in as little as 24 months.

Two attractive secured credit cards…*

•**Amalgamated Bank of Chicago Secured Standard MasterCard,** 800-723-0303.

Annual percentage rate (APR): 16.25% variable.

Annual fee: $50.

Minimum deposit: $500.

•**Orchard Bank Secured Standard Mastercard,** 503-245-9280.

APR: 8.90% variable.

Annual fee: $35.

Minimum deposit: $200.

Important: Don't respond to credit card offers in the mail if you just emerged from bankruptcy. You are unlikely to be approved, and applying increases the number of inquiries on your credit record, lowering your already damaged rating.

CAR LOANS

Car dealerships hate to turn away buyers—many are willing to make loans to those with problem credit or recent bankruptcies. This isn't as risky for the dealers as it might seem because the loan is collateralized by the car. *To obtain a car loan…*

•**Call dealerships and speak to the finance managers.** *Ask the following questions…*

What credit bureau do you use to make loan decisions? Most dealerships check with only one of the three credit bureaus. Go to a car dealer that uses the bureau with which you have the highest score. *To get your scores, contact each of the following…*

•Equifax, 800-685-1111, *www.equifax.com*. Cost: $7.95.

•Experian, 888-397-3742, *www.experian.com*. Cost: $6.

•TransUnion, 800-888-4213, *www.transunion.com*. Cost: $9.95.

Or you can obtain copies of all three credit reports, including scores from myFICO at 800-319-4433 or on-line at *www.myfico.com* for $49.95.

What's the minimum credit score I need to be approved for a loan? The dealer might overlook a bankruptcy, but only if your credit score is above the dealership's minimum. Interestingly, bankrupt people don't necessarily have the lowest credit scores.

*Rates and prices subject to change.

How does a recent bankruptcy impact your loan decisions? Many—but not all—dealers will look past recent bankruptcies and other credit problems.

What kind of company provides the financing? Steer clear of any dealership that uses a "finance company." Finance companies will typically charge high interest rates and should be considered lenders of last resort. Other lenders will view it as a negative if they see a finance company loan on your credit report. If the dealership uses "a bank," ask if it's spelled "B-A-N-K" or "B-A-N-C." When it is spelled with a "C," the firm may be a finance company in disguise.

•**Insist on a noncosigned loan.** You might be asked to have a relative cosign your loan. If you do it once, however, future lenders will be more likely to expect the same concession.

•**After screening dealerships, call the top contenders to apply for a loan.** Apply for all loans within a 14-day period—applications submitted within 14 days of one another count as one inquiry on your credit report, reducing their impact on your credit rating. (The same is true for mortgage applications.)

Helpful: If a dealership advertises a tent sale or other big event, ask if the manufacturer will have a financing representative present. If so, it's a sign that the dealership is anxious to finance vehicles in-house, which increases the odds that you'll qualify for a loan.

MORTGAGES

When your credit rating is poor, you're unlikely to qualify for a conventional mortgage at an attractive rate, but the Federal Housing Administration (FHA) mortgages, underwritten by the Department of Housing and Urban Development (HUD), do not take credit scores into account. They are available to those who have been in bankruptcy, as long as the bankruptcy was discharged at least 24 months before the loan is finalized. An FHA lender is likely to look very closely at your credit history since your bankruptcy, so responsible postbankruptcy use of a secured credit card or car loan can count for a lot.

FHA mortgages charge interest rates comparable to those available to home buyers with exceptional credit and require as little as 3% down. The amount you can borrow is capped, but in all except the highest-priced regions, caps are high enough to finance a midsized house. To find an FHA lender in your area and determine local mortgage caps, call 202-708-1112 or go to HUD's Web site, *www.hud.gov.*

Free Credit Report Scam

Don't be lured by a free credit report to sign up for subscription-based services sold by credit bureaus. Web sites such as MyFreeCreditReport.com will give you a onetime free copy of your credit report in exchange for your credit card number. You will be billed an annual fee of $79.95 automatically for ongoing credit reports and updates unless you remember to cancel the service.

Better and cheaper: You can obtain a truly free report from the congressionally mandated site AnnualCreditReport.com, which allows consumers to check their credit ratings once a year.

James Van Dyke, founder, Javelin Strategy & Research, Pleasanton, CA, and author of the report *Credit Monitoring and Identity Fraud Insurance: What Do Consumers Need?*

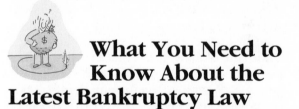

What You Need to Know About the Latest Bankruptcy Law

Donald W. MacPherson, Esq., head attorney for The MacPherson Group, PC, which practices criminal, tax and bankruptcy law, Glendale, AZ, *www.beatirs.com.*

The latest bankruptcy law went into effect on October 17, 2005, and it is a tough one, putting the dream of a "fresh start" beyond the reach of most debtors. *So, if you or someone you care about is thinking of filing for bankruptcy, here's what you should know…*

THE LATEST LAW

•**Chapter 7.** The big change is that under the new law, Chapter 7 generally is not available to persons with as little as $100 per month of disposable income. Instead, these persons are forced into Chapter 13.

This means that even many persons who have very little income against big debts will be unable to get a fresh start, but instead will be forced into a "workout" arrangement that lasts years.

●**Chapter 13.** *Two big changes with the new bankruptcy law...*

●Debt payoff plans last five years, instead of three to five. Many debtors have to make up to two extra years of payments.

●"Disposable income" is now figured using IRS "Collection Financial Standards," which permit a smaller amount for living expenses than many bankruptcy courts have in the past—this results in a greater amount of disposable income being deemed available to pay creditors, making it all the more difficult for individuals.

Note: IRS Collection Financial Standards by geographical location are available on the IRS Web site at *www.irs.gov*, in the section labeled "Individuals."

Net result: Debtors who formerly would have obtained a three-year payment period now not only have to make payments for five years—but probably have to make larger monthly payments as well.

●**The homestead exemption.** The new law makes it more difficult to increase one's homestead exemption by relocating to a different state in anticipation of declaring bankruptcy. Under the old law, there was a 91-day waiting period. Under the new law, if you relocate to a new state with a larger exemption—such as by moving from New York to Florida to obtain an unlimited exemption—you have to qualify as a resident of that state for *two years* before filing for bankruptcy.

In addition, under the new law, the amount that can be added to any existing homestead (such as by making improvements to it within the last 3.3 years) is limited to $125,000, unless the increase results from equity being rolled over from one house into another. If you put more money into your house than the limit, the money is not protected.

These changes made to the homestead exemption are already effective.

Of course, the details of the new law are much more complex than can be fully explained here, so expert help is a must.

Best: Even if you face no current liabilities that threaten your finances, include bankruptcy planning in your long-term financial protection strategies, especially if you own your own business or are a professional. In today's litigious society, an unexpected lawsuit or financial setback is always a possibility.

The True Cost Of Debt

Greg McBride, CFA, senior financial analyst, Bankrate. com, provider of interest rate and consumer finance information, North Palm Beach, FL.

How much is your debt actually costing you? *Answer the three questions below to find out...*

●**What am I paying after taxes?** The true cost of mortgage debt and home-equity loans is what they cost after you factor in the interest deduction, which you can take if you itemize. If you have a 6% mortgage and you're in the 28% federal income tax bracket, your interest rate after the deduction is only 4.32%.

●**How much of each payment goes toward principal?** My firm's site, *www.bankrate. com,* offers an amortization calculator to figure how much of each payment pays down principal and how much is eaten up by interest.

●**How much does it cost to make only minimum payments on credit card bills?** Another calculator on our site shows how long it will take to pay off debt and how much interest you'll pay if you make only the minimum payment each month (or any amount that's less than the total amount due).

Higher minimum payments recently went into effect that drastically decrease how long it will take to pay off debt.

Example: Under previous requirements, a cardholder with $2,000 in debt at an interest rate of 18% making a minimum payment of just 2% of the balance would have taken nearly 31 years to pay the debt. Interest cost would have been $4,931.15.

Now, if that same cardholder pays the new minimum—monthly interest and fees plus 1% of the principal balance, which will total more than 2%—it will take nearly 19 years to pay back. Interest cost will be $2,652.09.

More from Greg McBride, CFA...

Earn Miles When You Refinance

Some lenders offer frequent-flier miles when you refinance, purchase a car or take out a home-equity loan.

Example: United Airlines has a partnership with LendingTree.com.

These deals can be attractive, depending on the terms of the loan and the amount of miles or, in some cases, free airline tickets offered.

Caution: A borrowing rate that is one-quarter of a percentage point higher on a $250,000 mortgage would add about $50 a month to your cost, quickly eroding the advantage of "free" miles.

Common Myths About Today's Real Estate Market

Robert Irwin, investor and licensed real estate broker for more than 40 years, West Lake Village, CA. He is author of more than 50 books, including *How to Get Started in Real Estate Investing* and *How to Find Hidden Real Estate Bargains* (both from McGraw-Hill), and the *For Sale by Owner Kit* (Dearborn). His Web site is *www.robertirwin.com.*

Tales of big profits and fast, easy deals for sellers have seized the imaginations of home buyers in recent years. Low interest rates, "no money down" deals and fast price appreciation enabled some people to buy up several properties at once, quickly resell ("flip") them, then plow the profits into even more expensive houses, condos or town houses.

The dangerous myths of real estate...

Myth: **Home prices never decline.**

Reality: Real estate, like any class of assets, has up and down cycles. Prices do decline. As recently as the mid-1990s, in Riverside County, California, east of Los Angeles, housing prices fell by an average of more than 15%—and many other regions experienced very similar declines during that period.

In recent years, residential real estate has been especially hot on the East and West coasts. While a much larger percentage of Midwesterners still can afford the median-priced home, that is not true of pricey areas in California and the New York/New Jersey/Connecticut metropolitan area. These regions are now likely to see one to two years of flat or even falling values.

According to the National Association of Realtors, the national median existing single-family home price during the third quarter of 2006 was down 1.2% from a year earlier.

The trouble now: Mortgage rates are likely to rise, and sticker shock from the run-up in prices will slow appreciation and dampen demand.

Myth: **It's a good idea to borrow as much as you can.**

Reality: This is a risky strategy at any time, but especially at this point in the cycle. Interest rates for 30-year fixed-rate mortgages still average about 6%.* But once rates start rising, home owners with adjustable-rate mortgages will face higher monthly payments. Investment property owners might find that rental income no longer covers their costs.

The risk is magnified for those who now own two or more mortgaged properties. They might end up having to sell property at a loss if the market softens.

Myth: **Investing in real estate is better than buying stocks.**

Reality: All investments have their pros and cons, and timing is important.

Real estate's pluses...

•**Simplicity.** Real estate's big attraction is tangible. At the most basic level, houses do provide places to live. In comparison, stocks are financial instruments, not hard assets. The stock market also is intimidating to many investors.

•**Income.** When bought for investment purposes, a single-family home can produce generous income for the owner once the mortgage is paid down and rents increase. Until then, rental income can fund mortgage payments. Despite a trend toward higher dividends in the past 10

*Rates subject to change.

years, income from stocks is lower than it has been historically.

.Profit. Having little or no down payment means big profits are possible when the market is up. Such leverage also magnifies losses in a down market.

Real estate's downsides…

.Negative cash flow. Because of today's high prices, the rental income for a new purchase often cannot come close to matching expenses, which include mortgage payments, taxes, insurance, repairs and maintenance.

.Lack of liquidity. Unlike stocks, property cannot be sold quickly. Even in a red-hot real estate market, it can take several weeks to close a deal. In a weak market, it can take months or even years.

.Maintenance costs. As long as you own a property, you have to maintain it. Unless you hire a property manager—which typically costs about 12% of a property's monthly income—you have to take on the management responsibility yourself. If your properties aren't nearby, you also need to travel to them.

Personal story: One time I purchased several single-family houses in Phoenix, although I lived in Los Angeles. These were older properties that required frequent repairs. I purchased them just as the Phoenix housing market was weakening, which created tenant turnover as renters shopped for better deals. For these and other reasons, I had to fly to Phoenix regularly. This drag on my resources prompted me to hire a property manager. Eventually, I sold the properties without making a profit. From that experience, I learned to buy only newer properties that are close to home.

.Transaction costs. Closing expenses for the "round-trip" (both buying and selling) can be as much as 10% of the property's value. Stocks, in contrast, cost little to buy, hold and sell.

Myth: **A vacation home is a great investment because you always can rent it or sell it for a profit.**

Reality: Not so. People want these properties when the economy flourishes but back away when conditions sour. In a weak economy, it may be difficult to charge enough to cover your costs or to find a renter at all. When it is time to

sell, you'll find that demand for vacation homes is more volatile than demand for other residential properties.

Exception: Waterfront properties and homes in upscale resort areas, such as Vail, Colorado, attract extremely wealthy buyers. Prices in those areas are better able to withstand a softening in the market.

Myth: **You can sell your home free of capital gains taxes.**

Reality: To obtain a tax exclusion, owners must have lived in the house for two of the last five years. Single filers get an exclusion of up to $250,000 of gains, and married couples filing jointly can exclude up to $500,000.

Special concern: Flipping properties. Capital gains on properties held for less than one year don't qualify for the exclusion and are taxed at ordinary income tax rates, which typically are much higher than the long-term capital gains rate (15% for individuals in a 25% or higher bracket and 5% for taxpayers in the 10% and 15% brackets).

Myth: **Remodeling a home always boosts its value.**

Reality: Although improvements add to a home's resale value, they typically don't provide dollar-for-dollar increases. If an investor spends $100,000 on an addition, it might add only $50,000 to the resale value of the property. That's because the price for which you can sell your house is influenced more by the going rate for similar homes in the area than by the size and quality of the addition or improvement. Some enhancements—such as installing an in-ground pool—even may dissuade many prospective buyers.

Fixer-uppers are a special case. Remodeling one can definitely pay off, but finding a good candidate can be tricky.

Personal story: I have purchased homes at bargain prices because of outdated kitchens or bathrooms. After making the improvements, I was able to resell the houses, in many cases for sizable profits. Once, however, I bought a home that had structural problems. Its foundation cracked because the builder had neglected to put in steel reinforcing bars. Although I sold the home for $100,000 more than I had paid, I didn't come out ahead. It had cost me almost $100,000 to make the needed improvements.

Smarter Home Selling

Kendra Todd, president of My House Real Estate, Inc., a marketing organization in Boynton Beach, FL, *www.my housere.com*. Ms. Todd is the third-season winner of the TV reality show *The Apprentice,* starring Donald Trump. As an employee of the Trump organization, she oversees a project to renovate and market a $125 million estate on Palm Beach Island, FL.

Some home sellers are currently advertising price ranges not one asking price. But that strategy isn't wise in most cases.

Reason: When presented with a price range—say, from $300,000 to $350,000—a typical buyer naturally will want the lowest price. As a result, owners might end up with lower selling prices than they had hoped for.

However, using a price range can be rewarding if a seller wants to unload a property quickly.

Reason: A range increases the number of potential buyers who will consider a given house.

Example: If house shoppers could afford only the $300,000 properties, they might not become aware of houses in a database priced at $350,000, but such shoppers might learn of the availability of properties priced in a $300,000-to-$350,000 *range*. Meanwhile, buyers looking for houses priced at $350,000 and up will become aware of the house as well. The more potential buyers, the faster it can sell.

In certain locations, particularly where home prices have risen rapidly, this price-range technique could prove useful. There, a single price on a home may appear too high to many buyers, but a price range might make the property seem more affordable.

How to Tap the Hidden Wealth in Your Home

William Stanton, CFP, senior financial planner for J.P. Morgan Private Client Services in New York City, where the wealth management unit services more than 175,000 clients in more than 100 offices.

With the recent increase in property values, homes are the biggest source of wealth for many households, so it is important to make the most of real estate assets.

In a red-hot market, a home owner might be tempted to cash in by selling, but that can generate capital gains taxes—and after you sell the home, you still may have to spend money on a new place to live.

Top financial planner William Stanton has advised many clients on how best to tap the hidden wealth in their homes. *Here are some recent cases and the advice that he gave...*

DOWNSIZING

A 77-year-old grandmother owned a house worth $600,000, up from the $30,000 that she paid for it four decades earlier. Rising property taxes and maintenance costs had become a major burden, and she no longer needed such a big place, so she was considering selling. Because of the appreciation, any sale would produce a huge tax bill. A single person can exclude the first $250,000 in profits from the sale of a primary residence. After that, the home owner might pay federal capital gains tax of up to 15%, as well as state taxes.

Solution: The woman sold the house and realized a $550,000 capital gain. Her cost basis in the house was $50,000—the $30,000 purchase price plus $20,000 in capital improvements. Only $300,000 ($550,000 minus the $250,000 exclusion) was subject to capital gains tax at a rate of about 20% (state and federal).

She paid the $60,000 in taxes, then used the remaining assets to invest in a conservative portfolio and her grandchildren's savings for college. She put $60,000—the maximum allowable initial deposit without incurring federal gift taxes—into a 529 college savings plan for each child. The amount contributed to the plans as well as the accumulated investment earnings could be withdrawn from the account tax free as long as the withdrawal was used for qualified education expenses.

If the children decided not to attend college— or if the grandmother changed her mind—she could withdraw the money and pay a 10% tax penalty as well as taxes on the income and capital gains.

Alternatively, the grandmother could change the account beneficiary to another qualified family member to keep the account going and to avoid (or delay) taking taxable withdrawals.

To avoid buying a new house or paying rent, the grandmother chose to move in with her son and his family. Now she helps pay the family's housing costs. Freed from much of the burden of paying for his children's college, her son can afford to increase his savings. Now he is thinking about taking early retirement.

SUDDEN LAYOFF

A 52-year-old bank executive lived in a condominium with his wife and two children. With $500,000 in his 401(k) and IRA, a deferred-compensation plan and a good-paying job, the man saw no need to set aside cash for emergencies. Then his employer informed him that he would be laid off and that he would receive paychecks for only two months more. Unless the executive found a job quickly, he would need to raise cash for living expenses.

He considered selling the condo and moving to a cheaper area, but that would have forced him to put his children into a new school. He could have raised money with a second mortgage, but that would have meant taking on the long-term interest payments and paying closing costs. He also could have taken cash from his retirement or deferred-compensation plan.

Solution: As a temporary measure, the family obtained a home-equity line of credit. The executive, a longtime customer of the bank, easily qualified for the line of credit. (He was not required to disclose that he could be without a job in the future.) The credit line served like a credit card. If the executive needed to make a $300 payment on his car, he could tap the account by writing a check. He could draw up to $35,000.

Caution: Your home is collateral for a home-equity line. If you do not make payments, the bank will foreclose.

Interest on the credit line was 4.4% (prime minus 0.25%) and was tax deductible. While that rate could have risen if the Federal Reserve kept raising interest rates, it was still well below the typical rate on credit card debt.

Fortunately, the executive found employment within three months and did not have to use the line of credit, but he did realize the importance of establishing an emergency fund.

CHARITY BEGINS AT "HOME"

A doctor owned an investment property that had appreciated from $200,000 to $750,000. The doctor had an intense desire to pass wealth on to charity, but selling the property would have generated big capital gains taxes.

Solution: At my suggestion, the physician donated the building to a charitable remainder trust that benefited a public charity. Then he received an income tax deduction for the charitable contribution. The trustee sold the $750,000 property and invested the proceeds in a diversified portfolio. For the next 20 years, the trust will pay the doctor income of $37,500 every year (5% of the fair market value of the property transferred). Assuming an 8% growth rate on the trust, at the end of 20 years, $1,779,644 will pass to charity.

While utilizing the trust did not maximize the doctor's overall wealth, it provided a stream of income for his retirement and enabled him to donate money to charity.

EXTENDING A MORTGAGE

A 61-year-old attorney was worried that he would not have sufficient cash flow to finance his child's upcoming college tuition payments. He also wanted to be able to maintain his current lifestyle.

Solution: The attorney refinanced his mortgage. He extended the term of the loan, which lowered his monthly payment. In 1991, when he purchased the property, he had taken out a 30-year mortgage for $300,000. With an interest rate of 6.25%, the monthly payments were $1,847.

By 2006, the principal on the mortgage had shrunk to $215,000. By refinancing and taking out another 30-year mortgage at 6.25%—coincidentally, he was able to get the same rate 15 years later—he was able to reduce the monthly payments to $1,323. He used some of the cash for living expenses and tuition and invested the rest in stocks and bonds to raise money for future needs.

This approach was appropriate because over the long term, the lawyer believed that the return on his investments would outperform the after-tax cost of his mortgage. Furthermore, because he extended the term of his loan, his mortgage interest deduction would last for many years and could be taken against earned income.

Caution: While this plan increased monthly cash flow, it also significantly raised the amount of interest that the lawyer had to pay over the life of the loan.

If You're Looking for a Home Abroad...

To find a home overseas—for your personal use or investment purposes—use an Internet search engine such as Google. To get listings, type in "real estate" and the name of the country you want to search. Get listings and information on living and investing abroad at *www.escape artist.com* and at *www.internationalliving.com.* Search for real estate agents and for real estate listings at *www.worldproperties.com,* sponsored by the International Consortium of Real Estate Associations. Consider agents who are certified international property specialists—they tend to have more expertise than others.

Kiplinger's Personal Finance, 1729 H St. NW, Washington, DC 20006.

When Prepaying a Mortgage Makes Sense— And When It Doesn't

Paul Palazzo, director of financial planning, L.J. Altfest & Co., writing in *The Altfest Advisory Letter,* 425 Park Ave., New York City 10022, a newsletter free to clients.

Prepaying a mortgage has a financial effect much like buying a bond—with your return being the after-tax interest cost you

avoid paying on the mortgage, instead of the after-tax interest you receive from a bond.

Example: If you are in the 30% tax bracket and use $1,000 to...

•**Prepay $1,000 on a 6% mortgage,** you will avoid having to pay $42 after tax annually ($60 × 70%) on the $1,000 for the remaining term of the mortgage. So your return is $42 a year.

•**Purchase a $1,000 taxable bond paying 6% annually,** you will receive $42 of interest annually after tax ($60 × 70%) for the bond's term. So your return is the same $42 a year.

BEFORE PREPAYING A MORTGAGE CONSIDER...

•**If you have other, higher-cost debt outstanding**—such as on credit cards or consumer loans that accrue nondeductible interest—you'll save more by paying them first.

•**If your choice is between using money to prepay a mortgage and making another investment with it,** realize that prepaying a mortgage provides a secure return while most other investments are riskier. To justify investing in the riskier investment, you should expect a significantly higher return from it than from a mortgage prepayment.

•**After-tax return is what matters,** so contributions to your tax-favored retirement accounts may be better than prepaying a mortgage due to the various tax advantages they can offer.

•**Prepayment risk.** There is a downside to prepaying a mortgage in that it costs you liquidity—you lose use of the cash used to prepay the loan, which you could otherwise keep in a savings account or liquid investments.

If it later turns out that you need that cash, and interest rates have risen from today's low level in the meantime, you may have to take out a new loan at a higher rate to get it.

And you may pay more taxes, too—because only $100,000 of home-equity borrowing qualifies for the mortgage interest deduction. Thus, if you do prepay your mortgage, the maximum amount of deductible borrowing against your home will be reduced.

Example: Your home is worth $225,000 and your outstanding acquisition loan (mortgage) is $100,000. If a need to raise cash arises, you can use a home-equity loan to borrow an additional $100,000—for a total (with your mortgage) of $200,000 against your home, which will produce deductible mortgage interest. But if you prepay the mortgage balance down to only $50,000, then no more than $150,000 of total borrowing against the home ($50,000 mortgage plus $100,000 home equity) will produce deductible mortgage interest.

How to Get the Best Home-Equity Loan

Home-equity rates can vary significantly, so shop around. The interest rates for similar loans or lines of credit can vary by as much as two percentage points. And, don't automatically gravitate to lenders that advertise aggressively. Their marketing campaigns are costly, and the tab is passed on to borrowers. The best deals for home-equity lines of credit and loans often can be found at the smallest institutions. Contact credit unions and small banks and thrifts. You also may obtain a good deal through the financial institution where you maintain your checking account. Ask for more favorable terms if you agree to have payments automatically deducted from the account.

Keith Gumbinger, vice president, HSH Associates, publisher of mortgage and consumer loan information, Pompton Plains, NJ, www.hsh.com.

An Insider's Secrets to Getting More Financial Aid for College

Ben Kaplan, Oregon-located developer of ScholarshipCoach.com, which provides information on how to obtain college financing. He graduated from Harvard University debt-free in 1999 by using $90,000 in scholarships and is the author of 12 books and CDs on paying for college, including How to Go to College Almost for Free: 10 Days to Scholarship Success (ScholarshipCoach.com).

Many families fail to take full advantage of the financial aid available to them and lose out on tens of thousands of dollars in grants, scholarships and subsidized loans. Even households that have considerable incomes and assets can qualify. (Merit scholarships are available regardless of income.) *Here's how to get the most financial aid you can...*

•Defer your income in the calendar year before your child graduates from high school. The financial-aid eligibility clock starts ticking sooner than most parents expect.

Example: If your student graduates high school in 2008, your income during 2007 will serve as the basis for freshman-year financial-aid calculations.

Strategy: Ask that employers give year-end bonuses in early 2008 rather than during 2007. If you're self-employed, accelerate or postpone customer billing to minimize 2007 income. Avoid selling assets, such as stocks, bonds and rental property, in 2007 if proceeds will be taxed as income. (Delaying income from 2007 to 2008 might cause your aid to drop in the student's sophomore year, but you'll come out ahead, since the freshman "base" year sets the precedent for financial aid allocations.)

•To reduce cash reserves, make major expenditures—on home renovations, cars, computers, entertainment systems, etc.—before you apply for aid.

Reason: Colleges take most financial assets into account when they determine your need for aid but not other personal assets, such as cars or home electronics.

If your child has significant savings, urge him/her to spend his own money first—as opposed to yours—on big-ticket items.

Reason: When figuring out an aid package according to the federal methodology, colleges expect students to contribute 35% of their assets to college costs. Parents are expected to pitch in only about 5% of their assets. (You can, of course, pay the child back later without incurring gift tax as long as you do not exceed the maximum annual gift limit of $12,000 per recipient—$24,000 for couples in 2007.)

•Apply for aid as soon as possible. Many colleges distribute financial aid on a first-come, first-served basis, so money might be substantially depleted long before the official end of the application period. Submit the federal government's

Free Application for Federal Student Aid (FAFSA) form—as well as any additional forms required by private colleges—by January or early February of your child's senior year in high school to ensure the biggest share possible.

To assemble the necessary information, you will need to finish up your tax forms well before April. If you can't, use estimates on your college aid forms (identifying them as estimates) and follow up with actual figures as soon as possible.

•**If a school's aid offer is lower than you expected, explain special circumstances** that are not considered by the aid formulas—hefty medical bills...private-school expenses for your other children in grade-school...graduate school costs for your older kids, if you pay some of their bills...or an unusually high income year that is not representative of your typical earnings. Follow up with evidence, such as invoices, establishing that, for example, you are paying Grandma's hospital bills, or the last five years' tax returns to show that your income last year was much higher than normal.

•**Apply for merit-based scholarships from corporations,** foundations, associations, unions and community groups. Links to award databases can be found at my site, ScholarshipCoach.com.

Note: These scholarships may affect other financial aid.

•**Leverage offers from other schools.** If your top choice is X University, but Y University offers more aid, call X and ask to speak to the financial aid officer responsible for your file. Explain that your child really wants to attend, but Y's aid package makes going there more financially feasible. X might increase its offer. This works best when the schools involved are rivals or the student is particularly appealing to the college because of special credentials or talents.

Does Your Child Qualify for a PLUS Loan?

PLUS (Parent Loan for Undergraduate Students) is a federal college loan program in which parents can borrow up to the cost of attendance, minus any other financial aid the student receives. To qualify, your child must be a dependent, an undergraduate and enrolled at least half-time. These loans are available year-round and are not need-based. Applications are available from the school or from many banks. The interest rate is fixed at 8.5%.* Repayment begins in 60 days and must be completed within 10 years.

Starting July 1, 2006, graduate and professional students will also be able to borrow through the PLUS program.

More information: *www.finaid.org.*

Nancy Dunnan, a financial adviser and author in New York City. Her latest book is *How to Invest $50–$5,000* (HarperCollins).

*Rate subject to change.

Tax-Savvy Way to Save for College

Glenn Frank, CPA, CFP/PFS, senior vice president for Wachovia Wealth Management, and an adjunct assistant professor in financial planning and taxation, Bentley College, both in Waltham, MA. He was listed among America's top financial advisers by *Worth* in 2004.

If you only have a limited amount to invest for your child's college education, place the portion you want to keep in bonds in a 529 college savings plan instead so that interest income won't be taxed. You can withdraw money tax free to pay for higher education. Invest in stocks through a tax managed mutual fund that you hold in your own name. These funds are managed to minimize capital gains taxes, and you can deduct any losses from your taxes (you can't do that with a 529).

Better yet: Instead of taking gains in your own name, first give away appreciated stock to your children, who are probably in a lower tax bracket—they might pay only 5% tax (0% in 2008 through 2010) on gains when they are more than 17 years old. They then can use the proceeds to pay college bills.

Caution: Before making such gifts, check that your children will not qualify for need-based financial aid. By shifting assets to your children, you'll lower your family's eligibility for such aid.

Student Loan Relief

If you are a lawyer, doctor or teacher and perform some kind of public service, you can get a big chunk of your debt load trimmed or forgiven.

Good deals are increasingly available for lawyers willing to practice public interest law for a nonprofit agency or work as government prosecutors or public defenders (check with your law school)...doctors who specialize in high-demand areas of medicine, such as primary care, or who are located in underserved areas (check the Web site of the Association of American Medical Colleges, *www.aamc.org*)...teachers specializing in subjects where expertise is in short supply, such as math, science and special education, or those who work in schools that serve low-income students (check with your loan provider and your state department of education).

US News & World Report, 1050 Thomas Jefferson St. NW, Washington, DC 20007.

Student Loans for Postgraduate Degrees

Students seeking MBAs and medical and law degrees can apply for federal funds, such as Stafford and Perkins loans, but these may not cover the entire cost. Sallie Mae is offering additional loans. *Graduate business students* can apply for an MBA Stafford or MBA Private Loan, both sponsored by the Graduate Management Admissions Council. *Law students* may be eligible for a LawLoans Stafford or LawLoans Private Loan. Students studying for the bar may apply for a LawLoans Bar Study Loan. *Medical students* may be eligible for a MedLoans Stafford Loan.

Information: Sallie Mae, 800-891-4599, *www. salliemae.com.*

Raymond D. Loewe, CLU, ChFC, president and owner, College Money, Marlton, NJ, *www.collegemoney.com.*

Secrets to a Fair Divorce

Gayle Rosenwald Smith, JD, an attorney specializing in family and divorce law, Philadelphia, *www.smithondivorce. com.* She is author of *Divorce and Money: Everything You Need to Know* (Perigee).

Why do some people receive equitable divorce settlements while others get the short end of the stick? The answer lies in the ability to keep emotions in check. *Based on my legal experience and on interviews with hundreds of judges for my book, here are secrets to getting your fair share...*

●**Hire a top-notch divorce lawyer.** Get referrals from friends and relatives, your accountant or family attorney, or try *lawyers.com.*

●**Consider the end of your marriage as a business transaction.** This may not be easy emotionally, but tell yourself that your partnership didn't work out. You'll fare better if you wrap up loose ends and separate on good terms.

List dollar amounts for your important financial needs, such as housing, utilities, insurance, transportation, credit cards and other debt payments, retirement contributions and other savings. Refer to this list whenever you sense yourself becoming emotional or irrational. Don't waste time worrying about anything that isn't on your list.

Case study: A nonworking wife was battling her husband for the couple's $12,000, state-of-the-art home theater system. It was a hot button because they had spent months researching it. I pointed out that the top priority on her divorce list was health-care coverage. While federal law (COBRA) ensured that she would continue getting coverage under her husband's plan for 36 months after her divorce, she still would have to pay $200 per month. My client decided to let her husband have the home theater system, which was now worth much less than the purchase price, if he agreed to pay her premiums—potentially more than $7,000 for the three years.

●**Eliminate joint debt.** Pay off credit cards and nonmortgage-related loans from joint funds, or transfer balances to cards in your own name.

Reason: When you reach a property settlement that stipulates who is responsible for joint debts, it won't be binding on a third party, such as a bank. If your ex-spouse defaults on a credit obligation, the bank still can pursue you for the money it is owed.

Important: If you file joint returns, you are liable for your spouse's taxes. If you fear that your spouse has understated income or overstated expenses, ask your accountant about preparing your returns as "married filing separately." If you trust your spouse, ask your accountant if you can get a tax break by signing a joint return for the year of the divorce.

•**Protect assets you had before the marriage.** In most states, money, securities, property and gifts you brought into the marriage remain yours after the divorce, but you will need proof of ownership of those original assets.

Example: Say you owned a condominium prior to your marriage. After you got married, you sold it and put the sale price toward a home purchase with your husband. In many states, you may be able to get full or partial credit for that down payment when you sell your house, but you will need copies of statements showing withdrawals from your separate bank account that were deposited into a joint account or delivered to the bank or mortgage company. These should be with your closing documents for the home purchase.

List all your joint assets to ensure that they are included in the "marital estate." Include your home, vehicles, bank and investment accounts and often-overlooked assets—prepaid life insurance, frequent-flier miles, club memberships, season tickets to sporting events, upcoming tax refunds, vacation pay and stock options.

Smart: Hire an experienced accountant or a divorce planner to assess your assets and help you propose an appropriate settlement based on your financial situation. For a referral, contact the Institute for Divorce Financial Analysts, 800-875-1760, *www.institutedfa.com.*

Caution: If you suspect that your spouse is trying to hide personal or joint assets from you (see the following article), take action.

•**Opt for mediation** if you feel that you can negotiate directly with your spouse. It costs much less than divorce litigation.

How it works: A trained divorce mediator sits down with both parties, negotiates an agreement and prepares a memorandum of understanding, which then is reviewed by a lawyer and submitted to the court for a judge's approval.

Ask your attorney to recommend a local mediator or contact the Association for Conflict Resolution, 202-464-9700, *www.acrnet.org.*

•**Familiarize yourself with your state's divorce laws.** Unless you signed a prenuptial agreement or reached an agreement with your spouse out of court, your property settlement will be governed by the law in your state. In nine of the states—Arizona, California, Idaho, Louisiana, Nevada, New Mexico, Texas, Washington and Wisconsin—all wages, income and property acquired during the marriage are considered community property to be split 50-50, regardless of the length of the marriage or the financial contribution of each spouse.

In most other states, a judge can divide the assets in any way that he/she deems to be fair. To learn your rights where you live, check your state's chapter of the American Bar Association (800-285-2221 or *www.abanet.org*) or check out DivorceNet (*www.divorcenet.com*), a family law advice site with helpful links to state-specific information.

•**Transfer retirement assets in a way that avoids triggering tax penalties.** When figuring out how to divide retirement plans, courts look at the complete marital estate. If there are enough assets, one party can equitably take, say, the house and the sailboat, while the other can take the retirement accounts without having to divide them.

If the estate is small—a house and a pension—and the pension is worth more, it might have to be split. Your attorney may draft a qualified domestic relations order (QDRO), a court order that tells how retirement plan assets will be distributed in a divorce. It must be approved by your spouse's retirement-plan administrator and the divorce judge.

Once you receive your distribution from your spouse's qualified plan, you can roll the money into an IRA. If you take the proceeds in cash pursuant to a QDRO, you will owe ordinary income taxes but not a 10% early withdrawal penalty—even if you are under age 59½.

Resource: Dividing up assets in a traditional (defined-benefit) pension plan may require an evaluation expert. Get a referral from your lawyer or contact Pension Analysis Consultants, Inc., a fee-based service, 800-288-3675, *www.pension analysis.com.*

●**Make sure that your spouse purchases term life insurance** if you expect to receive child support or alimony. The insurance benefit should be enough to cover your agreed-upon income stream in the event of your spouse's death. He/she should make you the irrevocable beneficiary of the policy. And, the property settlement should stipulate that the supporting spouse will notify you every time a premium is due and every time one is paid.

●**Don't give up your right to sue.** Most settlements stipulate that each spouse must waive the right to file "known" claims against the other in the future. Don't waive your right to file unknown claims.

Example: After you settle your divorce, you discover that you have contracted a sexually transmitted disease as a result of your spouse's extramarital affair. You want to retain the ability to file a tort claim for money damages for this "unknown claim."

●**Include "cost-of-living adjustment" and "late fee" clauses** in child-support agreements. Otherwise, you will face expensive trips back to court if payments are late or if you want payments increased due to inflation.

More from Gayle Rosenwald Smith, JD…

How Divorcing Spouses Hide Assets

Besides shifting assets out of joint accounts, there are many creative ways to keep money out of the hands of a spouse—some legal and some not. *What to watch for…*

●**Asking an employer to put off payment of bonuses or raises until after the divorce.**

●**Setting up a custodial account that's in the name of your child,** using the child's Social Security number, and transferring the joint assets to that account.

●**Investing in municipal bonds or Series EE US savings bonds.** Interest does not need to be reported on tax returns.

●**"Repaying" bogus debts to friends or to family members,** who hold the money for the spouse until after the divorce.

●**If your spouse has a business, he/she could pay a "salary" to a nonexistent employee** to hide assets.

Self-defense: If you suspect that your spouse is hiding assets, you may need a forensic accountant. Ask your attorney for a recommendation…or when a business is involved, hire a business evaluator. The National Association of Certified Valuation Analysts at 800-677-2009 or *www.nacva.com* is a good place to start.

Pension Finder

Trying to locate a lost pension? Contact the Social Security Administration to obtain your earnings record. Your former employer's federal employer identification number (EIN) will be on record. Then use the EIN to search for the company at *www.freeerisa.com.* Also, check with the Pension Benefit Guaranty Corporation (*www.pbgc.gov*), the federal agency that insures corporate defined-benefit plans. Another place to check is the nonprofit Pension Rights Center at *www.pensionrights.org,* which helps employees and retirees understand and enforce their legal rights.

AARP Bulletin, 601 E St. NW, Washington, DC 20049. Free with membership.

8

Insurance Guide

Anyone Can Find Affordable Health Insurance: Here's How...

If you do not have health insurance—because of a layoff or other change in work, a divorce or a preexisting medical condition—do not give up. Efforts to expand health insurance coverage reportedly are becoming quite common. Proposals have been introduced in many US states, and Illinois and New York already offer low-cost health insurance to children.

Even under current law, it is possible to find coverage for you and your family, usually at a reasonable cost. *Options to consider if you need health coverage but are too young (under age 65) to qualify for Medicare...*

COBRA/STATE PLANS

For people who recently have lost group coverage, a smart choice may be to purchase a policy under COBRA, the temporary health benefits provision of the *Consolidated Omnibus Budget Reconciliation Act of 1986*. According to the rules, you can continue to be covered under your employer's insurance for up to 18 months at up to 102% of the former policy's expenses, depending on your circumstances. This amount includes both the employee and the employer's share, if your employer splits the expense with workers, as many do. (The extra 2% is for administrative costs.) COBRA usually is available only from companies that have at least 20 employees. (Your spouse and dependent children can be covered for up to 36 months.)

Paying the full tab can be a shock to someone who is accustomed to having an employer pick up most of the cost of insurance. However, while COBRA policies often are more expensive than those purchased privately on an individual basis, they usually have more comprehensive benefits.

What to do: Apply for COBRA through your previous employer. To get more information on

---

Jessica Waltman, legislative director of health policy research for the National Association of Health Underwriters, an insurance industry trade group, Arlington, VA, *www.nahu.org*.

127

COBRA, contact the US Department of Labor's Employee Benefits Security Administration, 866-444-3272, *www.dol.gov/ebsa.*

Helpful: Many states require smaller companies and others not bound by COBRA to offer some type of continuation of coverage to employees. For a database on health-care coverage options by state, go to *www.nahu.org/consumer/healthcare* or call 703-276-0220.

INDIVIDUAL POLICIES

Individual insurance is regulated on a state-by-state basis. You must buy a policy sold in your home state. Rules for individual health insurance outside a group plan vary among states.

•**Medical underwriting.** In the vast majority of states, insurance costs are based on the applicant's health status. He/she will be assigned a rate class by the company and put into a pool with similar individuals who will be charged the same premium. Also, many states allow health insurers to issue *elimination riders* to people who have preexisting medical conditions. These riders allow you the option of picking a policy that covers all conditions or a less expensive policy that excludes certain preexisting conditions.

•**Pricing based on guaranteed issue/community rating.** "Guaranteed issue" laws state that a health insurance company cannot reject you for coverage based on any preexisting medical condition. Community rating laws say that everyone in the same geographic area pays the same price for coverage, regardless of age or health. It may be easier for people with medical problems to obtain coverage in states with such laws, but there is a price involved.

These laws make individual coverage in the state more expensive, on average, because insurers do not have the medical information to appropriately spread risk among the applicants. In these states, healthy young people are much less likely to purchase coverage. This makes coverage more expensive for those who buy it.

Examples:* A healthy, 25-year-old man living in the New Jersey suburb of Haddonfield could pay $467.16 per month for a comprehensive individual policy with a $1,000 deductible. If he lived in Pennsylvania in the suburb of Wayne (20 miles away), he could buy the

*Using rates obtained from eHealthInsurance.com. All rates are subject to change.

128

same policy for only $58.86 a month. A healthy, 60-year-old man in Wayne would pay $289.82 for that policy. A man of the same age living in Haddonfield would be charged the same $467.16 a month that the 25-year-old pays for the plan. These vast price differences are due to the community rating and guaranteed issue laws affecting individual insurance in New Jersey.

What to do: Purchase private coverage from an independent health insurance agent licensed in your state. Access the agent locator at *www.nahu.org/consumer/findagent.cfm* or call 703-276-0220. You also can find quotes from Web sites such as *www.ehealthinsurance.com.*

HEALTH SAVINGS ACCOUNTS

For a tax-efficient way to pay for individual health insurance, consider a health savings account (HSA). For 2007, you must choose a policy with a high insurance deductible—at least $1,100 for individuals ($2,200 for families) and make deductible contributions to the HSAs up to a maximum of $2,850 for individuals ($5,650 for families). Each year you can make your tax-deductible contribution up to the amount of the deductible. You withdraw funds from the account to cover out-of-pocket medical expenses.

For people who create HSAs but don't need to tap them, the accounts can function like IRAs. The money can be invested to grow tax-deferred. After age 65, you can withdraw the money for any reason, but you will have to pay income tax if it is used for nonqualified expenses.

COVERAGE FOR SERIOUS MEDICAL PROBLEMS

In most states, you can be turned down for individual coverage if you have a serious medical condition (e.g., HIV or cancer). Fortunately, most states have developed some way to provide hard-to-insure people with access to private individual health insurance coverage.

Thirty-three states provide high-risk pools. You can apply for high-risk pool coverage through an insurance agent or directly to the state. Coverage costs more than private coverage because all the people in the pool have serious medical problems, but the rates are capped, usually between 125% and 200% of the average individual market premium. For instance, in a state where a healthy person pays $100 a month, someone of the same age in the risk pool might pay $150.

Twelve states use other means of providing hard-to-insure people with access to individual coverage (for instance, requiring coverage through a designated health insurance company of last resort). Five states—Arizona, Delaware, Georgia, Hawaii and Nevada—offer no individual coverage options for those who are hard to insure. For more information on insurance for those who cannot get coverage privately, go to *www.nahu.org/consumer/healthcare*.

What to Do If You Lose Your Health Insurance

Charles B. Inlander, a health-care consultant and president of the nonprofit People's Medical Society, a consumer health advocacy group in Allentown, PA. He is the author of more than 20 books on consumer health issues, including *Take This Book to the Hospital with You: A Consumer Guide to Surviving Your Hospital Stay* (St. Martin's).

An average day in a hospital costs about $2,000. The typical cholesterol-lowering drug can cost about $100 a month. It's no wonder that we value our health insurance so highly.

However, losing your health insurance is a real possibility. Many people lose insurance because of a job layoff, their employer drops health benefits completely or they retire early. Others become uninsured when they cannot afford the insurance premiums that their employer requires them to pay, or because of a divorce or the death of a spouse. If you lose your health insurance and you do not qualify for Medicaid or are not yet 65 and eligible for Medicare, there are ways to get temporary insurance or needed medical services and prescriptions. *See below...*

•**COBRA.** As noted on page 127, the Consolidated Omnibus Budget Reconciliation Act (COBRA) allows workers covered by an employer's group health insurance plan to continue to purchase that coverage for up to 18 months, at their own expense, if they have been laid off, taken voluntary leave or had their hours reduced to the point where they are no longer eligible for benefits. You may purchase that insurance for anyone in your family who was covered before you lost the insurance. Family members of an insured employee who dies also can purchase coverage under COBRA.

Important: COBRA only applies to companies with 20 or more employees. It does not apply if your former employer goes completely out of business. And it can be expensive. A typical employer-sponsored family health insurance plan, which includes hospital, physician, dental and prescription drug coverage, can easily cost up to $12,000 annually.

•**Hospital coverage for the uninsured.** Under both state and federal laws, you cannot be turned away from a hospital emergency room if you are uninsured. And if you require more than just emergency room care, you cannot be denied admission to the hospital. Last year, hospitals provided more than $25 billion in care to people who were unable to pay their bills, whether they were insured or not. In addition, many hospitals run free or low-cost clinics that can be used to help monitor chronic conditions, such as diabetes, asthma or heart disease.

•**Free or low-cost prescription medications.** More than 475 public and private assistance programs, including those offered by more than 150 drug companies, provide free or low-cost prescription drugs to qualified patients who lack prescription medication coverage. To find out about these programs—and which you qualify for—consult the Partnership for Prescription Assistance (888-477-2669 or *www.pparx.org*).

•**Negotiate with your doctor.** Losing your health insurance does not necessarily mean you cannot see the doctors you have always used. Most will work out reduced fees or extended payment arrangements for you and your family. But it's up to you to ask.

Beware of Insurance Through Associations

Group health insurance sold through associations could cost more than advertised.

Some associations claim to sell low-cost insurance at group rates, but they actually are selling individual policies, so rates rise quickly after the initial low teaser rate expires. They also may misrepresent the extent of coverage, leaving policyholders responsible for much higher costs than expected.

How to tell if an association is legitimate: Membership organizations, such as professional and trade associations, often offer other services as well, such as educational opportunities.

More information: At *www.familiesusa.org*, click on "Private Insurance."

Study by Families USA, consumer advocacy organization, Washington, DC.

Dietitian Visits May Be Covered

Visits to dietitians are covered by an increasing number of insurance plans. The most frequent reimbursement is for the treatment of conditions directly related to nutrition, such as obesity, hypertension and diabetes. Some insurers also will cover counseling for early warning symptoms, such as elevated blood sugar or cholesterol. Insurance coverage varies widely—check with your plan.

Cynthia Sass, MPH, RD, spokesperson, American Dietetic Association, Tampa.

HSA Know-How

A good way to locate companies that provide health savings accounts (HSAs) is to contact the HSA Insider at *www.hsainsider.com* or eHealthInsurance, *www.ehealthinsurance.com*. You will find information by state on insurers that offer HSAs, which are designed to let medical consumers pay health-care expenses with tax-exempt dollars.

Congress created HSAs as part of the sweeping Medicare legislation during 2003, but it took a while for the insurance companies to start offering them. You also can establish an HSA through an outside bank or another financial institution, such as Wellfund and American Chartered Bank. To qualify for an HSA, your policy must have a deductible in 2007 of at least $1,100 for an individual or $2,200 for a family.

Included on HSA Insider's list are some high-profile insurance companies, such as CIGNA, Aetna and UnitedHealthcare, that offer policies in dozens of states.

James Shagawat, fee-only investment adviser and principal at Baron-Financial.com, a wealth-management firm in Fair Lawn, NJ.

Traps in Medicare's Drug Benefit Program

Judith Stein, attorney and executive director of the Center for Medicare Advocacy, Mansfield, CT.

Medicare Part D, Medicare's drug benefit program, is extremely confusing. *Traps to avoid...*

•**The waiting pitfall.** Some people believe that delaying enrollment makes sense because their current drug costs are lower than their premiums would be under Part D. It may save you money initially, but if you enroll more than three months after your 65th birthday, when you become eligible for Medicare, you will be charged an extra 1% of the current monthly premium for every month you wait to enroll. This is in addition to the annual premium increases affecting all Part D enrollees.

Better: Enroll as soon as you are eligible. If your needs change, you can change plans one time without penalty and choose a new plan between November 15 and December 31 for the following year. When selecting a plan, factor in co-payments and premiums. Make sure your drugs are in the plan's formulary. If a drug isn't included but your doctor can show that it is necessary, you can appeal for an exception—however, there are no guarantees.

People who have "creditable" drug or other coverage—that is, employer, union or other benefits that are equal to, or even better than, the standard Medicare Part D plan—should receive a notice to this effect from their benefits department or insurer. If the creditable coverage is lost at a later time, they can enroll in a Medicare drug plan without any penalty—so long as they make their choice within 63 days of the loss of coverage. This protection is not available if you have purchased coverage individually.

•Snowbird pitfall. Most regional Medicare plans cover only drug purchases made in the region. (Some make exceptions for emergencies or have a mail-order option.) People who divide their time between two homes should choose a national plan.

•Nursing home trap. If your loved one is in a nursing home, make sure that the pharmacy used by the nursing home is in the plan that you choose.

•"Donut hole" trap. When Part D was originally being discussed, using a "standard plan" model, the plan would pick up a portion of expenses up to $2,250 in total drug costs, then the individual would pay 100% of expenses up to $5,100 (the so-called "donut hole"), then the plan would resume picking up 95% of the costs over this amount for the remainder of the year. In the end, there was no standard plan—so when the donut hole begins, what you pay depends on the plan you select. Read the various plans' rules to find out what they provide.

No matter when the coverage gap begins, once you reach $3,600 in out-of-pocket drug expenses in a calendar year—not including premiums, drugs that aren't included on the plan and drugs purchased at out-of-network pharmacies—"catastrophic coverage" kicks in and 95% of costs (not including the items above) are covered.

For additional information, access the Medicare Web site at *www.medicare.gov*.

How to Save Big on Long-Term-Care Insurance

Peter Gelbwaks, chairman of the National LTC Network, Inc., the largest marketer of long-term-care insurance in the US. He is president of Gelbwaks Insurance Services in Plantation, FL, *www.gelbwaks.com*.

The average annual cost of nursing home care is about $74,000—yet only 10% of Americans age 65 and above have long-term-care (LTC) insurance to cover this big expense. *How to find an affordable policy…*

THREE WAYS TO SAVE

•Choose a firm that has staying power. More than 100 companies sell LTC insurance, but only a few have done so for at least 15 years without increasing the premiums: Genworth Financial (888-436-9678 or *www.genworthcom*)…John Hancock (800-377-7311 or *www.johnhancock.com*)…MedAmerica (800-544-0327 or *www.yourlongtermcare.com*)…Metropolitan Life Insurance Company (800-638-5433 or *www.metlife.com*)…and The Prudential Insurance Company of America (800-843-7625 or *www.prudential.com*). Though premiums can increase with state regulatory approval, these firms have a history of stable pricing.

•Consider a policy that offers cash benefits. The traditional LTC policies specify exactly what types of care are covered and pay only for those services. "Disability model" policies pay cash and let policyholders who are eligible for benefits use the money as they choose—say, to finance a nursing home stay or for in-home care. You even can keep the money and let a family member look after you.

Important: Benefits in excess of a specific amount ($260 per day for 2007) may be taxed as income.

A few companies offer disability model LTC programs. Among them are MedAmerica's Simplicity, Met-Life's Premier and Prudential's LTC3 with cash-benefit rider.

•Buy a policy when you are young. The sooner you buy, the better the rates are for the life of the policy. If you do wait until your health begins to deteriorate, the expense will be higher still—if you are healthy enough to qualify at all. Although buying LTC insurance is worthwhile even for older people, attractive LTC rates are available to those in their 30s and 40s.

Example: A 40-year-old could buy a policy from one of the top companies that pays $6,000* per month in benefits for a total benefit amount of $360,000 (with a 90-day elimination period before benefits kick in). The annual premium would be about $300. The annual premiums for the same type of policy could be $1,500 at age 60 and $3,000 at age 70.

*Rates and offers subject to change.

Helpful: Most carriers allow a 30-day grace period after a birthday to get coverage based on your previous age.

SPECIAL OPTIONS FOR COUPLES AND FAMILIES

Get a couple's discount whether or not you and your partner are married. Insurers are offering discounts to unmarrieds—including same sex couples.

Examples: Genworth provides a 40% discount for couples who live together…Prudential offers a 30% discount to couples if both partners purchase policies. Prudential and MetLife even extend their couples' rates to multigenerational cohabitators, such as a mother and adult child who are living together. Smaller discounts typically are available when only one partner applies or qualifies for coverage.

•**Share the care with your spouse or partner** with a "shared-care" plan.

Example: You buy a shared-care plan with eight years of coverage. If you need only five years of long-term care, your spouse will have three years of coverage available. This should lower your cost, since one eight-year shared-care plan is cheaper than two separate policies.

John Hancock took this idea a step further with its Family Care plan. Up to four members of one family—grandparents, parents, siblings, spouses, etc.—sign up together, then share the benefits pool. The savings compared with individual policies can be considerable, but there is the risk that one member of the group will need extended care and exhaust the benefits.

Five Common Myths About Life Insurance

Thomas Henske, CFP, CLU, a partner at Lenox Advisors, Inc., in New York City, Chicago and San Francisco, *www. lenoxadvisors.com.* Lenox Advisors is a wholly owned subsidiary of National Financial Partners. Mr. Henske is a frequent speaker on life insurance topics.

The majority of American households do have some variety of life insurance. But so few of us understand how to get the most out of it. *Five of the most damaging myths that lead to costly life insurance mistakes…*

Myth 1: I just need enough life insurance to cover my family's future expenses.

Fact: If you really want to provide for your family's well-being, you'll need more than that. The good news is that this extra coverage won't set you back as much as you might think.

A typical family should combine the remaining portion of its mortgage…projected inflation-adjusted annual living expenses for the remainder of the spouse's life…and college costs if they are a factor (assuming that costs will rise by 3% to 5% per year) to determine the amount the family needs to get by. Subtract the amount the surviving spouse will earn if he/she expects to return to the workforce at some point.

Example: A 40-year-old man who's in good health would pay about $875* a year for a simple 20-year level-term life insurance policy that provides $1 million in coverage, and this would be enough to cover all his family's future expenses. And, for about $1,750, he could get a $2 million policy, enough to fully replace his lifetime earnings if his salary would have averaged $80,000 per year for the remaining 25 years of his career. An extra $875 per year (about $73 a month) is a small price to pay to ensure that his family won't suffer financially after his death.

To compare life insurance costs, contact your insurance professional or visit the Web sites *www. accuquote.com* or *www.quotesmithcom.*

Myth 2: Term life insurance is always a better deal than whole life.

Fact: Term life insurance policies will usually provide lower premiums than a permanent cash-value policy like whole life, which combines the pure insurance of a term policy with a tax-favored investment account. But under particular circumstances—if you plan to keep the policy for more than 20 years…can afford the premiums…and have maxed out other tax-deferred investments, such as a 401(k) plan and an IRA—whole life insurance makes more sense.

Assuming that you don't dip into your investment for at least 20 years, your total return from a whole life policy, including the death benefit and investment return, is likely to be higher than what you would earn by purchasing a similar

*Rates subject to change.

amount of term coverage and investing the cost difference in municipal bonds—which is a comparable investment in terms of both risk and tax treatment.

Other permanent insurance options include *variable universal life,* which might be appropriate for younger couples in their 20s or early 30s, since the investment component could be put in high-growth mutual funds…and *universal life,* which can be appropriate for those whose income can fluctuate significantly from year to year, such as sales professionals, since it allows the insured to determine the premium paid in any year.

Other benefits of permanent (cash-value) insurance: You can borrow against the cash value of your policy at reasonable interest rates. Also, withdrawals up to the amount of your investment are tax-free.

Of course, permanent insurance loses its appeal if you need access to your money before two decades or more pass. Life insurance companies front-load their fees, so if you withdraw the money before then, your investment return will suffer disproportionately.

Myth 3: **My wife does not work, so she doesn't need her own life insurance policy.**

Fact: Stay-at-home spouses might not produce income, but they often provide important services that are expensive to replace, such as cleaning, cooking and child care. Some spouses also find that their own ability to earn is temporarily reduced after the loss of a partner.

Example: A lawyer in private practice spent the year after his wife's death walking around in a daze, causing his income to plummet.

Couples with children should have at least $1 million in coverage for the nonworking spouse, more if the family is large or lives in an expensive area. You can consider decreasing that figure if the kids are in their teens and reducing it again once the kids are out of the house. A 40-year-old nonsmoking woman in good health should be able to get a $1 million 20-year level-term policy for about $730 a year.

Myth 4: **My term-life policy can be converted to whole life,** so I don't have to worry about losing coverage if I ever become chronically ill.

Fact: While it is true that more than two-thirds of term policies allow policyholders to convert over to whole life regardless of health problems, many "convertible" term policies can be converted only within a five- or 10-year window—and insurance companies may not warn you when that window is about to close. If you don't convert and the policy lapses, the insurance company gets to keep all the money you paid in premiums and won't have to pay out a dime on the policy.

It is not uncommon for policyholders who have developed serious health problems to unwittingly miss their opportunity to convert to whole life and then find themselves uninsured and essentially uninsurable.

Self-defense: Make a habit of reviewing your policy at least once a year so that you won't miss your chance to convert—or any other deadline.

Myth 5: **I'm retiring soon, so I don't need life insurance anymore.**

Fact: This might be true in some cases, but life insurance can be useful for retirement planning and/or estate planning. *Examples…*

•If your employer offers a defined-benefit pension plan, it probably has two payout options—a single life annuity, which provides income only during your lifetime, and a joint life annuity, which provides a smaller monthly payment until you and your spouse both die. In spite of these smaller payments per month, most married people choose joint life for the sake of their spouses.

Assuming that you are in good health, single life is a better choice if you also hold a life insurance policy with your spouse as the beneficiary. Should you die first, your spouse could live on the proceeds. It's best to purchase the insurance a decade or more before you retire to lock in an attractive age-based rate.

•If you expect to have a large estate—$3 million or more—it may be wise to use life insurance to pay the estate tax. Too often, people don't buy the proper insurance for this purpose. The usual choice is a "second-to-die" policy—one that pays out when the surviving spouse passes away. But when you crunch the numbers, second-to-die policies can be inferior deals for most couples younger than 60…and any couple in which the husband is more than five years older than his wife or the wife is more than 10 years older than her husband, since women live an average of five years longer than men. In such cases, it's better for each spouse to buy a separate policy.

Scenario: A husband and wife, each 45 years old and healthy, would pay an annual premium of about $11,000 for a $1 million second-to-die whole life policy. If they had bought separate $500,000 whole life policies, they would pay a total of about $17,500 in annual premiums. (The high cost reflects the lifetime coverage with this type of policy.)

At first glance, the second-to-die policy looks great, saving about $6,500 a year, but the insurer pays nothing until both spouses die. With separate policies, the insurer must pay out $500,000 upon the death of the first spouse. If the surviving spouse were to invest that $500,000, he/she could turn it into more than $800,000 in a decade—even at a 5% after-tax return.

Bonus: Once the first spouse has died, the premiums must be paid only on the remaining spouse's policy, reducing costs.

Second-to-die policies do make sense if both spouses are over age 60 and close in age. In this case, the odds are lower that they will die many years apart.

More from Thomas Henske, CFP...

Types of Life Insurance

There are four main types of life insurance. *Check them out below...*

●**Term life.** Coverage is for a particular period. Premiums may stay fixed for the term of a policy—from five to 30 years. No savings (cash-value) component.

●**Whole life.** Policy builds cash value and stays in force over the policyholder's lifetime—as long as premiums, invested by the insurance company, are paid. If you cancel the policy, you receive a lump sum.

●**Universal life.** Combines low-cost term insurance and a cash-value component. The policyholder earns tax-deferred money market rates on the cash value and can increase or decrease coverage and premium levels.

●**Variable universal life.** The policy's cash value is invested in a selection of mutual fund–like stock or bond portfolios provided by the insurer. Cash value and death benefit rise and fall based on investment performance.

Also from Thomas Henske, CFP...

LTC Insurance Rates Are Rising

Long-term-care (LTC) insurance rates are rising. Some of the rate hikes are very large—to compensate for faulty cost assumptions made by insurers when they started offering policies. New policies will be priced higher, but future rate hikes are possible—the longer the term, the greater the risk.

Self-defense: Consider limited-pay policies, which let you pay for a set period, for instance, 10 years, after which the policy is paid in full. If you have cash-value life insurance, find out if your insurer will allow you to tap into the benefits for LTC costs before you die.

 **Costly Home Insurance Mistakes Can Be Easily Prevented**

Kitty Werner, the author of *The Savvy Woman's Guide to Owning a Home: How to Care for, Improve and Maintain Your Home* (RSBPress) and publisher of RSBPress in Waitsfield, VT. Ms. Werner formerly worked for two of the world's largest insurers, GEICO and Lloyds of London.

A few precautions can help save you hundreds of dollars a year on your home insurance and maybe many thousands of dollars in the event of serious misfortune.

The effort is particularly important today because many insurance companies—concerned with boosting profit margins—are raising premiums and getting tougher on paying claims. *Traps to avoid...*

TRAP: THE WRONG VALUE

Most home insurance policies state the maximum amount that the company will pay out to rebuild a house in the event it is destroyed. All too often, however, that amount is less than it would actually cost. The problem typically occurs because an old policy hasn't been updated to reflect today's reconstruction cost.

Safeguard: Ask local real estate agents and contractors how much it would cost to rebuild your house. (This cost is less than the sales price—that includes the land and foundation, which can withstand most disasters.)

Then check to see whether your insurance policy is written so that it will pay the actual reconstruction cost. If it isn't, ask your insurance agent to amend the policy.

Some insurance companies may refuse to raise the ceiling on the full replacement value. You may want to shop around for another carrier.

Be careful, however, not to let an agent talk you into a policy that states a higher value for your house than it would cost to rebuild. That can hike your premium unnecessarily because the insurance company still will not pay more than the actual reconstruction cost.

Shopping for insurance is easier than ever because many companies help you compare rates by phone and/or on the Internet. Three of the larger rate-comparison companies are Insurance.com (866-533-0227), Answerfinancial.com (800-233-3028) and 2Insure4Less.com (800-647-2164).

To find others, enter "home insurance quotes" into Google or another Internet search engine.

TRAP: THE WRONG INSURER

Though overall insurance rates are rising, the ability to make easy comparisons of coverage has encouraged competition among insurers, resulting in a wide variation in premiums and a growing number of companies to choose from. Unfortunately, not all are reliable.

Safeguard: Prior to buying a policy, check out the company with your state's agency that oversees the insurance business.

Many states have consumer-friendly agencies that are eager to tell residents about the financial and claims-paying history of insurers. Some agencies have Web sites where this information is also available. To find your state's agency, check your state's Web site.

You can also check out the financial soundness of insurers through Weiss Ratings (800-289-9222, *www.weissratings.com*).

Price per company report: $14.99* on the Web and $19 by phone.

Insurers are rated on criteria that include financial stability and the number of customer complaints against them. A company is then given a grade of A for "excellent," B for "good," C for "fair" or D for "weak."

Choose a company with at least a B rating.

TRAP: HASTY COMPARISONS

Instead of comparing only homeowner's policies, ask for quotes on your total insurance needs, including auto insurance for all members of the household and business insurance if you have your own company.

Most insurance companies give reductions of 5% to 15% to customers who buy what they call "multiline" policies.

TRAP: GAPS IN COVERAGE

As a general rule, homeowner's policies will cover most common types of damage, including that caused by fire, smoke, rain, lightning, wind, hail, snow, ice, sleet, vandalism, theft, explosions, civil commotions, vehicles, planes and problems stemming from the malfunction of the electrical system, plumbing, heating, air conditioning or appliances.

Not covered in standard policies is damage from earthquakes and floods, both much more prevalent—and costly—than most home owners believe. For example, some of the nation's most destructive earthquakes in the last 200 years were centered in the Midwest, not California.

Hurricane coverage is tricky—you may find that you are covered for high winds, but not for flood. Check with your agent.

In areas where earthquakes are rare, insurance is usually available for under $50 a year with deductibles of $200. Premiums and deductibles rise fast, however, in areas where earthquakes are frequent.

Big mistake: Believing that coverage for rain damage will automatically reimburse you, say, if the back porch collapses after a two-day downpour. In fact, the insurers might argue that this type of damage is the result of a flood and not of the rain itself.

Safeguard: Even if you don't live in a flood-prone area, consider flood insurance.

*Prices and rates subject to change.

Information: The Federal Emergency Management Agency (800-480-2520 or 202-566-1600, *www.fema.gov/business/nfip*).

Premiums vary widely, from a few hundred to a few thousand dollars a year, depending on the location of a house, its age and type.

TRAP: THE WRONG DEDUCTIBLE

As you compare prices, it might seem that policies with a zero deductible or a very low one are the way to go. The additional cost of a low-deductible policy in some cases wouldn't even be as high as repairing one broken window caused by a kid who carelessly throws a baseball.

Trap: Home owners who have low-deductible policies often file a claim each time there's the slightest damage to the house or its contents.

The result is that the insurance company will hike premiums and may even cancel the policy. *Safeguards…*

●**Opt for coverage with the highest deductible you can afford.** You'll save a bit on premiums—perhaps 5% to 10%. Even more important, you'll make fewer claims, and this will help keep your rates from rising in the future.

●**Order a copy of your CLUE report,** the database that lists the claims history of home owners, from ChoicePoint Asset Company (866-527-2600, *www.choicetrust.com*). The insurers use this information in calculating your premiums. Federal law entitles consumers to one free report every 12 months.

If there's an error in the report, federal law also provides a procedure for home owners to correct it. Contact ChoicePoint Asset for an explanation of the procedure.

Data in CLUE reports are maintained for five years. If you can't escape high premiums because of your claims history, cut down on filing any new claims until your records expire. Then ask for new quotes, which are likely to be lower.

TRAP: IGNORING SAFETY DEVICES

Ask your insurance company or agent what home devices can reduce premiums. Most insurers offer lower rates for houses that have working smoke detectors, carbon monoxide detectors, fire extinguishers, burglar alarms that automatically notify authorities and sprinkler systems that fight fires. Installing safety devices can cut premiums by 5% to 15%.

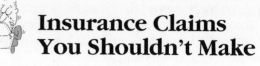

Insurance Claims You Shouldn't Make

Mary Hunt, editor of *Debt-Proof Living*, Box 2135, Paramount, CA 90723, *www.debtproofliving.com*. She is also author of *Live Your Life for Half the Price—Without Sacrificing the Life You Love* (DPL).

Always beware of making all these insurance claims—they might cost you more than they are worth because of subsequently increased premiums…

●**Small claims.** Insurance is intended to protect you against major losses that you can't afford. If you make small claims unnecessarily, you may increase your premiums so much that you can't afford the protection you need against major liabilities.

Best: Figure out what you can afford to pay for accidents and repairs out-of-pocket and then take the largest possible corresponding deductibles to minimize premiums.

●**"Moldy" claims.** Home insurers have become phobic about mold problems, which can be hugely expensive. A report of a mold problem in your home may do worse than raise your premiums—it may make the property uninsurable.

Best: If mold is not the real problem, don't even mention the word in a claim.

Example: A washing machine leak makes a carpet "smell moldy." The essential problem is water damage, not mold, so, again, don't mention mold.

●**Claims due to your own neglect.** Most insurers don't cover claims that they determine result from your lack of care.

So, if you neglect to care for your plumbing or roof, then make a claim for resulting water damage, the insurer may both deny your claim and increase your premiums.

Best: Be diligent about performing essential maintenance on your property.

Caution: A state law and/or your insurance policy may require that you report certain kinds of incidents and damage—so read your policy and follow the rules.

Should You Report That Fender Bender?

When and when not to report a fender bender to your insurance company…

•Determine who is involved. If another person is injured or his/her property is damaged, report the accident immediately. Your insurance company can help protect you from a future lawsuit.

•Know your deductible. If no one else is involved and repairs will cost less than your deductible, don't file a claim.

•Consider your driving record. If you have been in several accidents during the last three years, it may be better to fix the damage yourself. Multiple claims can increase your insurance rates.

Important: Review your insurance policy. Some companies require the insured to report all damage. Others leave the decision up to the insured.

Jeanne Salvatore, senior vice president of consumer affairs at Insurance Information Institute, New York City, www.iii.org.

Auto Insurance Savvy

Many people think that comprehensive auto insurance will protect against everything—including collisions with other vehicles—as the name implies. Insurers use the word "comprehensive" to refer to coverage of damage caused from events *other than vehicle collisions*—fire, flood, storm damage, animal collisions, theft or vandalism.

More little-known insurance facts: Getting car and home insurance from the same company doesn't always get you the best rates, so shop around. Rates don't always drop when a driver reaches age 25—it depends on his/her claims history, make of the car and other factors.

Rick Crawley, product development general manager, Progressive Insurance Companies, Mayfield Village, OH.

Car Insurance Cost Cutter

Decrease car insurance costs by opting for a family plan. More inclusive than individual policies, family plans cover everyone living in a household for one flat rate—generally only 8% to 10% more than for an individual driver policy. Check the Web site of your state's department of insurance for additional ways to keep premiums down. To find your state department, go to the National Association of Insurance Commissioners Web site *(www.naic.org)*.

Insurance Consumer Advocacy Network, Branson West, MO.

Specialty Insurance: What's Worth It… What's Not

Lee Rosenberg, CFP, founder, ARS Financial Services, Inc., a financial-planning firm based in Jericho, NY, www.arsfinancial.com. He is the author of Retirement Ready or Not (Career), and a frequent guest on CNBC.

Insurance marketers become creative geniuses when it comes to thinking up policies to pitch to consumers. *Here is the lowdown on some newer types—and if they are worthwhile…*

POLICIES WORTH HAVING

•Trip insurance. Many people don't realize that their health insurance may not cover them if they become ill when traveling overseas. Trip insurance reimburses you for emergency medical expenses and a medical evacuation. It also covers cancellation or interruption of a trip due to your illness or bad weather, such as a hurricane or tornado, as well as luggage that is lost or damaged in transit.

One source of trip insurance is Travel Insurance Center at *www.travelinsurancecenter.com,* 866-979-6753. Coverage typically runs between $100 and $200* per trip, depending on the destination and the traveler's age.

*Prices subject to change.

•**Pet health insurance.** This insurance is becoming cost-effective as more advanced—and expensive—treatments are made available for pets. A pacemaker for a dog could cost several thousand dollars.

Ask your veterinarian about the best policies. You can obtain coverage for dogs, cats and other critters. Premiums can run $200 to $1,000, depending on the pet's age and breed and where you live.

•**Credit card surveillance.** Although it isn't really insurance, credit card monitoring protection through your bank card issuer ensures that you are notified of any change in your credit profile—unusual spending, card applications or changes of address.

Cost: $30 to $75 a year.

New trend: Identity theft insurance. A credit card company will protect you against phony charges—you are liable for only up to $50. But they won't help you fix the mess that identity theft often creates. Identity theft insurance reimburses you for expenses such as lost pay while you are straightening things out.

According to industry research, the average ID theft victim spends hundreds of hours restoring his/her financial reputation. If you have credit card surveillance, you probably do not require personal identity theft coverage unless you have many cardholders in your household or business. Annual coverage costs vary. Check with your credit card issuer or insurance company.

A growing number of employers also are offering identity theft insurance as a perk.

POLICIES TO AVOID

•**Terrorism insurance.** This insurance started to appear after 9/11 to play into Americans' fears of a terrorist attack. Insurance that focuses strictly on terrorism is geared toward businesses and covers such costs as relocating a firm or replacing damaged equipment. Even then, business-interruption insurance is a better option—it also covers fires, floods, etc.

•**Water line protection.** Very few people need this niche coverage, which pays for damage caused by leaks in the water service line that runs from the curb valve into the home in towns that have public water. The coverage is worth considering only if your neighbors have experienced problems due to age of the pipes or geological issues.

Also: Check for duplicate coverage.

Example: One of my clients had to have his house jacked up to replace the water pipes below it, but he didn't need water line insurance because the $11,000 cost was partially covered by his homeowner's insurance.

•**Accidental death and dismemberment insurance.** This insurance pays out if you are killed accidentally. Don't waste your money on it. Regular life insurance covers you when you die.

•**Disease-specific coverage,** such as cancer insurance, also should be avoided.

9

Tax Update

The New Tax Law: Opportunities and Traps

President G.W. Bush signed into law another tax act in May 2006 called *The Tax Increase Prevention & Reconciliation Act of 2005*. The new tax law reinstates *some* of the more than three dozen deductions and other tax breaks that expired at the end of 2005. It provides $90 billion in tax breaks to individuals and businesses over the coming years, but also includes $20 billion in revenue raisers—meaning increased taxes.

Important: Many expired provisions were not addressed in this law and *may* be handled through a "trailer" bill to come.

BIG BREAK FOR INVESTORS

The cornerstone of the new law is a two-year extension of the favorable tax rates on long-term capital gains and dividends. The rates had been scheduled to expire at the end of 2008—they now run through 2010. *For 2008 through 2010…*

• **Individuals in tax brackets above the bottom two brackets pay only 15%** on dividends and long-term capital gains.

• **Low-bracket taxpayers, those in the 10% and 15% brackets, pay nothing** on long-term gains or dividends. They can receive this type of income entirely tax free.

Strategy: Shift assets to low-bracket family members who will pay no tax on dividends and long-term gains. An easy way to do this is to make use of the $12,000 annual gift tax exclusion.

AMT RELIEF

Some middle-income taxpayers, increasingly blasted by the alternative minimum tax (AMT), can breathe a sigh of relief, at least for 2006. The new law provides a temporary "patch" for the AMT that will free 15 million middle-income taxpayers who would have paid the tax in 2006. This AMT relief totals about $34 billion.

Barbara Weltman, an attorney based in Millwood, NY, and author of *J.K. Lasser's 1001 Deductions and Tax Breaks 2007* (Wiley). She is also publisher of the on-line newsletter, *Big Ideas for Small Business, www.barbaraweltman.com.*

Catch: The patch is only for 2006. Congress will have to revisit the AMT issue. *How the 2006 patch works...*

● **The exemption amounts for AMT are increased** for 2006 to $62,550 on a joint tax return and $42,500 for single taxpayers. In 2005, the exemptions were $58,000 (joint) and $40,250 (single). Without the new patch, the 2006 exemption amounts would have declined to just $45,000 on a joint return and $33,750 for singles.

● **The nonrefundable personal tax credits,** such as the education credit and the dependent care credit, can now be used to offset AMT liability. Without this change, the only personal credits that could offset AMT liability in 2006 would have been the adoption credit, the child tax credit and the retirement saver's credit.

Planning strategies: Because this fix is only temporary, individuals must continue to be proactive in minimizing or avoiding the AMT. This includes carefully timing the exercise of incentive stock options and payment (or prepayment) of state and local taxes. They are not deductible under the AMT.

MORE ROTH IRA CONVERSIONS

Currently, an individual can convert a traditional IRA to a Roth IRA only if his/her modified adjusted gross income for the year of conversion does not exceed $100,000. This limit applies to an individual taxpayer as well as a couple filing jointly. (A married person filing separately in most cases cannot convert regardless of his income.)

The new law waives this income limit, allowing anyone to convert a traditional IRA to a Roth IRA starting in 2010.

Bonus: When the conversion is made, the reporting of any resulting income is deferred from 2010. Income is reported 50% in 2011 and 50% in 2012.

Option: Individuals can elect to report all the income in 2010.

Strategy: With a Roth IRA conversion, you're choosing to accept a current tax bill on IRA withdrawals in exchange for future tax-free earnings from the proceeds.

As long as funds remain in the Roth account at least five years after the conversion and are not withdrawn prior to age 59½ (or for certain other permissible reasons), all money will come out tax free.

So, taxpayers who anticipate being in a higher tax bracket when they take distributions from their retirement accounts should consider conversion. Higher tax rates in general are not at all unlikely given the fact that many of the current tax rules are scheduled to expire after 2010.

Key: Use separate funds to pay the tax on a Roth IRA conversion so that the account is not diminished.

NEW TAX BREAK FOR SENIORS

Senior citizens who pay, or have paid, an entry fee to a continuing care facility that can be returned, in whole or in part, when they move or die had been required to recognize phantom interest income due to the below-market loan rules. The new law eliminates this requirement for 2006 through 2010.

To avoid any imputed interest income, the taxpayer (or spouse) needs to be at least age 62 before the close of the year, and the continuing care contract must entitle him to an independent-living unit as well as assisted living or nursing care as his health requires.

BAD NEWS, TOO

While most of the new rules are favorable to taxpayers, there are some revenue raisers that many won't like.

● **Rise in the kiddie tax age from age 14 to 18,** starting in 2006. Unearned income of a child under the age of 18 is now subject to the kiddie tax. Investment income, such as interest, above a threshold amount (e.g., $1,700 in 2006 and 2007) is taxed to the child at the parents' highest marginal tax bracket (up to 35%). Only when they reach age 18 is their unearned income taxed according to their own tax bracket, which may be no more than 10% or 15%.

Effective date: This change is retroactive to January 1, 2006.

Trap: Children and their parents are squeezed by this retroactive change (it applies to all of 2006 and beyond). For example, a parent who had been planning to sell a child's securities after age 13 to capture the child's low rate cannot do so now, without running afoul of the kiddie tax, until the child turns 18. This means that parents whose top tax bracket exceeds 15% will lose the zero tax rate on capital gains and dividends for 2008 through 2010.

Strategy: The only thing to be done is to apply the same kiddie tax strategies that had been in use for younger children prior to this law.

Examples: Have the child own non-income-producing assets, such as US savings bonds and growth stocks. Postpone sales until after the kiddie tax no longer applies to the child.

•**Increase in the cost of offers in compromise.** The cost to taxpayers trying to obtain an offer in compromise from the IRS, which allows them to pay less than the total amount of tax due, increases with the new tax law. Taxpayers are now required to pay part of the tax owed in addition to a user fee of $150 when requesting an offer in compromise.

For a lump-sum offer, this means paying 20% of the offer up front. For offers in compromise that will be paid in installments, all proposed installments must be made while the IRS is considering the offer.

One bright spot for taxpayers: If the IRS fails to process the offer within two years, it is deemed to have been accepted. This provision is brand new.

Effective date: Offers must have been submitted after July 16, 2006 (60 days after the date of enactment, May 17, 2006).

Common Tax Mistakes Can Cost You Big Bucks

Martin S. Kaplan, CPA, 11 Penn Plaza in New York City, *www.irsmaven.com.* He is a frequent speaker at insurance, banking and financial-planning seminars and is author of *What the IRS Doesn't Want You to Know* (Wiley).

The Internal Revenue Code is published in two jam-packed volumes which take up several inches of shelf space. It's no wonder that taxpayers make so many big mistakes when it comes to their taxes. *Here are some of the most costly ones...*

CLAIMING DEPENDENTS

Mistake: **Not having any money withheld from your paycheck.**

It is true that you can reduce or even eliminate income tax withholding by increasing the number of dependents you claim on the Form W-4 you file with your employer. However, you'll have to settle up with the IRS when you file your tax return for the year. At that point, having withheld too little will cost you interest and possibly penalties.

What to do instead: If possible, increase income tax withholding toward year-end to make up for shortfalls, since all withholding is considered to be paid evenly throughout the year.

Caution: If you are self-employed and owe $1,000 or more in federal income tax, failing to make equal quarterly payments of federal income tax, Social Security and Medicare taxes can lead to penalties.

SOCIAL SECURITY

Mistake: **Thinking that you won't have to pay any tax on Social Security benefits once you reach your full retirement age.**

Most people have to pay this tax, unless they have low "provisional income." *Provisional income is the total of...*

•**Adjusted gross income (AGI).**

•**Tax-exempt interest income** from municipal bonds and municipal bond funds.

•**One-half of your annual Social Security benefits.**

On a joint return, if your provisional income is more than $32,000 (but less than $44,000), up to 50% of your benefits can be taxed. For single filers, the threshold is $25,000 to $34,000.

If provisional income is greater than $44,000 on a joint return ($34,000, single), up to 85% of benefits will be taxed.

What to do instead: Reduce your AGI to help lower the tax on Social Security benefits. You might, for example, postpone taking withdrawals from your IRA.

SELF-EMPLOYMENT

Mistake: **Not paying tax if you don't receive a Form 1099.**

If you're self-employed, even part of the time, you are supposed to receive an IRS Form 1099 from every party who paid you $600 or more during the prior year. Those forms also are sent to the IRS. Some people think that if they don't receive a 1099 form, they don't have to declare the income.

What to do instead: You must report *all* of income that you earn. Some employers will send a 1099 to the IRS even if they do not send you a copy. Any discrepancy may trigger an audit. Even if a 1099 was not sent to the IRS, if your tax return is examined for any reason, the IRS agent may ask to go over your bank records. Deposits may be considered taxable income unless you can prove that they should not be.

DEDUCTIONS

Mistake: **Taking any deductions you want as long as they are not in excess of the "average" amount.**

The IRS publishes the average itemized deductions for certain levels of income. For those who had AGIs of $50,000 to $100,000 in 2004, for example (the last year for which figures were published), average deductions included $8,310 of interest expenses and $5,808 for taxes paid.

What to do instead: Take only the deductions that you can corroborate with supporting documents, such as receipts.

PERSONAL EXPENSES

Mistake: **Transferring assets to a trust so that you can deduct your personal expenses.**

Some trust promoters promise that personal expenses can be paid by the trust, which will effectively make these expenses tax deductible. Not true.

When a trust is created, any income generated by the trust is taxable to the creator ("grantor"), the beneficiaries or the trust itself, depending on the circumstances. Income that is taxable to the trust is taxed at higher rates than on a personal tax return.

What's more, personal expenses do not become deductible just because they're claimed by a trust. Only expenses that are legitimate can be deducted.

What to do instead: Use a trust for legitimate purposes only, such as an irrevocable life insurance trust for paying estate tax or a credit-shelter trust to pay income to your spouse for life and then pass the remainder tax free to other beneficiaries.

FOREIGN TAX SHELTERS

Mistake: **Holding investments offshore in order to shield them from US income taxes.**

Some people even get foreign credit cards because they believe that they can then spend the money without Uncle Sam finding out. Some unethical advisers tell clients to have earned income paid to an offshore bank, where it won't be reported to the IRS.

What to do instead: Report any income you earn anywhere in the world to Uncle Sam—that is what is legally required. You might get an offsetting credit for income taxes paid to foreign governments, but you must first report offshore income to the US.

Having an offshore credit card won't shelter money either—the IRS now requires credit card issuers to report activity by US residents holding offshore cards.

More from Martin Kaplan, CPA...

Very Smart Tax-Planning Moves to Make in the New Year

Here are six ideas to use now to cut your total taxes and ease the cash-flow cost of taxes you do owe...

1. Use carryovers. Look at your 2006 tax return to find items that carry over into 2007.

Example: If you have a capital loss carryover from 2006, you could take an offsetting amount of capital gains in 2007 tax free.

Other carryovers that may impact 2007 tax planning include those for net operating losses, investment interest expense, charity deductions and various tax credits. Check your 2006 tax return to identify all of them.

2. Make IRA contributions as soon as possible. If you have an IRA or a Roth IRA, make contributions to it for both 2006 *and* 2007 early in the year.

The deadline for an IRA contribution is the April 15 after year-end. But making a contribution early provides extra tax-favored investment returns in the IRA.

Example: An IRA contribution for 2007 made in January 2007 instead of April 2008 will provide 15 additional months of tax-favored investment returns. If you will not withdraw your IRA assets for 20 years, those extra returns will compound for those 20 years.

If you make IRA contributions for both 2006 and 2007 at the same time, do so by separate checks to avoid mixups at the IRS.

Don't worry that at year-end you may prove ineligible to contribute to an IRA due to changes in your circumstances. If that happens, you can withdraw the funds from your IRA before the due date of your tax return without penalty (although earnings would be taxable).

3. Make bigger pretax retirement plan contributions during 2007. The maximum contribution from salary to a 401(k) plan increases in 2007 to $15,500 (from $15,000 in 2006). For persons age 50 and older, the maximum "catch-up" contribution is $5,000 in 2006 and 2007.

Elect at the beginning of the year to contribute the new maximum.

Important: Many employers match a portion of employee contributions to a 401(k) plan—this is literally free money for the employee. Be sure that you contribute enough to a 401(k) to take full advantage of any employer match.

If your employer has a retirement program other than a 401(k), ask its administrator about its contribution limit for year 2007—and plan to make it.

The contribution limits for other kinds of plans will be up in 2007 too. The maximum contribution for a profit-sharing or simplified employee pension plan was $44,000 in 2006 and is $45,000 in 2007.

4. Maximize use of flexible spending accounts (or FSAs). These are savings accounts to which employees can contribute a portion of salary tax free to be used to pay medical costs not covered by the employer's medical benefit plan.

Examples: Co-payments and deductibles, plus noncovered items that might include eyeglasses, dental services, and the like.

The effect of an FSA is equivalent to making expenditures on such items deductible.

Key: Employees are required to elect how much they will contribute to an FSA for the year. This means projecting medical expenditures for the full year ahead. Take some time to do this as accurately as possible, so you contribute neither too little nor too much to the FSA.

New: Generally, FSA funds are "use it or lose it" by year-end—which is why you don't want to contribute too much. But new IRS rules let employers amend an FSA program to permit funds to be spent by employees as late as March 15 of the following year.

If you have an unspent balance in an FSA at year-end, check with your employer to see if its plan now gives this extra time to consume the unspent funds.

5. Make income-shifting gifts during the beginning of the year. This is another strategy that many don't use until the end of the year even though it is much more effective at the start.

Gifting income-producing assets to the family members in lower tax brackets (such as children age 18 and over) can reduce the family's total income tax bill. Doing so at the start of the year can lower taxes for the full year—while doing so at year-end puts off tax savings until the following year.

The annual gift tax exclusion allows gifts of up to $12,000 each in 2007 to be made free of gift tax to as many recipients as you wish. The limit is $24,000 when gifts are made jointly by a married couple.

Example: A married couple can give a child and the child's spouse $48,000 in 2007 (a $24,000 joint gift to each recipient spouse).

Opportunity: If the income-producing asset transferred is a minority holding in a private business or investment real estate held in an LLC, then "minority" and "lack of marketability" valuation discounts can be applied to transfer even more. For instance, with a 33% discount, each gift can transfer ownership of $18,000 of assets tax free.

Example: You own real estate that's worth $100,000 through an S corporation. Using a 33% minority discount, you can transfer shares representing 18% ownership of the property, not merely 12%, to each gift recipient. The shares transferring $18,000 of the property, when discounted by 33%, are worth just about $12,000.

Such gifts can also be used to avoid future estate taxes by reducing the gift maker's estate, and for other estate planning purposes, in addition to reducing current family income taxes.

6. Update wage withholding and planned estimated tax payments. Project your tax bill for 2007 at the start of the year, considering all of the items you expect to change from 2006.

Examples: Expected salary increases…realized investment gains or losses…marriage or divorce…purchase of a home…new use of tax-saving strategies such as those above.

If you will receive a big tax refund for 2006, avoid doing so again—it means that you made an interest-free loan to the IRS.

To avoid penalty, your combined withheld and quarterly estimated tax payments for 2007 must equal at least the lesser of…

• **90% of your actual tax bill for 2007,** or…

• **100% of 2006's final taxes** (110% if 2006's adjusted gross income is $150,000 or more).

So, if you expect that your tax liability…

• **Will rise in 2007,** you can minimize tax payments throughout the year by basing withholding and estimated tax payments on your 2006 tax bill. But you must then be prepared to pay a "make-up" payment by April 15, 2008.

• **Will fall in 2007 from 2006,** you should base tax payments on your actual 2007 income.

Adjust wage withholding by filing a new Form W-4 with your employer.

Helpful: The IRS provides a W-4 withholding calculator on its Web site. At *www.irs.gov,* click on "Individuals" and then "IRS Withholding Calculator."

If you will have nonwage income, including investment gains, you can pay the taxes on it through withholding on wages as well. This can be easier than calculating and paying quarterly estimated payments on top of withholding—and if such nonwage income turns out to be different in amount than you expect, you can compensate by adjusting withholding later in the year through a new W-4.

20 Year-End Tax-Saving Ideas

Laurence I. Foster, CPA/PFS, consultant and former partner at Eisner LLP, 750 Third Ave., New York City 10017. Mr. Foster is former chairman of the Personal Financial Specialist Credential Committee for the American Institute of Certified Public Accountants.

You can slash your 2007 tax bill by acting as late as December 31. *Here are 20 year-end ideas to consider that may help you do so…*

1. Check liability for the alternative minimum tax (AMT). This tax hits more people as a surprise every year. It is most likely to affect you if you live in a state with high taxes, and as a result have a large deduction for state taxes on the federal return.

The AMT is very complex and can affect the use of other normal tax strategies, such as those mentioned in this article. So if you are at risk for AMT, be sure to check the consequences with an expert.

2. Use credit cards to pay your deductible expenses. Deductible costs placed on a credit card are deductible this year if the charge is made by year-end, even if the charge isn't paid off until a later year.

Rule: The credit card must be a general use card, not a store card.

3. Use up flexible spending account (FSA) balances. Many employers provide FSAs, which act as tax-free savings accounts that employees can use to pay medical expenses not covered by the employer's medical plan.

Trap: Most FSAs are "use it or lose it" by year-end, with any funds in the FSA not used being forfeited. So, spend unused funds at year-end on items such as eyeglasses and/or contact lenses, dental visits, medication purchases and similar items.

Note: Employers can amend their plans to extend the deadline to two-and-a-half months after the close of the plan's year. Check with your employer.

4. Pay college tuition, fees and student loan interest by year-end. Deductions and credits for these items are taken in the year paid—so even if they aren't due until January and the beginning of the new term, pay them by December 31 to get a deduction this year.

5. Maximize the sales tax deduction. This provision allows state sales tax to be deducted on the federal return, instead of state income tax, when it provides a larger tax benefit (such as for those in states with no or low state income tax).

To take advantage of the sales tax deduction, you would want to make purchases by year-end—especially of big ticket items such as a car, boat and home-building supplies. Instructions to Schedule A of Form 1040 provide a list of the items for which you can deduct the tax.

6. Prepay all deductible state and local taxes not due until 2008. Paying them off by the end of 2007 gets you a federal deduction for these taxes this year.

Caution: Don't prepay if you are subject to the AMT.

Examples: Property taxes…estimated state income tax payments due in January…the final state income tax payment for 2007 due on April 15, 2008.

7. Move by year-end. If you will be moving to take a new job early next year, pay moving expenses by year-end to get a deduction for them this year.

8. Convert a regular IRA into a Roth IRA. If you later decide the conversion was a mistake, you can reverse it as late as October 15, 2008. However, if you do not make your conversion by year-end, the chance to do so for 2007 will be lost forever.

9. Adjust withholding on your last paychecks. If you've overpaid taxes to date this year, reducing withholding saves taxes for you now without your having to wait to claim a refund on your tax return. If you have underpaid taxes, then increasing your withholding may prevent a tax penalty.

10. Make tax-free gifts. For 2007, gifts of up to $12,000 per recipient can be made free of gift tax—the limit is $24,000 when gifts are made jointly by a married couple.

Example: A couple can give up to $48,000 a year tax free to a child and the child's spouse, plus pay for certain education and medical expenses.

The chance to make tax-free gifts for 2007 is lost if they aren't made by year-end.

11. Sell off near-worthless stocks and investments. If you've made an investment that's gone bad, it will be deductible when it becomes completely worthless—and not until then. But legal disputes, such as those involved in bankruptcy, may delay that determination for years.

What to do: Sell the investment in an arm's-length transaction—even if only for a nominal amount such as $1—by year-end to be able to deduct your loss this year.

12. Offset capital gains and losses. If you've realized taxable capital gains to date this year and have unrealized losses in your portfolio, you could incur gains tax needlessly. Avoid the tax by realizing offsetting losses.

13. Take the teacher's tax deduction. This provision enables teachers or educators to deduct up to $250 of out-of-pocket classroom instruction expenses.

14. "Double up" deductions with AGI floors. Medical expenses are tax deductible only to the extent that they exceed 7.5% of adjusted gross income (AGI), and miscellaneous expenses (including employee business, investment and legal expenses) to the extent that they exceed 2% of AGI.

If you will be over these AGI floors, accelerate expenditures into 2007. If not, delay them into 2008.

15. Time marriage for tax effect. Project the tax effect of a turn-of-the-year marriage. If it will reduce taxes and you have the flexibility, marry by December 31. If it will increase them, wait until January 2008.

16. Defer income. Postpone receipt of income that's under your control—such as optional IRA distributions, investment gains, distributions from a private corporation—until after year-end.

17. Put business equipment in service by year-end. If you own a small business, use "Section 179 expensing" to deduct the full cost of equipment acquired as late as December 31.

Important: The equipment must be placed in service by year-end, not merely purchased, to be deductible this year.

18. Make charitable contributions. Be sure that charitable gifts are completed by December 31 to be deducted this year. If you own a business using accrual accounting, special rules apply to certain corporate donations.

19. Pay discretionary business expenses. Buy supplies, renew business subscriptions and memberships, make repairs and so on by December 31 in order to deduct business expenses or employee business expenses this year.

20. Take a gambling holiday. If you have net gambling winnings near year-end, you can receive a tax subsidy for further gambling—since losses are deductible against winnings.

Therefore, if you take a last-minute gambling holiday and win, you win, while if you lose, you get a tax deduction that helps offset what you already won (assuming you itemize deductions) and subsidizes the good time you had.

Note: You must itemize deductions to benefit from gambling losses.

More from Laurence Foster, CPA/PFS...

Hot Tax Breaks for College And Other Schools, Too

The expense of education keeps going up faster than the rate of inflation, but Congress has created new tax breaks to help with education expenses.

GOOD NEWS, BAD NEWS

The good news is that so many tax breaks exist for education costs that there's probably at least one to help you. The snag is that Congress limits them with complicated rules and restrictions and sets a general rule that more than one can't be used for the same expense.

The basics of the various education tax breaks are given here. After identifying the breaks that may help you most, explore their details with a tax- or college-planning expert.

•**Hope tax credit.** This can be worth up to $1,650 per student in 2006 and 2007.

Key: A tax credit is worth more than a deduction of an equal dollar amount because it cuts taxes on a dollar-for-dollar basis. For a person in the 15% tax bracket, a $1 deduction saves 15 cents of tax—but a $1 credit saves a full $1.

The amount of the Hope credit is 100% of the first $1,100 of education costs plus 50% of the next $1,100. *Limitations...*

•The credit is available only for the first two years of postsecondary education per student.

•The student must be pursuing a degree or other recognized education credential and be enrolled at least half-time.

•The credit is phased out as your 2006 modified adjusted gross income (MAGI)* increases from $45,000 to $55,000 on a single tax return, and from $90,000 to $110,000 on a joint return. The phaseout for 2007 is from $47,000 to $57,000 on single returns and from $94,000 to $114,000 on joint returns.

•**Lifetime Learning credit.** This can be as much as $2,000 per tax return, with rules that differ from the Hope credit...

•This credit equals 20% of the first $10,000 of education expenses (maximum credit per taxpayer regardless of the number of students).

•The credit may be claimed for a student for any number of years.

•The student need not be pursuing a degree and may be taking only one course. *Example:* A person who takes a single nondegree course to improve his/her job skills may qualify for the Lifetime Learning credit.

The credit is phased out at the same income levels as the Hope credit.

Credit planning: The Hope credit and Lifetime Learning credit can't both be claimed for the same student in the same year, but both can be claimed on the same return for different students (such as a child in college and a parent taking a work-related course).

Generally, if expenses eligible for the credit are less than $7,500, the Hope credit will be worth more, while if they exceed $7,500, the Lifetime Learning credit will save the most (20% of $7,500 equals $1,500, the maximum amount of the Hope credit).

•**Student-loan interest tax deduction.** This is available for up to $2,500 of loan interest even for those who don't itemize deductions on their tax returns. Loan origination fees are deductible as well.

Snag: Those who do not itemize often overlook this deduction.

The deduction is available for interest on a loan used to finance tuition, fees, room and board, books, equipment and other necessary expenses

*MAGI is adjusted gross income with some technical adjustments described in IRS Publication 970, *Tax Benefits for Education.*

(such as transportation) at virtually all accredited postsecondary and vocational schools.

Limit: The deduction is phased out as 2006 MAGI increases from $50,000 to $65,000 on a single return and from $105,000 to $135,000 on a joint tax return. The phaseout for 2007 is from $55,000 to $70,000 on single returns and from $110,00 to $140,000 on joint returns.

•Student loan cancellations and repayment assistance. Some student loans contain terms saying that the loan will be forgiven if the student, after graduation, provides specified services for a governmental or nonprofit entity for a period of time. When the loan balance is canceled, the amount of the debt forgiveness is normally considered taxable income.

But under the tax law, such debt forgiveness can qualify as tax free for the student. (See Tax Code Section 108(f).)

New: Some *states* have programs that will provide funds to pay off normal student loans, conditioned on the student providing such services. This type of repayment assistance can qualify as tax free as well.

•Tuition and fee deduction. This tax deduction is also available for accredited postsecondary schools, including vocational schools, to people who don't itemize. It can be up to $4,000 on returns with MAGI up to $65,000 single or $130,000 joint…and up to $2,000 if MAGI is greater but not more than $80,000 single or $160,000 joint.

This deduction is useful for taxpayers whose MAGI is too high to take the Hope or Lifetime Learning credits.

It can be taken for expenses paid with borrowed funds (together with a student loan interest deduction for interest on the borrowing).

•Coverdell Education Savings Accounts or ESAs. Formerly known as Education IRAs, these can receive up to $2,000 per year for any single beneficiary under age 18. ESAs earn tax-deferred investment returns which can be used tax free to pay education expenses.

Advantage: ESAs can be used to pay for elementary through high school, not just college education.

To contribute to an ESA, one must have MAGI not exceeding $110,000 on single tax returns or $220,000 for married filing jointly. Anyone can contribute to an ESA for an individual, so if parents are unable to, a friend or other relative may contribute.

•Qualified tuition programs (Section 529 plans). These plans can hold funds that earn tax-deferred investment returns which can be spent tax free on college education costs. Or they can be prepaid tuition plans allowing a person to buy tuition now at today's prices

Advantage: These plans can hold far more than ESAs—being set up with as much as $55,000 free of gift tax—and therefore can be used for estate planning. Yet a person who contributes funds to the plan can withdraw them in case of need—a unique instance of being able to "keep while giving away" under the Tax Code.

Snags: In some states, savings plans fees are high and investment options are limited. Consult with an expert before using one of these plans.

•Early IRA distributions. The 10% penalty for early withdrawal normally incurred on IRA distributions taken before age 59½ does not apply when the funds are used to pay for tuition, fees, books, supplies or room and board at a postsecondary or vocational school.

•Education savings bonds. Interest received when Series EE and Series I savings bonds are cashed in can be taken tax free when used to pay postsecondary tuition and fees—or to fund a Coverdell or Section 529 account.

The limits are…

• The owner of the bond must be at least 24 years old when it is issued.

• The exclusion is phased out as 2006 MAGI increases from $61,200 to $76,200 on a single return and from $91,850 to $121,850 on a joint one. The phaseout for 2007 is from $65,600 to $80,600 on single returns and from $98,400 to $128,400 on joint returns.

•Employer-paid education assistance. This can be tax free as an employee benefit when provided under a written company educational assistance program. The education need not be work related. The maximum amount is $5,250, regardless of income.

•Business deduction for work-related education. When education improves your skills in your current line of work, related costs may be deducted as a business expense on Schedule

C if you are self-employed, or as an itemized employee business expense on Schedule A.

•**Tax-free scholarships, fellowships and need-based grants.** These forms of aid generally are tax free when funds received are applied to tuition, fees and required course-related expenses (such as books, supplies and equipment).

Beware: Funds applied to the cost of room and board, travel or research are taxable.

Scholarships also generally are taxable to the extent that students are required to provide services (teaching, research or clerical work) as a condition of receiving them.

For more help with education breaks, see IRS Publication 970, *Tax Benefits for Education.*

Laurence Foster on deducting your fun…

Turn the Hobby You Love Into Great Tax Breaks

With longer and healthier retirements, more and more people want to stay financially productive. But they also want to do something fun—something that is both personally and financially rewarding.

Perfect solution: Turn a hobby or pastime you enjoy into a moneymaking sideline or second career. The IRS will even help you do it. *Here's how…*

FOR STARTERS

Most new businesses incur start-up losses. You can write these off against income from other sources, such as bond income or salary from your day job, so your business acts as a legal tax shelter.

Starting a business can provide valuable new deductions, too—for home-ownership costs, previously nondeductible commuting, travel and other items.

Then, when your business becomes profitable, you can use some of the profit to generate tax-favored income. You can fund retirement accounts, for example, that will reduce your current tax bill while building future wealth.

A BUSINESS IS A BUSINESS

Many different kinds of hobbies can be developed into sideline businesses or second careers—collecting (antiques, pottery or stamps), photography, writing, gardening, jewelry making—practically anything.

Key: To qualify a hobby as a business, you need to demonstrate a profit motive. Without a profit motive, it will still be deemed a hobby, and loss deductions and other business deductions won't be allowed.

You do not have to actually make a profit from an activity to qualify it as a business—but only show that you *intend* to make a profit. When courts have been satisfied that taxpayers had profit motives, they have allowed many consecutive years of loss deductions, even for businesses that *never* made a profit.

Of course, courts are not mind readers, so they look for evidence of profit motive in the way an activity is conducted—whether or not it operates in a businesslike manner. *Evidence of profit motive…*

•**Complete business books and records are kept.**

•**Business funds are segregated from personal funds** with separate bank accounts.

•**The business is registered with the local authorities.**

•**There is a formal business plan** that maps out how the business intends to make a profit.

•**It advertises its product or service.**

•**The owner consults with experts in the field.**

•**The owner spends a significant amount of hours working in the business.**

•**If profits don't result, the business plan is modified in light of experience.**

The IRS publishes audit guides for dozens of businesses. See the IRS Web site at *www.irs.gov.* The guide will tell you what the IRS is looking for in a particular business.

No one item is determinative, but the more businesslike the manner in which an activity is run, the more likely a profit motive will be deemed to exist—even in the face of continuous losses.

Helpful: If an activity shows a profit in three out of five years, it is presumed to have a profit motive. (Separate rules do apply for breeding, showing and racing horses.)

When starting a new business, you can file IRS Form 5213, *Election to Postpone Determination,* to postpone determination of business status for five years.

Pro: This filing gives you five years to show your activity's profit motive, and allows you to deduct all losses and business deductions in the meantime.

Con: You notify the IRS that you are conducting such an activity, and so increase risk of an audit five years in the future. If the IRS then decides you had no profit motive, it can disallow all five years of deductions and charge you interest. By contrast, in a normal audit, the IRS can go back only three years.

Bottom line: If you are very certain that you won't have a profit for the first three years, file a Form 5213. Otherwise, it's better not to.

Once you can show a genuine profit motive, you can then reap a host of tax breaks from your new business.

HOME-OFFICE DEDUCTION

If you run your business out of your home, you can deduct those expenses associated with the part of your home used for the business, which would otherwise be nondeductible...

•**Equipment used in your home office,** such as computers, copiers, phones, furniture, chairs, desks and other items, are subject to generous deduction rules. Their total cost may be fully tax deductible when purchased under Tax Code Section 179 expensing rules. If you convert personally owned equipment to business use, the equipment cannot be expensed but it can be depreciated (using the lower of cost or fair market value at the time of conversion).

•**Commuting to a regular job may become deductible.** Travel between two work locations is tax deductible—so if your home qualifies as a work location, travel between it and other work sites (formerly nondeductible commuting) becomes deductible.

Other write-offs can include insurance, repairs and maintenance, utility bills and depreciation on that part of the home you own that is used as an office—a noncash expense that produces cash tax savings.

Deduction requirements: A home office must be used exclusively for business, as the primary place you conduct your business or as a place needed to maintain records for a business activity conducted elsewhere due to the lack of any other office. The home office needn't be an entire room—a portion of a room may qualify.

Safety: Take photos of the office or work area so that you can show an auditor who may inquire about it years later.

TAX-FAVORED BENEFITS

A sideline business can provide the same tax-favored benefits as a full-time business. *For instance...*

•**A solo 401(k) account** that you set up can receive up to the first $15,500 of business income ($20,500 from a person age 50 or above) plus 25% of additional amounts, up to $45,000 ($50,000 if age 50 or older) in total in 2007. That much income becomes tax free today while increasing future retirement wealth. Other kinds of retirement plans are available, too, such as Keogh plans and SIMPLE IRAs.

•**Health insurance** is 100% deductible when it's obtained through your own unincorporated business.

TRAVEL DEDUCTIONS

When you take a trip primarily for business, the cost of travel and lodging and 50% of meals is deductible even if the trip has a pleasure element. Only separate "pleasure" expenses (such as theater tickets) are nondeductible.

If you travel with someone else, the cost you would incur if traveling by yourself is still deductible—the extra cost for the additional person is not. But the extra cost may be slight. If a single room costs $100 and a double costs $120, you can deduct the $100.

SHIFTING INCOME

When you have your own business, you can hire children and other low-tax-bracket family members, and deduct their wages at your high-tax-bracket rate while having them taxed at their low bracket. They can then use the wages to fund Roth IRAs or deductible retirement savings plans, increasing their financial security.

LEGAL PROTECTION

You can protect yourself against the business's potential liabilities by organizing it as a limited liability company or a similar entity under your state's laws and by getting appropriate insurance. These measures shouldn't be complicated or expensive, but always consult legal and tax advisers before starting a business.

SECURITY AND HAPPINESS

The best benefits of a new business may be the additional financial freedom and personal satisfaction it provides—and it is entirely yours, to do with as you please.

Deduct a Vacation Home Abroad

The same tax rules for the mortgage interest deduction for a personal residence apply whether it is located within the US or abroad. So, if you would be eligible to claim the deduction for your second home if it were in the US, you can if it is located abroad.

William G. Brennan, CPA/PFS, CFP, principal, Capital Management Group, LLC, a wealth management firm for high-net-worth individuals and families, 1730 Rhode Island Ave. NW, Washington, DC 20036.

Slash Your Rising Property Taxes

Martin H. Abo, CPA, CVA, Abo & Company, CPAs, Plaza 1000 at Main St., Voorhees, NJ 08043. Mr. Abo has advised clients on the property tax appeals process for more than 35 years. He also has served as the president of the Estate and Financial Planning Council of Southern New Jersey and has chaired the Litigation Services Committee of the New Jersey Society of CPAs.

Home owners are feeling wealthier these days, as prices remain high in most parts of the country. But that's bad news, as well. While you might be enjoying paper profits, you likely are suffering increased costs as property taxes rise along with housing values.

And, not only might you have to pay higher property taxes, you might not be able to deduct them on your tax return.

Why: State and local taxes are not deductible against the federal alternative minimum tax (AMT), which an increasing number of taxpayers must pay.

Fight back. Don't accept a higher valuation on your home, and the higher taxes that result, without a challenge. A tax appeal might lower your tax bill. What's more, receiving tax relief from a lower valuation this year will pay off in the future. You will owe less tax each year as a result of your reduced valuation.

OVERVALUED, OVERTAXED

According to the nonprofit National Taxpayers Union, as much as 60% of all taxable property in the US is overassessed. Overassessment, in turn, leads to unnecessary tax payments.

Key: Property taxes do need to be the same percentage of the property's value, from one property to another, within the same jurisdiction. However, equivalent properties commonly are assessed at different levels of their value.

Owners who can show that their properties are assessed at a higher percentage of value than similar property often can obtain tax reductions.

Many taxpayers are reluctant to question an assessment that they believe is below the current market value of their property. However, a low assessment may still be unfair.

Example: Your home is worth $500,000, and the jurisdiction's regulations state that such property is assessed at 100% of fair market value. If the assessed value shown on your real estate tax bill is $400,000, you might be inclined to accept the assessment and pay the tax.

However, if other houses worth $500,000 in the same jurisdiction are being assessed at an average of $350,000, you would definitely be paying more than your fair share of the real estate tax burden. A protest might lower your tax bill.

TIMING IS CRITICAL

In most jurisdictions, the procedure for protesting an assessment is fairly straightforward. Periodically, typically it's annually, you will be mailed an assessment of your home's value from your local taxing authority. There is a deadline to file an appeal and a specific process that must be followed.

Step one, then, is to learn how soon an appeal must be filed. If the date is not on your assessment notice, call your local assessor's office to find out.

Caution: Missing the deadline by even one day means that you have accepted the assessment and cannot appeal until the next round of notices, which might be a year or more away.

You should send your request for an appeal by certified mail with a return receipt requested, in order to prove that you have complied with the deadline.

INDICATE THE INACCURACIES

Once you've filed your protest, you need to build a case that will reduce your tax bill.

One way to lower your assessment is to show that it contains actual errors. *Examples...*

•**Your home is assessed at a higher rate than authorized by law.**

•**Your home's square footage was incorrectly calculated.**

•**Your home is listed as newer than it really is.**

•**Your home is listed as having more bedrooms or bathrooms than is the case.**

Ask the assessor's office for a copy of your property record card to check to see if the information is accurate.

FINDING FLAWS

In some parts of the country, age, square footage, number of rooms, etc., matter very little, if at all. Instead, your assessment will be based on recent home sales in your locality.

You can locate information on comparable homes and their recent selling prices at the assessor's office. If this search shows that your assessment is not equitable compared with other valuations of similar property, you have grounds for a protest.

In addition, make sure that you have received all exemptions for which you qualify. These exemptions, which vary by locality, may remove a portion of your property's value from taxation.

Exemptions may apply to the elderly, home owners with disabilities, veterans, or widows or widowers, to name a few.

LEARN THE PROCEDURE

In some jurisdictions, informal meetings with the assessor are allowed. You might point out any errors and the resulting overvaluation, then walk away with a tax cut.

If such meetings are not allowed, or if one proves to be fruitless, you'll have to file a formal protest.

Find out about all the required procedures and be sure to follow them to the letter. You do not want your protest to be denied because of a simple technicality.

You will likely get a hearing date, so be sure you are well prepared. If your local hearings are open to the public, sit in on several other protests, preferably several days before yours. Check out the process and try to get a feel for which arguments are most effective.

When the day comes for your appearance, you might bring...

•**A statement from a reputable third party,** such as a highly regarded local real estate agent, who has measured your living space, for instance, or counted your bathrooms.

•**Photographs.** For example, if your home has value-lowering problems (such as a cracked foundation), photos accompanied by a contractor's statement saying that you have a cracked foundation that needs repairing, along with the cost of repair, will help.

•**A chart showing recent sale prices along with data that compares your house with those sold.**

Once your evidence is all lined up, prepare a presentation that will make your points clearly and succinctly. Some hearing boards enforce a time limit for testimony, so be sure that you will be in compliance.

FINAL FLING

In some locations, a negative decision from a hearing board may be appealed to a local or state court. Again, learn all of the requirements and follow them carefully.

If you prefer not to do all the legwork yourself, consider hiring a property tax consultant.

Some consultants will take a percentage of the first-year tax savings if they succeed in lowering your assessment. Others will charge flat fees or charge you by the hour.

Best: Ask a local real estate professional, such as an experienced agent or real estate attorney, for a recommendation.

For additional information on protesting your property tax, visit the Web sites of the American Homeowners Association (*www.ahahome. com,* 800-470-2242) and the National Taxpayers Union (*www.ntu.org,* 703-683-5700).

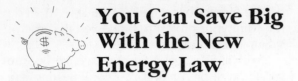

You Can Save Big With the New Energy Law

Bob D. Scharin, Esq., editor of RIA-Warren, Gorham & Lamont's *Practical Tax Strategies*, a monthly journal for tax professionals, New York City, *ria.thomson.com*. He has edited leading tax publications for more than 20 years.

The $14.5 billion in tax breaks from the new energy law will mainly benefit corporations, but owners of homes and car buyers can save hundreds to thousands of dollars, too. The catch is that you need to spend the money soon.

BUY A HYBRID VEHICLE

If you buy one between now and the end of 2010, you might qualify for a tax *credit* of $250 to $2,600. This replaces the previous $2,000 tax deduction. All else being equal, tax credits are more appealing than tax deductions because the savings are dollar for dollar rather than just reductions in taxable income.

This tax break has many limitations…

•Many hybrids don't conserve as much fuel as you might expect—so the tax credit for them will be small. Credits will be determined by a formula based on the size and fuel economy of the hybrid.

Examples: The 2006 Honda Accord Hybrid and the 2006-2007 GMC Sierra Hybrid (4WD) each qualify for a tax credit of as high as $650. On the other hand, a 2006-2007 Toyota Prius buyer could receive a tax credit of $1,575…2007 Camry Hybrid buyers can receive about $1,300. Visit *www.fueleconomy.com* for more information.

•The tax credit might disappear quickly. Credit amounts phase out for a given manufacturer once it has sold over 60,000 eligible vehicles. Manufacturers of the most popular hybrids are likely to run out of credits long before the 2010 deadline. For example, sales for the Toyota Prius passed this figure in June 2006, so the credit was reduced for sales after September 2006.

Before buying a hybrid, make sure that you will be able to obtain a credit—and find out, in writing, how large it will be.

BUY ENERGY-EFFICIENT PRODUCTS

If you buy such products for your principal residence during 2006 or 2007, you could earn a tax credit of 10% of the costs, to a maximum of $500. Qualifying products include insulation, windows, exterior doors, central air-conditioning systems, heat pumps, water heaters, furnaces and boilers. Only the most energy-efficient units qualify. No more than $200 of your credit can be for windows and no more than $300 for air-conditioning, heat pumps and water heaters. You can claim the $500 once—not, for instance, in 2006 and again in 2007.

Helpful: The energy bill includes tax credits of $75 to $125 for new energy-efficient dishwashers, washing machines and refrigerators. These credits go to the appliance maker, not the buyer, but manufacturers are likely to pass along some of the savings to consumers.

CONSIDER A SOLAR WATER HEATER

If you purchase a solar water heater in 2006 or 2007, the new energy bill allows you to take an additional tax credit equal to 30% of its cost, up to $2,000. Solar water heaters are proven money savers, particularly in regions with high energy costs, and this 30% credit will significantly offset the cost. This credit does not apply to water heaters used to heat pools or hot tubs.

AMT alert: You can't use these tax credits if you are subject to the alternative minimum tax (AMT). This tax prevents millions of taxpayers from claiming all the tax deductions and credits they otherwise could. If you expect large deductions and credits, the AMT may apply to you. For information, see IRS Form 6251, *Alternative Minimum Tax—Individuals* (available by calling 800-829-3676 or visiting *www.irs.gov*).

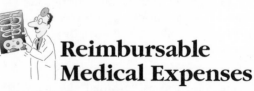

Reimbursable Medical Expenses

Lisa N. Collins, CPA/PFS, retired vice president and director of tax services at Harding, Shymanski & Co., PSC, Evansville, IN.

IRS-deductible medical costs often are reimbursable through a flexible spending account (FSA). Unless your company's rules are more strict than IRS regulations, any medical expense considered deductible on Schedule A of Form 1040 should be reimbursable under an FSA.

Example: The IRS allows deduction of the cost of specialty foods for a medical condition, so if you have celiac disease, which requires a gluten-free diet, you can deduct the amount by which the cost of gluten-free foods exceeds the cost of the same foods containing gluten.

The catch: Medical-expense deductions are allowed only when they exceed 7.5% of adjusted gross income. Higher food expenses probably are not enough to meet the threshold, but the costs still should be reimbursable through your FSA. Talk to your FSA administrator.

Information: IRS Publication 969, *Health Savings Accounts and Other Tax-Favored Plans*, is available at 800-829-3676 or *www.irs.gov.*

Generous Tax Breaks That Help You Support Your Aging Parents

Sandy Soltis, CPA, tax partner, Blackman Kallick Bartelstein, LLP at 10 S. Riverside Plaza, Chicago 60606. Ms. Soltis provides tax-consulting services to middle-market businesses and their owners.

As baby boomers age, so do their parents. In many cases, middle-aged children will help to support parents or other elderly loved ones—and those costs can be extensive.

Opportunity: Tax credits and deductions can help reduce the effective cost of supporting your parents. Also, making some minor adjustments in spending patterns or behavioral habits, such as switching investment and savings accounts, can bring you major tax savings.

DEPENDENCY EXEMPTIONS

One possible tax break is being able to claim one or both of your parents as dependents.

Each dependency exemption you can claim provides a $3,400 deduction in 2007, up from $3,300 in 2006.

Limits: This break may not mean much for upper-income taxpayers. In 2007, couples filing jointly start losing the benefit of dependency exemptions (and deductions) when their income exceeds $234,600.

Required: Even if you are generally eligible for the dependency exemption, certain tests must be met for a parent to be a "qualifying relative," as defined under the new law…

•**Income.** Your parent's income cannot exceed the dependency exemption, which is $3,400 for 2007.

This quantity refers to the taxable amount. For low-income parents, Social Security benefits aren't taxable, so this won't be a problem.

Tax-exempt interest doesn't count, either, so you might want to switch your parent's bank accounts, taxable bonds and bond funds to tax-exempt bonds or funds.

•**Support.** You must provide more than half of a parent's support during the year.

Key: If your parent lives with you, put a fair market rental value on the housing you provide, as well as food, medicine, transportation, etc., that you pay for.

If your parent does not live with you, money you pay toward rent or housing costs can be included in support along with other expenses, such as those mentioned above. Optional items —clothing and entertainment, for example—also can be included.

Strategy: Keep good track of this calculation throughout the year and make sure that you wind up paying at least 51%. Urge your parent to defer year-end spending of personal funds if it's a close call.

•**Other tests.** In addition to meeting all the above income and support tests, a dependent needs to be a US citizen or a resident of North America. He/she can't file a joint tax return, unless the return is filed only to receive a refund for taxes paid.

The person must be a relative (parent, stepparent, parent-in-law, grandparent, great-grandparent, aunt, uncle) or a full-time member of your household.

MULTIPLE SUPPORT AGREEMENTS

If you have siblings, it's only natural that you share the burden of supporting, say, your widowed mother. In such situations, it is possible that all the siblings together provide more than

50% of the parent's support, but no one sibling does alone.

Strategy: You and your siblings can agree to file Form 2120, *Multiple Support Declaration,* with your tax return.

Required: Each signer needs to contribute at least 10% of the parent's support for the year, and the total must exceed 50%.

The siblings can agree that one brother or sister will take the dependency exemption in a given year. For example, have the sibling who provides two-thirds of the support claim the exemption in two years out of three.

Wrinkle: A high-income sibling should not be included in the rotation because he will get little or no tax benefit, as explained earlier.

Note: Starting in 2006, the deduction cutback for high-income taxpayers described above will start to be phased out. The cutback will disappear entirely in 2010.

DEPENDENT CARE CREDIT

If you pay someone to care for your parent so you can work, you might be eligible for a dependent care tax credit. As much as $3,000 that you spend for such care is eligible for the credit.

What it's worth: Assuming your family income is more than $43,000, the credit rate is 20% (lower incomes get a credit rate as high as 35%).

What's covered: Home care as well as fees paid to an elder care day care center.

Example: You and your spouse both work and your joint income is more than $43,000. You spend more than $3,000 to have someone care for your widowed mother during the day.

Your tax credit would be worth $600 (20% of $3,000). If you hire someone to care for two people, that 20% credit can be applied to $6,000 in expenses, for $1,200 in tax savings.

Note: You can claim this credit even if you don't meet the 50%-plus support test. However, the qualifying relative must live with you for more than half the year.

Opportunity: Some employers offer a flexible savings account (FSA) that covers dependent care. Up to $5,000 can be contributed to the FSA and used for dependent care expenses, tax free.

If you're in such a plan and your parents are included as qualifying dependents, you probably will be better off using the FSA and forgoing the dependent care tax credit. If you use $5,000 in an FSA and you're caring for one parent, you can't also claim the $3,000-per-person credit. If you're caring for two parents, spending at least $6,000, use $5,000 from the FSA, then you can figure the credit on $1,000 worth of expenses.

MEDICAL COSTS

If you pay some or all of an elderly relative's medical bills, they might be deductible as long as the relative is a dependent.

Loophole: Even if you can't claim a relative as a dependent, you still may be able to deduct medical payments made for that person. You need to be able to meet all the dependency tests except for the $3,400 income limit, mentioned earlier.

Adding medical bills paid for a parent may put you over the 7.5%-of-income requirement for medical deductions.

Situation: Your total income for this year is $100,000, so you must spend more than $7,500 on medical expenses to deduct any of them. However, the total of your own unreimbursed medical outlays is only $4,000, so no deduction would be allowed. (Your unreimbursed medical outlays equal the amount you would normally claim on your tax return, without counting outlays for a parent.)

Suppose you provide more than 50% of your widowed mother's support, including $10,000 you spend on her medical bills. That brings your total to $14,000, allowing you a $6,500 medical deduction ($14,000 − $7,500).

Do not forget to include any premiums that you pay for a parent's Medigap or long-term-care insurance.

If you and your siblings file a multiple support declaration, the sibling that claims the exemption should pay all the medical expenses for that year. The other siblings can pay different expenses to even out the total support costs for a given year.

That will maximize all the deductible medical expenses for the year. The other siblings relinquish parent-related tax benefits for the year so any medical bills they pay won't be deductible.

Trap: Money you spend on dependent care also may qualify as a medical expense, but you can't take both the credit and the deduction for the same outlays.

Strategy: Work the math both ways to see which provides the greatest tax benefit. If you're able to deduct medical expenses and you're in a 25% tax bracket or higher, that's a better deal. If you can't take medical deductions because you're below the threshold, or if your tax bracket is 15%, you're better off with the 20% credit.

HEAD OF HOUSEHOLD STATUS

If you are not married and you help to support a parent, you may claim head of household filing status. The requirements here are less stringent than those for claiming a parent as a dependent.

Benefit: You will owe less than you would as a single filer.

Required: To qualify, you need to provide more than half of your parent's housing costs or nursing home costs. Alternatively, your parent can live with you for more than half the year.

Various other tax rules are much more favorable for head of household filers than for single filers, so this can be a valuable tax break.

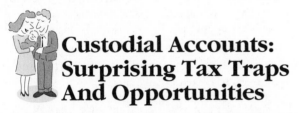

Custodial Accounts: Surprising Tax Traps And Opportunities

Julian Block, a tax attorney and nationally syndicated columnist, Larchmont, NY. He is author of *Marriage and Divorce: Savvy Ways for Persons Marrying, Married, or Divorcing to Trim Their Taxes to the Legal Minimum* (it's available from Mr. Block at *julianblock@yahoo.com*).

Parents with young children often create custodial accounts, which may be set up under the Uniform Transfers to Minors Act (UTMA) or the Uniform Gifts to Minors Act (UGMA). Most of the states have now adopted the UTMA. Once a state adopts the UTMA, you can no longer establish an UGMA for a child living in that state.

There is not much difference between UTMA and UGMA accounts. UTMA may permit a wider variety of assets to be held, but either account will enable minors to own bank accounts and securities, the most common holdings in custodial accounts. Usually, only cash, mutual funds, securities and insurance policies can be held in an UGMA. The UTMA generally allows almost any asset to be held for a minor.

Compared with the other vehicles that permit minors to own assets, such as trusts and guardianships, custodial accounts are simpler and less expensive to create and maintain.

TAX TRIMMERS

Transferring income-producing assets to a child's custodial account can save taxes, year after year.

Situation: Abby and Ben Carson, who are in the 35% federal tax bracket, hold $12,500 worth of taxable bond funds yielding 4%. These funds generate $500 worth of taxable income each year, and a $175 tax bill.

If the Carsons transfer their shares in the bond fund to a custodial account for their baby daughter, Daisy, the income tax bill is transferred to Daisy as well. The result may be less tax, or no tax at all.

Avoiding the gift tax: Between them, the Carsons can give up to $24,000 worth of assets to Daisy in 2007 tax free because of the annual gift tax exclusion. Such gifts will not eat into either parent's $1 million lifetime exemption from gift tax.

Key: The income tax bill for such transfers will be determined by the "kiddie tax" rule.

How it works: Children under age 18 pay no income tax in 2007 on up to $850 of unearned income such as interest and dividends. They'll owe only 10% tax on the next $850 of interest income (or 5% if the income is in the form of dividends or long-term capital gains).

Trap: What if young Daisy has $1,900 in interest, dividends and net realized long-term capital gains from her custodial accounts this year? The first $1,700 will generate $42.50 to $85 in taxes, as explained above, but the excess $200 will be taxed at her parents' rate, 35% in this example (15% in dividends or long-term gains), because of the kiddie tax.

Strategy: For children under age 18, custodial accounts should be structured so that income does not exceed the kiddie tax limit.

Even so, the tax savings can be meaningful. Parents who would owe $595 in tax on $1,700 in investment income this year at a 35% rate can cut that obligation to as little as $42.50 by transferring the assets to custodial accounts.

These tax savings can be enjoyed for each child under age 18.

OUTGROWING THE KIDDIE TAX

Once your children reach age 18, the potential tax savings are even greater.

Loophole: After reaching age 18, a youngster is treated as a regular single taxpayer rather than a "kiddie." As a single taxpayer, he/she will be taxed at 10% or 15% on up to $31,850 in taxable income in 2007.

Within that income level, capital gains will be taxed at only 5%.

Strategy: Once children reach age 18, give them appreciated assets you intend to sell.

Situation: Edward and Cynthia Foster own shares of ABC mutual fund that they wish to sell. But instead of selling them outright, they transfer $24,000 worth of those shares to a custodial account for their 18-year-old son, Greg.

Those shares were bought many years ago, and the Fosters' cost basis in the transferred shares is $10,000.

Loophole: If the Fosters had sold the shares themselves, they would have had a $14,000 long-term capital gain and a $2,100 tax bill at 15%.

After the transfer, their son Greg will retain his parents' holding period and cost basis. But when Greg's custodian sells the shares, Greg's tax rate will apply.

Outcome: The $14,000 gain will be taxed at only 5% for a $700 tax bill. The after-tax sales proceeds of $23,300 can remain in Greg's custodial account, where further investment income will be taxed at Greg's low tax rate.

Subsequently, the money in this account may be used for Greg's higher education, the down payment on a home or other benefits for Greg.

Opportunity: The 5% tax rate on long-term gains for low-bracket taxpayers will go down to 0% from 2008 through 2010. Thus, you should plan for sales of appreciated assets from custodial accounts in these years.

NOW THE NEGATIVES

While custodial accounts can offer large tax savings, they also have disadvantages.

Coming of age: Custodianship ceases when a child attains the age of majority, which is between 18 and 21, depending upon the law in your state. At that point, the youngster automatically acquires control over any assets in these accounts.

Thus, money intended for college may be gambled away in a casino, used to buy a sports car, etc.

Strategy: Avoid making very large transfers to very young children. As your kids mature, assuming that they seem to be responsible, more money can go into their custodial accounts for tax savings.

A lemon for aid: Transfers to custodial accounts work against families who apply for college financial aid. If you expect your children to be eligible for need-based aid, keep your assets in your own name.

Estate tax issues: Any parent concerned about potential estate tax liability may want to name someone besides himself as custodian of a child's account.

Trap: When a parent acting as custodian dies while the account is still effective, the account's assets may go back into the decedent's taxable estate and increase the estate tax obligation.

In essence, the IRS might contend that the parent/custodian retained control over those assets.

Parents living in community property states may need to be especially careful because if one spouse is custodian and the *other* spouse dies, assets in custodial accounts may be included in the decedent's estate.

Lack of support: Depending on state law, custodians may run into a tax trap if they tap a custodial account for items they're obligated to spend as a parent.

Situation: As custodian, you tap into Junior's bank account to pay for his school clothes and school lunches. The IRS may say that the custodial account really was used for your benefit, not for Junior's, so the taxable income generated by that account should be reported on your tax return.

Key: Your economic status plays a role here. Tapping Junior's custodial account to pay for private elementary school might be allowed for Joe Sixpack but not for Dr. Big Bucks, for whom private schooling could be considered a normal support obligation.

Before using funds in a custodial account for expenses that might be considered a parental responsibility, check with a professional adviser about your state's rules.

Summer Day Camp Can Provide a Tax Credit

If you sent a child to day camp this past summer, you may be eligible for a tax credit of 35% of up to $3,000 of expenses ($6,000 for two or more children). To be eligible for the credit, parents must show that it is necessary to provide care for a child under age 13 (at the time expenses are incurred) while they work—so the general rule is that in a two-parent household, both parents must work or be full-time students. You'll also need the taxpayer ID number of the summer camp and a record of expenses.

Details: See IRS Publication 503, *Child and Dependent Care Expenses.*

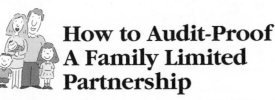

How to Audit-Proof A Family Limited Partnership

David A. Handler, Esq., a partner in the law firm of Kirkland & Ellis LLP, 200 E. Randolph Dr., Chicago 60601. He is author of *Drafting the Estate: Law and Forms* (CCH).

The IRS recently announced that it is stepping up its audits of family limited partnerships (FLPs). If you currently own an interest in an FLP or are thinking of setting one up for your family, take steps now to protect the tax benefits you expect to reap from the arrangement. Assume that your FLP will be scrutinized and act accordingly.

FLP BASICS

A family limited partnership is an entity typically set up to own realty, securities and other assets of a senior member of the family (referred to throughout this article as "parent") and members of his/her family.

Usually, interests in the FLP are gifted to the junior family members, such as the children and grandchildren. In valuing gifts of these interests, substantial valuation discounts (in general from 20% to 40%) are used to reflect minority ownership and lack of marketability, decreasing the amount of each gift. Often, gifts occur over a period of years to shelter each gift by the annual gift tax exclusion ($12,000 for 2007) and/or the $1 million lifetime gift tax exemption.

Situation: Say a parent transfers to an FLP a rental property valued at $1 million. He wants to share ownership of the FLP with his 10 children and grandchildren, so his first step may be to start gifting limited partnership interests. If he uses a 40% discount, he can give each person a $20,000 interest annually at a gift tax value of $12,000 ($20,000 × 40% discount). There is no gift tax on the transfer each year of these interests worth $200,000 ($20,000 × 10 recipients).

Result: In five years, the parent has transferred all of the interests without any gift tax. Assuming the valuation holds up and the IRS views the arrangement as legitimate, the parent has effectively transferred to his heirs property worth $1 million at *no* gift or estate tax cost.

However, if the FLP is not properly structured and operated, the IRS can essentially disregard the entity as a sham or assume that the person setting it up has not really given up control of the property.

Result: All of the property held in the FLP becomes taxable in the senior member's estate and all transfer tax advantage is lost.

Strategy 1: Don't keep a general partnership interest. If the parent keeps a general partnership interest, then he can effectively decide when to make the distributions and otherwise influence the beneficial enjoyment of the property by the limited partners. Again, this can be viewed as retention of an interest that warrants inclusion of the property in the parent's estate.

Better way: Recognize that you can't have your cake and eat it, too—you can't retain control and avoid estate tax. Don't retain a general partnership interest. If you have already set up an FLP, relinquish this interest now.

Instead of retaining the general partnership interest, name an independent third party as a general partner. For example, use a "friendly" general partner, such as a sibling.

Strategy 2: Run the FLP like a business. If a parent continues to buy, sell or otherwise make decisions about assets after they have been placed in the FLP in the same way as he did before the FLP, the IRS can successfully argue that the parent retains control of the assets. As such, the value of the assets is included in the parent's estate upon his death.

Better way: Whether you are just setting up an FLP or have owned one for years, don't treat the assets as if they were your own personal assets. Handle them like you would any business assets—like you would any other business activity.

Tips: Have partnership meetings regularly, keep minutes of topics discussed, and prepare and distribute quarterly and annual statements to all owners.

Strategy 3: Keep personal assets out of the FLP. If the partnership holds a parent's vacation property and other highly personal assets, this makes it more likely that the IRS can view the entity as a sham and disregard it for estate tax purposes.

Better way: Only put into the FLP property what can be managed through it. For example, it may make good sense for administrative purposes for the FLP to own various real properties or securities. But it wouldn't make sense to have your jewelry in an FLP.

Strategy 4: Form the FLP later rather than sooner. One of the key problems with FLPs is the valuation of interests being gifted to junior family members. Valuation is subjective and is often disputed.

Better way: Set up trusts for junior family members before inaugurating the FLP. Fund the trusts for the benefit of these relatives so that there is sufficient capital for the trusts to invest

in the FLP. In essence, this creates a joint investment vehicle. The "gift" issue is avoided because the interests are purchased.

Strategy 5: Don't form the FLP too late. Some FLPs are set up just months or weeks before the parent's death. Agents acting under a durable power of attorney create the FLP on behalf of the parent, using the parent's assets, as a way to make last-minute gifts to family members in order to take advantage of substantial valuation discounts.

Better way: If you want to set up an FLP, do it yourself while you are in good health. Don't wait until there is a serious illness. The longer the FLP has been in operation (and run in a businesslike manner), the easier it becomes to withstand IRS attack.

Note: The IRS warns that it may scrutinize a parent's medical records or interview his doctors to determine if an FLP was created when he was near death. The IRS is likely to argue that the only motivation for the FLP in this situation was to save taxes, and the IRS may then disregard the transfers as a sham.

Divorce Loopholes

Edward Mendlowitz, CPA, shareholder in the CPA firm WithumSmith+Brown, 120 Albany St., New Brunswick, NJ 08901. He is author of *Estate Planning* (Practical Programs).

Below are some tax loopholes that can have a tremendous effect on divorcing and divorced couples...

Loophole: Structure property settlements correctly to avoid income taxes. In general, transfers of residences, shares of stock and other assets are not taxable to the spouse transferring the property or the spouse receiving it. In contrast, alimony payments are deductible to the payer spouse and taxable income is deductible to the payee spouse.

How to do it: Property settlements can be made in a lump sum or in periodic payments. If they are made periodically, there is no tax effect unless the payments are considered to be alimony. Often, the only difference between alimony and property-settlement payments is the label the couple attaches to the payments.

Key: The designation must be clearly spelled out in the separation agreement.

Loophole: **Account for capital gains taxes when you calculate property settlements.** While income and gift taxes do not apply to property settlements, the person receiving property may owe capital gains taxes. When an asset received in settlement of divorce is sold, capital gains tax is owed on the difference between the sales price and the asset's tax cost.

What to do: To minimize taxes, the person receiving property wants assets with a high tax cost (basis).

Example: In their settlement, one spouse receives $100,000 cash and the other spouse receives shares of stock worth $100,000. The tax cost of the shares is $20,000. When the stock is sold, capital gains tax will be owed on the $80,000 difference between the sales price and its tax cost, decreasing the actual value of the shares compared with the cash.

Strategy: If you receive property in a divorce settlement, the total settlement value received should cover the capital gains tax that will be owed when the property is sold.

Loophole: **Write "remarriage bonuses" into your property-settlement agreement.** In some divorce settlements, one ex-spouse offers the other a bonus when he/she remarries because the obligation to make alimony payments ceases upon remarriage. By definition, remarriage bonuses are not deductible alimony, because alimony payments stop when the recipient remarries or dies. Instead, make the remarriage bonus part of your property-settlement agreement, which is neither deductible nor taxable income and is gift tax free.

Loophole: **Use "head of household" filing status when you prepare your tax return.** Couples who are legally married on the last day of the year must file a joint tax return for that year, or separate returns as married people filing separately. But someone who has lived apart from his/her spouse for the last six months of a year and has a dependent child can use head of household status to file the return.

Reason: The tax rates that apply to head of household are lower than those for married filing separately.

Loophole: **Noncustodial parents can claim dependency exemptions for their children.** A divorced parent who has custody of the couple's children is automatically entitled to claim dependency exemptions. However, the custodial parent can transfer dependency exemptions to the ex-spouse either in the divorce agreement or on a year-by-year basis.

Reason: The exemption is worth more to the spouse who pays taxes in a higher bracket, or whose adjusted gross income is not too high to have the exemptions phased out.

How to do it: Use IRS Form 8332 to sign over exemptions to a noncustodial parent for one tax year, a specified number of years or all future years.

Best practical way: One year at a time.

Loophole: **You can deduct medical insurance payments on behalf of your children even if you do not claim dependency exemptions for them.**

Reason: Under IRS rules, a child living with one parent is considered a dependent of both for purposes of the medical expense deduction. Therefore, the insurance payments are deductible medical expenses for the parent who paid them.

Loophole: **When a couple decides to sell a jointly owned primary residence as part of a divorce settlement, profits from the sale can be sheltered** by the full $500,000 income exclusion even if one spouse moved out of the house before the property was sold.

How to do this: Your divorce or separation agreement needs to state that the spouse who owns the house (or holds joint title) retains title and the former spouse is awarded temporary possession. Legally, the spouse who owns the house but doesn't occupy it is treated as if he did occupy it during the time the former spouse lived there.

Cut Taxes and Lock In Income with a Charitable Gift Annuity

Gloria S. Neuwirth, Esq., a partner in the law firm of Davidson, Dawson & Clark LLP at 60 E. 42 St., New York City 10165. The firm specializes in tax, trust and estate law and not-for-profit organizations. Ms. Neuwirth lectures and writes on estate planning and trust and tax issues.

If you are thinking of making a sizable philanthropic contribution, consider a charitable gift annuity (CGA). *With this form of giving, you can...*

● **Receive an immediate tax deduction.**

● **Lock in guaranteed lifetime income** for yourself and perhaps your spouse.

● **Remove assets from your taxable estate** with no gift tax consequences.

● **Enjoy the satisfaction of making a charitable contribution** as well as the recognition that comes with it.

KEEP THE CASH FLOWING

As the name suggests, with a CGA you make a gift to a charity or nonprofit organization. In turn, the charity promises to give you a stream of cash flow.

The annuity is a general obligation of the charitable organization, which means that it backs up the contract with all of its assets.

Typical arrangement: The payments may continue over your lifetime, no matter how long you live. Alternatively, the cash may keep flowing while either you or your spouse is alive.

Someone besides you or your spouse can be named as an annuitant or coannuitant, but gift tax liability may be incurred if payments are going to, say, your child or your nephew.

Terms: Payments are fixed, not variable. To set rates, many charities use a table supplied by the American Council on Gift Annuities (ACGA), a not-for-profit organization that on-line provides actuarially sound gift annuity rate recommendations and advocates consumer protection. To see this table, which covers ages zero to 90 and older, access its Web site at *www.acga-web.org/gift rates.html.*

The older you are when you enter into the contract, the higher your fixed payment will be.

Example: Using the table, if your nearest birthday is 65, you would receive 6%—or $6,000 a year from a $100,000 contribution. And someone age 80—whose life expectancy is shorter—would receive $8,000 per year from the same $100,000 contribution.

An annuity covering two lives will pay less. If that 65-year-old donor includes a 60-year-old spouse, the ACGA rate today would be 5.5%. A couple aged 75 and 80 would receive 6.6%.

Note: These rates, set by the ACGA, are effective through June 2007.

They have changed seven times in the past six years. The ACGA has its own formula.

Caution: Rates on CGAs are lower than you would receive from a purely commercial annuity from an insurance company. While you give up some income with a CGA, you'll support a favored cause and enjoy tax benefits.

Example: The 70-year-old who is giving away $100,000 might receive $6,500 per year with a CGA versus $8,500 with a commercial annuity. However, with the CGA, there would be, say, a $40,000 tax deduction that saves $14,000 in tax up front at a 35% tax rate, so the donor would be financially ahead for seven years or so with a CGA.

The longer you live, the more you give up financially with a CGA. Even so, CGA rates are probably higher than the dividends or interest you would currently receive from a straight portfolio of stocks or bonds, so this type of contract may appeal to retirees living on a fixed income. In essence, CGAs provide a means to tap into principal as well as investment income. You tap from principal with a CGA because the money that you've invested is being returned to you, along with imputed earnings, with every check you receive.

TAX CONSEQUENCES

As is the case with any form of annuity, the money received from a CGA will be partially a tax-free return of principal and partially ordinary income. Any immediate (or "payout" or "income") annuity that you have acquired with cash or other assets will be subject to this type of tax treatment. If the donation is made with appreciated assets held for more than one year, some of the income will be favorably taxed as a long-term capital gain.

Up-front deduction: With a CGA, you'll get an immediate charitable deduction, too.

How it works: The present value of the annuity is computed, based on interest rate tables provided by the IRS. This value, which equates a flow of future payments to a lump sum received today, is subtracted from the fair market value of the property donated, and the difference may be taken as an immediate income tax deduction.

Key: If you donate appreciated assets held more than a year, the current value, which is the market value of the donated assets on the date of the contribution, will be included in this calculation, increasing your up-front deduction.

Example: You bought stock many years ago for $10,000. On the date you donate this stock to a CGA, you hold 1,000 shares trading at $25 apiece, so this donation will be valued at $25,000 when calculating your up-front tax deduction.

What to expect: Depending on current interest rates, donors in their 60s and 70s might qualify for up-front deductions of 35% to 45% on a single-life CGA. With a $100,000 CGA, that would be a charitable deduction of between $35,000 and $45,000. (These numbers are approximate and will change as interest rates fluctuate.)

The deduction will be bigger for older donors, smaller if the CGA covers two lives.

Trap: Some up-front deductions may be too large to use immediately.

Here is why: In general, you can take a charitable deduction of up to 50% of your adjusted gross income (AGI) every year. But for gifts of appreciated assets (often the case with a CGA), your charitable tax deduction cannot top 30% of your AGI.

Loophole: Charitable donations you can't deduct right away may be carried forward up to five years.

Nevertheless, you may not want to fund a CGA for an amount so large that you can't use all the tax deductions in six years. (Six years equal the year of the donation plus the five years an excess contribution may be carried forward.)

Strategy: In such a situation, agree to a CGA that will provide tax deductions you reasonably expect to use within six years. After that six-year period, you can fund another CGA if you wish.

PAY ME LATER

CGA payments may begin immediately, but donors often choose to have them deferred, perhaps until retirement age.

Situation: Alice Jones gives $100,000 to her alma mater in 2006, when she is age 50. The university agrees to pay Alice an annuity starting in 2021, when she will be 65 and expects to no longer generate earned income.

Tax-free buildup: With a deferred CGA, the amount of the original gift is compounded annually, at a predetermined interest rate, during the deferral period. The eventual annual payout is based on the anticipated sum. This is the amount that your donation is expected to become by the time payments start. The imputed buildup rate is locked in at the time of the donation, and expressed as a payout rate in the future.

As illustrated below, a CGA that would have paid 6%, starting immediately, will pay 12%, with a 5% assumed growth rate on the donation and a 15-year deferral.

Thus, you can lock in a future income stream today based on projected (but not realized) returns. What's more, the projected return will not be reduced for taxes.

Example: When Alice gives the $100,000 to her alma mater, the buildup rate is just under 5%. With a 15-year deferral, the annuity rate—the payout rate on the original donation—will be roughly doubled.

As explained above, the ACGA rate for a 65-year-old is currently 6%. By doubling that rate with a deferred gift, Alice will receive around 12% a year ($12,000) starting in 2021. She may be in a lower tax bracket then, which would enable her to keep more of that cash flow in her pocket.

CGA VS. CRT

Some of the benefits offered by a CGA also can be provided by a charitable remainder trust (CRT). With a CRT, you transfer assets into a trust, specifying a stream of payments to a beneficiary or beneficiaries you name, depending on the age of the beneficiary or beneficiaries. The trust may be instructed to make payments as long as an income beneficiary is alive. When the income beneficiaries no longer are receiving cash flow, the assets left in the trust (the "remainder") go to a charity or charities you've named.

CGA advantages: A CGA generally is simpler and less expensive to create and maintain than a CRT. In fact, many nonprofit institutions will make annuity arrangements for contributors free of charge.

Also, the annuity payments are the legal liability of the charity issuing the contract, which isn't the case with a CRT. CGA payments are secure if the charity is financially solid. The trust you've created is responsible for making payments. If the money runs out, it runs out.

CRT advantages: Although CRTs are more expensive, they leave more control in the hands of you, the donor. For example, you can change the charitable beneficiary.

There's more financial flexibility with a CRT, too. You can design a CRT so that payments will increase over time, if investment performance is sound, while CGA payments remain fixed.

Key: Not all charitable organizations provide CGA programs, so a CRT may be the only viable way to get an up-front deduction and ongoing cash flow while making a donation to your favorite charity.

Bottom line: The more you are concerned with cost saving, simplicity and secure cash flow, the more appealing a CGA will be.

For more information on CGAs, visit *www. acga-web.org*.

Giving Stock vs. Collectibles

The very best charitable gifts are of appreciated long-term capital gains property, such as stock shares or collectibles. That's because you get a deduction for their full value while avoiding ever paying capital gains tax on their appreciation (such as if you sold them and then donated the cash proceeds).

The most tax can be saved on collectibles, because the long-term gains rate on them is 28% rather than the 15% top rate as on stock shares and other investments. Talk to your tax adviser about special rules that may apply to donations of your collectibles.

Bob Carlson, editor, *Bob Carlson's Retirement Watch*, PO Box 970, Oxon Hill, MD 20750. His Web site is *www. retirementwatch.com*.

Taxpayers Win! IRS Loses

Taxpayers have been victorious in some great cases against the IRS. *These winners may help you save taxes on your 2006 returns and beyond...*

TRACI A. TOMKO, TC SUMMARY OPINION 2005-139.

IRS loses: **Gambling losses deductible in spite of insufficient records.** A married couple who regularly played the slots in a casino reported $44,000 of winnings against which they offset more than $46,000 of losses. But the IRS disallowed all of their losses as unsubstantiated because they had not kept a journal or any other daily record of their gambling results.

Tax Court: The couple's records "leave something to be desired." But when the court believes deductible expenses must have been incurred, it can estimate a permitted deduction. Here, the couple's credit card statements showed $46,500 of cash withdrawals during their gambling trips. On the basis of this, combined with the fact that the odds are against the player, $40,000 of gambling loss deductions are allowed.

NARIMAN TEYMOURIAN, TC MEMO 2005-232.

IRS loses: **Company's advances to its CEO/owner are tax-free loans, not income.** A private corporation regularly made cash advances to its CEO/co-owner and also paid bills on his behalf. Over two years, these amounts totaled $1.6 million, which the CEO/co-owner treated as a tax-free loan. But the IRS objected that there was no written loan agreement security for the loan or fixed repayment schedule, and thus held the amount to be a taxable dividend distribution.

Court: The organization had treated the $1.6 million as a loan on its financial statements…the CEO/co-owner had paid $440,000 back to the company, and both he and the company had treated $40,000 of this as interest…the CEO/co-owner had sufficient resources to repay the full amount…and the company's other owner said that he considered the amount to be a loan. All this indicated that the intention of the parties was to create a loan arrangement, so that's how it will be treated.

MAGUIRE THOMAS PARTNERS—FIFTH & GRAND, LTD. ET AL., TC MEMO 2005-34.

IRS loses: **The cost of zoning variances for new construction is depreciable.** A business paid large fees to obtain zoning variances that enabled it to construct a new building. It then added the cost of the variances to the depreciable cost of the building. But the IRS said that costs related to obtaining zoning rule changes are not deductible.

Court: The zoning rule changes apply permanently to land. Here, however, the variances applied only to the particular building and not to subsequent construction that might occur on the same site. Thus, the benefit received from the variances will run only for the life of the building, and the expense of obtaining them may be added to the depreciable cost of the building.

LETTER RULING 200521003.

IRS loses: **Special schooling for a dyslexic child is a deductible medical expense.** The cost of a child's education is not deductible. But the cost of a program designed to remedy a medical condition is deductible, even if it provides education as an incidental benefit. So when parents send children to a school with a special education program that has the primary purpose of remedying dyslexia, their tuition cost is a deductible medical expense.

DAVID JACKSON, TC SUMMARY OPINION 2005-12.

IRS loses: **IRS can't charge interest for time its own actions prevented payment of tax.** An individual who owed a tax bill intended to use a home loan to pay it—but then the IRS issued a lien against his home. The bank wouldn't make the loan until the IRS wrote it a letter saying it would lift the lien after the loan proceeds were used to pay the tax. The IRS delayed several months before sending the letter—and then added interest to the tax bill for the entire period. The individual protested.

Court: The IRS itself is responsible for delaying the tax payment during the time until it issued the letter, so it cannot charge interest for that period.

IN THE MATTER OF: CHARLES PETERSON, BNKR. D NEB., NO. BK03-40948.

IRS loses: **IRS must consider offers in compromise (OICs) from persons in bankruptcy.** An individual declared bankruptcy in large part because of a big back tax bill. He then made an OIC to the IRS to settle the bill for a lesser amount. The IRS responded that it has a policy of not considering OICs received from persons in bankruptcy, and the individual protested.

Court: The US Tax Code and Treasury Regulations authorize the IRS to consider OICs in all cases, and these two sources of legal authority are superior to the IRS's policy of not doing so, which is in no way legally binding. So, the IRS must consider the individual's offer in good faith under its own standards for accepting OICs—even if these offer better terms to the individual than the bankruptcy court would.

JOHN E. MORRISSEY, TC SUMMARY OPINION 2005-86.

IRS loses: **Sideline drag racing losses are deductible.** A full-time bank officer owned a car that he drove in drag races, incurring losses nine of the 10 years he did so. He deducted the losses, but the IRS said that the continuous losses showed the racing was only a hobby and disallowed his deduction.

Court: The individual had long experience in racing, won races (if not enough to make a profit), and, after consulting with experts, had drawn up a business plan to make his racing profitable. Moreover, his racing had actually become profitable when he obtained a sponsor in accord with the plan. The unexpected loss of the sponsor caused additional losses—but the taxpayer then changed his activity to minimize his losses and obtain a new sponsor. All of this indicated that there was a profit motive behind the racing, so the losses are deductible.

Should You File Separately or Jointly?

Here are the pluses and minuses of joint tax returns…

•**Joint filing usually is better** when one spouse makes a lot more money than the other. The combined income will most likely end up in a lower tax bracket.

Also: Some credits and deductions, such as the child-care credit and higher education expenses, are available only when filing jointly.

•**Filing taxes separately can be better** if one spouse has high medical expenses, miscellaneous itemized tax deductions and/or casualty losses, such as uninsured damage to a vacation property owned by that spouse. These are deductible only to the extent that they exceed a certain percentage of the adjusted gross income (AGI)—so the deductions will be higher if AGI is calculated separately. Filing jointly makes both spouses liable for the full amount of tax.

Consult your tax adviser.

Sally Schreiber, JD, tax analyst, RIA, provider of information and software to tax professionals, New York City, ria.thomson.com.

Inside the IRS

In the following articles, Ms. X, Esq., a former IRS agent who is still well connected, reveals inside secrets from the IRS…

WHAT'S THE SAFEST TIME TO FILE?

The date you file your tax return can mean the difference between getting audited and not getting audited, though the IRS will never admit there's a connection. But my understanding, as a former IRS insider, is that the IRS fills its quota of tax returns to audit on a "first-in basis." This means that the vast majority of the returns selected for the next audit cycle will have already been identified by the end of September in any given year.

Impact: The safest time to file your return is as close to the October 15 extended filing deadline as possible.

CLAIMING TOO MANY DEDUCTIONS CAN SPELL BIG TROUBLE

There's a distinct line between taking all the deductions you are entitled to and overstating or inflating the deductions to materially reduce your tax liability. Many taxpayers that find themselves in serious trouble with the IRS do not realize that their troubles could have been avoided by being less aggressive. Making up numbers or encouraging your tax preparer to make up numbers is a recipe for disaster.

Example: Suppose claiming an additional $10,000 of deductions you know you can't prove will save $2,500 in tax. This extra $10,000 of deductions could very well trigger an audit, resulting in interest and penalties on tax not paid.

Best advice: Don't be greedy or allow your tax preparer to get you back any more money than you are entitled to.

WHAT IF YOU DON'T SHOW UP FOR YOUR AUDIT APPOINTMENT?

Not appearing for a scheduled appointment could be the smartest approach to a tax audit, especially if you failed to report a substantial amount of income or overstated your expenses and the IRS doesn't know this. Generally, if you don't appear for an appointment, the auditor assigned to your case will submit a report disallowing all of the expenses he was prepared to examine.

Strategy: You can always appeal the findings contained in the report. Meanwhile, the auditor will not have the opportunity to ask you questions.

Best approach: Contact a knowledgeable tax attorney if you have failed to report income and are being audited.

10

Investment Adviser

These Money Myths Can Cost You Big— What to Do Instead

Falling for an investment myth can cost you big. *Here are the most common myths—about mutual funds, stocks, bonds and gold…*

Myth: Stick with index funds.

Reality: It is true that over long periods (10 years or more), the returns from S&P 500 Index funds exceed the returns from more than 80% of actively managed large-cap funds. However, investors need to consider a mutual fund's risk, not just its return. For example, between 2000 and 2002, a large-cap index fund would have lost almost half of its value. If that fund constituted a major portion of your portfolio, could you have stomached that loss? Would you have kept adding money without bailing out?

Smart strategy: Consider an actively managed fund that is effective at handling downside risk, especially if you invest over periods shorter than 10 years.

Before investing, find out a fund's Sharpe ratio, a measure of risk. The higher a fund's Sharpe ratio, the better its returns have been relative to the amount of risk it has taken.

For example, the Vanguard 500 Index Fund offers a Sharpe ratio of 1.09. Actively managed large-cap funds that I have recommended to my clients have even higher Sharpe ratios. They include AllianceBernstein Value (ABVAX), with a Sharpe ratio of 1.38 (*performance:* 9.96%,* 800-221-5672)…and Van Kampen Growth & Income (ACGIX), with a Sharpe ratio of 1.58 (*performance:* 9.53%, 800-847-2424).

Sharpe ratios can be found at *www.morning star.com.* Search using a fund's ticker symbol, then click on "Risk Measures."

*The performance figures, from Morningstar, Inc., are the funds' five-year annualized rates of return ending November 15, 2006.

Robert J. Reby, CFP, president of Robert J. Reby & Co., Inc., a wealth preservation firm in Danbury, CT. He is the author of *Retire Without Worry: Simple, Straightforward Answers to Serious Financial Questions* (Reby).

Myth: To figure out how much to invest in stocks, subtract your age from 100—so a 55-year-old would keep 45% (100 minus 55) in stocks and the rest in bonds.

Reality: Simple formulas are appealing, but this one won't help most investors meet their goals. In the above example, the 55-year-old might not have enough in stocks to allow for growth in his/her nest egg, since his life expectancy is 30-plus years.

Instead, decide what return you will need to reach your goal and how much fluctuation you can bear. Then develop an asset allocation that has produced that return over long periods. The wealthier you become, the more conservative you can afford to be.

Helpful: The retirement income calculator at *www.troweprice.com.*

Myth: Gold is a safe investment.

Reality: At its height in 1980, one ounce of gold was worth $870. Today, it is worth $645* in dollar terms and only about $300 in inflation-adjusted terms—even though its price is at a 25-year high.

As a buy-and-hold investment, gold has been disastrous. It costs money to store and insure, yet gold provides no income. And gold-related stocks are extremely volatile. As a hedge against inflation, a weak American dollar and the possibility of worldwide terrorism disrupting oil supplies and wounding Western economies, it has made some sense for large institutional investors with decades-long time horizons to keep a small amount in gold.

For the average investor, there are less risky ways to diversify a stock portfolio—commodity funds, which may have some exposure to gold but also own copper, oil, soybeans and other commodities.

A favorite fund of mine: Oppenheimer Real Asset Fund (QRAAX), 888-470-0862.

Myth: Never invest in bonds when the Fed is raising interest rates.

Reality: Because bond values move in the opposite direction of interest rates, the value of most bonds or bond funds will go down (you will lose principal) when interest rates rise. But it still may make sense to hold bonds as rates rise.

*Price subject to change.

If you plan to hold a bond until maturity, the loss in value won't matter. You also can estimate a fund's sensitivity to interest rates. The rule of thumb is that for every one percentage point rise in interest rates, the value of shares drops by that percentage times the "duration" of the fund. The longer the duration, the more shares will drop in price if rates rise. For example, if interest rates rise by one percentage point and the duration of your fund is six years, your fund shares should decrease in value by about 6%. (Duration can be found at *www.morningstar.com.*)

If you switch to a fund that has a shorter duration, it will lose less if rates rise.

High-yield ("junk") bonds are not as affected by changes in interest rates as comparable Treasury, investment-grade corporate or municipal bonds. They trade largely on the basis of their credit ratings and corporate cash flows. Keeping some money in high-yield bond funds—say, 5% to 10% of your bond portfolio—can soften the effects of rate increases.

Myth: It pays to invest in foreign stock mutual funds only when the dollar is starting to weaken.

Reality: It's true that foreign stock funds do well when foreign currencies gain value against the dollar—but not all stocks benefit. And over time, a falling dollar can hurt profits of foreign companies that export heavily to the US because their products become more expensive relative to American-made goods.

Instead of waiting to take advantage of any currency gain against the dollar, investors should always keep 8% to 20% in foreign stocks, especially small- and mid-caps, which don't move in lockstep with US stocks. For example, in 2005, foreign indexes had double-digit returns—the benchmark MSCI EAFE gained 13.5% in US dollar terms—while the S&P 500 Index gained 4.9%.

You can increase your portfolio's total return over time without increasing your overall risk by adding foreign stocks.

Inflation Protection

Nancy Dunnan, a financial adviser and author in New York City. Her latest book is *How to Invest $50–$5,000* (HarperCollins).

The following calculators spell out how inflation affects your savings and stock portfolio—*www.calculatorweb.com/calculators/inflationcalc.shtml* and *www.american century.com/workshop/tools.jsp.*

You might want to consider buying Treasury inflation-protected securities (TIPS). Issued by the government in multiples of $1,000, the principal you'll eventually get back is adjusted according to the Consumer Price Index (CPI). While you hold the bond, interest payments rise or fall in conjunction with the principal. For more on TIPS, visit *www.publicdebt.treas.gov.* TIPS are best held in tax-exempt accounts.

And, while specific stocks in some industries do suffer during inflation, many do not. Aspirin, toothpaste, soap and medicines continue to be in demand, regardless of the state of the economy. So, stocks in well-run pharmaceutical companies, as well as food and beverage companies, are often inflation fighters. The same is true for solid public utility and health-care companies. Ask your financial adviser or broker for specific recommendations.

More information: *www.inflationdata.com.*

Free Help with Investing, Budgeting and College Planning

Lynn O'Shaughnessy, a syndicated financial columnist in San Diego, and author of *Retirement Bible* and *Investing Bible* (both from Wiley).

There are numerous on-line calculators for personal finances. Here is a list of five of my favorite…

•**General finance.** *Money Chimp.* This fun, educational financial site provides a stock-valuation calculator that features a more sophisticated measure of a stock's worth than tools such as price-to-earnings ratios. Money Chimp also offers an inflation calculator that measures the potential effect of rising prices on investments. Another calculator explores the virtues of Roth versus traditional IRAs. *www.moneychimp.com*

•**US savings bonds.** The *Bureau of the Public Debt* has a calculator that determines what your US savings bonds are worth. Features include current interest rate, final maturity date and year-to-date interest earned. *www.treasurydirect.gov* (click on "Individual/Personal," then "Tools").

•**Fixed income.** *Yahoo! Finance Bonds Center.* The fixed-income calculators here can provide answers to these kinds of questions: "Should I buy a tax-exempt or taxable bond?" and "What is my yield-to-maturity?" (The yield-to-maturity is the rate of return anticipated on a bond that is held until it matures.) *finance.yahoo.com/bonds/calculator_index*

•**Mortgages.** *Dr. Calculator.* A variety of calculators for mortgages, including one that lets you determine how fast your mortgage would shrink if you made extra payments. Other calculators estimate how much your savings will be worth in the future and compare the terms of different loans. *www.drcalculator.com*

•**Planning for college.** *FinAid.* This college-funding information site offers dozens of tools for calculating college costs, loan payments, your expected family contribution and more. *www.finaid.org*

Lessons from the Master Investors

Mark Tier, an investment analyst and adviser, Hong Kong. He is author of *Becoming Rich* (St. Martin's). The book examines the wealth-building secrets of Warren Buffett, Carl Icahn, Sir John Templeton and other master investors.

For years, my portfolio returns barely kept pace with the major stock market averages. Then I began studying the strategies of legendary investors, such as bargain hunter Warren Buffett, corporate raider Carl Icahn and emerging-markets pioneer Sir John Templeton.

Although they used different strategies, they all had habits that allowed them to implement their techniques with conviction and consistency. After researching their habits for my book, I incorporated their practices into my own strategy. In the eight years since, my personal portfolio has gained an average of 23.7% a year.

Here are the habits of superstar investors and the master who best represents each one...

HABIT: HAVE INFINITE PATIENCE

Master investor: Warren Buffett, Berkshire Hathaway Inc.

If you have stringent investment criteria, there naturally will be extended periods of time when you can't find anything to invest in.

In February 1973, the US economy was in recession and the Dow had fallen by 40% from its highs. Other blue chips also had declined sharply. Stock in The Washington Post Company had fallen so far that Wall Street valued the company at only $80 million. Mr. Buffett estimated that if the company sold its newspaper and magazine businesses to a private publisher, it would get around $400 million, so he began buying shares at an average of $22.75. Even so, the price of the stock kept falling. It took two years before Mr. Buffett even got back to his original purchase price, but he did not care how long he had to wait. His stake is now worth nearly $2 billion.

Lesson: It's not necessary to always be doing something in the market. You get paid for being right, not for actively trading.

HABIT: PASSIONATELY AVOID RISK

Master investor: Carl Icahn, Icahn & Co.

It's hard to believe that an aggressive investor such as Carl Icahn would shun risk, but this has been fundamental to his accumulation of wealth.

He focuses on high-probability situations—for which his analyses indicate that potential profits are large and potential losses minimal. By insisting on this margin of safety, he doesn't always score wins, but the odds are in his favor.

Classic example: In the 1970s, Mr. Icahn set his sights on a real estate investment trust called Baird & Warner. He estimated that the company's liquidation value was, conservatively, $20/share. He started buying this stock at $8.50/share, a nearly 60% discount to his fair value estimate for the stock. This was his margin of safety.

After building enough of a stake to get a seat on Baird & Warner's board, Mr. Icahn launched a proxy battle for control of the company. He vowed not to take a penny in compensation if he won. Meanwhile, managers of the company paid themselves generous salaries while refusing to pay dividends to shareholders.

Mr. Icahn won control of the company and sold off its real estate. Shareholders who stayed onboard made piles of money. (This company still exists, but it is now a real estate brokerage. Mr. Icahn no longer has a stake.)

Lesson: Preserving capital should always be your first priority.

HABIT: ACT INSTANTLY

Master investor: Sir John Templeton, John Templeton Foundation.

Sir John Templeton concentrates on emerging countries—ones with developing stock markets and economies—and refuses to buy any stock that does not meet his rigorous, value-oriented criteria. One of his best-known criteria is to invest based on a "trigger"—a dramatic event that could favorably impact his return. When such triggers occur, he acts instantly.

Classic example: In the late 1990s, Sir John was shocked, like many value managers, to see tech stocks reach absurdly high prices. Based on the stocks' high valuations, many of his peers bet on a price decline by short-selling them. (Short sellers make money when the stock price goes down, and they lose if the price goes up.) But the short sellers suffered huge losses on those positions as tech stocks climbed.

Not Sir John—he waited until he found a specific trigger for tech-stock prices. Typically, corporate insiders are restricted from selling shares they receive in initial public offerings until a 180-day period has elapsed. He used the end of this "lockup period" as his trigger. He figured that the increased supply of stock from insiders rushing to cash out would depress prices. For many technology stocks, the end of the lockup occurred at the beginning of 2000, three months before the tech-heavy NASDAQ composite peaked.

Sir John initiated short positions in 84 different dot-com companies just a few days before the lockup period for each stock expired. Within a year and a half, he had made $86 million shorting dot-com stocks.

Lesson: Do not procrastinate. Once you have made a decision based on thoughtful analysis, take action.

The Warren Buffett Way, by Robert G. Hagstrom (Wiley).

The Real Warren Buffett, by James O'Loughlin (Intercultural).

Berkshire Hathaway annual shareholder letters, *www.berkshirehathaway.com/letters/letters.html.*

King Icahn: The Biography of a Renegade Capitalist, by Mark Stevens (Dutton).

Sir John Templeton: Lessons from the Legends of Wall Street, by Nikki Ross (Kaplan).

Helpful: Compare your investing habits with those of the master investors at *www.marktier. com/IQ-test.htm.*

Sane Investing in An Insane World From Jim Cramer

Jim Cramer, cofounder of TheStreet.com and host of CNBC-TV's *Mad Money* and the syndicated radio show *RealMoney*. Located in Englewood Cliffs, NJ, he is also the author of three books, including most recently, *Jim Cramer's Real Money: Sane Investing in an Insane World* (Simon & Schuster).

You may chuckle at Jim Cramer's outrageous, in-your-face TV antics such as the "lightning round," during which he shouts "buy," "sell" or "hold" for one stock after another. He also adds crazy special effects, such as a man jumping out of a window or strains of the "Hallelujah Chorus." But nobody is denying that this hedge-fund-manager-turned-TV-personality knows how to invest.

During his 13 years running a private hedge fund, Mr. Cramer achieved a 24% compounded return after fees. His secret wasn't so much masterfully picking winners as avoiding losses. *Here are his portfolio defense strategies…*

•**Buy best-of-breed companies.** Amateur investors can be suckers for cheaper alternatives to quality stocks. Too many choose Safeway over Whole Foods Market and pick Hewlett-Packard or Gateway over Dell.

There are very few bargains in the world of second-rate players. When I have the choice of a few companies in an industry, I go with the best one—even if the stock's price-to-earnings multiple makes it more expensive.

Reason: High-quality businesses will hold up much better in downturns. The underdog hardly ever wins the game.

•**Defend your picks.** Take several minutes and explain to someone else—your spouse, a friend, a coworker—why you're buying a particular stock. Having to put your thinking into words this way can help you spot flawed logic and avoid mistakes.

Questions I force myself to answer: What's the catalyst that will make this stock rise? Have I already missed a lot of the move up? Should I wait until it comes down a little in price? Do I like this stock more than every other one I own—and why do I like it more?

This last question is critical because you can keep track of only so many good ideas at once. In fact, many professional investors discipline themselves by refusing to add a stock to their portfolios unless they like it enough to sell one that they already own.

•**Don't buy based on earnings "preannouncements."** Nothing is more tempting than a stock that has fallen in price after its CEO preannounces that the company's quarterly earnings aren't likely to meet expectations. Professionals know it is foolish to buy one of these.

Reasons: Companies hate to preannounce and aren't required to do so. They won't make negative preannouncements if there is any hope that performance will get better in the month before actual earnings are released.

•**Pay taxes willingly.** Gains can be ephemeral. Never use taxes as an excuse to hold a stock if the price has gone up rapidly. Long-term gains on stocks held for more than one year are taxed at a maximum rate of 15%, while short-term gains are taxed at a rate of up to 35%—but waiting to sell is foolhardy if a stock has weakening fundamentals or has become overvalued.

Helpful: Minimize your taxes by using losses on bad picks to offset gains.

•**When a CEO or CFO leaves suddenly, so should you.** Don't let company press releases fool you. High-level executives don't resign for "personal" or "family" reasons. They got their fabulous jobs after sacrificing much of what other people enjoy.

Competition is so fierce for these positions that a company must have serious problems before a CEO would step down without another equally good situation available. For instance, I wasn't smart enough to cash out of Enron when it was $90 per share, but when CEO Jeffrey Skilling resigned in 2001, I sold immediately at $47. Ultimately, the stock went to zero.

●**Never subsidize losers with winners.** Amateurs hate selling their dogs. Rather than take their medicine—the loss—they rationalize that other investors soon will see the company's hidden value. They raise cash by selling some of their winning shares to buy more of their losers.

My rule of thumb: When a stock's price deteriorates, sell it if the company fundamentals, such as earnings, market share, etc., also are deteriorating. Buy more shares only if such fundamentals are solid or improving.

●**Don't buy all at once.** When I first started as a professional trader, I was arrogant about my stock-picking ability. If I wanted 5,000 shares of Caterpillar, I would buy them all at once.

But after purchasing billions of shares in my career, do you know how often I got in at the very lowest price? Probably once in 100 times—and I'm pretty good at spotting bottoms.

Now I buy and sell in increments, spacing out trades to avoid letting my emotions get in the way. For example, every year for my 401(k) retirement account, I decide how much I will contribute and put ½ of that to work each month.

Exception: If the stock market is down by 10% one month, I put in the next month's contribution as well. If the market is down by 15%, I put in the entire next quarter's contribution. Should the market decline by 20% in a month—which has happened twice in the past decade—I invest my entire year's contribution.

How to Invest in Stocks Without a Broker and Beat the Market

Vita Nelson, publisher of *DirectInvesting* and editor and publisher of *The Moneypaper*, newsletters devoted to dividend reinvestment plans (DRIPs) in Rye, NY, *www.directinvesting.com*. She is comanager, with David Fish, of the MP 63 Fund (DRIPX), a no-load mutual fund.

Since the first dividend reinvestment plan (DRIP) was introduced in 1969, hundreds of companies have offered investors the alternative of buying shares directly—and reinvesting dividends into more shares—without a broker. Now there's evidence that these plans (also known as direct reinvestment plans and direct stock purchase plans) are a smart way to identify winning stocks and beat the market as well.

Since its inception, the MP 63 Index of DRIP stocks, developed by my company, is up by 284%, versus 172% for the S&P 500 Index. That gap would be even wider if you factored in stock transaction charges, which can be avoided with DRIPs.

Why should companies that let individuals invest directly outperform the rest of the market?

Likely reason: The companies that go out of their way to make buying their shares cheap and convenient also go out of their way to deliver good returns to shareholders. Plus their shares are widely held, and investors tend to buy their products and services.

INVESTING IN DRIPS

More than 1,300 companies offer some form of DRIP, but only 722 are no- or low-fee plans (which charge up to $2.50*). For a list of no-fee DRIPs, go to *www.directinvesting.com*, click on "Find Companies," check both "No fee" boxes, then click on "Search." You must own at least one share of a company's stock to enroll in its no-fee DRIP. Once enrolled, you can invest as often as you wish with no further fees. You'll have to pay a brokerage fee on your initial purchase of the company's stock, however.

To obtain an initial share (or shares), you can ask a broker to buy a share for you or have a

*Prices subject to change.

share you already own reissued in your name. The share must be in your name, not the brokerage's "street name," so that the company recognizes you as the shareholder.

In addition to the commission fee, expect a broker to charge $25 to $100 to transfer ownership—then you have to enroll in the DRIP yourself with the issuer's DRIP transfer agent.

Easier way: My brokerage affiliate (Temper of the Times, 800-388-9993) handles all the steps for a 50-cent commission for one share plus a $40 enrollment fee.

More from Vita Nelson...

Hidden Cost of Buying Stocks on Margin

Buying on margin means borrowing money from your broker to buy stock. Dividends on stocks bought on margin may not be taxable at the favorable 15% rate. The broker is allowed to lend out shares from a margin account. If the shares are out of the account when a dividend is paid, you will get a cash payment in lieu of dividends from the company. This cash payment is treated as ordinary income instead of qualified dividend income and taxed at the ordinary income rate, which may be 25% or more.

Giving a Gift Of Stock

Here are the tax rules for giving stock as a gift—when the gift is made while you are alive, the recipient receives the *carryover basis* and, after selling, calculates gain based on the price you paid for the shares. If the gift is a bequest, the recipient gets a *stepped-up basis,* usually figuring tax based on the value of the shares as of the date of your death.

Barbara Weltman, an attorney based in Millwood, NY, and author of *J.K. Lasser's 1001 Deductions and Tax Breaks 2007* (Wiley). She is also publisher of the on-line newsletter, *Big Ideas for Small Business, www.barbaraweltman.com.*

What to Do with Worthless Stock

When a stock becomes worthless, you can claim your entire purchase price as a loss for tax purposes. Report the loss on Schedule D as if you sold the stock on December 31 of the year it became worthless. If a stock became worthless and you did not report it at the time, you will have to file an amended return to claim the loss in a later year.

Example: Enron stock was officially cancelled on November 17, 2004. If you did not report it when filing your 2004 return, then you must file form 1040X to amend the return and claim the loss. You can file an amended return within seven years from the original due date of the tax return.

Sidney Kess, Esq., attorney and CPA, New York City.

A Hedge Fund Manager's Secrets to Picking Winning Stocks

Patrick O'Neil, manager of the Loring Stock Fund in Minneapolis, a $10 million hedge fund for wealthy investors. His Web site, *www.stockbook.com,* features a free on-line newsletter and stock and mutual fund evaluation tools.

For 30 years, I ran a trucking company in the Midwest. Because it's a business with razor-thin profit margins, I had to watch all my pennies and take only calculated risks.

I brought this same perspective to long-term stock investing, which I first began to do professionally in 1994, after my children were grown. Unlike managers of most hedge funds, I don't short stocks, buy options or try to get the inside track on hot initial public offerings. Instead, I own stock in 15 to 20 stable-growth companies that have shrewd management and increase their profits year after year, through bull and bear markets. Such consistency limits risk.

To develop your own top-performing stock portfolio, look for companies with some or all of these winning traits...

FINANCIAL PERFORMANCE

●**Reliable earnings.** I look for companies that have had earnings growth of at least 20% a year over the last two years. There's no sure thing on Wall Street, but rising profits usually mean rising stock prices.

Look at the companies supporting companies in risky sectors. Their earnings are more consistent than those of the companies they service.

For example, drug-company stocks are volatile—the prices soar or sink depending on FDA approvals—but all drugs are sold through the prescription department of drugstore chains.

Another area to look for reliable earnings is e-commerce. Successful companies are outsourcing Internet service operations so that they can concentrate on their core businesses.

●**A stock price above $10** with at least five million shares available for daily trading (called the "float").

Reason: Thinly traded stocks priced below $10 do not attract investments from mutual funds —such investments make a stock's price more stable. Ask your broker for the float, or search under the ticker symbol and click "More Key Statistics" to find out shares outstanding at *finance. yahoo.com.*

Also look for significant ownership by leading mutual funds. When a stock's top shareholders include shrewd investment firms such as Fidelity and TIAA-CREF, its share price is less likely to drop on temporary bad news. (For information on finding institutional owners of stocks, see "My Favorite Resources" in the next column.)

●**Higher-than-projected earnings per share.** I like to see management offer higher earnings predictions in its reports to shareholders for the coming year than the consensus estimates of Wall Street analysts.

●**Little or no long-term debt.** You can find this figure on the company's balance sheet.

●**Good performance in bad times.** Did the company remain profitable during the most recent bear market? Did it steal market share from failing competitors? Did its stock price hold up—or even increase?

OTHER GAUGES

●**A history of share buybacks.** I like to see companies buying back their own stock—with at least a 3% reduction in total shares outstanding from the prior year. This is a vote of confidence—management is telling you that the best dollar-for-dollar value for excess corporate cash is investing in the company's future.

●**A top-notch CEO.** Get to know the name and performance record of a company's chief executive officer. Judge for yourself whether you like what he/she has to say about the condition of the company and its future.

Red flag: Any CEO who never acknowledges tough times or never admits to bad decisions. Trust your gut—you'll recognize talent, leadership and vision when you encounter it.

Example: eBay (EBAY). This on-line leader is looking beyond auctions and buying on-line classified-ad companies in the US, Europe and Asia. CEO Meg Whitman admits to mistakes, such as not marketing aggressively in Japan.

Audio interviews with CEOs are available on the Internet. Use a search engine to find Webcasts by company (type in the CEO's name, company name and the word "interview"), or check conference call sites or the company's site.

Important: Always have a sell strategy. I evaluate long-term positions four times a year, but only consider selling if a stock fails to meet earnings expectations for two consecutive quarters.

More from Patrick O'Neil...

My Favorite Resources

Below are some of the best Web sites for investment information...

●**Analysts' estimates of earnings.** *www.zacks. com.* Free.

●**Conference calls.** *www.bestcalls.com.* Free.

●**Financial data on companies.** Every Monday, *Investor's Business Daily* (*www.investors.com*) lists 100 stocks that are profitable. It also offers access to stock statistics. Basic information is free. Or check a company's quarterly filings at *www. sec.gov/edgar/searchedgar/webusers.htm.* Free.

●**Institutional ownership.** Locate top holdings by fund at *www.morningstar.com.* Free.

●**Stock buybacks.** The *Online Investor* lists stock buybacks at *www.theonlineinvestor.com/ buybacks.phtml.* Free.

Mutual Fund Research

Mutual funds are easier to research thanks to new regulations. Each fund prospectus must include policies regarding heavy trading by its fund investors…the fund manager's compensation…and how much he/she has invested in the fund. Load funds must explain eligibility for sales charge discounts. Funds also must disclose portfolio holdings every quarter.

Mercer E. Bullard, president and founder, Fund Democracy, a shareholder advocacy group, Oxford, MS. His Web site is *www.funddemocracy.com.*

Easy Way to Find Old Stock Certificates

To locate old stock certificates, find the company's transfer agent at StockTransfer.com for free. A company's transfer agent can tell you where shares that were held in the "street" name (i.e., at the brokerage firm) currently are being held. The number of shares you now own may have changed as a result of mergers, stock splits or reverse splits.

Gary Schatsky, JD, an attorney and principal in the fee-only financial advisory firm The ObjectiveAdvice Group, New York City, *www.objectiveadvice.com,* and past chairman of the National Association of Personal Financial Advisors.

Dividend-Paying Stocks Are Better Than Ever

Gary E. Stroik, CFP, vice president and portfolio manager at WBI Investments, Little Silver, NJ, *www.wbiinvestments.com*. He is coauthor of *All About Dividend Investing* (McGraw-Hill).

John Buckingham, president and chief portfolio manager, Al Frank Asset Management, Laguna Beach, CA, which manages $700 million, including the Al Frank Fund (VALUX). Go to *www.alfrankfund.com* for more information.

Stocks that pay dividends produce strong returns in all kinds of markets. Over the past 15 years, large-cap dividend-paying stocks posted a 13.4% average annual return, compared with 11.7% for stocks of large-cap companies that did not pay dividends. Stocks paying dividends also were 40% less volatile. And, dividend investing is even more compelling with today's tax rate of only 15% on dividend income.

Opportunities in dividend-paying stocks…

THE CASE FOR DIVIDEND INVESTING
Gary E. Stroik, CFP

Holding dividend stocks will be particularly important over the next decade for several reasons which are outlined below…

•**Stocks will have limited gains.** I expect a prolonged period of weak market performance. How can I be sure? Ruled by human emotion, markets have long followed predictable patterns. As investors grow more confident, they bid up stock prices for years. Then markets drop, and investors shun stocks for long periods. Historically, the pendulum swings in one direction for about 17 years before shifting.

The last lengthy period of underperformance was the 16 years from 1966 through 1981, when the market fell by 9.7% (excluding dividends). In that time, the Dow Jones Industrial Average went down—the only gain came from the dividends. From 1981 to 1999, stocks surged, producing average annual price gains of more than 15%. In 2000, a new era of weak performance began. During the five years ending in November 2006, the Dow provided an annualized return of 4.41% (excluding dividends).

•**Dividends provide steady income.** Unlike stock price increases, dividend income is steady. Once companies start to pay out dividends, they are reluctant to curtail payments. Any reduction is seen as a sign of serious problems, and many investors immediately dump the stock.

•**Demand for dividends will increase.** The dividend-paying stocks should enjoy exceptional performance due to demand from baby boomers. In the 1990s, these investors sought growth stocks in an effort to boost retirement savings. Their appetite for capital gains helped push up prices of technology shares. Now that the oldest members of the baby boom generation are turning 60, the group will increasingly look for ways to protect savings and produce steady income.

TODAY'S BEST DIVIDEND PAYERS
John Buckingham

If you look back over the past 15 years, stocks that paid dividends produced higher annual returns with substantially less risk than those that didn't. Why are dividend stocks so steady? Many of them are mature companies that have predictable earning streams.

Every time you receive a dividend, think of the check as a reduction in your risk. Say a stock pays a 6% dividend. Even if the stock price drops by 10%, you have offset six percentage points of that loss with the dividend.

Choose companies that regularly raise their dividends. Those that have increased dividends annually for at least three decades include Johnson & Johnson, Masco Corp. and Procter & Gamble Co.

Caution: Rich yields can be a sign of trouble. A company's dividend yield rises as the share price drops. Companies that yield 8% or more in today's market could be about to cut their dividends.

 # The Entertainment Revolution: Today's Big Tech-Stock Opportunity

Christopher K. McHugh, vice president, Turner Investment Partners, a firm that has $21.2 billion in assets under management, specializing in growth and technology investing, Berwyn, PA. He's portfolio manager of Turner Midcap Growth Fund (TMGFX).

Within four years, household gadgets will be enhanced and connected so that a home owner can take care of all his/her household and entertainment needs with a single remote control.

One "superbox"—a networked computer or standalone digital device—will allow the remote control to connect all cell phones, TVs, music devices (such as MP3 players and iPods), DVD players, digital video recorders and household appliances, including refrigerators. Heating, cooling, lighting and security systems also will be linked to this centralized system. The result will be fully digital homes, a trend that promises big gains for investors.

AN ENTERTAINMENT REVOLUTION

The digital home will include entertainment systems with picture and sound quality that far exceeds what exists in state-of-the-art theaters today. Already, TV viewers can watch programs that they have downloaded from the Internet, videos on demand from their cable providers and programs that have been recorded on digital video recorders.

Consumers also can download entertainment to "smart phones," handheld personal digital assistants (PDAs) and game consoles. Apple's new video iPod is just the beginning. Segments of an ESPN sports recap or a two-minute news update from CNBC on the financial markets will give way to full-feature video programming of the caliber now available on TV and cable networks.

The industry's challenge will be maximizing battery life and storage capacity to meet consumers' growing appetite for these services.

DIGITAL FRIDGE

Another emerging trend is refrigerators outfitted with video screens. Instead of using magnets to keep shopping lists and photos on fridge doors, consumers will be able to display interactive messages and digital photographs. Home owners could use the fridge to surf the Web, send e-mails, watch TV and play DVDs.

Also, a monitoring system on the refrigerator will tell you when you are low on supplies. It can be programmed to send e-mails to grocery stores and have the items delivered.

FAVORITE STOCKS

As the demand for electronic gadgets climbs, sales should increase steadily for the next five years. The prices of consumer goods continue to come down. Today's 42-inch flat-panel TVs are much cheaper than they were just a year ago.

Rising interest rates would have little effect on these purchases—most electronic gadgets cost less than $300.

At press time, the following companies are at the center of the digital home...

•**Apple Computer, Inc.** (AAPL). Long a great innovator, this company scored a huge success with its iPod digital music player. More than 35 million were in use by the end of 2005. Besides downloading music from the Internet, music lovers use the system to store tracks from CDs. With certain iPod accessories, users can listen to their handpicked favorite songs on their automobile sound systems or connect iPods to stereo-quality speakers in their homes.

●**Avid Technology, Inc.** (AVID). This company provides the equipment and software that movie producers need to deliver digital effects. Television broadcasters also are relying more heavily on the company for digital technology.

●**Best Buy Co. Inc.** (BBY). The leading consumer electronics retailer in North America.

●**Circuit City Stores, Inc.** (CC). This consumer electronics retailer has more than 600 US stores.

●**Comcast Corporation** (CMCSA). The leading US provider of cable-TV and broadband Internet service will be able to charge more per household as it adds new profitable services, such as digital TV and video on demand.

●**Marvell Technology Group Ltd.** (MRVL). This company manufactures small semiconductor chips for the digital storage, communications and broadband industries. Sales are booming because gadgets are getting smaller and the latest chips can provide the same power as bigger units used on gadgets in the past.

●**Microsoft Corporation** (MSFT). The software giant is developing Media Center, which can integrate a computer with a TV. Using one remote-control device, consumers can download games and photos from their personal computers onto their TVs. Putting your photos or camcorder videos on TV gives you more incentive to create your own slide shows, customize your videos with your favorite music and integrate pictures with video. And Microsoft's game system has more lifelike features than ever.

●**Texas Instruments Inc.** (TXN). This company's semiconductors help produce clear digital TV images. The company's chips for wireless phone systems are likely to experience strong sales growth.

●**Trident Microsystems, Inc.** (TRID). This company makes video processors used by leading digital-TV manufacturers, such as Sony and Philips, for flat-panel and high-definition TVs. The small-chip producer should grow quickly as the industry leaders prosper.

Best Biotech Stocks— From a Fund Manager Who Is Also a Doctor

Kris H. Jenner, MD, vice president of T. Rowe Price Associates, Inc., Baltimore, *www.troweprice.com*. He is portfolio manager of T. Rowe Price Health Sciences Fund (PRHSX).

The next decade promises to be an exciting one for investors in the biotechnology sector. In the race to bring new medications to market, biotech sector leaders—such as Amgen, Genentech and Gilead Sciences—now compete directly against such traditional pharmaceutical powerhouses as Pfizer and Bristol-Myers Squibb.

Biotechs have done well lately, but they have not reached the highs we saw in the 1990s. This means that careful investors still can find attractive opportunities. The vast majority of biotech companies won't make it to the top ranks. *Here's how to separate the winners from the losers…*

A THREE-TIERED SECTOR

Due to the speculative nature of the sector, only a few biotechnology stocks are even worth considering. *I classify stocks in the sector according to their level of risk…*

●**Highest risk.** The companies in this group all have little chance of delivering a commercial product in the next three years. How can you tell? They don't have any drugs in late-stage human trials, so no products will be approved by the US Food and Drug Administration (FDA) any time soon. This pocket of the stock market truly resembles a lottery. A handful of investors will win big, but most will emerge empty-handed. Even top biotechnology experts have a hard time forecasting which companies will deliver solid products.

●**Lowest risk.** These big companies, which include Amgen and Genentech, have strong pipelines of products and growing earnings. You can evaluate these stocks the way you would any stock. For instance, look for solid growth prospects based on analysts' consensus earnings estimates. You can find these estimates at financial Web sites such as *www.zacks.com* and *finance. yahoo.com.*

Caution: It can even be risky to own champions in this particular industry. Investors periodically fall in love with the biotech sector and push prices up to unsustainable heights. These booms are inevitably followed by busts.

●**Medium risk.** This is the sweet spot—these biotech stocks are especially promising. Many small and midsized companies are likely to produce strong profits within the next one or two years. Because the stocks sell at moderate valuations, medium-risk companies have the potential to rise sharply in price. Some have products in late-stage human clinical trials, which means that the drugs may be less than two years from FDA approval. Other companies' drugs have approval but have not yet had commercial success.

My favorite stocks from the low- and medium-risk groups are Cephalon, Inc., Genentech, Inc., Gilead Sciences, Inc. and Sepracor Inc. But be sure to consult with your financial adviser for stocks that are best for your particular portfolio.

How to Protect Your Portfolio from Global Warming

Jack Robinson, founder and president of Winslow Management Company, a Boston-based firm specializing in environmentally effective investing. The company features the Winslow Green Growth Fund (WGGFX), a no-load mutual fund. For more information, go to *www.winslowgreen.com.*

Global warming may already be affecting your stock portfolio. In August 2003, my research team put together two hypothetical portfolios made up of stocks in the utilities, oil and automotive sectors, all of which are likely to be strongly affected by global warming. One portfolio held shares of firms actively searching for ways to decrease carbon dioxide emissions, which contribute to global warming. The other included shares of companies in the same sectors that were ignoring the issue.

One year later, the stocks of companies that were confronting global warming, either by decreasing emissions during their manufacturing processes or by switching over to products that have lower emissions, were up by approximately 30%—10 percentage points more than stocks of those companies that were not taking such steps. This suggests that consumers and investors favor products that make global warming a priority, and investors fear government regulation of companies that don't.

How to prepare: Concentrate on forward-thinking businesses that stand to benefit from environmental-protection measures.

Sectors on which global warming has the biggest impact…

●**Automotive.** Cars are a major contributor to the carbon dioxide emissions that lead to global warming. Two Japanese giants already offer a range of environmentally friendly high-mileage and hybrid gas/electric vehicles, and customers are lining up to buy them—Toyota and Honda.

●**Oil.** Two oil companies have invested significant amounts in researching alternative fuels and solar energy—BP and Royal Dutch Shell.

●**Utilities.** Green Mountain Power and Florida Power & Light—controlled by the holding company FPL Group—have invested substantially in technologies that emit less carbon dioxide.

Easy way to profit from renewable energy: The exchange-traded fund PowerShares Wilder-Hill Clean Energy Portfolio, which now invests in nearly 40 stocks of companies focused on this specialty area.

●**Natural foods.** Also expect firms that promote healthy living—through vitamins, supplements and organic foods—to fare well as more Americans experience respiratory problems associated with global warming.

Natural foods retailer Whole Foods Market has been growing earnings at close to 20% per year, while many other grocery store chains have remained stagnant.

United Natural Foods, the country's largest distributor of natural foods, should post double-digit earnings growth as demand increases for these products.

Helpful: For information on mutual funds engaged in environmentally responsible investing, contact the Social Investment Forum (202-872-5319, *www.socialinvest.org*).

Be sure to check with your financial adviser for stocks that are best for your particular portfolio.

How to Profit from High Energy Prices...and Cut Your Tax Bill, Too

Jack Hollander, chairman of Investment Program Association, an organization which represents both sponsors and brokerages in the alternative investment arena, New York City, *www.ipa-dc.org*. He is a tax attorney who has 20 years of experience in limited partnerships.

Want to convert high energy expenses to an advantage? Consider investing in a natural gas drilling limited partnership fund. In addition to protecting against inflation, these funds can provide big initial tax deductions—as much as 85% or more of the invested amount—and might even provide partially tax-sheltered income from ongoing cash flows. They also will diversify your portfolio—energy prices and prices of stocks in general tend to move in opposite directions.

The minimum limited partnership investment can be as little as $10,000, but because tax advantages are needed to balance out the risks, these funds are most appropriate for people in high tax brackets. They're typically used by investors with high income in a given year, perhaps due to a large bonus, sale of a business or exercise of stock options.

Caution: Write-offs from this investment may trigger alternative minimum tax (AMT) liability. Consult your tax adviser before investing in an energy drilling partnership.

BUYING INTO A PARTNERSHIP

It's safest to invest in "developmental drilling" partnerships, which search for gas in regions where it's already known to exist. About 90% of wells in developmental drilling partnerships, on average, produce at least some natural gas.

Energy limited partnerships are sold through financial planners. Ask your financial professional to choose a reputable partnership sponsor that has been in the business for years.

If you decide to invest, act in the first quarter of the year. Many partnerships are in heavy demand starting in the second quarter of the year, when investors get a feel for the amount of a tax write-off that they will need to offset income for that year. Each fund offers a limited number of shares.

DRAWBACKS

Energy partnerships should not make up more than 10% of any portfolio. In addition to the risk that the partnership might find little or no gas, you could lose principal if the price of gas falls.

There is no active secondary market for partnership units, so you are stuck with them once you acquire them. (Some sponsors do allow limited partners to sell back units at big discounts.)

Expect to own your partnership for as long as the wells are producing gas. That is likely to be at least five years, and it could be more than 20 years. This information and performance history are in the partnership offering documents.

Royalty Trusts for Cash Flow and Tax Benefits— A Smart Play on Energy

Timothy W. Chase, CPA/PFS, CFP, CLU, principal, WMS Partners, 305 Washington Ave., Towson, MD 21204. WMS has consistently been ranked among the largest of wealth managers according to *Bloomberg Wealth Manager* magazine. Mr. Chase has been named one of America's top financial advisers by *Worth* magazine.

Investors can put themselves on the receiving end of soaring energy prices by buying shares (known as "units") in royalty trusts. Although US royalty trusts may be found, yields generally are higher in Canadian royalty trusts.

American royalty trusts, as well as some Canadian royalty trusts, are available on the US exchanges, where they trade like common stocks.

ESSENTIALS

If oil or gas is discovered on someone's land, the landowner will get a royalty—a specific portion of a property's revenue stream. A royalty is pure profit to the landowner. It's a share of the gross income, with no reduction for any operating or development costs.

Some landowners prefer cash up front, rather than a long-term revenue stream. Thus, they'll sell all or part of their revenue interest.

Spin-off of royalty interests: In some cases, energy companies own royalty interests as a result of their operations.

Due to capital-raising or internal tax reasons, these companies may sell off their royalty interests or distribute them to existing shareholders.

No matter how they're created, royalty trusts own a top-line income stream that's unaffected by any costs. As long as the oil wells continue to produce revenues, royalty trusts will collect income.

Royalty trusts amount to a pure play on the price of oil or natural gas. Some trusts emphasize one or the other while some are balanced between the two.

If prices shoot up, and production remains steady, royalty income will rise. On the other hand, a drop in prices will reduce royalty income.

Caution: Although royalty trusts produce income, they are not bonds with fixed coupon payments. Investors should expect royalties to fluctuate—perhaps wildly.

PASS-THROUGH POLICY

Typically, royalty trusts are structured as simple trusts.

How they work: After the costs of administering the trust, all income usually is passed through to investors.

Royalty trusts won't owe income tax in these circumstances. That can leave substantial income for distributions to investors.

Examples: Canadian royalty trusts such as Pengrowth Energy (PGH), Provident Energy (PVX) and PrimeWest (PWI) all trade in the US on the New York Stock Exchange or the American Stock Exchange. Currently, these trusts pay out 14.8%,* 11.50% and 12.40% respectively.

This is higher than the distributions from US-based royalty trusts, which currently average a 9% yield.

Explaining the difference: In general, US investors may be reluctant to invest in foreign securities. This reluctance lowers the price and drives up yields. Also, Canadian trusts may carry more debt, have other risk factors, such as foreign currency risk, and may be more difficult to trade because most do not trade on US exchanges. But, for US investors, the dividends qualify for the 15% tax rate, which is not the case with US trusts.

*Rates subject to change.

Trap: With either Canadian or US royalty trusts, the highest payout does not necessarily equate to the best investment. Some trusts may hold royalties on short-lived reserves that will cease production within a few years.

Strategy: Do not invest in a publicly traded trust before reading the research report. (Your broker can provide these reports.) Look for a trust with an extensive estimated reserve life— the longer the better.

TAX ANGLES

Energy investors enjoy substantial tax breaks, and royalty trusts are no exception.

Loophole: **Royalty trusts qualify for a depletion allowance.** That's the equivalent of depreciation deductions in other industries.

Reasoning: When you invest in oil and gas, your income stream will decline as the reserves play out. Each payment you receive is literally a partial return of your principal as the underlying assets are sold.

There are different methods of calculating depletion, based on factors such as purchase price, estimated reserves and depletion previously taken. For investors in publicly traded royalty trusts, the trustee will provide the data necessary to calculate depletion.

Loophole: **Calculate depletion in different ways and use the method that maximizes the tax deduction.**

Situation: You invest $20,000 in the hypothetical ABC Royalty Trust. This year, you receive distributions of $1,800 (9%).

Based on data from the fund, your tax pro calculates $1,200 (6%) worth of depletion.

Result: Only $600 of income from ABC Royalty Trust will be taxable to you this year—$1,800 in distributions minus $1,200 in depletion.

As previously mentioned, these trusts typically are structured so that payments made to investors in the US will qualify for the special 15% tax rate on dividends.

Outcome: You would owe 15% federal income tax on $600 worth of dividends in the above example. That would be $90.

And, you would net $1,710, after taxes, for an 8.55% payout, cash-on-cash, on your $20,000 investment.

Strategy: Royalty trusts should be held in a taxable account so that you can take advantage of these tax breaks.

Trap: If you hold a Canadian royalty trust in an IRA or another tax-deferred retirement plan, you will lose the credit for foreign taxes withheld.

In addition, royalty trusts (US or Canadian) might generate unrelated business taxable income (UBTI). Be sure to consult with your tax pro before investing.

PAYBACK TIME

Distributions sheltered by the depletion allowance reduce your basis in royalty trust units.

Situation: Suppose, like above, you invest $20,000 in a royalty trust. You hold these units for four years, using a total of $4,800 worth of depletion to shelter cash flow. Then you sell the units for, say, $22,000.

Tax treatment: You would have a $2,000 long-term capital gain, taxed at 15% under current law. That's your $22,000 selling price minus the $20,000 you paid.

In addition, the $4,800 worth of depletion will be recaptured as ordinary income.

Benefit: In essence, the depletion allowance enables you to defer tax on the cash flow you receive from a royalty trust.

Loophole: If you don't sell your units in a royalty trust, you can keep collecting cash flow and never pay the deferred tax.

Under current law, if you hold those units until death, your heirs will inherit with a basis step-up to market value, and the deferred tax will never be paid.

Strategy: As long as it's feasible, hold on to a royalty trust investment. Sell other investments to raise spending money for retirement. Selling a security is primarily an investment decision. If there's no compelling reason to sell, you might as well hold on to these trusts as long as possible for tax reasons.

If you must sell a royalty trust at some point, it's best to wait until you're retired and in a lower tax bracket.

Bottom line: Royalty trusts are a direct energy play. If you believe that high prices for oil and gas are here to stay, these investment vehicles provide you with an attractive way to collect a generous income stream that's lightly taxed.

Note: We have mentioned the primary risks—oil/gas prices may fall and reserves may be depleted. In addition, there is always the potential for complications (currency fluctuations, tax reporting) when buying foreign securities.

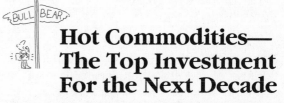

Hot Commodities— The Top Investment For the Next Decade

Jim Rogers, author of *Hot Commodities* and *Adventure Capitalist* (both from Random House). Based in New York City, he currently is a private investor and a frequent guest on *Fox News*. A fund based on his index is the top-performing index fund in the world since its 1998 inception.

After he wrote his best-selling memoir *Investment Biker,* in which he traveled on his motorcycle through 52 countries in 22 months chronicling moneymaking opportunities, *Time* magazine dubbed Jim Rogers "The Indiana Jones of Finance." Indeed, Mr. Rogers, who cofounded Quantum Fund in 1970, is no stranger to the back roads—in investing as well as touring.

Mr. Rogers believes that investments in commodities will soar for at least the next 10 years, while stocks and bonds will stagnate. *Here is why, plus his favorite opportunities now...*

THE HIDDEN BULL MARKET

Over the past century, stocks and commodities have followed somewhat predictable cycles of about 18 years. Stocks enjoyed a bull market, while commodities experienced a bear market, for most of the 1980s and 1990s. Then the roles reversed. Since 1998, commodities have soared, on average, while stocks have stagnated.

We now are less than halfway through a long-term commodities bull market. Prices of many commodities have more than doubled, and they should continue to rise until at least 2015.

It is no coincidence that stocks and commodities follow opposite paths. When the commodity prices rise, corporate profits suffer and, as a result, so do stock prices. During periods when commodities are cheap, corporate profits climb, pushing up stock prices.

Example: The giant cereal maker Kellogg Company does best when prices for its commodities—wheat, corn and sugar—are low. In the 1980s and 1990s, when commodity prices fell, Kellogg enjoyed fat profits. Its shares rose from $2 to $40 during the 20 years ending in 1999. Since then, commodity prices have soared and Kellogg stock has gained little, trading recently at $49.95.*

THE CHINA EFFECT

Demand for commodities is growing rapidly because of the economic expansion of China and other emerging markets. Chinese consumers are racing to buy an array of finished goods, from televisions and computers to town houses. China now consumes one-third of the world's steel supplies, more than the US and Japan combined. China had been exporting commodities a decade ago, but now the country is forced to import most of its iron ore and oil.

China is not alone in its appetite for raw materials. Developing markets throughout Asia, Latin America and Eastern Europe are consuming more lead, copper and aluminum. US consumers are playing their part, too, buying gas-guzzling cars (still!) and houses that are bigger than ever.

GLOBAL SHORTAGES

Supplies are not keeping pace with this rapid consumption. Eventually, new production will depress prices, but this will take many years. To build a new copper mine, for instance, capital needs to be raised and government permits obtained before production can even begin—this is a multiyear process.

All the current shortages began developing two decades ago. With investors excited about computers, technology companies issued stock and borrowed billions of dollars to increase their production. Investors were not interested in financing lead mines or sugar fields. As a result, little was spent on expanding production of commodities.

Examples: Virtually no new mine shafts have been opened in 20 years.

Oil production spending is now dangerously low. The US has not built a new oil refinery since 1976. The number of rigs exploring for oil

*Prices subject to change.

in the US dropped from 4,530 in 1982 to 1,668 in 2006. With limited exploration, no major oil field has been discovered in the world for about 30 years.

Many veteran oil fields now are running dry. US production peaked in the early 1970s, while North Sea production—in Norway and the UK—has been declining since 1999. For 25 years, the UK was a big oil exporter, but it will be forced to import oil in the next decade.

INFLATION DANGERS

Rising inflation is another sign of the strength of commodities. US consumer prices are officially climbing by only about 3% annually, according to government figures, but those figures are unrealistic. The low numbers result from adjustments by the Bureau of Labor Statistics.

According to the number crunchers, housing costs really have not increased much because the higher prices are based on improvements in quality—but anyone who goes to the supermarket knows that inflation is back. With commodity prices climbing, the costs of many goods and services are soaring, including health care, entertainment, education and energy.

Inflation hurts stock and bond performance. Stock prices suffer because manufacturers must spend more on production. This is only partially offset by companies' ability to charge consumers higher prices. Bond investors are hurt even more than stock investors because coupon interest payments are fixed, while investors' purchasing power continues to decline.

THE DECLINING DOLLAR

Besides hurting stocks and bonds, inflation will take a toll on the dollar. When prices rise, dollars are worth less, making imported goods more expensive. The dollar will further weaken against the Japanese yen and the euro because the US government is running a huge budget deficit. To pay its debts, Washington is creating more dollars. With the supply of money growing, the value of each dollar falls.

Smart strategy: To protect against a collapse of the dollar, consider opening a bank savings account in a foreign currency. If you travel to Canada, stop in a bank and open an account. To open a foreign-currency account on-line, contact the Internet bank EverBank (*www.everbank.com*). The account is FDIC-insured but not protected from currency losses versus the dollar.

FAST-CLIMBING PRICES

Once commodity prices begin to rise, they can record huge, protracted gains.

Examples: Gold increased from $35 per ounce during the 1960s to $870 in 1980. Though it subsequently plummeted, it now is at $645. Sugar climbed by about 1,200% between 1969 and 1974. Oil rose by a factor of 15 in the 1970s, to $40 a barrel.

To participate in these price gains and protect long-term investments against inflation, all investors should own some commodities. The highest returns are from futures contracts on individual commodities, such as copper and sugar—but trading futures is tricky.

Smart, easy strategy: Stick with diversified mutual funds that invest in commodities, such as Oppenheimer Real Asset (QRAAX, 800-525-7048) and PIMCO Commodity RealReturn Strategy (PCRAX, 800-426-0107).

Caution: Commodity prices are more volatile than stock and bond prices. Once you have invested, don't panic over periodic setbacks. Keep in mind that bull markets generally don't end until prices reach record levels, and many commodities have not yet come close to hitting their all-time highs.

Example: Oil was recently just over $60 a barrel, but crude will not hit an inflation-adjusted record until its price tops $90, set in 1979.

You will know that the market has peaked when commodity investments proliferate. Television financial news programs will talk about commodity mutual funds, and brokers will aggressively push commodity opportunities. These days, brokers and TV reporters emphasize stocks and bonds. There are very few commodity mutual funds on the market.

Targeting Real Returns In a Tricky Market

John Mauldin, president, Millennium Wave Investments, a money-management firm, Arlington, TX. He is author of *Bull's Eye Investing: Targeting Real Returns in a Smoke and Mirrors Market* and editor of *Just One Thing: Twelve of the World's Best Investors Reveal the One Strategy You Can't Overlook* (both from Wiley).

Yes, we all have been taught that stocks provide high returns over the long haul. But stock prices also can stay flat or decline for long spans. We now are embarking on such a period.

During such frustrating times, investors must look beyond the broad market to find opportunities for decent returns.

BEARISH SIGNS

Here's why I am convinced the market will not suddenly rise by 15% to 20%...

•**Stocks remain pricey.** Historically, price-to-earnings ratios (P/Es) of major benchmarks such as the S&P 500 Index have declined to an average of 15 during prolonged bear markets. During the last downturn from 2001 to 2002, the P/E rarely fell below 20. The last peak stock valuation came in early 2000, when the average P/E of the S&P 500 soared above 40. Since then, we have drifted down to the current level of 18.51.* Based on historical patterns, the P/E will have to continue dropping—which can happen as a result of falling stock prices and/or rising corporate earnings—before another bull market can begin.

•**The last bear market never ended.** Investors should look at bull and bear market cycles in terms of valuation, not price. There may be price rallies, but not enough to break the value cycle. By this measure, it has always taken a minimum of eight to a maximum of 17 years after a peak for the market's P/E to hit bottom. Since we are only four years into the current bear period, if history is a guide, we can expect at the very least four more years before the P/E on the S&P 500 reaches a cycle low.

With the economy growing now, won't stocks soon rise? That isn't likely. It can take years of economic growth before stocks benefit.

*Prices and rates subject to change.

Example: From 1964 to 1981—a period of nearly 20 years—gross domestic product rose by 371%, yet the S&P 500 and the Dow Jones Industrial averages both stayed relatively flat.

WHEN BULL MARKETS BEGIN

The greatest bull markets start during periods of low P/Es. In late 1980, the P/E of the S&P 500 was only 8.9. It peaked at 42.1 in early 2000. During this period, investors enjoyed annualized returns of 14% a year, the best 20-year performance on record.

If the market were to take off tomorrow, we would have had the shortest bear market on record (in terms of value, not price)—and the first bull market to be launched from such a high P/E.

BULL'S EYE STRATEGY

Today, many advisers continue to recommend stocks, arguing that if you buy and hold for 30 years, you will get decent results. That is sensible advice for big pension funds, but many individual investors cannot tolerate a prolonged period of poor results. After a few years of dismal returns, they typically sell a stock or mutual fund. The result is that many investors buy high and sell low, a guaranteed formula for poor returns.

Better strategy: Keep about 45% in bonds or bond funds. For the rest of your portfolio, *Here are my favorite allocations...*

●**25% hedge fund lookalikes.** True hedge funds set out to make money every year, even when the stock market is down. They do this by using strategies such as selling short—hoping to profit from a bet that a stock will decline in price. Most hedge funds have high minimum investments and high fees. *To enjoy the benefits of hedge funds with lower fees and smaller minimum investments, try mutual funds that act like hedge funds...*

●Hussman Strategic Growth Fund (HSGFX) sells short when the market appears overvalued. 800-487-7626, *www.hussman.net. Minimum initial investment:* $1,000.

●The Calamos Market Neutral Income Fund (CVSIX) engages in short sales of the stocks underlying convertible securities. 800-582-6959, *www.cal amos.com. Minimum initial investment:* $2,500.

●**10% foreign-currency CDs.** With Americans' huge appetite for imports, foreign currencies should rise in value against the dollar. That will boost the value of foreign investment holdings. To limit risk, stick with foreign certificates of deposit (CDs) available through Everbank. I like Everbank's Commodity Index CD, which includes a variety of holdings from commodity-rich countries—Australia, Canada, New Zealand and South Africa. (Though FDIC-insured, the accounts can decline in value based on currency moves.) 800-926-4922, *www.everbank.com.* The minimum initial investment is $20,000.

●**20% gold/natural resources.** When the dollar falls in value, gold and other hard assets tend to go up in price. *Choose from one or more of my favorite funds...*

●US Global Gold Shares Fund (USERX). 800-873-8637, *www.usfunds.com.*

●Tocqueville Gold Fund (TGLDX). 800-697-3863, *www.tocqueville.com.*

●Pimco All Asset Fund D (PASDX). The fund holds a mix of commodities, foreign bonds and other assets. 800-426-0107, *www.allianzinvestors. com.* The Pimco fund is offered in no-load form through discount brokers.

Higher Mutual Fund Fees

Small investors may face higher mutual fund fees. Many funds are increasingly charging "account maintenance" fees on all accounts that drop below a certain minimum, such as $10,000.

Small investors also miss out on discounts. It is common for fund firms to waive IRA account maintenance fees—for example, for shareholders with $50,000 or $100,000 in assets. Vanguard has even created a separate class of funds with lower expenses depending on how long you've invested and the size of your account.

Self-defense: Consolidate your portfolio into a handful of funds, preferably with one provider, to reduce costs.

Mercer E. Bullard, president and founder, Fund Democracy, a shareholder advocacy group, Oxford, MS. His Web site is *www.funddemocracy.com.*

How to Disaster-Proof Your Municipal Bond Portfolio

Marilyn Cohen, president of Envision Capital Management, investment advisers specializing in fixed-income investments, 11755 Wilshire Blvd., Suite 1140, Los Angeles 90025, *www.envisioncap.com.* She is author of *The Bond Bible* (Prentice Hall).

Hurricanes, earthquakes, floods, fires and terrorist attacks all can seriously affect the state and local entities that issue tax-free bonds. But there are ways for investors to protect themselves.

•What is the worst effect that disasters can have on municipal bonds? Investors buy munis based on the expectation of a stable or growing tax-paying population. If residents don't return after a disaster, the state and local authorities will have a smaller tax base from which to pay bondholders. Or a disaster could destroy entire projects, such as construction of roads, which also may be financed with muni bonds.

With a worst-case scenario, the bond issuer might default on coupon payments. But even if that doesn't happen, the credit rating could be downgraded, meaning that investors who want to sell their munis before maturity would get lower prices than they paid.

•Are bondholders often hurt in this way? Not so far. The default rate for munis has been low, and most bonds are insured, meaning that they automatically qualify for a top AAA rating.

For example, prior to Hurricane Katrina, the Mississippi Development Bank, a state agency, had issued bonds to finance the renovation of municipal buildings, parks, streets and the sewage system in the city of Waveland. The town was virtually obliterated by Katrina, but the bond issue was insured, so investors have continued to receive coupon payments.

Though muni owners have rarely lost money in the past, they shouldn't be complacent. The severity and frequency of hurricanes and floods seem to be increasing, and no one can predict if or when the country will again be affected by terrorist attacks.

So far, insurance companies have been able to protect bondholders, but there's no way to know if all insurers can do this in the future.

•How else can investors protect themselves? Buy bonds that are insured or rated A or better. Diversify your portfolio among several state and local authorities. This will protect you in the event that any one issuer gets into financial difficulty.

Also, check each prospectus to make sure that your munis aren't all insured by the same company. The largest insurers—Ambac, FGIC, FSA and MBIA—have performed well in the past, but there's no guarantee that they will continue to do so. Alternatively, buy shares in insured municipal bond funds, virtually all of which diversify among insurers.

Opportunity for bargain hunters: While it is risky to buy individual bonds in disaster zones, muni funds that include bonds from the affected states can be a good value. These bonds often are inexpensive because the disaster may have hurt the issuer's credit rating. Once the disaster recovery is under way, such bonds might appreciate and offer generous yields.

Big New Tax Traps And Big New Tax Opportunities for Landlords

Martin Nissenbaum, Esq., CPA/PFS, CFP, national director of personal income tax planning, Ernst & Young LLP, 1285 Avenue of the Americas, New York City 10019. He is also coauthor of *Ernst & Young's Personal Financial Planning Guide* (Wiley).

Buying a house or duplex and renting it to tenants may demand some time and effort, but it also can be very rewarding financially.

Tax advantages add to the appeal of owning rental property. But it's vital to know all the possible tax consequences when you're trying to calculate the potential returns from this type of real estate.

For landlords, returns may come from current cash flow, from long-term appreciation, or from both.

Example: Say that you buy a duplex for $300,000, which you rent to tenants. In year one, your net cash flow—after mortgage payments, taxes and operating expenses—is $7,000.

If you had purchased the property with a $60,000 (20%) down payment, $7,000 would be a return of nearly 12%, in terms of cash flow.

Note: This example is hypothetical and such returns certainly are not guaranteed. Nevertheless, they are possible with a well-chosen real estate investment.

Loophole: If you do pocket cash from rental income, some or all of that cash might be tax free.

PROFIT AND LOSS

Where do the tax benefits come in? Because you're holding the duplex for investment, you can take noncash deductions, including depreciation.

In this simplified example, you might write off $10,000 per year. The exact amount will depend on the allocations to land, building, furnishings, fixtures, etc.

So, if you have $7,000 in net cash flow and take $10,000 worth of noncash deductions, you would have a loss of $3,000 for tax purposes.

Payoff: With a tax loss, you would owe no income tax on this real estate investment. You would pocket your $7,000 in cash flow tax free.

DETERMINING THE DEDUCTION

Besides your tax-free cash flow, can you deduct the loss?

For most landlords, who are not real estate professionals, such a loss would be classified as a passive activity loss. Its deductibility would be determined by whether you actively participate in the activity and by your adjusted gross income (AGI).

Passive losses from rental real estate are deductible by joint filers, up to $25,000 per year if your AGI is no more than $100,000 per year. (For married filing separately, the deduction is up to $12,500 and the AGI limit is $50,000.) Also, you must actively participate in the rental activity by making decisions on tenant selection, lease terms, capital expenditures, etc.

If your AGI is more than $100,000, deductions are phased out, $1 for every $2 over the threshold, until they vanish at $150,000 in AGI. *Examples...*

•**Suppose Bill Smith owns and participates in the decisions regarding the rental property described above.** This year, Bill's AGI is $99,000. He can deduct the entire $3,000 loss against his other income.

•**Suppose Bill's AGI increases to $146,000 next year.** He will be over the threshold by $46,000, which will drop his maximum deduction by $23,000—from $25,000 to $2,000.

Assuming that the duplex shows the same $3,000 tax loss, Bill could deduct only $2,000 worth of that loss this year.

•**Suppose that Bill's AGI is $151,000 the following year.** He'll be over the $150,000 limit, so no losses from the rental property will be deductible against his other income.

Tax-free cash: Regardless of whether the loss is deductible, all cash Bill receives from rental income will be untaxed in the above examples.

The tax law becomes more favorable if you can qualify as a real estate professional.

Required: You must spend more than half of your working time on real estate and your real estate efforts must take up more than 750 hours a year.

If so, you are entitled to deduct your rental property losses right away, regardless of your AGI, assuming that you materially participate in those ventures, as described.

DELAYED GRATIFICATION

What happens to any losses that can't be deducted immediately?

They are carried over into future years, when they can offset any passive income, including taxable income from rental properties.

When the properties are sold off, any unused losses can be deducted. Upon sale, any depreciation deductions you have taken will be taxed ("recaptured"), up to the extent of any gain. The tax rate will be no higher than 25% under current law.

Thus, this provision allows you to avoid paying tax now, at rates up to 35%, and instead pay that tax years from now at 25%.

REFINANCING REWARDS

If your property appreciates, you stand to gain from yet another big tax break—tax-free refinancing.

Generally, lenders will provide 80% loan-to-value financing.

Situation: If your $300,000 duplex grows in value to $400,000, you might increase your mortgage to $320,000.

If you originally borrowed $240,000 to buy the building, you can pay off that loan with the new one.

Result: The extra $80,000 can go right into your pocket. You'll owe no tax on the loan proceeds.

It's true that you'll be paying off a $320,000 loan instead of one for $240,000. However, if the property has appreciated, that probably indicates rents have increased, so you may be able to carry the extra debt service.

The interest on the additional proceeds you get on the refinancing may or may not be deductible, depending on what you do with the money. For instance, if you use the money to pay for a vacation, it's not deductible. If you repair the house, it is.

LIFE-AND-DEATH MANEUVERS

If rental property has been held more than one year, any profit on a sale will qualify as a long-term capital gain. You'll owe federal tax at a maximum rate of 15% under current law, and 25% on recaptured depreciation.

Trading places: You don't necessarily have to pay any tax on rental property appreciation. Instead, you can enter into a like-kind exchange for another investment property.

Typically, this is a three-way exchange. You sell your property, have an unrelated qualified intermediary hold the proceeds temporarily, and use the proceeds to acquire replacement property that you've designated.

Key: To make sure that this transaction is tax free, you should never have access to any cash.

Loophole: If you do hold on to the original property or replacement property until you die, your heirs may inherit it with a step-up in basis to market value. If so, all prior appreciation will escape capital gains tax. (There might be an estate tax, though.)

The tax law currently offers a one-year only (2010) period in which this basis step-up will be partially repealed. However, previous attempts to annul the basis step-up provisions have proven to be impractical, and that may indeed be the case again.

Home sweet home: Another zero-tax strategy is to move into your rental property and convert it to your principal residence.

After you've lived there for two years, you can sell it and exclude up to $250,000 worth of capital gains, or $500,000 if you're married. (You'll owe tax on any gain attributable to depreciation taken after May 6, 1997.)

Worth waiting for: If you obtain rental property through a tax-free exchange and subsequently make it your principal residence, you can use the $250,000 or $500,000 exclusion. However, you have to own the home as your residence for at least five years after the swap to make the sale.

Make Money When Real Estate Values Fall

Firms such as Merrill Lynch are offering financial products that rise in value if the price of a basket of housing-related stocks, such as home builders and real estate investment trusts (REITs), declines. Early in 2006, HedgeStreet Inc., an on-line derivatives exchange, launched "hedgelets," which also pay off if real estate prices dip. And, the Chicago Mercantile Exchange now provides futures contracts based on housing price movements in 10 cities.

Keith Gumbinger, vice president, HSH Associates, publisher of mortgage and consumer loan information, Pompton Plains, NJ, *www.hsh.com.*

Real Estate Opportunity

Buying tax liens can provide good yields. To raise cash, local governments auction off unpaid property tax bills, which gives holders a legal claim, or "lien," on the property. Investors then must try to collect the taxes owed. If they succeed, they get the taxes owed plus 12% to 24% interest, depending on local laws. If the taxes are not paid, investors can foreclose on the property on which the taxes are owed—and potentially sell it for a huge profit.

Caution: This is a high-risk investment that requires knowledge of the local laws regarding lien sales.

Information: The National Tax Lien Association, 877-470-9007, *www.ntlainfo.org*.

Denise L. Evans, Esq., commercial real estate broker, Tuscaloosa, AL, and author of *How to Make Money on Foreclosures* (Sphinx).

How to Avoid the 10 Costliest Tax Mistakes Investors Make

Janice M. Johnson, CPA, JD, A.B. Watley Group at 50 Broad St., New York City 10004. Ms. Johnson has more than 25 years of experience in advising high-net-worth investors, hedge funds and broker dealers about the tax consequences of investing.

R eturn from investments after taxes is what matters to investors. *Avoid these 10 common tax mistakes to keep your after-tax returns as high as possible...*

1. Not counting reinvested dividends in the basis of mutual fund shares. If you reinvest mutual fund dividends (and capital gains distributions) to buy additional fund shares, the dividends become part of the cost of your shareholdings and reduce your taxable gain. But investors often neglect to count reinvested dividends in the cost of their shares. Instead, they figure gain on a sale of shares by subtracting only the original cash price they paid for the shares from the sale price of the shares.

Result: Taxable gain is mistakenly increased (or deductible loss mistakenly reduced).

2. Not separating brokers' fees for investment advice from transaction costs. Many brokers will charge a single "wrap fee" that covers the cost of both executing transactions and investment advice provided by the broker.

Trap: These items are subject to different tax rules. Transaction costs are added to the asset's basis on Schedule D, which serves to minimize gain and maximize loss. But the cost of investment advice is included among miscellaneous itemized deductions, which are deductible only to the extent they exceed 2% of adjusted gross income, so they may not be deductible at all.

If these items aren't separated, you can't deduct them properly and they may be challenged if you're audited.

Best: Ask your broker for a written statement of how much of his/her fee is for each of the two items.

3. Not tracking gains and losses throughout the year. It's commonly known that investment gains and losses when you sell stocks can be advantageously offset—if you have a net loss for the year to date, you can realize an offsetting gain tax free, and if you have a net gain, you can voluntarily realize losses to shelter it from tax.

To use these offsetting strategies wisely, you must consistently know your gains and losses for the year to date—including realized results from transactions, unrealized gains and losses in your portfolio, and loss carry forwards from the previous year.

The more often you trade, the more important this information is.

Helpful: You can get computer spreadsheets and investment-tracking software that make it easier to manage your investments.

4. Not identifying particular stock and fund shares to sell. When you have purchased shares of the same stock or mutual fund at different times, you probably paid different prices. When selling some of them, you can select for sale the particular shares that will produce the best tax result.

Example: You purchased shares of a stock at both $20 and $40. It's now worth $35, and you intend to sell some. You have the choice of selling shares to obtain a $15 per share gain or $5 per share loss—while receiving the same $35 per share cash either way. Which choice is best will depend on your other gains and losses.

Rule: When using the "specific identification" method of selling shares, you must keep records sufficient to identify the purchase price of all your shares, inform your broker in writing of the shares you wish to sell and receive an acknowledgment that they were sold.

5. Giving cash rather than appreciated securities to support low-bracket family members. If you pay cash to help support an individual who is in a low tax bracket—such as a retired parent or other family member—you probably can do better by giving appreciated securities instead of cash and having the individual sell them for his own account.

Why: The tax due on long-term capital gains is 5% when incurred by someone who is in the 10% or 15% tax bracket—that's almost tax free (from 2008 through 2010 it will be completely tax free). When you give long-term investments as a gift, your holding period carries over to the recipient.

Payoff: By cutting the tax on the securities' sale by having the taxpayer in the lowest tax bracket sell them, you can use fewer securities to provide the same amount of support.

6. Donating cash rather than appreciated securities to charity. Even if you want to keep owning appreciated securities, you'll do best by donating the shares you own to charity and then repurchasing new shares in the market.

Advantages: When you donate appreciated securities that you've owned for at least a year, you get the same deduction as if you had donated cash of equal value—but avoid paying gains tax on the securities.

By then repurchasing like shares, you reset your tax basis in them at their higher current value, up from the cheaper price at which you originally purchased them. The end result is two tax breaks—a charitable contribution deduction now *and* a smaller taxable gain when you sell them in the future.

7. Buying tax-exempt securities through retirement accounts. This is an expensive mistake in two ways—first, tax-exempt bonds pay less interest than taxable bonds, so they will provide less income to the retirement account. Second, distributions from traditional IRAs, 401(k)s and other tax-deferred accounts are taxed as ordinary income. So, income from tax-exempt securities that would be tax free if held outside the retirement account is taxed at top rates when taken from the retirement account.

The smartest investment tax-wise for a tax-deferred retirement account is a regular bond or similar item paying a high rate of taxable interest. The tax-deferred nature of the account lets the high interest compound on a pretax basis.

Strategy: Strive to have a diversified portfolio with the fully taxable investments held in tax-favored retirement accounts, and tax-favored investments held outside tax-favored accounts.

8. Investing in mutual funds to the exclusion of exchange-traded funds (ETFs). ETFs are much more tax efficient than most mutual funds. An ETF is like an index mutual fund in that it owns a portfolio of stocks or bonds. It is traded like a stock.

Tax key: A mutual fund may generate taxable gains for its investors every year as it sells shares that it holds to fund redemptions by other investors and balances its portfolio. These tax liabilities are distributed to its investors. But ETFs generally create tax liability for their investors only when the ETF shares are actually sold.

ETFs also have much lower management fees than mutual funds—lower even than almost all index funds.

9. Not checking 1099 forms. These forms report taxable investment income to the IRS. They have significant error rates—those filed by brokerage firms have been reported by the IRS to have error rates as high as 10%.

So check 1099s carefully to be sure that they do not report more income than you received.

10. Holding on to investments just to avoid paying tax on gains. People often delay selling an investment that they know they should sell simply because they don't want to pay tax that would result from the sale. Or, they may want to pass it on to heirs with a stepped-up cost basis.

However, the goal of minimizing tax should never compromise the top priority of holding sound investments—especially with the long-term capital gains tax rate now reduced to an historic low of 15%.

If it is time to sell an investment and you have no way to avoid paying the tax, sell and pay it—rates may never be lower than today. It's much cheaper to pay tax on a gain than to end up with a loss by holding an investment too long.

Tax Loopholes For Investors

Edward Mendlowitz, CPA, shareholder in the CPA firm WithumSmith+Brown, 120 Albany St., New Brunswick, NJ 08901. He is author of *Estate Planning* (Practical Programs).

Here are some important tax strategies to consider when you make investment decisions...

Loophole: **Use the "specific identification method" to minimize capital gains taxes** when you sell part of your holdings in a stock, mutual fund or other investment.

Example: Say you decide to sell some of your Microsoft holdings and maintain a reduced stake. If you acquired the shares at various times for various prices, you'll want to sell the highest-cost shares first. That way, you'll trigger the lowest possible capital gain (or the biggest possible capital loss).

By using the specific identification method, you select the particular shares you want to sell. If your securities are held by a broker, IRS regulations say that you must identify the shares you want sold by reference to their purchase date and per-share price. The broker must then issue a written confirmation of your instructions.

Warning: Many discount and on-line brokers will not issue the IRS-required confirmations.

However, the Tax Court's 1994 decision in the Concord Instruments Corp. case (*Concord Instruments Corporation*, TC Memo 1994-248) seems to allow investors who give oral instructions regarding the shares to be sold to use the specific ID method to calculate their gain...even though there is no written confirmation.

Self-defense: Protect yourself against potential audits by documenting your sell instructions. Make notations of them on the written transaction statements received from your broker. Follow up with a confirming letter.

Loophole: **Give profitable stocks to children and to family members.** You can make these gifts in conjunction with an overall program of decreasing the amount you invest in stocks. *Here's how to get the best tax results from your generosity...*

●**Do not give losing investments (that are currently worth less than what you paid) to relatives.**

Better: Sell the shares and use the capital losses to shelter other capital gains or income from other sources. Then give the cash to your family members.

●**Do give appreciated shares to lower-tax-bracket children or grandchildren** whose lower income would have them taxed at rates lower than the 15% maximum capital gains tax.

Note: Someone in the 10% or 15% ordinary income bracket is taxed at 5% on capital gains of securities if the combined holding period of you and the gift recipient together is more than one year.

If the shares were held one year or less, the gift recipient will pay tax at his/her ordinary income tax rate.

By contrast, if you sell appreciated stock, you will owe 15% on any long-term gains, and short-term gains will be taxed at regular income tax rates, as high as 35%.

Caution: Gains recognized by children under age 18 may be taxed at their parents' marginal income tax rates under the so-called kiddie tax rules. However, the kiddie tax does not apply starting in the calendar year in which a child turns 18, and affects only children who report more than $1,700 of unearned income from capital gains, interest or dividends in 2006 or 2007.

Loophole: **Maximize charitable donations of stock.** *How...*

●**Sell shares for a loss,** deduct the capital losses on your return, and then give cash to the charity. You get the capital loss write-off plus the charitable deduction, which is a double tax benefit.

●**Donate profitable shares directly** instead of selling them and donating cash.

Reason: You can deduct the full current market value of publicly traded shares that you've owned for more than one year. Plus, when you give the appreciated stock away, you get rid of the built-in capital gains tax liability. And you might also save any AMT. So this idea could be a triple tax saver.

11

The Savvy Shopper

Save Big Money on Big Purchases

Big-ticket purchases can put a strain on your budget for years. *Below is how to save hundreds, maybe thousands, of dollars on appliances, electronics and many other expensive items...*

•**Anticipate big purchases.** Many people do avoid thinking about when they might need to make a large purchase. And then once the time comes, they make a hasty decision. Instead, you should plan ahead.

All reputable dealers will gladly tell you how long a big-ticket item is likely to last.

Examples: Dishwasher, 10 years...top-load washer, 10 years...front-load washer, 14 years ...refrigerator, 12 to 15 years...mattress, eight to 10 years...laptop computer, three years (if you use the computer every day).

As soon as you buy a big-ticket item, earmark a portion of your monthly savings for its replacement, based on how long you expect it to last. When an item is approaching the end of its useful life, keep an eye out for sales on new models.

Smart: Add years to the life of big-ticket products with regular maintenance. Service the lawn mower each year—change the oil and sharpen the blade. Run a gallon of vinegar through the washing machine every few months to remove mineral buildup from hard water. Flip mattresses regularly to even out the wear patterns.

•**Use credit only if you expect the item to last more than three years.** Also, make sure that you can pay it off in less than three years— you don't want to run the risk of problems before you finish paying for the item.

Items that you shouldn't buy with credit: Laptop computers, baby cribs, MP-3 players and

Mary Hunt, editor of *Debt-Proof Living*, Box 2135, Paramount, CA 90723, *www.debtproofliving.com*. She is author of many books, including *Everyday Cheapskate's Greatest Tips: 500 Simple Strategies for Smart Living* (Running Press) and *Live Your Life for Half the Price—Without Sacrificing the Life You Love* (DPL).

video game systems. After three years, all these items are likely to be worth less than the amount you still owe on them. You never want to get trapped into making monthly payments on an expensive product that you rarely use.

•**Match quality to need.** Buy only big-ticket items that you truly need, and avoid paying for features that you'll never use.

Example: Two years ago, I needed to get a new vacuum cleaner. I saw an ad for a high-end model ($500) that had received a top-quality rating. It turned out to be the vacuum that rated best in picking up animal hairs and dander from deep-pile carpeting. Since I have neither pets nor thick carpeting, I decided on another model with good ratings that cost half as much, and it does everything that I need it to do.

•**Negotiate for discounts.** Big stores need to turn over their inventory regularly. Hand the salesperson your phone number or a business card and say, "If you need to meet a sales quota in the next month or two and you can help me get a better discount on this stereo system or tell me when it will be on sale, give me a call." Also ask for free shipping and/or free assembly.

Once you have agreed on a price, request a further discount—for instance, 10%—for paying in cash. You're more likely to get this discount from local retailers, who want to avoid the fees they have to pay when you use your credit card, than from national chains, which have bigger sales volume. While you will miss out on credit card company protections, these are typically very limited and a discount for paying cash is hard to beat.

•**Look for a "price guarantee" policy** that promises to match any competitor's price on the same item for at least 30 days following the purchase. Keep an eye out for sales during this period. Most national retail chains have price-match guarantees.

•**Avoid extended warranties.** Service contracts are tempting because big-ticket items can be very costly to repair or replace. But these agreements cover the middle years of a product's life—after the initial warranty but before "old age" sets in—when it is unlikely to experience problems. It rarely pays to purchase extended warranties for long-lasting appliances, such as dishwashers, washers and dryers.

Only take the extended warranty on items that are known to have high failure rates in the first few years, such as treadmills and laptop computers. The warranty should last at least as long as you plan to use the item—in some cases, this might require you to renew the warranty. The cost of the warranty should not exceed 20% of the purchase price.

Helpful: If you make a purchase with your American Express card, one year is added for free to any manufacturer's warranty that covers less than five years.*

•**Comparison shop on-line.** *Here are my favorite resources…*

• *www.consumerreports.org,* which provides product ratings (a one-year subscription is $26).

• *www.epinions.com.* Offers customer reviews of products.

• *froogle.google.com,* a product search engine. Type in the specific item, and get a listing of all prices for the item on the Internet, including prices from on-line auctions.

• *www.salescircular.com.* Lets you search for the best price in your state at Best Buy, Circuit City, CompUSA, Kmart, Office Depot, OfficeMax, Radio Shack, Sears, Staples, Target and Wal-Mart, as well as local-area retailers.

• *www.gotapex.com.* Super deals on computer equipment.

*Prices, rates and offers subject to change.

Save Hundreds on Electronics, Appliances, Cell Phones and More

Robert Silva, an expert on consumer electronics based in La Mesa, CA. Since 1999, he has written for About.com and currently serves as its home theater guru (*hometheater. about.com*). He tests and reviews hundreds of new products each year and has worked in electronics sales, video production and computer animation.

Each year, there are billions of dollars worth of brand-name appliances and electronics returned to the retailers and manufacturers. Consumers return items because of shipping damage and minor problems or simply because they changed their minds. In the past, since these products could no longer be marketed legally as "new," they were destroyed or sent to liquidators. But retailing has become so competitive that manufacturers now "refurbish" the goods that are returned—repairing and repackaging them—and then sell them as high-quality, used merchandise.

Savings: Up to 80% off retail price.

"Refurbs"—from cameras and laptop computers to DVD players and golf clubs—come with a limited choice of features and colors and may not have the latest technology, but their prices make them attractive bargains.

The best deals can be found in January.

Reasons: Holiday returns pile up. And, electronics retailers must clear shelves of old demo models and stock to prepare for new products following the industry's Consumer Electronics Show, held every January.

HOW TO SHOP FOR "REFURBS"

• **Find out how the manufacturer or retailer defines "refurbished."** There are no federal regulations for labeling these goods, which also may be called "factory reconditioned," "open-box" or "preowned," but many sellers will tell you if you ask.

The best refurbs are…

• Items that have been returned unused. Most major retailers have a 30-day return policy for their products.

• Otherwise-sound goods that had cosmetic damage, perhaps scratches or dents. The original internal components usually are put into a new cabinet or casing.

• Overstock items. These typically are older models that need to be cleared off store shelves.

Less desirable refurbs…

• Demonstration units. These floor models are used in stores, at trade shows or for product reviews. They often have suffered substantial wear and tear.

• Defective products. These items already have been repaired, which may or may not have fixed the problem.

• **Look for a strong parts-and-labor warranty and return policy.** The product should come with a 45-day warranty and a 14-day return policy.

Caution: You may be able to get a warranty only if you buy through the manufacturer or a manufacturer-authorized reseller.

• **Make sure the refurb comes with all the basic components of a new product.** Check the model and configuration of the newest version of the product on the manufacturer's Web site or in the owner's manual to make sure that your model comes with everything you need. For instance, some refurbished electronics may be sold without necessary cables, headphones, software, etc.

POPULAR SOURCES FOR REFURBISHED GOODS

My favorite Web sites for refurbs…*

• **Electronics…**
  • Apple, *store.apple.com* (see "Special Deals")
  • Dell, *www.delloutlet.com*
  • Hewlett-Packard, *www.shopping.hp.com*
  • *www.officemachinesolutions.com*
  • The Palm Store, *store.palm.com*
  • *www.refurbelectronics.com*
  • Frys, *shop1.outpost.com*
  • *www.smalldog.com*

• **Appliances…**
  • *www.kitchencollection.com*
  • *www.shopkitchenaid.com*

• **Sports gear…**
  • Callaway Golf, *callawaygolfpreowned.com*

• **General merchandise…**
  • *www.amazon.com*
  • *www.ebay.com*
  • *www.costco.com*
  • *www.nextag.com*
  • *www.overstock.com*
  • *www.refurbdepot.com*
  • *www.shopping.com*
  • *www.ubid.com*

• **Cell phones…**
  • Find them at cell phone stores or at *www.ebay.com*.

*Click on "refurbished" or enter "refurbished" plus the product in the search window unless the site is just for refurbs. In most cases, you also can enter "refurbished" plus the brand in an Internet search engine.

Get Money for Your Old Cell Phone

Your old cell phone may be worth up to $200, depending on the model and on its condition. Sell it to firms that resell old phones elsewhere in the world or have other uses for them. Check CellforCash.com (800-503-8026)... OldCellPhone.com (888-877-1113)...or CashMyPhone.com.

Satellite TV Trap

Before you sign up for satellite TV, know the hidden costs. The price quoted usually covers just one TV set—you pay a separate monthly fee for each additional set. Determine the cost of connecting all the TVs in your home before signing anything.

Also: Because you may not be happy with satellite reception, sign up for as short a period as possible. And, make sure you understand what you must do to get out of your contract when the trial ends. For instance, the company could charge a hefty fee to retrieve its equipment if you cancel when the trial period is over.

Jack Gillis, director of public affairs for Consumer Federation of America, Washington, DC, *consumerfederation.org.*

Get Great Deals on Used Stuff on the Internet

Hillary Mendelsohn, author of *thepurplebook: The Definitive Guide to Exceptional Online Shopping* (Warner), an annual directory of the best shops found on the Internet. She also has a subscription Web site, *www.thepurplebook.com,* where you can find reviews from the most recent edition of *thepurplebook,* as well as customer-service ratings. Ms. Mendelsohn lives in Los Angeles.

Buying used items on-line is a great way to save money, often big money—in some cases as much as 80%. Lots of items, including golf clubs, home gyms, designer accessories, hand tools, books, CDs and musical instruments, can be purchased used from various Web sites. New technologies make it easier to compare prices between new and used items.

Used merchandise is often just as good as new, and many items are factory reconditioned—and many of these come with money-back guarantees (if you buy from the right seller).

RECONDITIONED/REFURBISHED

Factory-reconditioned or refurbished products are products that have been returned to the authorized factory service center and restored to meet all original manufacturer quality standards. Refurbishing may be as simple as replacing an electrical cord, or as major as replacing a hard drive on your computer. These products carry a manufacturer warranty that is as good as the warranty on the item if it were new, and are usually repackaged like new. They should also include the same accessories and manuals as would be included with new products.

You can buy refurbished items at savings up to 80% at RefurbDepot (*www.refurbdepot.com*). Here you can find items such as home theaters, portable digital music players, digital copiers, camcorders and power tools.

Hint: Not every type of refurbished item is a good bargain—especially computers, plasma TVs and certain appliances. For example, you can buy a new Dell Dimension 3000 desktop computer for about $400,* so why even consider buying refurbished? A similar refurbished desktop computer will cost about 15% less, but you probably won't get up-to-the-minute technology and cannot customize it to your exact specifications. Similarly, the newest technology in plasma screen TVs is much better than that of slightly older models—and prices are coming down all the time, so it pays to wait until a new model fits your budget. It may be tempting to look on-line for washers, dryers, dishwashers and refrigerators, but in many cases, newer models with higher energy efficiency will save you more money on monthly energy bills than the savings you could reap from the purchase price of a refurbished model. *Some good buys...*

•**Home gyms.** High-end workout equipment for the home is constructed so well that you can get terrific merchandise at bargain prices, with a

*Prices, rates and offers subject to change.

warranty. Lots of sites that sell new stuff have a used and reconditioned section as well. Try *www.gymcor.com* for treadmills, exercise bikes, elliptical cross trainers, rowing machines, etc. A reconditioned StairMaster Stepmill 7000PT costs $2,795 compared with $4,999 new, a savings of 44%.

•Hand tools. Check out factory-reconditioned tools, like those from top manufacturer Bosch, at *bosch.cpotools.com/reconditioned_tools.* A wide variety of tools, such as circular saws, belt sanders, routers and drills (corded and cordless) are featured for 20% to 30% less than the cost for new tools.

•Musical instruments. Secondhand instruments, both used and reconditioned, are a bargain at *www.musiciansbuyline.com,* where you can find violins, guitars, banjos, keyboards, drums —even pianos—and more.

•Boats. The Web site *www.iboats.com* offers more than 100,000 marine products at low prices, including used sailboats and reconditioned powerboats. Before purchasing a used or reconditioned boat, have it checked out by a qualified marine mechanic. Find one at the Society of Accredited Marine Surveyors, Inc. (800-344-9077 or *www.marinesurvey.org*).

•Photography equipment. At B&H Photo-Video (*www.bhphotovideo.com*) you can find used and reconditioned cameras, camera lenses, darkroom and video equipment, binoculars and more. This site's in-house service department (the company has a large bricks-and-mortar retail store in New York City) inspects every piece of used equipment and a warranty is included for each item.

WHAT TO BUY USED

Dramatic price savings make buying used (but not refurbished) worthwhile for certain items…

•Golf clubs. Deals on used drivers, woods, iron sets, individual irons, wedges and putters can be found at Callaway Golf Pre-Owned (*callawaygolfpreowned.com*), which, in addition to their own label, sells other brands, such as Titleist and TaylorMade. A set of Big Bertha 2004 irons in average condition costs as little as $400, versus $760 for the set when it was new.

•Designer accessories. You can get great discounts on formerly very pricey scarves, designer handbags, sunglasses and belts from such designers as Prada, Gucci and Ferragamo. Visit *www.luxuryvintage.com* where, for example, you can buy a $690 (when new) Gucci tote handbag for $388—a savings of 44%.

•Books. You can get today's best-selling books for 30% to 40% off the suggested retail price simply by going to the giant on-line retailer Amazon.com, which lists some used books alongside new ones. For much larger lists of used books, check Alibris (*www.alibris.com*), which lists more than 60 million used and out-of-print books. Abebooks at *www.abebooks.com* also lists approximately 60 million used and out-of-print books. At these Web sites you can also find rare old books and used textbooks.

•DVDs and CDs. You can buy a wide variety of movies and music CDs at *www.secondspin.com* for 30% to 50% off retail prices. Everything is backed by a 100% money-back guarantee if you receive a CD or DVD that is defective.

BUYING ON EBAY

eBay (*www.ebay.com*) is the world's largest Internet marketplace for the sale of used goods and may be the first site that comes to mind when you want to purchase something. There are sound reasons to buy here, as well as a reason to steer clear.

Advantages: eBay offers an incredible range of items—on an average day, there are millions of items offered on eBay. Buyers may purchase items in an auction format or at a fixed price through a feature called "Buy It Now."

Disadvantage: According to the Federal Trade Commission (FTC), the on-line auction format at eBay and some other sites can be shaky—complaints arise from late shipments, products that aren't the same as advertised, no shipments and bogus on-line payment and escrow services. Although eBay provides a limited fraud protection program, buying from the Internet sites of bricks-and-mortar stores provides a safer buying environment than buying from individuals.

Suggestion: Read the FTC guide to Internet auctions, free at *www.pueblo.gsa.gov/cic_text/computers/internet-auction/internet_auctions.htm.*

SHOPPING SAFELY ON THE INTERNET

•Look for the padlock icon to be in the locked position in the lower right-hand corner of your browser window. The padlock indicates that the site uses encryption technology to transfer information from your computer to the on-line merchant's computer. Never send your credit card number or bank account number via e-mail. If you must, break up the number into two messages so that hackers are less able to get your whole account number.

•**Verify the display of seals of approval.** Sites often suggest that they are reliable by displaying a credential from third-party firms in the form of seals of approval. Make sure these seals, such as those of the Better Business Bureau, actually link to the sponsoring organization.

•**Use a credit card for on-line buying.** If you're offered a choice, always pay with a credit card. *The Fair Credit Billing Act* protects your transaction—you can withhold payment of your credit card bill at least temporarily if there is a problem with the transaction.

•**Watch shipping charges carefully.** The price of items may be low, but sellers often charge you an arm and a leg for shipping.

•**Read the "fine print" warranty language.** Find out what it covers, how long the coverage lasts and where to send the product for repairs, a refund or replacement. Ideally, you want a warranty that covers the product for a relatively long time and offers repairs and/or replacements.

Luxuries For Less

Sue Goldstein, creator of The Underground Shopper, a multimedia outlet that includes a Dallas-area call-in radio program on shopping and an Internet shopping site, *www.undergroundshopper.com.*

High-quality goods are available now at discounts on the Internet. *My favorite sites for luxury items...*

•**Designer clothing and accessories.** Save at least 50%* on new and gently used designer products, including handbags, sunglasses, jeans, pants, tops, dresses, footwear and belts. Brands include Christian Dior, Fendi, Prada and Yves Saint Laurent. Rodeo Drive Resale, 888-697-3725, *www.rodeodriveresale.com.*

*Prices, rates and offers subject to change.

Recent special: A black Versace velvet zip-top tote with organizer sold for $489.99. Similar ones retail at Versace Boutiques for $800 to $1,000.

•**Gourmet coffees and teas.** Cavallini offers the same exotic blends used at five-star restaurants and resorts. 214-353-0328, *www.cavallini coffee.com.*

•**Linens.** Bedsheet.com sells high-thread-count sheets for up to 70% off retail prices. 800-965-5558, *www.bedsheet.com.*

Recent special: A queen-sized supima cotton sheet set with a 1,000-thread count, which typically retails for $499.99, went for $199.99, plus $39.99 for two pillow cases.

•**Skin-care products.** This company offers skin-care and cosmetic products that usually are available only at spas and doctors' offices. Popular lines include Babor, Bare Escentuals, Blinc and Cellex-C. 800-709-1865, *www.spalook.com.*

•**Jewelry.** Order reproductions of the jewelry worn by Hollywood starlets in legendary films. 800-788-5600, *www.thehollywoodcollection.com.*

Recent special: Vivien Leigh's Southern emerald earrings—synthetic green emerald earrings, each stone 1.03 carats, set in gold-plated sterling silver and surrounded by 10 cubic zirconia stones—for $60.

•**China, crystal and flatware.** Great prices on sterling silverware, stainless flatware, and silver home accessories, including such top brands as Lenox and Noritake. 800-426-3057, *www.silver superstore.com.*

Smarter Eyeglass Buying

Glasses in the $100 to $150 range often are made of more durable plastic or metal and hold their shape better than $75 frames. More expensive frames, priced at $200 or more, typically are not worth the money—you usually are paying extra for the style or designer name.

Melvin Schrier, OD, vision consultant and retired New York City optometrist, Rancho Palos Verdes, CA.

Get the Best Deal...and Help Charity

Browse the discounts, closeouts, giveaways, multiple rebates, coupon codes and in-store promotions at DealTaker.com. Visitors to the site trade links, information and other tips. There's a "Free Stuff" user forum, in which visitors share information about free magazine subscriptions, cosmetics, T-shirts, software, recipes and even long-distance phone cards. A portion of all proceeds from purchases made through these links is donated to breast cancer research.

Why Coupon Users End Up Spending More

People who use coupons spend an average of 8% more money than people who don't use coupons.

Possible reason: Coupon users often reward themselves for using coupons by purchasing luxury items.

Ambar Rao, PhD, Fossett Distinguished Professor of Marketing, Olin School of Business, Washington University, St. Louis, and leader of a study of people's spending patterns, published in *Journal of Marketing Research*.

Cut Spending by Bartering

Tom McDowell, executive director, National Association of Trade Exchanges, Mentor, OH.

The Internet has spawned electronic barter exchanges, making it easier than ever before to barter goods and services. If you're handy at making something that people want or can offer a service, you can avoid running up credit card charges and spending cash, and you can obtain items at discount prices.

Example: A piece of jewelry costs you $25 to make but has a market price of $75. Through barter you can trade it for an item worth $75—in effect, paying only $25 for it.

One can barter services (babysitting, pet care, photography, writing, etc.) as well as goods. So barter can be a great resource for a small home-based or sideline business.

One can also barter excess personal belongings—such as the accumulated contents of an attic or garage—and perhaps get much better terms than from selling them in a lawn sale.

Barter is possible through local groups, national exchanges or among friends and associates.

To learn more about barter or to find a barter group located near you, visit the Web site of the National Association of Trade Exchanges, *www.nate.org*, or phone them at 440-205-5378.

You can also find specialty barter exchanges on-line using a search engine. Enter the word "barter" and the name of the item you want to trade or acquire.

Caution: Bartering doesn't avoid income or sales taxes, which you still must pay.

Cheap and Easy Ways to Cut Home Energy Bills

Harvey Sachs, PhD, director of buildings program, The American Council for an Energy-Efficient Economy, Washington, DC, a nonprofit organization that promotes energy efficiency, *www.aceee.org*.

A typical home owner in the Northeast—where two-thirds of oil-heated homes are located—can expect huge increases in bills over last year. And, home owners who use natural gas will see an even bigger jump. Finally, electric bills are up as well.

What to do: You can easily shave hundreds of dollars off your energy bills this coming winter by taking a few no-cost and low-cost energy-saving steps.

SAVE ON HEATING BILLS

Furnace and fans...

•**Use ventilating fans in the kitchen,** bath and other areas prudently. In just one hour of use, they can pull out a houseful of warm air.

•**Check furnace filters monthly and clean or replace filters.** Dirty filters block airflow, increasing your energy bill and shortening the equipment's life.

•**Clean registers, baseboard heaters and radiators with a damp rag** or vacuum cleaner about once a month. Don't block them with furniture, carpeting or drapes—leave at least a few inches of space.

Thermostats…

•**Set your thermostats to the lowest comfortable level**—a good target is 65°F during the day and 60°F for sleeping.

•**Turn your thermostats down to 55°F in little-used rooms** if the system includes multiple zones.

•**Install a programmable thermostat** that you can set to lower the heat to 55°F when you are not at home.

Cost: About $35 to $100* for certified Energy Star (*www.energystar.gov*) models. (Energy Star is a government rating program—it shows which items are more efficient than typical models.)

Windows and doors…

•**If you have old single-pane windows, add storm windows.** They can decrease heat loss by 25% to 50%. For a quick, temporary fix, insulate your windows with plastic sheeting, sold for this purpose in home-supply or hardware stores, taped on the inside. Or replace single-pane windows with Energy Star–qualified windows. An Energy Star–qualified window has at least two panes and a low-emittance (Low-E) glass coating, and some have odorless, nontoxic gases, such as argon or krypton, between the panes to improve the insulating property of the window.

•**Seal up your windows and doors with weather stripping** if there are air leaks.

Ducts…

•**Use mastic (a gooey substance that will not degrade or shrink and is applied easily with a paintbrush) to seal seams and gaps** in all exposed ductwork in areas such as the attic, crawl space and basement. The mastic seals the joints and protects against warm air loss. If

*Prices subject to change.

your pipes are not already insulated, add preformed pipe insulation that can be cut to fit your hot water and steam pipes.

•**After sealing, insulate ducts** that are in the attic and crawl spaces. Duct-wrap insulation is available at home supply and hardware stores.

Other helpful things to do…

•**Keep draperies and shades on south-facing windows open** during the day, to admit solar heat, and closed at night to reduce heat loss and keep you from feeling chilly.

•**Keep the damper closed on your fireplace when not in use.** Use fireplaces sparingly—they suck heat from the house and send it up the chimney.

•**Consider buying a small electric space heater** that's approved by Underwriters Laboratories Inc. (*www.ul.com*)—with the UL symbol—to supplement inadequate heating in a room.

SAVE ON ELECTRIC BILLS

Appliances…

•**When using the washing machine and dishwasher, do only full loads.**

•**Clean out your dryer's lint filter after every load** to improve air circulation.

•**In the winter, circulate the warm air** that would otherwise stagnate at the ceiling, using a ceiling fan with the blades moving in reverse.

Lighting…

•**Energy for lighting accounts for about 10% of your electric bill.** Incandescent lightbulbs are out of date—95% of the power used to light them is wasted as heat (and they add unwanted heat to your home in the summer).

Substitute the five most used lightbulbs you have with Energy Star compact fluorescent bulbs. These are four times more efficient than incandescent bulbs and provide the same light levels. As other bulbs burn out, consider replacing them with compact fluorescents.

•**Use timers and motion detectors** on both indoor and outdoor lighting.

•**Maximize the power of daylight by keeping window shades and blinds open during the day,** and consider light wall colors to minimize the need for artificial lighting.

Water use…

•**Wash clothes in cold water.**

- **Take a quick shower instead of a bath.**
- **Install low-flow aerating showerheads,** which cut water use in half.
- **Check the temperature on your water heater**—it should be turned to "warm"—a thermometer held under running hot water should show a reading of no more than 120°F.
- **Hot-water tank insulation wrap costs about $20 and helps hold heat**—it will pay for itself in about one year. (This is not as important on very new, highly insulated models.)
- **Add preformed fiberglass pipe insulation to hot-water pipes** coming out of your water heater.
- **Turn off everything not being used**—lights, televisions, stereos, computers.

FREE COST-CUTTING GUIDE

The American Council for an Energy-Efficient Economy publishes the *Consumer Guide to Home Energy Savings* ($8.95), which includes tips, diagrams, charts and explanations on nearly every facet of home energy use—insulation, dish washing, laundry, cooking, heating and cooling, food storage, windows, lighting and more.

This guide also lists which investments in energy efficiency pay for themselves, which energy-saving products work and which are more hype than savings. Call 202-429-0063 to order or visit *www.aceee.org/consumerguide/mostenef.htm* for a free condensed on-line version.

New Ways To Cut Your Heating Costs

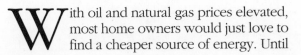

Amber Thurlo Pearson, biodiesel specialist, National Biodiesel Board, Jefferson City, MO, *www.biodiesel.org*.

Kirk Golden, president, Quality Solar Concepts, Rochester, NY, *www.solar4me.com*.

Heather Rhoads-Weaver, small-wind consultant for the American Wind Energy Association, *www.awea.org*, and founder of Seattle-based eFormative Options, LLC, which oversees renewable energy projects.

With oil and natural gas prices elevated, most home owners would just love to find a cheaper source of energy. Until now, alternatives were limited and expensive. That has changed, thanks to new technology. Rebates and federal/state tax credits also may be available. Check the Database of State Incentives for Renewable Energy (*www.dsireusa.org*) to find out.

Cutting-edge ways to save energy…

BIOFUEL
Amber Thurlo Pearson

How it works: A home owner uses a blend of heating oil and biodiesel, nontoxic fuel that's made from vegetable oils, such as soybean and canola. Biodiesel produces less soot and carbon monoxide than traditional oil.

Cost/savings: From six to eight cents* less a gallon than conventional heating oil. That is a savings of about 3%, based on current heating oil prices.

Additional savings: Biofuel acts like a detergent when it burns, unclogging heating units so that they run more efficiently, which means that you spend less on maintenance and service calls. Biofuel can be used without any modifications to an existing oil heating system.

Availability: For a list of biofuel distributors in your state, go to *www.biodiesel.org* (click on "Buying Biodiesel," then "Biodiesel Distributors Map") or call the National Biodiesel Board at 800-841-5849.

SOLAR HEATING
Kirk Golden

Solar heating systems can supplement your existing system. The more sunlight you have, the less you need to rely on conventional heating. Solar panels don't only generate electricity or heat water—they can heat rooms, too.

How it works: An eight-foot-high solar collector mounted on a south-facing exterior wall or your roof can generate 10,000 BTUs of energy. That is enough to comfortably heat 1,000 square feet as long as you have 15 minutes of sunlight per daylight hour.

The sun heats a plate on the panel, which in turn heats the air in a collector. An electrically powered fan blows the air from the collector into your home through ductwork or a portable vent.

*Prices and rates subject to change.

Cost/savings: A basic system with venting costs $2,500 installed, but federal and state tax credits can reduce that amount to about $1,500. The average home in the Northeast or Midwest can reduce its heating costs by 10% to 15%. Assuming it uses an average of 650 gallons of heating oil every winter, costs can be recouped in about 16 years at today's energy prices—more quickly if energy prices rise. Systems last up to 20 years.

Quality brands: Cansolair, 709-229-4387, *www. cansolair.com*...Your Solar Home, 866-556-5504, *www.yoursolarhome.com*.

HOME WIND TURBINES
Heather Rhoads-Weaver

How it works: A turbine that has four-foot blades is mounted on a 40- to 80-foot tower on your property. The turbine connects to your local utility's power grid. Wind power can sharply reduce a home's electrical usage, including electric heating and cooling costs.

Requirements: Your property must be big enough to include the free-standing or lattice-design steel tower. Your region must have an average wind speed of at least nine miles per hour. Residential wind turbines have been installed in almost every state, but most are in states with incentive programs, such as California, New York and Iowa. The local utility grid will maintain a constant energy supply to your home if the wind is not strong enough. Check state wind resource maps to find your area's wind potential—*www.eere.energy.gov/windand hydro,* click on "Wind Powering America," then on the map.

Cost: About $7,000, including the tower, plus $2,000 for installation.

Savings: One micro wind turbine generates about 3,000 kilowatts of electricity a year, one-third of the average home's demand. If your utility charges 15 to 20 cents per kilowatt hour, that's a savings of $450 to $600 per year, so you can recoup your cost in about 15 years.

Quality brands: Bergey Windpower, 405-364-4212, *www.bergey.com*...Southwest Windpower, 928-779-9463, *www.windenergy.com*...or browse a list from the American Wind Association, *www. awea.org/faq/smsyslst.html*.

Phone Company Tricks

Rate hikes hidden as fees are spreading from regular phone bills to cell phone and high-speed–Internet bills. The national cell phone service providers impose fees—with such names as "regulatory cost recovery fee" and "federal universal service fund fee"—which they claim are to recover the costs of complying with specific government rules, such as maintaining number portability for wireless phones. But the government does not require these separate fees, and companies can collect the money and use it as they like—so the fees are rate hikes in disguise.

Report on telecommunications fees by Center for Public Integrity, Washington, DC, *www.publicintegrity.org*.

Home Scam Alert

Scams related to home repair are more prevalent than ever. *Protect yourself from...*

●**Cut-rate chimney cleaning/repair companies** that offer low prices, then claim to find structural damage. Get a second opinion, preferably from a sweep certified by the Chimney Safety Institute of America (800-536-0118, *www. csia.org*), or consult with a masonry contractor or a home inspector. In some areas, the fire department will inspect a chimney for free.

●**Some basement-waterproofing companies** recommend expensive interior perimeter drainage systems. Look into less costly solutions, such as gutters that drain to a drywell, improved drains and landscape changes that direct water away from the house.

Danny Lipford, a contractor in Mobile, AL, and host of the syndicated TV program *Today's Homeowner with Danny Lipford.* He is a regular contributor to *The Early Show* on CBS.

Cut Health-Care Costs Now

David Nganele, PhD, president of DMN Healthcare Solutions, a health education company, 527 Third Ave., New York City 10016. He is a former product management executive for Pfizer Inc. and author of *The Best Healthcare for Less* (Wiley).

Medical costs are rising so fast that many patients are postponing treatments or tapping their retirement savings to pay the bills. Last year, half of all personal bankruptcies were due to serious illness—and most of those people *had* health insurance.

Great ways to save thousands of dollars each year on health care…

•Choose the right health insurance plan. Don't make the big mistake of focusing only on keeping monthly premiums down. Try to realistically factor in deductibles and co-payments. Many employers offer a choice of health insurance plans. *Here's a snapshot…*

•HMO. A *health maintenance organization* is best if you and your family generally don't have complex medical issues and mostly use general practitioners…you are satisfied with the selection of doctors in the plan's network…and/or you need a lot of routine care, such as checkups for young children.

•PPO. A *preferred provider organization* is best if you have a medical problem that requires you to see specialists…and/or your favorite doctors are out of network. PPOs cover non-network doctors, although co-payments and deductibles are higher than with HMOs.

•POS. A *point of service plan,* which combines features of HMOs and PPOs, is best if you and your family are healthy and need routine care but want the flexibility of going out of network. With a POS, you can see any doctor you want. Your share of the cost usually is a percentage of the total bill.

Resource: Planforyourhealth.com provides worksheets to help you "guesstimate" your future health-care spending and choose the insurance plan that fits you best.

•Think about a health savings account (HSA). Many large companies now offer HSAs, which combine a high-deductible ($1,050/year or more for individual coverage and $2,100 for family coverage in 2006; $1,100 and $2,200 respectively in 2007) and a low-premium health insurance plan for large hospital bills with a tax-free savings account for smaller medical costs, such as doctor visits.

HSA holders can contribute up to $2,700 a year ($5,450 for families) in 2006 and up to $2,850 and $5,650 respectively in 2007. Unused money can be carried over from year to year and invested where it can grow without being taxed.

An HSA is particularly good for older workers who want to accumulate money for postretirement health-care costs or for long-term-care insurance premiums. Self-employed people can write off health insurance premiums and HSA contributions as business expenses. For more information, check out IRS publication 969, *Health Savings Accounts and Other Tax-Favored Health Plans,* available from the IRS, 800-TAX-FORM, *www.irs.gov/publications.*

The deadline for establishing and contributing to an HSA is April 16, 2007 for 2006 and April 15, 2008 for 2007. For more information and a list of banks, brokerages and insurance companies that offer HSAs, contact HSA Insider at 202-558-2303, *www.hsainsider.com.*

•Get more out of your flexible spending account (FSA). With this employer-sponsored plan, you can choose to have up to $5,000 in pretax dollars deducted from your paycheck to reimburse you for out-of-pocket medical costs. Under new rules, your company can grant you two and a half months beyond the end of the year to use the money you set aside. The unused balances can't be carried over beyond that date —the money is forfeited.

Many people know that they can use FSAs for prescription drugs, but few realize all that it covers, including health insurance deductibles and co-payments…acupuncture…eyeglasses… contact lenses…flu shots…laser eye surgery… over-the-counter drugs, such as allergy medication…air conditioners/air purifiers (if prescribed by a doctor)…crutches…bandages…and certain cosmetic surgeries, such as breast reconstruction.

Important: Your plan may not cover all expenses that the IRS permits.

•Increase the odds that your insurance claims will be paid. An appeal can take two months or longer and disrupt your budgeting because you must pay out-of-pocket while you wait. Many patients don't bother fighting a denial if, say, only $350 of a $400 claim is reimbursed, but these costs add up. *My suggestions…*

•Use in-network providers as often as possible. It's difficult to predict how much your insurer will cover for a visit to an outside provider. Many plans say that 80% of such charges are covered—but, in fact, insurers pay 80% of what they consider "reasonable and customary." Most consumers don't have access to what insurers will pay, but you can request the figures from your insurer.

•If you go out of network, have your doctor's visit precertified by your insurer. Ask your doctor's office manager for the billing code for your particular exam, test and/or treatment. With this code, your insurer can better estimate how much it will reimburse. Or ask your doctor to agree to treat you on an AWIP (accept what insurance pays) basis.

•Review your doctor's invoice immediately. Make sure you received each treatment/test.

•**Keep track of medical expenses for a possible tax deduction.** You can deduct only those medical expenses that exceed 7.5% of your adjusted gross income. This may seem to be an unreachable amount, but the listing of allowable itemized medical deductions has now expanded. They include the transportation costs to and from medical facilities (for automobiles, the rate is 18 cents per mile in 2006 and 20 cents per mile in 2007)…home-improvement projects for medical purposes, such as lowering counters, adjusting electrical outlets, installing grab bars in bathrooms and grading exterior landscaping for easier access to the house…physician-advised weight-loss programs for obesity or hypertension…costs for alcohol- or drug-abuse treatment programs…and vasectomies.

For a complete list of deductible expenses, see IRS Publication 502, *Medical and Dental Expenses (Including the Health Coverage Tax Credit)*.

•**Watch out for hospital billing errors.** In my experience, the vast majority of hospital bills contain errors. *Self-defense…*

•Ask a family member to keep a log of your medications, procedures and specialists' appointments, including dates.

•Before leaving the hospital, request an itemized bill. Federal law requires that you receive one within 30 days of your request. Ask for explanations of vague terms such as "lab fees" or "miscellaneous

fees." Compare the bill to your log and the explanation of benefits (EOB) from your insurance company. If the hospital billing department doesn't correct discrepancies, speak to the patient ombudsman.

•Hire a professional medical claims advocate if your bill is very high and complex. You can find one in your area by contacting Medical Billing Advocates of America at 304-645-6389, *www.bill advocates.com*…or Alliance of Claims Assistance Professionals, 873 Brentwood Dr., West Chicago, Illinois 60185, *www.claims.org. Typical cost:* $30* or more an hour. Initial consultation is free.

*Price subject to change.

Give Your Medical Bills A Checkup

Charles B. Inlander, a health-care consultant and president of the nonprofit People's Medical Society, a consumer health advocacy group in Allentown, PA. He is the author of more than 20 books on consumer health issues, including *Take This Book to the Hospital with You: A Consumer Guide to Surviving Your Hospital Stay* (St. Martin's).

My mother-in-law recently spent 20 days in the hospital with a near-fatal bout of pneumonia.

Her bill was more than $30,000. Although the hospital had billed her insurers directly, when she checked out, I insisted that we be given a fully itemized hospital bill—one that listed *every single charge*. After reviewing the bill, I discovered at least $3,000 worth of questionable charges. I called the hospital's billing office and challenged the bill. It was changed. I'm still waiting to see if Medicare and my mother-in-law's supplemental insurer got the correct bill.

Companies that review hospital bills report finding errors in at least 80% of them. Not surprisingly, most errors favor the hospital or doctor. Hospitals are not the only culprits. If you receive a medical bill for a visit to your doctor or an outpatient surgical procedure, chances are good it is incorrect. And don't assume that it's only your health insurer's problem. These errors contribute to skyrocketing health-care costs that are passed on to *you* in the form of higher insurance rates and out-of-pocket costs. *Most common errors to watch for…*

•Double billing. Getting charged twice for the same service, product or medication is by far the most common error in both doctor office and hospital bills. This can happen because a nurse or doctor writes the same thing twice on a record or a clerk hits the wrong computer key.

•Up-coding. This frequently happens in hospitals when the charge for a lower-cost service is shifted to one that costs more. For example, you are charged for the brand-name medication when you were given a generic drug.

•Unbundling. This happens when a doctor performs just one procedure but charges for two separate ones. A dermatologist did this when my father had two small growths removed from his forehead. The doctor snipped both of them off in less than 30 seconds. When we got the Medicare benefit explanation, he had charged the government $400 for the two separate surgeries. What he did was illegal, and we reported him to the federal government. In such cases, doctors can be dropped by their insurance companies and Medicare—and lose their licenses.

•Services never rendered. Frequently, doctors and hospital personnel order a medical service and then decide against it—but they fail to correct the record. If you are hospitalized, you can guard against this by asking for a daily bill.

To protect yourself against these errors, question any billing that you think may be wrong. If the doctor or hospital ignores your inquiry, contact the fraud department of your insurance company to report the problem. If you are a Medicare beneficiary, call 800-633-4227 and say that you want to report a billing problem. Both the insurer and Medicare will look into it. If you suspect major fraud, contact your state's attorney general's office to report it.

How to Save Big on Drugs

Rebecca Shannonhouse, editor of *BottomLine/Health*, Boardroom Inc., 281 Tresser Blvd., Stamford, CT 06901.

Americans spend an average of $885 on their prescription and over-the-counter (OTC) medications annually. But when it comes to cost, you have more options than you might think.

Example: An average daily dose of the popular cholesterol-lowering statin Lipitor costs about $98* per month. *Lovastatin*, a generic of the statin Mevacor that is used in lower-risk patients, is available for $37 a month.

The next time your doctor writes you a prescription, be sure to ask the right questions to save money, advises Diane Nitzki-George, RPh, clinical pharmacist in Evanston, Illinois, and author of *Generic Alternatives to Prescription Drugs* (Basic Health)…

•Is a generic available? On average, generics, which have the same active ingredients as brand-name drugs, cost 52% less.

•Is there a cheaper medicine in the same class? The newest—and most expensive—drugs sometimes represent a significant advance over older medications in the same chemical class. But many people do just as well with the older, less-expensive medications.

Or physicians may prescribe expensive drugs that are more convenient for patients to take.

Example: The blood pressure drug Toprol-XL (about $65 per month) is taken only once per day, while the generic version, *metoprolol* ($10 per month), is taken twice a day.

Finally, ask your health insurer if a prescribed drug is listed in its formulary, the list of drugs covered by an insurance plan. Patients usually must pay full price for medications that do not appear on the formulary.

*Prices subject to change. For more on cost-saving generic drugs, go to the FDA's Web site at *www.fda.gov/cder/consumerinfo/generic_text.htm*.

Save Hundreds of Dollars Buying Drugs On-Line

Rick Melcher, RPh, a registered pharmacist in Yakima, WA, and coauthor of *Smart Buys Drug-Wise* (Harbor). The publisher's Web site, *www.smartbuysdrugwise.com*, is updated monthly with the latest information on drug recalls, new generic products, etc.

Internet pharmacies can provide big savings for people who require prescription drugs. Prices average 18% less than even discount retail store prices. For some drugs, the savings are as high as 45%.

How it works: A patient orders a drug on-line. The patient or his/her doctor sends a written prescription to the Internet pharmacy. The pharmacist reviews and fills the prescription, which then is shipped through the mail.

Many over-the-counter products are available at Internet pharmacies, too. Most Internet pharmacies also accept phone orders if you do not have computer access...or you can go to your library and use the computer there.

Both the convenience and savings of Internet pharmacies have led many patients to abandon brick-and-mortar stores—but you have to make sure the pharmacy is reputable and shop wisely to get the best deals. *Here's how...*

•**Look for the VIPPS seal.** Internet pharmacies that advertise themselves as Verified Internet Pharmacy Practice Sites (VIPPS) have been inspected by the National Association of Boards of Pharmacy (NABP). NABP evaluates participating pharmacies on the quality and consistency of their procedures.

Caution: Some unscrupulous Internet companies display the VIPPS seal even though they haven't been inspected. Check out a company's status at *www.nabp.net.* Some reputable pharmacies, such as AARP's and Costco's, are not VIPPS members—be sure you are familiar with the company's reputation.

•**Check insurance participation.** Most Internet pharmacies work with a limited number of insurance companies. Some bill the insurers directly...others do not. You can find this information on the pharmacy Web sites, or call your insurance company to find out which, if any, Internet pharmacies are part of its network.

•**Figure in extra costs.** Some Internet pharmacies offer free shipping for standard ground delivery. This usually takes two weeks, so order well in advance. Fees for overnight delivery can be high.

A few Internet pharmacies, such as AARP's, charge patients annual membership fees. If you need many prescriptions over a year, the savings can more than offset the extra fee.

•**Buy in bulk.** Some insurance companies allow people to get a three-month supply of medication for a single co-payment when they order from Internet pharmacies, cutting costs by 67%.

Patients also can save by buying up to a year's supply at a time.

Example: One woman ordered a year's worth of the thyroid hormone *levothyroxine.* She skipped her insurance company entirely—and still saved $80. In addition, some pharmacies offer free shipping on big orders.

•**Pick a company that has a "live" pharmacist.** Avoid any Web-based pharmacies that don't provide customer support. Look for one that has a pharmacist available to answer questions, either via e-mail or telephone.

•**Ask a pharmacist.** Some drugs, such as the anticoagulant *warfarin* and the heart drug *digoxin,* are sensitive to extremes in temperature and so can degrade while they're in the mail. Ask the Internet pharmacist whether your medications can withstand all the rigors of mail travel before ordering on the Internet.

Take the Savvy Consumer Quiz

Elisabeth Leamy, an Emmy Award–winning television investigative reporter in Washington, DC. She is author of *The Savvy Consumer: How to Avoid Scams and Rip-Offs That Cost You Time and Money* (Capital). For more quizzes, visit *www.thesavvyconsumer.com.*

As a TV investigative reporter, I see even smart people being ripped off for thousands of dollars every day.

To avoid being a target, be the hunter, *not* the hunted. Ignore any company that pursues you too aggressively—the contractor who knocks on your door claiming to be working on other houses in the neighborhood...the broker who cold-calls you with must-own stocks...the carpet cleaner who sends you a coupon offering steep discounts. Always conduct your own research first, then hire someone that you have sought out.

To test just how knowledgeable you are as a consumer, take my quiz. *Answer true or false...*

•**If your home-improvement contractor rips you off or does shoddy work, some states will pay you back.**

True. Many states have "construction recovery" or "contractor's guaranty" funds that reimburse consumers for as much as $50,000 or more. The fund covers general contractors, plumbers, electricians, etc. Check with the state board of contractors or department of licensing to see if such a fund is available.

Important: To be eligible for a reimbursement, you must have hired a contractor who is licensed in your state. (Thirty-six states require contractors to be licensed, and nearly all states license plumbers and electricians.)

You can present your case yourself at a formal hearing and be reimbursed by your state in as little as 60 days.

Helpful evidence: Photos of shoddy work and an inspector's report.

To avoid unlicensed contractors, know the warning signs...

•An unmarked vehicle. Most states require license numbers to appear on vehicles, estimates and advertising.

•The only contact information for him/her is through a post office box, a pager or an answering service, instead of a permanent street address.

•He has a "business" or "occupancy" license, not a contractor's license. A business license is not proof of competency and requires no testing or apprenticeships. An occupancy license is for zoning—it simply grants permission to conduct a certain type of business at a particular address.

•If you receive unsolicited merchandise in the mail, you are legally obligated to send back the product or pay for it.

False. Federal law makes it illegal for companies to send you something that you didn't order and then bill you for it. You are allowed to keep the item as a gift, give it away or throw it out. *Other steps to take...*

•Send a certified letter to the company notifying it that you have received unwanted merchandise and will not be burdened with the time and expense of returning it. While you are not required by law to send such a letter, by doing so you establish a paper trail in case the company ever tries to come after you with collection notices.

•If it does appear that you received a product through an honest error—such as a customer mix-up at a legitimate merchant—write or e-mail the seller saying that you're giving it a reasonable

amount of time (15 to 30 days) to send a courier to pick up the product or else you reserve the right to keep it. If you receive a bill for the item, contact your local US Postal Inspector's office to report the company.

•A coupon to clean four rooms of carpeting for $29.95 is a good deal.

False. Based on all my investigations of carpet cleaners, initial low prices with these common come-ons always are followed by hefty "upcharges." Typically, you'll be charged extra for pretreatment solutions, deodorizers and protective spray...moving furniture...and cleaning carpeting in closets. *To avoid rip-offs...*

•Use a reputable carpet cleaner. These companies tend to charge by the square foot, not the room. You also may want to hire a cleaning contractor that uses truck-mounted equipment, which is more powerful than the self-contained equipment used by cut-rate carpet cleaners.

•To find a reputable carpet cleaner in your area, contact the Institute of Inspection, Cleaning and Restoration Certification at 800-835-4624 or *www.iicrc.org.*

•When you get an unwanted telemarketing pitch, you should say, "Take me off your list."

False. That request has no legal teeth. *Better...*

•Ask the telemarketer to put you on the company's "do-not-call" list. Laws require telemarketers to maintain and honor such lists.

•Have your home and cell phone numbers put on three do-not-call lists—The Direct Marketing Association list, 212-768-7277, *www.thedma. org*...your state's registry (contact your state consumer protection agency office to find out if your state has one)...the FTC's National Do Not Call Registry, 888-382-1222, *www.donotcall.gov.*

•Parking-garage time clocks are accurate.

False. When I investigated parking garages around Washington, DC, I discovered that 75% of them skewed their clocks in their favor by at least six minutes.

Typical result: A customer checks in, returning just before an hour has elapsed, only to be charged for some or all of the second hour.

To avoid rip-offs...

•Make a note of the time on your own watch as you enter and exit, and show the attendant. It doesn't matter whether the garage clocks match yours. What matters is the time elapsed.

•If there is any discrepancy, complain and threaten to contact the department of consumer affairs in your city or town. Most garages will back down rather than risk having an official complaint lodged against them.

•You can improve or repair your credit score within 24 to 72 hours.

True. While the credit repair industry is riddled with scams, "rapid rescoring" is a legitimate service offered by local credit bureaus when you apply for a home loan.

How it works: Rescorers work directly with the three major credit bureaus. Not only will they correct errors on your credit report, they restructure your debt in ways that boost your credit score.

Cost: About $200.* This might seem high, but by raising your credit score, you often can qualify for a lower mortgage rate and save thousands.

How it might work: A rescorer notices that you have three credit cards. One is near its limit, while you hardly use the other two at all. By transferring some debt to the underused cards, you improve your score by 5%. Why would this be? Scoring models are biased against consumers who are near any of their credit limits.

If you want assistance from a rapid rescorer, ask your mortgage broker or lender to refer you to one—rapid rescoring firms don't work directly with consumers. If you get an unsolicited offer for overnight credit repair, it's a scam.

*Price subject to change.

Getting Through to A Customer Service Rep

Paul English, cofounder and chief technical officer of the travel Web site Kayak.com, Concord, MA. Out of frustration, Mr. English published on his Web log ("blog") a dozen bypass codes he figured out by trial and error. The rest of them came from other disgruntled individuals. You can view his list at *www.paulenglish.com*. He is a former vice president of software giant Intuit.

It is becoming harder and harder to reach live phone representatives at companies. In fact, almost 40% of the phone calls to customer service operations now are handled by interactive voice response (IVR) systems that lead callers through all those annoying, time-consuming series of keypunch menus—"So that we may better serve you, please press or say 'one' for…"

There is an escape from this maze. I have compiled a list of shortcuts for major consumer companies that allow you to bypass the electronic technology and speak with a human being right away.

GENERAL STRATEGIES

•Avoid pressing 0 to get an operator. Callers try this so frequently that many companies have eliminated the option. In fact, hitting 0 just once is likely to send you right back to the beginning of the main menu or in some instances will disconnect the call.

If you want to try guessing at a shortcut, do the following…

•Try hitting 0# or 0* on your phone keypad.

•Press the menu options for opening or canceling an account, such as "sales" or "new service." A human always seems to answer these options promptly. Then ask to be transferred to the department you need.

•Press nothing. The IVR system will think you are calling from a rotary phone and may transfer you to a live person.

•Ask for the secret code when you reach a customer service rep. Tell him/her, "I'm a loyal but very busy customer. Is there a way I can navigate your menu to reach a live person directly?"

Also ask about unpublicized toll-free numbers that the company might have that will connect you to an operator immediately.

•Make sure you are not being charged for speaking with a live person. Some companies, including Wells Fargo bank and the banking and financial holding company KeyCorp, charge some customers between $1 and $2 if they talk to an agent more than a set number of times in a month. Most airlines charge $5 to $10 to make a reservation over the phone with a customer service rep rather than on the Internet. Usually, you will be notified about the charge up front, but be sure to ask.

12

Worry-Free Retirement

Top 10 Places to Retire

When choosing a place to retire, it is easy to neglect features of a town that might not seem immediately important but that could be significant later on. In my studies of retirees, I have discovered that the happiest ones nearly always live in areas with certain characteristics in regard to climate, community services, crime rate, cost of living, cultural and educational activities, employment and volunteer opportunities, health care, landscape, recreational activities, retail services and transportation. *Based on these criteria, here are 10 of the leading cities for retirement, selected to represent different geographical areas...*

PORTLAND, OREGON

The Portland metropolitan area has a population of about 1.95 million, but the city often seems much smaller because of its uncongested downtown and its beautiful residential neighborhoods. Many retirees are also attracted to the city because of its excellent public transportation and medical facilities.

Apart from a wide range of cultural and recreational activities, Portland has first-rate basketball and hockey teams, making it a great town for sports fans.

Located between two mountain ranges in the Willamette Valley, Portland averages only about 36 inches of rain a year, far less than the deluge that many newcomers might expect. Temperatures vary from an average daily high of 46°F in January to 81°F in August.

A house in an upscale neighborhood near public transportation typically costs about $350,000,* and retiree living costs are slightly above the national average.

Smaller houses and those in less fashionable neighborhoods are, of course, less expensive, as are condominiums.

*Prices subject to change.

Warren R. Bland, PhD, professor of geography, California State University at Northridge, and author of *Retire in Style: 60 Outstanding Places Across the USA and Canada* (Next Decade). Professor Bland intends to retire this year to Ithaca, NY.

Information: Portland Oregon Visitors Association, 800-962-3700, *www.pova.com.*

BOULDER, COLORADO

Unlike many other US cities, Boulder has a low-crime downtown area where people stroll among upscale shops, street markets and restaurants. Parking is easy, and there's little traffic congestion.

Recreational opportunities include skiing and nature hiking, and the University of Colorado provides an abundance of cultural activities for this city of just over 100,000 residents. Boulder is only 35 miles from Denver, where a major airport and Amtrak trains make it easy to reach other parts of the country.

The city gets about 83 inches of snow a year, but temperatures are surprisingly mild. In January, the daily high averages about 45°F, and in July, it's 88°F.

Drawback: Boulder is expensive. A house suitable for a retired couple can easily cost $500,000, and the cost of living is about 20% above the US average.

Information: Boulder, Colorado Convention and Visitors Bureau, 800-444-0447, *www.boulder coloradousa.com.*

ASHEVILLE, NORTH CAROLINA

Located on a 2,100-foot-high plateau near the Blue Ridge Mountains, Asheville is a sophisticated city that has attracted retirees for many decades. The city, which has about 70,000 residents, provides excellent health care, shopping and entertainment, and a wide variety of outdoor activities.

Using a variety of data, I estimate that the cost of living in Asheville is near the national average. A three-bedroom, 1,800-square-foot house in great condition in an upscale neighborhood costs about $275,000.

Many Northerners enjoy Asheville because it has the familiar four seasons but without the bitter cold. Southerners like the city because summers are not oppressively hot. In January, the average daily high is 47°F, and in July, it's 83°F.

Drawback: To fly from Asheville to many major cities, you must transfer in Atlanta or take a plane at the Greenville-Spartanburg International Airport in South Carolina, which is about 50 miles away.

Information: City of Asheville, 828-251-1122, *www.ci.asheville.nc.us.*

SAN ANTONIO, TEXAS

This riverside city of 1.8 million has first-class health care, and there's excellent transportation within the city and to other regions of the country, including Amtrak routes to Chicago, Los Angeles and points in Florida.

Retirees are attracted to San Antonio's upbeat rhythm and friendly people. Its vibrant Mexican heritage is reflected in local restaurants and music festivals in many of San Antonio's cultural centers, including the San Antonio Museum of Art.

The city is a bargain. The cost of living is 7% below the national average, and houses suitable for retired couples cost about $200,000.

Drawbacks: Temperatures climb to 90°F or more on an average of 116 days a year. Air pollution in the summer can be a problem for people with respiratory ailments.

Information: San Antonio Convention and Visitors Bureau, 800-447-3372, *www.sanantonio cvb.com.*

VICTORIA, BRITISH COLUMBIA

Just across the border on Vancouver Island, off Canada's west coast, Victoria is a sophisticated city with excellent museums, theater and recreation opportunities. Three colleges in the area provide a wide variety of cultural activities.

Nearby mountain ranges act as a barrier to rain clouds, so Victoria averages only 30 inches of rain a year. The average high temperature is 44°F in winter and 70°F in summer. The greater metropolitan area has a population of approximately 325,000.

Drawbacks: The cost of living is about 20% above the average for North America. A three-bedroom house located in an upscale neighborhood typically costs about $400,000.

Information: City of Victoria, 250-385-5711, *www.city.victoria.bc.ca.*

TALLAHASSEE, FLORIDA

The capital of Florida is only 30 miles from the Gulf of Mexico, but is high enough above sea level to protect it from flooding in the event of a hurricane.

Population 151,000, Tallahassee combines old Southern charm with a variety of cultural and recreational activities at Florida State University. Tallahassee also has excellent health-care facilities. Its cost of living is near the national average. The typical price of a three-bedroom house is as low as $200,000.

Information: Tallahassee Visitor's Guide, 800-628-2866, *www.seetallahassee.com.*

More from Warren Bland, PhD...

Four Lesser-Known Great Cities

Below are some frequently overlooked cities that are wonderful places to live for retirees…

BLOOMINGTON, INDIANA

Located in the rolling hills of southern Indiana, Bloomington is the epitome of a university town—in this case, Indiana University. Retirees like the city's many outdoor activities and cultural and athletic events.

Population: 70,000.

Cost of living: About 5% below the national average.

Housing: An upscale house costs as little as $200,000.

Information: City of Bloomington, 812-349-3400, *www.bloomington.in.gov.*

THOMASVILLE, GEORGIA

Retirees are rediscovering this southern Georgia city. They like its antebellum charm, outdoor activities, downtown boutiques and architectural remnants of the late 19th century. It has first-rate health-care facilities.

Population: 18,000.

Cost of living: About 10% below the national average.

Housing: The three-bedroom homes start at about $150,000.

Information: Thomasville/Thomas County Conventions & Visitors Bureau, 866-577-3600, *www.thomasvillega.com.*

ITHACA, NEW YORK

Sure, it's cold in the winter, but the city offers lots to compensate for the climate. Ithaca is located at the south end of Cayuga Lake and close to scenic mountains. Cornell University and Ithaca College provide many free and low-cost activities, including theater, concerts and classes.

Population: 30,000.

Cost of living: Just above the national average.

Housing: An upscale house typically costs $275,000.

Information: City of Ithaca at 800-284-8422 or *www.ci.ithaca.ny.us.*

BURLINGTON, VERMONT

Situated on the shore of Lake Champlain with the Green Mountains in the background, Burlington offers many outdoor activities as well as the boutiques, cafés and craft vendors at the Church Street Marketplace. And, health-care facilities are excellent.

Population: 40,000.

Cost of living: About 12% above the national average.

Housing: About $300,000 in an upscale area.

Information: City of Burlington at 802-865-7000 or *www.ci.burlington.vt.us.*

Wonderful New Options In Retirement Living

David Savageau, the author of *Retirement Places Rated: What You Need to Know to Plan the Retirement You Deserve* (Wiley). Mr. Savageau has researched retirement locales since 1982 and is a consultant on the subject to many organizations, including the US State Department. He lives in Washington, DC.

When Americans looked for retirement locales a few years back, they often put a high priority on sunny beaches, line dancing and buffet dinners. Those are still fun, but today's retirees are more demanding.

Many people at or near retirement age now look for towns with exciting culture and a sense of history—places that are a short walk or quick drive from arts centers, vibrant college communities, top-quality entertainment and, not incidentally, medical facilities. Climate still matters, of course, but so does an opportunity to make interesting friends.

If these objectives are important to you, take a close look at some of the best retirement options today…

COLLEGE TOWNS

They might sound like the last places that people over age 50 should consider, but college towns actually have many features that today's retirees are seeking.

Examples: Top-notch medical facilities, big libraries, many cultural organizations, concerts, sporting events and art galleries.

The property market is another big plus. The steady turnover of faculty, students and staff usually makes it easy to find a residence to buy or rent. Many retirees in college towns supplement their incomes by renting rooms to students and faculty.

Among the very best college towns for retirees are Austin (University of Texas), Boulder (University of Colorado), Charlottesville (University of Virginia), Iowa City (The University of Iowa) and the areas surrounding Medford and Ashland (Southern Oregon University).

In addition to chambers of commerce and real estate agents, details on college towns are usually available from the universities themselves. If you contact a university, ask whether it has services specifically designed to help retirees, as many now do.

Example: The North Carolina Center for Creative Retirement in Asheville (828-251-6140, *www.unca.edu/ncccr*), which offers a program that encourages seniors to continue learning and to share their knowledge with the community.

BLUE-COLLAR TOWNS

Though college towns have big advantages, some areas once associated mainly with blue-collar industries are also attracting retirees who enjoy the small-town atmosphere and affordable housing.

Example: Wenatchee, Washington, a town of about 30,000, is located in a beautiful apple-growing region and for many decades has been home to an aluminum factory. Today, there's also an emerging wine industry.

Retirees are especially attracted to Wenatchee's sunny weather, turn-of-the-century architecture and newly invigorated cultural life.

Information: 509-664-3300, *www.cityofwen atchee.com.*

Other working-class towns that are attracting retirees include both Hamilton, Montana (406-363-2101, *www.cityofhamilton.net*), and Berkeley Springs, West Virginia (800-447-8797, *www.berke leysprings.com*).

Hamilton was originally a mining and farming community. Today, it's attracting residents who like its beautiful mountain scenery and recreational opportunities that include fishing, hiking and hunting.

In the West Virginia mountains, light manufacturing and mining are often the major industries. Berkeley Springs, however, has one of the country's oldest warm-spring spas, which today is the center of a growing community with a theater and live music events.

NEW URBAN VILLAGES

While some retirees like big cities, the demand for a small-town lifestyle is so great that developers are creating "new urban villages" all over the country.

Celebration, Florida, founded in 1994 by The Celebration Company, a subsidiary of Disney, is the best known, but about 650 others have been built or are in the planning phases. Most have fewer than 5,000 residents.

Often designed to look like American towns of a century ago, new urban villages are typically built around a downtown with shops, restaurants, offices, schools, theaters, medical centers, religious organizations and nearby recreation facilities.

Many communities have features designed to attract retirees, such as apartment buildings with elevators and houses with bedrooms on the first floor. Most of the houses are within a 15-minute walk of the downtown area, but public transportation is available in nearly all communities.

Among the most popular of the new urban villages…

•**Celebration, Florida** (407-566-1200, *www. celebrationfl.com*).

•**Fairview Village, Oregon** (503-669-9125, *www.fairviewvillage.com*).

•**Kentlands, Gaithersburg, Maryland** (301-926-6636, *www.kentlandsusa.com*).

•**Stapleton in Denver** (303-355-9600, *www. stapletondenver.com*).

NORCs

Naturally occurring retirement communities—NORCs, for short—is a term that urban planners and government officials often use to describe downtown areas that are home to a growing number of retirees.

Some of these retirees have lived in their apartments or townhouses for many years, sticking it out despite urban decay, which, in many cases, has been replaced by a beautiful urban renewal.

Still other retirees have recently moved into downtown areas, often after cities encouraged developers to convert unused office buildings into residences for retirees and gave financial incentives to restaurants, supermarkets and other resident-friendly businesses to move in.

Today, friendly and thriving NORCs can be found in nearly all major cities.

Examples: Lincoln Square, a grouping of about 14 apartment buildings on the west side of Manhattan, and the Cleveland Park neighborhood of Washington, DC, where a growing number of retirees take advantage of nearby restaurants, a library, movie theater, supermarket, upscale shops and easy access to the city's subway system.

Disadvantages of NORCs can include higher rent or condominium prices than those in suburbs or traditional retirement communities. High crime rates do, of course, persist in some urban areas.

Some municipalities, such as New York and Chicago, provide NORC residents with free services that can include on-site health counseling and transportation.

To find more NORCs, contact mayors' offices, chambers of commerce or real estate agents in the towns you're considering for retirement. Though the NORC acronym still is not widely known to the general public, most urban real estate agents are familiar with it.

UNLIKELY COUNTRIES

Costa Rica, Belize and Mexico are still popular foreign retirement destinations for Americans, but so are some countries that weren't on many retirees' lists until very recently—Bolivia, Croatia, Thailand, Turkey and Uruguay.

They all provide temperate climates, low-cost housing and the excitement of exploring new cultures. In many parts of Bolivia, for instance, a retiree might pay less than $500 a month to rent a modern two-bedroom house in a quiet and safe neighborhood.

You can often cut expenses by living overseas, but don't overlook the trade-offs. Medicare, for example, doesn't normally pay for health care outside the US. And what you save on housing might not compensate for the additional cost of airfare to make visits to the States.

There's also no guarantee that prices won't rise once the local economy improves, as it has in Ireland.

There are tax considerations, as well. You don't lose your obligation to pay US taxes just because you live in another country. But, under some circumstances, overseas residents can exclude foreign earned income from being taxed by the IRS (up to $85,700 in 2007). The rules are tricky, so consult your tax accountant.

Smart: Before considering a move overseas, contact a US expatriate organization, which can be found through the US embassy in the country you're considering.

Embassies can be located at *usembassy.state.gov* or by calling 202-647-4000.

Expatriate groups can generally recommend real estate agents and relocation firms that don't take advantage of Americans who might be unfamiliar with local markets, laws or customs.

Helpful: International Living, a Web-based company that offers information on living and buying property overseas at *www.internationalliving.com.*

More from David Savageau...

City and Town Resources

For more information on retirement cities and towns, see the resources below...

•**More details on college towns** are available at *www.collegetownlife.com*, a noncommercial Web site that compiles data and resources on college towns.

•**For information on US cities,** visit *www.citydata.com.*

•**For a list of urban villages in the US,** go to *www.newurbannews.com.* The Web site of the publication *New Towns* (*www.tndtownpaper.com*) is also a great resource for information on urban villages.

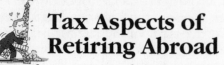

Tax Aspects of Retiring Abroad

Even if you retire to a foreign country and reside there all 365 days of a calendar year, you can't escape US income taxes for that year.

As long as you remain a US citizen, you are liable for taxes on all of your worldwide income.

Moreover, while there is a "foreign income exclusion" that can protect the first $85,700 of income earned abroad in 2007 from taxes, this applies only to wages and earned income, not retirement income.

Saver: This does not mean that your retirement income will be double taxed by the IRS and the foreign country. The US has tax treaties with many foreign nations that set specific negotiated rules for taxing persons who are subject to tax by both. These rules could be favorable for you.

Details: See IRS Publication 54, *Tax Guide for US Citizens and Resident Aliens Abroad.*

Lawrence Berland, CPA, partner, Mahoney Cohen & Company, CPA, PC, 1065 Avenue of the Americas, New York City 10018.

The Biggest Mistakes Seniors Make with Their Money Can Be Avoided

William G. Brennan, CPA/PFS, CFP, principal, Capital Management Group, LLC, a wealth management firm for high-net-worth individuals and families, 1730 Rhode Island Ave. NW, Washington, DC 20036.

Even the smartest people can run into trouble managing their finances. *Serious mistakes can be hazardous to your wealth…*

Mistake: **Becoming too conservative.** Seniors may feel that they must quickly shift their investment portfolio from stocks to bonds and other income-oriented instruments.

Reality: At age 60 or 65, your investment portfolio might have to last for 30 or 40 years, or even longer. Married couples, in particular, face the probability that at least one spouse will live for many years.

Over long periods, stocks have outperformed bonds, and that probably will be true in the future. Giving up on stocks can mean crimping your future lifestyle.

Strategy: Early in retirement, the best portfolio is a blended one that includes a large portion of stocks or stock funds.

With an average risk tolerance, a 60-40 split, stocks to bonds, might be appropriate. As you grow older, gradually tilt your portfolio toward bonds and other fixed-income investments to reduce the risk of incurring heavy stock market losses that you won't be able to make up. A retiree with a 60% allocation to stocks at age 65 might drop that to 55% by age 70, 50% at 75, etc.

Mistake: **Tapping retirement accounts too soon.** Many people start to withdraw funds from their IRAs and other retirement plans as soon as they retire.

Trap: Such withdrawals will reduce the tax-deferred growth enjoyed with a retirement plan. Also, withdrawals before age 59½ may be subject to a 10% penalty tax.

Strategy: Assuming that you have enough other assets to leave your retirement account in place, tap taxable accounts for spending money throughout the year. In November or December, once you can project your taxable income (and tax bracket) for the entire year, take low-taxed withdrawals, if possible.

Example: At year-end, your tax pro tells you that you can withdraw $10,000 from your IRA this year and remain in the 15% federal tax bracket. You should take the money out at the 15% rate, because future withdrawals may be taxed at higher rates, depending on your personal circumstances and changes in tax law.

This strategy can be repeated each year (after you turn 59½ and the 10% penalty no longer applies). After you pass age 70½, though, you'll have to take minimum withdrawals from most retirement accounts to avoid a 50% penalty.

Mistake: **Ignoring Roth IRA conversion opportunities.** In any year that your modified adjusted gross income (MAGI) is no more than $100,000 on a single or joint return, you can convert all or part of a traditional IRA to a Roth IRA (in 2010 only, the MAGI limit will not apply).

Advantages: After five years, all withdrawals will be tax free, assuming that you're at least

59½ years old. (Contributions can be withdrawn tax free at any time.) Also, there are no minimum required withdrawals from Roth IRAs.

Trap: Some seniors fear Roth IRA conversions because they think a total conversion is necessary, which will require a large tax payment to gain eventual tax-free distributions and/or relief from required distributions. In fact, partial conversions are allowed.

Situation: Len Johnson has $200,000 in a traditional IRA. His MAGI (before any conversion) is less than $100,000, so he's eligible for a Roth IRA conversion.

However, converting Len's entire IRA would generate $200,000 in additional taxable income and cost him around $66,000 in tax, assuming a 33% effective rate. Len does not have $66,000 in cash, so he chooses not to convert.

Strategy: Len can do partial conversions, year after year, as long as his AGI does not exceed $100,000.

Example: Len converts $40,000 of his traditional IRA to a Roth IRA each year. Even if he still owes tax at 28%, that would be an annual tax obligation of only $11,200. After five years, Len's entire IRA will be a Roth IRA.

The five-year period to make tax-free Roth IRA withdrawals starts on January 1 of the year of the first partial conversion. The five-year test, which applies to each separate conversion, is met five years from January 1 of the year of the first partial conversion. Assuming that the Roth IRA owner is beyond age 59½, the account can be tapped at will, tax free.

Mistake: **Overspending.** You may be tempted to spend as much after retirement as you did while you were working. However, chances are that your retirement income is substantially less than when paychecks were coming in.

Best: Be realistic. You might spend what you receive from pensions, Social Security, part-time earnings, etc., after paying income tax.

It also makes sense to withdraw no more than 4% of your total investment portfolio for spending in Year One of retirement, then increase that withdrawal amount annually to keep pace with inflation. Academic studies have indicated that such a drawdown rate, accompanied by a well-balanced investment plan, is likely to keep the portfolio viable for 30 years or more.

If you already have been retired for some time and your age is around 65, you can start this year to take 4% from your portfolio. Next year, adjust what you take to keep up with inflation.

If you are around 70, you can start with a 5% withdrawal, then increase for inflation. Older retirees might start with 6% or even 7%.

Mistake: **Stopping retirement plan contributions.** Many "retirees" actually earn money from part-time employment, self-employment, director's fees, etc. This allows you to contribute to any of a number of retirement plans—defined-benefit, simplified employee pension, profit-sharing and 401(k) plans, for example.

Advantages: Contributions decrease the tax that you'll owe today and the retirement fund will provide an additional stream of income for your later retirement years.

Mistake: **Canceling your life insurance prematurely.** Once all your children are living independently and you have enough assets to provide for yourself and your spouse, you may wish to stop paying insurance premiums.

However, you might want cash from your life insurance at your death to pay off taxes, funeral costs, unpaid medical bills, etc. In addition, if you are going to leave one asset (such as your house) to one of your children, cash to other heirs can make for a fairer division. Life insurance can play other valuable roles, such as benefiting your favorite charities.

Best: Talk with a financial adviser and proceed cautiously before letting coverage lapse.

Rule of thumb: If you can enjoy your desired lifestyle while still paying insurance premiums, you might as well keep paying.

Mistake: **Giving away too much, too soon.** Affluent retirees may give assets to children or grandchildren to help them and to reduce their own taxable estate.

There might even be pressure from the family members to start doing this. However, such gifts should not begin too early, from a personal comfort standpoint. You may be concerned that you or your spouse will need those assets someday.

Strategy: Alternatively, make formal loans, as needed, to your children. As they prosper, they may be able to repay the loans, providing you with additional retirement assets.

A formal loan is one that's written down and signed by all the parties involved in the transaction. Terms (interest rate, repayment obligations) should be similar to loans made from an unrelated lender.

Bonus: If you determine one day that you really don't need the loan money back, you can forgive the loans and elect to treat the transactions as gifts.

Don't Save More Than You Should

Widespread emphasis on retirement planning has led some people to "save" more than they can afford. They put money away and then finance everyday expenses with credit cards, home-equity loans or other forms of borrowing.

Result: They are not saving at all. In the long run, retirement funds are used to pay off large debts.

Self-defense: Figure out your current financial needs before deciding how much to save or invest.

Kay Bidwell Aronowitz, financial counselor, FISC Consumer Credit Counseling Service of Northeast Wisconsin, Menasha.

It's Not Too Late! You Can Still Build a Solid Nest Egg

Ben Stein, an economist, attorney, actor and comedian who resides in Beverly Hills, CA, with his wife and teenaged son. He was a speechwriter for Presidents Richard Nixon and Gerald Ford. His most recent book is *Yes, You Can Become a Successful Income Investor! Reaching for Yield in Today's Market* (Hay House).

Only 18% of American workers have retirement savings of more than $100,000. Less than half have even calculated how much they will need for retirement.

Rectifying this situation has become a personal mission for economist Ben Stein. Notoriously frugal, he based his Emmy Award–winning TV game show, *Win Ben Stein's Money*, on his passion for saving. More recently, he served as spokesman for National Retirement Planning Week, sponsored by a coalition of financial education organizations, and testified before Congress about America's retirement savings problem.

Below, Mr. Stein discusses America's growing retirement problems and how he likes to invest his money…

•**Can Americans count on the Social Security privatization plan to boost their savings?** Privatization does not look probable. It is actually a distraction from real retirement planning. Squeezing extra returns from your government benefits—the average payout for retirees currently is just $958* per month—is not going to enable you to retire comfortably. That will happen only if you make saving an everyday priority.

•**How much do you put away?** I have been worrying about my retirement since I was 13. I am 61 now, and although I expect a modest pension from the Screen Actors Guild, I'm also trying to save very aggressively on my own— about 20% of my annual income.

•**Few people can afford to save that much. How can the average person squirrel away more money?** Look, people in China, which has only 14% the gross domestic product per capita that we have, save 40% of their incomes. Americans save roughly just 1%, so we can do a lot better.

A clear-cut goal makes it easier to deprive yourself of indulgences. You can calculate how much you will need in retirement at the AARP Web site, *www.aarp.org/money/financial_planning*. Be sure to use 100% of your current living expenses as your goal.

You can live on less—but a man of 65 today is likely to live to 80…a woman of 65 is likely to live to 83½. Prices could increase by 75% or more by then, so you must generate income in excess of what you need today.

•**Where do you invest additional money after you have maxed out retirement plan contributions?** Any additional money is put

*Rates subject to change.

into variable annuities. That advice came from my father, who served as chairman of the Council of Economic Advisors under Presidents Nixon and Ford. He did not earn a lot of money in his lifetime, but he had a comfortable retirement because owning annuities meant that he never had to worry about outliving his money.

•Haven't a lot of people been burned by variable annuities? Annuities have taken a lot of heat in recent years because of overaggressive selling by the insurance industry and lots of hidden fees. But if you do your homework, you'll realize that transferring the financial risk of living a long life to the insurance company and away from yourself is worth a look. For a primer on annuities, visit *www.sec.gov/investor/pubs/varannty.htm* or research all the inexpensive offerings from TIAA-CREF (800-842-2252, *www.tiaacref.org*) and at The Vanguard Group (800-523-7731, *www.vanguard.com*).

•How do you invest your retirement money? I have always been very diversified, so I have never suffered a catastrophic loss. I spread my money around the way a large institutional investor does. I use a variety of brokerage firms. I manage some of my accounts myself...I hire money managers for others. I own wide-ranging global asset classes—from emerging-market bonds to real estate investment trusts (REITs).

•What mistakes have you made? Most of the mistakes I have made as an investor have come from ignoring my own advice. I bought Berkshire Hathaway when it was cheap—$900 a share—but I didn't buy with conviction and should have scooped up a lot more. It's now worth $82,800 a share. I also got caught up a bit in the quest for Internet stock riches, even though my indicators told me that the market was overvalued.

•You detailed those indicators in your book, *Yes, You Can Time the Market*. How do you use this strategy for retirement investing? My definition of market timing bears no resemblance to that of most financial gurus. No one can consistently predict what will happen in the stock market within the next year or the next five, but you can identify when stocks are cheaper by historical standards. If you buy stocks in those periods, your likelihood of making money over 20 years or longer is far better than if you

dollar cost average into stock investments year after year, as many advisers recommend.

•Tell us more about your research. I sifted through 100 years of stock market data and found four simple measurements, or "metrics," that indicate with uncanny consistency when the S&P 500 was over- or undervalued. They include the current inflation-adjusted average price of stocks in the index...the index's average price-to-earnings ratio based on the trailing 12 months...average dividend yield...and average price-to-book value. You can find current figures, along with historical returns, on my book's Web site, *www.yesyoucantimethemarket.com*.

Next, I compared each of these measurements to their own 15-year moving averages. The optimal time to buy is at market lows—when the dividend yield is above its moving average and the rest of the metrics are well below theirs. You avoid stocks when the situation reverses itself.

By following this strategy, you would have bought stocks in 15 out of 15 of the best years to invest since 1926 and would have avoided the worst 15 years.

•What do you do during overpriced stock market cycles? Stay invested in the stocks I own, but I use new money to buy bonds (or bond funds), REITs (or REIT funds) and shares in a money market fund.

Web Sites for Seniors

Seniors are the fastest-growing segment of Internet users, and the Web offers them more all the time. *Some great sites for seniors...*

•*www.seniorlaw.com.* Provides information about a range of legal issues for seniors—Medicare and Medicaid, Social Security, insurance, wills and trusts and more.

•*www.50plusfun.com.* A portal to information about many kinds of fun and healthful diversions for seniors—the arts, dancing, hobbies, games, sports, etc.

•*www.festivalfinder.com.* More than 2,500 music festivals in North America, everything from bluegrass to classical.

●***www.golf.com.*** The most popular site on the Internet for golf news plus help in finding local golf courses, buying equipment, obtaining instruction and more.

●***www.cyberparent.com/gran/.*** Gives tips on grandparenting—camping, unusual activities, information about legal rights and much more.

●***www.acbl.org.*** Learn all about bridge and play against other real players on-line via the Web site of the American Contract Bridge League.

James Glass, Esq., a contributing writer to *Bottom Line/ Retirement* on information technology topics.

Safeguard Your Savings: Very Shrewd Strategies to Minimize Taxes

Frank Armstrong III, CFP, founder, Investor Solutions, Inc., Coconut Grove, FL, *www.investorsolutions.com.* He is author of *The Informed Investor* (American Management Association).

For tax savings, the years between the age of 59½, when you can take money from your IRAs and other tax-deferred retirement accounts without penalty, and 70½, when you *must* start taking distributions from traditional IRAs, are golden. *Here are strategies to shield the most money from Uncle Sam…*

●**Maximize IRA withdrawals** when you are in the lowest possible tax bracket.

Situation: Harrison and Margaret Smith are both 60 years old. As joint tax filers, they project their taxable income to be around $45,000 this year. To remain in the 15% tax bracket in 2007, their taxable income cannot exceed $63,700 (see the table at end of article). This means that they can withdraw approximately $18,700 from their IRAs by the end of the year.

Trap: If Harrison and Margaret neglect to prune their IRAs in this manner, the money in the accounts would continue growing tax deferred. By the time required minimum distributions began after age 70½, they would be large enough to push the Smiths into the 25%—or higher—tax bracket.

If you are nearing retirement age, your IRA is well into seven figures and your taxable income puts you into the 25% or lower federal tax bracket, it is probably smart to make withdrawals to benefit from the low bracket now. They might even spare you from future tax rates as high as 35% once minimum required distributions begin.

●**Convert some or all of your traditional IRAs over to a Roth IRA** instead of withdrawing money from your IRAs. Then you will never pay taxes on withdrawals. You can convert an IRA to a Roth this year if your modified adjusted gross income does not exceed $100,000, married or single. In 2010 only, the limit will not apply.

Example: Instead of withdrawing $18,700 from their IRAs, the Smiths could convert that amount into Roth IRAs. Roth IRA withdrawals are tax free five years after January 1 of the year in which the account was created—assuming that you are over age 59½ at the time you begin taking withdrawals. (Contributions—excluding earnings—may be withdrawn tax free at any time.)

●**Leave IRA money you don't need to your heirs.** They can stretch out minimum withdrawals over their lifetimes.

Situation: A 20-year-old granddaughter will start taking withdrawals at a rate of less than 2%, based on her remaining life expectancy of 63 years. Next year's distribution will be based on her life expectancy reduced by one (62 years) and so on. The rest of the money can accrue tax free for generations. With a Roth IRA as opposed to a traditional IRA, these withdrawals are never taxed.

●**Invest in a tax-efficient manner.** Many retirees aim to boost retirement income by investing in municipal bonds and municipal bond funds. Such funds generally are suitable only for investors in the highest tax brackets—33% and 35%.

In the lower tax brackets, your after-tax yield is likely to be higher from both taxable bonds and bond funds.

Even better: Invest in a diversified portfolio of stocks and bonds, which will provide growth potential while meeting income needs.

TAX BRACKETS FOR 2007

FEDERAL BRACKET	Single	Married Filing Jointly
	TAXABLE INCOME LIMIT	
15%	$31,850	$63,700
25%	$77,100	$128,500
28%	$160,850	$195,850
33%	$349,700*	$349,700*

*Same for single or married filing jointly. Additional income subject to 35% rate. Alternative minimum tax (AMT) brackets differ.

A High-Yield Strategy for a Low-Yield World

Marc J. Minker, CPA/PFS, RIA, managing director, private client and family office services at Mahoney Cohen & Company, CPA, PC, a full-service accountancy and personal advisory firm, 1065 Avenue of the Americas, New York City 10018.

Andrew S. Pincus, Esq., CPA, managing member of Regal Wealth Advisors, LLC at 513 Warrenville Rd., Warren, NJ 07059. Mr. Minker serves on the executive committee of the AICPA's Personal Financial Planning Division. Mr. Pincus is actively involved with the New Jersey State Society of CPA's Financial Planning Resource Group.

Even though investment yields are higher than they were a few years ago, they are still not impressive.

The yield on taxable bonds is low today. And municipal bond funds, generally the best tool for high-income taxpayers to earn strong tax-exempt yields, now yield less than 4.3%** on average. In order to get such middling yields, you must invest in long-term bonds or bond funds, which lose principal when long-term interest rates rise.

To protect yourself against rising rates, you can invest in a short- or an intermediate-term muni fund. But these funds offer even lower tax-exempt yields.

TWO FOR THE MONEY

One innovative strategy can provide the opportunity for higher after-tax yields—combine a single-premium immediate annuity (SPIA) with a universal life (UL) insurance policy. Assuming that you're in relatively good health, you can enjoy high current cash flow after tax.

**Rates subject to change.

This parlay also can provide a substantial inheritance for your loved ones.

LIFETIME CASH FLOW

An immediate annuity is a contract that provides you (or you and another party, such as a spouse) with a stream of income that begins right away. Generally, these payments are fixed. The price of an immediate annuity depends on the recipients' ages, the number of people covered and the specific terms of the contract.

Hypothetical example: Based on today's prices, George Williams, 70 years old, might be able to buy a single-life annuity for $1 million (covering only his life) from ABC Life Insurance Co. that will pay him $13,333 per month, which equals almost $160,000 per year.

These monthly payments continue as long as George is alive.

Key: Many retirees today are concerned that they will run short of money if they live into their 90s or reach triple figures. Their investment portfolios may decline as the cost of living rises.

With an SPIA, you're guaranteed, to the extent of the issuer's solvency, to keep receiving checks, no matter how long you live.

Strategy: If you're interested in an SPIA, buy from an insurer that's rated A or better by AM Best…AA or better by Standard & Poor's. You want to be confident that the annuity issuer is in good financial condition so that you can count on receiving checks for decades to come.

Among well-rated annuity issuers, shop around for the best deal. There may be sizable differences in payouts from one insurer to another.

TAX TREATMENT

With an SPIA, for many years, part of the cash flow you receive will be tax free. This will be based on your age.

Situation: At age 70, the IRS puts your life expectancy at 17 years. Therefore, you are treated as if you will be getting a return of your investment (a return of principal) over the course of 17 years.

With a $1 million investment, this 17-year return of principal equals $58,824 per year. If you are receiving a total of $160,000 per year from your annuity, then only $101,176 ($160,000 minus $58,824) will be taxable.

Assuming an effective 30% tax rate, your annuity cash flow will be subject to $30,353 in tax each year (30% of $101,176).

After paying this tax, you will net $129,647 ($160,000 in cash flow minus $30,353 in tax). This is a return of more than 12.9% per year, after tax, on your $1 million outlay, which is far higher than you would get with municipal bonds.

What's more, you're locking in this cash flow for your lifetime. There's no risk of lower before-tax income or a loss of principal due to interest rate fluctuations.

Caution: In this example, after 17 years, you will have received all of your principal back, as far as the IRS is concerned. If you're still alive after age 87, all future annuity payments will be fully taxable.

Using the same assumptions as above, you will net $112,000 per year, after tax. This 11.2% is more than you would get from municipal bonds now—though, of course, there is no knowing future interest rates.

Be aware that you will not get inflation protection with this SPIA.

PROTECT YOUR HEIRS

The above strategy may be fine if you have no loved ones for whom you would like to provide at your death. However, few people fall into this category.

Trap: Upon your death, a single-life annuity such as the one described above will cease payments. If this happens after one month, you will have paid $1 million and received just one monthly check.

Your heirs will get nothing.

Strategy: You can protect your heirs by buying $1 million worth of life insurance (or buying the same amount of life insurance that you invested in the annuity). For true lifetime protection, you can choose a permanent life insurance policy such as universal life, with a guaranteed death benefit.

Cost: The amount you will pay for insurance will vary by insurer and according to your age and health. In some cases, a healthy 70-year-old might buy a $1 million universal life policy with annual premiums around $85,000.

If this is the case, the after-tax income in our example will exceed the premium outlays by $44,647 for the first 17 years.

Bottom line: With this example, the person buying the SPIA and a UL policy would receive 4.46% per year, after tax, on a $1 million investment. That's still higher than today's returns from municipal bonds.

What's more, that cash flow is locked in, no matter how long you live or what happens to interest rates in the interim.

This strategy also protects your loved ones. When you die, even if you have received only one annuity payment, a beneficiary or beneficiaries you name will receive $1 million from the UL policy.

Alternative: You could buy a joint annuity, mentioned above. You might get payments for the life of yourself and your spouse, for example. Joint annuities will have a lower monthly payout. A joint annuity with, say, a 10-year minimum payout will have still lower monthly payouts.

Caution: This type of setup might negate your goal of beating today's bond yields—and might not be worth it.

MORE TAX BREAKS

Premiums you pay for a universal life policy are not tax deductible. However, buying a UL policy provides several tax advantages.

As is generally the case with life insurance, the $1 million death benefit will not be subject to income tax.

UL policies also have a cash value. This investment account will grow at a rate comparable to short-term bond yields, without any income tax obligation.

One drawback to buying an SPIA is that you won't have access to the money you invest beyond the monthly checks. If you might need access to additional capital, then you might want to consider a UL policy that has more significant cash value as an alternative. Be aware, though, that such a policy might impact the net cash flow described above.

Trap: Even though UL policies offer all of these advantages, the death benefit may be subject to estate tax. If you think that your estate will be taxable, you may be better off if the policy is outside of your possession, perhaps held in an irrevocable trust. Be sure to consult with your estate attorney.

The Right Investments To Put in Your Retirement Accounts…and Those To Leave Out

Christopher J. Cordaro, CFP, CFA, chief investment officer, RegentAtlantic Capital, LLC, One Main St., Chatham, NJ 07928. He has served as an adjunct faculty member at Fairleigh Dickinson University and at the County College of Morris and has been named one of the nation's top financial advisers by *Worth* magazine. Mr. Cordaro is also a past president of the New Jersey Chapter of the Financial Planning Association and serves on the Advisory Board of Financial Advisors for TD Waterhouse.

Most investors lead two lives. They hold some investments in taxable accounts, while others are allocated to an IRA, a 401(k), a simplified employee pension (SEP) plan or some other tax-deferred account. *The difference…*

.**With your taxable accounts,** you pay current income tax on dividends and interest, and gains tax on net realized capital gains. You can use capital losses, the low long-term capital gains rates, investment tax credits and other tax benefits.

.**Inside a tax-deferred account,** investment income and gains generally are untaxed. However, in most cases (a Roth IRA is one exception) all withdrawals will be taxed as ordinary income—you'll lose the other tax benefits offered to investors.

Strategy: To make the most of tax deferral, put your least "tax-efficient" investments inside your retirement accounts. The most tax-efficient investments—those that generate the lowest current tax or are tax free—should be held in taxable accounts.

With all of the different investment choices, it may be hard to know how they compare, in terms of tax efficiency. *Here's a guide…*

THE INSIDE STORY

These *tax-inefficient* assets should go inside your retirement accounts…

.**Actively traded accounts.** When you move in and out of stocks or stock funds, such trading should be done inside of a retirement plan.

You won't be reluctant to take short-term gains (which are highly taxed as ordinary income) because such gains won't be taxed immediately.

.**Tax-inefficient mutual funds.** Some funds have appealing records, yet tend to make distributions of capital gains realized by the fund but which don't necessarily benefit investors. They work best inside a retirement plan. (To identify such funds, check the history of capital gains distributions per share in relation to net asset value per share.)

.**Real estate investment trusts or REITs.** Shares in REITs and mutual funds that invest heavily in REITs also belong "on the inside."

Trap: Most of the money REITs pay to investors is taxable at ordinary income rates. Therefore, they belong inside a retirement plan, where the tax can be deferred.

.**Small-cap stocks.** Investors often access this asset class through mutual funds that have substantial portfolio turnover, leading to short-term gains. Again, tax deferral is available inside a retirement account.

.**Taxable bonds.** Both corporate bonds and mortgage-backed securities pay out substantial yields, subject to federal, state and possibly local income tax. Such tax can be deferred inside a retirement plan.

If you have a long-term allocation to fully taxable high-yield (junk) bonds, it's important to hold them inside a plan, where the tax on interest income is deferred.

.**Hedge funds.** Increasingly popular among investors, hedge funds, which are typically managed for returns, not tax efficiency, may do well, but their gains can be short term because of rapid trading. Any net short-term gains are passed through to investors and taxed at ordinary income rates.

Therefore, most hedge fund shares are best held inside a tax-deferred account. This means finding a hedge fund that will accept IRAs and qualified plans as investors.

.**Commodities.** Like hedge funds, commodity investments, such as options and futures contracts as well as managed futures funds, tend to be tax inefficient. Gains on some contracts are effectively taxed at 23%, a blend of short- and long-term rates.

217

Thus, commodities may belong inside a retirement plan.

Note: Some new forms of commodities investing have appeared, offering a buy-and-hold strategy that defers tax until sale. Such vehicles may be better held in taxable accounts because you can get long-term capital gains from them and they don't generate a great deal of taxable income. Newer forms of commodities investing include "real asset" mutual funds, such as Oppenheimer Real Asset Fund (QRAAX) and PIMCO Commodity Real Return Strategy Fund (PCRDX), and the gold-bullion-based exchange-traded funds (ETFs), such as streetTRACKS Gold Shares (GLD).

ON THE OUTSIDE

Investments that work best outside retirement accounts…

•Cash reserves. Investors generally are advised to hold, say, six months' worth of spending money in cash equivalents such as money market fund shares. These reserves should be held outside of a retirement account for tax-free access if they're needed. You do not pay tax if you need to tap your cash reserves held on the outside. If your cash reserves are inside your retirement plan, you would have to pay tax to take them out of the plan and put them in your pocket.

•Large-cap domestic equities. If a company is paying out a low dividend, not much taxable income will be generated per year. On the other hand, even if a company is paying high dividends, that income will be taxed at only 15% under current law.

Therefore, holding such stocks "on the outside" will not generate a lot of current taxable income, as long as you're a buy-and-hold investor. By holding these stocks in taxable accounts, you eventually may be able to take favorably taxed long-term capital gains on them.

Large-cap index funds, including ETFs, are especially tax efficient, so they should go in your taxable account. The same for mutual funds that are explicitly "tax managed."

•Municipal bonds. Many high-bracket investors prefer these tax-exempt issues. Holding munis or muni funds inside a retirement plan would be a major mistake—you would convert untaxed interest income to taxable income upon withdrawal.

•US Treasury securities. From a tax point of view, T-bills, T-notes, T-bonds and savings bonds should be held by investors in high-tax cities and states because the interest that they produce is exempt from both state and local income taxes. Such investors should hold Treasury investments in taxable accounts, in order to utilize the tax exemption.

Exception: Treasury inflation-protected securities (TIPS), a type of federal security which adjusts principal semiannually for inflation, are best held inside tax-deferred accounts.

Reason: The inflation adjustment is subject to current taxation in outside accounts.

•International stocks. Generally, both foreign stocks and stock funds are tax efficient, so they belong on the outside. (Foreign stocks tend to be tax efficient because many don't pay large dividends. Foreign stock funds tend to hold large-company stocks, and they haven't made substantial capital gains distributions, as a group.) Check the distribution history of a foreign-stock fund as you would any fund.

Also, you may get tax credits for foreign taxes withheld on these investments. Such credits have no value inside a retirement plan, so you would wind up paying both the withheld foreign tax up front and US income tax on withdrawals.

Exception: The small-cap foreign stock funds tend to be tax inefficient, generating short-term gains. These funds should be held inside your retirement account.

•Deferred annuities. These type of investments, which may be fixed (paying a specific return) or variable (returns fluctuate with market performance), might appeal to people with lengthy time horizons and a desire for guaranteed income. It does not make sense to retain these tax-deferred vehicles inside of a tax-deferred retirement account.

ACTION PLAN

The above lists of which investments belong inside a plan and which go outside may seem cut and dried—but implementation is not always easy.

Trap: If you participate in an employer-sponsored 401(k) or similar plan, the menu might not include tax-inefficient entries such as REITs, hedge funds and commodities.

In such a case, look first for the plan's best investment choices in terms of performance, low costs and suitability to your investment goals. Among these acceptable investments, put your money into the least tax-efficient ones.

Examples: Small-cap funds, taxable bond funds, stock funds you may trade actively.

Some tax-efficient investments may have to be held inside your retirement account, too, to give you the overall asset allocation that you want.

New Tax-Free Savings Option: The Roth 401(k)

Barry C. Picker, CPA/PFS, CFP, Picker & Weinberg, CPAs, PC, 1908 Avenue O, Brooklyn 11230. He is author of *Barry Picker's Guide to Retirement Distribution Planning* (800-809-0015) as well as chair of the New York State Society of CPAs' Employee Benefits Committee, a member of that society's Estate Planning Committee and technical editor of *Ed Slott's IRA Advisor*, 100 Merrick Rd., Rockville Centre, NY 11570.

Roth IRAs have been available for building up tax-free retirement funds since 1998. But in January 2006, the particular tax-free aspects of Roth IRAs were extended to 401(k)s, creating a brand-new retirement savings vehicle—called the Roth 401(k). *The Pension Protection Act of 2006* made Roth 401(k)s permanent (they were slated to expire after 2010). Traditional 401(k)s and Roth IRAs continue to be available.

AN OVERVIEW

The basic practical difference between 401(k)s and Roth IRAs has been that with a 401(k), salary contributions and appreciation are tax deferred while withdrawals are taxable…and with a Roth IRA, contributions are made with after-tax dollars, and under certain circumstances, withdrawals are tax free. Now, if a 401(k) plan offers a Roth option, a participant can put some—or all—of his/her annual contributions into a separate account designated as a Roth. The portion of total contributions that goes to this account will be taxable to the participant as current compensation. But if the funds are held for a requisite time (discussed below), withdrawals will be entirely tax free.

What you should know…

• **Contribution limit.** The maximum amount that can be contributed to a Roth 401(k) each year is the same as for a regular 401(k). In 2006, this limit is $15,000, or $20,000 for those age 50 and older by the end of the year ($15,500 or $20,500 in 2007). The Roth IRA income limits to making contributions do not apply to Roth 401(k)s.

Strategy: Participants can split their 401(k) contributions between a traditional and a Roth 401(k). For example, a participant may decide to put $10,500 into a traditional 401(k) to obtain tax deferral on this portion of salary, while contributing $5,000 to a Roth 401(k) for future tax-free income.

• **Separate accounts necessary.** Funds need to be held in separate accounts for regular and Roth 401(k) contributions. This will mean a little more effort on the part of participants to coordinate and track investments in the two accounts.

Important: If companies offer matching contributions, they can't be made to a Roth 401(k), but instead have to be made to the regular 401(k).

• **Tax-free withdrawals.** Like Roth IRAs, funds in Roth 401(k)s are available for tax-free withdrawal if they are held more than five years and are taken after age 59½, or because of disability or death, or to use for up to $10,000 in first-time home-buying expenses.

• **Rollovers.** When employees leave the job, they can roll over funds from a Roth 401(k) into a Roth IRA. This means that departing employees will have two potential rollovers when they leave, one for the rollover funds from a regular 401(k) to a traditional IRA and the second for funds from a Roth 401(k) to a Roth IRA.

Caution: Unlike IRAs that can be converted to Roth IRAs, funds from a regular 401(k) cannot be converted to a Roth 401(k).

• **Distributions.** In contrast to the Roth IRAs that have no lifetime distribution requirements, funds in a Roth 401(k) are subject to mandatory lifetime distribution rules. This generally means that withdrawals must commence at age 70½.

IS A ROTH 401(K) FOR YOU?

To obtain future tax-free treatment available from the Roth 401(k), a person must give up the current tax-deferral benefit. Not everyone will be willing to do this, despite the potential big payoff. *Who should consider this new option…*

●**Younger workers.** Those with a long time until retirement may be willing to sacrifice current tax deferral for future tax-free income. They will have many years to build up a retirement fund that will generate tax-free income.

●**Low-tax-bracket taxpayers with bright futures.** Those who are in lower tax brackets do not save much in taxes by opting for current deferral. They might be better off with a Roth 401(k) so that future withdrawals will be tax free when they presumably will be in higher tax brackets.

●**Higher-income taxpayers closed out of Roth IRAs.** The maximum contributions to Roth IRAs are limited to taxpayers with adjusted gross incomes (AGIs) below $95,000 on a single return or $150,000 on a joint return for 2006 and below $99,000 single or $156,000 joint in 2007.

The annual contribution limit starts falling for those who have AGI above the limits and reaches zero for those with AGI above $110,000 on a single return or $160,000 on a joint return for 2006 and above $114,000 single or $166,000 joint in 2007. With Roth 401(k)s, there are no AGI limits.

●**Those betting on higher tax rates in the future.** These taxpayers might want to gamble on future tax-free income from a Roth 401(k).

Generally, Roth 401(k)s are not suitable for workers within five years of age 70½, or those close to retirement at a younger age, when funds from the account will be needed to live on.

Reason: The accounts will not have time to qualify for tax-free-withdrawal treatment.

WHAT TO DO NOW

Small-business owners and self-employed individuals should determine whether to set up Roth 401(k)s.

Employees need to be alert to whether their employers are offering them Roth 401(k)s. Roth 401(k)s can also be set up by 403(b) plans used by schools and charities, but not by 457 government plans.

Note: Companies are not required to expand their 401(k)s to include the Roth option, and it remains to be seen which will act upon this option.

If employees learn they will be able to make Roth 401(k) contributions, they need to consult with a financial adviser to decide whether, and the extent to which, they will take advantage of this opportunity.

Protect Retirement Funds From Creditors

Federal bankruptcy law now makes funds held in an employer-sponsored qualified retirement plan immune from creditor claims in unlimited amount—and it extends the same treatment to funds from such a plan that are rolled over into an IRA. But other "regular" IRA funds and the earnings on them are exempt only up to $1 million.

Safety: Keep funds rolled over from an employer plan in a segregated IRA that holds only those funds. That way, no matter how many years pass and how high your IRA balances rise, you will always be able to identify those funds as being protected in full.

Seymour Goldberg, Esq., CPA, Goldberg & Goldberg, PC, 100 Jericho Quadrangle, Jericho, NY 11753, on the Web at *www.goldbergira.com.*

Direct Deposit Pays

When wired directly into a bank account, Social Security funds arrive more quickly, can't be lost in the mail and the retiree is saved the trouble of taking the check to the bank to deposit it. Moreover, in the event of a disaster (such as a hurricane) that disrupts mail service, it prevents a check from being delayed when the retiree may need it the most. To sign up for direct deposit, call the Social Security Administration's "Go Direct" at 800-333-1795 or visit its Web site at *www.godirect.org.*

How to Unlock Your Retirement Accounts Before Age 59½

Ed Slott, CPA, editor, *Ed Slott's IRA Advisor,* 100 Merrick Rd., Rockville Centre, NY 11570. Mr. Slott is a nationally recognized IRA distributions expert. His Web site is *www. irahelp.com.*

The tax law encourages you to build up money in your retirement plans by imposing a 10% penalty on withdrawals taken before age 59½. But what if you need the money before then? Can you get your hands on it without paying a penalty? And how can you avoid tax?

BORROW FROM THE PLAN

If you need money quickly—for a down payment on a home, to cover large medical bills or for other major expenditures—consider borrowing from your company retirement plans, including your 401(k). Most plans permit borrowing. Since the money you receive is a loan, not a plan distribution, you aren't taxed on it. Nor are you penalized.

Limit: You can borrow up to half of your account balance or $50,000, whichever is less.

Example: Your 401(k) shows a balance of $82,000 and you don't have any other outstanding plan loans. You can borrow up to $41,000.

Contact your plan's administrator to request the loan. You'll be required to repay the funds in level payments within five years—longer if the money is used to buy a home. If you fail to repay, it's a taxable distribution and may be subject to penalties.

The interest that you pay is credited back to your account. As long as you're not a "key employee" (owner or executive earning more than $140,000 in 2006 or more than $145,000 in 2007), the interest may be deductible, depending on how the money is used. *If you use the money...*

•**To buy a home,** the interest is fully deductible if the loan is secured by the home.

•**For investment purposes,** the interest is deductible to the extent of your net investment income for the year.

•**For personal reasons**—including payment of medical expenses—you cannot deduct any of the interest.

You can't borrow from your IRA. But you can take distributions before age 59½ without a 10% penalty to pay for...

•**Medical expenses exceeding 7.5%** of your adjusted gross income.

•**First-time home-buying costs**—up to a maximum of $10,000.

•**Health insurance if you're unemployed** and have received unemployment benefits for at least 12 consecutive weeks (or would have received benefits but for the fact that you're self-employed and aren't entitled to unemployment benefits).

The tax-free Roth way: If you funded your Roth IRA in 2000 or earlier, either through contributions or a conversion of your existing IRA, you can withdraw the earnings tax free because five years have passed—as long as you are at least 59½, or disabled, or use the funds to pay first-time home-buying expenses up to $10,000. Contributions to the Roth IRA can be withdrawn penalty free at any time for any purpose.

RETIRE EARLY

If you retire early, but after you have reached age 59½, and find that you need more income, consider taking distributions from your retirement accounts. They can tide you over until you start collecting Social Security benefits. While you won't pay a penalty, the withdrawals are taxable.

You can withdraw as much as you need. But keep in mind that your savings—in both personal and retirement accounts—must provide you with income for the rest of your life.

There's no early distribution penalty for...

•**Withdrawals from your traditional IRA** after you reach age 59½.

•**Distributions from company plans,** including 401(k)s, after age 55 following separation from your job.

•**Pre-59½ withdrawals from an IRA** or company plan taken in a series of substantially equal periodic payments. The payments must continue until you reach age 59½ but for no less than five years.

Example: You're age 57 and want to tap into your IRA for extra retirement income. You must continue distributions under this method until age 62—five full years.

There are three ways to calculate substantially equal periodic payments. These rules are complex, so it's best to work with a tax or benefits expert. If you make a mistake—for instance, if you stop distributions too early or take too little or too much—you can be subject to the early distribution penalty on all the distributions you've taken.

DIVORCE

If you divorce, and your retirement accounts are a marital asset subject to a property division, don't simply withdraw funds from the accounts and pay them to your spouse. Doing so will result in a taxable distribution, even if you owe your spouse money under the terms of your divorce. *To avoid taxes, follow these rules when transferring funds to your ex-spouse...*

•**For company plans,** the transfer must be pursuant to a qualified domestic relations order (QDRO). This is a court order that directs the plan administrator to pay the benefits to your ex-spouse.

•**For IRAs,** transfer funds into your spouse's IRA incident to the divorce. By having your IRA custodian make a direct transfer to the custodian of your spouse's IRA, you never have control over the funds, so you're not taxed on them.

INHERITANCE

If you inherit a retirement account, you must take distributions even if you do not need the money and you would prefer to let the funds continue their tax-deferred compounding. You can, of course, take all of the funds immediately in a lump sum and pay the resulting tax. But if you don't want to do so, in most cases, you can spread distributions over your single life expectancy at the time of the decedent's death. The first distribution must be made by the end of the year following the year of death.

Exception: If you're a surviving spouse and inherit an IRA, you can roll the funds over to your own retirement account. Ordinarily, distributions would begin the year following the year of death. But, in this event, you can delay taking distributions until age 70½. And you can name your own beneficiaries to inherit the account after you die.

Give Your Pension a Boost

Retirees who have a traditional defined-benefit plan usually will have a choice of distribution alternatives—"single life option" or "joint & survivor option." The first pays more per month, but only during your lifetime—your spouse will get nothing after you die. The second pays less but continues to pay out as long as you or your spouse is alive.

To maximize your pension, you can choose the single life option and buy life insurance with your spouse as the beneficiary. The earlier you buy it, the cheaper it is. You receive a higher pension for the rest of your life, some of which can be used to pay the insurance premium. The death benefit replaces your spouse's lost pension benefit if you die first. Be sure your policy is approved and in force before electing the single life option.

Byron Udell, JD, ChFC, CFP, founder/president, Accu-Quote, consumer life insurance information service, Wheeling, IL, www.accuquote.com.

Pay Less Tax on Your Social Security Benefits

Richard Vitale, CPA/PFS, chairman of Vitale, Caturano and Co., 80 City Sq., Boston 02129. He is also chairman of the legislation committee and former director and vice president of the Massachusetts Society of Certified Public Accountants, Inc.

Some people receiving Social Security retirement benefits find that they're untaxed. Others, though, are taxed heavily.

Savvy tax planning may prove to be a win-win strategy. Not only may you be able to reduce the haircut that the IRS will give your Social Security benefits, but in the process, you can trim the tax on your other income as well.

THE FORMULA

The tax on your Social Security benefits depends on the amount of your "provisional income," which generally is the total of...

1. Adjusted gross income (AGI), as reported on your federal income tax return, excluding your Social Security benefits, and…

2. Tax-exempt interest income from municipal bonds and municipal bond funds, and…

3. One-half your annual benefits.

A married couple filing jointly could have provisional income up to $32,000 and owe no tax on their Social Security benefits. Single filers with provisional income up to $25,000 also pocket Social Security benefits untaxed.

Over the limits: If your provisional income is more than $32,000 (married filing jointly) or $25,000 (single), up to 50% of your benefits can be taxed. Once your provisional income exceeds $44,000 (joint) or $34,000 (single), up to 85% of your benefits will be taxed.

TOO MUCH OR TOO LITTLE

When your provisional income is below the $32,000 (or $25,000) threshold, you won't owe any tax on your Social Security benefits.

But if your provisional income is far above the $44,000 (or $34,000) thresholds—say, at $60,000 or more—there might not be much opportunity to do anything to reduce taxes on your benefits. You'll have to resign yourself to having up to 85% of your Social Security benefits subject to income tax.

Important distinction: This does not mean that your Social Security benefits will be taxed at an 85% rate. Instead, it means that 85% of your benefits will be subject to income tax.

Example: Suppose you receive $15,000 in Social Security benefits this year, your provisional income is far above the threshold and you are in the 28% federal tax bracket.

In this scenario, 85% of your $15,000 in benefits ($12,750) will be subject to income tax. If you're in the 28% bracket, you would owe the IRS $3,570 this year, on that $15,000 worth of benefits, so your effective tax rate on the benefits would be 23.8%.

Exception: If you're married filing separately, and you have resided with your spouse at any time during the year, up to 85% of your Social Security benefits will be included in taxable income, no matter what your provisional income.

WIGGLE ROOM

If your provisional income is neither too little nor too large, there are steps that you can take to lower it that might, in turn, reduce the tax on your benefits.

Crucial: If your provisional income is in the range where tax planning is a possibility, as described above, any additional income you might have will be especially highly taxed.

Reason: You'll owe income tax on this additional income and you'll also owe more tax on your Social Security benefits.

Any steps you take to bring down provisional income will have a powerful tax reduction effect.

Double loophole: Maryann and John have $30,500 of AGI (excluding Social Security), no tax-exempt interest and $16,000 of Social Security benefits. They reduce their AGI by $500 (to $30,000) by shifting assets from a high-yield bond fund to a tax-managed equity fund.

Not only do they reduce their taxable income by $500, they also remove $250 worth of Social Security (50% of $500) from the reach of the IRS. Trimming their investment income by $500 lops $750 off their overall taxable income!

TAX-CUTTING STRATEGIES

To decrease your AGI (and your provisional income)…

• **Maximize retirement plan deductions.** If you still have earnings while you collect Social Security, contribute as much as possible to tax-deductible IRAs, 401(k)s, etc.

• **Favor stocks.** As long as you do not need bond income and you can stand some volatility, tilt your portfolio toward stocks, especially low-dividend stocks. Left alone, such issues will generate little if any current income and thus won't boost your AGI.

Tax-efficient stock funds also can plump your portfolio without generating income.

• **Harvest losses.** Try to wind up each year with at least $3,000 worth of net capital losses from your investments. This is the most that you can deduct each year against your other income (thus reducing your provisional income).

• **Buy savings bonds.** For part of the bond allocation of your portfolio, invest in EE or I savings bonds, which permit you to opt to postpone interest income recognition until redemption or maturity, whichever comes first.

•Depend on deferred annuities. Inside of these insurance contracts, which are designed as savings vehicles, earnings will build up, tax deferred, so they won't provide any taxable income and will not augment your AGI.

Substantial fees are involved. Expect to pay 0.5% to 1.5% of your investment in fees each year. However, if you can get along while deferring investment income rather than spending it, these vehicles can be tax-efficient wealth builders.

•Borrow when you need spending money. You might, for example, put your money into an investment-type insurance product, such as whole life, universal life or variable life insurance. Your cash value can build up, tax free, and you can take tax-free loans that won't be reflected in your AGI.

Similarly, a reverse mortgage (a special type of home-equity loan used by older Americans), can generate untaxed cash from borrowing that you won't have to repay during your lifetime. (For more information on reverse mortgages, go to the AARP Web site at *www.aarp.org/money/ revmort.*)

Caution: Borrowing always has a cost, which might include less in life insurance proceeds or less home equity to leave to heirs.

More from Richard Vitale, CPA...

The Penalty for Working

While you're planning to reduce the tax on your Social Security benefits, don't neglect another "tax"—the penalty for working that reduces benefits.

Current limits: From age 62 to full retirement age, you lose $1 in Social Security benefits for every $2 you earn over $12,960, in 2007.

The year that you turn 65, you'll face a smaller earnings penalty for a little while until you reach "full retirement age."

Example: Those born during 1942 turn 65 this year but don't reach their official full retirement age until 65 years and 10 months. Between their 65th birthdays and the age of 65 and eight months, they'll lose $1 in benefits for every $3 earned in excess of $2,870 a month.

Strategy: If you earn in excess of these ceilings (which increase every year), defer receiving Social Security benefits until you reach full retirement age, when there's no penalty for income that's earned.

If you still don't require the funds, you can wait even longer—until age 70. The longer you wait to begin receiving benefits, the higher the monthly check will be for you (and perhaps a spouse as well).

If you're already receiving benefits, you can stop them coming to avoid the penalty. But to do this, you must give back all the Social Security payments you've received from day one.

A Paycheck for Retirement

To make retirement money last, create your own "paycheck." Arrange for your investment institution to direct-deposit to your bank the amount needed to cover your monthly expenses on the first day of each month. It will feel as if you are getting a paycheck and help you with budgeting.

Also, aim to withdraw no more than 4% to 5% from your nest egg each year so that the rest can keep growing and generating income. Set aside 24 to 36 months' worth of your income needs in a bank savings or money market account or in laddered CDs. Then every six to 12 months, rebalance your portfolio by taking gains from the best-performing assets to replenish the cash account.

Derrick Kinney, senior financial adviser for Ameriprise Financial, Arlington, TX.

13

Estate Planning Answers

How to Turn $100,000 Into Millions: Top Financial Adviser's Estate Plan

Older Americans will bequeath trillions of their hard-earned dollars to descendants in the coming decades.

Sadly, much of this money will be wasted—estates often pay unnecessarily high taxes when assets are transferred, and heirs often don't handle their newfound wealth responsibly.

Financial adviser Paul Merriman, age 62, has devised a multigenerational strategy—what he calls a "500-year plan"—that addresses both of these concerns. You can set up a plan with as little as $100,000.* *Mr. Merriman explains to us how it works...*

*If your estate will be worth less than six figures, this plan probably is not worth the time, effort and attorneys' fees.

A GIFT THAT KEEPS GIVING

Rather than hand my children the money that I have worked a lifetime to accumulate, I will give them something similar to a pension. After my death, they will receive ongoing financial support from my estate based on my instructions. When my children pass away, the remainder of my estate will be used to support charities that I believe in. (If I had chosen to leave the bulk of my money to future generations rather than charities, I would have created dynasty trusts.) Your attorney can help you do this. *Personal and financial advantages to my strategy...*

• Peace of mind. I don't have to worry about my children's financial futures because they'll have annual incomes from my estate.

• Asset protection. A child won't be able to squander his/her inheritance, nor could he lose it because of a costly lawsuit or divorce.

Paul Merriman, founder and president of Merriman Capital Management, which manages more than $900 million in assets, Seattle, *www.merrimancapital.com*. He is publisher of FundAdvice.com, a free electronic newsletter, and the author of *Live It Up Without Outliving Your Money!* (Wiley).

.Charitable legacy. My memory will remain alive because my children and, later, my favorite charities will receive annual gifts in my name, not just a lump sum after my death. Thanks to the long-term growth that my investment plan should provide, my money will do far more good hundreds of years from now than it would in the near future.

A CHARITABLE REMAINDER TRUST

My estate plan relies mainly on a type of financial entity called a charitable remainder trust (CRT). When an appreciated asset is put in a CRT, it can be sold without paying tax. The CRT pays the beneficiary income for life, and the remainder goes to the charity upon his death.

With the help of an attorney, I created four CRTs, one for each of my children. When I am gone, these trusts will be funded with money from my estate and each year, 5% of the trusts' value will be distributed to my children. Since the money is invested for growth, the amount in the trusts and the size of the payouts should increase over time, even after withdrawals and inflation (see table below). When my children pass away, the 5% annual payments—in cash and/or securities—will go to the charities that I have selected.

A Century of Growth

Year	Trust Assets*	Annual Distribution
2007	$100,000	—
2027	$180,611	$9,030
2052	$378,159	$18,908
2077	$791,782	$39,589
2107	$1,921,863	$96,093

CRTs provide two major tax benefits. They generate a deduction for estate tax purposes, and the money grows tax free. Only distributions to my heirs will be taxed—at regular income tax rates.

All community foundations—nonprofit organizations designed to facilitate charitable giving—have attorneys on staff to draft up CRTs for free. Otherwise, setting one up costs $500 to $1,500.**

After my children pass away, the community foundation I have chosen will take control of my trusts and make the 5% distributions to the charities. (If one of my charities goes out of business

*Assuming an 8% return and 5% distribution annually.

**Prices subject to change.

after I'm gone, the foundation will replace it with a charity that has a similar goal.)

To learn more about community foundations or to locate one in your area, contact the Council on Foundations (202-466-6512, *www.cof.org*).

THE 500-YEAR PORTFOLIO

Investments, whether in mutual funds or variable annuities, should be for the long haul—centuries, not decades. If your investment doesn't continue to earn a good amount of money after you're gone, it will be eaten away by inflation, administrative expenses (up to 1% of assets per year) and payments to heirs and charities. On the other hand, if your investment plan is too risky, it could be crippled by market downturns.

The best strategy is used by most pension funds—invest 60% in a diversified stock portfolio and the rest in bonds. The trustee will rebalance allocations annually. Even after accounting for inflation and for 5% annual withdrawals, my portfolio's value should double within 30 years of my death. Although I am not tremendously wealthy, my estate will have a significant impact on the future.

Choose mutual funds with low expenses and good, consistent long-term performance. (Model portfolios are available at my Web site, *www. fundadvice.com*.)

PROVIDING FOR GRANDCHILDREN

I have a separate estate plan to provide for my grandson, Aaron. Minors who inherit significant amounts from their grandparents typically gain full control of the money on their 18th or 21st birthdays, depending on state law. However, money received at such a tender age often is squandered, and large inheritances can rob young people of a solid work ethic.

You can provide for a child at any age, but rather than give my grandson a pile of money when he reaches 21, I decided to give him the likely guarantee of a comfortable retirement. With the uncertain state of Social Security and fewer employers offering old-fashioned, reliable pension plans, this should be a gift that he will appreciate one day—and it cost me only $11,000.

How it works: When Aaron was born, I made a one-time gift of $10,000 to an irrevocable trust with Aaron as beneficiary and his parents as trustees. (Setting up this trust cost me about $1,000 in attorney's fees.) The money in the trust is invested in a low-cost variable annuity, a type of investment account that lets assets compound tax deferred (so a tax return doesn't need to be filed each year).

Firms that provide no-load, low-expense variable annuities include Charles Schwab (866-855-9102, *www.schwab.com*), Fidelity (800-343-3548, *www.fidelity.com*), T. Rowe Price (800-225-5132, *www.troweprice.com*) and The Vanguard Group (800-523-7731, *www.vanguard.com*). For maximum growth, I selected a variable annuity that invests entirely in stocks—through mutual fund–like "subaccounts."

Starting at age 65, Aaron will receive annual payments of 7% of the trust's value. Historically, the equity investments I have selected have produced an average annual return of 11.2%. Assuming that return, my $10,000 should be worth about $10 million by the time Aaron reaches age 65. That means that his first annual 7% payment should be about $700,000. When adjusted for inflation, that's $131,000 in today's dollars, enough to set the stage for a comfortable retirement. When Aaron dies, the remaining funds will be given away to a charitable organization that he will select.

An Estate Tax Savings Triple Play

Lee Slavutin, MD, CLU, chairman, Stern Slavutin-2 Inc., an insurance and estate-planning firm at 530 Fifth Ave., New York City 10036. Dr. Slavutin is the author of *Guide to Life Insurance Strategies* (Practitioners).

The current now-you-see-it, now-you-don't, now-you-might-see-it-again estate tax situation makes planning difficult. No one knows when—or if—Congress will act on the estate tax, or what the outcome might be. The threshold and rates could go way down...or way up...or stay about the same.

Likely result: As I see it, it's probable that moderately wealthy taxpayers (say, couples who have up to $4 million in net worth) will owe little or nothing in federal estate tax, provided they do some basic planning, such as dividing assets between spouses and leaving some to their children at each death.

Wealthier families, though, may wind up with steep estate tax bills unless they take more specific, proactive measures.

Strategy: To maximize after-tax transfers to heirs, one powerful option for affluent families is to combine three tax-favored vehicles—the family limited partnership (FLP), grantor-retained annuity trust (GRAT) and irrevocable life insurance trust (ILIT). *Here's how and why to do it...*

THE THREE BUILDING BLOCKS

1. Family limited partnership. An FLP consists of general partnership and limited partnership interests.

Loophole: If you create an FLP and transfer assets into it, the limited partnership interests will be valued at discounts for lack of liquidity and lack of marketability.

Caution: The partnership agreement should set out reasons for creating an FLP, beyond tax avoidance. Creating a partnership with a legitimate business purpose, like owning and managing real estate, is a possibility.

2. Grantor retained annuity trust. With a GRAT, the trust creator retains the right to receive annuity payments. At the end of a specified trust term, whatever is left in the trust passes to named beneficiaries.

Key: The present value of the assets transferred minus the present value of the annuity payments will be considered a taxable gift by the trust creator.

Situation: You give assets which are valued at $3 million to a GRAT and specify an income stream valued at $2.5 million. You have made a $500,000 gift to the GRAT—the $3 million transfer minus the $2.5 million present value of the income you'll receive.

Loophole: In a relatively low interest-rate environment, such as the one we're still in today, the present value of the future income stream will be relatively high, which results in a smaller taxable gift. Receiving, say, $100,000 per year is more valuable if interest rates are at 5% rather than 7%.

3. Irrevocable life insurance trust. A life insurance policy held in an ILIT will be out of any individual's taxable estate.

Loophole: Life insurance death benefits are usually not subject to income tax. If the policy is held in an ILIT, where estate tax also can be avoided, the insurance proceeds can be totally tax free, even if the amount is $5 million, $10 million, or more.

PUTTING THEM TOGETHER

By artfully combining these strategies, affluent taxpayers can trim their estates and pass on tax-free wealth to their heirs.

Situation: Jane Williams has a large estate she wants to pass to her three children and six grandchildren. She places $5 million worth of assets (investment real estate, securities) in an FLP.

The way the FLP is structured, there is a 1% general partnership interest (face value of $50,000) and a 99% limited partnership interest ($4.95 million). Jane starts out holding both interests.

Discounts: Jane can then transfer the limited partnership interest to a GRAT she has created. A reputable appraiser might value the transfer at $3.2 million, representing a 35% discount for illiquidity and lack of control because the assets are held inside an FLP.

Caution: In recent years, discounts people have tried to claim with FLPs have been challenged in Tax Court. Consult with a trusts and estates lawyer when setting up your FLP to avoid any future problems.

GRAT term: In our example, Jane selects a nine-year trust term and a $300,000 annual distribution from the GRAT back to Jane.

Vital: The creator of a GRAT should pick a trust term that he/she is likely to outlive. If the creator dies while the GRAT is still in effect, the trust assets will go back into the creator's taxable estate.

In this example, the present value of the nine years' worth of $300,000 distributions might be $2.2 million, depending on interest rates in effect at that time.

Result: If Jane transfers assets to the GRAT valued at $3.2 million in return for payouts valued at $2.2 million, she has made a $1 million gift to the GRAT.

Loophole: Everyone has a $1 million gift tax exemption. Thus, Jane owes no federal gift tax from this transfer.

Key: The trust distributions can be set so that the taxable gift will be $1 million, sheltered by this lifetime gift tax exemption.

WINNING THE ENDGAME

At the end of the trust term, the assets left in the GRAT will go to the GRAT beneficiary. In this strategy, that would be the life insurance trust.

Payout: The amount of this distribution will depend on how the assets grow over the nine-year trust term.

In our example, where assets with a face value of $4.95 million are transferred to the GRAT, and $300,000 is paid to Jane each year, the trust could grow to around $7 million, assuming 9% to 10% annualized returns.

(Such returns are not guaranteed, but they're possible if the underlying real estate and securities perform well.)

Benefits: Depending on Jane's age and her health at the time of the initial steps, the assets transferred into the ILIT from the GRAT might fund an $18 million life insurance policy for the rest of Jane's life.

Outcome: In this example, Jane has removed nearly $5 million from her taxable estate while paying no gift tax.

She has shunted $300,000 per year back to herself for nine years—a total of $2.7 million. (See below for how Jane might be able to get some or all of this out of her estate.)

At her death, the ILIT will receive $18 million in insurance proceeds, tax free. That $18 million can be distributed to Jane's children and grandchildren, the ILIT beneficiaries.

Alternatively, the $18 million can stay in trust. Then a trustee named by Jane can distribute the funds, as needed, to the ILIT beneficiaries.

MEETING THE CHALLENGE

In this example, the challenge will be to pay for the life insurance until the GRAT terminates and moves a lump sum into the ILIT. The premiums would have to be enough to carry an $18 million life insurance policy for nine years. Premiums for such a sizable policy will be large. They must be paid by the ILIT in order for the death benefit to be out of Jane's taxable estate.

Getting large sums into the trust without paying gift tax is the challenge.

Strategy: A savvy life insurance professional can help with the policy design. Inexpensive term life might be used up front, with a conversion to a permanent life insurance policy after the GRAT payout.

Embracing the exclusion: The annual gift tax exclusion might be used to help provide money for the insurance premiums. In 2007, each individual can give $12,000 worth of assets to any number of recipients, per year, free of gift tax.

In our example, if Jane names her three children, their three spouses and all six grandchildren as ILIT beneficiaries, those 12 beneficiaries can receive $144,000 in gifts this year tax free—12 × $12,000. With proper counsel, Jane could transfer $144,000 to the ILIT for premium payments on the life insurance policy. The distributions Jane receives from the GRAT each year might be used to fund these transfers.

Loan arrangers: Instead of or in addition to such transfers, the ILIT might borrow money from a bank or other lending institution to fund the life insurance premiums for the first nine years, in our example. Then the transfer from the GRAT could repay the loan, if that's desirable.

Loophole: Borrowing by the ILIT won't create a gift or generate a gift tax.

Using these various strategies together can create powerful wealth-transfer leverage. But be sure to work with knowledgeable advisers to avoid costly missteps.

Protect Your Family for Generations with a Dynasty Trust

Gideon Rothschild, Esq., CPA, partner in the law firm Moses & Singer LLP, 1301 Avenue of the Americas, New York City 10019. He is adjunct professor in estate planning and wealth preservation at New York Law School and at University of Miami Law School. For additional articles on asset-protection strategies, go to *www.mosessinger.com*.

Properly structured trusts can provide several advantages, including tax savings and asset protection. However, those benefits may be lost when the trust terminates and the assets are distributed.

In recent years, nearly half of the states have passed laws allowing trusts to last for hundreds of years, or even in perpetuity, something that was not permitted in the past. The advantages of these "dynasty" trusts may be extended over many future generations. Setting up a dynasty trust properly will eliminate gift and estate tax and shield the assets from creditors.

Caution: Highly publicized research indicates that $100 billion worth of assets has flowed into personal trusts in those states in the past two years. In response, the staff of the Congressional Joint Committee on Taxation has proposed limits on these long-lasting trusts.

Strategy: There is no certainty that any legislation will pass. However, if you are interested in a dynasty trust, you may want to act before any restrictions are put in place.

TAX TACTICS

A dynasty trust is an irrevocable trust, typically funded with a substantial amount of assets. Currently, each individual can transfer up to $1 million to such a trust (assuming no other taxable gifts have been made), without having to pay a gift tax.

Situation: John and Mary Smith are married. Each may transfer $1 million to the Smith Family Trust without paying gift tax.

If John does not have the ability or the inclination to make a gift to the trust, Mary can make a $2 million gift. As long as John consents to a spousal gift, no tax will be owed.

Drawback: Any tax-free lifetime gifts will reduce the donor's eventual estate tax exemption, dollar-for-dollar. If Mary makes a $1 million gift and dies when the estate tax exemption is $3.5 million, her estate will have a $2.5 million exemption remaining.

Exclusions: By using the annual gift tax exclusion, both gift and estate tax consequences may be avoided. In 2007, anyone can give up to $12,000 worth of their assets to any number of recipients.

In the case of gifts to a trust, the recipients are the trust beneficiaries. Special care is needed, though, if the gifts are to qualify for the annual gift tax exclusion.

Situation: Suppose that John and Mary Smith fund a trust, as described previously. Their three children and six grandchildren are beneficiaries. John and Mary can give away $216,000 worth of assets to the trust this year—$12,000 times two donors times nine beneficiaries—with no gift tax obligation.

Such tax-free gifts can be made each year. In fact, the number will increase as the annual gift tax exclusion is raised in order to keep pace with inflation.

Required: To qualify for the gift tax exclusion, each trust beneficiary must be notified of the gift. He/she must be given a time period in which the gifted assets can be withdrawn from the trust—$24,000 per beneficiary in this example.

Key: After the withdrawal window closes, the assets can remain in the trust and no gift tax will be assessed, provided the proper formalities have been followed.

GENERATION SKIPPING

In the above example, grandchildren have been named as trust beneficiaries. That's often the case with a dynasty trust.

Trap: If grandchildren or great-grandchildren are trust beneficiaries, the generation-skipping transfer (GST) tax must be considered.

This is an extra level of transfer tax levied on bequests or gifts that "skip" at least one generation. In 2007, the GST tax rate is 45%!

Fortunately, each individual now receives a $2 million exemption from the GST tax.

Thus, if John and Mary Smith transfer $2 million to a trust, they can *each* designate $1 million worth of their GST tax exemption. No GST tax will be paid.

Transfers to trusts that are in excess of the $2 million-per-person ceiling will incur the GST tax, though.

SEEKING SHELTER

By following all the above rules, substantial amounts can be transferred to a trust, with little or no tax obligation. If the trust is irrevocable, created in a state that allows long (or perpetual) trust terms, the assets can remain in trust for numerous years. *Reasons for creating and funding such trusts...*

•**Eliminate estate tax.** Once assets are properly transferred to a trust, they don't belong to

any individual. Thus, they will not be taxed at anyone's death.

Situation: John and Mary Smith fund a trust with $2 million, as above. At John's death, suppose the trust fund has grown to $4 million.

No estate tax will be due.

Key: The same is true at Mary's death, the deaths of their children, etc. Their original $2 million gift could grow to $20 million, even $200 million over the years, and never be reduced by gift, estate or GST tax.

•**Curbing creditors.** Just as assets that don't belong to any individual will be out of the reach of transfer taxes, they also will be protected from the creditors of John, Mary and the other trust beneficiaries.

Thus, the trust assets won't be exposed to divorce settlements, bankruptcy, judgments, etc.

A BENEVOLENT BANKER

Just because the assets are beyond the reach of creditors and tax collectors does not mean that John's family will get no benefit from the trust assets.

In dynasty trusts, the trustee typically has the discretion to distribute trust assets among the beneficiaries.

These assets might be available to help a child pay medical expenses, fund a grandchild's college education, purchase a home (to be retained in the trust) for a great-grandchild and so on.

Motivating beneficiaries: A popular wrinkle is the "incentive trust." The trust can include language saying that the trust beneficiaries will receive distributions based on certain achievements, such as educational degrees or reaching specified amounts of earned income.

FINE POINTS

If dynasty trusts remain in existence for decades (even centuries), they may grow unmanageable, as future beneficiaries are added. If one trust has to provide for 50 beneficiaries in 22 states (just a hypothetical instance), that might be hard for one trustee to handle.

Solution: The original trust may be designed to divide into "subtrusts" at some future date, perhaps one for each of the grantor's children. Then those subtrusts can subdivide further, as more beneficiaries arrive on the scene.

State selection: You don't have to live in a state that offers long-term trusts in order to create one. Generally, all that is necessary is that you use an in-state trustee and keep some trust assets in the state.

Strategy: When choosing among states for a dynasty trust, you may want to consider the lack of a state income tax (Alaska, Delaware, Florida) or a long history of settled trust law (Delaware). (While these trusts are estate, gift and GST tax free, they're subject to income tax on trust income.)

Eight states—Alaska, Delaware, Missouri, Nevada, Oklahoma, Rhode Island, South Dakota and Utah—permit the grantor of a dynasty trust to be a beneficiary. Thus, assets may be returned in the case of a financial setback. But under the bankruptcy law that took effect on October 17, 2005, there's a new 10-year limitation period for transfers to these trusts, transfers within this period may not be protected.

In any case, be sure to consult with an attorney experienced in trusts and estate planning if you are considering a dynasty trust.

Recheck All Beneficiary Designations Now

James Glass, a tax attorney in New York City and a contributing writer to *Tax Hotline,* a newsletter published by Boardroom Inc. that covers traps and opportunities in the latest tax laws, rules and regulations.

I frequently advise people to check all beneficiary designations on employer-provided retirement plans, IRAs, insurance and other such financial assets.

Why: To be sure not only that they are up to date, but also that they haven't been lost or mistakenly recorded by the financial institution involved.

Now a *Tax Hotline* reader writes us of his experience…

"Last year, I thought I would review my IRAs and life insurance policies to be sure that they were all current with respect to beneficiary designations. What I found shocked me.

"It turned out that of five IRAs, three had the wrong information. And one life insurance policy was also incorrect. All the discrepancies were the fault of the companies involved—the mistakes were so far off base that I would never have made these choices.

"One IRA had no beneficiary listed, but my wife and children were listed initially—14 years ago. (I had saved a copy of the original application.)

"Your readers need to check these. Don't assume that they are correct no matter how the original application was filled out."

—Doug Sweet, Birmingham, Alabama

A mistaken beneficiary designation could be hugely expensive—causing funds to pass differently than you intended and greatly increasing taxes on them.

Critical: Be sure to check them out now.

You've Got to Give to Save

Give away your life insurance policy to save your heirs thousands of dollars in estate taxes. Life insurance proceeds (cash surrender value or death benefit) are considered part of your taxable estate—but if you don't own the policy, proceeds are not taxable.

Giving the policy to your spouse is not usually a good idea—if he/she dies first, the proceeds become part of his estate and the problem remains. If you have adult children, give them the policy. You must report any policy value above $12,000 per recipient for gift tax purposes, since currently $12,000 per year is the most anyone can give anyone else tax free, but the policy's eventual proceeds will not be taxed.

Caution: You cannot continue to pay policy premiums after making the transfer, but you can give the new owners up to the annual gift limit without any tax consequences—and they can use that money to pay premiums.

Ralph C. Wileczec, CPA, CFP, vice president and senior private client adviser, Wilmington Trust, Wilmington, DE.

Plan for State-Level Estate Taxes

The cost of state-level estate taxes used to be covered by a credit against the federal estate tax, but this credit was eliminated in 2005. In addition, although the amount that's exempt from federal estate tax has been increased (from $675,000 for 2001 to $1.5 million for 2005 and to $2 million for 2006 and 2007), many states have not increased their exempt amounts accordingly—so state-level estate taxes now are an extra concern to plan for.

For Your Sake and Your Family's...Plan Now for Possible Future Incapacity

B. Dane Dudley, Esq., partner in the law firm of Day, Berry & Howard LLP, Town Center, 29 S. Main St., West Hartford, CT 06107. He specializes in estate planning and trust and estate administration.

People are living a lot longer these days, but increased longevity may have its drawbacks. Chances are, a parent, a sibling or other older loved one may reach a point where he/she no longer can manage his own affairs. You and/or your spouse also may become incompetent some day.

If incapacity strikes, assets may be at risk. Family members might have to petition a court to appoint a fiduciary to act on behalf of the incompetent individual. Such proceedings can be expensive, time consuming, exposed to public scrutiny and, most important, may result in the appointment of someone who would not have been your choice.

Strategy: To help avoid this scenario, work with a qualified lawyer to put an incapacity plan into place while you are still competent. And, remind your parents and siblings to implement their own plans, too.

What might go into an incapacity plan? *Some key elements...*

JOINT OWNERSHIP

Maybe the simplest and least expensive tactic for dealing with potential incapacity is to put some assets in joint ownership, with right of survivorship.

Situation: Marie names her niece Linda as joint owner of her bank account. If Marie becomes incapacitated, Linda can pay bills from that account, handle deposits, etc.

Trap I: At the death of one co-owner, the survivor automatically inherits the balance of the account. That's true no matter what it says in the will of the person who dies.

In our example, Linda would inherit the bank account while all other nieces, nephews and other possible beneficiaries would be excluded. The same would be true if Marie named Linda co-owner of brokerage accounts or real estate.

Trap II: For wealthier families, joint ownership may interfere with an estate plan designed to reduce or defer estate taxes.

Another problem with joint ownership is the absence of protection against poor judgment. If Aunt Marie decides to empty the joint bank account to invest in some questionable scheme, there is nothing Linda can do to prevent it.

Still other problems may arise. For example, niece Linda might spend Marie's money improperly. Also, if Linda is co-owner of the account, her creditors may have access, as they would to any of her assets. This includes the IRS.

Strategy: Arrange for automatic deposit of investment income and Social Security checks as well as automatic payment of utility and other bills. This will reduce the need for joint ownership of a bank account because investment income will be deposited and bills will be paid even if one co-owner becomes incapacitated. Automatic deposit and payment can be arranged right away. It's safe and convenient. Bills won't go unpaid because they're paid immediately from a bank account.

If some joint ownership is still desired, it usually is best to limit it to a bank account with modest deposits. Name a person you trust as joint owner.

POWERS OF ATTORNEY

A power of attorney is a document authorizing someone (an "agent" or "attorney-in-fact") to act on behalf of someone else (the "principal"). Be sure to include one in your incapacity plan.

A power of attorney shouldn't interfere with your estate plan the way joint ownership might.

Situation: If you name your son Charlie as attorney-in-fact, he can sign contracts on your behalf, buy and sell investments, and so on.

For this purpose, be sure to execute a "durable" power. Otherwise, a power of attorney will not be recognized if a court finds that you have become incompetent. The durable power will remain in force.

You will want to name someone you trust as your agent. Even so, you may be reluctant to have a power of attorney in someone else's hands while you are still competent.

Solution: Many states recognize "springing durable powers of attorney." These take effect only under specified circumstances.

Example: Your springing power might take effect only after two doctors, including your personal physician, have determined that you have become incapacitated.

No matter what type of power you choose, review it every few years, as your circumstances may change, leading you to want to change provisions or name another agent.

Also, some financial institutions are leery of "outdated" powers of attorney.

Important: Check with your bank, broker and mutual fund company to see if they will accept your power or if they'll insist that their own forms be used.

Don't confuse the legal/financial powers of attorney described above with *health-care* powers of attorney. The latter, also known as "health care proxies," allow someone else to make medical decisions for you if you can't.

A health-care power also belongs in your incapacity plan.

The agent you name in your health care power does not have to be the same person named in your durable power of attorney. If someone in your family is especially knowledgeable about medical issues or is more attuned to your personal wishes, he might be given the health care proxy. Your durable power of attorney should be entrusted to someone likely to make sound *financial* decisions.

REVOCABLE TRUSTS

Another component of your incapacity plan might be a revocable trust. These are sometimes known as "living trusts." These trusts can be used to avoid probate and provide for management of trust assets in case of incapacity.

Work with an estate-planning attorney to create a revocable trust and then consider whether to transfer none, most, some or all of your assets into this trust during your lifetime.

You can be both the trustee and beneficiary of the trust. You make the decisions about trust assets, and you collect any cash paid out by the trust. You will be responsible for the income tax on any earnings of trust assets.

Life goes on, pretty much as before, although the trust—not you—holds title to the assets in it.

Escape clause: If you become unhappy with your trust for any reason, you can scrap it and retake personal ownership of the assets. That's why these trusts are "revocable."

Where incapacity protection comes in: When you create your revocable trust, you can name a cotrustee or successor trustee, perhaps your spouse or child. If you become incompetent (as determined under the terms of the trust document), the individual you have named as co- or successor trustee will take over the management of trust assets.

The entire process can occur seamlessly, without court involvement and the risk that assets won't be managed for a period of time.

Advantage: Your replacement trustee will have a fiduciary responsibility to preserve the trust assets and use them to provide for you, the trust beneficiary.

What's more, your estate plan need not be disrupted. A revocable trust can fit in with your overall estate plan—along with your will, beneficiary designations, etc.

Negate probate: At your death, trust assets avoid probate, which can be time consuming and expensive. The trust assets can be directed in the manner you desired, as expressed in the trust document.

Trap: All of these advantages apply only to the assets actually held in the trust. A surprising number of people create revocable trusts and then fail to transfer assets to them during their lives or at death.

Strategy: If you do create a revocable trust, make sure you consider re-titling at least some of your assets so that they're owned by the trust. As with the rest of your plan, it's wise to work with a knowledgeable attorney to ensure that the transfers accomplish your objectives.

In addition, don't assume that creating a revocable trust alone will provide tax advantages. You still need to consult with your professional advisers to reduce income, estate and other taxes.

More from B. Dane Dudley, Esq....

Living Wills

The emotional story of Terri Schiavo back in 2005 created intense interest in living wills. Generally, a living will directs that certain artificial life-sustaining measures doctors and hospitals are normally expected to take be withheld if you have a terminal medical condition or are in a permanent coma. Each state describes these threshold medical conditions in general terms, and it's left to doctors to determine whether a person's condition falls within that description. Talk to your doctor now about your particular preferences.

You also might opt for a do-not-resuscitate (DNR) order, another form of advance directive, which directs doctors and other hospital personnel not to revive you if you stop breathing.

It's important that your personal physician have a copy of any type of advance directive. Loved ones should know your wishes, too, so that they don't have to guess what you would want to happen at this difficult time.

Talk to your attorney. The more clear you are in making your wishes known, the greater the chances that they'll be followed by family members, doctors and hospitals.

A living will may also keep your assets from being dissipated for expensive medical care that has no hope of success. Treat a living will as you would any other legal document. It should be drawn up and signed according to the requirements of your state's law.

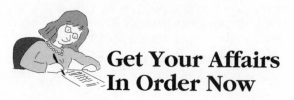

Get Your Affairs In Order Now

Make your passing easier for loved ones. Indicate in writing who should be notified of your death, the type of funeral or memorial service desired, whether you prefer flowers or charitable contributions, etc. Also, list where loved ones can find your will, living trust, insurance policies, bank accounts, annuities, mutual funds and investments, real estate holdings and related documents, and safe-deposit boxes and keys.

Melanie Cullen, a consultant in management and technology, Davis, CA, who spent 20 years in corporate management. She is author of *Get It Together: Organize Your Records So Your Family Won't Have To* (Nolo).

14

Bon Voyage

The Seven Best Tours In America

One way to cut down on travel hassles is to sign up for a tour and leave all the driving, decision making and problem solving in the capable hands of the tour operator.

Tours can also be moneysavers. Tour companies negotiate group rates on hotels, meals, admission prices and transportation. In general, you can expect to spend approximately 30% less with a package tour than you would following the very same itinerary on your own in a rental car.

Tours are best for those who like to keep busy on vacation and enjoy meeting new people, not for those who prefer to relax on the beach or travel with only a few companions. Most people who sign up for tours are in their 50s or older, so younger vacationers might feel out of place (except on tours specifically designed for families or young people).

To make sure you're dealing with a quality tour company, confirm that it is a member of the American Society of Travel Agents at 703-739-2782, *www.travelsense.org*…it has been in business for at least five years…and there aren't numerous complaints about it lodged on travel Web sites, such as Trip-Advisor.com, or with the Better Business Bureau.

Here, seven domestic tours that deliver a lot for the money…*

• **Yellowstone & Grand Teton National Parks.** See the wonders of the West, including the magnificent glaciers, forests and stone pinnacles of Grand Teton National Park…the dramatic canyons and geysers of Yellowstone National Park…and the grandeur of Mount Rushmore on

*Prices subject to change. Prices are also per person double occupancy and do not include travel expenses to and from the tour's departure point. Packages typically include some but not all meals. Contact the tour operator for details.

Mike Putman, founder of Travel Team Consulting, Inc., which advises airlines, hotel chains and others in the travel business, *www.travelteamconsulting.com*. He is president of Putman Travel, Inc., a Greenville, SC, travel agency that has been in business for 20 years.

this 10-day journey. You'll also explore some of the historic towns of the West and take a raft trip on the wild Snake River. Tauck World Discovery (800-788-7885, *www.tauck.com*). $2,480.

●**Southern Charms and the Great Smokies.** This wide-ranging eight-day tour starts in Tennessee with stops in Memphis and Nashville, ventures north into Kentucky bluegrass country, then south through the Great Smoky Mountain National Park and finally east into the beautiful Carolinas, ending with a dinner cruise off Charleston. Globus (866-755-8581, *www.globus journeys.com*). $1,349.

●**Colorado Rail Adventure.** Take a scenic nine-day rail tour through the Rocky Mountains, staying in quality hotels along the way. Rail lines go places that cars can't, hugging the sides of mountains and tracing the course of rugged rivers. You'll tour spectacular Mesa Verde National Park and also explore New Mexico's enchanting Taos and Sante Fe. Maupintour (800-255-4266, *www.maupintour.com*). $2,529.

●**Arizona and the Canyons.** This eight-day guided tour takes you to unforgettable sites—Zion National Park, Monument Valley and the magnificent Grand Canyon. Maupintour, $2,299.

●**Coastal California Vacation.** The Pacific Coast Highway, also known as Route 1, is often called the greatest driving road in America. This nine-day tour lets you sit back and enjoy the views. You'll visit some of America's greatest cities, including San Francisco, Los Angeles and San Diego, and explore picturesque towns such as Carmel, Monterey and San Juan Capistrano. The package includes short cruises in San Francisco Bay and San Diego Bay. Globus, $1,749 to $1,799.

●**Alaska: A Family Adventure.** This 11-day family-oriented tour isn't cheap, but considering what you get, it's a good value. You take a private guided tour of Denali National Park…meet an Iditarod competitor and her dog team…fly on float planes and bush planes…visit remote locations that are inaccessible by road…take a raft ride on the Sheridan River…and enjoy the whale watching, panning for gold and campfires. Abercrombie & Kent, Inc. (800-554-7016, *www. abercrombiekent.com*). $6,835 per adult/$3,535 per child under age 12, sharing with two adults.

●**The Best of Hawaii.** It isn't easy to see all of Hawaii in one visit—you have to arrange flights from island to island and secure a rental vehicle and hotel room on each island. This 12-day package offers an easy way to visit the four most popular islands—Kauai, Maui, Oahu and the Big Island. You will explore volcanoes, tour harbors and villages and visit coffee farms and historic sites, such as Pearl Harbor. Plus there's plenty of time for snorkeling, golfing and all the other things people associate with Hawaiian vacations. Tauck World Discovery, $3,890 (with an additional charge of $195 for flights between islands).

Quick and Affordable Getaways to Exotic Places

Joan Rattner Heilman, an award-winning travel writer located in New York State. She is author of *Unbelievably Good Deals and Great Adventures That You Absolutely Can't Get Unless You're Over 50* (McGraw-Hill).

Need a complete break from your everyday routine? Want a fresh perspective on life? Think exotic. Right now there are some remarkably inexpensive getaways to unusual destinations all over the world.

All of the short vacations here offer you plenty for your money. None are longer than six nights. Pay a little more, however, and you can add extra days.

MACHU PICCHU, PERU
THE LOST CITY OF THE INCAS

On this tour, you'll spend six nights in Peru, starting with one night in Lima, the capital, a city filled with colonial architecture and Indian markets. The temperatures are in the 70s during the winter. You'll then fly to Cuzco, the capital city of the Incas, high in the Andes, to stay four nights. There you'll wander through old palaces and temples built around 1200 AD. You'll take a four-hour journey on the famous Backpacker Train that climbs up a series of switchbacks to Machu Picchu, "The Lost City of the Incas," which escaped discovery and plundering by the 16th-century Spanish invaders, and remained hidden from the rest of the world until Yale archeologist Hiram Bingham stumbled on its ruins in 1911. Your last night is spent in Aguas Calientes before you go back to Lima.

Cost: From $999.* Includes round-trip airfare from Miami and between Lima and Cuzco, hotels, tours, breakfasts and some other meals.

Information: Traveland.com (800-321-6336, *www.traveland.com*).

TAHITI AND MOOREA
PAUL GAUGUIN AND SOUTH PACIFIC

A little vacation in French Polynesia in the South Pacific might be exactly what you crave right now. Think about Air Tahiti Nui's six-night visit to Tahiti and the nearby island of Moorea, where the temperature averages about 85°F during the day and 70°F at night.

You'll stay overnight in Tahiti, time enough to explore much of this lush, mountainous island of waterfalls, coral reefs, beaches and blue lagoons. You'll then fly 11 miles across the Sea of the Moon to Moorea, the inspiration for author James Michener's mythical island of Bali Hai. Luxuriate on the beach, explore the island by outrigger canoe, view the twin bays from Belvedere lookout and visit pineapple plantations.

Cost: From $1,341. Cost includes round-trip airfare from New York, hotels, interisland air, breakfasts and dinners.

Information: Air Tahiti Nui (866-456-6000, *www.airtahitinui-usa.com*).

TO GALWAY AND BEYOND
GALWAY BAY AND BLARNEY CASTLE

This five-night fly/drive tour of Ireland starts from Shannon Airport on Ireland's west coast. You stay the first night at the Clare Inn in Newmarket-on-Fergus, a quaint little town in County Clare, just a few miles inland and home of Dromoland Castle. You'll spend the last night at the five-star Glenlo Abbey Hotel in Galway, with dinner included at one of the property's two award-winning restaurants. Galway is a big city with some of the best seafood restaurants in Ireland.

In between, you'll drive a small rental car (with unlimited miles) wherever you please—

*Prices are per person, double occupancy and may vary depending on the level of accommodations and time of year. Airport taxes are not included. In most cases, you can add extra nights.

places like County Killarney, the Ring of Kerry or County Cork and its famous Blarney Castle. You get vouchers for bed-and-breakfasts and make reservations a day ahead as you go, choosing from a list of 450 sprinkled throughout Ireland. Prices include a standard shift car (an automatic is available for a small fee). Temperatures are chilly from January to about April, with average highs in the 40s.

Cost: Five-night packages run from $383 to $461, depending on the season. Cost includes lodgings, economy car and coffee reception.

Information: Sceptre Tours (800-221-0924, *www.sceptretours.com*).

PANAMA CANAL
THE MIRAFLORES LOCKS

Fly to Panama for a guided tour of the Panama Canal, one of the most phenomenal engineering feats of recent history. The canal took 75,000 workers more than 10 years to complete. You'll learn the secrets of its construction and watch huge vessels pass through the renowned Miraflores Locks.

On this three-night getaway, you'll also tour Panama City, a modern, cosmopolitan city with one of the world's largest duty-free zones, gourmet restaurants, casinos, nightclubs, shops and markets. Of special interest are its historic areas, Casco Viejo and Panama Vieja, where you'll find plazas, old narrow streets, churches and handicraft markets.

On the outskirts of Panama City is a rain forest, home to monkeys, sloths and 200 species of birds. You can also tour mangrove swamps and coral reefs.

Cost: A three-night package starts at $629, depending on the hotel. This package includes round-trip airfare from Miami, daily breakfast, hotel accommodations, tours and admission to a nightclub.

Information: Go-Today (800-227-3235, *www.go-today.com*).

ESCAPE TO FINLAND
HELSINKI AND THE ARCTIC CIRCLE

Helsinki, the dynamic, sophisticated, ultramodern capital of Finland, is one of Europe's hippest cities. Close by the Arctic Circle, daylight is scarce and temperatures are chilly (around 32°F), in the winter, but attractions are plentiful, ranging from symphony concerts, opera and ballet performances, more than 80 museums, art galleries, spas and gourmet restaurants to pubs, heavy-metal karaoke bars, nightclubs and amusement parks. You'll also find avant-garde clothing, accessories and furniture at chic shops in the Helsinki Design District.

Cost: Starts at $549 round-trip airfare from New York or $639 from Boston. Includes three nights hotel, including a Saturday night and daily breakfast. Extra nights cost about $66.

Information: Nordic Saga Tours (800-848-6449, *www.nordicsaga.com*).

OFF-SEASON VENICE
ST. MARK'S SQUARE AND THE GRAND CANAL

Venice in the off-season (November to March) may be chilly, around 40°F, but it is more alluring than ever because you'll almost have the place to yourself. This is a city to explore on foot, and you can wander in any direction and find treasures.

A four-night stay gives you enough time to get acquainted with this fantastically beautiful, historic city surrounded by water and crisscrossed with canals, and even to visit its famous islands of Murano, known for glassmaking…Burano, for lacemaking…and Torcello, an idyllic outpost of the traditional way of life. Hang out in St. Mark's Square, visit the Doge's Palace and the Basilica of San Marco, then take the elevator to the top of the 325-foot Campanile for a view of the whole city. Follow the Grand Canal to the Rialto Bridge to see miles of opulent palaces. Tired of walking? Hop on a gondola or a vaporetto (water bus) for a return to your hotel.

Cost: Four nights with a departure between November 1 and February 3 starts at $579 from New York City. Includes round-trip airfare, four nights of accommodations and breakfasts. Your stay must include a Saturday night.

Information: Virgin Vacations (888-937-8474, *www.virgin-vacations.com*).

More from Joan Rattner Heilman…

Great US Bird-Watching Sites

Avid birders can be found in the strangest places. They'll grab their binoculars and go almost anywhere to spot birds, especially in the spring and fall when many birds migrate.

Bird-watching is the fastest-growing outdoor recreational activity in the country, according to a US Fish and Wildlife Service survey. If you want to take part but are not experienced enough to chase birds on your own, join one of the many excursions run by local clubs or Audubon Society chapters, or you can choose a commercial tour. *Among the top birding destinations…*

MATAGORDA COUNTY, TEXAS

For the last eight years, Matagorda County, on the Gulf Coast of Texas 80 miles south of Houston, has ranked number one in the Audubon Society's annual Christmas bird count. That means more species of birds—songbirds, such as warblers and catbirds, as well as shore and water birds—were spotted there on that one day than at any other place in North America. Situated on the "central flyway," Matagorda County is a major migration route for birds flying north or south between Central and South America and the US and Canada, with its flat plains, bays, salt marshes, forests, streams and sandy shoreline.

Great spots for watching birds include the Matagorda County Birding Nature Center and the Mad Island Marsh Preserve, managed by the Texas Nature Conservancy.

Information: The Bay City Texas Chamber of Commerce, 800-806-8333, *http://baycitychamber. org*…Palacios Chamber of Commerce, 800-611-4567, *www.palacioschamber.com*.

MONTEREY COUNTY, CALIFORNIA

A few years ago, the American Birding Association named this county on the Pacific coast in California the "Birdiest County in North America."

Although there are many good viewing areas, Elkhorn Slough is probably the most renowned. An area of tidal wetlands, coastal prairie and woodlands located close to the city of Monterey, it is full of migratory birds and rare species, such as the brown pelican, peregrine falcon, Caspian tern and snowy plover.

It's a good habitat for seabirds and shorebirds, such as ducks, loons, grebes, gulls and terns. It also boasts the Rookery, an area that is home to a large breeding colony of great blue herons and great egrets that nest each spring in the treetops above a marsh. Guided walks are available.

Another top birding site is Andrew Molera State Park on Highway 1 in the spectacular Big Sur area. This 5,000-acre park consists of many types of habitat, and has large numbers of vagrant species (birds rare in the West but blown off course during migration), as well as its own native birds.

From April through October, Tuesdays through Saturdays, Big Sur Ornithology Lab bands birds that have been caught in mist nets. Visitors are welcome to observe.

Information: Monterey County Convention & Visitors Bureau, 888-221-1010, *www.monterey info.org*...Elkhorn Slough, 831-728-2822, *www. elkhornslough.org*...Andrew Molera State Park, Big Sur Ornithology Lab, 831-624-1202, *www. ventanaws.org/lab.htm.*

CAPE MAY, NEW JERSEY

Cape May Point, literally the southern tip of New Jersey, is another premier hotspot, best known for its concentrations of hawks and songbirds during fall migration when birds heading south along the East coast stop in or fly by in the millions. At its annual autumn hawk watch, an average of 60,000 birds of prey—hawks, ospreys and falcons—have been tallied.

In the spring, sightings include large numbers of shorebirds feeding on horseshoe crab eggs on the beaches of Delaware Bay...seabirds, such as loons, cormorants and ducks, flying along the coast...and songbirds on their way north. The prime source of information and programs that include daily walks, workshops, field trips and talks is the Northwood Center of the Audubon Society's Cape May Bird Observatory.

Information: Cape May Bird Observatory at 609-884-2736, *www.njaudubon.org/centers/cmbo.*

EVERGLADES NATIONAL PARK, FLORIDA

A vast "river of grass" that once covered more than three million acres in the southernmost part of Florida, the Everglades, though greatly reduced in size by development, still attracts more than 300 species of birds.

The Everglades has a rich bird life—especially large wading birds, such as roseate spoonbills, white pelicans, wood storks, herons, egrets and ibis. It abounds in hawks and bald eagles, and serves as a temporary haven for migratory species, including orioles and many varieties of warblers.

Among the best spots to observe: Eco Pond in the Flamingo area and the Anhinga Trail in the Long Pine Key area.

Information: National Park Service, 305-242-7700, *www.nps.gov/ever*...Flamingo Lodge & Marina, 239-695-3101, *www.flamingolodge.com.*

GIBBON, NEBRASKA

Located on the banks of the Platte River in south-central Nebraska, Gibbon is well-known for the world's largest concentration of sandhill cranes, huge birds that stop to rest and feed on their way north in March and April. About a half million sandhill cranes pass through every year, along with several million geese and ducks.

The most popular place to observe them is at Audubon's Rowe Sanctuary. It offers two-hour guided trips ($20 per person, no children under the age of eight) to a series of observation blinds set up along the river's edge. The tours leave at 5:30 am or 5:30 pm during the six weeks of crane season. A spectacular sight, each adult crane stands three to four feet tall, weighs six to 12 pounds and has a wingspan of about six feet.

At other times of the year, other waterfowl, prairie chickens, bald eagles and many varieties of songbirds can be found in abundance.

Information: Rowe Sanctuary, 308-468-5282, *www.rowesanctuary.org.*

Less Waiting at Disney Attractions

RideMax (*www.ridemax.com*) PC software helps users plan trips to Disneyland in California and Walt Disney World in Florida. Users can select the attractions they wish to visit, and the program will create a personalized schedule that minimizes the amount of time spent waiting in line.

Recent example: A visitor rode six of Disneyland's most popular rides in just over two hours, with an average waiting time of only 13 minutes per ride.

Cost for Disneyland: $14.95* for a 90-day subscription or $24.95 for a one-year subscription.

Cost for Disney World: $18.95 for a 120-day subscription or $29.95 for a one-year subscription.

*Prices subject to change.

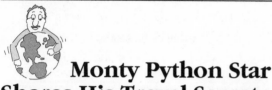

Monty Python Star Shares His Travel Secrets

Michael Palin, London-based member of the Monty Python comedy troupe. His book, *Himalaya* (St. Martin's), was the subject of a TV series on the Travel Channel. His Web site, *www.palinstravels.co.uk,* offers travel information and free access to his books.

Actor and comedian Michael Palin is an avid traveler whose journeys have been chronicled in books and on television. Since being bitten by the travel bug in 1988, he has visited more than 80 countries, logging enough miles to fill a half-dozen passports.

His latest journey was to the Himalayas—from the Pakistani-Afghan frontier through India, Nepal, Tibet, Assam, Bhutan and Bangladesh.**

While between trips, Mr. Palin shares some of his travel secrets…

●**Few people have the time or money to visit Tibet, Nepal or the headwaters of the Amazon, as you have done. Can you recommend some equally thrilling—but more accessible—locations?** Almost everyone lives within a short journey of out-of-the-way places that are fascinating because of their history, culture and natural beauty. To find these places, get a guide on local history or on a particular subject you are very interested in, such as folk art. Then plan a short trip.

Not too long ago, for instance, I discovered Glencoe in Scotland. Glencoe is one of the most

**US government travel advisories are available from the Department of State, 888-407-4747, *travel.state.gov/travel/warnings.html.*

pristine places in the British Isles—mountainous and beautiful. Whenever I hike around the area, I get the feeling that no one else has ever been there, much as I have felt in the middle of the Sahara. In fact, Glencoe is only a half-day trip from London and several other big cities.

●**Many travelers never see much more than their hotels and a few well-trodden tourist sites. How can they get a real understanding of a place?** Ask people you meet—local residents as well as other tourists—to suggest interesting side trips. Sometimes you'll be disappointed, but you'll often have the satisfaction of seeing people and places that others miss.

In Tibet, for example, a local resident recommended that we meet a yak herder who could show us more about their ancient way of life than any guidebook could. The yak herder even prodded me into milking one of the animals.

Of course, what anyone derives from a travel experience is up to the individual. In this case, I derived just enough yak milk for a cappuccino.

●**You have retraced the steps of Ernest Hemingway's journeys. Did you enjoy that? Is there another famous writer you would recommend following?** Following in the footsteps of a famous person can be a great way to get insight into both the individual and the places he/she visited. I might never have thought to visit some interesting parts of Havana if I had not read Hemingway's accounts of them. After seeing the running of the bulls in (Pamplona) Spain, I gained a much better understanding of his novel *The Sun Also Rises.*

Robert Louis Stevenson is another writer who can point the way. In *Travels with a Donkey in the Cévennes,* he wrote wonderfully about journeying through the central southeast region of France. It remains a beautiful and fairly remote part of the country. I would strongly recommend his book as well as a visit to the Cévennes.

●**Which places are your favorite alternatives to the familiar tourist spots? What makes them special?** For some of the best music in the world, go to Dakar in Senegal, located on the west coast of Africa. For exotic scenery, you can't beat the interior of Colombia. Both countries don't attract many tourists, but it's not difficult to find comfortable accommodations.

•**Any last-minute advice for country-hoppers like yourself?** Remember to bring proper documents. The old UK passports had names and numbers on the front and were bigger and harder to lose than the current European Community (EC) substitutes. The EC covers all look alike, which once landed me in an embarrassing spot. When leaving Paris, I handed over my EC passport only to receive a strange look from the immigration officer. He peered again at greater length, then frowned and shook his head. When I asked what the problem was, he held up the passport and I found myself looking at my wife's picture. I realized with horror that we kept all the family passports in the same drawer, and I had taken the wrong one.

Fortunately, I was helped by his colleague, who recognized me from Monty Python and therefore assumed it was quite natural for me to be dressed as a woman. But if you weren't in Monty Python, this could be a problem.

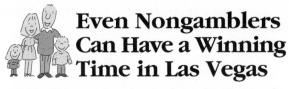

Even Nongamblers Can Have a Winning Time in Las Vegas

Mary Herczog, a travel writer located in Los Angeles who has written numerous books on Las Vegas, including *Frommer's Portable Las Vegas for Non-Gamblers* and *Frommer's Las Vegas 2007* (both from Frommer's).

Most people go to Las Vegas to gamble—but even if gambling isn't your thing, there's still plenty to do and see…

ATTRACTIONS

•**Secret Garden and Dolphin Habitat at the Mirage Hotel.** Observe Atlantic bottlenose dolphins in this well-designed habitat.

Admission: $15* for adults…children are less. See Web site for hours. Includes access to the Secret Garden of Siegfried & Roy, a small zoo. 3400 Las Vegas Blvd. South, 702-791-7188, *www. miragehabitat.com.*

•**Liberace Museum.** A truly enjoyable collection celebrating the late performer.

*Prices subject to change.

Admission: $12.50…$8.50 for students and seniors. Open 10 am to 5 pm Monday through Saturday…12 pm to 4 pm Sunday. 1775 E. Tropicana Ave., 702-798-5595, *www.liberace.com/museum.cfm.*

•**King Tut's Tomb & Museum.** A meticulous full-scale re-creation of King Tut's tomb at the Luxor Hotel and Casino.

Admission: $5. Open 9 am to 11 pm Sunday through Thursday…9 am to 11:30 pm Friday and Saturday. 3900 Las Vegas Blvd. South, 800-557-7428, *www.luxor.com.*

•**Las Vegas Mini Gran Prix.** This extensive go-cart track and arcade provides great fun for families—it has go-carts for kids and adults.

Tickets: $6 per ride. Open 10 am to 10 pm Sunday through Thursday…10 am to 11 pm on Fridays and Saturdays. 1401 N. Rainbow Blvd., just off US 95 North, 888-259-7223, *www.lvmgp. com.*

SHOWS

Vegas draws such big-name performers as Celine Dion, Elton John and Jerry Seinfeld. For listings, check *Las Vegas Online Entertainment Guide* (*www.lvol.com*). *Current shows include…*

•**Blue Man Group.** Hilarious performance art by a blue-faced troupe.

Tickets: $71.50 to $121. Shows at 7:30 pm daily, plus a 10:30 pm show on Saturdays at the Venetian, 702-414-4300, *www.venetiantickets.com.*

•**Cirque du Soleil's KA.** The newest show combines astounding acrobatics, martial arts and puppetry, all on a moving stage.

Tickets: $69 to $150. Shows Tuesday through Saturday at 7:30 pm and 10:30 pm at the MGM Grand, 877-264-1844, *www.cirquedusoleil.com.*

ART

•**Bellagio Gallery of Fine Art.** This is one of the best small art galleries in the country.

Admission: $15…$12 for seniors, students and Nevada residents. Open 9 am to 10 pm daily. Reservations suggested. 3600 Las Vegas Blvd. South, 877-957-9777, *www.bellagio.com.*

•**Guggenheim Hermitage Museum.** This is a world-class museum located in the Venetian Hotel and Casino.

Admission: $19.50…$15 for seniors…$12.50 for students. Open 9:30 am to 8:30 pm daily. Reservations suggested. 3355 Las Vegas Blvd. South, 702-414-2440, *www.guggenheimlasvegas.org*.

•**The Arts Factory.** This large group of art galleries and artists' workspaces is the center of the artistic community.

Admission: Free. Most galleries are open 12 noon to 4 pm, Tuesday through Saturday. 101-109 E. Charleston Blvd., 702-676-1111, *www.theartsfactory.com*.

SURROUNDING AREA

•**Hoover Dam.** The scale of this massive engineering feat makes it worth the 45-minute drive from the city.

Tour: $11…$9 for seniors or military personnel…$6 for children ages seven to 16. Parking is $7 per vehicle. Tours from 9 am to 5 pm daily. Located southeast of Las Vegas right on Route 93, 866-730-9097, *www.usbr.gov/lc/hooverdam*.

•**Red Rock Canyon.** Drive the 13-mile loop through the natural rock formations. Just 40 minutes from Las Vegas.

Admission: $5 per vehicle (or $12 per night to camp in the park). Open 6 am to 8 pm. Located west of the city off Nevada Route 159, 702-515-5350.

•**Valley of Fire State Park.** About an hour from town, the park, with its red sandstone, has been used as a setting for sci-fi movies.

Admission: $6 per vehicle (or $14 per night to camp). Northeast of Las Vegas on Route 15, 702-397-2088, *parks.nv.gov/vf.htm*.

Best Cruise Fares

Cruise ships are sailing full these days, so last-minute bargains are becoming rare. The best savings now come from booking early—and can be as much as 40% off.

Other opportunities: Travel during "shoulder season," at the edge of the busy season when demand for rooms falls off but weather is still good at your destination.

Or take a "repositioning cruise" on a ship as it moves between seasons from one cruise route to another.

Example: From the Caribbean to the Panama Canal and up the Pacific Coast to Alaska.

Sherri Eisenberg, freelance travel writer, *Travel + Leisure*, 1120 Avenue of the Americas, New York City 10036.

Airport Parking at a Discount

Reserve an airport parking space on-line to save 10%. Some of these services also offer perks, like baggage service, valet parking and car washes.

More information: *www.airportparkingreservations.com…www.longtermparking.com… and www.parknflynetwork.com*.

Money, Time-Life Bldg., Rockefeller Center, New York City 10020.

Cut Your Waiting Time At the Airport

US air travelers wait longer than they need to. More than half of fliers wait 19 minutes to check in at airlines' main counters. Only 18% use self-service kiosks, where the wait averages eight minutes…10% check in curbside and wait 13 minutes.

Decrease waits by printing boarding passes from airline Web sites—only 5% of passengers actually do this.

Global Airport Satisfaction Index Study, JD Power and Associates, Westlake Village, CA, *www.jdpower.com*.

An Airline Pilot Answers Your Questions

Meryl Getline, a pilot in Elizabeth, CO, with 32 years of flying experience, including 15 years as a captain with a major airline. She now maintains the aviation Web sites FromtheCockpit.com and FlyingFearless.com. She is author of *The World at My Feet: The True (and Sometimes Hilarious) Adventures of a Lady Airline Captain* and the e-book *Ground School for Passengers* (both available at FromtheCockpit.com and FlyingFearless.com).

We trust our lives to airplanes and the pilots who fly them, but there is a lot that the average passenger does not realize about modern aircraft. *Here, a veteran airline captain answers some of the most common passenger questions…*

•**Where is the best place to sit on an airplane if you are prone to airsickness?** The best spot is over the wing or a few rows in front of the wing. When a plane climbs or descends, it pivots on its center of gravity, which tends to be just in front of the wings. The closer you are to this point, the less you'll feel the movement, just as sitting in the middle of a seesaw subjects you to less movement than sitting at the end.

•**How do you prevent jet lag?** I really don't suffer much from jet lag. I always observe local time, though many pilots keep their watches set to their hometown time and try to sleep accordingly. If you're traveling on business, this may be impractical.

The best advice is to stay well-hydrated and rest on the plane if you are traveling overnight and arriving in the morning. If you are traveling during the day, plan to read or watch a movie en route so that you're ready to sleep that night after you arrive.

•**Could the "autopilot" fly or land a plane without the pilots?** Not really. Autopilot can't do much more than fly a programmed route or maintain the last heading or altitude entered by the pilots. Pilots are needed to manage the autopilot during the flight.

The autopilot sometimes plays a role in landings—it can keep the plane lined up with the centerline of the runway and it can even land the plane under certain conditions—but the pilot must control the air speed (even if autothrottles are used, they must be programmed and the speed monitored), flaps and landing gear. The autopilot plays no role at all during takeoffs, although some airplanes may employ autothrottles during takeoff.

•**How do I know that I can trust my pilot?** Airline pilots are among the most thoroughly trained and tested professionals in the US. They also must go through a rigorous retraining each year to remain certified. Any pilot at any airline in this country can be trusted to be a proficient flier.

The pilot certification process may not be as rigorous in some less developed countries, however. Before you board a flight on a small airline in another country, consider checking the airline's safety record on the Web site *www.airsafe. com.* You can view accident reports and other statistics and reach your own conclusions.

•**Are air pockets dangerous?** Not only are they not dangerous, they don't exist. The term "air pocket" was coined by a journalist during World War I, but he really just was referring to turbulence—irregular air currents that can shake aircraft around a bit.

When a plane "hits an air pocket" and seems to drop 1,000 feet, it really has just run into a little turbulence and probably dropped or climbed no more than 10 to 20 feet. Light turbulence is so common and inconsequential that experienced pilots scarcely notice it.

There is such a thing as "severe turbulence," which can be strong enough to injure passengers who aren't wearing their seat belts, but this is so rare that I have never encountered it in my 32 years of flying. Modern radar is advanced enough that pilots usually can steer clear of areas that have a high probability of moderate or severe turbulence.

Even when a plane does experience severe turbulence, it won't crash because of it. When was the last time you read or heard of an airplane accident blamed on turbulence? If you're worried that a little turbulence will bring down your flight, watch one of those Discovery channel documentaries on "hurricane hunter" planes that fly right into the middle of huge storms and come out unscathed on the other side. A modern passenger jet is just as sturdy.

●**In the movies, whenever a plane hits severe turbulence, the baggage compartments open up and luggage tumbles out. Would that happen in a real plane?** On occasion, if it gets really rough, an overhead compartment could open, especially if it isn't securely latched. I have never witnessed more than one compartment at a time come open due to turbulence, and I have only seen this once or twice.

●**How dangerous is it when a plane gets struck by lightning?** My plane has been struck at least three times in my career. There's sometimes a bang, like a cannon going off, but it's not all that dangerous. The lightning charge simply travels around the plane's metal exterior, then off the "static wicks" (pencil-like protrusions) on the trailing edges and tips of the wings and tail.

It is true that lightning can cause problems for a plane's electrical systems. Once, on a flight from Los Angeles to Denver, a lightning strike knocked out my plane's power, but only for a few seconds. Even if the plane's main electrical system had been permanently disabled, we still had standby power. Some modern planes are now outfitted with Ram Air Turbines (RATs), which use the airstream to power onboard electrical backup generators and hydraulic systems.

Between the emergency power systems and the extensive training that pilots receive, there's no reason to think that a plane would crash just because its main electrical system went out.

●**What advice do you have for people who are afraid to fly?** I suggest that you consider the statistics regarding flying. It really is true that the drive to the airport is many, many times more dangerous than the flight. Personally, I feel far safer in a plane than I do in a car.

●**Are some airports safer than others?** All US airports are safe, but some are more modern than others and thus probably a little safer.

Modern airports often have longer runways, easier-to-navigate approaches and more sophisticated electronics that allow pilots to land even with limited or no visibility. The ultramodern airports include Denver International Airport and Los Angeles International Airport.

Older airports, such as Chicago's Midway International Airport, Jackson Hole Airport, San Diego International Airport, New York City's LaGuardia Airport and Ronald Reagan Washington National Airport, are not this advanced, but I certainly wouldn't call them unsafe.

●**Has air travel security improved since 9/11?** Yes, mostly because the passengers themselves now are part of the security force. In the past, if a passenger started acting oddly, those seated near him/her would just mind their own business. These days, if a passenger starts doing anything halfway suspicious, other passengers quickly alert a flight attendant.

Fly in Comfort

The most comfortable plane seats (flatbeds) are on nonUS air carriers. Researchers found the best seats for sleeping, based on dimensions and contouring, in first class on Air France, All Nippon, British Airways, Cathay Pacific, Emirates, Gulf Air, Malaysia Airlines, Qantas Airways, Qatar Airways, Singapore Airlines, South African Airways, Swiss International Airways, TAM Brazilian and Thai Airways.

Study by Skytrax, an airline-quality research firm based in London.

Inside Information On Airfares

Get the inside information on airfares and on first-class upgrades at ExpertFlyer.com and FlyerTalk.com. Using fare codes which explain restrictions, travelers can search for special offers, frequent-flier award seating and upgrades that do not show up on the popular travel sites Travelocity, Expedia.com and Orbitz.

ExpertFlyer.com's premium service is offered for $99.99/yr.* FlyerTalk.com is a travelers' message board that you can search to locate code information. Flights cannot be booked through these sites, but travelers can use the code information to get the best deals through other Web sites or travel agents.

The Wall Street Journal, 200 Liberty St., New York City 10281.

*Price subject to change.

More Airfare Advice

To get the lowest fares, clear your computer of cookies left behind at travel and airline Web sites. Cookies may automatically take you to the last price you saw, rather than to the latest —and possibly better—deals. See your browser's "Help" file for instructions.

Kiplinger's Personal Finance, 1729 H St. NW, Washington, DC 20006.

New Way to Get Great Travel Deals

Wonderful travel bargains may be available when pricing errors occur on travel Web sites. FareAlert.net tracks down errors, including mistyped flight or hotel rates, on such travel sites as Travelocity and then e-mails the information to its subscribers.

Example: $20 for a flight to London instead of $200. In many cases, airlines and hotel chains honor the incorrect rates.

Planes for Hire

Private flights have traditionally involved small corporation-owned jets seating six to eight people—but "fractional" ownership of planes by several parties and charter planes, known as on-demand "air taxi" services, have given more travelers access to private flights. Some charter planes offer "jet card" programs, in which travelers prepay for flight hours. Private flights can access up to 5,300 noncommercial US airports.

Costs vary but are at least several hundred dollars more per person than those of commercial first-class flights. However, more convenient schedules and arrivals closer to final destinations mean that air travelers can forgo hotels or rental cars in some cases.

How to find charter companies: The National Business Aviation Association provides a free *Aircraft Charter Consumer Guide* (202-783-9286, *www.nbaa.org*).

Dan Hubbard, vice president of communications, National Business Aviation Association, Washington, DC.

Rent a Car By the Hour

Rent cars by the hour in major cities—to visit tourist sites or just run errands. Flexcar (877-353-9227 or *www.flexcar.com*) has by-the-hour rentals in Los Angeles...Portland, Oregon...San Diego...Seattle...and Washington, DC. Zipcar (866-494-7227 or *www.zipcar.com*) operates in Boston...Chapel Hill, North Carolina...metropolitan New York...Washington, DC...Minneapolis ...Toronto...and San Francisco.

Application charges and annual membership fees vary depending on the city. Rental rates start at $8/hour.* Initial membership fees run about $75. Cars can be reserved via phone or on-line. Fees for both companies include gas, insurance, maintenance and parking at reserved spots.

*Prices subject to change.

Luxury Rental Car Trap

The cost of renting luxury cars is lower than ever—but there's an insurance trap. If you rent a car that is more costly than the car you own, your personal auto insurance might protect you only up to the amount of your own vehicle's value. So if you crash a more expensive rental car, you may be liable for the difference. Insurance obtained through a credit card may not help because cards often cap coverage and exclude very expensive cars outright. So check your insurance before renting a luxury car—this is one case where you might want to pay for the rental firm's collision damage waiver.

SmartMoney, 250 W. 55 St., New York City 10019.

Hidden Hotel Fees

Hotels are charging for almost every convenience they offer.

Among the fees on bills: $2 for maid service…$2 for coffee used in the "complimentary" coffeemaker…$9.50 for porter service, even if you carried your own bags…even $50 to get packages at the front desk.

Self-defense: At the time of booking, ask the agent if there are charges other than room occupancy and sales tax. If there is a charge on your bill that you don't agree with, ask the manager to remove it.

Survey of visitors to ConsumerReports.org, conducted by *Consumer Reports,* 101 Truman Ave., Yonkers, NY.

Sleep Well at Hotels

Many hotels are now making an effort to improve their beds and bedding. Radisson bought 90,000 Select Comfort mattresses, which allow for different degrees of firmness on each side. Sheraton Four Points is now offering Sealy Posturepedic plush-top beds. And, Marriott is replacing the bedding in its chains with high-quality sheets, more pillows and a softer mattress cover. Westin launched this trend six years ago with its Heavenly Bed campaign.

Consensus of hotel executives, reported in *The Wall Street Journal.*

Passport Savvy

Kelly Shannon, press officer, Bureau of Consular Affairs, US Department of State, Washington, DC.

It's best to keep your passport up-to-date—even though the US government doesn't require its citizens to maintain valid passports. Some countries require a passport to have been valid for at least six months before your travel date. Others require that it be valid for at least six months after the date of your arrival. This is especially important if there is any chance that you may have to travel abroad with little notice.

Example: If you have ill or elderly relatives abroad and may have to get to them quickly. Countries' passport regulations change, so check with the embassy or consulate of each country you may visit.

Helpful: Register with the US Department of State prior to traveling so the government can more easily help you in—or notify you of—an emergency. Registration is free and secure at *https://travelregistration.state.gov,* and lasts for six months.

Note: Since December 31, 2005, Americans traveling to Canada, Mexico and other Western Hemisphere countries are required to have a passport or other security document.

Information: *travel.state.gov.*

Passport Alert

Americans visiting Canada, Mexico, Bermuda, the Caribbean and Central and South America will need to show their passports to reenter the US starting in 2008. These guidelines were created to deter terrorists from entering the US. Previously, Americans could show a driver's license or a state identification card.

US Customs and Border Protection, Washington, DC.

Make Dinner Reservations Before You Travel Abroad

You can make dinner reservations at popular restaurants in Europe and Asia on the Internet at *www.eat2eat.com* for Asia…*www.cuisine net.co.uk* and *www.toptable.co.uk* for the United Kingdom, Paris, Dublin, Barcelona and New York…and *www.restaurantrow.com* worldwide (which charges $4.95* for each reservation).

*Price subject to change.

Best Way to Get Foreign Currency Before a Trip

American Express charges a flat fee (usually $3*) for currency purchases at its branches or $15 for on-line orders. It has a wide currency selection and offers favorable exchange rates.

Alternative: Travelex, the biggest currency-exchange company, lets travelers pay $5 to guarantee the same exchange rate if they return the currency within 31 days after buying it. Travelex fees are higher—$5.50 or 1% of the total, whichever is higher—and exchange rates are not as favorable. AAA members receive a 25% discount.

More information: *www.travelex.com.*

*Prices subject to change.

Tipping Basics

Wondering how much to tip the concierge? What about the front-desk clerk? *Some tipping basics…*

•**Give a doorman $1 to $2 per bag** for carrying luggage and $1 to $4 for hailing a cab—more in bad weather.

•**Give the bellhop $1 to $2 per bag.**

•**Tip a concierge $5 to $10 for each special service** immediately, not when you check out.

•**Leave at least $2 each day for the housekeeper.**

•**Airport shuttle drivers do not need to be tipped** unless they help you with bags—then tip $1 to $2 per bag.

•**There is no need to tip the front-desk clerk…**bed-and-breakfast owner…or room-service waiter if a gratuity is included on the bill.

Peggy Post, great-granddaughter-in-law of etiquette pioneer Emily Post. She is a director and spokesperson for the Emily Post Institute in Burlington, VT, and author of *Emily Post's Etiquette, 17th Edition* (HarperCollins). Her Web site is *www.emilypost.com.*

Avoid Expensive Phone Charges While Traveling

Both hotel phone charges and cell phone roaming charges can be very high.

New alternative: Internet phone calls using Voice Over Internet Protocol (VoIP) may cost only a fraction as much (from about $15* per month). All that's needed is a high-speed connection for the Internet (now routinely provided in many hotels) and an adapter that connects a phone (yours or the hotel's) to the Internet, which is supplied by the VoIP service provider. Such providers include Vonage (*www.vonage. com*), Packet8 (*www.packet8.net*) and a growing number of conventional phone companies. VoIP can be used abroad as well.

*Price subject to change.

Restrooms When You Are on the Go

Where to Stop & Where to Go: A Guide to Traveling with Overactive Bladder in the United States lists public bathrooms in 19 leisure travel destinations and four national parks. To obtain your free copy, contact Novartis at 877-786-7465 or *www.wheretostopwheretogo.com.*

Keep Your Plants Alive

To keep houseplants moist while on a trip, soak plant soil with water, then seal plants in clear perforated plastic bags, such as those often used by dry cleaners. Water rises up inside the bags during the day and drips down at night…air penetrates through the holes. Also, place plants out of direct sunlight. Plants will stay healthy for up to 12 weeks.

Marion Owen, master gardener, Kodiak, AK, and coauthor of *Chicken Soup for the Gardener's Soul* (HCI).

Is Airplane Air Bad?

In one study, air in a plane was no more likely to transmit disease than air in an office building. Infection risk rose only if participants sat within two rows of a contagious passenger for more than eight hours.

Mark A. Gendreau, MD, emergency medicine specialist, Lahey Clinic Medical Center, Burlington, MA, and co-author of an airplane air study, published in *The Lancet*.

To Be on the Safe Side...

To avoid catching a cold or the flu after flying, take the dietary supplement *lactoferrin*. People who travel on airplanes often get colds within a week of travel. The supplement, which is made from whey, is identical to the lactoferrin protein that occurs naturally in the gut. This protein boosts the production of immunoglobulins, compounds that fight bacteria and viruses.

Helpful: Take 200 mg of lactoferrin twice daily two days before you fly, and continue taking it for three days afterward.

Erika T. Schwartz, MD, an internist in private practice in New York City.

Diarrhea Prevention

One antibiotic that is used to treat traveler's diarrhea, *rifaximin* (Xifaxan), may prevent it without causing the resistance that eventually makes other antibiotics ineffective.

Recent study: Rifaximin prevented traveler's diarrhea in 85% of US students who took it daily for their first two weeks in Mexico.

Diarrhea, an ailment triggered by bacteria in food and, to a lesser degree, water, affects about 20 million international travelers a year.

Herbert L. DuPont, MD, professor and director, Center for Infectious Diseases, University of Texas School of Public Health and chief of internal medicine, St. Luke's Episcopal Hospital, both in Houston. He is lead author of a study of 210 travelers, published in *Annals of Internal Medicine*.

Dengue Fever Alert

Dengue fever is a serious health concern for travelers to tropical locations, such as Central America, the north of South America, India, Southeast Asia and parts of coastal Africa. There is no treatment or vaccine for this severe, flu-like illness, which lasts for one to two weeks. A second dengue infection may result in dengue hemorrhagic fever, a potentially fatal disease. The mosquitoes that carry the dengue fever are widespread in warm regions, especially in cities, and are most active at dawn and dusk.

Self-defense: Make sure you wear protective clothing on which you have sprayed the insecticide permethrin, and use mosquito repellent that has a DEET content of 30% to 35%. Consult a travel-medicine specialist before your trip.

Mayo Clinic Health Letter, 200 First St. SW, Rochester, MN 55905.

Pickpocket Protection

Pickpockets are worse than ever in Europe. A simple thought to keep in mind all the time—pickpockets do not make a move until they know where your money is. That means every time you pay for something, you let them know where you carry cash and cards.

Therefore, separate your cash and credit and debit cards, keeping them in at least two, preferably three, separate places, such as in different pieces of clothing...in various pockets of your jacket, slacks, shirt...in zippered compartments in your purse, briefcase or tote...in a fanny pack worn under clothing. Then, should you be targeted, the thief will not be able to take all your money nor all of your cards.

Additional defense: Always carry enough traveler's checks to cover an emergency—and keep the issuer's phone number and the serial numbers of the checks separate from the checks. The issuer will replace your checks at no charge if they are lost or stolen.

Nancy Dunnan, editor and publisher of *TravelSmart*, *www.travelsmartnewsletter.com*.

15

Fun Times

Seven Big Gambling Myths from a High Roller

I n casinos, the odds will always be against the gambler, but the odds grow even more dim when gamblers hold erroneous beliefs about the games that they play. *Seven of the most common—and the costliest—gambling myths...*

Myth 1: **Higher-limit slot machines offer better odds,** so they're a smarter play. In major casinos, the quarter slots typically return about 91% of the money bet...the dollar slots, 94% to 95%...and the $5 slots, upwards of 95%. But in this case, the better odds are not your best bet. The 91% average return on the quarter slots means that over time, you'll lose an average of 2.25 cents per play, assuming that you risk just one coin at a time. The 94% to 95% return on the dollar slots translates into an average loss of five to six cents every time you insert a coin, so you'll lose your money more than twice as fast. And with $5 slots, you'll lose an average of at least 25 cents per play—more than 10 times as fast as with the quarter machines.

Reality: It's true that, statistically, you stand to win most at the highest-limit machines, but unless you have lots of money that you can afford to lose, the only time it's wise to move up to the dollar slots is if you have been playing the quarter slots three quarters at a time.

At an average loss of between six and seven cents per pull, you would be better off switching to the dollar machines—assuming that you want to restrict yourself to a single dollar coin per play.

Warning: The worst slot odds are on "progressive" or "linked" machines that offer escalating jackpots, up to six figures or higher. These machines typically return only 85% of the money bet.

Frank Scoblete, Malverne, NY–based author of 20 books on gambling topics, including *Casino Gambling: Play Like a Pro in 10 Minutes or Less!* and *The Craps Underground* (both from Bonus). He spends more than 100 days each year at casinos and leads the very popular Golden Touch seminars. He maintains a craps Internet site at *www.golden touchcraps.com.*

Myth 2: **This slot machine is due.** Some slot players continue to pour money into slot machines that have not been winning on the theory that the machines are "due" to hit. Conversely, players who have won money on one machine sometimes continue to play, thinking that the machine is "hot." Still others believe that when all the symbols for a big jackpot appear in view, but not in line, the machine is close to a major payout.

Reality: What a slot machine has done on past spins has absolutely no bearing on what it does on future spins. Each spin is independent and random.

Myth 3: **Single-deck blackjack gives gamblers a fighting chance** against the casino. At a typical casino blackjack table, six or eight decks of cards are shuffled together. But now many casinos also offer single-deck blackjack, where only one deck is in play at any given time. With just 52 cards to account for, it seems easier for gamblers to calculate their best strategies.

Reality: Casinos have structured the single-deck game so that it's harder than ever to beat the house. At the normal blackjack tables, the casino pays three to two when you get blackjack—$15 on a $10 bet. At single-deck tables, the payout is only six to five, or $12 on a $10 bet. That lower payout means that over time, even if you are able to win a few more hands because you have kept track of the cards that have been played, you can expect to lose your money nearly three times as fast as you would at a multideck table.

Myth 4: **Play the trend at the blackjack table.** Gamblers like to search for trends, even where none exist. They'll bet more at the craps table when the dice are running "hot" or bet a number that has hit a few times on the roulette wheel, though a modern wheel in a major casino is extremely unlikely to be biased.

In general, betting the trend in the casino is no worse than any other bet, but blackjack is an "antitrend" game.

Example: When a lot of small cards have been dealt, there are fewer small cards left to be played, making it smarter to assume that the trend will reverse.

Reality: At the blackjack table, betting the trend is a costly mistake.

Myth 5: **If I can win in poker games with my friends, I can win in the casino or on-line.** In casinos and at on-line gambling sites, you are not just playing against the other players at the table—you're also playing against the "rake," the house's cut of anywhere from 2% to 20% of the winning pots. And unlike in home games, you're not playing against people you know, so you can't expect to read your opponents. On-line, you might even come up against some pro gamblers with computer programs and teamwork to up their odds.

Reality: The best way to survive is to play tighter than you would at a friendly home game, folding most hands and risking your money only when your opportunities are greatest.

Myth 6: **Fast play is good play.** At the table games, experienced gamblers typically make quick decisions and become frustrated with novice players who move slowly and drag down the pace of play.

Reality: It's in a gambler's best interests to move slowly. Not only does slower play give you more time to think, it reduces the number of hands that you'll play on a given night. Because the odds are in the house's favor on every hand, fewer hands played means greater odds that you'll walk away a winner—or at least that you'll lose less. The only downside to taking a little time is the dirty looks you'll receive from the dealer and your fellow gamblers. If you're at a casino with friends, play at the same table, so you won't feel outnumbered and bullied into fast play.

Myth 7: **Comps are a way to "win" at the casino.** After you sign up for a rewards card at the casino, you might earn complimentary meals, show tickets—even hotel rooms. Many gamblers view these comps as a way to recoup their losses at the gambling tables. Casinos view them as a way to keep gamblers happy as they lose money.

Reality: Whenever you receive great comps, it means that based on how you are betting, the casino expects you to lose a large amount of money.

Don't Use the ATM In Casinos

ATM machines in casinos often charge inflated fees. Some have been known to charge more than double what an average ATM charges. If you want to use a credit card for a cash advance, the fees are even higher. Avoid ATMs by getting cash before you enter the casino…or bring your checkbook—many casinos cash personal checks for free.

SmartMoney, 250 W. 55 St., New York City 10019.

She's Won Over 450 Contests: How She Does It

Carol Shaffer, author of *Contest Queen* (Truman). This book has helped many readers win prizes in local and national contests. She is based in Columbia, IL.

Carol Shaffer was over age 50 when she decided to get her degree in marketing. While at Southwestern Illinois College, she chose to do her thesis on contests and promotions, a subject that few people had studied. Ms. Shaffer's thesis led to more than a degree. She has won more than 450 contests in seven years and has written a book that shares her strategy with others. *Some of her best advice is outlined below…*

Think twice before you pass up an opportunity to enter a contest or sweepstake. Your chances of winning are often far better than you imagine.

Apart from cash, you can win automobiles, computers, dinner out with a celebrity, gift certificates, tickets to shows and games, toys, trips and chances to appear on television.

The myth is that so many people enter contests that the odds of winning are very long. But in reality, organizations that hold sweepstakes often have trouble convincing people to enter.

Advantage: A large number of contests are free, while it costs money to enter the lotteries where you have only a remote chance to win.

Reminder: Taxes are due on the fair market value of your prizes.

GREAT OPPORTUNITIES

Here's where your odds of winning prizes are best…

• **Local contests and sweepstakes.** National events may have bigger prizes, but they usually attract many more entrants than local contests, some of which have surprisingly few entries.

Exception: National contests with a long list of prizes. The top prize might be a vacation for two in Hawaii, for instance, but there could be dozens of lesser prizes.

Many would-be entrants stay away because they know chances of winning the top prize are slim. They forget that the overall odds are much better for winning one of the many smaller prizes. And as a general rule, the shorter the entry period is, the better your chances are because there's less time for competitors to get in the game.

• **Essay contests and competitions that require you to fill out a questionnaire.** Despite the allure of prizes, many people do not want to spend the few minutes that it takes to meet the requirements.

WINNING TACTICS

A couple of years ago, I entered a contest sponsored by CBS and Venture Stores, a regional discount chain. To win a top-of-the-line TV set, contestants had to answer questions about CBS television shows. The winner was then selected by a random drawing of correct entries.

Because there were nearly a dozen Venture stores in the area, I entered at each one. I won *three* TV sets.

This contest is a great example of two winning strategies…

• **Enter the contests that allow duplicate entries** or entries at more than one location. Sure, some other contestants may also submit more than one entry, but you'll have an edge over the vast majority who don't.

Advertisements for contests often ask you to fill out an entry form supplied with the product. The fine print, however, may explain that you don't actually have to buy the product to enter. That makes it easier to enter many times, which increases your odds of winning.

•**Read the rules very carefully,** and stick to them. Just by doing that, you can boost your chances enormously.

If the Venture contest was like most others, about 25% of entries were disqualified for not following the fine print.

Typically overlooked: Requirements to list your Zip code, to use an envelope of a certain size or to print instead of writing in longhand.

BEATING THE ODDS

More winning strategies…

•**Choose contests that require long essays** over those that ask for short essays. Long-essay contests have better odds because there are generally fewer entrants. Also, in an essay of 100 to 200 words, judges are more likely to spot phrases they like than they are in an essay of, say, 25 words.

•**Go beyond the obvious.** One of my local TV stations, for example, held a contest for viewers to write about their favorite soap opera. I won with an essay on *The Young and the Restless*—because I was the only one who wrote about the female villain on the show, rather than the main characters as everyone else had done.

The prize? I got to tape an actual TV commercial for the local station—and they even used passages from my essay in the commercial!

And when National Foods held a recipe contest in the St. Louis area, I won $100 for using the company's ranch dressing—not in a salad, which would have been obvious, but in a hot side dish of potatoes, green beans, bacon and cheddar cheese.

•**Give your essay a title.** If a contest requires you to write an essay, put a short title on your entry that can catch the judges' attention. (Titles usually aren't included in the word count, but check the rules to make sure.)

If an airline, for instance, asks all contest entrants to write an essay on why they like to fly, you could write about flying to baseball games and then improve your chances with a title like "Take Me Out to the Ball Game."

The title is upbeat, mentions a national pastime and suggests a reason to fly that airlines may have overlooked. It could go a long way in making your entry stand out from the others.

Smart move: Pick up brochures of the sponsoring company, which are typically available where its product or service is sold. Or go to the company's Web site. Then try to make your entry a part of the marketing strategy that you read about. The baseball theme, for example, would be appropriate for an airline that's trying to attract families, especially during summer months. Football could work in the fall.

Be careful, however, not to mimic the exact words that a company uses in its ads—you will lose originality points.

•**Make your entries physically stand out.** Instead of mailing an entry in a standard white envelope, use a colored one of an odd size.

Caution: Make sure your entry conforms to the rules.

Or for a drawing, fold some of your entries like an accordion, or crumple them so they stand out to the touch when someone reaches into the container. Entries prepared in these ways are also less likely to settle unnoticed at the bottom.

I used the crumpled-entry strategy a few years ago in a big contest sponsored by the Sherwin-Williams Co. I won a Chrysler LHS sedan.

Similarly, don't submit all your entries on the same date in sweepstakes where the winner is drawn from a bowl or other container. By staggering entries, you cut the risk that all of yours will be in one section of the container.

And unless rules specify otherwise, consider writing your entry in colored ink or on colored paper. A small drawing at the top of the page can also make it stand out, and so can writing the entry in a unique style.

My grandson, for example, won a trip to the St. Louis Cardinals' spring training camp in Florida by writing an essay on why his mother was a good soccer mom. He wrote it as a poem!

To find out about contests, check local papers, ask store managers, tune in to the local radio and TV stations or go to their Web sites. A listing of nationwide contests is provided at *contests. about.com.*

Caution: The number of Web-based contests is soaring. Though most are legitimate, beware of scam contests with the purpose of collecting e-mail addresses and personal data.

Safeguard: Don't enter a contest unless it's sponsored by a company you've heard of and have no reason to distrust.

Smart Lottery Playing

In lotteries that are fair, each number has the same chance of coming up—but some numbers are picked by lottery players much more often than other numbers.

Examples: "Lucky" numbers like seven numbers in a sequential pattern, and numbers corresponding to calendar dates (one to 31). If you wager on such popular numbers, you're more likely to share any prize you win with a number of other people.

Instead, choose unpopular numbers—your chances of having the winning numbers will be just the same, but since you'll be less likely to share a prize, if you do win, you will win much more.

Larry Lesser, PhD, associate professor of mathematics, University of Texas at El Paso.

How to Prevent Golf Injuries

Frank Rabadam, a DPT (doctor of physical therapy), who is certified by Back to Golf, the PGA- and LPGA-approved fitness and golf biomechanics program. He also is a certified Yoga for Golfers instructor, senior physical therapist at Portsmouth Regional Hospital in NH and owner of Back Under Par, a golf performance enhancement program.

The sedate pace of golf would appear to leave little room for injuries—but that is not so. According to one study, as many as one-third of the more than 25 million golfers in the US sustain significant injuries of the back, spine, shoulders, elbows or wrists while playing the sport. *Important...*

•**Warm up properly.** A study in the *British Journal of Sports Medicine* found that nearly 46% of golfers don't warm up. Those who do warm up usually perform little more than a few "air swings" before hitting the ball. Inadequate warm-up is a leading cause of injury. *How to do it properly...*

•Allow two to five minutes of aerobic warm-up activity—jogging in place, fast walking, etc.

•Follow the aerobic workout with five to 10 minutes of gentle stretching—torso twists, chest stretches, etc. Include neck turns. Neck stiffness interferes with smooth body rotation during swings. Also, do stretches that target the hamstrings, such as lying leg lifts. Poor hamstring flexibility is a common cause of back pain.

•Stretch one or two muscle groups at each hole while waiting for your turn. For more information on the best stretches and exercises for golfers, go to *www.yogaforgolfers.com,* which is run by fitness consultant Katherine Roberts. She is author of the book *Yoga for Golfers* (McGraw-Hill).

•**Be careful when lifting.** Golfers often get hurt before the first tee because they jerk their clubs out of the car trunk. Use your legs as well as your back when lifting the bag. On the course, pick up balls by kneeling rather than bending.

•**Practice good balance and posture.** Most neck and shoulder stiffness occurs when players hunch over the ball excessively, with their neck and shoulders too far forward. Work with a golf pro to optimize your posture and stance when addressing the ball. You want to maintain a neutral spine position, without excessive bending or extension.

•**Limit your swing.** Amateur golfers tend to "overswing"—using greater force than necessary. Instead, shorten your swing. End the backswing at about the 1:00 position, instead of 3:00.

•**Strength train.** Lifting weights to increase strength and endurance can significantly reduce the risk of golf injuries. Focus on strengthening the shoulders, upper back, and "core" muscles in the abdomen and lower back.

•**Consider graphite clubs.** They have more "give" and generate less vibration and shock than clubs with steel shafts. This is important when you accidentally hit the ground during hard drives, a cause of wrist and elbow injuries.

Father–Son Baseball Camps

If you are a baseball-loving family, check out these great father–son weekend camps…

●**Bucky Dent's Baseball School in Delray Beach, Florida,** 561-265-0280, *www.dentbaseball. com,* $350* for a father and one son age five or older.

●**Lions Baseball Camp, Southeastern Louisiana University, Hammond,** 985-345-5504, *www.i-55.com/slubaseballcamp,* $325 for a father and one son age eight and older.

●**Virginia Baseball Camps, Syria, Virginia,** 434-982-5775, *www.vabaseballcamps.com,* $425 for a father and one son age seven to 12.

●**Virginia Baseball Club, Frostburg, Maryland,** 703-698-5599, *eteamz.active.com/baseball camp,* $430 for a father and one son age nine to 14.

*Prices subject to change. Also, they are for early registration and include lodging but not transportation. All of these camps will take extra sons and/or grandfathers for an additional cost.

Hooked on Fly-Fishing

Michael Shook, a fly-fishing guide and instructor based in Colorado (800-781-8120 or *shook@flyfishguide.com*). He has fly-fished throughout the US as well as in Africa and Asia. Mr. Shook is on the board of governors of Trout Unlimited, a leading trout and salmon conservation organization, 1300 N. 17 St., Arlington, VA 22209, *www.tu.org.* He is author of *The Complete Idiot's Guide to Fly Fishing* (Alpha).

Men, women and children of all ages are taking up fly-fishing. Being outdoors, surrounded by nature, enticing fish to bite on an artfully crafted fly can be peaceful for the soul and challenging for the mind. It's just what the doctor ordered for these stressful times. It's a serene, even spiritual, sport.

It's different from other types of angling: The lures are constructed to resemble insects or other small natural prey of gamefish. They usually incorporate feathers and thread and are often quite beautiful. There's no slimy bait, dead or alive.

Rather than simply dropping a hook into the water, you cast your line over a pond, brook, river, stream or ocean and then gently manipulate the fly to imitate an insect's movement—or lack of it.

Trout are the most popular quarry for fly fishermen because they're very plentiful, challenging and live in beautiful locations with clean water. But you can fly-fish for almost any gamefish—bluegill, pike, tarpon, bass, salmon, carp, crappie, perch, bonefish, snapper, marlin, etc.

Many fly fishermen remove the hook and release the fish back into the water. Others, of course, put their catch on the menu. Catch-and-release rules vary from state to state. Check with your local fish and game department.

To get a good idea of what fly-fishing is about, read *A River Runs Through It, and Other Stories,* by Norman Maclean (The University of Chicago). Or rent the movie based on this true story of two fly-fishing boys growing up in Montana.

GETTING STARTED

It can take years to become an expert fly fisherman, but less than an hour's practice can bring lots of enjoyment—and probably even success. And though experts spend thousands of dollars on gear, it only costs about $500 to $600 to get started—or just rent what you need. *How to learn…*

●**Buy an instructional video or DVD** at a sporting-goods shop, Amazon.com, a fly-fishing Web outlet such as the Fly Shop (*www.flyshop. com*) or a specialty fly-fishing store.

Example: Mel Krieger's *The Essence of Flycasting,* 60 minutes of basic instruction, much of it in slow motion.

Price: $29.95,* VHS or DVD.

●**Take lessons** from a professional at a fly shop or sporting-goods store. Most lessons last less than two hours.

Cost: Less than $50.

●**Ask friends or relatives** who fly-fish to take you along.

●**Read a book** by an expert. In addition to my own, I recommend *The Orvis Guide to Prospecting for Trout* by Tom Rosenbauer (Delta) and *Fly Fishing in Salt Water* by Lefty Kreh (The Lyons Press).

*Prices subject to change.

•**Attend a fly-fishing school** where you can actually go fishing.

Cost: $100 to $400 for a day of instruction. *Some examples…*

•Fishcamp, near the town of Weed in Northern California, offers a four-night, five-day family fly-fishing camp, starting at $650 per person (800-669-3474, *www.flyfishcamp.com*).

•Fran Betters Adirondack Sport Shop near Lake Placid in New York, offers free daily lessons with one-on-one casting instruction or an all-day class, including lunch and a box of flies, for $195 (518-946-2605, *www.adirondackflyfishing.com*).

•The Little Missouri Fly Fishing Arkansas Schools in Murfreesboro, Arkansas, offer Sunday afternoon family lessons at $60 for the first person and $40 for each additional family member (870-285-2807, *www.littlemissouriflyfishing.com*).

•**Join a club.** Many local groups offer instruction and hold shows and other events. Clubs can be found through the Fly Fishing Club Directory at the Web site *www.flycaster.com*, or by contacting The Federation of Fly Fishers (406-222-9369, *www.fedflyfishers.org*).

EQUIPMENT

You can buy a decent fly rod, reel and fly line for about $300. Ask the salesperson to suggest several rods that are appropriate for the type of water you plan to fish and the fish you plan to pursue. Choose the rod with which you're most comfortable. *You'll also need…*

•**Waders** (long leg garments that keep you warm and dry—stocking-foot style requires a separate boot…boot-foot style has the boot already attached). The best waders are made of breathable synthetic material, such as Gore-Tex.

•**Boots** with felt soles to give good traction on riverbeds.

Note: Even though you wade in the water to fly-fish, you don't necessarily need to know how to swim as long as you don't venture into deep water or swift currents.

•**Polarized sunglasses** that reduce glare and let you see into the water.

•**Light-colored hat,** also to reduce glare.

•**Vest with pockets** for flies and other gear, and a rain jacket that's loose enough to permit easy motion but also warm enough for several hours of fishing. Avoid white clothing, which can spook fish on a sunny day.

•**Leader,** a very fine piece of line that connects the fly to the main line.

•**Forceps and clippers** to unhook flies (both from the mouth of the fish and your clothes or skin) and cut the leader when needed.

•**Flies.** You'll need about 40 to 50 flies, which are easily lost to bushes or trees or when a fish breaks the line.

Cost: $1.50 to $2 each.

The total cost of clothing, flies and tools will run about $200 to $300.

CASTING

Some fly shops have space for customers to practice casting. Or practice in your backyard, empty schoolyard or other open space where there's no risk of snagging anyone with a hook.

You're casting correctly when you can send the line parallel to the ground at least 20 to 30 feet in front of you. Most people get the knack of casting in 30 to 60 minutes.

Learning the basics will let you cast the line so that the fly gently hits the water without splashing—in a manner that makes fish mistake it for a snack.

TYING ONE ON

To get started, it is important to know two knots—the "surgeon's knot" for tying leader to leader, and the "improved clinch knot" for fastening the fly to the leader. Most fly-fishing books and videos show how to tie the knots, and the staff in most fly shops can also be helpful.

GO FISH!

For a novice, bluegill, crappie and sunfish are usually the easiest to catch because they're indiscriminate feeders that aren't easily spooked. They typically inhabit the freshwater ponds and other still water throughout most of the US.

Trout are much more challenging. Some of the best trout streams are in Colorado, Pennsylvania and Montana.

For bass, another fish that's challenging, try out the Mississippi River area, the Great Lakes or the southeastern US where these fish are native. The Florida Keys are tops for bonefish, tarpon and permit, while Cabo San Lucas (the tip of the Baja peninsula) is the best for larger gamefish, such as sailfish and marlin.

Important: Check with state and/or local governments about license requirements. The fee for out-of-state residents is usually under $50.

Good strategy: When you reach the water, observe the surface for a few moments to see which kind of insects are hovering and whether the fish are biting. Then match your fly with the type of insect the fish are eating.

If this is not possible, use the trial-and-error method until you find the fly that the fish will rise to. Experiment with different sizes of flies until you have success. Most anglers fish with flies that are too large.

Local fly shops can be a gold mine of information in regard to which flies are best to use in the area.

One of the biggest novice mistakes is not taking enough flies. Without an ample supply, you risk running out of the type of fly that attracts the particular fish in the stream where you're casting—and that would be a shame when you've gone to so much trouble to get there.

Best Way to Land a Fish

To land a fish, set the hook by squaring your shoulders, twisting to the right and pulling your rod toward your right hip. With your left shoulder facing the fish, reel in the slack, then snap your wrist to set the hook. If the fish fights, keep the line taut so the hook is not dislodged. When the fish is next to the boat, place your left hand eight inches above the reel and your right hand six inches below. Pull up with your left hand and push down with your right to lift the fish out of the water. If the fish is big—and not a pike or pickerel, which have sharp teeth—reach down and grab it by sticking your thumb in its mouth and putting your fingers under its lip. Remove the hook carefully.

Alton Jones, a professional competitive bass fisherman, quoted in *Men's Health, www.menshealth.com.*

Easy Ways to Try Birding

To get started in birding, join a local club, or go on a nature-center bird walk. These low-pressure activities have a strong and enjoyable social component. If you find that you enjoy birdwatching, buy a good pair of binoculars and plan to watch early in the morning or late in the day—the best times to see birds.

More information: Cornell Lab of Ornithology, *www.birds.cornell.edu*...American Birding Association, *www.americanbirding.org*...and for expert advice on binoculars and other birding gear, Christophers, Ltd., *www.birdbino.com.*

Scott Weidensaul, ornithologist, Schuylkill Haven, PA, and author of *Living on the Wind: Across the Hemisphere with Migratory Birds* (North Point).

Find Out What Your Collectibles Are Worth

Thanks to the success of the on-line auction Internet site eBay, which holds hundreds of collectibles auctions every hour, collectors who previously relied on guidebooks to determine collectible values currently use real-time on-line prices for greater accuracy. eBay auctions have redefined "scarcity"—numerous collectibles once thought to be rare are quite common, and prices are reduced due to the increased supply. Rely on "field-based" values (prices that buyers actually are paying).

To review the recent price history of a collectible, go to *www.ebay.com* and click on "Advanced Search," then "Completed Listings Only." If you insure your collectibles, stay current with eBay prices and periodically adjust the coverage based on the market value of your collection.

Malcolm Katt, owner of Millwood Gallery, specializing in militaria and other collectibles, Millwood, NY, and an eBay PowerSeller since 1998.

Make Sure Your Baseball Memorabilia Is Authentic

The baseball memorabilia authentication program run by Major League Baseball (MLB) guarantees that sports items are genuine. Experts estimate that 50% to 90% of sports memorabilia items are counterfeit. MLB's program—the first of its kind in professional sports—combines on-site authentication by an independent party at all MLB games, events and signings with a serial numbering system, a hologram of the item and an on-line verification process.

More information: At *www.mlb.com,* click on "Auction," then on "MLB Authentication Program" at the bottom of the pull-down menu.

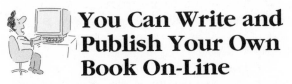

You Can Write and Publish Your Own Book On-Line

Angela Hoy, author and publisher in Bangor, ME. She has written eight e-books as well as nine printed books, including *How to Write, Publish and Sell E-Books* (Booklocker.com). She is co-owner of Booklocker.com, which offers more than 800 e-books for sale as well as products and services that help authors publish and market their own works.

One of the hottest trends in publishing is electronic books, or e-books. They are sold on the Internet directly to readers who download them to read via a computer, laptop or personal digital assistant (PDA). Unlike with traditional publishing, e-book authors don't need to hunt for agents, entice publishers or suffer the wait between acceptance and publication of their works.

And best of all, a large portion of every sale—about $10 per book, on average—goes directly into the writer's pocket. The eight e-books that I have written generate a steady income of about $5,000 a month. *My secrets...*

WRITING THE BOOK

•**Choose a nonfiction subject that helps people improve or enrich their lives.** Smart, original self-help information is the hottest market for e-publishing.

Example: One of my company's top-selling e-books is *Play Piano in a Flash* ($9.95),* written by professional musician and teacher Scott Houston. Mr. Houston's learning techniques are faster and simpler than traditional piano lessons.

•**Find your niche.** Traditional publishers must pursue sizable audiences in order to cover their overhead costs, but you can write an e-book for a very specific readership and still do well.

•**Use your favorite word-processing program** to write and organize your manuscript. All e-books should run at least 75 single-spaced pages—otherwise, customers feel that they have bought a pamphlet, not a book. Download a free e-book template for Microsoft Word from my company at *www.booklocker.com/samplebook.zip* to see how a typical e-book is organized.

•**Illustrate your book with an interesting cover and graphics.** You can get software from *www.dynamitecovers.com* or *www.coverfactory. com.* Prices start at $40. For graphics, I suggest using *www.gettyimages.com,* the world's leading provider of on-line images with millions of low-cost choices. Keep the digital size of your e-book under three megabytes for faster customer downloads. You can determine the file size of your book by right-clicking on the document or the document folder and viewing "Properties."

•**Convert your work to a PDF file** that can be sent to customers once the writing, editing and layout are complete. PDF files are a standard format for e-books. You can convert up to five files for free at *createpdf.adobe.com.*

Resource: *www.ebookapprentice.com* offers a free, comprehensive tutorial on creating and publishing e-books.

SELLING YOUR E-BOOK

•**Let others do it for you.** Some e-publishers will handle the technical tasks of putting your work on a Web site, filling orders and processing payments. Authors get to keep up to 70% from e-book sales.

Try: *www.booklocker.com* (my company)... *www.ebooks.com...www.ebookjungle.com.*

•**Create your own Web site** to sell your book. This requires more time and motivation, but you keep 100% of sales. For a how-to, go

*Prices subject to change.

to *www.publishyourownebooks.com* and download Gary McLaren's book with a great chapter on building your own Web site.

●**Get your site listed on search engines and directories**—Google, Yahoo!, MSN and Alta Vista. *www.selfpromotion.com* teaches you how to submit your site to search engines for maximum effectiveness.

Suggested reading: *Search Engine Visibility* by Shari Thurow (New Riders) and *Search Engine Optimization for Dummies* by Peter Kent (Wiley).

Movie Tickets for Less

Save on movie tickets—buy in bulk. Regal Entertainment Group (800-784-8477 or *www.reg movies.com*) sells tickets in blocks of 50 for $7* each—good for any movies showing at Regal, United Artists or Edwards movie theaters. Other discount packages are available.

*Price subject to change.

Download Movies

Download movies legally from *www.cinema now.com* and *www.movielink.com*. It generally takes less than one hour to download a film if you have a high-speed Internet connection. You can start watching on your computer screen just minutes after the download begins.

Renting a new movie will cost $3.99.* To purchase a movie, it will cost between $9.95 and $19.95. Rented movies must be viewed within a specified period—usually within 24 hours after you first open the file for CinemaNow. Movielink allows you to store rented movies for up to 30 days and watch them during any 24-hour period. Movies can be downloaded only from computers equipped with Windows formats.

*Prices subject to change.

Scoring a Reservation

Get a dinner reservation at a popular restaurant by phoning around lunchtime the day before. This is when many people call to cancel their reservations for the next evening.

New York, 444 Madison Ave., New York City 10022.

Gifts You Should Never Give

Sherri Athay, coauthor of Present Perfect: Unforgettable Gifts for Every Occasion *(Mobius). She and her husband, Larry, founded Present Perfect Gift Consultants, gift selection advisers, Essex, CT, www.giftelan.com.*

The best gifts can nurture the relationship between the giver and recipient. The worst gifts "say" inappropriate things. *Don't give gifts that are...*

●**Inducements to improve.** Although you might think such gifts are exactly what the recipient needs, he/she may resent their implications—and you.

Examples: A treadmill given to a couch potato...time-management classes to someone who is disorganized.

●**Beneath the recipient's standards.** If your sister wears only solid gold jewelry, don't present her with costume jewelry. Just because you can't tell the difference doesn't mean she will appreciate an impostor.

●**Assembly required**—unless you're certain the recipient is willing or able to do the job (or you'll do it for him). You wouldn't give a child an unassembled bicycle, and you shouldn't leave Uncle Ned's bookshelf in pieces in the box.

●**Living creatures.** Giving any pet to a child without consulting his parents or to an adult without being certain the animal is wanted can backfire. The recipient might resent having to take care of the pet and may give it away.

●**Intended for family use,** or your own use, but disguised as a gift to an individual. The recipient will be on to you as soon as the wrapping is off.

Example: A high-definition TV to your wife when you're the one who loves to watch TV.

16

A Smooth Ride

***

How to Get a Great Deal On a New Car

Toward the end of the year is the perfect time to give yourself a gift—a new car at a great price. Reason? This is crunch time for dealers who want to make their sales quotas for the whole year. And, this puts them in the mood to move cars off the lots—even if it means selling them cheaper than they would like.

Here are the steps to gaining control of the entire car-buying process so that you can get a better deal…

•Decide between a 2007 and 2008 model. Dealers want to clear old models off their lots to make way for new ones, so automakers will offer plenty of rebates and low-interest financing on 2007 models.

Many people may hesitate to buy a 2007 model late in the year because of concerns about resale value, buyers will see the car as a year older than

it actually is. But savings on 2007 models versus comparable 2008 models can range from a few hundred to a few thousand dollars or more.

If you plan to keep the car longer than five years, the difference in resale value between a 2007 and a 2008 of similar condition will be minimal. If you plan to keep your new car for fewer than five years, buy a 2008 model.

•Check financing options before you go car shopping. If you think that you will need financing, compare rates on car loans at *www.bankrate.com* or get quotes from local lending institutions. Their rates generally are one to two percentage points below those offered by car dealers. If your credit score is 650 or higher (out of 850), you should ask for the lowest available interest rate, whether you decide to finance with the dealer or a local lender. If your score is below

***

Ken and Daria Dolan, authors of five books on personal finance, including *Don't Mess with My Money* (Currency Doubleday). They are frequent guests on national television news programs, including NBC's *Today* show. They were money editors on *CBS This Morning* and *CBS News Saturday Morning* for several years and also hosted their own show on CNBC. Their Web site is *www.dolans.com*.

650, be prepared to pay at least one or two percentage points more.

Request a free copy of your credit report at *www.annualcreditreport.com,* or call 877-322-8228. You can purchase a copy of your credit score here or through one of the credit reporting agencies, usually for $15 or less.*

•**When considering a specific car, check the white label on the driver's-side door or doorjamb**—it shows the month and year in which the car was manufactured. In most cases, the older the car is, the more anxious the dealer will be to sell it. In fact, you can save money by looking for "slow sellers"—models whose national "days' supply" (a projection of how long the current on-hand inventory will last) exceeds 60 days. You can find this figure in *Automotive News,* a trade publication available at major newsstands and in large public libraries. Or you can subscribe for $149 per year (52 issues). 888-446-1422, *www.autonews.com.*

•**Drive a hard bargain.** Salespeople know that most new-car buyers walk into dealerships unprepared to negotiate one of their largest purchases ever.

Smart strategy: Instead of negotiating *down* from the sticker price, negotiate *up* from the car dealer's invoice (what the car costs the dealer).

Some dealers might sell you a car *below* invoice price. How is this possible? Some invoice prices quoted in car-pricing guides are above the actual cost to the dealer because they include holdbacks (a portion of the manufacturer's suggested retail price or invoice price repaid to the dealer after the sale) and dealer rebates from the manufacturer. However, if the invoice price includes regional marketing fees—which increase the dealer's cost—you may have less negotiating room. For pricing information, go to *www.edmunds.com* or check *New Car Buying Guide 2007–2008* (Consumer Reports), available at libraries and bookstores.

Other sources: www.carsdirect.com, www. autousa.com and *www.invoicedealers.com.*

•**Don't be a "turnover"**—a customer who is passed along to another salesperson because the first one couldn't get you to sign a contract. A more aggressive salesperson will then try to

*Prices subject to change.

close out the sale. To better control this process, keep negotiating with the salesperson you started with—or go to another dealership.

•**Don't trust a dealership to give you a fair trade-in price for your old car.** To get the best price, do your best to sell your car to a private party. Check out prices that thousands of other sellers are asking for different cars at *www.kbb. com* and *www.autotrader.com.*

•**Don't give your Social Security number to a salesperson.** He/she often will use that information to check a shopper's credit history. Unnecessary credit checks can hurt your score.

•**Hand over your driver's license only when you go for a test drive,** and then only for it to be photocopied. Write on the copy, in bold letters, *Credit Checks Not Authorized!* The Federal Trade Commission forbids unauthorized credit checks. By doing this, you have made it clear that you won't allow one. Your credit rating is none of the dealer's business unless you decide to discuss financing.

Important: Don't let anyone from the dealership hold on to the original license. You can't make a quick exit without your license in hand.

•**Explore dealer financing only after you have settled on a price.** Don't be suckered by the question "How much of a monthly payment can you afford?" Many times, the salesperson is trying to divert your attention from the actual price of the car. By manipulating the loan terms, he can get you the monthly payment you ask for and still get the highest overall price for himself.

Nor should you fall prey to "If you spread out the payments over 72 months (or more), you'll be able to afford this beauty." If you can't afford to pay off the car in 36 or 48 months, it's probably beyond your budget. Find a less expensive car.

Important: If you don't need financing, don't sit down with the "F&I" (finance and insurance) person. One of his/her jobs is to sell you expensive—and often unnecessary—add-ons, such as undercoating, an overpriced extended warranty, a security system or paint sealant.

•**Put your deposit on a credit card.** Don't use cash or a check. If something goes wrong between contract and delivery, it might be hard to get back your cash or check. With a credit card deposit, you can get the card issuer in your corner in the event of a dispute.

- **Never forget the ultimate weapon**—every salesperson's greatest fear—your ability to walk out of the showroom.

LEASE OR BUY?

Consider leasing if…

- **You are willing to pay extra,** in the long run, for a new car every three or four years.
- **You have a legitimate business use for the car**—some costs may be tax deductible.
- **Your priority is to keep up-front costs down**—they may be lower for a lease than for a purchase.

More information at *www.leaseguide.com.*

Is It a Lemon?

James Turner, executive director, HALT, an organization for legal reform, Washington, DC, *www.halt.org.*

A new car is considered a lemon if it must be returned repeatedly to the dealer for the same repair and the dealer is unable to fix it satisfactorily. Specific laws vary by state. Generally, defects must show up within 12 to 24 months or 12,000 to 24,000 miles from the time of purchase. State lemon laws allowing you to return the car for a full refund or a replacement apply only if the defect is repeatedly unfixable. Car dealers usually have one or two chances to fix a serious safety problem, such as defective brakes or steering…and three or four chances to fix any other serious problem, such as engine failure or violent shaking.

If you disagree with the manufacturer's proposed settlement—let's say you want a refund, not a new car—you might need to go through arbitration. Just because a vehicle has multiple defects requiring frequent service doesn't mean that it will legally be considered a lemon.

Find out all about your state's lemon law at *www.lemonlawamerica.com.* For help with getting a manufacturer to comply with lemon laws, contact your state consumer protection office or use the Better Business Bureau's Auto Line (800-955-5100, *www.dr.bbb.org/autoline/index.asp*).

You Can Save Thousands Of Dollars on a Used Car

Eric Peters, a Washington, DC–based automotive columnist, and author of *Automotive Atrocities! The Cars We Love to Hate* (Motorbooks International).

If you're in the market for a used car or truck, vehicle auctions may be your best low-cost alternative to dealerships, used-car lots and classified ads. The auctions used to be "insider-only" events—restricted to buyers representing dealerships and other professionals. Cars would be bought wholesale, then resold to consumers with a dealer's markup. Now, with a glut of used vehicles for sale as they come off leases, many vehicle auctions are open to the public. *The main types…*

- **Government auctions.** Federal, state and even some local governments hold auctions to dispose of cars that they no longer need or vehicles that have been seized. Auctions are advertised on local radio and TV stations, or you can contact town officials for information. For information on federal auctions, access the US General Services Administration's auction Web site, *www.autoauctions.gsa.gov,* or write to GSA Fleet Vehicle Sales, 1941 Jefferson Davis Hwy., Arlington, Virginia 22202.

- **Charities** such as Goodwill Industries (800-741-0186, *www.goodwill.org*) and The Salvation Army (800-725-2769, *www.salvationarmyusa.org*) auction cars they have received as donations.

- **Car wholesalers** auction dealer trade-ins as well as excess inventory.

Attending most auctions is free, although you may have to register in advance. If you do buy a car, you typically take it home the same day.

ADVANTAGES

Why buy at an auction? In most cases, you'll pay less for a given make and model than you would elsewhere. The bidding generally starts at or below the average wholesale value of the car or truck in question. At a lot or dealership, your starting point for negotiation is the full retail price. The savings at auction can be as much as 40% off the dealer price, depending on the car and the number of bids.

DRAWBACKS

●**Potentially shabby appearance.** An auction company's costs are lower than a dealership's, in part because it doesn't service, clean up or otherwise "detail" the vehicle to make it presentable.

●**Hurried pace.** You have to make a quick decision when the moment arrives.

●**Mechanical problems.** You will have a few hours at most to check out a vehicle. You can start the engine and hear it run, but test drives are seldom granted, so it is difficult to gauge a vehicle's mechanical condition. There are legal protections and, depending on the auction, there even may be a guarantee of some kind—but if you are not satisfied with the car, it's harder to seek redress against an auction firm, which is likely to be based out of state, than a local dealership or private seller in your community.

AUCTION STRATEGIES

To boost your chances of getting a fair deal at an auction…

●**Arrive early.** This will give you time for a thorough "walk-around" inspection of any car you're interested in. (You can open up the hood, crawl underneath the auto, etc.) Jot down the car's make, model, vehicle identification number, year of model, mileage, features and other information that might affect its price. If you are not familiar with cars and where to look for signs of trouble, bring a car-savvy friend or ask a mechanic to accompany you for a fee—say, $100 for two hours.

●**Bring a laptop computer or a personal digital assistant,** if possible, so that you can research cars on the Internet.

Alternative: Arrange for a friend to look up helpful information when you call from your cell phone. Never bid on a car until you have checked its value with such sources as the National Automobile Dealers Association's used-car pricing guides (800-252-6232, *www.nada.com*).

●**Run a check with Carfax.com** to instantly find evidence of odometer fraud, flood damage, accidents, etc.

Cost: $19.99.*

*Price subject to change.

●**Check out the car's title** before any money changes hands. Don't buy a car that lacks a clean, lien-free, transferable title.

●**Keep a clear head**—don't overbid.

ON-LINE AUCTIONS

On-line auctions such as those on eBay Motors have increased in popularity. They run for several days—giving you ample time to check a car's vehicle identification number. You can make arrangements with a buyer to see a car before purchase, but that might involve traveling. You can use the site's escrow service to hold your down payment, which will vary by lender, and pay the balance when the car and paperwork are transferred.

More from Eric Peters…

Cars with the Highest Resale Value…and the Lowest

The conventional wisdom used to be that the "blue chip" brands, such as Mercedes-Benz, were the smart car buys because they held their value longer than other vehicles. But brands that were once the standard for value are not necessarily good investments today, and relative up-and-comers, such as Lexus, will hold their value better than the average car.

Understanding depreciation (how well or how poorly a vehicle retains its value over time) is key to making a smart car-buying decision—it will affect how much (or little) you'll recoup when you sell or trade in the vehicle. Depreciation is impacted by the vehicle's reliability record and the brand's reputation. Undesirable models can lose as much as half their retail value within two years. The average vehicle loses 20% of its value within the first year of ownership. For depreciation ratings, check out *Kelley Blue Book* or go to its Web site at *www.kbb.com.*

American cars (especially GM and Ford models) have among the highest depreciation rates, while Japanese imports (especially Honda and Toyota) hold their value very well. Hyundai and Kia—the two major Korean automakers—have made great strides quality-wise (and offer superb warranties) but tend to depreciate faster than average.

Among European imports, there is often great variation even within the same brand of vehicle.

For example, the Mercedes-Benz M-Class SUV has suffered high rates of depreciation (probably as a result of quality problems with early vehicles), while the C-Class compact sedan has done well. Land Rover's LR3 SUV has held its value, while the smaller Freelander has not. Jaguar's reliability problems have hurt the brand's resale value.

BEST

According to the *Kelley Blue Book*, 2007 vehicles that have lower-than-average depreciation rates include the Acura TSX; Toyota Scion tC; BMW 5 series; MINI Cooper two-door coupe; Volkswagen GTI and Volkswagen Eos; Lexus IS; Pontiac Solstice; Honda Civic and Toyota Prius Hybrid.

WORST

Vehicles for 2006 with higher-than-average depreciation rates include the Kia Rio sedan; Kia Optima sedan; Chrysler Sebring sedan; Jaguar X-Type sedan; Mercury Monterey van; Chrysler Town and Country van and Pontiac Montana van.

Also from Eric Peters…

Hybrids vs. Diesels

Overall, the diesel vehicles get better mileage versus similar-sized gas engines, but they are best for highway driving.

The hybrid is best for city driving. It is designed to operate at optimal efficiency at lower speeds, especially stop-and-go traffic. Some hybrids, such as the Toyota Prius, are able to operate on electricity alone at low speeds—which cuts way down on the fuel consumption. Other hybrids automatically shut off their gasoline engines when the vehicle is stopped so that no fuel is wasted on an idling engine.

If you consult the EPA fuel efficiency ratings, you'll see that a hybrid's gas mileage rating will be higher for city driving than highway—the reverse of a conventional gas- or diesel-only car.

Finally from Eric Peters…

The Truth About No-Name Gas

While some name-brand gasolines do have more than the required minimum detergent/additive mixture (which keeps your fuel system clean), you will not harm your engine by going with an off-brand "no-name" fuel. All gasoline—regardless of the brand name—must conform to specific (and tightly enforced) federal and state laws governing additives, octane ratings, etc.

Some off-brands are identical to name-brand gasolines. They're just sold to different franchise owners who then resell to consumers, but under their own brand names.

Caution: Be wary of off-the-beaten-path stations in low-traffic rural areas. If the fuel that's in their underground storage tanks is not frequently used up and replaced with fresh fuel, there may be problems with excess water buildup.

Cut Costs on Gasoline

Bankrate, Inc., *www.bankrate.com* or 561-630-2400.

Here are gas savers from the experts at Bankrate, Inc., a wonderful resource for moneysaving advice…

• **Drive smoothly.** Accelerate slowly and anticipate stops—let up on the accelerator, coast and brake gently.

• **Follow the speed limit.** Driving 75 mph instead of 65 mph will decrease fuel economy by 10%…70 mph instead of 55 mph lowers it by 17%.

• **Drive with the air conditioner off in stop-and-go traffic.** Use the air conditioning when driving over 40 mph—that's when open windows can create drag and decrease fuel economy.

• **Combine errands**—and plan your route before leaving home.

• **Check out your local gasoline prices** at *www.gasbuddy.com* or *www.gaspricewatch.com*. Bankrate has a calculator to determine whether you would save money by driving to a cheaper station. Log onto *www.bankrate.com/brm/calc/gas price.asp*.

• **Fill up before you are low** on gas so you can choose an inexpensive station.

• **Use the lowest octane fuel rated appropriate** by your car's manufacturer.

More Gas Savers

Here are five additional smart ways that help you save on gas…

•**Use regular gas** if your car is designed for it—using higher grades wastes money.

Caution: Most cars designed for premium gas also can use regular, but they will not operate as efficiently.

•**Buy from busy gas stations**—fresh gas will burn more cleanly and produce fewer engine deposits than older gas.

•**Use a gas additive** to help increase fuel economy and keep fuel injectors clean.

•**Check tire pressure seasonally.** Inflating tires by five pounds above the amount listed in the owner's manual will increase fuel mileage but with the trade-off of a rough ride.

•**Use synthetic oil in your engine** for an increase of as much as 10% in fuel mileage.

C.J. Tolson, editor, MotorWatch.com, a consumer automotive membership organization, Box 123, Butler, MD, 21023.

Also from C.J. Tolson…

Overlooked Signs of Odometer Fraud

Don't overlook these common indications of odometer fraud…

•**Replaced tires, belts, hoses or spark plug wires** on a vehicle that supposedly has less than 30,000 miles.

•**A worn driver's seat or interior door scuffing.**

•**Unusually low mileage,** given the age of the car—on average, cars travel about 15,000 miles per year.

Helpful: Ask the dealer or current owner for all service records, and check odometer readings listed on them. You also can order a vehicle history report at *www.autocheck.com* or *www.car fax.com.*

Cost: $19.99.*

*Price subject to change.

What Auto Repairs Should Really Cost

David Solomon, a certified master auto technician and chairman, MotorWatch.com, a consumer automotive membership organization, Box 123, Butler, MD 21023.

When your car is on the blink, will you know if your mechanic is taking you for a ride? Although today's vehicles are now built better than ever, sooner or later all cars need a trip to the shop.

Select a repair shop that specializes in your type of vehicle so that the mechanic will be able to pinpoint any problem. Consider an independent repair shop—they score consistently higher than dealers in customer satisfaction surveys.

Repair costs do vary widely, and hourly labor costs can be as much as 50% higher in certain large cities and throughout California. The parts for European and luxury models generally cost much more than for domestic models.

Here's a guide to what common maintenance and repairs should cost, taking into account parts and labor for each service…

REPAIRS

•**Transmission.** $2,000 to $4,000.* As a rule, expect a $2,000 bill to replace a transmission in an American car…$3,000 in a Japanese car… and $4,000 in a European car.

•**Timing belt.** $300 to $500—if you replace the belt before it breaks. The timing belt synchronizes engine functions. If you wait for it to fail, the resulting damage to certain engines may inflate your bill to $1,500 to $5,000. Follow the replacement schedule in your vehicle's owner's manual. To save on labor, replace your timing belt when you are replacing your water pump and/or fan belt.

•**Head gasket.** $800 to $1,200. Head gasket failure will often result from overheating, so in addition to replacing the part, you might need to repair some underlying condition, such as a plugged radiator.

•**Evaporative emissions/misfires.** $500 to $1,500. When your "check engine" dashboard

*Prices subject to change.

warning light comes on, it generally signals either an evaporative emissions system problem, which can be time-consuming to fix, or a misfire problem, which can be tricky to diagnose.

Helpful: Fill your gas tank with the engine turned off, and be sure to tighten the gas cap with at least three clicks. This will solve many "check engine" problems.

MAINTENANCE

•**Oxygen sensor.** $80 to $250 each (there may be as many as four). The life span of this device, which regulates gas consumption, is 100,000 to 150,000 miles, but it can be shortened considerably if you use an inappropriate additive.

•**Thermostat.** $50 to $100. The thermostat might be replaced during a 60,000-mile service or coolant flush. If not, ask for it to be replaced.

•**Brake pads.** $150 to $215 for two wheels. If new disc brake rotors are needed, you'll pay an extra $50 to $125 per wheel—the price of rotors varies widely from vehicle to vehicle.

Caution: Chinese manufacturers are flooding the auto-parts market with substandard brake rotors. Insist that your mechanic use rotors labeled as meeting the D3EA standard.

•**Brake fluid flush.** $100 to $150. Have this done every three years or 36,000 miles, or you may have to replace your antilock braking system components, which can cost as much as $1,500 to $2,000.

•**Coolant flush.** $100 to $150. Modern coolants are said to last five years, but it's safer to change them after three years or 36,000 miles. Putting it off too long means that you might cause serious engine problems or need to replace the radiator at a cost of $300 to $500.

•**Fuel injector cleaning.** $100 to $150. If you do not have this done every 60,000 miles, you might need to replace injectors, at a cost of $250 each—that's $1,500 for a V-6 engine.

Front Seat Danger For Kids

Front seats of cars are not safe for children under age 14. Previously it was thought that children over 12 could sit safely in the front seat.

But, younger children are up to six times more likely to be injured than older kids when air bags deploy.

Reason: Bones and lean muscle protect the body, and age—not height or weight—determines their development.

Craig D. Newgard, MD, MPH, Center for Policy and Research in Emergency Medicine, Oregon Health and Sciences University, Portland, and author of a study of the effects of motor vehicle crashes on 3,790 children, published in *Pediatrics.*

Dangerous Driving Advice

William Van Tassel, PhD, manager of driver training operations, AAA, Heathrow, FL, America's leading not-for-profit drivers' organization, *www.aaa.com.*

Driving in harsh winter weather is never easy, but it is even more difficult and hazardous when you believe in the following common myths…

Myth: **Steer in the direction of a skid.** The best strategy in any skid is to look and steer in the direction that you want the car to go—in other words, align your front wheels with your intended direction of travel. In either a front- or rear-wheel cornering skid, let your eyes help you, and keep looking in the direction where you want the car to go. If your skid occurs while you are going straight and trying to slow down, not when turning a corner, smoothly apply your brakes until you reach the threshold of wheel lockup. This method works whether your vehicle is equipped with antilock brakes or not.

Myth: **I'm safe as long as I stay behind the salt truck.** Salt takes time to melt snow and ice, so driving right behind a municipal salt truck will not ensure traction. In fact, driving closely behind any large vehicle in winter weather can block your view of the road and blind you with slush and debris kicked up by the tires. Stay even farther away from these vehicles on slick roads than you would when trailing a smaller car.

Myth: **The safest speed is the speed of traffic.** Though you don't want to be the one vehicle driving much more slowly than everyone else on a busy, icy highway, you shouldn't automatically drive at the same speed as those around you. The roads are full of people who drive too fast in poor conditions. If one of these people is tailgating you on a snow-covered road, find a safe place to pull over and let him/her pass.

Myth: **I can go a little faster than other drivers on snow or ice because my vehicle is big and heavy.** You can't safely drive any faster on slippery roads with a big car than a small one. A heavy vehicle, such as an SUV, only has an advantage over a lighter car when it comes to *starting* from a stop on snow or ice—but stopping a heavy vehicle takes longer.

Myth: **My vehicle has four-wheel drive, so it will easily handle the snow.** Four-wheel or all-wheel drive will help your vehicle start off and corner on snowy roads, but it will not help it stop any faster. You still must drive conservatively.

Myth: **Adding weight above both rear wheels will help me to get traction in the snow.** If your car has front-wheel drive, adding sandbags or cinder blocks in the storage space over the rear wheels can make a rear-end skid *more* likely. If you have rear-wheel drive, adding weight over the rear wheels might help you get started from a standstill on a slick surface, but it also will increase the distance that you need for stopping. Add weight over rear-drive wheels only if your vehicle has very little weight in the back, as with a rear-wheel-drive pickup truck.

Myth: **If I deflate my tires slightly, they'll become wider and I'll have more traction on snow or ice.** Car tires are designed to be most effective at their prescribed tire pressure, regardless of driving conditions. Not only are under-inflated tires less fuel efficient and less durable than properly inflated tires, they're likely to provide less traction because they'll probably cup inward, putting less tread on the road.

Important: Tire air pressure drops with the temperature, so double-check that your tires still are properly inflated.

Some people believe that wide snow tires are better for traction, but these may slide on top of snow or slush when narrower tires would cut through. Select the tires recommended for your particular vehicle.

Myth: **Hot water will melt the ice on my windshield or door lock.** Maybe—or maybe the sudden heat will crack your windshield and the added water will freeze your lock even tighter. Deicer, available at auto-supply stores, is a safer option. If you don't have deicer, dip your car key in rubbing alcohol before inserting it into the lock. The alcohol should help melt the ice inside.

Myth: **I should let my engine warm up for a long time in cold weather.** It's better to warm up a car up by driving conservatively for the first 15 minutes than to let it sit and idle. Prolonged idling can lead to premature exhaust corrosion and engine contamination from incomplete fuel combustion, and idling warms up only the engine, not other components, such as the transmission. Let your engine idle for only a minute or two so that your windows don't fog up as you drive.

Lock Out Car Thieves

Stop car thieves with the AutoLock. The steel pedal-clamping system (which is impervious to drilling and sawing) fits around your brake or clutch pedal so that it can't be depressed. The lock has an encrypted, four-sided key that can't be duplicated.

Cost: $49.95* at auto-parts and hardware stores.
*Price subject to change.

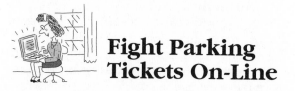

Fight Parking Tickets On-Line

The parkingticket.com Web site employs former judges and police officers to assist its clients in getting tickets dismissed.

How: Ticket data is entered on the Web site and users then receive a customized dismissal request letter to file, citing the exact reason(s) why the ticket should be dismissed.

Guarantee: If the fine is not dismissed or reduced, you pay nothing. If it is, the fee is half the amount saved.

Service currently is available in New York City, Washington, DC, San Francisco, Boston and Philadelphia, and is expanding.

17

Home and Family Matters

Dangerous Toxins May Be Lurking in Your Home

As long as you breathe, eat and drink, you cannot entirely escape environmental toxins. Research on the risks associated with these toxins is ongoing, but many scientists believe that existing evidence suggests that toxic build-up in our bodies contributes to the development of Parkinson's disease and may increase risk for some types of cancer and other serious conditions.

A Centers for Disease Control and Prevention study that tested 10,000 men and women for the presence of 116 chemicals, including *phthalates* and *dioxin*, concluded that most Americans carried some combination of these toxins in small amounts in their blood.

TOXICITY IN THE HOME

Household sources of toxins that are under investigation...

•**Home furnishings.** *Polybrominated diphenyl ethers* (PBDEs), the common ingredients in flame retardants that are used to treat upholstered chairs and sofas, foam mattresses and cushions, may be carcinogenic. PBDEs also may disrupt thyroid function and brain development.

What to do: When buying foam mattresses, upholstered furniture, etc., ask whether PBDEs were used during manufacturing.

•**Pressed wood and fiberboard,** which often are used in furniture and shelving, are common sources of *formaldehyde,* a gaseous compound that is used as a disinfectant. Formaldehyde has been found to be a probable carcinogen.

What to do: Look for solid wood products or those carrying the seal of the American National Standards Institute (ANSI), which certifies that the item is low in formaldehyde emissions.

Mitchell Gaynor, MD, an assistant clinical professor of medicine at Weill Medical College of Cornell University, and founder and president of Gaynor Integrative Oncology, both in New York City. He is the author of *Nurture Nature/Nurture Health: Your Health and the Environment* (Nurture Nature).

To find furniture and other products that are low in potentially dangerous chemical emissions, consult the Greenguard Environmental Institute, a nonprofit, independent organization that certifies low-emitting products, 800-427-9681, *www.greenguard.org.*

•**Cleaning products.** Most people utilize a wide variety of cleaning products and many of these do contain toxic chemicals. Chlorine bleach is potentially carcinogenic and can damage the respiratory system. Among its by-products are the *chlorinated hydrocarbons, chloroform* and *trihalomethanes,* all of which act like weak estrogens and can cause breast cells to divide more rapidly. These by-products have been shown to cause breast tumors in animals.

What to do: Use commercial cleansers that are free of chlorine and most chemicals. Seventh Generation and Sun & Earth are two brands that are widely available at health-food stores.

Or use natural cleaning alternatives—baking soda to scrub sinks, tubs and toilets…white distilled vinegar in a pump-spray bottle to clean mirrors and windows. If you really need to use chlorine-containing cleaners, make sure that the room is well-ventilated.

•**Pesticides.** Research has shown that pesticides increase risk for Parkinson's disease—and may be a cause of some cancers.

What to do: Use baits and traps instead of sprays. Try organic alternatives to toxic bug killers, including oil sprays, such as Sharpshooter, an all-natural insect killer containing plant oils… Burnout II, a natural herbicide that contains vinegar, clove and lemon…and corn gluten meal, a natural weed killer. All of these products are available at most garden centers that carry organic products.

For more information on pesticides and other toxic household products, visit the Web site of Earth Share (a nationwide network of environmental organizations) at *www.earthshare.org.*

•**Cosmetics.** *Paraphenylenediamine,* which is found in some darker hair dyes, increases the risk for bladder cancer in humans, according to a finding in the journal *Carcinogenesis. Other toxic ingredients used in cosmetics…*

•*Phthalates,* typically used as a solvent and plastic softener, have been linked to cancer and to birth defects of the male reproductive system. They are found in many shampoos and other hair products, cosmetics, deodorants and nail polish. To learn more about phthalates and get a list of products that contain them as well as those that don't, go to *www.nottoopretty.org,* a Web site of several consumer environmental groups. Click on "United States" and then on "US Products."

•*Talc,* in talcum powder, has been linked to a 60% increase in the risk for ovarian cancer in women who use it in the genital area.

•*Propylene glycol,* an ingredient that's found in some moisturizing products and skin creams, is absorbed through the skin, and high levels may damage the kidneys and liver.

What to do: Read labels carefully. By law, cosmetic ingredients must be listed on the label, starting with those in largest amounts. Choose all-natural alternatives, such as products made with olive oil, safflower oil or oatmeal, whenever possible.

SELF-DEFENSE

Antioxidants, such as vitamins C and E, are known to promote health by scavenging free radicals (harmful by-products of metabolism), which damage our cells and contribute to cancer and other diseases.

But antioxidants have another role that is possibly even more important in protecting against environmental toxins. The antioxidants stimulate an area of the DNA known as the *antioxidant responsive element* (ARE), which activates a gene that produces detoxifying enzymes. This is the body's way of breaking down carcinogens and other toxins.

In addition to commonly known antioxidant sources, such as brightly colored produce (carrots, beets, kale and tomatoes), make sure your diet contains…

•**Cruciferous vegetables,** such as cauliflower and brussels sprouts, which contain the potent enzyme inducer, *sulforaphane.*

•**Green tea,** an antioxidant source that is 20 times more potent than vitamin E, according to the American Chemical Society. Try to drink two to five cups daily.

•**Rosemary,** a source of *carnosol,* which has antioxidant and anticarcinogenic properties. Use rosemary in cooking, or drink one cup of rosemary tea daily.

• **Curry,** which contains curcumin and turmeric, two potent cancer-fighting herbs. Cook with curry three times a week.

Nature's Air Filters

Research shows that having plants in a room can reduce airborne mold and bacteria by as much as 60%, as well as improve indoor air quality by absorbing pollutants into their leaves. Plants also promote healthful humidity levels. They can be particularly useful in reducing "indoor air pollution" in energy-efficient buildings that are largely sealed with little ventilation from outdoors. If you work in such a building, keep a plant on your desk or within a few feet of where you spend most of your time.

B. C. Wolverton, PhD, retired NASA research scientist, John C. Stennis Space Center, Picayune, MS.

Room Freshener Danger

Room fresheners may cause headaches, depression and other maladies. A recent study discovered that "volatile organic compounds" found in aerosols such as air fresheners are associated with increased incidence of headache and depression among women, and higher levels of diarrhea, earaches and other symptoms among young children. The study authors warn that this may indicate heightened risk for other groups who are home a large percentage of their time, such as the elderly.

Safer: Use baking soda, lemons and other natural odor remedies. Do not use aerosols in confined spaces.

Alexandra Farrow, PhD, course director for the School of Health Sciences & Social Care, Brunel University, Isleworth, England.

Solutions for Home Moisture and Water Leakage Problems

Bill Keith, a remodeling contractor for 25 years in the St. John, IN, area and now host of the *Home Tips Show* on Chicago PBS-TV and radio stations. His Internet site, *www. billkeith.com,* offers free answers to remodeling questions.

Moisture can be a home owner's greatest enemy. When problems aren't addressed quickly, the cost of repairs can reach well up into the thousands. The resulting mold and mildew can bring on health problems as well.

Common trouble spots in the home…

ATTICS

There are three major causes of attic moisture. *See below…*

• **Leaky roof.** Leaks often occur where the roof meets chimneys, vents, skylights and other openings. Roofs also may leak when leaves and branches collect on top of or in the gutters. This debris forms dams that prevent rainwater from flowing freely. When the water pools and backs up under the shingles, it seeps through the roof and into the attic.

• **Ice dams** can cause wet attics in winter and spring. These dams form when heat escaping from the interior of the house melts ice and snow on the roof. The resulting cold water rolls down the inclined roof until it reaches the eaves, where it refreezes. This ice can back up under the shingles or cause water to pool and get under the shingles. Either way, water can work its way through the roof and into the attic.

Solution: Increase the thickness of the attic insulation that you have in your home. The correct amount of insulation for most regions is between R-38 and R-49, which translates to 12 to 20 inches of fiberglass.

• **Poor air circulation.** If your attic does not vent the air when it is hot out, it can turn into a sweatbox. Poorly installed insulation is the most common culprit. Home owners add insulation to trim energy bills without realizing that they must leave three- or four-inch-wide gaps in the insulation at the eaves to permit air flow.

Solution: Cut two- to three-foot lengths of drain spout or use Styrofoam baffles, available in home-improvement stores, to keep air channels open.

It is best to insert the baffles before installing insulation, but if necessary, you can force them into place between or alongside existing pieces of insulation. Free airflow must be possible through at least every second rafter pocket (that is, through at least half of the eaves).

Adding or adjusting insulation isn't technically difficult, but it's easier and safer to have a handyman install it for you. For more information, consult the "Ceilings and Attics Technology Fact Sheet," from the US Department of Energy (available at *www.eere.energy.gov/buildings/info/ publications.html*).

Arrange to have a checkup by a roofing professional every two or three years so that leaks don't develop in the first place. These checkups cost $75 to $150,* or more if you have a large, multipitched or difficult-to-reach roof.

Caution: Falls from ladders result in many injuries. To be safe, hire a roofing professional for repairs and a gutter-cleaning service for maintenance.

INSIDE THE HOME

If your home's interior humidity gets above 65%, mold and/or mildew problems are likely to develop. You can monitor moisture with a humidistat, available from a home-improvement store for less than $50. *Common causes of humidity problems...*

•**Showering or cooking in poorly ventilated areas.** Bathroom fans should be on while you are showering and for at least five minutes after, or you can open windows to provide necessary ventilation. Stove ventilating fans should run while cooking and for at least five minutes after. Don't use them longer—you'll be throwing away expensively heated (or cooled) air.

If humidity problems persist in a bathroom, you might need a more powerful exhaust vent, for $30 and up plus the cost of installation.

If the persistent humidity problem isn't tied to a specific bathroom, a dehumidifier placed in the utility room (where your furnace and water heater are kept) might be the solution.

*Prices subject to change.

Cost: About $200 for a high-quality Energy Star model. Set it to come on whenever humidity climbs above 50%.

•**Leaky pipes** are the second major source of in-home moisture problems. They are most common in bathrooms, kitchens and laundry rooms—but water pipes can be located behind any wall.

A leaky pipe can be tricky to find because the problem is more likely to be slow seepage than a large, obvious drip. If the leak is in an out-of-the-way spot, the first sign might be a mildewy smell that won't go away no matter how well you clean. You also might see swelling or a chalky discoloration around the base of bathroom or kitchen cabinets that sit directly on the subfloor. Tile floors often hide the worst water damage, but wood cabinetry that is in direct contact with a wood subfloor can wick the moisture upward until the problem is visible.

To find a leaky pipe: Head down to your basement, and shine a flashlight up at the flooring beneath the trouble area to see if there's discoloration. Feel all the exposed water pipes in the vicinity of the musty odor to see if any are moist. If you suspect the leak is hidden behind a wall, use a moisture meter, which registers the moisture content of the wood or drywall next to it. These are available at hardware stores for as little as $80.

Expect to spend several hundred dollars to replace one leaky pipe, plus several hundred more for drywall repair if the plumber has to cut through your wall to reach the problem. Cutting through tile, of course, can cost even more—but leaks must be fixed.

•**Shutoff valves for toilets and sinks** are a common source of leaks. Replacement valves are available at home-improvement stores for about $4 each and are easy to install with a pair of large wrenches—just remember to shut off your home's water first.

•**Toilets.** If your toilet rocks back and forth, gently tighten the bolts that hold it down.

Caution: If you make it too tight, you could crack the ceramic bowl. If the toilet still rocks, the floor underneath might be uneven. Plastic shims, available at home-improvement stores for less than $1 apiece, might solve the problem. Stick a shim or two between the toilet and the floor in front or in back as needed until it no longer rocks. Then trim the shim so that it does not extend beyond the edge of the toilet. Seal with mildew-resistant caulking, available for a few dollars a tube at hardware stores. This prevents moisture from getting in and keeps the shim from showing.

If the toilet leaks but does not rock, the wax ring, a gasket between the base of the toilet and the floor, might need to be replaced.

Cost: About $5.

BASEMENT

Numerous sealants claim to offer moisture-proof barriers for basement walls, but they seldom work well.

If a hill or slope near your property is funneling water down into your basement, try one of these strategies...

•Extend gutter downspouts. Extend them further from the home to prevent water from seeping inside.

•Install a French drain. Dig an 18- to 24-inch-deep trench at least four feet away from the house on the uphill side. Then line the new trench with a plastic drain tile. These perforated plastic tubes (sold in 50- to 100-foot-long rolls) are placed in French drains as well as alongside a home's foundation and covered with gravel. Position the drain tile to steer water away from your house. Plant flowers on both sides of the trench to improve its appearance. If you would prefer not to do the digging, a professional excavator should be able to do the job for perhaps $200 to $400.

•Replace the original drain tile around your home's foundation. Persistent leaks might mean that this drain tile needs to be dug up and replaced. A professional excavator typically charges $3,000 to $5,000 to do this—the tile itself is cheap, but labor costs are considerable.

You also might have to replace any landscaping that needs to be pulled up in the process. If the exterior of your home is extensively landscaped and your basement is unfinished, it might be more practical to have the new drain tile installed below the *interior* perimeter of your basement. An excavator accomplishes this by digging a trench just inside your foundation walls. Costs are comparable to putting the trench outside of the house, only without the landscaping issues.

Helpful: If you're having a new home built, remind the contractor to include drain tiles around both the outside and inside perimeter of the home. For an extra $100 to $200, you'll have a great insurance policy against future basement moisture.

•Use a sump pump. These devices remove accumulations of water from the lowest point in a drainage system, typically the basement. If your home is built on a hill, your drain tile might use gravity to divert water away from the home. Otherwise, the drain tile will be angled to bring the water to a sump pump—ideally one with a battery backup in case the power goes out in a storm. Sump pumps cost around $80...battery backup systems, around $200. Expect to pay a plumber about $200 to install the pump.

More from Bill Keith...

Give Your Home the Look of Luxury Without Spending a Lot

You can make your home look more luxurious, even when you are on a budget. *Here are eight inexpensive items that can add elegance...*

INTERIOR

•Ceramic tile flooring. In entryways, hallways, kitchens and bathrooms, no flooring offers a more luxurious look per dollar spent than ceramic tile. Quality tiles typically cost $2 to $3* each, but home-improvement stores usually have discontinued or overstock tiles marked down to as little as 65 cents per tile. If you are handy, you can lay the tile yourself. If you aren't, installation typically is $2.50 to $3.50 per square foot.

Buy tiles that are at least 12" × 12" in size—big tiles make rooms appear larger. Neutral colors, such as beige, tan or taupe, never go out of style. Avoid white tile, which shows dirt and looks institutional.

•New kitchen cabinet handles and knobs. Give your kitchen a classy, fresh look. For timeless elegance, favor handles and knobs that have simple, clean lines and a brushed nickel finish. Prices start at $2 per piece at home centers.

*Prices subject to change.

●**Crown molding.** Adding molding where walls meet the ceiling brings an air of old-fashioned elegance. New polystyrene crown molding looks like wood, and do-it-yourself kits make it easy to install. Corners are premade, eliminating the need for a miter saw. Fill any gaps with painter's caulk before painting. A kit large enough for an average-sized room costs less than $200 at a home center.

●**Fresh coat of store-brand paint.** Despite what you may have heard, store-brand interior paint available at a reputable store is every bit as attractive and long lasting as a brand-name product. A five-gallon bucket starts at $30, about the cost of one gallon of designer paint.

Helpful: Home-improvement stores often offer free classes on techniques such as rag or sponge painting, which give walls a stylish, textured look. Or search the Web for "faux painting."

●**Off-brand overhead light fixtures.** For every designer lamp that costs $200 or more, there likely is an attractive imitation for much less. Because overhead lights are on the ceiling, no one is ever close enough to see that yours is made of plastic or plated metal. "Contractor packs" of four to six fixtures are available at big home-improvement stores for about $10 per fixture.

EXTERIOR

●**Entryway planter.** Put a large planter by your home's entryway. Use it to grow several plants, such as tall grass with ivy hanging over the side. Home stores sell large plastic planters that mimic limestone or terra-cotta for less than $50 each. Bigger is better here—it looks more luxurious. The planter should be at least 18 inches tall. Don't clutter your entryway with hanging plants or other small decorations.

●**Asphalt sealer.** Applying a coat of jet-black sealer to your asphalt driveway for about $100 to $200 (more for long driveways) makes your home look neater and more expensive.

If you have a concrete driveway, rent a pressure washer every year or two to remove grass stains and tire marks. A one-day rental costs $50 to $80. It shouldn't take more than a few hours to clean a driveway, so you may be able to split the cost with one or two neighbors.

●**Shutters.** Today's high-quality vinyl shutters look like wood and add a wonderful accent for about $35 a pair (installation averages an additional $50 per pair). They come prefinished in a myriad of colors. A good pair of wood shutters costs about $100 and needs to be painted or stained every six to eight years.

The color of your front door usually is the best color to select for shutters. If you would like to test a few colors, use a digital camera to take a picture of the front of your house, then print out a few copies. Using markers or colored pencils, draw in the colors you're considering. Post the pictures on the fridge, and see which you like at the end of a week. Don't waste money putting shutters on side or back windows—few people see them.

Time to Get Organized! Strategies That Make It Easy

Peter Walsh, a professional organizer on *Clean Sweep*, TLC's home makeover show, Los Angeles. He is author of *How to Organize (Just About) Everything* (Free Press).

Good intentions to finally get organized often end in failure and frustration. *Here is how to make your efforts a success...*

GET HELP

Schedule a "declutter day" at least a week in advance, and warn everyone in the household to keep that day free. Making this a joint effort divides the work and can even make it fun.

●**If your children are old enough,** ask them to help. Begin by assigning each person a room to declutter. Set a time limit to keep everyone on track. Give each family member two large garbage bags. They are not done until they have filled one with trash and the other with unneeded clothes or personal items to give to charity or sell at a garage sale. If you hold a garage sale, use the proceeds to fund an enjoyable event as a reward for everyone's efforts.

●**If your kids are grown and out of the house,** consider teaming up with close friends for spring cleaning. This Saturday, they help you clean the garage, then you buy dinner. Next

Saturday, you help them and they treat. Cleaning won't seem so tedious with friends around, and you'll be less likely to stop before the job is done.

•**If you can't find the time to devote a full day to spring cleaning,** clean only one area per day. Today you might tackle the piles on the kitchen counter...tomorrow, clean up your desk...Saturday, the basement shelves. Don't stop until the whole house is done.

•**If you have difficulty staying motivated,** consider that it isn't just a question of neatness—it also may affect the health of your family. A cluttered home usually is a dusty home, and dust can cause or exacerbate respiratory problems, including asthma and allergies.

CLOSETS

•**Sort through your wardrobe.** Odds are, there are plenty of garments that you wouldn't miss if they were gone. Most people wear 20% of their clothes 80% of the time. Therefore, I recommend a 4:1 ratio—for every four items you keep, donate one to charity or set it aside for a garage sale.

•**Move winter garments to storage.** Put them in a dry location, such as the attic or a spare closet. Clean clothes before storing them—moths and other insects are drawn to the smell of dead skin and body odor. Don't put leather garments in plastic suit bags or garbage bags—when leather can't breathe, it dries out.

•**Take the clothes that remain and turn the hangers in the opposite direction.** After you next wear an item, return it to its place with the hanger in the normal direction. Anything still backwards when you clean next spring is a prime candidate for removal.

•**Clear closet floors.** Shoe racks on the floor or shoe caddies that hang from closet doors or hangers are wonderful organizational tools.

•**Store rarely worn shoes and seasonal items,** such as scarves and gloves, in shoe boxes on high closet shelves. Take a picture of the contents of each box, and staple it to the box front so you can find what you need without digging. At the least, write the contents on each box in large letters.

PAPERWORK

•**Limit periodicals.** There's usually no reason to have more than two issues of any publication in your home. If the April and May issues of a magazine have arrived and you haven't gotten around to reading the March issue, you probably never will—throw it out.

Designate a place in your home for publications, such as a magazine rack near a favorite chair. Otherwise, they will spread to cover every available surface.

•**Buy an accordion-style 12-month file** at an office-supply store to organize your bills, receipts and account statements. When you pay a bill or get a receipt or a statement, just drop it into the appropriate month's pocket. More intricate filing systems only encourage paperwork to pile up, since no one finds time to put every last scrap in its proper place.

GARAGE, ATTIC AND BASEMENT

These areas often become household dumping grounds.

•**Pull out everything and sort by theme**—holiday items, sporting goods, gardening tools, cleaning products, luggage, etc. Discard or give away things that you never use. When you return the rest, keep the thematic groups together to reduce the time needed to find things later.

•**Call your town office to find out how you should dispose of leftover paint,** pesticides and other household chemicals that you'll never use. These things often clutter up homes for decades because people do not know how to discard of them safely.

•**Take advantage of vertical space.** The Container Store (888-266-8246 or *www.container store.com*) and other home-improvement stores sell a wide range of rack systems that organize things along walls rather than in piles on the floor. There also are rack systems designed to hang from garage or attic rafters.

BATHROOMS

Bathroom clutter lets mold get a foothold because it's difficult to clean properly around bottles, tubes, etc.

•**Assign each family member a portable shower caddy** to hold personal grooming items. The caddy can be stored in the person's bedroom and brought into the bathroom when needed. Also, if possible, assign each person a bathroom drawer or a section of a shelf so that there are no excuses for leaving things on the counter.

●**Throw out old medicine.** You would be surprised at how many people don't do this.

Safe Ways to Control Outdoor Pests

Bernice Lifton, author of *Bug Busters: Poison-Free Pest Controls for Your House and Garden* (Avery). A freelance writer and researcher located in Pasadena, CA, she has never used a chemical pesticide inside her home.

Check the warning label on most insecticides and you are likely to see that they are not only toxic to pests—but also potentially harmful to your own health.

And, because insects develop a resistance to insecticides over time, even harsh chemicals offer only a temporary respite.

Better: Minimize breeding grounds of insects, and make your house—and yourself—less attractive to them. *Here's how...*

MOSQUITOES

As disease carriers, mosquitoes are the most dangerous of insects. Worldwide, the mosquito-borne disease malaria kills one million people a year. In the US, the most common mosquito threat is West Nile Virus, which can cause flu-like symptoms and even death.

Removing *all* sources of standing water is key. That's because mosquitoes need only one-quarter inch of water in which to lay their eggs. Most people recognize obvious pools of stagnant water, such as those found in birdbaths and tires used in playgrounds, but gutters, garbage can lids and the trays under planters are commonly overlooked. Empty water in all of these places. If you have a swimming pool and drain it, make sure that no water remains. A partially filled up swimming pool can be a source of mosquitoes for an entire neighborhood.

Candles and lanterns that burn citronella oil have been touted as effective outdoor mosquito repellents, but they work only when the air is still.

Otherwise, opt for a commercial repellent that contains N,N-diethyl-meta-toluamide (DEET). Although DEET products are effective, they should be used with caution. Apply a DEET insecticide to exposed skin only—never to skin that will be covered by clothing. Also, applying a sunscreen and a DEET product at the same time can reduce the sunscreen's effectiveness by as much as one-third. Wait 15 minutes after applying sunscreen before applying a DEET repellent.

HOUSEFLIES

Flies rank second as carriers of human disease. Houseflies pose a particular threat because they transmit germs from sewage and garbage to our household food, dishes, skin and other surfaces. Diarrhea outbreaks have been linked to warm-weather surges in the housefly population.

Tight-fitting window screens (16-mesh is recommended) and outward-opening, self-closing screen doors are the best defense. If a door leading outside is used often, install a ceiling fan as close as possible to the opening. Find one that moves at least 1,500 cubic feet of air downward per minute.

Outdoors, garbage pails should have tight-fitting lids. Research has found that tight covers reduce local fly populations by 90%, while a single improperly sealed container breeds an average of 1,000 flies per week.

If flies still get into your house, try growing the herb tansy, which repels flies. Plant it outside near your kitchen door or wherever flies tend to cluster.

ANTS

Ants do more good than harm. Besides enriching the soil with their droppings and dead bodies, they also prey on cockroaches, fly larvae and other pests. But, a home invasion of ants is never pleasant.

To to keep ants out of your house, trim tree and shrub branches several feet away from the house...patch all wall cracks both inside and out...don't overwater outdoor plants (ants often invade a home after their nest is flooded by a hose or heavy rain)...keep cupboards clean... wipe up spilled foods immediately...rinse dishes before putting into the dishwasher...and store food in closed containers. Another trick is to sprinkle wet coffee grounds around the house perimeter—the odor repels ants.

If you spot an ant indoors, wipe or vacuum it up, then wash its scent trail with household detergent.

Secrets for a Perfect Lawn from the Boston Red Sox Groundskeeper

David R. Mellor, master groundskeeper at Fenway Park in Boston and author of *The Lawn Bible* (Hyperion) and *Picture Perfect: Mowing Techniques for Lawns, Landscapes, and Sports* (Wiley). He also has cared for grounds for the San Francisco Giants, the Los Angeles Angels at Anaheim, the Milwaukee Brewers and the Green Bay Packers.

I f you think that you've lost the battle with your lawn, do not surrender! You can give your yard a first-class makeover without investing a lot of time or money. *Here are simple steps from David Mellor, master groundskeeper for the Boston Red Sox...*

•**Be wise when you fertilize.** Fertilizing your lawn is an important step, so do it at the right time—in the fall for cool-season grasses, such as Kentucky bluegrass and perennial rye...and twice (once in spring and once in early fall) for warm-season grasses, such as Bermuda grass. It's best to fertilize when the lawn is dry and water afterward. Use a rotary or broadcast spreader to apply the fertilizer. Ask your garden center to recommend a quality product for your area, and follow label directions carefully. Don't use a handheld crank spreader unless your lawn is small—it won't provide an even application.

Caution: Fertilizing too frequently can lead to explosive lawn growth, which may look great temporarily but will stunt growth over the long term. You'll end up with a shallow root system that won't be able to last through drought or other difficult weather.

•**Don't "scalp" your lawn.** Never cut more than one-third of the height of grass blades when mowing—if grass is three inches tall, cut no more than one inch. Scalping harms the lawn's ability to support its own root growth. In general, you want grass to be at least three inches tall for the cool-season grasses or three quarters of an inch tall for Bermuda grass.

Tall grass retains moisture, so you will not need to water as often. Higher grass also shades the surface of the soil, minimizing the growth of weeds.

•**Water at dawn.** For the best results, water between 4 am and 7 am. If you water later, the water will evaporate quickly. There is no need to get up early—if you don't have in-ground irrigation, buy timers for your spigots.

•**Do not bag clippings.** I leave them on the field at Fenway Park and on my lawn at home. They release nitrogen into the newly cut grass, making your lawn healthier and more lush.

•**Check your lawn mower blade.** The Red Sox grounds crew checks the blade every week. For home owners, every month should suffice. The blade can become dull from use or be dented when the lawn mower rolls over branches and children's or pets' toys.

If your blade is dull, the tips of your grass blades will look gray and dried up. Disconnect your lawn mower's spark plugs, and remove the blade with a wrench. Place the blade in a vise, and sharpen with the beveled edge of a file, or get the blade sharpened at a hardware store or lawn center.

•**Test your soil.** A soil test will determine the levels of pH, phosphorus, potassium and organic matter in your soil, as well as the percentage of sand, silt and clay. The test will also tell you if your lawn's nutrients are unbalanced and explain what you need to add to your lawn.

Test soil every two or three years because its composition can change.

Best: Your local agricultural extension service, found in the blue pages of your phone book, can supply an inexpensive test kit with instructions on how to collect soil samples.

Gardening Danger

Tetanus spores live in almost all soils as well as in compost. Adults who are not up to date on their tetanus immunization could contract the disease through even a small cut received while gardening. Tetanus boosters are recommended every 10 years—ask your doctor when you last had one if you can't remember.

Susan Rehm, MD, clinician, department of infectious disease, The Cleveland Clinic Foundation, OH, and medical director, National Foundation for Infectious Diseases, Bethesda, MD, *www.nfid.org.*

"All You Need Is Love"...and Other Lies About Marriage

John W. Jacobs, MD, a psychiatrist and couples therapist in private practice in New York City who has counseled hundreds of couples over the past three decades. He is an associate clinical professor at New York University School of Medicine and the author of *All You Need Is Love, And Other Lies About Marriage* (HarperCollins).

Marriage is more fragile today than ever before, as evidenced by the shockingly high 48% divorce rate among American couples over the past year. With so many marriages breaking up, it is clear that some of our basic assumptions about the modern institution are misguided—and even outright wrong. *Understanding the realities of marriage today can help make your relationship more satisfying...*

Myth: All you need is love.

Reality: Love is not enough to keep you together. Marital love is conditional and it's based on how you behave toward one another day in and day out.

What to do: First, be clear to your spouse about what you need from the relationship—what you can live with and what you cannot live with.

Ask your partner to think about that, as well. Then share your views and negotiate how you each can fulfill each other's wishes.

Example: You may feel the need to go out with friends regularly without your partner, but your partner may feel hurt by this. You might negotiate to go out one night with friends in exchange for one night out with your partner.

Myth: Talking things out will always resolve problems.

Reality: Communication has been oversold as the key to a better marriage. Many couples actually make things *worse* by talking things out. Brutal honesty often backfires, causing a spouse to dig in his/her heels instead of making changes in behavior.

What to do: Learn how to communicate skillfully by focusing on problems rather than fault. Use "I language," not "you language." With "I language," you take the responsibility for your emotional experience rather than blaming it on your partner.

Example: "I feel anxious when we do not have things planned in advance, and it would be a big help to me if we could make dates with friends as far in advance as possible." That is better than making accusatory statements such as, "You always wait until the last minute to make plans, and then our friends are too busy to see us."

Myth: People don't change.

Reality: Change is *always* possible, and small changes often can produce big results. But most people go about trying to change their relationships in unproductive ways—by trying to get their spouses to change. Marital problems are rarely the fault of just one partner, and the biggest impediment to change is the belief that you aren't the one who needs to change.

What to do: Change your own behavior—this often is the best way to prompt shifts in your partner's behavior.

Example: If your spouse always seems to criticize you, try praising his actions on a regular basis. Eventually, he may reciprocate by praising you.

Myth: Our culture's shift in gender roles has made marriage easier.

Reality: The modern marital arrangement—in which both husband and wife work outside the home, and family responsibilities and decisions are handled by both partners—may be "fairer," but it has created its own problems. Confusion about roles, as well as mutual feelings of being taken for granted, can lead to resentment and conflict.

What to do: When discussing your expectations of your relationship, be on the alert for gender stereotypes, such as the idea that women cook and men take out the garbage. Apportion your duties and responsibilities fairly.

Example: You cook two days each week, and your spouse cooks two days a week. Order takeout on the other days.

Myth: **Children solidify a marriage.**

Reality: The stress of having children is a serious threat to a couple's harmony. Even when you feel that you are prepared for their impact on your relationship, your natural devotion to them will leave little time and energy for your marriage.

What to do: If you really want to preserve your marriage, the children cannot always come first. Commit to regular alone time as a couple with weekly or biweekly date nights and occasional trips away from the kids.

Myth: **The sexual revolution has made great sex easier.**

Reality: Movies, television shows and advertisements have raised our expectations about sex, making it seem like everyone is enjoying great sex on a regular basis and you're abnormal if you're not. But many married couples have sexual problems—they just do not talk openly about them.

What to do: Expect ebbs and flows in your sex life, and don't buy into the Hollywood image of what your sex life should be. Consider seeking help from a couples counselor or sex therapist if you cannot resolve sexual problems on your own.

To locate a qualified practitioner, contact...

•**American Association for Marriage and Family Therapy,** 703-838-9808, *www.aamft.org.*

•**American Association of Sexuality Educators, Counselors and Therapists,** 804-752-0026, *www.aasect.org.*

Little Tricks to Make Your Marriage Much, Much Happier

Harville Hendrix, PhD, a therapist and president of the Imago Relationship Therapy Institute, New York City, a nonprofit organization devoted to couples communication therapy, www.imagotherapy.com. He is author of several books on marriage and coauthor, with his spouse, Helen LaKelly Hunt, PhD, of Receiving Love: Transform Your Relationship by Letting Yourself Be Loved (Atria).

It doesn't take a major change to improve a marriage. The path to a more loving relationship is tread with small steps—with an unexpected compliment...the touch of a hand ...or a phone call just to say "hello." You can spend thousands of dollars on a big anniversary bash for your spouse, but the celebration won't mean much if you haven't said "I love you" on the other days of the year.

Some little things that can make your marriage better...

•**Honor "otherness."** The longer we're married, the more we tend to forget that we're married to another person. We begin to think of our spouses as simply extensions of ourselves—then we get frustrated when they act in ways that we wouldn't. We say things like, "Why would you do something like that?" or "How can you think that?" These reactions overlook the fact of difference, that our partners are not a part of us and that they have their own reality.

"Otherness" is part of being married—no two partners are completely compatible. Be curious about the differences, and not critical. Ask your spouse why he/she holds an opinion or took a certain action. Do not make him feel that he is wrong. Validate the opinion or action with a response such as, "I can see the sense of that."

•**Eliminate negativity.** If there's something about your relationship or your partner's behavior that you don't like, it rarely helps to complain about it. Instead, ask for what you want.

Examples: Rather than say, "You never take me out to eat," try, "I'd like it if we went out to eat more." Instead of "We don't have sex anymore," say, "I'd like us to have sex more often." Then turn your statement into a dialogue by adding, "What do you think?"

This approach makes it less likely that your partner will feel attacked and more likely that you'll get what you want. Strive to eliminate negativity—it injures your partner and ruptures your connection. Requests change behavior more often than complaints.

•Make the bedroom a problem-free zone. Everyone needs a place where he can feel safe and happy. If you and your spouse agree to ban arguments and serious discussions from the bedroom, you will end each day together in a place of serenity. Select another place in your home for serious discussions, such as the living room—and set a time limit on those discussions.

•Acknowledge the little things your partner does for you. Perhaps your spouse makes you breakfast every morning or changes the oil in your car. You might consider such chores to be his responsibilities, but that doesn't free you from your responsibility to express thanks. It's wonderful to have someone in your life who does things for you. The fact that your partner helps you out on a regular basis makes his efforts even more worthy of praise, not something to be ignored.

Helpful: When you express gratitude for your spouse's contributions, say it like you mean it and be specific about what you appreciate. A heartfelt statement such as, "I love that you look at me when I am talking. Thank you," means more than an offhand, "Thanks."

•Take the initiative. We forget that feelings of tenderness between partners do not just happen—we must take the initiative to remind our spouses that we still love them.

What you do to accomplish this isn't terribly important, so long as you do something daily that shows your spouse you're thinking of him. Call him from work on your lunch hour just to say "hello"...bring him a cup of coffee in the morning...or touch his shoulder and say, "I love you," as you walk by.

•Touch your partner the way he likes to be touched. Sharing a touch makes us feel closer to each other—yet few couples take the time to enjoy each other's touch in nonsexual ways. Some people like back rubs...others prefer foot rubs or just a touch on the face. If you're not sure what your partner likes, ask him. Make

touch an everyday routine until it becomes second nature.

•Laugh together. Share a funny anecdote or cartoon. Do whatever it takes to laugh with your spouse on a regular basis, even if it is simply watching a humorous movie or television show together.

Emotional memories stay with us on a much deeper level than other memories. If you laugh often with your partner, the whole emotional center of your lives together will improve.

•Receive compliments well. Many people don't know how to handle a compliment. If you say that you like his shirt, he might say, "Oh, it's old."

People brush off compliments because they have inner doubts about their abilities or they're trying to be modest. If you regularly dismiss the compliments from your spouse, you will hurt his feelings, strain your relationship and bring all the compliments to an end. Instead, say, "Thank you. I like hearing that and appreciate your noticing." Let your spouse's compliment in and accept the warmth being sent your way.

How to Care for Mom and Dad When They Live Many Miles Away

Penelope S. Tzougros, PhD, ChFC, CLU, a principal at Wealthy Choices LLC, a financial-planning firm located in Waltham, MA. She is the author of *Wealthy Choices: The 7 Competencies of Financial Success* (Wiley) and host of a nationally syndicated radio talk show on financial advice and planning. Her guide, *How to Care for Mom—When She's Miles Away,* is available from her company at 800-631-1970 or *www.wealthychoices.com.*

A doctor phones to say that your father, who resides in Arizona, has fallen and fractured his hip. The doctor wants to know your plan for when your father gets out of the hospital.

You visit your mother in Florida, and she appears very thin. She admits that she sometimes forgets to eat.

About seven million American adult children face such scenarios as they try to provide care for elderly parents who live far away. As a financial- and estate-planning specialist for 20 years, I have helped hundreds of families manage long-distance caregiving. The key? *Devise a plan before a crisis arises...*

ACTIONS TO TAKE NOW

•**Keep medical, financial and legal information at hand.** For example, it is helpful to have the names and telephone numbers of your parent's physician, pharmacy and health-care plan, including member ID number. Also, prepare a list of medications, supplements and dosages. Update it frequently.

Download a checklist of vital information at *www.aarp.org/families* (just click on "locate valuable documents").

•Set up automatic deposit to a checking or savings account for checks from the Social Security Administration, the Veterans Administration and/or your parent's pension plan administrator. Or, become a "representative payee" who is authorized to receive your parent's monthly benefits.

•Arrange for automatic payment of recurring bills. Ask your parent to share passwords and account numbers with you so that you can arrange for payments.

•Ask your parent to make you an "interested party" on his/her investment accounts so that you can get copies of monthly statements.

•Consider asking your parent to provide you power of attorney to handle financial matters.

•If your parent needs help writing checks and managing household accounts, you may want to hire a third party to handle the record keeping and check signing. The responsibility is time-consuming, and you'll need to keep careful records. Such services are provided by the American Association of Daily Money Managers (814-238-2401, *www.aadmm.com*). *Cost:* $35 to $100* an hour. Expect it to take two to 10 hours or more a month.

Important: Don't become a joint owner of your parent's accounts. Many caregivers find this convenient because they can pay bills or prevent scammers from coaxing money from Mom—but it's risky. If you are sued or go through a divorce, assets in a joint account are legally considered yours—and, therefore, fair game.

•**If your parent lives alone,** subscribe to a personal emergency response system (PERS). The

*Prices subject to change.

emergency response center will provide a radio transmitter (a help button carried or worn by your parent) and a console connected to the phone. Your parent can summon help 24 hours a day.

Cost: $200 and up for the transmitter, plus a monitoring fee ranging from $15 to $30 per month. (Cost may be covered by long-term-care insurance.)

For more information on providers, contact a social worker or SeniorCitizens.com (*www.seniorcitizens.com/k/eprs.html*).

•**When you visit your parents,** assess their needs and gather information.

•Take home the local phone book and Yellow Pages, or order copies from the phone company.

•Do a home-safety inspection. Make sure that smoke detectors work, and change the batteries. Look for potential accident zones—loose rugs, exposed extension cords, excess clutter on the floor, unstable banisters and furniture, needed items on high shelves. Replace regular lightbulbs with the long-life kind. Check the refrigerator for expired foods. *Resource:* Get a free home-safety checklist for seniors from the US Consumer Product Safety Commission (800-638-2772, *www.cpsc.gov/cpscpub/pubs/701.html*).

•Check your parent's car and assess his driving skills. Ask a mechanic to check the oil, brakes and tires and do a general inspection. Ask your parent to drive you to the service station so that you can assess his driving skills. If you are worried, encourage him to take a driving test—these are offered by senior centers. If you think that he poses a danger to himself or others, ask his doctor to evaluate his reflexes, vision and cognition.

•Evaluate the need for in-home help. *Signs that your parent may require help daily or periodically:* A breakdown in personal appearance and cleanliness...unusually messy or disorderly surroundings...outside doors that are unlocked...food left cooking on the stove unattended...short-term memory failure, including the inability to recount daily activities or carry out necessary tasks such as bill-paying...inappropriate food choices or failure to eat regularly...failure to take prescribed medicines.

Signs that a parent may no longer be able to live on his own include failure to perform daily activities without help, including moving from a bed to a chair, dressing, bathing, eating and toileting. *Resource:* For a checklist of trouble signs, go to *www.aging-parents-and-elder-care.com.*

WHEN A PARENT NEEDS MORE HELP

•**Assemble a "care team," those who will check in with him regularly.** Get a parent's approval first. Enlist trusted observers who are willing to call you when problems arise. Some churches and synagogues have volunteers who do this. *Also consider...*

•Neighbors. Give a neighbor a key to your parent's house or apartment. Ask him to drop by once a day. Offer to pay him a small monthly stipend.

•Mail carrier. He will know if the mail is starting to pile up.

•Clergyman or spiritual adviser.

•Gardener/handyman.

•Physician who makes house calls. To locate one, contact the American Academy of Home Care Physicians (410-676-7966, *www.aahcp.org*). The doctor can coordinate care with your parent's primary physician. Ask your parent if he will sign a release so that the doctors can discuss health issues with you.

Resource: For a free handbook on assembling a team, contact Family Caregiver Alliance (800-445-8106, *www.caregiver.org*, click on "Fact Sheets & Publications," then "Consumer Guide").

•**Identify community services.** There are numerous free or low-cost resources for seniors, including adult day care facilities, transportation and activities.

Resources: Faith in Action (877-324-8411 or *www.fiavolunteers.org*) and Senior Corps' Senior Companions Program (800-424-8867 or *www.seniorcorps.org*) make visits to the elderly, helping with simple chores and providing transportation to medical appointments.

IF PROFESSIONAL CARE IS NEEDED

Ask your parent's doctor or a social worker at the local hospital to recommend a local home-care agency.

Cost: $50 per hour and up—it may be covered if your parent has long-term-care insurance or qualifies for Medicaid.

Going through a reputable private agency is more expensive than hiring someone directly, but it can save you headaches. Agency aides are bonded (insured against theft, loss and injury in a home), you don't have to pay their taxes as an employer and the agency provides replacement workers quickly, if necessary.

Also: Retain a geriatric care manager. These licensed social workers and/or nurses can recommend solutions to short-term problems or develop long-term-care plans for your parent. For example, one can act as the family's advocate with hospitals and physicians, fill out the proper forms for benefits programs and help smooth your parent's transition to an institutional setting.

Cost: $300 to $800 for an initial assessment, $75 to $150 per hour after that.

To locate a professional in your area, contact the National Association of Professional Geriatric Care Managers (520 881-8008, *www.caremanager.org*).

TAX BREAKS FOR CAREGIVING

If you support one or more of your parents financially, no matter how far apart you live, the IRS may allow you to claim him as a dependent and save on your taxes.

To qualify: You must pay more than 50% of his expenses.

For more information, check IRS Publication 17, *Your Federal Income Tax,* Table 3-1.

More from Penelope Tzougros, PhD...

Helpful Resources for Caregivers

If you care for an elderly relative, be sure to check out these resources for guidance...

•**National Association of Area Agencies on Aging** (202-872-0888, *www.n4a.org*). Your local chapter of this federally funded clearinghouse can refer you to government programs for housing, transportation, etc.

•**National Long Term Care Ombudsman Resource Center** (202-332-2275, *www.ltcombudsman.org*). This agency investigates complaints by nursing home residents and provides information on residents' rights. Available in every state.

•**US Administration on Aging's Eldercare Locator** (800-677-1116, *www.eldercare.gov*) lists a variety of social service programs in your area, including insurance counseling, prescription and legal assistance, abuse prevention, etc.

US Adoptions Are Getting Easier

Some adoption agencies now have more babies than applicants.

Major reason: Growing interest in open adoptions, in which birth and adoptive parents stay in touch. Pregnant women who might not have given up babies if they would lose contact with them now are more willing to consider open adoption.

Consensus of adoption agencies, reported in *The Wall Street Journal.*

Smart Way to Pay for Summer Camp

Save on kids' summer camp by booking it a year in advance. A typical sleepaway camp costs about $3,400* for four weeks, and prices are rising by 5% to 10% each year. Many camps offer early bird sign-ups at the end of the summer—you can lock in the current year's rate for the following year. A few camps allow you to lock in a lifetime rate. If the camp does not advertise an early-bird rate, ask for one.

Jeff Solomon, executive director, National Camp Association, New York City, *www.summercamp.org.*

*Price subject to change.

A Shoulder to Cry On

To help your teenager with a romantic breakup, lend a willing ear and shoulder to cry on —don't give advice or commentary.

Do not minimize a teenage romance by calling it "puppy love" or saying anything else that a teen would perceive as demeaning. Don't tell your child that he/she is overreacting and will get over the breakup in time. Also, do not give your own opinions of the former boyfriend or girlfriend, and don't try to reassure a teen that he will look back on the breakup with a better perspective in the future.

All these well-meaning comments will only help to push a teen away and possibly trigger depression.

Best: Simply be there for your child, let him initiate any conversation and be sympathetic and nonjudgmental.

Deborah P. Welsh, PhD, associate professor, psychology, University of Tennessee, Knoxville.

Easy Way to Monitor Your Kids Computer Use

Limit kids' on-line time with *ComputerTime* software. Parents can specify limits for each child. When the time is up, the computer automatically logs off. ComputerTime also controls the time of day the computer may be used. The cost is $39.95.*

More information: SoftwareTime, 203-481-1222, *www.softwaretime.com.*

*Price subject to change.

Cell Phone for Kids

The *Firefly* cell phone is designed for children ages eight to 12. Only 22 phone numbers (including the numbers for Mom and Dad) can be preprogrammed into the phone, and they are the only numbers that can be called or from which calls can be received. The five large buttons allow for easy dialing. The Firefly phone, available nationwide, costs $99.99,* including 30 minutes of air time. Additional minutes cost 25 cents each.

More information: 800-347-3359, *www.fire flymobile.com.*

*Price subject to change.

The Great Outdoors

Children who have attention deficit hyperactivity disorder (ADHD), a neurological condition, usually are treated with medications, but these can have side effects and do not work on all ADHD kids. An alternative treatment for ADHD kids is spending time outdoors.

New finding: Exposing ADHD kids to the outdoors after school and during weekends can help to reduce symptoms.

Exposure to nature could supplement but not replace other forms of treatment. Clinical trials and additional research are needed to confirm the benefits of this approach.

Frances E. Kuo, PhD, associate professor, department of natural resources and environmental sciences and department of psychology, University of Illinois at Urbana-Champaign, and coauthor of a study of 452 children with ADHD, which was published in the American Journal of Public Health.

Petting Zoo Danger

Petting zoos and farms can make children seriously ill. Bacteria in the feces of cattle, sheep and goats can jeopardize health.

Most dangerous: A strain of *E. coli* (O157: H7), which can cause bloody diarrhea and lead to life-threatening kidney disease.

Self-defense: Children shouldn't bring food, drinks, sippy cups, pacifiers, etc. into the enclosures. They should wash hands immediately afterward. If manure is abundant, reach over the fence to pet animals. If a child suffers fever and/ or diarrhea soon after visiting a petting zoo, see your pediatrician immediately and tell him/her that your child was recently at a petting zoo.

Jeff Bender, DVM, assistant professor, veterinary public health, University of Minnesota, St. Paul.

 # Pets That Don't Make You Sneeze

Most people who are allergic to dogs or cats react to the animal's dander—the dried, flaky material that typically comes off when a dog or cat sheds. There are no allergen-free cats or dogs, but some breeds produce less dander than others, and, in general, female pets cause fewer allergic reactions than male ones.

Best dog breeds: Small basenji…soft-coated Wheaten terrier…bichon frise…poodle…Portuguese water dog…Chinese crested…or the mixed breeds, such as the labradoodle or other poodle mixes.

Cat breeds: Cornish Rex…Devon Rex…Siberian…or Sphynx (a mostly hairless breed). Dark cats cause allergic reactions more frequently than lighter-coated cats.

To lessen your chance of allergy, bathe your pet once per week with a quality pet shampoo and feed your pet a premium diet, as recommended by a veterinarian.

Marty Becker, DVM, Twin Falls, ID–based author of The Healing Power of Pets *(Hyperion). His Internet site is* www.drmartybecker.com.

Food Dangers for Dogs

The following foods have been known to be harmful to dogs. *Grapes* and *raisins* have been associated with kidney failure in dogs. The symptoms include vomiting and diarrhea. *Chocolate* can be toxic, and the darker the chocolate, the more dangerous. *Sugarless gum* and *candies* made with the sweetener *xylitol* can trigger a rapid drop in blood sugar, which could lead to loss of coordination and seizures. *Onions, garlic* and *other allium* species may damage dogs' blood cells. And, *macadamia nuts* can bring on temporary paralysis of a dog's hind legs as well as vomiting, loss of balance and tremors.

If you suspect that your dog has ingested a toxic food, contact your local veterinarian or the ASPCA Animal Poison Control Center (888-426-4435).

Steven Hansen, DVM, senior vice president, ASPCA Animal Poison Control Center, Urbana, IL. Their Web site is www.aspca.org/apcc.

18

Your Personal Coach

How to Enjoy Life Much, Much More

Do you remember the last time that you said, "Wow, I love my life!"? It might have been when you got married…your child was born…or you received a big promotion.

Those hallmark milestones are rewarding—but they're also few and far between. We can't use them to define our lives. We need to make the small moments count.

Over the years, I have learned some simple rules for loving life more…

•**When you notice the "pink in the rug," shift your focus.** We tend to obsess over the 1% in a situation that bothers us and overlook the 99% that's fantastic.

Example: My friend Donna ordered a custom-made rug with a purple background but received a rug with a pink background. She had waited so long to get it that she decided not to return it. But instead of seeing all the beauty in the room, all she could focus on was "the pink in the rug," wishing it were purple. We had a good laugh, and it didn't take very long for her to change her focus to all that was wonderful in her life.

When you are upset by something in your life, shift your focus from what is negative to what is positive about the situation.

•**Ask yourself, "If I really were important, what would I be doing with my life?"** Many of us feel invisible, as if our actions don't matter. Instead, play the "act as if" game. Start acting as if your actions truly make a difference—and soon they will.

Example: Peggy hated her job and complained that she was bored. I urged her to try an experiment for one week—to act as if she

Susan Jeffers, PhD, a psychologist in Santa Monica, CA, and best-selling author of many books, including *Life Is Huge! Laughing, Loving and Learning from It All* and *The Feel the Fear Guide to Lasting Love* (both from Jeffers). She is a sought-after public speaker and a guest on many radio and television programs. Her Web site is *www.susanjeffers.com.*

really were important in her job. Reluctantly, she agreed. She began by perking up her drab office space…being much friendlier to her coworkers…improving the company in any way she could. In just a few days, she began to feel more connected to the organization and to enjoy her job, realizing that she truly was important.

●**Say yes to adversity.** Yes is more than a word. It's a state of mind, a choice that says, "I'll make something wonderful of my life, no matter what happens." When I discovered that I had breast cancer, I vowed to find the good in my situation—even though I couldn't fathom what that might be. And I did—I now appreciate life so much more. Also, the experience deepened my relationship with the man I was dating and led to my wonderful marriage of more than 20 years. If you look for the good in whatever happens, you will find it.

●**Don't let rejection stop you.** My first book, *Feel the Fear and Do It Anyway,* was rejected by many publishers. One even wrote, "Lady Di could be bicycling nude down the street giving this book away, and no one would read it." Discouraged, I put the book aside—but three years later, I pulled it out of the drawer and resolved to get it published. This time, my agent found a buyer. The book now has sold millions of copies worldwide, and I have published many others.

●**Feel the fear, and do it anyway.** As the title of my first book says, don't wait until you're less afraid to do something, whether it's going on a trip by yourself or acquiring a skill. Learn the tools to help you move past the fear. If you wait to conquer your fear, you'll always be waiting. By doing something despite your fear, you empower yourself.

●**When you feel terrible, help someone else.** You can choose to wallow in your misery, or you can take the attention off yourself by helping others, such as visiting the elderly in a nursing home or reading to children in a hospital. Giving to others is the key to happiness because it helps you realize that you have meaning and purpose in this world. It is a feeling that we all yearn to have, and it is so easy to achieve.

●**Live in the now.** Notice the little things that comprise life—the raindrops on your windowpane…your spouse's laughter…the way it feels to climb into a warm bed at night. If we pay attention to those small moments, we are able to flip the light switch to "on" and find the joy in everything.

Dr. Bernie Siegel's Happiness Boosters

Bernie S. Siegel, MD, a retired surgeon and well-known proponent of alternative approaches to help heal the body, mind and soul. Based in Woodbridge, CT, he is the originator of Exceptional Cancer Patients, a form of individual and group therapy, *www.ecap-online.org*. He is author of several books, including *101 Exercises for the Soul: A Divine Workout Plan for Body, Mind, and Spirit* (New World Library) and the best-seller *Love, Medicine & Miracles* (Harper).

In everyday life, it's easy to lose touch with your soul. I define "soul" as the authentic self that lies deep within you.

Your soul needs regular attention because it enables you to live with enthusiasm, vigor and joy. It also increases your ability to overcome difficulties that you encounter in your life. *Here's how to strengthen your soul…*

●**Access your creative side.** Take up painting, writing, sculpting or other creative endeavors. Expressing your creativity distracts you from emotional and physical pain. It also helps bring to the surface what is trapped within you so that you are able to heal emotionally and physically.

Example: More than 25 years ago, when I painted a self-portrait, I painted my face with a surgical mask. That helped me to realize that I was covering up my emotions even in the painting. Doctors aren't trained to deal with loss and pain—so we bury it. I knew that I needed to uncover my feelings and express them.

●**Define your fears.** By specifically defining your fears, you can come up with solutions so you don't feel so powerless and frightened by them.

Example: If you're afraid of losing your job, dig deeper to find what that really means. Perhaps you're afraid that you'll end up homeless. If so, you can take steps to secure your home, such as setting aside enough savings to cover your mortgage for a year.

•Get rid of the clutter in your life. Release some of the negativity of the past, and make room for emotional growth by periodically cleaning your environment and letting go of belongings.

•Get regular massages. Being touched is therapeutic for your body and soul because it releases muscle tension, enhances the immune system and suppresses pain. Go to a massage therapist, or exchange massages with your partner. Touch can be a tool to help enhance your relationship.

•Focus on the joyful. All too often, we remember only painful experiences—the annoying client, the traffic jam—rather than the happy moments. Carry a small journal to record happy moments in your life. Share funny stories at dinner. Watch funny movies and listen to comedy CDs while driving. My favorite is Mel Brooks's *2000 Year Old Man*.

•Carry your baby picture in your wallet. Most likely, it will elicit feelings of joy when you look at it. Remind yourself that even though you're all grown up, there's still a happy, lovable child inside.

•Find your chocolate—and eat it, too. Chocolate, particularly the dark variety, stimulates the release of natural endorphins that boost mood. If you do not like chocolate, find "your chocolate"—whatever helps you to feel good when you're feeling low. It could be music, gardening, reading or talking with a loved one.

Stop Obsessing... And Start Enjoying Your Life

Edna B. Foa, PhD, professor of psychology in psychiatry and director of the Center for the Treatment and Study of Anxiety at the University of Pennsylvania in Philadelphia. She is coauthor of *Stop Obsessing! How to Overcome Your Obsessions and Compulsions* (Bantam).

Thousands of thoughts enter our minds every day, and some of them are distinctly unwelcome—unpleasant ruminations on what happened yesterday, or fears about what might happen later today or tomorrow.

No one escapes such thoughts altogether—but sometimes they take on a particularly troubling and persistent quality.

You can defend yourself against such painful obsessions—with an understanding of why you have them and what you can do to eliminate them.

AM I OBSESSING?

Ordinary worries shift frequently—you worry that you're not dressed warmly enough and will get sick…or you fret about running out of money when you get your credit card statement. But then your mind moves on.

Obsessions, on the other hand, have a fixed quality with the same fearful thoughts recurring over and over, sometimes for years. The threat of harm—sometimes to oneself, but many times to others—is one common theme.

Examples: You're afraid that you'll forget to turn off the stove, cause a fire and burn down your house…or afraid that you'll fall under the spell of an uncontrollable impulse, and attack and hurt someone you love.

Often the harder you fight obsessions, the more frequently they return and the longer they stay in your mind.

Here's why: Experiments show that people are generally not successful at suppressing ordinary thoughts on command, let alone obsessions. In fact, trying to drive away a thought actually pours energy into it and keeps it alive.

Example: If someone says to you, "Don't think about red turtles. Think about anything else, but not red turtles…," the image becomes difficult to suppress. And if you were told that thinking about red turtles would put your family in grave danger, the image would probably haunt you even more.

THE POWER OF ACCEPTANCE

As illogical as it may seem, to get rid of obsessions, you must accept them. This doesn't mean believing them. To the contrary, it's essential to recognize that thinking about something won't make it happen.

Rather than running from an obsession, you look at what is happening objectively: "Okay, I'm having this thought, and it is alright." Believe it or not, your fear diminishes, and its grip on you begins to loosen—even if just a little.

With time, you will discover that even when you don't fight the unpleasant thought, you do not, in fact, follow through on it.

Other strategies to help you gain control…

●Postponement. When a familiar obsession enters your mind, instead of trying to drive it away forever—what you've probably tried and failed to do so many times in the past—make a compromise.

Tell yourself you'll pay full attention to the thought—only sometime later. Put it off, maybe for just five or 10 minutes at first.

Return to whatever you are doing, and set a timer, if you wish, for obsessing. When the time comes, let yourself obsess. Or if you can, put it off again.

In so doing, you've exerted some level of control over obsessing and have broken the pattern of automatically obsessing as soon as the thought enters your mind.

●Worry time. Make a commitment that at a certain time each day, you'll sit down for 15 minutes and do nothing else but think about your obsession. Turn it over in your mind again… and again. You'll be surprised at how hard it is to obsess, nonstop, for all that time. By giving it your undivided attention, you'll also see how irrational the worry is.

EXPOSURE THERAPY

The best technique to get over your obsessions is called exposure therapy. The basic principle—when you face what you're afraid of, the fear fades away.

How it works: Using a tape recorder, describe what you are worried about. *Narrate in detail, moment by moment, exactly what happens in your fantasy…*

I'm driving my car, and I feel that I have driven over a bump on the road. I think that I might have inadvertently run over a person. I want to stop driving and check, but I decide not to yield to my obsession. I continue to drive. Then I see a police car behind me, and the police officer pulls me over and I am arrested for hit and run. I am put in jail. My wife and parents disown me.

It can't get much worse than that, can it? Play the tape, over and over, for 45 minutes each day. Let the terrible feelings it provokes wash over you…watch them crest, then recede. After five to 10 repetitions, you'll no longer respond to the terrible thoughts.

Alternative: Write down the scenario in full detail. Read the story to yourself repeatedly, for 45 minutes each day.

PROFESSIONAL HELP

Sometimes an obsession is too powerful to conquer on your own. You have used self-help techniques for several weeks or months, and your obsessions still impair your ability to enjoy life to its fullest.

In this case, psychotherapy can be extremely helpful. Medications, typically selective serotonin reuptake inhibitors, such as *fluoxetine* (Prozac) and *paroxetine* (Paxil), work too, often in conjunction with therapy.

To find a mental health professional skilled in this area, contact the Obsessive Compulsive Foundation at 203-401-2070 or on the Internet at *www.ocfoundation.org.*

Wayne Dyer's Simple Plan for a Stress-Free Life

Wayne W. Dyer, PhD, renowned thinker and speaker on the subject of self-development. He is the best-selling author of more than 20 books, including *The Power of Intention: Learning to Co-Create Your World Your Way* and *Getting in the Gap: Making Conscious Contact with God Through Meditation* (both from Hay House). He lives in Hawaii and his Web site is *www.drwaynedyer.com.*

S tress has become so ingrained in modern life that many people assume that tension and anxiety are normal and unavoidable. Not true.

There is nothing natural about living a life filled with stress and anxiety. Our bodies react with elevated blood pressure, increased heart rate, indigestion, ulcers, headaches, breathing difficulties and other negative responses.

Believe it or not, our natural state is joy. *Here's how to return to that state and live a more tranquil life….*

●Understand that you are the source of your stress. Stress and anxiety are choices that we make to process unpleasant events rather than entities that are waiting to invade our lives.

If you blame outside forces for making your life stressful, you'll only make stress more difficult to beat.

When you admit that your own mind is the source, stress becomes manageable. You always have a choice—do I stay with the thoughts that produce stress within me or do I work to activate thoughts that make stress impossible?

For example, I had to drop off a prescription at the drugstore, and the customer ahead of me was asking the pharmacist a series of, what seemed to me, inane questions. I started thinking, *There's always someone just ahead of me in line who asks silly questions or fumbles with money or can't find what's needed.*

I knew that was a signal to change my inner dialogue. I reminded myself of my intention to live a stress-free life. I stopped judging and actually saw the virtue in having to take a moment and slow down. My emotion shifted from discomfort to ease, making stress impossible at that moment.

•Expel stressful thoughts. Stress can feed upon itself when left unchecked. Break the cycle of anxiety by banishing a stressful thought from your mind. Take a deep breath, and visualize yourself stamping "Next" or "Cancel" across the thought and pushing it out of your way.

If you're in a bad mood, repeat "I want to feel good" until you believe it. Then say, "I intend to feel good" until you feel better. These new responses eventually will become habitual and replace your old habit of responding in stress-producing ways.

Sometimes, particularly worrisome thoughts run through your head. *Here is what you could say to yourself instead....*

•I have so many things to do that I can never get caught up. Instead, say, "I'll only think about the one thing I'm doing right now and will have peaceful thoughts."

•I can never get ahead with this job. "If I choose to appreciate what I am doing, I'll attract even greater opportunities."

•I worry about my health problems. "I live in a universe that attracts healing, and I refuse to focus on sickness."

•I can't be happy when the person I love has abandoned me. "I choose to focus on what I have rather than on what I'm missing. I trust that love will return to my life."

•I feel uneasy about the economy. I have lost so much money already. "I choose to think about what I have, and I will be fine. The universe will provide me with what I need."

•My family members are making me feel anxious and fearful. "I choose thoughts that make me feel good, and this will help me uplift those family members in need."

•I don't deserve to feel good when so many people are suffering. "I didn't come into a world in which everyone is going to have the same experiences. I'll choose to feel good, and, by being uplifted, I will help eradicate some of the suffering."

•Return to your happiest moment. Visualize a scene from your past that brings you joy. For me, it's a dock on a Michigan lake where I spent time with my family as a child. For others, it might be the greatest moment of a high school athletic career...the face of a loved one...a tree-lined road...even making love.

When you feel overwhelmed by stress, picture this wonderful image for several moments. Your mind naturally will return to the joyous mental state that you experienced originally.

•Stop taking yourself so seriously. Next time you are anxious about something trivial, take a step back and laugh at yourself for thinking that the problem is worth getting worked up over.

Example: Feel the anxiety building inside you because you're stuck in traffic? Ask yourself what you were going to do with the five minutes you lost that was so important.

The world operates on its own time, and not on yours. If you plant tomatoes in your garden, they'll ripen when they ripen—wanting a tomato any sooner won't change anything. Yet in many phases of our lives, we expect the world to operate on our timetable and we become stressed when it doesn't.

•Realize you will never get it all done. There always will be something else to do or to accomplish. Your desires, goals, hopes and dreams will never be finished—ever. As soon as you realize one dream, another will most assuredly pop up. The secret is to live more fully in the moment.

•**Live in a state of gratitude.** It's impossible to be stressed and appreciative at the same time. Consider all the things that you have achieved in your life—your family, career success, anything that makes you proud and happy—and be grateful for them. Then search for a way to appreciate whatever currently is causing you stress. Perhaps the person in front of you who is driving too slowly is saving you from a speeding ticket or a traffic accident.

•**Meditate.** Nothing else relieves stress, anxiety and depression like silence and meditation. The stillness of meditation relaxes the mind and gives us strength. Take time every day for moments of relaxation and quiet contemplation.

Stress Kills Brain Cells

Stress causes *adrenaline* and *cortisol* to kill brain cells and damage endorphin receptors, which register feelings of pleasure.

Result: Good feelings do not have as much effect as they once did.

Self-defense: Make a conscious, ongoing effort to feel good so that your brain becomes more receptive to positive feelings.

Richard O'Connor, PhD, a psychotherapist in private practice in New York City and Canaan, CT. He is author of *Undoing Perpetual Stress* (Berkley).

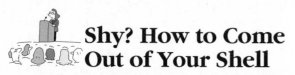

Shy? How to Come Out of Your Shell

Martin M. Antony, PhD, director and founder of the Anxiety Treatment and Research Center, St. Joseph's Healthcare, and professor of psychiatry and behavioral neurosciences at McMaster University, both in Hamilton, Ontario, Canada, *www.martinantony.com*. He is the author of *10 Simple Solutions to Shyness: How to Overcome Shyness, Social Anxiety & Fear of Public Speaking* (New Harbinger).

It's normal to feel nervous before attending a party, giving a speech or meeting with new people. But for shy people, social engagements can be fraught with anxiety.

Shyness is the tendency to be withdrawn or uncomfortable in situations that involve contact with others. Anyone, whether shy or extroverted, may sometimes experience the more intense form of shyness called social anxiety—extreme nervousness in situations that involve being observed or judged by others. You may experience both mental distress and the physical symptoms, such as a pounding heart or shaking hands.

More than five million of Americans, almost equally divided between women and men, have social anxiety disorder. In extreme cases, a person with social anxiety disorder may stop going out altogether. Millions more are shy. They cope socially, but with difficulty.

If shyness disturbs or disrupts your life, be assured that the pain can be conquered. Standard treatments for social anxiety disorder will likely work for shyness, too.

GETTING STARTED

Use a journal to record your experiences…

•**Note your general observations about what's happened before.** Then describe anxious thoughts as they occur or as soon as possible afterward. Think about where these thoughts came from and how to refocus them.

•**Classify what alarms you.** Do you fear big gatherings…one-on-one encounters…perhaps public speaking?

•**Identify all your symptoms.** Shyness has three components…

•*Physical:* Blushing…perspiring…shaking…palpitations…shortness of breath…dry mouth.

•*Cognitive:* Negative thoughts, such as, "I will make a fool of myself" and "No one will like me."

•*Behavioral:* Avoidance of all social situations …hiding out in a corner…increased consumption of alcohol.

•**Assess the situation.** In your journal, write a page on how shyness interferes with your life.

•**Set a goal.** Your immediate goal may be long term or short term, general or specific.

Example: A shy woman sought help from our clinic to increase her social comfort level three months before her daughter's wedding.

STRATEGY #1: EXPOSURE THERAPY

Shy people often fear rejection and can feel uncomfortable even during personal encounters that do not faze others. By deliberately exposing yourself to low-threat versions of alarming social situations, you'll learn that even if things don't work out this time, the consequences will be minimal and you'll be OK. Building your confidence over time will encourage you to break out of your shyness.

In developing exposure exercises for yourself, recall situations that created unacceptable levels of distress. List them from most distressing to least distressing. Address one of the least upsetting scenarios first and work your way up.

First, expose yourself to situations in a safe environment through role play. Ask friends to be your simulated audience at a group presentation…a relative can pretend to be a stranger at a party where you both arrived early.

Before the role play, imagine everything about such a situation—sights, sounds, smells…your thoughts, emotions and feelings. Record these in your notebook. What anxious thoughts, predictions or assumptions do you have regarding this exposure? What do you expect to happen during the exposure practice? What evidence do you have that your fearful thoughts are true?

After the role play, write up what happened and how accurate your original thoughts and predictions were.

When it feels safe, face your fear in the real world, but in a low-key way.

Example I: If you strongly dislike drawing attention to yourself, do just that by intentionally dropping your keys in a mall. People will look up for a second, then ignore you. That wasn't so bad. Slowly, you'll condition yourself to relax.

Example II: If making small talk intimidates you, say hello to a neighbor.

STRATEGY #2: SOCIAL SKILLS TRAINING

People who spend most of their time alone may feel anxious around others. At gatherings, they stand in the corner, talk quietly and look down. They remember parties as negative experiences and may stop going.

Start fitting in better: Talk to an amiable stranger, making eye contact, at the gym…give a short presentation at your book club.

Be patient with yourself. Give yourself assignments and follow them. (A therapist can help with this.) If one attempt doesn't work out, another will.

STRATEGY #3: COGNITIVE THERAPY

Cognitive therapy with a professional therapist makes you more aware of the beliefs and the assumptions that influence your emotions… helps you learn to view your negative beliefs as hypotheses, not facts…replaces your assumptions with more realistic, more positive ways of thinking. As you explore your reactions to ordinary situations, you will discover ways to protect yourself from anxiety. Working with a therapist can be very useful for beating shyness.

What a therapist might suggest: When you notice your anxiety level shifting up or down, ask yourself, "What am I thinking right now? How did my thoughts just change?" Record these observations in your notebook.

Most anxious thoughts can be phrased as predictions. Ask: "What do I think will happen? What might this person be thinking about me? How does that make me feel?"

Criticism and comparisons assail us from all sides. You may be afraid you aren't perfect, but can you name anyone who is? The same traits that make one person like you will make another person dislike you.

Example: Susan fears returning shoes to a store because "the saleswoman will think I'm an idiot." I ask Susan, "Can everybody like everybody? Does it matter what the sales clerk thinks of you?"

Assess the probable consequences of others' negative judgments—"Even if my friend never goes on vacation with me again, is that the end of the world?"

STRATEGY #4: MEDICATION

Drugs, best when used along with psychological approaches, can reduce even severe cases of social anxiety.

Advantage: Medication will often work more quickly than psychological therapies, which may not take effect for a couple of months.

Disadvantages: Medications may cause side effects, sometimes including weight gain, low sex drive and fatigue…may have to be taken for years, eventually becoming much more expensive than a few months of counseling…may interact with other drugs or alcohol…may have unpleasant withdrawal effects.

Three medications have been approved by the Food and Drug Administration for treating social anxiety disorder—*paroxetine* (Paxil), *venlafaxine* (Effexor XR) and *sertraline* (Zoloft). All are antidepressants, an umbrella term covering five drug classes. (The word "antidepressant" was coined for their initial use, to treat depression. They can do much more.)

Also effective: *Clonazepam* (Klonopin), *alprazolam* (Xanax) and other *benzodiazepines.* For some people, a combination of drugs works best. Ask your doctor whether any such drugs are appropriate for you.

SLOW BUT STEADY IMPROVEMENT

If you follow these winning strategies, you'll probably notice improvement in a few weeks or months. You may still be anxious at the end of treatment, but far less than before.

Don't be shy. Try.

Tanya Tucker and Friends on How To Beat the Blues

Tanya Tucker, one of the most successful vocalists in the history of country music. She has released 30 albums and is the author of *100 Ways to Beat the Blues* (Fireside), a compendium of her friends' blues-beating techniques. She lives on a farm outside of Nashville. Her Web site is *www.tanyatucker.com.*

No one is immune to the blues. The rich and famous have down days just like everyone else. Country music star Tanya Tucker says her three children are "the best three ways I ever found to beat the blues." *Her friends have other great ways to pull themselves up when they're feeling down...*

•**Psychologist Dr. Joyce Brothers** turns to comfort food when she's feeling down. The foods that cheer us up tend to be the ones we enjoyed the most as children, says Dr. Brothers. For her, that's tapioca or rice pudding. "There is research that shows comfort food really does comfort," she says.

•**NASCAR driver Geoff Bodine** sweeps away his blues by cleaning. "I'll polish the entire house, clean out the garage, reorganize my office, wax my car and groom my animals. My two dogs are never brushed as much as when I'm feeling bad."

•**Actor Burt Reynolds** seeks out people who make him laugh. You can't feel bad if you're laughing. "Dom DeLuise can always make me laugh," says Reynolds. "As can Charles Nelson Reilly. Charles Durning always works. And I've found two new ones: Adam Sandler and Chris Rock."

•**Stand-up comic James Gregory** does "hospital math." He starts by counting the number of hospitals in the area. Then he estimates the number of patients in each of those hospitals, many of whom are in great pain or have little hope of survival. Finally, he reminds himself that despite whatever has got him down, any of those people would trade places with him in a second. "By the time I'm that far into the conversation with myself, I stop feeling depressed."

•**Former First Lady Barbara Bush** turns to prayer when things seem most bleak. She isn't a woman to give in to the blues easily. When her husband or one of her sons is criticized, she tells herself, "This too will pass." But back in the early 1950s, tragedy struck—her four-year-old daughter died of leukemia. "I found that prayer helped enormously."

•**Country singer Brenda Lee** helps others. She says that when we do a favor for a loved one, a friend or even a stranger, we do a favor for ourselves as well. "Providing a helping hand to another person will lift you up faster than anything."

•**Rock-and-roll legend Little Richard** reminds himself that all people have problems. Often, the blues are brought on by feelings of disappointment that we're not getting more out of our lives—or by feelings of jealousy for those who seem to have it all. "Just keep this in mind," says Little Richard. "The grass may look greener on the other side. But believe me, it is just as hard to cut."

•**Country singer Loretta Lynn** says that when she is blue, she thinks about her husband Doolittle Lynn, who died in 1996. "I think about how tough my husband was, how nothing kept him down for too long. And I tell myself that if Doolittle was standing there with me, he would get gruff as an old bear: 'Loretta, get yourself out of the night air, fix yourself a fried baloney sandwich and say to hell with the blues!' So that's what I do."

•**Singer Taylor Dayne** goes on a hike. No problem seems quite as bad after taking "a hike in nature, a walk in a quiet neighborhood, looking at the clouds and trees, admiring the beauty around you."

Finding Love Again... At Any Age

Sol Gordon, PhD, a psychologist, educator on sex and professor emeritus of child and family studies at Syracuse University in Syracuse, NY. He resides in Chapel Hill, NC. A former love advice columnist, he is the author of numerous books, including How Can You Tell If You're Really in Love?, *and coauthor, with Elaine Fantle Shimberg, of* Another Chance for Love: Finding a Partner Later in Life *(both from Adams Media).*

As a therapist, I have heard it all: "Love cannot work anymore"..."It's too late"... "I have passed my prime." What these people didn't understand was that pessimism about finding a mate could become a self-fulfilling prophecy.

Whether you are widowed, divorced or never married, you can find love, companionship and happiness at any age. In just this country by itself, there are 35 million single people over age 40 and 28 million over 60. One of them is waiting for you!

DON'T CALL IT DATING

I hear countless stories about older people who thought they had found the perfect mate through a dating service. Just a few dates later, they were disillusioned.

Example: The guy was married and just wanted sex.

In my view, the on-line dating services and matchmaking organizations don't work well for the senior crowd.

While love at first sight exists, it rarely endures. After a short time, people who have proclaimed themselves "madly in love" just get mad. Mature love, on the other hand, grows as it's gently nurtured. And there are ways to find it.

FRIENDSHIP IS THE KEY

Love promises intimacy—but passionate friendship delivers it. Friends can give us what we need most at this time of our lives. For the best chance at love, focus on friendship first, not on whether you're "in love" or could love this person. *Look for these traits...*

•**Empathy and trust.** A friend listens…keeps confidences…offers support and understanding …expects the same of you.

•**Shared value systems.** Seek out someone who shares your ethical or spiritual (not necessarily religious) goals. Your sense of right and wrong and of what is fair and moral should correspond.

•**Solid communication skills.** Communicating effectively is a major indicator of a couple's ability to sustain a caring, trusting relationship through good times and bad.

Example: Carol admits that instead of expressing her feelings early during her 40-year marriage, "I would just shut down or cry, which didn't help. My husband patiently encouraged me to say what I felt. Now we can talk about everything."

•**Cooperation and respect.** Couples who are friends can discuss amicably the countless decisions of life, respect each other's wishes and make decisions as a team.

Bonus: Starting a relationship later in life, without the gender-specific baggage of an earlier, less-equitable era, opens opportunities for a full sharing of household chores from the very beginning. Many women over age 50 have had an entire lifetime of being the chief cook and bottle washer and are no longer willing to assume that role.

Men who prefer a more traditional distribution of labor and who question the value of equality may profit from reading books by Terrence Real, including *How Can I Get Through to You? Closing the Intimacy Gap Between Men and Women* (Scribner).

•**A humorous outlook.** This important trait can compensate for deficiencies in other areas. Laughter reduces blood pressure and stress… improves blood circulation…lightens sadness. A person who can laugh at the craziness of life is a treasure. Laughter is appealing, too.

HOW TO FIND A SPECIAL PERSON

•**Get out there.** Frequent a senior center…join a coed hobby group…do community service. Browse in bookstores and strike up conversations. Share recipes at the grocery store.

For safety's sake, women shouldn't give an address or phone number to a stranger (an e-mail address is OK). If you want to meet again, do so in public places for a while.

•**Learn something new.** Take a class…work for a political party…environmental group…local theater. Energy, confidence and enthusiasm are attractive.

Example: At the Voters for Choice benefit during 1999, the feminist Gloria Steinem, who had doubted she would ever want to marry, met David Bale, the South African–born father of actor Christian Bale. The following year they married—he, at 59, for the third time and she, at 66, for the first.

•**Ask your friends and relatives to fix you up.** To get the most out of blind dates, focus on your interests. Tell your matchmakers that you're looking for a skiing companion or tennis partner…a theater or movie buddy…someone with whom to hike or try new restaurants.

Also, joining a religious institution provides a time-honored way to meet people with whom you'll have at least one thing in common.

•**Attend reunions.** Contact an old flame—you may rekindle the spark.

Famous old flame: Actress Carol Channing, at 82, married her junior high school sweetheart, Harry Kullijian, age 83, in 2003. After seeing his name several times in her memoir, *Just Lucky I Guess: A Memoir of Sorts* (Simon & Schuster), a mutual friend suggested that he get in touch with her. And, he did.

I know lots of couples who got together many years after they first met. In fact, I was motivated to write *Another Chance for Love*, a book about finding a partner in later life, by my own story.

In 1991, Judith, my dear wife of 40 years, died of cancer. Seven years later, I reconnected with Marlene at the 50th-anniversary celebration of the founding of an Israeli kibbutz where we had met as teenagers. She, too, had been widowed. We've been together ever since.

You can find almost anyone through the Internet. Visit *www.switchboard.com…www.anywho.com…www.whitepages.com…www.whowhere.com…www.411.com.*

FIGHT PRECONCEIVED NOTIONS

People like to tick off the imperfections of each potential partner. If you're tempted to do this and then dismiss someone as an "otherwise perfect person," identify the sticky points. Could you overlook or learn to live with them…or are they "deal breakers"? Don't try to be too logical about it—go with your gut feeling. Do you have a good time together…feel relaxed around this person…feel able to be yourself? If so, compromise may be worth a try.

Keep an open mind about your partner's age. Reject the stereotype that the man must be older than the woman. I know of many happy couples, including several good friends, consisting of an older woman and younger man.

Another common mistake is expecting to find someone who is just like a beloved departed spouse. No one will fit that bill. Instead, enjoy the aspects of a companion that are unique.

IT'S UP TO YOU

Man or woman, you can make the first move. Ask someone to join you for coffee, go for a bike ride or help you with your golf swing. Forget that Mother said, "Nice girls don't call boys." Today, they do. Remaining active and "out there" keeps you young and interesting.

My philosophy: If you have plans, you never get old. At 81, I'm still lecturing and writing books…and planning a trip to Czechoslovakia with Marlene.

Better Listening

Listen quietly when someone is talking. Don't spend the time formulating your response or you will miss some of his/her message. Welcome his ideas with an open mind. This helps you personally and professionally—people want someone to care about what they say.

Gary D. Danoff, executive coach, Rockville, MD, *coach garyd@aol.com.*

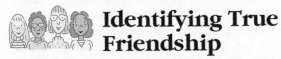

Identifying True Friendship

Laverne Bardy-Pollak, author of the humor column titled "Laverne's View" for *50 Plus Monthly*, a regional NJ newspaper, and a columnist for the nationally syndicated Senior Wire news service. Her essays, articles and poems have appeared in many magazines and anthologies. A resident of Newton, NJ, she has compiled a book of her columns and is writing a novel.

Potential friends are attracted much as lovers are—through both chemistry and body language…the recognition of similar temperaments, intelligence, sense of humor, experiences, tastes and interests. The more that two people have in common, the deeper their relationship promises to be.

How you will know a true friend…

•**Friends are people you genuinely look forward to sharing time with** and miss when you're apart for too long.

•**Friends reveal their weaknesses.** At our age, we (finally) know we're not perfect. Recognizing the same faults in ourselves strengthens the bond.

•**Friends accept each other's quirks and value their strengths.**

Example: My friends know that as a writer, I have an inordinate personal and professional craving for solitude. An old pal confided, "It's a good thing I understand your needs. Otherwise, this relationship wouldn't have lasted so long."

•**Friends reveal truths that you may not want to hear.** In turn, you can say what's on your mind without being hurtful or insulting. A solid friendship can withstand well-intended criticism.

Bonus: Those who know us best may offer better personal advice than anyone else could.

•**Friends are generous and flexible.**

Example: Two old pals and I choose activities to share on our own birthdays. They love museums, plays and visits to the big city…I prefer craft shows, antiquing and being pampered at a spa. Obliging each other is part of the fun—and opens us to new experiences.

How to Be Persuasive: A Top Lawyer's Negotiating Tricks

Laurie Puhn, JD, an attorney, mediator and communication expert in New York City. She owns a professional and personal development training firm and is author of the best seller *Instant Persuasion: How to Change Your Words to Change Your Life* (Tarcher/Penguin). Her Web site is *www.smartcomments.com*.

A conversation offers a chance to convince someone else to like you…or believe in your ideas…or help you succeed. But to achieve these positive results, you must learn to be persuasive. *Here's how…*

•**Hear people out.** If you immediately voice disagreement, you'll only encourage your conversation partner to get defensive. Instead, ask him/her to explain his position. This shows respect for the person's thoughts, which encourages him to show respect for yours. It also gives you a chance to hear his reasoning, which puts you in a better position to tailor your rebuttal.

•**Be a positive gossip.** When you hear something nice about someone you know, pass along the compliment to the person praised.

Example: You overhear your employer praising a colleague's work. Let the colleague know that he has scored with the boss. You will build a good relationship with a coworker who is going places.

Though all you have done is relay someone else's kind comments, the recipient will associate you with good news and positive feelings. This "positive gossip" technique also sends the message that you're rooting for this person's success, which should encourage him to root for yours.

•**Complain constructively.** The more we complain, the more others tend to tune us out, decreasing the odds that we will ever be able to persuade them of anything. When you have no choice but to complain, present your complaint together with a potential solution and you'll be thought of as a problem solver, not a complainer.

Example: Your company's morning meeting always runs long. Rather than moan about it, offer to take charge of the meeting's agenda.

Suggest that copies of the agenda be distributed in advance and that time limits be placed on every topic. Not only will you keep things moving, you'll have a powerful role—shaping the agenda.

•**Stay in touch.** Most of us have acquaintances we think to call only when we need something. Sooner or later, these people feel that they're being used and no longer respond to our requests. To prevent this, occasionally call or e-mail when you don't need anything or, better yet, when you have something to offer.

Example: You find a newspaper article that you think your old boss would be interested in. Call to tell him about it, or drop it in the mail.

•**Get their attention.** You cannot convince people when they're not paying attention—and most people aren't paying full attention most of the time.

Rather than rush ahead with an important discussion because the moment suits you, ask the person you're trying to persuade whether it is a good time for him/her to discuss an important matter. If he says yes, your question has alerted him that this is something serious and he should pay attention. If the answer is no, ask him to pick a better time.

•**Don't take sides.** It's tempting to voice an opinion when a friend is involved in a disagreement. We think our wisdom is required and our friend needs our support. Usually it's wiser to keep out of it. By taking sides, we cost ourselves points with the person we sided against—and we might cost ourselves points with the person we sided with as well.

Example: Your best friend has a big argument with his wife. You tell him that he is right—his wife is unbearably bossy. Eventually, husband and wife reconcile—and your friend is angry with you for badmouthing his wife.

•**Balance the conversation.** Our conversations are most persuasive when both parties speak approximately 50% of the time. Do too much of the talking, and your listener might become disengaged and not pay enough attention to be persuaded. Let the other person do too much talking, and you might not get your point across.

If you're having a conversation with someone who won't give you a chance to speak, say, "I'd like to tell you something because I value your opinion." This should encourage him to let you speak. If you do find yourself doing too much of the talking, ask questions to encourage balance.

•**Close the deal.** People sometimes become so relieved or excited when they think they have secured an important agreement that they end the conversation without hammering out the details. Then it becomes difficult to raise the subject again without seeming like a pest.

Example: You persuade a difficult neighbor to split the cost and effort of planting a hedge between your properties—but you don't pick a specific date to do it. If you call him the next day, he may think you're harassing him. If you wait a week, he may have changed his mind.

After persuading someone of your point of view, cement your success by securing an agreement on when and how to take the next step.

Building Brain Power With Super Foods

Arthur Winter, MD, assistant professor of neurosurgery at New Jersey Medical College and director of New Jersey Neurological Institute, both in Livingston. He is coauthor of *Brain Workout* and *Build Your Brain Power* (both are from St. Martin's).

W hat you eat has a direct effect on your brain. Some foods improve your ability to concentrate. Others aid memory and facilitate the ability to solve problems. Still others generate hormones that stabilize mood and enhance concentration.

Here are important brain nutrients and the foods that contain them....

CHOLINE

Choline is a fatlike substance related to the B vitamins. It is converted in the brain into *acetylcholine*, a neurotransmitter linked to memory and cognitive function. You should make every effort to get adequate choline as you age because the level of the enzyme required to produce it, *N-acetyltransferase,* declines as we age. People with Alzheimer's disease have been found to have significantly reduced levels of acetylcholine.

In laboratory studies, animals given choline-enhanced diets for several months were able to form new long-term memories more efficiently than animals on standard diets. It's not clear if supplemental choline is beneficial to humans, but adequate dietary amounts are essential for normal brain function and may play a role in preserving brain function in people with Alzheimer's and other neurological diseases.

Recommended: One or more servings daily of high-choline foods—egg yolks, dairy, soy, beef, liver, wheat germ, oatmeal, brown rice, peanuts and fish.

VITAMIN B-12

Vitamin B-12 is used to produce *myelin,* the sheathing around nerve cells. A deficiency can cause impaired transmission of nerve signals as well as declines in memory and other cognitive functions.

New finding: B-12 inhibits activity of *monoamine oxidase* (MAO), an enzyme that breaks down brain chemicals. Alzheimer's patients given supplemental B-12 have improved memory and communication skills.

Recommended: Two to three servings weekly of B-12-rich liver, red meat, eggs or dairy. Everyone should take a daily multivitamin and mineral supplement for insurance. People who follow a strict vegan diet (no animal foods) should also supplement with 6 micrograms (mcg) of B-12 every day.

Ask your doctor to check your blood level of vitamin B-12 if you're experiencing memory problems. More than 20% of older adults have low levels of vitamin B-12 because they lack *intrinsic factor,* a stomach protein required for B-12 absorption. Deficiencies of B-12 are thought to account for 10% of non-Alzheimer's memory loss cases. People who have inadequate intrinsic factor need to receive a monthly intramuscular B-12 injection.

AMINO ACIDS

The brain is almost completely regulated by amino acids, the 20 different building blocks of protein. Nine of these—the essential amino acids—can be derived from diet only. People who eat a well-balanced diet almost always get adequate amino acids. Supplemental amounts may offer additional protection, but this hasn't been established. The promising amino acids include *tyrosine* (involved in alertness), *phenylalanine* (linked to memory) and *methionine* (involved in motivation and focus).

Recommended: From 45 to 75 grams (g) of dietary protein daily—about three servings. Protein from animal foods, such as beef, chicken, fish and dairy, are complete and contain all of the necessary amino acids. Vegetable proteins (with the exception of soy) don't contain all of the essential amino acids. Vegetarians should eat a variety of high-protein foods daily, such as combining nuts with legumes, to achieve the proper balance.

FOLIC ACID

Another B vitamin, folic acid, appears to affect brain function. One study found that older adults with dementia or other mental disorders were three times more likely than normal adults to have low levels of folic acid. Deficiencies of folic acid have been linked with declines in memory and abstract thinking ability.

Recommended: Along with a multivitamin, eat two servings daily of the foods high in folic acid—asparagus, leafy green vegetables, lentils, wheat, fortified cereals, meat and broccoli.

As little as 200 mcg of folic acid (the amount in three-quarters of a cup of cooked spinach) has been shown to improve mood and relieve depression and fatigue in elderly people who are healthy.

VITAMIN C

The brain and adrenal glands are the body's main repositories of vitamin C. Because the adrenal glands produce stress-related hormones, it is suspected that vitamin C may play a role in modulating physical and emotional stress.

Stress elevates levels of the hormone *cortisol,* which can over time damage cells in the hippocampus, the portion of the brain involved in memory. Vitamin C is a powerful antioxidant that can minimize physical stress to brain tissue caused by such factors as smoking, alcohol consumption and air pollution.

Vitamin C also assists in the production of neurotransmitters and participates in the processing of glucose, the brain's primary fuel. One study found that people with low blood levels of vitamin C scored lower on memory tests than those with normal levels.

Recommended: Two daily servings of vitamin C–rich foods—which include citrus fruits and juices, tomatoes, strawberries and potatoes. Most Americans should receive at least 100 milligrams (mg) of vitamin C per day—more if you smoke or drink alcohol. One orange has about 70 mg.

COMPLEX CARBOHYDRATES

The brain depends almost entirely on glucose—derived from the breakdown of carbohydrates—for energy. Glucose provides the energy that the brain needs for concentration and other cognitive functions, and it has been shown to enhance memory and improve performance on standardized tests.

Caution: A diet high in simple sugars (from pastries, soft drinks, candy, etc.) triggers hormonal changes that cause drops in blood glucose—this increases fatigue and impairs memory and concentration. Stroke patients with excessive blood sugar suffer more nerve and brain damage than those with lower levels.

Recommended: Avoid sugar. Obtain glucose from the complex carbohydrates, such as whole grains, legumes, fruits and vegetables. Approximately half of your daily caloric intake should come from these foods.

THE TOP 10

The best foods for your brain include…

- **Low-fat milk or yogurt.**
- **Eggs.**
- **Lean meats, such as flank steak.**
- **Poultry.**
- **Spinach and other leafy greens.**
- **Whole-wheat bread.**
- **Oranges.**
- **Black beans and other legumes.**
- **Enriched brown rice.**
- **Salmon.**

Grown-Ups Need Naps Too

Napping not only refreshes you, it also improves mental performance.

New study: Healthy men and women, ages 55 to 85, either napped or stayed awake between 2 pm and 4 pm each day for three days. Those who napped for 10 minutes to almost two hours performed up to 15% better on computerized mental tests than those who only relaxed. The improvement, which was seen immediately following the nap, was maintained throughout the next day.

If you feel decreased daytime alertness: Try adding a nap to your routine.

Scott S. Campbell, PhD, sleep expert, department of psychiatry, Weill Medical College of Cornell University, White Plains, NY.

Five Proven Ways to Keep Your Memory Very Sharp

Lynn Stern, MSW, a senior clinical social worker who helps people overcome memory problems, University of Michigan Health System, Ann Arbor. She is coauthor of *Improving Your Memory: How to Remember What You're Starting to Forget* (Johns Hopkins University).

Unlike the memory experts who perform tricks on stage and on television, Lynn Stern spends many hours each week actually helping people who experience memory problems. During her 20 years at the University of Michigan's Turner Clinic, Ms. Stern has determined what works—and what doesn't—to improve memory. *Here's her advice…*

Scientists do not understand exactly how it happens, but nearly everyone's memory slowly undergoes certain changes as they age…

- **It becomes harder to remember words that were once familiar to you**—a friend's maiden name, for example, or the type of dog your uncle had as a pet.

• **Learning something new takes more effort than it used to.**

• **You increasingly forget items on your schedule,** such as the need to pay a bill by a certain date.

• **You have more difficulty in paying attention to more than one thing at a time—** carrying on a conversation while watching TV, for instance.

While these memory changes are common, it still may be wise to consult your physician. In most cases, the doctor will reassure you that some memory difficulties are normal as you age. In some instances, physicians may recommend medical tests when they suspect the onset of Alzheimer's disease or another serious condition.

PROTECTING MEMORY

You can't reverse normal memory changes, but here are five sure ways to dramatically slow them down…

• **Learn something new.** Scientists are not certain of the reason, but research indicates that learning a new language, craft, game or other skill slows memory loss.

It's generally more effective to learn a new skill than to enhance one you already possess. An accountant, for instance, probably wouldn't benefit as much from learning calculus as from studying a foreign language, while a person who already knows two languages would not benefit as much from studying a third one as he/she would from, say, learning to play bridge.

Challenge: Motivating yourself to learn something new.

Choose a skill that you'll enjoy using once you learn it. If you learn a language, arrange a trip to a country where it's spoken. If you learn bridge, join a bridge club where you can meet new people.

• **Play challenging games.** Games such as bridge, Go (an ancient Chinese board game), crossword puzzles and Scrabble can strengthen memory, especially the type of memory required for the game itself.

Working crossword puzzles, for instance, has been proven to assist with verbal recognition. Such proficiency at crosswords is unlikely to help with remembering the phone numbers of close friends and relatives. If that is a problem for you, devise a challenge by writing down the phone numbers and then trying once or twice a week to repeat them from memory.

Or if you have trouble recalling names of new people you meet, jot them down and test yourself periodically in the same way.

• **Socialize with friends, new and old.** Socializing—no matter how you do it or how often—helps slow down memory changes because it always requires the use of memory.

It's all but impossible, for instance, to carry on a conversation without referring to people and events that you have stored in memory.

Moreover, talking to friends about what you've read in the newspaper or seen on TV reinforces those facts in your mind.

• **Stay physically active.** According to researchers here at the University of Michigan and elsewhere, people who engage in physical activity—regardless of the type or amount—are more likely to maintain their memory and other mental abilities.

• **Organize important activities around your most alert time periods.** Almost everyone has a time of day when he is most alert. It's usually impossible to cram all important activities into that time slot, but as often as possible, reserve that period for important tasks, such as caring for a grandchild or driving.

Also try to learn new skills during your most alert times. For example, if you want to study acting and have a choice between a morning or an afternoon class, choose the time when you customarily feel more alert.

Smart move: Ask your doctor whether any medication you are taking can impair memory. This effect occurs most often with the prescription medications for sleeping problems, anxiety, muscle tension, allergies, colds and pain.

If the answer is yes, ask if another drug without the side effect is available. Should you opt to continue the medication, at least you'll know that related memory problems are likely to stop when you cease taking it.

MEMORY TRIGGERS

Fortunately, most memory changes happen over a period of many years, and this usually gives you some time to adapt before they become very serious.

Successful strategies to improve memory…

•**Do something unusual to trigger your memory.** For example, to remember to stop at the grocery store on the way home from work, switch your watch from one wrist to the other earlier in the day. The mild but nagging discomfort acts as a reminder.

Yes, you may occasionally forget what it was you were supposed to remember, but with a little thought it usually will come back.

Other memory triggers: Get organized—always put your glasses, keys, etc., in the same place. Say what you want to remember aloud or write it down—both actions will reinforce it in your memory.

•**In one compact notebook, write down information you may need in the future.** If you order a product over the phone, jot down the phone number and name of the person you spoke with. And if you meet interesting people at a party, put their names and phone numbers in the notebook.

Information like this too often winds up on scraps of paper stored in dozens of places around the house. By using a single notebook, however, you can easily refer to it as the information becomes necessary.

Also helpful: A date for each entry to make it easier to look up information. And when one book fills up, store it in a designated place and start another.

•**Write down other information next to names in your personal phone book,** such as birthdays, anniversaries and names of children that are too easy to forget as families grow larger and grow apart, too.

•**Avoid procrastination.** If you put off doing something, chances increase that you will forget it altogether.

There's no simple way to change the habits of a lifetime, but if you're prone to procrastination, post reminders of appointments and upcoming events on the bathroom mirror and in other places where you regularly look.

Memory Booster

The very first supplement that's proven to enhance short-term memory—a neuropeptide known as MemoProve—is now available. The supplement has shown in clinical trials that it can improve short-term memory in middle-aged and older adults by an average of 15%, which is the equivalent of reversing 12 years of age-related memory decline. It can boost concentration, increase mental alertness and improve the ability to retain new information.

More information: Visit *www.memoprove. com.*

Thomas H. Crook III, PhD, a clinical psychologist, memory researcher and president of the research company Psychologix, Inc., Fort Lauderdale, FL, *www.psychologix.com.* He is author of *The Memory Cure* (Pocket).

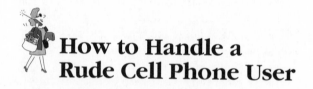

How to Handle a Rude Cell Phone User

To handle rude cell phone users without being rude yourself…

•**Be forthright and polite**—"Could you please set your phone on vibrate? The ringing is disturbing us."

•**Act as if the user does not know what he/she is doing**—"I'm sure you don't realize it, but you are speaking loudly. Could you please lower your voice?" If the user gets annoyed, explain that you are not trying to offend him/her—just asking him to lower his voice.

•**Be direct if the user is someone you know**—"Please hang up so we can talk to each other." Complain to a manager if a cell phone user is ruining an experience for you, such as a movie or a meal.

•**Do not apologize for bringing up the problem…**but don't use hostile language.

Barbara Pachter, an authority on business communications and etiquette, Cherry Hill, NJ, *www.pachter.com,* and coauthor of *The Jerk with the Cell Phone* (Marlowe & Co.).

Amazing Cell Phone Tricks

Dylan Tweney, a technology journalist located in San Mateo, CA. He has contributed to many publications, including *PC World* and *Business 2.0*.

Modern cell phones can do much more than simply make calls, thanks to text-messaging technology. (Instructions are on your phone provider's Web site or in your owner's manual.) *Here is how to use your cell phone to...*

•Communicate even if the cellular network is overwhelmed. Most cell phones sold since 2002 let users send and receive short text messages. In an emergency, these messages may be your best way to communicate.

Example: London's cellular phone system was so overwhelmed following terrorist bombings in July of 2005 that many voice callers got only busy signals—yet text messages still made it through.

You might have to pay a few cents per message if text messaging isn't included in your cellular calling plan. Typing on a cell phone takes time, so practice using text messaging periodically. In an emergency, try calling out before resorting to text messaging.

•Get helpful information. Google's Short Message Service (*www.google.com/sms*) will send you driving directions...local business listings...stock quotes...weather forecasts...and even word definitions to any cell phone equipped with text-messaging capability. To get any of the following, type the information listed and send it as a text message to the number 46645.

•Store or restaurant. Want to find a nearby Thai restaurant or hardware store? Just type the word "Thai" or "hardware" and the local zip code into your phone as a text message and send it. (If you don't know the local zip code, Google will accept the town/city and state instead.)

•Weather report. Type and send "weather" and zip code for a forecast.

•Directions. Type and send "from" and an address and "to" and an address for driving directions (include city and state in each address).

•Movie times and theaters. Send the film's name and your zip code.

•Stock price. Send a ticker symbol to get a stock quote.

•Word definition. Just send "define" and any English word.

A text message containing the information will be sent to your cell phone within a minute. A printable, wallet-sized "tips sheet" with details is available on the Google SMS Web site. The service is free, but your service provider might charge a few cents per message.

•Find a job, home, etc. Get updates on new job openings, real estate listings and used cars for sale. A service called Feedbeep (*www.feedbeep.com*) will scan classified advertisements appearing on the Craigslist Internet site (*www.craigslist.org*) and forward any that meet your preset criteria to your cell phone as text messages.

Feedbeep also can be used to alert you to bargains on the discount shopping sites such as DealCatcher.com or Overstock.com. The basic package costs $3* per month. Your provider also might charge a few cents per message.

•Take a memo. Most cell phones do contain some variety of voice recorder or a text memo function. Your phone's manual should have details on locating and using these tools, or just scroll through the phone's menu. If your phone doesn't include a memo tool, you can use its address book or calendar to save notes to yourself as text messages.

•Identify a song. Want to know the name of the song you're enjoying on the radio or in a store or restaurant? Dial 866-411-SONG on your cell, and hold the phone up to the music for 15 seconds—the call will disconnect on its own. You'll get a text message back from 411-Song (*www.411song.com*) identifying the artist and title. The first ID is free—subsequent song IDs cost 99 cents each. There's no charge if a song is too obscure or its sound quality is too poor for an ID.

*Price subject to change.

How to Spot an E-Mail Virus

An easy way to spot an e-mailed virus that could infect your system is to look at the file extension of any e-mail attachment. The file extension is found after the document name.

Example: If you have a file named "letter.doc," the ".doc" is the file extension.

Beware of any unexpected e-mail attachments with the extensions ".exe," ".scr" or ".pif"—the most common extensions of viruses. If you don't know the sender, delete the e-mail.

David Boyer, research editor and resident computer guru, *Bottom Line/Personal,* Boardroom Inc., 281 Tresser Blvd., Stamford, CT 06901.

How to Calculate A Tip in Seconds And Other Math Tricks

Mark Ryan, founder of The Math Center, a math teaching and tutoring organization in Winnetka, IL, *www.themathcenter.com.* He is also author of *Everyday Math for Everyday Life: A Handbook for When It Just Doesn't Add Up* (Warner). A free on-line course based on the book is available through Barnes & Noble University (*university.barnesandnoble.com*).

Everyday math does not have to be hard. There are tricks to make common calculations easy. *Here, simple ways to...*

•**Calculate a tip.** If the check is more than $30, lop off the last three digits, and double the remaining number. The resulting tip always will fall between 15% and 20%.

Example: If the check is $87.46, take out the 7.46 and you're left with 8. Double it for a $16 tip (18.3%).

To calculate the tip if the check is less than $30, round up to the next highest dollar (so $13.27 becomes $14), then double that and insert a decimal point for the tip ($2.80, or 21%).

•**Translate Celsius to Fahrenheit.** Double the Celsius temperature and add 30 to get a fairly accurate Fahrenheit estimate.

Example: If it's 12° Celsius, double to 24, then add 30 for roughly 54° Fahrenheit. The exact temperature is 53.6°F.

•**Make metric conversions.** Remember just one number—1.1—and you will never be confused by metric measures again. Roughly speaking, there are 1.1 yards in a meter and 1.1 quarts in a liter. Add up those two 1.1s to remember that there are around 2.2 pounds in a kilogram.

If distance is the issue, consider that the White House has kept the country off the metric system—so 1600 Pennsylvania Avenue is to blame for the fact that you can't remember there are approximately 1,600 meters (or 1.6 kilometers) in one mile.

•**Estimate any weight.** People and animals have roughly the same density as water. If you remember that one pint of water weighs one pound and that there are eight pints in a gallon, you can estimate the weight of most things.

Example: Want to know how much a dog weighs? Try to picture the number of gallon jugs of milk necessary to form the dog's body. For a midsized, three-gallon dog, multiply three times eight—the dog weighs around 24 pounds.

•**Put government spending into perspective.** Just how outraged should we be by $100 million in government waste? $100 billion? For every billion the government spends, the average taxpayer is on the hook for between $7 and $8. That $100 million pork project likely cost you less than a cup of coffee, but a $100 billion boondoggle is $700 to $800 out of your pocket.

19

Best Bets in Business

Starting Your Own Business? Costly Mistakes to Avoid

Don't be fooled by the stop-and-go economy. *This is a great time to launch your own small business due to several factors that are outlined in the following paragraphs...*

•**Corporate America's controversial outsourcing trend isn't just directed overseas.** An increasing number of large companies are contracting out noncore operations to small US businesses and entrepreneurs, especially in such fields as graphic design, public relations, computer services, bookkeeping, payroll services and sales training.

•**Low-cost technology makes it cheaper than ever to launch a business.** For less than $3,000, you can buy a computer, software, a phone system, high-speed Internet access and basic office supplies.

•**The Internet provides small businesses access to customers,** suppliers and information from all over the world.

Example: eBay, the on-line auction site, has made it possible for hundreds of thousands of individuals to start up businesses. Yahoo! and Register.com provide low-cost Web start-up kits. Lower fixed costs for on-line businesses have spurred start-ups in thousands of specialty markets, such as picture frames, T-shirts and many other types of collectibles.

So get going! *But watch out for these common mistakes...*

MISTAKE—NOT TESTING THE WATERS

Most people research the competition before launching a product or service, but it's just as important to know your target market. Successful

Jeff and Rich Sloan, founders of StartupNation, which provides both information and services to new businesses and entrepreneurs, Birmingham, MI, 866-557-8278, *www.startup nation.com.* They host the weekly radio show StartupNation Radio on 55 stations across the country and are coauthors of *StartupNation: America's Leading Entrepreneurial Experts Reveal the Secrets to Building a Blockbuster Business* (Currency).

entrepreneurs spend months or years learning about customers' needs and wants. You do not have to wait years, but don't fly blind.

If you're targeting business clients, approach local entrepreneurs—your potential customers—for input. Describe how your product or service could help them, discuss its price and ask how they think they might use it.

If you're focusing on consumers, ask for permission to poll shoppers at nearby malls. If possible, bring samples or information for them to see for themselves.

Also ask store owners if they would be interested in the product or service. If they do say no, ask what changes they would recommend. Such exercises are useful even if you plan to sell on-line. Another fast, low-cost way to assess demand and determine pricing is to post products for sale on eBay.

MISTAKE—GOING IT ALONE

Ask an experienced businessperson to be your mentor. The best mentors ask tough questions, offer moral support and help you attract financing by introducing you to lenders and investors. It's a plus when your mentor has been in the same business, but that's not essential—many start-up challenges are common across the business spectrum.

To find a mentor, consider former colleagues or people you meet at trade associations or in social and religious groups, or ask for recommendations from your attorney or accountant.

Resources: Two organizations that can help entrepreneurs find a mentor are SCORE, which works in partnership with the US Small Business Administration (800-634-0245, *www.score. org*) and the Ewing Marion Kauffman Foundation (816-932-1000, *web.kauffman.org*).

MISTAKE—LACKING A DETAILED BUSINESS PLAN

To attract capital, you'll need a business plan to show to bankers and investors. It should include start-up expenses as well as revenue and cost projections. Beyond the numbers, developing a plan can reveal weaknesses in your original concept. Sample business and cash-management plans are available from accountants, commercial banks and on our Internet site, *www.startup nation.com.*

Make sure your plan includes…

•**A clear description of what makes your company unique.** A T-shirt company, for instance, may be the first to sell a particular design on-line or may have a desirable store location.

•**Evidence that the marketplace wants or, better yet, needs your product or service.** Show that your product solves a problem that you or others often complain about…that shoppers you surveyed wanted to pay for it on the spot…that it will help save time or money or provide a new form of enjoyment or entertainment.

Example: Several years ago now, Gretchen Schauffler, an entrepreneur in Lake Oswego, Oregon, created a successful new line of paints called Devine Color. She was the first to offer paint in small pouches instead of swatches. The pouches give prospective buyers just enough paint to see if the colors are right for their projects.

•**Biographies of the management group,** even if you're the only one on it. You must demonstrate why your team is well equipped to succeed. Include education, professional experience and achievements, especially those that illustrate leadership and the ability to meet challenges.

•**Description of each department.** Include the sales and marketing, manufacturing and administration tasks—even if you handle them all.

MISTAKE—RELYING ON BANK FINANCING

Banks shouldn't be the first stop for start-up capital—some will not even lend to businesses whose track records are less than two years old. *Alternatives…*

•**Friends and family.** Treat the transaction as formally as you would any other loan. Have an attorney draw up an agreement.

•**Credit cards.** They have long been a popular source of start-up capital, especially for people who have good credit. Just watch out for high rates.

•**Home equity.** If you have sufficient home equity and income to make the monthly payments, using a home-equity loan or refinancing your first mortgage and "cashing out" some of the value can be a good source of capital. You maintain control and 100% ownership.

Downside: Unlike credit cards, home-equity loans put your home at risk.

•**Angels.** These high-net-worth individuals desire an equity stake in the company and are patient about getting a return on their investments. Angels often belong to networks which can be located through banks, accountants and trade groups. You also can find them by keying "angel networks" and the name of your city and state into an Internet search engine. If you know a company that has secured this type of financing, ask its CEO for the angel's name. Many entrepreneurs are eager to share this information.

Bonus: Angels also can be mentors.

•**Venture capitalists.** These professional investors typically invest in fast-growth companies with demonstrated revenues in exchange for an equity stake. Before making a deal with a venture capitalist, hire an attorney who has experience with these agreements. Business attorneys and accountants can recommend venture capitalists.

Also helpful: The National Venture Capital Association, 703-524-2549, *www.nvca.org.*

•**Government.** For information on the federal loan programs, contact your local office of the Small Business Administration (800-827-5722 or *www.sba.gov*). For state and local programs, contact your area's chamber of commerce.

Time for a New Career? The Best Home-Based Businesses Now

Paul and Sarah Edwards, California-located cohosts of the *Entrepreneur Magazine Home-Based Business Show* on WSRadio.com and columnists for *Entrepreneur.* They are also coauthors of *The Best Home Businesses for People 50+* (Tarcher/Penguin). Their Web site is at *www.working frombome.com.*

Whether you are searching for a different or more interesting work life or looking for a way to supplement your income, a home-based business can be a wise option.

Other advantages: By owning a home-based business, you turn your maturity into an advantage—even people as young as 40 may face discrimination when they apply for jobs.

Ageism works in favor of older business owners —potential clients and lenders consider age a sign of reliability and experience.

There are financial benefits, as well. You can keep expenses down—there is no need to rent office space—and enjoy generous tax breaks.

To boost your chance of success, choose a business that is suited to your skills, schedule and interests. Is there a hobby that you could turn into a full- or part-time profession? Do you have a skill that is highly coveted, a service that companies might want to outsource?

If nothing springs to mind, look into one of these ideas that are in big demand in today's marketplace…

•**Errand service.** There are 29 million two-career couples in the US. Most of these families have little time for such everyday tasks as taking vehicles in to be serviced…waiting at home for repairmen to arrive…or picking up clothes from the dry cleaner. Small businesses also might outsource such tasks for certain busy executives or the company as a whole during hectic times.

Getting started: Most of your business will come through word of mouth, but you can attract clients initially by taking out inexpensive ads in local publications…posting flyers on community bulletin boards…and/or soliciting work directly from small businesses.

Helpful: Ask a friend with a flexible schedule to help you out occasionally when you get two rush assignments from important clients at the same time.

Potential earnings: $15 to $25 per hour.

Important: Purchase insurance for liability to protect you in the event of a lawsuit, particularly if you'll be driving other people in your own car or theirs. The cost of auto insurance varies greatly from state to state, but your insurer should be able to add an appropriate business rider to your policy for $1,500* or less per year. A special driver's license should not be necessary.

•**Medical coder.** Medical coders translate physicians' written diagnoses and lists of procedures into the codes that insurance companies use for billing. Most medical coding is done at hospitals or clinics, but outsourcing is becoming more common.

*Prices subject to change.

The job requires a good memory, a meticulous personality and the unique ability to read bad handwriting.

You'll need to pass the Certified Professional Coder (CPC) exam before you get into the profession. The best way to prepare for this test is to enroll in a 12- to 18-month course, typically through a community college. Expect to spend at least 20 hours per week studying. The Medical Training Directory site has links to reputable colleges that offer coding courses. At *www.medicaltrainingdirectory.com,* click on "Become a Medical Coder" under "Medical Career Guides" on the right-side menu.

You'll need to get liability insurance, which should cost between $250 and $700 per year, depending on your state. Contact the American Academy of Professional Coders (AAPC) for additional information about the profession (800-626-2633, *www.aapc.com*).

Getting started: Contact doctors' offices and hospitals in your area to find out if they need freelance coders, or check the AAPC's on-line job database.

Potential earnings: $20 to $45 per hour, or $1 per item in piecework from hospitals, though this varies by region.

●**Caretaker.** House-sitting for home owners who are out of town can be an easy way to earn extra money. It is also fun, because most people who hire caretakers live in big, attractive homes. Caretakers over age 50 are in particular demand because of their perceived reliability—older married couples all the more so because clients consider them stable, honest and dependable.

Liability insurance generally is not necessary, though if a home is full of expensive antiques or other valuables, insurance or bonding could help to reassure the home owner and clinch the job for you.

Getting started: Post ads on Web sites such as *www.caretaker.org* or *www.craigslist.org*. Or place classified ads in local newspapers.

Potential earnings: Most caretaking jobs provide only free housing, but some pay hundreds of dollars or more per month. If the home owner does offer to pay you, get the deal in writing. The paying jobs also generally involve garden or pet care. The more effort the job requires, the more you can charge.

You can distinguish yourself from other applicants if you have specialized knowledge of plants, animals or home maintenance.

Helpful: Some successful caretakers decide to sell their homes and furniture, freeing up cash and slashing expenses. This only makes sense if you have someplace to stay between jobs or if business takes off and you land consecutive assignments that last six months or longer.

●**Résumé writer.** Résumé writing is a wonderful part-time business, especially if you have experience in human resources and/or communications. Clients expect customized work, not computer-generated résumés.

Unlike most home-based businesses, résumé writing is recession-proof—when the economy falters and people lose their jobs, high-quality résumés are in particular demand.

You must have very strong writing skills and a firm grasp of what employers like to see on a résumé. People skills are important as well—a résumé writer must interview clients to draw out crucial information about them.

Getting started: Network with professional or trade organizations. The more active you are in the organization, the more likely others will steer potential clients your way. If you have a Web site or advertise your services on-line, focus on a particular profession. To stand out, buy an ad on the industry association Web site rather than on general job search sites. Leave your business cards with print shops, such as Kinko's, that handle résumés…make contact with executive recruitment or placement firms…and/or place an ad in the Yellow Pages.

Potential earnings: A flat fee of $50 for the typical résumé, but as much as $150 per hour for an executive résumé. Cover letters can bring another $30 to $65 apiece.

●**Personal coach.** Successful people can market their experience. Coaches help clients make decisions. Some coaches specialize in life decisions, others in career decisions. Many coaches concentrate on a particular industry or on a type of decision.

Examples: A corporate coach might specialize in supply-chain issues or in management training…a personal coach might specialize in parenting skills or retirement goals.

The job requires strong interpersonal skills, good judgment and an impressive life or career history that will convince clients that your advice has merit. For example, you might have risen to a high position in a well-known corporation.

Getting started: To find clients, network in professional or social organizations…post a listing on Findacoach.com…volunteer to speak before professional or community groups or give free workshops and seminars…and offer free 30-minute initial consultations during which you either focus on one specific issue or speak in broader terms to get to know a potential client.

Potential earnings: Coaches typically charge $200 or more for three or four 30- to 50-minute sessions, either in person or on the telephone. If you meet in person, it might make sense to do so at the client's home or office so that you don't have to have a special rider added to your homeowner's insurance in case a business visitor is hurt on your property. The more coaching experience you have and the more impressive your résumé is, the more you can charge. Business coaches generally earn more than personal coaches.

●**Home inspector.** Home inspectors examine houses that are on the market for any hidden flaws or problems that could affect the value. Most inspectors have backgrounds in home building or maintenance, but if you're a longtime home owner with the skills to do a remodeling job on your own and a willingness to study up on what you don't know, that should be sufficient.

Home inspectors must have knowledge of all of the systems in a home—heating, plumbing, electric, etc.—and must be physically fit enough to inspect attics and crawl spaces and to climb ladders to examine roofs. They must pass an exam to be certified by the American Society of Home Inspectors.

Liability insurance is a must and could cost thousands of dollars each year, depending on your state.

Getting started: After being certified, develop relationships with local real estate agents. Visit open houses, and introduce yourself when the host agents have a slow moment. Let them know that you'll deliver your reports quickly. Advertise in the real estate sections of all local newspapers. Also, join the American Society of Home Inspectors (ASHI) and take part in its "Find an Inspector" program (call 800-743-2744 or go to *www.ashi.org*).

Potential earnings: $250 to $300 per day, assuming one inspection per day.

One-Stop Resource for Small Businesses

There is an expanded IRS Web page to assist small businesses. It includes an on-line classroom with self-directed programs and streaming video…retirement plan resource information… help with employment taxes…tax advice when starting or closing a business…and many more resources for small businesses. Go to *www.irs. gov* and click on "Businesses" then "Small Business/Self-Employed."

IRS News Release IR-2005-51.

Doing Business on the Web? Avoid the New and Costly Traps

Joel Gensler, CPA, partner in charge of business services at Eisner LLP, 750 Third Ave., New York City 10017. Mr. Gensler specializes in providing services to growing businesses and start-ups, including addressing day-to-day issues on structuring partnership agreements and retirement and life insurance options.

The Internet makes it easier than ever to run a small business—enabling any entrepreneur to make sales across the nation and get good prices from on-line suppliers.

But tax traps face businesses that make sales and purchases over the Internet. *What you need to know to avoid the pitfalls…*

SALES TAX

For firms that begin making on-line sales, the first complication is collecting sales tax—at potentially many different tax rates.

A bricks-and-mortar store collects sales tax only at the rate imposed at its location. But an on-line seller must do so at the rate imposed at the location of the purchaser, if the purchaser is within a state in which the seller has a physical presence (see below).

Interstate sales trap: Plus, on-line sellers risk needlessly incurring sales tax liabilities in *states other than their own*—greatly complicating matters by adding many more tax rates to account for and jurisdictions in which sales tax returns must be filed.

There are more than 8,000 sales tax jurisdictions in the US, so a small business that unwittingly creates liability for itself among many of them could face a nightmare.

Key: A business can't be required to collect sales tax within a state if it has no physical presence there and conducts no activity there other than soliciting orders—such as by mail or phone or over the Internet.

But even a *slight* presence could be enough to incur collection responsibility. In fact, merely using an Internet server in a state is enough to do so.

Example: A New York firm making on-line sales nationwide contracts with an Internet Service Provider in California to use a Web server there to improve its connection to the West Coast. The New York firm will become liable to collect tax on all sales made in California.

Tax-collection responsibility also can be created by other relatively slight forms of presence in a state, such as by storing inventory or having a sales or service agent based there.

Personal risk: Business owners are personally liable for sales tax obligations, even if the business is run as a corporation that shields them from personal liability generally. This is because sales taxes are deemed paid by the purchaser and held "in trust" for them by the seller.

Moreover, if a sales tax return isn't filed, the statute of limitations never runs out on the tax liability and the state can collect it any number of years later—plus interest and penalties.

Safety: Before starting to make on-line sales, realize that sales tax obligations may be much more complicated than for sales that are made

from a physical store. Consult with an expert on e-commerce taxes for advice.

You will want your Web site to automatically collect the right tax for all the jurisdictions in your own state—commercial software may be available to help. It may be possible to plan interstate sales in a way that avoids needless tax liabilities.

Also, you may be able to take advantage of the fact that specific tax rules do vary by state. *Examples...*

●**Five states have no statewide sales tax** (though some localities within them may have a sales tax). Oregon is one, along with Alaska, Delaware, Montana and New Hampshire. So an East Coast firm that desires to have a server on the West Coast might position one in Oregon without the problems caused by having one in California.

●**New Jersey imposes no sales tax on clothes.** So a firm selling clothes over the Internet will owe no sales tax there, and will be able to locate a server in New Jersey without sales tax problems.

INCOME TAXES

When a firm begins selling over the Internet, it also risks incurring income tax liability in multiple states.

Again, the key determinant is the degree of its presence in the state. If the firm has no physical presence in a state but only solicits orders there, it will not owe income tax there—though even a slight presence may create liability.

And again, when tax returns that should be filed aren't filed, then the statute of limitations will not apply.

A smart strategy, again, is to limit activity outside one's home state to avoid unnecessary tax-filing liabilities—or to use differences in state tax rates and specific tax rules to your business's advantage. If a business has a choice of states in which to locate or expand, and these states have equal business merit, it makes sense to choose a state with a low income tax rate.

Example: Nevada has no income tax. So a firm in nearby, high-tax California that makes on-line sales may move inventory and other elements of its business to Nevada. Therefore, some of its income is allocated there—reducing its overall income tax bill.

PURCHASES

Firms increasingly make purchases (such as of business supplies) over the Internet.

Trap: When a purchaser's home state has a sales tax and an out-of-state vendor doesn't add the tax to the sales price, the purchaser still owes tax to the home state.

This "use tax" is the equivalent of sales tax that state residents must pay on purchases from out-of-state vendors. Every state that has a sales tax has a use tax, which purchasers are legally required to self-report and pay.

Mistake: Individuals often think on-line purchases from out-of-state vendors that don't add sales tax are tax free. However, many states are aggressively enforcing their use tax. Some even require individuals to report use tax liabilities on their income tax returns.

But if such a person starts a business and in this mistaken belief doesn't pay tax on on-line business purchases, a big tax risk arises.

Audit snare: State tax auditors know that use taxes often go unpaid, and it is easy for them to check a business's purchases and tax payments—so business use taxes have become a top audit target in many states.

Sales tax mistake: Sometimes vendors will charge sales tax when the purchaser does not owe it, or they charge too much. *Scenarios...*

• **The buyer will resell the goods,** so the purchase is legitimately tax free.

• **The goods are subject to a special sales tax exemption**—such as the clothing exemption in New Jersey.

• **An out-of-state vendor simply makes a mistake with state tax rules.**

So, if invoices are simply paid as received without checking for these errors, taxes may be overpaid.

SELF-MONITORING

Check your firm's practices for both paying and collecting taxes. It could be possible that the firm is overpaying and underpaying taxes at the same time.

State tax auditors will find taxes that you are underpaying—but won't advise you on how to change practices that cause tax to be incurred needlessly. You must take on that task yourself.

How to Value Personal Use of A Company Car

Alan J. Dlugash, CPA, partner, Marks, Paneth & Shron LLP, 622 Third Ave., New York City 10017. He is chair of the Taxation of Individuals Committee of the New York State Society of Certified Public Accountants.

One of the most common fringe benefits is the right to use a company car for personal purposes—including commuting. Unlike medical coverage, group term life insurance and certain other fringe benefits that are tax free, the company must report personal use of the car, other than nominal use, as income to employees.

GROUND RULES

There are five IRS-provided valuation methods for personal use of the company car—fair market value, annual lease value (ALV), cents-per-mile value, commuting value and fleet average value, all of which are explained below.

No matter what method is used for valuing income charged to the employee, the company can deduct the full costs of owning or leasing the automobile.

It's up to the employer to choose the valuation method. But when the employee is the company owner, the method to use is the one that is most favorable to both the company and the owner.

Method #1: **Fair market value of a comparable lease.** The value of personal use is based on what it would cost to lease a similar car in your geographic area. First, find out what the car is worth. *There are two IRS-approved methods for this...*

• **Manufacturer's suggested retail price minus 8%.**

• **Manufacturer's invoice price (including options) plus 4%.**

Then, find out what it would cost to lease a car of this value. (Ask a dealer.)

This determination of lease value is made at the start of the personal use—it remains constant for the years that the car is used.

If the employee uses the car for less than the full year, the annual imputed income amount is prorated.

Method #2: **Annual lease value.** The value of personal use is listed in an IRS table for annual lease value. The table can be found in IRS Publication 15-B, *Employer's Tax Guide to Fringe Benefits* (visit *www.irs.gov* or call 800-829-3676). For example, when the car's fair market value is $25,000, the imputed income under the ALV table would be $6,850. The employee would report this amount as income if he/she used the car for the full year. (ALV amounts are prorated if the car is used less than the full year.)

The ALV amount includes maintenance of the car, but not fuel consumption, which must be added to income if the employer pays for gasoline (e.g., via a company credit card). The add-on can be based on an IRS rate of 5.5¢ per mile.

Requirements: If the company wants to use the ALV method, it must elect it no later than the first pay period in which the car is used for personal purposes. The election is made by including the appropriate amount in the employee's income for this pay period.

Important: Compare the fair market value of a comparable lease with the ALV and choose the method that produces the smaller amount of imputed income for the employee.

Personal or total use? *Whether using the fair market value or ALV method, the employer can choose to include in the employee's income either of the following...*

•**Only the value of the employee's actual personal use.** The employee in this situation must provide adequate records to the employer to show business and personal use of the vehicle.

•**The full value of the car's use for the year** (personal and business). In this case, the employee reports the value of both personal and business use of the car—this amount is listed on the employee's Form W-2. The employee can then deduct the portion of imputed income representing business use as a miscellaneous itemized deduction on his personal return—to the extent that total itemized deductions exceed 2% of adjusted gross income (AGI) and assuming that the employee has records substantiating business use.

Making a choice: Generally, it makes sense from both the company and the employee perspectives to include only the actual personal use in income. Because all imputed income to the employee is subject to payroll taxes, the company saves money if it pays payroll taxes only on actual personal use. The employee reports less income and avoids the need to claim a deduction for business use—a deduction that may be useless in view of the 2% of AGI limit for regular tax purposes. Also bear in mind that such amounts are not deductible for alternative minimum tax purposes.

Method #3: **Cents-per-mile value.** Personal use is valued based on the IRS standard mileage rate (44.5¢ per mile for 2006 and 48.5¢ for 2007). For example, if an employee drives a company car 12,000 miles for personal purposes in 2007 (1,000 miles per month), the income to the employee is $5,820 (12,000 × 48.5¢).

Requirements: This method can be utilized only if the car is driven a total of at least 10,000 miles during the year and only if the car is valued at no more than $14,800 for a passenger car during 2006 or 2007. The company must elect to use this method no later than the first pay period in which the car is used for personal purposes.

Important: The cents-per-mile method can be used only if the employee is not a "control" employee—a director, an officer with compensation over $85,000 in 2006 or over $90,000 in 2007, an owner with at least a 1% interest in the company or any employee earning at least $175,000 in 2006 or at least $180,000 in 2007.

When to use it: If an employee uses a car that meets all the mileage and value conditions above and personal use is modest, this method can produce the lowest imputed income to the employee. Once personal use becomes substantial, however, the cents-per-mile rate can result in more imputed income than would the fair market value or ALV method.

Example: If the car is driven 6,000 miles for personal purposes in 2007 (500 miles per month), the imputed income would be only $2,910. But if the car is driven 24,000 personal miles (2,000 miles per month), the imputed income would be $11,640. In comparison, the imputed income under the ALV method for a $14,500 car (regardless of miles driven) is $4,100.

***Method #4:* Commuting value.** Personal use of commuting is valued at the flat rate of $1.50 per one-way trip ($3 per day). Total up the days the employee drives to and from work in the year and multiply that number by $3 to find the annual amount reported as income.

Restrictions: This method can be used only if the company requires the employee to commute in the car. And there must be a written company policy that the automobile cannot be used for personal purposes other than commuting or nominal personal use. This valuation method cannot be used for control employees.

***Method #5:* Fleet average value.** There is an additional method that can be used if the company has 20 or more cars in its fleet, but only for cars that have a fair market value of no more than $16,500. This method cannot be used for control employees.

TRUE TAX-FREE PERK

While business use of a company car generates imputed income, it is possible to give employees a real (no tax cost) benefit by grossing up compensation to account for the tax cost on their personal use of company cars. For example, if imputed income to an owner in the 33% tax bracket is $10,000, salary can be bumped up by $5,000 to cover the tax on the imputed income as well as the tax that results from this additional income.

Note: When grossing up salary, do take into account the impact on payroll taxes. If an employee is below the Social Security wage base for the year ($94,200 in 2006 or $97,500 in 2007), then every dollar of additional salary costs the company and the employee each 7.65% in FICA.

Caution: Depending on the value of the car, miles driven and employee tax bracket, use of a company car may in some circumstances be too expensive a fringe benefit. The employee may be better off leasing or buying his own car and forgoing the company's offer of the use of its car.

Audit-Proof Your Compensation Package

The IRS says that abuses in compensation programs for top-paid executives have made them a new audit target. To assist its auditors in examining them, it has created six new audit guides for them to use in tax examinations. *Subjects...*

- **Executive compensation as well as fringe benefits.**
    - **Golden parachutes.**
    - **Nonqualified deferred compensation.**
    - **Split-dollar life insurance.**
    - **Stock-based compensation.**
    - **IRC 162(m) salary deduction limitations.**

Self-defense: These guides are also available to the public for free. Obtain and use them to draft an audit-proof compensation package, or to defend against a challenge if the auditor calls. Go to *www.irs.gov/businesses* and click on "Audit Techniques Guides (ATGs)."

Vital Year-End Strategies for Businesses

Martin S. Kaplan, CPA, 11 Penn Plaza in New York City, *www.irsmaven.com.* He is a frequent speaker at insurance, banking and financial-planning seminars and is author of *What the IRS Doesn't Want You to Know* (Wiley).

Owners of small businesses should review business results for the year and consider the following smart year-end strategies...

C CORPORATIONS

- **Declare dividends.** The top tax rate on dividends is currently 15%—and only 5% for persons in a 15% or lower tax bracket.

This makes it more attractive than ever to distribute profits through dividends, especially if shares in a family business are owned by family members who will pay the low 5% tax rate. And, in 2008 through 2010, these family members may pay *zero* tax on dividends.

Many businesses got into the habit of not paying dividends during past years when they were taxed at top rates. Reconsider this now.

Opportunity: Make gifts of shares to lower-bracket family members before declaring a dividend as part of a larger plan of shifting ownership of the business to the younger generation.

●**Justify accumulated earnings.** A professional service corporation (such as accounting, law, consulting) that has retained earnings exceeding $150,000 risks incurring the accumulated earnings penalty tax.

Defense: Record in your corporate minutes a business reason for retaining earnings during the year—such as to finance future expansion. Doing so now, as the earnings are retained, is much safer and more persuasive than doing it later after the auditor calls.

●**Manage the capital gains.** Corporate capital gains are not tax favored as gains taken by individuals are—they are taxed at ordinary rates up to 35%, while net losses are not deductible.

If a corporation has taken net gains during the year, look for offsetting losses to realize by year-end to save the gains from high tax—and to get a tax benefit from the losses.

●**Prepare to claim a quick refund.** If the corporation paid too much in estimated tax during the year, get a fast tax refund by filing IRS Form 4466, *Corporation Application for Quick Refund of Overpayment of Estimated Tax,* as soon as possible after year-end, prior to filing the company's tax return. The IRS will respond within 45 days.

Being prepared by year-end to file will get you the refund at the earliest possible date.

PASS-THROUGH ENTITIES

Pass-through entities, such as partnerships and S corporations, have their income taxed on their owners' personal tax returns. *Year-end keys...*

●**Increase basis to deduct losses.** The losses of a pass-through entity are deductible only to the extent that the owner has basis in the entity—as may be obtained by investing in it or making a loan to it.

If you are planning to deduct such losses this year, check to be sure you have adequate basis in the business. If you do not, take steps to in-crease your basis by year-end, for instance, by lending money to your S corporation.

●**Adjust personal tax payments to pay business taxes.** Tax on business income earned by a pass-through entity must be paid through personal payments of estimated or withheld taxes made by the business's owners.

Thus, it is important for the firm's owners to know the amount of income they will receive from the business in order to avoid over- or underpaying their taxes for the year. Minority owners and passive investors should get this type of information from the controlling owner/manager.

Strategy: If you find as year-end approaches that taxes are underpaid, increase the wage withholding for you and/or your spouse if you file jointly to cover the shortfall. Withholding is treated as if it takes place at an even rate through the full year—so a late increase in it can avert penalties for an earlier shortfall in a way that a late extra estimated tax payment cannot.

●**Beware of a surprise alternative minimum tax (AMT) hit.** Items on a business's tax return may generate liability for personal AMT when passed through to its owners.

Example: Large deductions for accelerated depreciation.

This may come as a costly surprise to minority or passive investors who aren't knowledgeable about the business's operations. They need to be informed about the business's potential AMT items long enough before year-end in order to take the steps necessary to manage their personal AMT exposure.

ALL BUSINESSES

●**Make last-minute equipment purchases.** Up to $112,000 of new equipment purchases that are made as late as December 31, 2007, are fully deductible for the year using the Section 179 expensing election.

Exception: SUVs weighing more than 6,000 pounds have a deduction limit of $25,000 each.

Equipment purchases in excess of $112,000 generally provide a half year's worth of depreciation deductions even if the equipment is placed in service as late as December 31 (as long as no more than 40% of all such acquisitions are made in the year's fourth quarter).

•**Prepare inventory write-downs.** If the firm owns inventory that has lost value, prepare to deduct the loss by documenting the inventory's lower value as of year-end.

Example: Make a bona fide offer to sell some of the inventory at a lowered price within 30 days of year-end.

•**Take abandonment losses.** If the company owns equipment it no longer needs that has not been fully depreciated, abandon it by year-end to get a deduction for the remaining tax basis in it.

Example: Computing equipment will often lose value faster than at the rate given in IRS depreciation schedules.

Important: Equipment must be physically abandoned, not merely written off the books, to get the deduction. For this purpose, abandoned means permanently giving up use and ownership without giving it to anyone else (throwing it away).

•**Time your discretionary expenditures.** Purchase supplies, make repairs and incur other discretionary deductible expenditures prior to year-end to maximize this year's deductions.

•**Time income.** Cash-basis businesses can delay sending out invoices near year-end, so that income won't be received until after year-end and thus won't be taxable this year.

•**Identify bad debts.** These are deductible by firms using accrual-basis accounting. Generally, bad debts cannot be estimated but must be specifically identified to be deducted. So examine receivables to find amounts that have become uncollectible.

•**Set up deductible retirement accounts.** A Keogh plan, 401(k) or "solo 401(k)" (for a one-person firm) must be set up by December 31 to receive deductible contributions for 2007. Other kinds of plans can be set up after year-end—but make your choice among all possible options before then.

•**Pay owner's salaries.** Firms using accrual accounting generally can deduct liabilities incurred by year-end even if they are not paid by then—but salaries and bonuses of shareholders who own 50% or more of the company must be paid by December 31 to be deductible.

•**Create or revise a flexible spending account (FSA).** This lets employees pay medical costs with pretax dollars saved from pay in a tax-favored savings account. The business saves employment taxes on these amounts and gets more for its compensation dollar by providing a tax-favored benefit. If you have an FSA, amend it prior to the end of the year to give employees an extra 2½ months to use up this year's contributions.

Secrets to Avoiding Business Tax Return Filing Mistakes

Steven Hurok, CPA, director, BDO Seidman, LLP, 90 Woodbridge Center Dr., Woodbridge, NJ 07095. He has appeared on television and radio regarding a wide range of tax matters.

B eware of all these key return-preparation errors that trip up more businesses than you might imagine…

NEW SNAGS

The "domestic production activities deduction," which was new on 2005 returns, is very complex and poses the risk of being mishandled by many firms.

The basic rule: Businesses may deduct an amount equal to 3% of their net income derived from production activities within the US. The deduction increases in future years, reaching 9% in 2010.

Key areas where mistakes may arise…

•**Accounting.** The tax deduction is available only for income from production activities. But a firm engaged in production may also engage in nonproduction activities—such as distribution, retailing, consulting or other services.

Since this tax deduction never existed before, such a firm may never before have summarized its information identifying income and expenses related solely to production, as it needs to do to claim the deduction now.

Make sure that your accounting records break out all required information—including separate allocations for items such as overhead costs attributable to production. Performing the needed accounting may be a complex task.

●**Identifying "production activities."** While the deduction sounds like it applies to manufacturing, other activities qualify for it as well.

Examples: Construction, engineering and architectural services, and the production of software sound recordings and films.

Snag: For 2006 and 2007, the tax deduction is limited to 3% of a corporation's taxable income. So if nonproduction activities produce a tax loss, the deduction will be reduced or eliminated. A second limitation is 50% of W-2 wages paid (for wages attributable to qualified activities).

Action: Businesses that intend to take this deduction should be doing the required accounting now. The rules are complex, so expert help is advised.

Going forward, use what was learned while preparing your previous tax return to track and plan to make the most of the deduction in future years when it will be more valuable.

Example: Owners of a company with a profitable production business intend to expand into a new nonproduction business that is expected to incur start-up losses. They may wish to organize the new activity in a separate legal entity to keep the losses from offsetting production profits on the original firm's tax return—and thus save the deduction. However, there are special rules for affiliated companies.

PASS-THROUGH ENTITIES

Businesses organized as S corporations, partnerships and limited liability companies have their income "passed through" and taxed on the personal tax returns of their owners.

Trap: Many such businesses obtain filing extensions to get more time to compute their income. But their owners must pay the tax they owe on that income by April 15—incurring a tax penalty if they underpay, or making an interest-free loan to the IRS if they overpay tax. (Obtaining a personal filing extension does not extend the time to pay tax.)

Moreover, items that pass through from the business's return may have an unexpected effect on an owner's personal return—and affect different owners in different ways.

Example: When a business uses accelerated depreciation on its assets, this may create liability for the alternative minimum tax (AMT) on the owner's return. This is because the difference between accelerated and straight-line depreciation amounts is a "preference item" that can trigger AMT. Because AMT is not indexed for inflation, this may occur on the 2006 or 2007 return even if it has not in the past and the business has not greatly changed its practices.

What to do: The managers of a pass-through entity should estimate its tax results for the year as closely as possible, and give the result to the entity's owners as soon as possible, so they can plan their April 15 tax payments in light of their personal tax situations.

Going forward, the managers should keep the owners informed of actions that may affect the owners' tax liabilities—such as use of accelerated depreciation. This is especially important in the case of passive investors who have little knowledge of how the business is being managed.

DEPRECIATION/EXPENSING

If new business equipment was placed in service by the end of 2006 or 2007, its cost can be deducted either through immediate "expensing" or through depreciation deductions taken over a series of years.

The expensing limit on 2006 returns is $108,000 ($112,000 on 2007 returns). Many businesses automatically use expensing—but this can be a mistake for them.

Example: If the firm is in a low tax bracket, expensing may produce little current tax savings. Moreover, expensing may reduce or eliminate the domestic production deduction (because it reduces your income).

In such cases, it may be better not to elect expensing but to use depreciation instead. Deductions for the cost of the equipment will be deferred in time but may save taxes at a higher tax bracket—with the domestic production deduction preserved.

Check what is best by running the numbers both ways (making your best estimate regarding the future).

Obsolete equipment: Firms that meticulously add new equipment to depreciation schedules sometimes forget to remove abandoned equipment from them. Especially with technology, it can happen that equipment loses its value and is "junked" before the conclusion of its depreciation period.

When equipment is abandoned early, its entire undepreciated cost is deductible immediately. *What to do…*

•**Check depreciation schedules** to locate items that have been abandoned, and claim deductions for them.

•**Physically dispose of any equipment** for which an abandonment deduction is claimed, and keep a record of how this was done.

The deduction is not available for equipment that the firm keeps, perhaps in storage, even if it sits unused. It must be removed. And proof of the date of disposal may be needed to meet an auditor's request in a later year.

INVENTORY

Common valuation mistakes…

•**Writedowns.** When inventory stops moving and loses value, the firm may want to take a deduction for the loss. But this can't be done simply by estimating a new value—there must be evidence supporting the new lower value.

Example: A bona fide offer to sell some of the inventory at the reduced price.

•**Abandonment.** When inventory becomes worthless, the firm may wish to take a full loss tax deduction for it. But, as with equipment, this cannot be done with items that remain in the firm's possession. The inventory must be physically disposed of and the fact documented.

•**Donations.** When a firm donates inventory to charity, it may mistakenly claim a deduction for the inventory's full market value—although only cost basis in the inventory is deductible.

Exception: When items are donated for use by the "ill or needy"—such as bread donated to a food pantry—the cost basis plus 50% of the difference between market value and cost basis (not to exceed twice the cost basis) may also be deductible. There are special documentation requirements.

More information: See the instructions to Form 1120, *US Corporation Income Tax Return.*

AUDIT RISK

Audit risk may be increased by many tax return mistakes that are unique to the particular kind of business. To avoid these errors, review the IRS's "audit technique guides." These are the same guides that IRS auditors follow when examining a business. To see if there is a guide for your business, go to *www.irs.gov* and click on "Businesses," then "More Topics" (under "Business Topics"), then "Audit Technique Guide."

IRS Now Requires Electronic Filing

The IRS now requires large corporations to file their tax returns electronically. Corporations with total assets of at least $50 million, who file Forms 1120, *US Corporation Income Tax Return,* and 1120S, *US Income Tax Return for an S Corporation,* had to file electronically for tax year 2005. The program has been expanded to include corporations with $10 million or more in assets for tax year 2006.

What this means to the small-business owner: Expect a further expansion of the electronic filing requirement to smaller corporations if the program proves successful. Electronic tax filing will enable the IRS to process tax return information faster and to more efficiently determine which corporation tax returns are likely to produce extra tax if audited.

Ms. X, Esq., a former agent with the IRS who is still well connected.

SEP vs. Profit-Sharing— Choose the Right Plan

Richard Vitale, CPA/PFS, chairman of Vitale, Caturano and Co., 80 City Sq., Boston 02129. He is also chairman of the legislation committee and former director and vice president of the Massachusetts Society of Certified Public Accountants, Inc.

If you're self-employed or run a small company, you may be considering, or already have, a profit-sharing plan. Such plans are flexible and permit sizable tax-deductible contributions.

Strategy: Look into using a simplified employee pension (or SEP) plan instead. The maximum contribution is the same but there's much less paperwork with a SEP.

SEP plans are not for everyone. But, they may be particularly appealing to self-employed individuals as well as to business owners or professionals with few employees.

SIMPLE DOES IT

With a SEP, all of the funding comes from the employer. However, a SEP is not an IRS qualified plan (as is a profit-sharing plan), so record keeping is less demanding.

Key: A SEP is like an IRA that can receive more than $4,000, or $5,000 per year (the 2006 and 2007 limit for IRAs), with the employer making the contributions to employees' accounts. Indeed, SEPs are sometimes known as SEP-IRAs, with each individual controlling his/her own retirement investments.

Advantage: As the name suggests, SEPs are very simplified. To establish a SEP, an employer need only fill out IRS Form 5305-SEP, *Simplified Employee Pension—Individual Retirement Accounts Contribution Agreement,* and give a copy to each eligible employee—but need not file it with the IRS. This form is much less onerous than the lengthy plan and trust documents required by the profit-sharing plans or money-purchase plans.

An added advantage: Since a SEP is not a qualified plan, no trust fund is involved. (Creating a trust—which is required by all qualified plans—adds complication and cost.) A SEP is considered to be the employee's own IRA. Furthermore, no annual reports need be filed with the IRS.

Outcome: SEPs are easier and cheaper to set up and maintain compared to other employer-sponsored plans.

Many self-employed individuals and the small-company employers do think in terms of Keogh plans. But Keoghs (which can be either defined-contribution or defined-benefit plans) are more complex and costly to administer than SEPs.

With SEPs, employees make their own investment decisions for the money in their accounts. Employers don't have the same level of fiduciary responsibility as they do in other types of plans (such as profit-sharing plans), where the employer does all the investing.

Flexible plans: Like profit-sharing plans, SEP plans allow contributions anywhere up to the maximum each year, which is based on a percentage of compensation. This can be especially appealing if your business is cyclical and you're reluctant to make commitments to a retirement plan each year.

By contrast, some other types of retirement plans (defined-benefit, target-benefit and money-purchase plans) require a certain level of funding each year.

LEARNING THE LIMITS

How much can you contribute to a SEP? The answer can be tricky.

The 25% solution: Generally, contributions can be up to 25% of a participating employee's compensation. For the self-employed individual, however, the calculation is more complicated and the contribution limit becomes about 20% of gross compensation.

Bottom line: The maximum contribution to a SEP plan is $44,000 in 2006 ($45,000 in 2007), the same upper limit that applies to profit-sharing plans.

It's true that you might be able to contribute as much as $49,000 to a profit-sharing plan that includes a 401(k), if you are 50 or older in 2006 ($50,000 in 2007), but such plans tend to be complicated and expensive.

Required: In order to make the maximum contribution to your own SEP account, you would need to earn at least $220,000 in 2006 ($225,000 in 2007) as a self-employed individual (after reduction for one-half of the self-employment tax). And, if you're a company employee, your salary must be $176,000 in 2006 ($180,000 in 2007) or more to qualify for a top contribution.

LOOKING BACK

In addition to simplicity and flexibility, SEPs have yet another advantage over qualified plans that are not set up by the end of the year—the ability to accept retroactive contributions.

How it works: A SEP will be effective for a calendar or a fiscal year if it's adopted by the time that year's tax return is due, including any extensions.

Result: If you did not create a SEP for 2006 by December 31, 2006, it is possible to do so by April 16, 2007, when tax returns are due. It is even possible to do so by October 15, 2007, if you obtain a filing extension.

Thus, you can create a SEP and retroactively reduce the previous year's taxable income, or do so for 2006 income in 2007.

WIN-WIN

Employers also like SEPs because their fiduciary responsibility is reduced.

Strategy: If you're the owner of a company sponsoring a SEP, retain an investment adviser to help in coordinating the program. This adviser can develop a listing of investment options, then meet with participating employees to help them make their choices.

Such a system may offload some liability for employees' retirement accounts.

Key: The more independent the investment professional, the greater the professional's expertise, and the greater the number of available investment choices, the less fiduciary responsibility the employer is likely to have.

Because each employee makes his own investment decisions, SEPs usually appeal to the workers, too.

Theirs to retain: All SEP contributions are fully vested and portable. The money belongs to the employees, the same as with an IRA.

Thus, SEPs give you an opportunity to provide your employees with a low-cost, highly motivational retirement plan.

TAKING CREDIT

Eligible employers can receive a general business tax credit for some of the costs of establishing new SEP plans under a law that took effect in 2002. The credit equals 50% of the costs incurred to create or maintain the plan, up to $500 per year.

This credit may be claimed for qualified costs incurred in *each* of the first three years, including the tax year in which the plan becomes effective.

Required: To qualify for this tax credit, your company must not have employed more than 100 employees who received at least $5,000 of compensation from the company in the preceding year.

NOW FOR THE NEGATIVE

With all of these advantages to SEPs, what's the downside?

Expensive contributions: When you have a large number of employees, you must contribute to their accounts, just as you contribute to your own.

Example: You earn $180,000 in 2007 as a corporate employee and you want your company to contribute $45,000 (25%) to your SEP account. The company, therefore, must contribute 25% of pay to *all* eligible employees. That includes workers you would like to leave out, including part-timers and workers who left the company during the plan year.

Required: *SEP sponsors must contribute to the account of each employee who…*

• **Is at least 21 years old,** *and…*

• **Has worked for the employer** at any time during at least three of the preceding five years, *and…*

• **Has earned at least $500** during the year for which contributions are being made.

Example: If an employee worked in three years from December of 2005 through January 2007, you must make a 2007 SEP contribution for that employee by the extended due date of your return, assuming his 2007 earnings were at least $500.

(By contrast, qualified plans generally permit you to exclude employees who work less than 1,000 hours per year. Qualified plan contributions for employees who have left the company also are not required in many cases.)

Trap: If you choose to exclude some workers because of the three-year rule mentioned above, *all* workers who fail this test must be excluded. This may negatively affect morale.

Balancing act: Some types of profit-sharing plans allow you to skew contributions to older executives, including yourself—an option that's not available with a SEP plan. With a skewed profit-sharing plan, you might be able to maximize contributions to your account while minimizing contributions to employees.

Outcome: SEPs generally work best for employers with few, relatively low-paid employees. Contributions to their accounts may be modest.

The larger your workforce, the more issues you'll have to weigh in deciding whether the simplicity of a SEP plan and the employee motivation are worth the added outlays.

Your Own Six-Figure Tax Shelter: A Defined-Benefit Plan

John M. Peterson, CPA, partner, Goodman & Company, LLP, 500 E. Main St., Norfolk, VA 23510. A widely published author on retirement plan issues, he is an adjunct professor at William & Mary School of Law, Williamsburg, VA, and at Old Dominion University, Norfolk, VA, where he teaches courses related to ERISA (the Employee Retirement Income Security Act).

If you run your own small business, you can choose among many varieties of employer-sponsored retirement plans. While defined-contribution plans (such as 401(k)s, profit-sharing plans) receive a lot of the press these days, for the greatest up-front tax deductions, a defined-benefit (DB) plan may be your best choice.

Demographics make the difference: Ideal candidates for DB plans are employers in their mid-40s or older. DB plans work especially well if you have a younger staff that is not highly compensated and tends to turn over frequently.

CASH COMMITMENT

DB plans are traditional pension plans—employers promise to pay retired employees a specific amount of income (the "defined benefit") based on earnings and years of service.

If you are on the payroll of your own company, you will be among the employees to whom the promise is made.

Loophole: In order to fund the promised benefits, large tax-deductible amounts of money must be put aside each year.

In the situation described above (older owner, younger staff), most of the money going into the DB plan will wind up funding the pension of the owner while relatively little goes to other employees.

Example: In 2007, the maximum benefit payable by a DB plan, as set by law, is a pension of $180,000 per year at retirement. To fund a benefit of that magnitude, a sum of $2 million or more (the amount is determined by an actuary) might be needed at retirement.

If you are age 50, with a target retirement age of 60, your company might have to contribute $125,000 or more per year to fund your pension at that level.

Benefit: *This contribution will be deductible from your company's income...*

●**If you operate a regular C corporation,** its income tax will be reduced by this sizable deduction.

●**Alternatively, if your company is a pass-through entity,** such as an S corporation or an LLC, the deduction effectively will flow to your personal tax return.

CLOSE TO THE VEST

Another benefit of DB plans for owners: A DB plan can have, say, a three-year "cliff" (vesting begins at 100% after three years) or a six-year graduated vesting requirement. If an employee leaves before any vesting, the plan retains all the money previously contributed for that employee.

Payoff: This forfeiture money can be used to reduce future mandated contributions to fund the plan.

Even if employees stay long enough to become fully vested, a young and relatively low-paid departing employee probably would be entitled to a relatively small lump-sum amount. Much of the money contributed to the plan, and the investment buildup, would stay in the plan to benefit the remaining employees.

Added attraction: Even if you are covered by another type of employer-sponsored retirement plan at work, you can have a DB plan to shelter income from unrelated freelance consulting, from serving as an outside director of an unrelated company, from a sideline business, etc.

Such plans may also offer considerable tax deductions, more than those offered by other types of plans.

DEALING WITH THE DOWNSIDE

If you think that such an attractive tax shelter will also have drawbacks, you are correct. *Before you adopt a DB plan, you need to address these issues...*

●**Administrative expenses.** Due to the annual expense of hiring a professional actuary to determine how much you can contribute (and deduct), you'll spend more to create and maintain a DB plan, compared with other types of employer-sponsored plans. In the typical small business (10 employees or fewer), those extra costs might run $2,000 to $5,000 per year.

Strategy: Obtain bids from several different firms that administer DB plans.

Be sure that the extra tax benefits you'll receive will outweigh the added costs, as compared with other types of retirement plans.

• **Employee coverage.** If you have employees, you'll have to provide them with pensions, too, after a certain number of years of service.

On the other hand, if your employees are young, relatively low paid and likely to leave after a few years, your actual cost of providing their pensions may be modest. Meanwhile, DB plans can motivate and reward loyal, longtime employees.

• **Required contributions.** Once you adopt a DB plan, you are locked in to making specified contributions, good years and bad. (Any modifications will require additional effort and expense.) Fixed contributions will vary each year, determined by an actuary. If your investment results exceed projections, they'll go down.

Best fit: Companies with steady earnings may be most suitable for DB plans. This can include professional practices.

• **Tax penalties.** Overfunding or underfunding a DB plan may lead to tax traps. What's more, future contribution requirements are tied to investment performance and are unknowable.

Example: Suppose that contributions to your DB plan assume projected investment returns of 7% a year. Your plan invests in stocks and enjoys a few good years, with annual returns of 12%. At this point, your plan is ahead of projections and may not be able to make deductible contributions for a period of time.

Suggested: Work with a professional investment consultant, rather than try to manage the money yourself. A professional will set a reasonable return projection and use a mix of stocks and bonds to hold down volatility.

Loophole: If your actuary projects a relatively small return (projections are recalculated annually), you can make larger, tax-deductible contributions. That's because at a lower return, larger amounts need to be invested to reach the target amount that can generate the specified pension.

LAST CHANCE

If you're age 50 or older and you haven't made good headway saving for retirement, you'll face a tough challenge trying to build up a substantial fund with other types of retirement plans.

Limits: In 2006, profit-sharing and simplified employee pension (SEP) plans permit contributions up to $44,000 for those earning at least $176,000. In 2007, the maximum contribution is $45,000 for those earning at least $180,000.

With 401(k)/profit-sharing plans, the 2006 upper limit is $44,000 for those earning at least $116,000 ($49,000 for the 50-plus crowd). For 2007, the maximum contribution is $45,000 for those earning at least $118,000 ($50,000 for the 50-plus crowd).

Raising the roof: A properly structured DB plan, on the other hand, can allow you to put away upwards of $100,000 per year on a tax-deferred basis. Such plans may be the only way you can create a huge retirement fund at a late stage of your career.

FOR MORE INFORMATION

To find a professional who can help you create a defined-benefit plan, contact the National Institute of Pension Administrators (*www.nipa. org*). Check their chapters listing for a chapter in your area. Or check the directories on Benefits-Link (*www.benefitslink.com/yellowpages*).

401(k) Plans for the Self-Employed

For 2007, people with no employees can put away as much as $45,000 in pretax money for retirement in a solo 401(k) or uni-k. Those age 50 or older can put away $50,000. Contributions can be higher than those allowed in simplified employee pension (SEP) IRAs. Unlike the SEPs, these plans also can have loan provisions. They are easy to set up and administer. A number of mutual fund companies, brokerages, third-party benefits administrators and other financial services firms offer individual 401(k)s. Visit *www. 401khelpcenter.com* for a list of firms.

Vern Hayden, CFP, president, Hayden Financial Group, LLC, Westport, CT, and author of *Getting an Investment Game Plan* (Wiley).

A Prudent Way To Transfer Your Company to Your Heirs

Michael D. Cohen, CPA/ABV, CFE, a partner in the accounting and consulting firm Singer Lewak Greenbaum & Goldstein, LLP, 10960 Wilshire Blvd., Los Angeles 90024. Accredited in business valuation (ABV) and a certified fraud examiner (CFE), he is director of the forensic accounting, business valuation and litigation services group.

When you're preparing to transfer your company to the next generation, you have several alternatives.

The most obvious: You can give away shares to your children or other successors or you can sell them your stock in the company.

Both techniques may be costly, though, when taxes are considered. In these situations, a stock bonus plan might be a better solution.

PITFALLS OF GIVING

Giving company shares to your children can trigger a gift tax.

Situation: You own 100% of your company. Your two children have been active in management and you would like them to take over.

Therefore, you give each child 26% of your shares, decreasing your stake to 48%. Now, if your children can work together, they will control the firm.

Trap: Such a transfer will have gift tax consequences. You may have to pay gift tax at a 45% rate in 2007. You do have a $1 million lifetime gift tax exemption. But any gift tax exemption you use reduces your estate tax exemption.

What's more, a gift transfers basis as well as the shares, reducing the true value of the shares to your children.

Example: You have zero basis in your company, which you built from scratch. If you give 26% of your company to each of your children, they will have zero basis in their shares—and any subsequent sale of these shares will be fully taxable for them.

SELL YOUR SHARES

Another tactic is to sell 26% of your shares to each child. This will avoid the problems described in the previous scenario.

Advantages: No gift tax will be due if the sale is made at fair market value. Your children's basis in the shares will be the amount they've paid. This will be an offset to the selling price and will reduce tax on a future sale. Plus, you'll wind up with cash from the sale.

Downsides: *You* will owe tax if you sell the shares to your kids, even though you'll likely owe only 15%, the long-term capital gains rate. Perhaps more important, your children will have to come up with a substantial amount of money to buy control of your company. They may have to borrow heavily, which could adversely impact their personal finances and the way they run the business after they take over.

BONUSES MIGHT BE BETTER

Rather than give away or sell shares, you can use stock bonuses to transfer control.

How it works: As owner of your company, you authorize the issuance of additional shares, which can then be given to your children as compensation.

Situation: Your company creates 1,000 new shares which are issued to your son, John, and another 1,000 new shares that are issued to your daughter, Joan, as a bonus. Both children are on your company's payroll.

Your children will each owe income tax on the value of the shares received.

Strategy: Have a reputable third party value the new shares. Discounts for lack of marketability and lack of control can be applied.

Let's say that your company is valued at $2 million. After the stock bonus, each of your two children holds 5% of the outstanding shares.

Those shares are minority interests and probably not worth $100,000 (5% of $2 million) per recipient. The appraiser might value the shares at say $60,000 or $70,000 per recipient and each child will owe income tax on that amount.

Outcome: Even if your children have to pay income tax at, say, 25% or 35% rates, that's lower than the 45% tax you would have to pay on a gift. And it's certainly less costly than paying the full purchase price.

What is more, the value of the shares paid to your children is a compensation deduction for your company. Your organization could save as much (or even more) from this tax deduction as your children owe in tax.

Strategy: When paying a substantial stock bonus to your children, "gross up" their cash compensation. That is, give them extra compensation so that they'll be in roughly the same after-tax position as they would have been without the stock bonus.

Caution: The entire amount paid to your children, including the value of the stock bonus, must be "reasonable" for the work they perform.

If the IRS examines your company's tax return and it determines that unreasonable compensation has been paid, the excess (the amount over what's deemed reasonable) would be recast as a nondeductible dividend.

Strategy: Be prepared to demonstrate that total compensation is reasonable. You can rely on external evidence such as media reports or industry surveys showing that the totals paid to your son, John, the chief operating officer, or your daughter, Joan, the chief financial officer, are in line with the compensation levels at other firms.

A business valuation adviser should be able to help you in demonstrating that the compensation is reasonable.

When your company awards bonus stock to employees, and they pay tax on the fair value of the stock, their basis is equal to that value. This will reduce the tax on a future sale.

REDEEMING FACTORS

A stock bonus transfer plan may take years to implement.

Situation: You are sole owner of a $2 million company. To transfer control to your two children, the company will have to issue them $1 million-plus in stock.

You determine that you might be able to have your company issue your two children $200,000 worth of stock each year. This amount, and the gross-up of cash compensation necessary to pay off the tax bill, can be defended as reasonable compensation.

Outcome: At $200,000 per year, it will take at least five years to issue your children enough shares to gain control of a $2 million company. If the company grows in value over those five years, it will take even longer to transfer control via stock bonuses.

Required: Begin a stock bonus plan well in advance of the time you would like to hand over control.

Alternate strategy: Combine a stock bonus plan with a redemption.

Let's say that your company has two million shares outstanding, valued at $1 per share. You own all of those shares. As above, you authorize your company to issue each of your two children 100,000 shares of stock per year. After two years, they would have a total of 400,000 shares of your company's stock.

Sellout: At that point, or even before, you might have your company redeem all two million of your shares of stock from you. That is, the company would buy those shares. You can even receive an installment note from the company, which could provide years of income for your retirement.

Now, your children possess 400,000 shares. Therefore, you would have (1) transferred control and (2) pulled some cash from your company. Keep in mind that the rules are strict in this area.

Trap: You will not be able to continue working at the company after the redemption. If you do, you will lose the tax advantages of a redemption, such as the low tax rate on long-term capital gains.

CONVERT TO AN S CORPORATION

Yet another approach is to convert your company to an S corporation, which allows partnership-like taxation. Then issue new S corporation shares to your children as a stock bonus in addition to their salaries.

Advantage: Any excess compensation is not an issue with an S corporation because double taxation (corporate plus personal income taxes) doesn't apply.

Pitfall: Conversion from a C corporation to an S corporation requires valuation of the built-in gains. There is a 10-year holding period to avoid double taxation if the assets of the company are sold in that time frame. Careful planning is required.

Strategy: Your children can receive cash if the S corporation distributes its profits to stockholders. And, this cash can be used to buy your shares from you.

If the purchase is made on an installment basis, the children can obtain your shares immediately while making payments over several years.

Result: You'll relinquish control while pocketing cash, paying tax at favorable long-term capital gains rates.

Big Mistakes Owners of Family Businesses Make

Paul Sessions, director of The Center for Family Business at the University of New Haven in New Haven, CT, *www.newhaven.edu/cfb.*

Daniel Smith, principal at Gowrie, Brett & Young, an estate- and retirement-planning firm in Westbrook, CT.

Family business failures rarely are due to downturns in the economy. *Most happen when the owner makes one of the following financial mistakes....*

•**Not having an estate plan.** The typical entrepreneur is a mover and shaker. The last thing he/she wants is to slow down long enough to create an estate plan to distribute business assets upon his death. If you don't have an estate plan, you place a burden on family members involved in the business.

Example: The owner of a New Jersey paper company died with his will unsigned and no estate plan. His family home and his business had to be sold to pay estate taxes. Because it was a distress sale, the $5 million business went for just $900,000.

What to do now: Create an estate and distribution plan with the help of a lawyer who works with family businesses.

Resource: Center for Family Business (203-932-7421).

•**Believing a terrible accident, illness or injury will never happen.** Most family business owners understand that they must have a succession plan to determine who will run the company upon their death, but they don't plan for disability. Until you reach age 65, you are five times as likely to be disabled as to die.

What to do now: First, purchase disability insurance to cover your living expenses if you can no longer work. Next, formulate a business contingency plan in case someone else must take over your company at a moment's notice.

•**Planning to work forever.** Some succession plans fall apart because owners cannot stay away even after children or other designated managers are put in charge of the business.

What to do now: Start thinking about how you will spend the rest of your life long before your succession plan is implemented. Will you pursue new hobbies? Travel? Start another business? Then phase yourself out of the business over three to five years—and commit to a deadline. This will allow you to train managers and give you a stake in ensuring the company's future success.

•**Assuming that the business will pay for your retirement.** The line that I often hear is, "I don't have to save—the business will provide for my retirement."

Owners assume that after living comfortably on their business's income for 20 to 30 years, they will continue to do so until the day they die. But what happens if a new manufacturing process renders your product obsolete? Or a foreign company with deep pockets buys up three of the biggest players in your industry? Now you are facing horrendous competition, and the business you counted on to fund your retirement is producing a fraction of its former income. And because it's weak now, you can't sell it at a decent price.

What to do now: Create a simplified employee pension plan (SEP), savings incentive match plan for employees of small employers (SIMPLE), Keogh or 401(k) plan to provide for your retirement years, no matter what happens to the business.

Help for E-Mail Overload

Marjory Abrams, publisher, newsletters, Boardroom Inc., 281 Tresser Blvd., Stamford, CT 06901.

Recently I heard about a financial news correspondent who had 23,276 new e-mail messages waiting for him when he returned from vacation.

My situation has never been that horrific—but e-mail often places overwhelming demands on my time. *I have a number of tricks to keep it from ruling my life, including…*

●**Limiting the number of times a day that I check my new mail**—and closing the e-mail window and turning off the sound on my computer in between so that I am not tempted to take a look.

●**Categorizing my e-mail address book by color**—coworkers, personal, e-letters, etc.—so I know immediately which messages are important and which ones can wait. (You also can set up rules so that e-mail is automatically filtered into folders. Your "Help" file will show you how to do this.)

●**Promptly stopping e-mail subscriptions** that I no longer want.

●**Printing out long e-mails** so I can read them at a more convenient time.

●**Using the phone** for questions that are better suited to conversation than a lot of back and forth messages.

There is an even more drastic step—opting out of e-mail completely. Trends forecaster Edie Weiner bit that bullet after her e-mail in-box spiraled out of control. Ms. Weiner, president of the firm Weiner, Edrich, Brown, Inc., New York City, is a futurist, so you might expect her life to be filled with the latest technology. Wrong! Besides not having e-mail, she also doesn't have a Blackberry, Palm Pilot or pager. She keeps a paper calendar. She doesn't have a computer at home. And, she leaves her cell phone off except when she is making a call.

When Ms. Weiner gives one of her frequent speeches, her "no e-mail policy" will generally pique the strongest interest from the audience. She says, "Some people enjoy technology and find that it works well for them. If not, no one should feel forced to use it in order to remain part of the human race."

Although Ms. Weiner misses the ease with which e-mail crosses multiple time zones, she has no real regrets. Her clients know how to get a hold of her. Phone calls, "snail mail" and even faxes keep things more personal, which is just how she likes it.

Better Meetings

Put heated issues aside during meetings. Return to them at the end of the meeting, when tempers have cooled. If emotions remain high, delay the topic for a future meeting—unless it is a time-sensitive matter. If it is, schedule a special meeting for the next day, devoted solely to the difficult issue.

Robert L. DeBruyn, president, The Master Teacher, educators' resource, Manhattan, KS.

Be a Better Boss

Thomas J. Neff, chairman, and James M. Citrin, managing director of global communications and media practices, Spencer Stuart, an executive search firm in New York City and in Stamford, CT. They are coauthors of *You're In Charge—Now What?* (Random House).

You've been named new head of the division! To succeed as the new boss, try out the helpful strategies below…

●**Listen**—ask open-ended questions to learn about the company.

●**Resist the savior syndrome**—don't make drastic changes. Instead, study what needs to be changed first.

●**Keep it simple**—don't overload employees with a long "to do" list. Focus on a few concrete priorities.

●**Pause**—think before answering questions, and get back to employees if you don't know the answer immediately.

●**Look for quick wins**—fix a few problems quickly to establish credibility.

●**Spell it out**—use management meetings to communicate your philosophy.

●**Don't bad-mouth your predecessor**—everyone who works at the company worked with the old boss.

●**Give feedback**—share what you learn with your employees.

Good News for Older Workers

The Supreme Court's decision on age bias boosts older workers' ability to claim discrimination when policies that seem neutral in their companywide impact actually hurt employees over age 40.

Example: A firm hires only associates who got their MBAs within the last five years.

If a practice seems disproportionately harmful to older workers, consult a lawyer who has expertise in age discrimination—you can find one in your area at *www.lawyers.com.*

Debra L. Raskin, an attorney specializing in employment law and a partner in the firm of Vladeck, Waldman, Elias & Engelhard, PC, New York City.

Flattery Pays

In a job interview, go ahead and flatter your prospective employer.

New study: Job applicants who flattered interviewers scored more points than those who just flaunted their own abilities. This includes making positive statements regarding or paying compliments to the organization and/or the recruiter...agreeing with statements made by the recruiter...and behaviors such as good eye contact and smiling.

Theory: Interviewers believe that those who flatter them are more likely to share their beliefs and attitudes.

Timothy A. Judge, PhD, eminent scholar chair, department of management at the Warrington School of Business, University of Florida, Gainesville, and coauthor of a study of 116 students actively seeking full-time employment, published in *Journal of Applied Psychology.*

Help Kids Launch Their Careers

Adele Scheele, PhD, a career strategist in New York City, *www.dradele.com,* and former director of the career center at California State University of Northridge. She is also author of *Launch Your Career in College: Strategies for Students, Educators, and Parents* (Praeger).

Internships are not the only way to get a career rolling during college. *Here are some often-overlooked career-building opportunities your child should take advantage of...*

●**Get to know the professors.** Few students speak to their professors outside of class, so it won't take much for your child to turn a professor into a mentor. Encourage your child to meet with the professors whose subjects are of the greatest interest. He/she could ask how to explore the field further...which other classes to take...even how to build a future in the field.

If these meetings go well and your student's interest in the subject deepens, he could obtain part-time work in the department...volunteer to help the professor with research—even earn a coauthor mention on one of the professor's papers...ask the professor to put him in contact with others in the field...or accompany the professor to relevant conferences to make contacts.

●**Bring guest speakers to campus.** College clubs often bring in speakers who are successful business leaders, politicians, entertainers, etc. If your child makes the effort to be the one arranging these speaking engagements for a club, he often will have opportunities to interact with these speakers one-on-one. That time can be used to impress speakers with his enthusiasm or knowledge of the field or to ask questions about launching a career. If handled correctly, such contacts can lead to valuable insight, letters of recommendation, internships and jobs.

●**Write for the college newspaper.** Even if your student isn't interested in a journalism career, writing for the school paper is a proven way to make contacts. He should angle for assignments interviewing successful alumni or local business leaders. Writing for the paper also helps hone communication skills that are vital in any profession.

20

Safe and Secure

Are You Prepared for the Next Wave of Terrorism?

Juval Aviv, the internationally renowned security adviser, formerly with the Israeli secret service, believes that a new kind of terrorism will hit the US this year or next.

He predicts that terrorists will try to hit about six towns and cities simultaneously to demoralize Americans with the message that we aren't secure anywhere in the US. There will be bombings in public areas where there are large concentrations of people. The Mall of America in Minnesota could be a prime target. Las Vegas is another possibility.

The federal government's ability to gain intelligence on these kinds of attacks is limited, so you and your family should prepare by taking these security precautions...

BEFORE A CRISIS

•**Carry a few items whenever you use mass transportation,** including a small bottle of water and a hand towel. Many victims in the London subway bombings died from inhaling toxic fumes, not from the actual blast. It can make the difference in your survival if you wet a towel, put it over your mouth and nose as a filter and stay low—heavy smoke and poisonous gases collect along the ceiling first.

Also consider: Filter masks (meeting the N95 standard) for home, work, your luggage, briefcase and/or vehicle glove compartment. These block almost all particles in the air, are lightweight and compact and cost less than $2 each. Various brands are available at medical-supply stores and on the Internet.

•**Avoid the highest-risk situations.** These include commuter areas, such as bridges, tunnels, train stations and transportation hubs at the

Juval Aviv, president and CEO of Interfor, Inc., an international corporate intelligence and investigations firm based in New York City. Formerly, he served as a counterterrorism officer with the Mossad, the Israeli secret service...a security adviser for El Al Airlines...and a special consultant to the US Congress. He is the author of *Staying Safe: The Complete Guide to Protecting Yourself, Your Family, and Your Business* (HarperResource).

323

height of rush hour, particularly from 8:30 am to 9 am and 5:30 pm to 6 pm. Terrorists like these times because it is easy to blend in and bomb damage is maximized. Obviously, you need to get to work and back home, but adjusting your travel time by as little as 30 minutes can greatly decrease your vulnerability.

Also avoid hotels and office buildings that have underground garages for parking. The terrorists love car bombs because they cost little and can bring down an entire structure. Terrorists also target glassed areas at airports because they can be a source of lots of deadly shrapnel in an explosion.

●**Be careful handling mail at home and the office.** When you open your mail, do it conscientiously. Look for any crystals or powder on the surface, discolorations of the wrapping or envelope and any oily spots or stains. Inspect the item for protruding wires or aluminum foil. Other signs of suspicious letters and packages include excessive postage…noncanceled postage…return labels that don't match the stamped postmark…unexpected mail that's from an overseas address.

Use a letter opener instead of tearing open an envelope with your fingers. Never blow into an envelope to open it or sniff its contents.

If you are suspicious of a letter or package, do not take it to show others or to a police station, fire department or doctor's office. Leave it where it is, and cover it with anything that's handy—clothing, newspaper, a trash can. Call 911. Exit the room, and close the door behind you. If possible, turn off all radios and cell phones in the area because they could be used to transmit a signal that could trigger a bomb.

●**Always have plenty of gas in your car.** Your tank should never be less than half full. In an emergency evacuation or a crisis, you may not have the time or opportunity to get gas.

●**Prepare for getting stuck at work.** During a crisis, you may not be able to go home or even be allowed on the street. Stash nonperishable food, water, a small flashlight, a portable radio and a first-aid kit in your office in case you're trapped there overnight.

In Israel today, every floor of a new building or addition to an existing building must be equipped with a floor protected space (FPS)—a room that has a blast door, a filtered ventilation system and emergency lighting as well as phone and radio reception.

DURING/AFTER A CRISIS

●**Question instructions that do not seem right.** Numerous survivors of the attack on the World Trade Center reported hearing repeated announcements over the public-address system to remain in their offices. When it comes down to a split-second decision between following anonymous advice or following your gut, go with your gut. Each of us has natural instincts that help keep us safe.

●**Stay away from the middle of the flow of pedestrians** when you are evacuating from any crowded public place. You are likely to get trampled if you fall. Your best bet is to get behind a counter or next to a wall or pillar, then scan the area for exits that aren't blocked.

●**Don't automatically run from an explosion or sounds of gunfire.** Running could expose you to stray bullets or flying, shrapnel-like debris. It's usually better to hit the ground first and assume a tucked position. Pull your upper arms and elbows to your sides to guard your heart and lungs. Cup the palms of your hands over your ears to protect the arteries in your neck and your hearing. If you do have children with you, cover them with your body.

If need be, try to locate a safe place to move to—for example, behind a pillar or a wall. When you move, stay as low as you can and get to the location as quickly as possible.

If you are a short distance from a protective barrier, roll along the ground with your arms over your head until you reach it.

●**Beware of second bombs.** Terrorists often plant a second explosive, typically in a parked car, near the vicinity of an initial bomb. The goal is to kill or injure emergency-aid workers as well as curious onlookers attracted by the first explosion. Clear out of the area as soon as you can.

●**Call your children's school before rushing there after a crisis.** Students may already have been evacuated. If you can't reach the school, call the local police station. Also, insist that school officials have an evacuation policy in place. For example, how will you be alerted if the school cannot get through by telephone?

Where will the children be taken in the event of evacuation or injuries?

.Conserve energy if you are trapped in debris. Concentrate on slowing your breathing to help calm your nerves and lower your blood pressure. Try not to shout too much—this will weaken you and cause you to inhale dust. Alert rescuers by tapping on a wall or pipe. In extreme situations, urinating can help rescue dogs pick up your scent.

HELPFUL RESOURCE

Invaluable information on how to care for yourself and others in the event of a biological, chemical or nuclear attack is available from the US Department of Homeland Security, 800-237-3239, *www.ready.gov.*

Facing Down Fear

Rabbi Shmuley Boteach, formerly of Oxford University, and the author of *Face Your Fear: Living Courageously in a Culture of Caution* (*www.shmuley.com*).

We live in an age of fear, a time when we no longer feel safe. Most people now blame terrorist attacks and the threat of natural disasters, such as the deadly tsunami or the Gulf Coast hurricanes, for our current sense of unease. But I believe that the root of the problem really lies within each of us.

In the past, Americans' sense of security was founded on their strong families and faith in God, things that could not be taken away. But these days, many people equate the word "security" with financial security instead. And, financial security *can* be taken away. In other words, we're fearful because we've lost our emotional and spiritual security.

Here are helpful strategies to help lessen the fear we feel...

.Separate caution from fear. *Caution* is an intelligent response to a real threat. *Fear* is an exaggerated response to an imagined or exaggerated threat. The trick is telling the difference. When an apparent threat looms, remain calm and take a dispassionate look at the true danger. Then take reasonable precautions.

Example: We all know that we are more likely to die in a car crash than in a terrorist attack. Therefore, wearing a seat belt is a sensible precaution. Building a $10,000 bomb shelter in the backyard is surrendering to fear.

.Be a leader. Fear is selfish—it turns us inward. When we take responsibility for others—our families, our friends, even total strangers—it forces us to turn outward, to realize that there is something beyond ourselves and our fears.

Examples: Richard Picciotto, a New York City fire chief, led 20 injured civilians and several firefighters to safety while the World Trade Center collapsed around them. When I asked him how he had overcome his fear, he told me that the others needed him and he couldn't let them down. The late Christopher Reeve faced tremendous fear when he was paralyzed. Rather than surrender to that fear, the actor became a leader in the efforts to find a cure for paralysis.

.Choose righteousness. How is the Dalai Lama able to stand up to the Chinese government? He believes his good causes are more important than his own life. His righteousness gives him courage. If we are scrupulous in our behavior, we gain strength and courage.

.Do something. Fear can make us immobilized. Forcing ourselves to do something—anything—can change our focus and free us from fear.

When soldiers are asked whether they are frightened during battle, they often answer that they're not while they're fighting but they are while they're sitting around waiting for the fighting to begin.

.Remind yourself that fear can hold you back. Fear makes people afraid to marry, so they remain lonely. It makes people afraid to explore the world, so they remain disconnected. It makes them afraid of dying, so they don't allow themselves to live fully. And it makes them so fearful about their children that they raise kids who are fearful themselves. We must each do our part to face down fear.

How to Disaster-Proof Your Belongings

Martin Kuritz, San Diego–based author of *The Beneficiary Book: A Family Information Organizer* and coauthor, with Alvin H. Danenberg, DDS, CFP, of *My Business Book,* a binder that has fill-in forms for business owners. Both are available from Mr. Kuritz's company, Active Insights, 800-222-9125, *www.active-insights.com*.

Several years ago, a wildfire threatened my family's home in California. We were caught unprepared, so we had to evacuate quickly without taking our photographs and important papers. Fortunately, we escaped safely and our home was spared, but I agonized about what could have been lost, including my father's letters home from World War II and my grandson's first work of art.

Last season's hurricanes served as reminders that the danger my family faced is hardly unique. Each year, many families confront earthquakes, floods and tornadoes.

To help protect important items, I developed a strategy that anyone can implement...

SECURING DOCUMENTS

Purchase a notebook, several portable plastic file boxes (available in legal and letter size) and a fireproof (and preferably waterproof) home safe. In addition, arrange for a safe-deposit box at a bank.

Make copies of all important items, including deeds, credit cards, insurance policies and health directives (living will, health-care proxy, etc.). Do not forget to copy keepsakes, including photos, diplomas, letters and children's report cards. Put these along with spare keys, valuable jewelry and irreplaceable objects, such as coin collections, in your home safe. (Don't keep loose photo negatives or stamp collections in the safe—conditions may be too moist. Consult an expert on collectibles for the proper storage.)

Keep the originals of documents in your safe-deposit box.

Off-site, perhaps at a friend's house, keep a current list of passwords and personal identification numbers, the combination of your home safe and a spare key to your safe-deposit box.

PORTABLE STORAGE

You can store digital or scanned photos on a CD. Copy this information from your computer frequently onto CDs, and store the CDs in your office or safe-deposit box.

Items that can't be copied and must be stored at home, such as family heirlooms, should be kept in portable file boxes. Mark the tops and sides of the boxes "Take." Store them where they can be reached if you must evacuate.

Keep an empty file box near the home safe in case you need to pack up the valuables quickly—or if there is room, keep them in a file box in the safe.

KEEPING TRACK

To prepare for any insurance claims, keep a room-by-room inventory or a video record of possessions. Don't forget items stored in garages, attics and basements. For major items, such as appliances and electronic gadgets, include the serial numbers, dates of purchase and prices. Store the inventory list or video record in your safe-deposit box.

In a notebook, keep instructions on where to find your documents and keepsakes, as well as names and phone numbers of emergency contacts, such as close family members, physicians, lawyers, insurance agents, etc. List all important family medical information and health insurance ID numbers. Make sure the notebook is accessible—say, on a shelf near the front door—so that you can grab it if you must evacuate.

More on Disaster Planning

David Shaw, enrolled agent and chair, California Society of Enrolled Agents Public Information & Awareness Committee, Yuba City, *www.meyershaw.com*.

The devastation caused by Hurricanes Katrina and Rita shows the importance of being prepared for disaster.

To protect yourself and your family...

•**Tell your loved ones, in advance, where you will go** and how you will get there if you have to evacuate your home.

•**Have a list of all important telephone numbers**—work locations, schools, etc.—that you may need to contact family members and relatives on short notice. Also, have a list of telephone numbers for police, fire department and ambulance service.

•**Keep a current list of all prescription medications and medical conditions,** plus contact numbers for your medical providers. Bring it with you if you must relocate, so you can obtain proper medical care at a new location.

To protect your finances, retain the following in an easy-to-carry box or at a safe off-site location…

•**Copies of all insurance policies** (home, life, auto, etc.).

•**Video, CD or photos of your house and its contents,** to document insurance claims.

•**Copies of all important papers,** such as birth certificates, green cards, wills, trusts and so on.

•**Copies of tax returns for the past four years,** including business returns and other filings (such as for payroll and sales taxes) if you own a business.

Helpful: A step-by-step guide, *Disaster Services and Preparedness*, is available from the California Society of Enrolled Agents. Just go to the "Taxpayer Help" section at its Web site, *www.csea.org.*

•**A survival kit.** Water is most important—one gallon per person per day for at least three days—but you also should have canned food (including food for pets), maps, water-purification tablets, medications, flashlights and batteries. Complete survival-kit instructions are now available from the US Department of Homeland Security (800-237-3239, *www.ready.gov*) or on the Internet sites of the Federal Emergency Management Agency (*www.fema.gov*) and the Red Cross (*www.redcross.org*).

•**Hand-cranked radio** that includes shortwave or TV audio band in addition to AM and FM. Shortwave transmissions carry such long distances that you may be able to get your information from overseas if necessary. Hand-cranked AM/FM radios, such as the Grundig FR200 with shortwave capability and Eton FR300, offer both light and unlimited reception time.

Cost: About $40 to $60.*

•**Cash.** In a box that's fireproof, put enough money for food, lodging and gas for a few days at inflated prices. Also keep a list of your bank and investment account numbers handy.

Helpful: Select a friend or relative who lives in a different part of the country to act as your emergency coordinator. Calling out of a disaster area can be easier than making a local call. You might be able to exchange information through this person. All members of the family should have this information.

*Prices subject to change.

Your Home Emergency Kit

John H. Fenimore V, retired US Air Force Major General, currently operating manager of The Fenimore Group LLC, a preparedness and homeland security consulting company, Schenectady, NY. He previously served as Adjutant General of New York State, and as chairman of the New York State Disaster Preparedness Commission and the National Guard Bureau's Weapons of Mass Destruction Advisory Board.

Here's a listing of what you really should have at home to be prepared for an emergency…

Home Safety Now

Nifty gadgets to help you monitor your home all the time…

•**Eaton's *Home Heartbeat*** checks for water leaks…open doors and windows…and whether appliances are in use. You are alerted to problems via e-mail or your cell phone. (*www.homeheartbeat.com,* $150*).

•**iControl Networks' *Home Monitoring System's* cameras and sensors** monitor the temperature of the whole house and activities

*Prices subject to change.

of, say, children, babysitters, etc. You receive e-mail or text message notification that, for example, your child has arrived home from school (650-322-2300, *icontrol.com,* $599, plus a $14.95 monthly fee).

●**Sylvania's *ZWave Wireless Lighting System*** controls the lights in your house via remote control. (Smarthome, 800-762-7846, *www.smarthome.com,* $129.99).

Money, Time-Life Bldg., Rockefeller Center, New York City 10020.

Burglar-Alarm Savvy

K eep your burglar alarm on at all times, even when you're at home in the daytime—simply disarm motion sensors—and especially at night when you are asleep. Many burglaries take place because alarms have not been turned on. And, don't skimp on coverage. Most systems cover entry doors but no windows. The systems that cover all doors and windows are best.

A preliminary alert should sound immediately but for no more than 20 seconds after a door or window is opened. If the system is not deactivated within 20 seconds, the full alarm should sound. Any longer, and a burglar could disarm the system or at least have enough time to steal something. Consult the system's manual for instructions on changing the delay times—or call the provider. A last bit of advice—do not write your alarm pass code either on or near the alarm keypad.

William F. McCarthy, PhD, president, Threat Research, Inc., an international security consulting firm, Alexandria, VA, *www.threatresearchinc.com,* and former commander of the New York City Police Department bomb squad.

Most Secure Door Locks For Every Budget

A ny of the following locks provides more security than the standard key-in-knob entry set found on most home doors...

●**High-security deadbolt** has hardened cylinders and unique pin configurations to better thwart burglars.

Cost: About $200.*

●**Double-cylinder deadbolt** has inside and outside keys and is easy to install.

Cost: About $60.

●**Single-cylinder deadbolt** has a metal collar outside and thumb-turn handle inside. It is inexpensive (about $25) and easy to install but not a good choice for doors with glass that a burglar could break.

●**Surface-mount interlocking deadbolt** is difficult to break by hammering or sawing but looks bulky and can be difficult to install.

Cost: About $20.

Consumer Reports, 101 Truman Ave., Yonkers, NY.
*Prices subject to change.

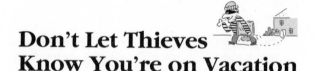

Don't Let Thieves Know You're on Vacation

W hen you are on vacation, don't set up an automatic e-mail response that mentions your vacation.

Problem: Thieves who send out an e-mail to your account and receive the automatic response may use your e-mail address to figure out where you live and then rob your home while you are away.

Best: Set up a generic auto-response e-mail that simply says you will respond shortly. The same is true for telephone answering machines.

MastermindLounge.com, on-line information and discussion site for marketing professionals.

How to Use a Fire Extinguisher

T o use a fire extinguisher properly, remember PASS...

●**Pull** the pin to discharge the material.

•**Aim** low, pointing the spray at the bottom of the blaze.

•**Squeeze** the lever above the handle to operate, and release it to stop the spray.

•**Sweep** the extinguisher from side to side until the flames are out.

Russell E. Sanders, executive secretary, Metropolitan Fire Chiefs Section, National Fire Protection Association, Quincy, MA, *www.nfpa.org.*

 **Fire Safety Tip**

Check smoke detector batteries when changing clocks for the end of daylight saving time on October 29.

Danger: 20% of all smoke detectors do not work because of rundown batteries—putting millions of families needlessly at risk if there is a fire.

Safety: The International Association of Fire Chiefs advises families to get into the habit of changing the batteries in their smoke detectors every time they set their clocks forward for daylight saving time or when they set them back for standard time.

Chief Bill Killen, president, The International Association of Fire Chiefs, Fairfax, VA, *www.iafc.org.*

Better 911 Calls

Too often, 911 calls from cell phones can't be traced by emergency personnel. Ten years ago, the Federal Communications Commission (FCC) ordered all cellular companies to upgrade technology so that cell phone callers could be located—but most municipal call centers can't afford this upgrade.

Best: Use a landline phone in an emergency. If traveling, provide street intersections and other landmarks to identify your location.

John Walls, vice president, public affairs, CTIA, wireless industry trade group, Washington, DC.

Cell Phones Can Explode

During the past two years, 130 cell phones have caught fire or exploded because of incompatible or faulty batteries or chargers.

Self-defense: When removing a cell phone battery, do not let it touch metal. Don't expose the battery to water or to extreme temperatures. Avoid crushing or dropping the battery. Make sure that the battery and charger are compatible with the phone model. Buy parts from an authorized dealer, carrier or legitimate outlet.

Scott Wolfson, spokesperson, Consumer Product Safety Commission, Washington, DC, *www.cpsc.gov.*

Big Rip-Offs That Target Seniors

Hal Morris, veteran Las Vegas–based consumer affairs journalist who writes widely about scams, schemes and other rip-offs.

Wallet-depleting fleecings continue to plague both seniors who use the Internet and those who do not. *Knowledge is your best defense—so here are some of the scams and rip-offs now making the rounds...*

"PHARMING" FOR PERSONAL INFO

Computer users going on-line for shopping, banking or bill paying should be on the alert for the newest menace on the Web—"pharming." Unlike "phishing"—the use of bogus e-mails to seek personal financial information—pharming doesn't rely on you unwittingly opening a scammer's e-mail. Instead, it redirects Internet users, *without their knowledge*, from sites they frequently use, such as financial institutions and credit card firms, to bogus look-alike sites where identity thieves capture log-in names, passwords, account numbers and other data. Pharmers inject a malicious code that infects your PC through an e-mail attachment that you open or when you inadvertently make a one-letter typo when typing in a popular Web address.

Another pharming threat is domain name system (DNS) "poisoning," which in one swoop can herd a large group of Internet users to counterfeit sites.

Self-defense: Only open an attachment when it comes from a source known to you. Make sure the Web address starts with "https"—indicating it's a secure sight—not "http." Check with your computer store for the latest antivirus and anti-spy software being offered to combat pharming. Ask your Internet service provider (ISP) what kind of measures it is taking to thwart pharming poisoning, such as upgrading its own computers' software.

DISASTER BILKERS

During hurricane season, fast-buck operators posing as legitimate contractors prey on property owners, especially the elderly, who will be anxious to get their homes back in shape if damage occurs. Other natural or man-made disasters—floods, fires, earthquakes, explosions, etc.—also trigger bilkers into action. So how does one distinguish the good guys from the scammers?

Word of mouth from trusted sources is very dependable—so ask for recommendations from family, business associates, your banker or your insurance agent. It is best to be prepared with recommendations for likely services needed prior to a disaster. With an insurance company, a good time to obtain a list of providers is when renewing a policy.

Self-defense: Seek to verify the names and track records of providers with your local Better Business Bureau and homebuilders association and with your insurance company's claims adjuster. Make sure there's no charge for a repair estimate—a classic rip-off. Also be wary of a bid that's significantly lower than others.

Deal only with licensed and insured contractors. (Contact county building and licensing departments to confirm a contractor's credentials.) Avoid those who show up at your door unannounced. Sign a contract only after carefully reviewing it and having an attorney review it if it's not all clear to you. Nix any contractor who asks for full up-front payment rather than the standard one-third. Never pay in cash—you'll have no legitimate record that you ever paid. A prime sign of a shady operator is a contractor who pushes for a cash transaction. (It also

indicates the guy is attempting to avoid paying taxes—not a good citizen.)

HOTEL BILL PADDING

Competition in the travel industry keeps on getting fiercer, particularly with Web shoppers insisting on rock-bottom prices. So, rather than charge higher room rates, many hotels and resorts are sneaking onto bills new items that hit unsuspecting guests at checkout time.

Examples: "Energy surcharges," supposedly to compensate for higher electricity costs, and "resort fees" linked to upkeep of essentials ranging from swimming pools to tennis courts.

Other pesky padding: Internet and fax fees, room safe fee and porterage charge (even if you carry your own bags), mandatory maid service gratuity, administrative fee and minibar restocking fee. New ones seem to pop up monthly.

These stealthy add-ons, seldom disclosed in ads or when booking, are in addition to ever-increasing sales and room taxes. Add them all up and rooms can easily cost an additional $35 or more a night.

Self-defense: Prior to picking a hotel, inquire about additional fees, surcharges and taxes. Say that you want to know about *all* fees, and take notes. Bring them with you to the hotel. If you see a surprise charge at the hotel, ask the desk manager or general manager to delete it. Show your notes if necessary. Usually, just complaining about these surprise charges leads a public relations–minded manager to adjust your bill.

SHADY DEBT SERVICES

As US consumer debt loads grow, senior citizens squeezed by mushrooming bills and facing difficulty in making payments need to use caution in selecting debt-counseling services.

Many operations are shady and won't bring the desired relief. And in fact, they could make things worse. Three debt-service operations recently scammed consumers out of $100 million through aggressive marketing. They promised to negotiate debt downward, stop creditors' collection efforts and eliminate debts. In most cases, they did nothing.

The National Foundation for Credit Counseling will help you find legitimate debt-help companies. To locate the closest agency, visit *www.nfcc.org* or call 800-388-2227.

Another nonprofit organization that provides information and also assists consumers with debt difficulties is American Consumer Credit Counseling at *www.consumercredit.com* or 800-769-3571.

Self-defense: Red flags are raised if any debt-negotiation organization guarantees removal of your unsecured debt, seeks high monthly fees and claims to be able to delete negative information from your credit reports. Make sure a written agreement includes price and services to be performed. Contact creditors to make sure they will work with the selected debt-counseling firm.

THE CASKET RACKET

Caskets are a big business, racking up billions of dollars in sales in the US each year. The average price tag of caskets—sold primarily for visual appeal—is slightly more than $2,000.* Some funeral homes charge up to six times wholesale price, increasing the cost of a traditional funeral to $6,000 to $10,000.

No wonder families are buying caskets from sources other than funeral homes. People are turning to discounters that sell caskets at prices starting at around $825 including next-day delivery. Major casket discounters include Costco Wholesale (*www.costco.com*) and Web-based *www.funeraldepot.com*, which offers free next-day delivery.

If you buy from a discounter, be aware that the funeral home may elevate prices of other services to make up for the loss of the casket sale. Compare charges with prices you were quoted.

Important: Legally, a funeral-service provider can't refuse a job because the casket is bought elsewhere, nor can it jack up other charges.

Ask for a list of services, with prices, before you start talking with the provider. The "Funeral Rule," enforced by the Federal Trade Commission, requires funeral directors to itemize prices in person, and, if asked, by telephone. That includes providing descriptions of available selections and prices before showing caskets. Comparison shop other funeral-service providers.

Self-defense: Curb funeral overspending that your family might experience by making your own arrangements while you're still alive.

*Prices subject to change.

Another Senior Scam

Telemarketing scams victimize seniors more than other age groups because they're more likely to be at home to answer the phone and are less likely to hang up on intrusive callers because of loneliness.

Self-defense: Do not accept anything for free or fill out sweepstakes forms, which is how con artists get your telephone numbers and, in some cases, Social Security number and credit card information. In addition, it is OK to hang up on telemarketers.

The Federal Trade Commission (FTC) has several pamphlets on telemarketing scams (*www.ftc.gov* or 877-382-4357).

Linda Foley, executive director of the nonprofit Identity Theft Resource Center, San Diego, *www.idtheftcenter.org.*

 # Beware of Consumer Scams

The most common, and the most expensive, consumer scams in the US today...

Most victims: Credit scams, according to the Federal Trade Commission.

Examples: Guaranteed loan and credit offers, credit repair promotions, insurance against charges on stolen credit cards—all promised in exchange for an advance fee.

Most expensive: False claims that the victim has won a lottery (average loss—more than $5,500) or a sweepstakes or other prize offer (average loss—more than $2,400) that the supposed winner has to pay to collect, according to the National Consumers League.

Self-defense: Never act on any offer that is unsolicited and requires that you make an up-front payment to an organization or person that you don't know.

Money, Time-Life Bldg., Rockefeller Center, New York City 10020.

Protect Your Phone Records

Home and cell phone records are not private. At least 50 Web sites can deliver cell phone records for about $100.* Some also can provide landline records. These records may be sought by private investigators and criminals.

Self-defense: Contact your local, long-distance and cell phone companies, and insist that your calling records be password-protected. Companies often use your mother's maiden name as the password for records access—make up a name instead of using the real one, in case someone has found out the true name. Insist that requests for records be confirmed by a written notice mailed to you. Opt out of marketing and information-sharing agreements.

John Featherman, a personal privacy consultant based in Philadelphia.

*Price subject to change.

More from John Featherman...

Password Security

To keep your password secure, follow these guidelines...

•**The safest computer passwords combine letters, numbers and other characters,** such as dollar signs and exclamation points—and are changed every six to 12 months.

•**Avoid passwords with common words.** These are easily guessed by hackers and fraud artists—even if you add a number.

•**Avoid using personal information,** such as the names of friends, family members, pets and birthdays, as a password or security code.

•**Never write down passwords,** and don't store them in your wallet or purse or on the flip-side of your keyboard.

Phishing for Information

Ron Hiner, Connecticut-based computer consultant at *www.softstonegroup.com.*
Dana Blankenhorn, Internet business consultant, *www.a-clue.com,* Atlanta.

Phishing is one of the biggest and most insidious e-mail scams, according to computer consultant Ron Hiner. Phishing e-mails purport to be from Citibank, eBay, PayPal and other popular, legitimate companies that conduct business on-line. Usually these e-mails contain links to Web sites that look exactly like the company's site. You then put in your user names, passwords and other confidential information, which crooks gather and then use on the legitimate sites—stealing your identity as well as your money.

If you do suspect that an e-mail message is a scam—or if it's from an organization with which you don't do business or a service that you have never used—don't open it at all. If you do open such an e-mail and then think better of it, don't click on any of the links that it contains.

If you think that you may have fallen victim to a scam and passed along confidential information, change your user names and passwords immediately. Also contact all the companies involved to alert them to potential problems.

Other ways to protect yourself from Internet trickery...

•**Keep your antivirus program up-to-date** —preferably with software that does it automatically every week.

Mr. Hiner's favorite antivirus software: AVG. A free edition (*Windows* and *Linux* only) for home use can be downloaded at *free.grisoft.com/freeweb.php.*

•**Make sure you have a good antispyware program.** Spyware programs "spy" on your computer and collect data about you, which is sent to reputable companies—or identity thieves. Mr. Hiner uses Ad-Aware Personal (*Windows* only). Download it for free at *www.lavasoftusa.com.*

Internet business consultant Dana Blankenhorn notes the evolving sophistication of phishers. As Citibank and other big guys strengthen their defenses, phishers are moving to smaller financial institutions and retailers.

Virus-infected e-mail is becoming more sophisticated, as well. Mr. Blankenhorn uses the *MailWasher* program to "clean" his messages—available from *www.mailwasher.net.* It allows you to read your e-mail before it is delivered to your computer and download only what you want to keep. There is a free version and a version that costs $37* per year.

Bottom line: Don't let your guard down, even for an instant. Crooks are always devising new and improved ways of getting your money.

*Price subject to change.

Cyberthieves Target On-Line Stock Investors

Thieves are finding ways to get personal data from investors who sign into their accounts with a user name and password. The SEC will not give details of the scam or say how widespread it is, but the agency offers precautions for better on-line security at *www.sec.gov/investor/pubs/onlinebrokerage.htm.* Some on-line brokerage firms are changing their sign-in procedures to protect against thieves.

Susan Wyderko, investor education director, Securities and Exchange Commission, Washington, DC, quoted in *USA Today.*

Gas Station Identity Theft Threat

Wrongdoers have invented a way to hijack card information when a credit or debit card is used to buy gasoline at a pump. The information is electronically stored in the machine until the hacker returns to the gas station and collects the information.

Safety: Use only credit cards at gas pumps.

Why: Credit cards offer much better protection, with credit card companies generally removing disputed charges right away. Debit cards

take money right out of your bank account, and it can be more difficult to get that money back.

Luci Duni, director, consumer education, TrueCredit, San Luis Obispo, CA, *www.truecredit.com.*

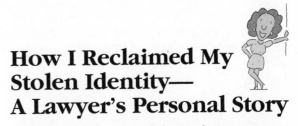

How I Reclaimed My Stolen Identity— A Lawyer's Personal Story

Mari J. Frank, Esq., a workplace-mediation attorney as well as a privacy consultant in Laguna Niguel, CA. She is the author of *Safeguard Your Identity* and *From Victim to Victor,* a step-by-step guide in book or CD format for victims of identity theft (both from Porpoise). Her Web site is *www.identitytheft.org.*

As many as 10 million Americans become victims of identity theft each year. It is awful—and I know because I was one of the earliest victims.

Back in 1996, I was 48 years old and living in Southern California with my husband and two children. I was a successful attorney. I had no debt, kept excellent financial records and thought I knew how to protect my personal information. When my identity was stolen, I had no idea at first how to get it back and reclaim my credit standing. *I hope my experience can help others avoid the emotional and financial pain...*

MY STORY

One afternoon, a bank called me, wanting to know why I had missed the payments on my $11,000 Visa bill. I thought it was a prank call.

In fact, someone had opened new credit card accounts in my name and charged more than $50,000 over 10 months before anyone notified me. I found out that a Ford Mustang convertible had been purchased by using credit in my name, and a rental-car company was suing me for damages to a vehicle that my impostor had rented. Though I was not held responsible for the charges, my credit was ruined.

Worst of all, this wasn't just a financial crime—the thief was stealing my professional identity as well. She was handing out business cards with my name on them to people who were looking for an attorney.

Because of my legal expertise, I figured that stemming and repairing this damage would take several weeks. Instead, it wound up taking almost a year. I met resistance at every turn. The credit card issuer told me that the bills for the fraudulent charges had been going to an address in Ventura County, four hours north of my home, and that it would investigate. Instead, the card issuer turned over my account to a collection agency, which inundated me with threatening calls.

UPHILL BATTLE

Local police refused to take the case because I wasn't responsible for the charges. The FBI informed me that it does not get involved with financial crimes against consumers (a federal law that I lobbied for has since changed that). The US Postal Service was so slow to grant my request to cease delivery to the thief of preapproved credit card offers in my name that I approached the local mailman in the thief's neighborhood. I pleaded with him to stop delivering such mail. He said that he would try to help but couldn't guarantee what would happen on his days off.

In desperation, I called up the Ventura County Police Department again and got lucky. One of the officers I spoke with had been a victim of identity theft himself. He investigated and then arrested the thief—a paralegal who had stolen my credit report from a law office where she worked as a temporary secretary. The law firm had a subscription to an information service, enabling my impostor to download my credit reports. Eventually, the woman pleaded guilty to six counts of felony fraud. Because she had not committed a violent crime, she was sentenced to probation and community service.

Meanwhile, it took me $1,500 and 500 hours of work to clean up the problem. (The national average for identity theft victims is $1,400 and about 600 hours.) During that time, I was barraged with calls from creditors and was not able to get new loans or credit. *Here's what I learned from the experience...*

IF SOMEONE STEALS YOUR IDENTITY

•**Contact the three main credit-reporting agencies.** Ask that a notation called a "fraud alert" be attached to your accounts. It is free, good for 90 days and hopefully (if the creditor

is diligent) means that you will be telephoned for verification whenever credit is applied for in your name. If you want to maintain the alert for up to seven years, you need to mail proof of identify theft, including a police report (see below) and affidavit, to each agency.

If you reside in a state that allows a security freeze, you can lock your report so that no one can get it without your permission secured by a password. To find out which states now have security freeze laws, visit *www.pirg.org/consumer/credit/statelaws.htm*.

While the reporting agencies, major banks and credit cards now offer credit-monitoring services that provide early notice of fraud, these services are quite expensive—as much as $200 a year. It's more cost effective to take advantage of a new federal law that requires each of the big reporting agencies to issue you one free credit report a year. That way, you can get a report every four months and monitor your credit record yourself. Visit *www.annualcreditreport.com* or call 877-322-8228 for more information.

•**Get an identity theft report** from the local police in your area documenting the fraudulent accounts and other illegal actions the thief has taken. It also should include the thief's address (if you know it). The police will take a full set of your fingerprints and your photo if someone committed a crime in your name.

Important: Few police departments have the resources to investigate identity theft, but every state gives you the right to get a victim's report "for informational purposes only." A report establishes the date that you became aware of the crime and makes it easier to get information and clear your name with financial institutions and government agencies. For example, federal law requires that once any creditor receives your identity theft report, it's illegal for it to sell, transfer or turn the debt over to a collection agency.

Caution: Do *not* contact the impostor yourself. He/she may be violent or may retaliate by threatening or harassing you. In addition, contacting him also could compromise any criminal case against him.

•**Contact the security/fraud departments at your bank** and all institutions from which you had credit—not just Visa and MasterCard issuers, but also stores, gas stations, brokerages, mortgage companies, etc. You also will need to contact any institutions that granted credit to the thief. All fraudulent accounts need to be closed and noted on your record as "Account Closed at Consumer's Request," not as "Lost or Stolen Card," which could lower your future credit score. Ask that new accounts opened by the perpetrator be "permanently removed" from your record, not simply closed—often, accounts are given a "soft" close, which means that they can be reopened with a request by phone.

Helpful: Identity theft victims tend to cancel all of their accounts to protect themselves, but you should keep open those that were not affected by the identity theft. Your credit record may be damaged due to the fraud, which will make getting new loans or credit almost impossible.

●**Reassert control of your bank accounts.** In addition to reporting stolen checks or account numbers to your bank, also report the theft to the major check guarantee/verification companies.

Reason: Merchants use these databases to learn whether you have a history of writing bad checks. Your bank may not update this information right away.

●**Conduct civil and criminal court checks** to make sure that the thief hasn't incurred any lawsuits, civil judgments or criminal charges in your name. For example, say that an impostor fails to pay his landlord, who sues and wins a case against "you" for past-due rent, or a large check bounces and a warrant is issued for your arrest. These problems are very serious because, for obvious reasons, they can escalate as time goes on.

To look up civil judgments, see *www.knowx. com* (free to search, reports cost $7.95*). If you discover a lawsuit against you, contact the court where the suit was filed to request a copy of the court records. Also contact the office of the attorneys involved in the case for instructions on resolving the matter.

For criminal cases, have your local police run a criminal background check on you. If your name surfaces, you'll need to hire an attorney to contact the police and/or district attorney's

*Price subject to change.

office where the crime was committed to get help. Also contact the US Department of Justice (202-514-2000, *www.usdoj.gov*) to check if your name is in the National Criminal Database. If it is, officials will tell you how to get it removed.

●**Do not pay fraudulent bills.** After months or years of fighting collection agencies and watching the interest and late fees on unpaid bills soar, many victims figure that it's easier to pay off false credit card charges or even declare bankruptcy. But doing so can damage your credit and hurt your case as a crime victim should other fraudulent charges surface. You must send harassing bill collectors the identity theft report issued by the police. Inform them that continuing to call you violates federal law and you will take legal action if they persist.

●**Log the time and expenses involved in clearing your name.** Any fraud losses, out-of-pocket costs and work time lost may be tax deductible under IRS Tax Code Section 165(c). You also could have a case against your credit grantors or the credit-reporting agencies if they violated the *Fair Credit Reporting Act* by committing willful or negligent acts in violation of the law, such as failure to investigate the fraud that resulted in the identity theft. Your action must be filed within two years of the date of discovery but no later than five years from the date of violation.

Finally, you can help prosecute the impostor and ask for restitution for out-of-pocket costs. In my case, the judge ordered restitution of several thousand dollars, but all I received was $60— my impersonator was subsequently incarcerated for committing identity theft again.

More from Mari Frank, Esq....

Resources for Identity Theft Victims

The following resources provide invaluable help to identity theft victims...

CREDIT-REPORTING AGENCIES

●**Equifax,** 888-766-0008, *www.equifax.com.*
●**Experian,** 888-397-3742, *www.experian.com.*
●**TransUnion,** 800-680-7289, *www.transunion. com.*

CHECK GUARANTEE COMPANIES

- **Certegy,** 800-770-3792.
- **ChexSystems,** 800-428-9623.
- **CrossCheck,** 800-843-0760.
- **Global Payments,** 800-560-2960.
- **SCAN,** 800-262-7771.
- **TeleCheck,** 800-710-9898.

HELPFUL ORGANIZATIONS

- **Federal Trade Commission,** 877-438-4338, *www.consumer.gov/idtheft.*
- **Identity Theft Prevention and Survival,** 800-725-0807, *www.identitytheft.org.*
- **Identity Theft Resource Center,** 858-693-7935, *www.idtheftcenter.org.*
- **Privacy Rights Clearinghouse,** 619-298-3396, *www.privacyrights.org.*

Also from Mari Frank, Esq....

Protect Your Social Security Number When in the Hospital

Social Security numbers often double as identification numbers for patients in hospitals. They appear on wristbands and charts, making them accessible to identity thieves.

Self-defense: Ask the hospital at check-in to use a different number for you. If that request is denied, black out all but the last few numbers wherever your Social Security number appears. Don't give your number out loud when you can be overheard.

Americans Are Lax About Identity Theft

Social Security numbers (SSNs) are sought by identity thieves, but 47% of Americans still carry their Social Security cards in their wallets

...28% use their SSNs as employee identification numbers...and 16% report that their SSN appears on their personal checks.

Also: Nearly 60% have not checked out their credit reports in the last year.

American Express ID Theft Quiz, conducted through telephone interviews with 1,007 American adults.

PIN Protection

It's a very poor idea to write down a PIN anywhere that an unsavory person might find it.

Useful trick: Write your PINs in your address book by entering them as part of the phone numbers of fake friends or contacts. You might find it helpful if the "name" is connected with the financial institution you're dealing with. For example, John S. Bank, 212-777-1234. In this case, 1234 would be the PIN number for your bank account.

Nancy Dunnan, a financial adviser and author in New York City. Her latest book is *How to Invest $50–$5,000* (HarperCollins).

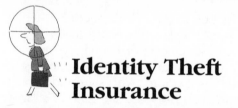 # Identity Theft Insurance

Identity theft insurance is now being offered by many employers to lower the cost of lost productivity when a worker is victimized. The average identity theft victim spends hundreds of hours restoring his/her credit, which requires time off from work. Insurance, which reimburses victims for the cost of restoring their identities and repairing their credit reports, can cost a few dollars per year per employee, depending on company size and level of coverage.

Nancy Callahan, vice president, AIG Identity Theft and Fraud Division, New York City, *www.aigidtheft.com.*

Index